Canada: The State of the Federation 2002

Reconsidering the Institutions of Canadian Federalism

Edited by

J. Peter Meekison,
Hamish Telford
and Harvey Lazar

Published for the Institute of Intergovernmental Relations
School of Policy Studies, Queen's University
by McGill-Queen's University Press
Montreal & Kingston • London • Ithaca

Canadian Cataloguing in Publication Data

The National Library of Canada has catalogued this publication as follows:

Canada : the state of the federation

Annual.
1985-
Continues: Year in review, ISSN 0825-1207.
ISSN 0827-0708
ISBN 1-55339-008-3 (2002 issue ; bound).—ISBN 1-55339-009-1 (2002 issue : pbk.)

1. Federal-provincial relations—Canada—Periodicals. 2. Federal government—Canada—Periodicals. I. Queen's University (Kingston, Ont.). Institute of Intergovernmental Relations

JL27.F42   321.02'3'0971   C86-030713-1 rev

The Institute of Intergovernmental Relations

The Institute is the only organization in Canada whose mandate is solely to promote research and communication on the challenges facing the federal system.

Current research interests include fiscal federalism, the social union, the reform of federal political institutions and the machinery of federal-provincial relations, Canadian federalism and the global economy, and comparative federalism.

The Institute pursues these objectives through research conducted by its own staff and other scholars, through its publication program, and through seminars and conferences.

The Institute links academics and practitioners of federalism in federal and provincial governments and the private sector.

The Institute of Intergovernmental Relations receives ongoing financial support from the J.A. Corry Memorial Endowment Fund, the Royal Bank of Canada Endowment Fund, Power Corporation, the Government of Canada, and the Government of Ontario. We are grateful for this support which enables the Institute to sustain its extensive program of research, publication, and related activities.

L'Institut des relations intergouvernementales

L'Institut est le seul organisme canadien à se consacrer exclusivement à la recherche et aux échanges sur les questions du fédéralisme.

Les priorités de recherche de l'Institut portent présentement sur le fédéralisme fiscal, l'union sociale, la modification éventuelle des institutions politiques fédérales, les mécanismes de relations fédérales-provinciales, le fédéralisme canadien au regard de l'économie mondiale et le fédéralisme comparatif.

L'Institut réalise ses objectifs par le biais de recherches effectuées par son personnel et par des universitaires de l'Université Queen's et d'ailleurs, de même que par des conférences et des colloques.

L'Institut sert de lien entre les universitaires, les fonctionnaires fédéraux et provinciaux et le secteur privé.

L'institut des relations intergouvernementales reçoit l'appui financier du J.A. Corry Memorial Endowment Fund, de la Fondation de la Banque Royale du Canada, de Power Corporation, du gouvernement du Canada et du gouvernement de l'Ontario. Nous les remercions de cet appui qui permet à l'Institut de poursuivre son vaste programme de recherche et de publication ainsi que ses activités connexes.

CONTENTS

FOREWORD

This year's *Canada: The State of the Federation* examines the role of institutions in the management of the federation. Although many of the institutions have been subject to analysis over the decades, it has been some time since all of the major institutions were considered in a single volume.

Institutions matter. They help to make some initiatives easy to pursue and constrain others. They are also often the visible manifestation of the way in which a federation balances the tensions between unity and diversity. As such, they have a symbolic significance as well as practical importance.

The volume begins with a consideration of the role of "traditional" institutions such as Parliament, Cabinet, the Supreme Court, and political parties. It has long been held that these institutions, as constituted, do not provide effective forums for inter-regional bargaining, and that this void has been filled at least in part by the institutions and practices of executive federalism. In this volume, we confirm the validity of this thesis. But we also argue that the performance of the traditional institutions, taken as a whole, has deteriorated over the last couple of decades. These institutions are even weaker today than they once were in bridging between the unity and diversity mentioned above.

The remaining parts of the volume focus on Canada's intergovernmental institutions. A theme that emerges from these chapters is that these institutions are poorly coordinated. Thus, we have found that relations among federal and provincial finance ministries are becoming more disjointed at a time when relations among line ministries remain highly interdependent. Given the connectedness between line and finance ministries, this inconsistency is highly problematic. To get more consistency requires direction from first ministers. Unfortunately, the First Ministers' Conference (FMC) has, in recent years, been a weak link in federation management. Not surprisingly, therefore, we conclude that there is a strong need for much improved leadership from first ministers, and that this in turn requires that they have a stronger institutional base.

Creating strong institutions of intergovernmental institutions, however, raises all of the pathologies associated with executive federalism. We therefore argue that a strengthened and better coordinated system of intergovernmental relations should be accompanied by an enhanced oversight role by Parliament and provincial legislatures. In short, both the traditional institutions and the intergovernmental institutions should be reformed together for optimal results in terms of federalism and democracy.

As in other years, we have included a chronology of major events. This volume covers the period from January 2002-December 2002. I would like to thank all the people who contributed to this volume. In particular, I want to make special note of the role played by my two co-editors. Peter Meekison wrote two chapters. Both break fresh ground. He also co-authored the introductory chapter, and played a large role in the editing of the volume. Hamish Telford was instrumental in developing this project, thinking through the structure of the volume, as well as playing a major role in the editorial process, and co-authoring the first chapter.

As in other years, Patti Candido and Mary Kennedy contributed their expertise to the conference that preceded this volume, and to the task of helping to prepare it for publication. The conference participants, including discussants and anonymous reviewers, provided crucial feedback to the authors. Valerie Jarus, Mark Howes and Kirsteen MacLeod managed the desktop publishing, cover design and copyediting, and collectively transformed the rough pages into the book.

The chapters in this volume were first presented at a conference at Queen's University in Kingston on 2-3 November 2001. I would like to thank those who participated in that event, as their feedback was instrumental to the processes that led to this volume.

Finally, I wish to acknowledge the financial support of the Social Sciences and Humanities Research Council and the federal Privy Council Office in helping to make this project and volume a reality.

Harvey Lazar
December 2003

CONTRIBUTORS

Jacques Bourgault teaches at Université du Québec and at l'École nationale du Québec in Montreal.

David Cameron is Professor of Political Science at the University of Toronto.

R. Kenneth Carty is Professor of Political Science at the University of British Columbia.

C.E.S. Franks is Professor Emeritus of the Department of Political Studies and the School of Physical and Health Education at Queen's University.

Roger Gibbins is Professor of Political Science at the University of Calgary.

Aaron Holdway is a Research Assistant at the Institute of Intergovernmental Relations at Queen's University.

Gregory J. Inwood is Associate Professor in the Department of Politics and School of Public Administration at Ryerson University, and Director of the Ontario Legislature Internship Programme.

Carolyn M. Johns is Assistant Professor in the Department of Politics and School of Public Administration at Ryerson University.

James B. Kelly is Assistant Professor of Political Science at Concordia University.

Harvey Lazar is Director of the Institute of Intergovernmental Relations at Queen's University.

Howard Leeson is Head of the Department of Political Science at the University of Regina. He has many years of experience in the Saskatchewan public service.

Peter Leslie is Visiting Professor of Canadian Studies at the Sorbonne Nouvelle (Paris), and a Fellow at the Institute of Intergovernmental Relations at Queen's University.

J. Peter Meekison is a Fellow at the Institute of Intergovernmental Relations at Queen's University, University Professor Emeritus of Political Science at the University of Alberta, and a former Deputy Minister of Federal and Intergovernmental Affairs for the Province of Alberta.

Nelson Michaud is Associate Professor of Political Science and International Relations at l'École nationale d'administration publique, Université du Québec.

Adele Mugford is a former Research Assistant at the Institute of Intergovernmental Relations, Queen's University. She is at present in Sweden on a DFAIT Internship.

Ronald H. Neumann is the Director of Intergovernmental Finance in the Province of Manitoba.

Patricia L. O'Reilly is Associate Professor in the Department of Politics and School of Public Administration at Ryerson University.

Martin Papillon is currently a PhD Candidate in Political Science at the University of Toronto. He previously worked for the federal Intergovernmental Affairs Secretariat.

Johanne Poirier is a Quebec lawyer and a senior researcher at the Center for Public Law of the Free University of Brussels. She specializes in comparative federalism.

Russ Robinson is a consultant specializing in strategic management and public policy reform in Ottawa.

Richard Simeon is Professor of Political Science and Law at the University of Toronto, and a former Director of the Institute of Intergovernmental Relations at Queen's University.

Julie M. Simmons is a Lecturer in the Department of Political Science at the University of Guelph.

Hamish Telford teaches political science at the University College of the Fraser Valley, and is a Research Associate of the Institute of Intergovernmental Relations at Queen's University.

Steven B. Wolinetz is Professor and Head of the Department of Political Science at Memorial University of Newfoundland.

I

Introduction

1

The Institutions of Executive Federalism: Myths and Realities

J. Peter Meekison, Hamish Telford and Harvey Lazar

Ce chapitre examine les institutions du fédéralisme canadien, non seulement les entités traditionnelles telles que le Parlement, le Cabinet, les partis politiques et les tribunaux, mais aussi les procédés et la machinerie du fédéralisme exécutif. Il émet l'hypothèse que ce dernier soit né de l'incapacité d'adaptation des institutions traditionnelles aux défis de l'interdépendance, et que lesdites institutions soient devenues encore moins efficaces au cours des deux dernières décennies. Les auteurs font voir que la forme prétendument «coopérative» de fédéralisme exécutif qui s'est développé dans les trois décennies suivant la Seconde Guerre mondiale se caractérisait par une dépendance intergouvernementale et par un fort leadership fédéral. Au cours de la dernière décennie, la fédération a semblé se diriger vers un type de fédéralisme exécutif qu'on prétend toujours «collaboratif», caractérisé cette fois par une dépendance entre gouvernements accrue et rehaussée, mais aussi par une plus grande parité entre les gouvernements fédéral et provinciaux en termes de leadership. Ils soutiennent que si cette tendance se maintient, les institutions qui adhèrent à une telle coopération devront rapidement évoluer en matière de réformes institutionnelles au niveau des premiers ministres. En même temps, ils reconnaissent que la création d'institutions intergouvernementales plus fortes entraîne tous les maux associés au fédéralisme exécutif. Ainsi, pour l'établissement d'un système mieux coordonné de relations intergouvernementales, on doit confier au Parlement et aux assemblées législatives provinciales un rôle de supervision accru.

INTRODUCTION

For the past six decades, Canadians have enjoyed the fruits and endured the pathologies of executive federalism. Canada has one of the most successful economies in the world, with a reasonably comprehensive social welfare system. Moreover, despite cultural and regional cleavages, Canada's internal affairs have been managed in a remarkably peaceful fashion. Many of these achievements have been managed through the institutions and processes of executive federalism. This suggests that executive interaction can be an effective and beneficial way to manage the federation. But executive federalism also has a well-known set of deficiencies. First, the processes of executive federalism have made it difficult to obtain an adequate degree of political accountability. Apart from proposals for major reforms to the constitution, Parliament and provincial legislatures have been almost totally excluded from the processes of executive federalism, and citizens have had trouble influencing its institutions. Second, executive federalism appears to be associated with excessive levels of intergovernmental conflict. While a degree of tension may lead to creative solutions, too much tension can be detrimental. In this chapter, we shall consider ways to remedy the deficiencies of executive federalism, as well as ways to make it a more effective and beneficial decision-making process.

The pathologies of executive federalism were abundantly clear to Canadian political scientists by the 1970s. Yet executive federalism has continued to expand and deepen, driven primarily by the functional need to respond to new challenges and opportunities in public policy. As executive federalism has become a routine feature of Canadian politics, notwithstanding numerous proposals to diminish it, one can say that it has become at least semi-institutionalized. The purposes of this volume are to describe and analyze the various institutions of federalism as they have evolved over the past 30 years. We deal mainly with the institutions of executive federalism, but we also examine the traditional institutions of the federation, such as Parliament and the courts. Our framework for analysis is based on two sets of factors. One has to do with whether the relationship between the two orders of government is based on *independence* or *interdependence*. The second factor is concerned with whether there is *hierarchy* or *parity* between the two orders of government. Where governments act largely independently, they do not need significant institutional support to manage their relationship. Where there is interdependence among governments, however, the need for institutional support is greater. In circumstances of both interdependence and parity, the need for decision rules, dispute resolution mechanisms, procedures for clarifying accountabilities, and bureaucratic support is greatest.

The 1950s and 1960s are sometimes characterized as the era of *co-operative federalism*. This was the period when many of the federal-provincial shared-cost social programs, as well as equalization, were introduced. Sometimes these initiatives entailed a significant measure of federal leadership and coercion (medical insurance), although in others the provinces were a driving force behind federal legislation (hospital and diagnostic services insurance). In yet other instances, such as the Canada Assistance Plan, there may have been more of a balance between federal and provincial initiative. In all cases, whether mutually agreed or hierarchical, the federal spending power was the instrument that enabled the governments to work together. The era of co-operative federalism was thus characterized by considerable policy interdependence among governments with varying degrees of hierarchy, and the co-operation of the provinces was frequently secured by the lure of "50-cent dollars."

Over the past quarter century, as Ottawa's fiscal contribution to provincial programs has declined and become somewhat less conditional, the federal-provincial relationship has become less hierarchical. This different kind of relationship, based on continued high levels of interdependence but greater parity among orders of government, has been styled *collaborative* federalism.[1] Both orders of government have indicated, at various times, some measure of support for this kind of federalism.[2] But the actions of both orders of government have not always been fully consistent with this rhetoric. Some premiers have moved to enhance the fiscal autonomy of their provinces, and Quebec has especially attempted to preserve the greatest degree of policy independence. With the Social Union Framework Agreement (SUFA), the federal government showed a willingness to collaborate, but it also sought to preserve the de facto status of its spending power. In sum, the first ministers have not fully committed themselves to the project of collaborative federalism. To the extent that collaborative federalism is being embraced, however, institutional development becomes more important. Whether or not there is a movement toward collaborative federalism, the federation will remain executive driven and there will therefore be a need to address the pathologies of executive federalism. Under collaborative federalism, however, this need becomes particularly pronounced as it entails an intensification of the executive-to-executive process.

In the next section we examine the theory and practice of executive federalism in more detail, and attempt to map the transition from co-operative to collaborative federalism. In the following section, we demonstrate that the traditional institutions of the federation are less capable on balance of resolving inter-regional disputes than they were in the past. We turn our attention next to the "peak institutions" of intergovernmental relations — the various forums in which first ministers meet — followed by an examination of the relationships between finance ministers and between line ministries, or what we term the "managing institutions" of intergovernmental relations. Then we examine the pressures created by global and continental integration and the deepening processes of urbanization in Canada. By way of conclusion, we suggest that executive federalism will remain a major feature of Canadian politics for the foreseeable future, but it is too early to determine if collaborative federalism will be fully embraced by the governments of Canada.

EXECUTIVE FEDERALISM IN THEORY AND PRACTICE

The economic havoc wreaked by the Depression demonstrated that modern economic issues transcend jurisdictional boundaries, and it compelled the two orders of government to provide social relief collaboratively. After World War II, government activity expanded, further blurring jurisdictional boundaries. As governments became increasingly interdependent, intergovernmental collaboration multiplied. "The result," as Richard Simeon explains, "is that the activities of each level of government often overlap; actions by one level can have major consequences for policies of the other. Even more important, it means that coherent policies in fields which cut across jurisdictions, or in which the policy instruments to deal with them are shared, can only be achieved if there is some degree of coordination, or of collaborative decision-making."[3] The fusion of executive and legislative power in Canada's system of parliamentary government meant that this intergovernmental process occurred at the executive level. Furthermore, as Ronald Watts has noted, "Of all the contemporary federations, Canada does the least institutionally to provide an adequate regional expression of views in national affairs through the structure of its central institutions."[4] In short, the combination of parliamentary government and federalism gave rise to what Donald Smiley termed "executive federalism."[5]

The development of executive federalism was characterized by (1) "the proliferation of federal-provincial conferences, committees, and liaison agencies, (2) the prominence of intergovernmental summitry as exemplified by the First Ministers' Conference, and (3) the concentration within each government of responsibility for intergovernmental relations in the hands of coordinating agencies and specialists."[6] For Watts, the importance of executive federalism stemmed not so much from the frequency of intergovernmental meetings but from the substantive decisions made by executives in these forums, including major social policies, economic and trade arrangements, and "the revision of the constitution itself."[7]

The processes of executive federalism also led to the creation of a welfare state. This was an extraordinary accomplishment. But there were also side effects that attracted criticism. Donald Smiley offered one of the most damning indictments:

> My charges against executive federalism are these: First, it contributes to undue secrecy in the conduct of the public's business. Second, it contributes to an unduly low level of citizen-participation in public affairs. Third, it weakens and dilutes the accountability of governments to their respective legislatures and to the wider public. Fourth, it frustrates a number of matters of crucial public concern from coming on the public agenda and being dealt with by the public authorities. Fifth, it has been a contributing factor to the indiscriminate growth of government activities. Sixth, it leads to continuous and often unresolved conflicts among governments, conflicts which serve no purpose broader than the political and bureaucratic interests of those involved in them.[8]

Following Smiley's indictment, Canadian academics expended considerable intellectual energy imagining ways to address the deficiencies of executive federalism.

In the late 1970s, Richard Simeon divided the various proposals into three general categories.[9] The first aimed at the *disentanglement* of the two orders of government; the second was directed at reforming federal institutions to better represent provincial concerns and interests within federal institutions; and the third included various proposals to improve the machinery of intergovernmental relations. While disentanglement conformed to the classical idea of federalism that had been advanced by the Judicial Committee of the Privy Council (JCPC), the benefits of disentanglement were thought to be limited because so many issues spilled over jurisdictional boundaries. Simeon thus concluded that the only avenues of reform were the reform of federal institutions and the improvement of the machinery of intergovernmental relations — avenues that were not mutually exclusive.

For much of the Canadian academic community, reforming federal institutions to better address provincial concerns was the preferred option.[10] The idea was to transform Canada from a pattern of *inter*-state federalism to a model of *intra*-state federalism. A variety of suggestions were made to realize the goal of intra-state federalism, including the adoption of a system of proportional representation, electoral reform of one form or another, the relaxation of party discipline in the House of Commons, a reformed Senate, and greater provincial input into the selection of Supreme Court of Canada justices. At the same time, Smiley and Watts lamented that such proposals for intrastate federalism paid insufficient attention to reforming the Cabinet. "The Canadian system of government," they wrote, "is dominated by the executive. Hence, if Ottawa is unresponsive to regional interests and concerns, the cause of the unresponsiveness is likely to be related in larger part to the structure and operations of the executive itself. Therefore, any remedies not directly involving the executive are not likely to be successful."[11] However, most of the proposals for intra-state federalism have to date fallen by the wayside. Ronald Watts eventually concluded, "as long as Canada continues to combine parliamentary and federal institutions, it will be difficult to eliminate 'executive federalism' and therefore, the focus should be on harnessing 'executive federalism' in order to make it more workable."[12]

While proposals to better disentangle federal and provincial governments and to improve intra-state federalism were making little or no progress, political decision-makers turned by default (and perhaps preference) to the third option for reforming executive federalism: improving the machinery of intergovernmental relations. In this vein, Stefan Dupré made a crucially important point: "Whether executive federalism works involves not whether governments agree or disagree, but whether it provides a forum (or more accurately a set of forums) that is conducive, and perceived to be conducive, as the case may be, to negotiation, consultation, or simply an exchange of information."[13] For Dupré, the "workability" of executive federalism depended on the establishment of "trust ties" among intergovernmental decision-makers and officials.

Dupré identified two types of executive federalism — "federal-provincial functional relations" and "federal-provincial summit relations" — and he analyzed how these distinct relational processes worked with different types of Cabinet structure. Dupré considered the traditional brokerage Cabinet was an institution of a bygone era, and focused instead on the transition in the 1960s and 1970s from *departmentalized* Cabinets to *institutionalized* Cabinets. In the departmentalized Cabinet, "ministers are endowed with a substantial measure of decision-making autonomy which redounds to the benefit of their departmental clients and bureaucracies."[14] By contrast, Dupré continued, "In the 'institutionalized' Cabinet ... various combinations of formal committee structures, established central agencies, and budgeting and management techniques combine to emphasize shared knowledge, collegial decision-making, and the formulation of government-wide priorities and objectives."[15] In sum, Dupré concluded that intergovernmental relations worked more effectively in the era of departmentalized Cabinets, but he acknowledged that "in one form or another, institutionalized Cabinets are here to stay."[16] While executive federalism was likely to be less efficacious with institutionalized Cabinets, Dupré also concluded that, in general, functional relations operated more smoothly than summit relations. He concluded though that summit relations could be improved by regularizing First Ministers' Meetings. Dupré's sage advice has never been fully heeded. Brian Mulroney agreed to regular annual meetings for five years of his term in office but subsequently discontinued this experiment. As for Paul Martin, before he assumed the office of Prime Minister at the end of 2003, he indicated that he was open to the idea of regular and frequent meetings of first ministers. Whether this turns out to be the case remains, of course, to be seen.

While the arrangements among first ministers have remained infrequent and *ad hoc*, some of the other relationships among federal, provincial, and territorial ministers have become somewhat more regular and institutionalized. In the social policy field, internal trade, and the environment, for example, framework agreements have been negotiated that appear to envisage a more *collaborative* relationship among governments than has been the recent experience at the level of first ministers. The Social Union Framework Agreement signed by the federal government, all the provinces (except Quebec), and the two territories in February 1999, may be regarded as a kind of "constitution" for collaborative federalism. Among other things, it was intended to define the relationship between the two orders of government in certain policy areas by providing a framework for joint decision-making and dispute resolution. It also made an explicit commitment to citizen engagement. While the agreement has not yet lived up to the expectations of many, following the three-year review of SUFA in June 2003, the Federal-Provincial-Territorial Ministerial Council on Social Policy Renewal concluded that "overall ... SUFA continues to provide a useful framework for governments in their efforts to respond to the social policy needs of Canadians,"[17] although the council also recognized "the importance of continuous improvement in intergovernmental consultations."[18] SUFA, however, is only a step toward collaborative federalism.

How does *collaborative* federalism differ from the *co-operative* federalism of the 1950s and 1960s? Co-operative and collaborative federalism both represent relationships of interdependence. In practice, co-operative federalism was characterized by a considerable degree of political and financial leadership by the federal government. Co-operative federalism thus entailed a degree of hierarchy. Collaborative federalism, by contrast, is supposed to reflect a situation of relative parity between the federal and provincial governments. Does Canada now have federalism based on equality and interdependence among governments? In reality, no federation is likely to conform strictly to any one model of federalism. At any given time in Canada, there may be elements of co-operative federalism, collaborative federalism, and classical federalism, and perhaps others types as well. Nonetheless, as will be discussed in later sections, we believe that the bulk of the evidence supports the idea that there has in fact been at least a modest shift toward a more interdependent, less hierarchical and thus more collaborative federation.

While the concept of collaborative federalism may capture the general tenor of intergovernmental relations of the 1990s and early 2000s, it should not be taken to mean that interdependence among governments is everywhere growing. Nor should it be taken to suggest that more collaboration is always better. In fact, the idea of disentangling program responsibilities within an interdependent policy framework is a step forward in answering the criticism that executive federalism confuses accountability relationships between governments and the citizenry. While key provisions of SUFA attempt to address the issues of accountability and the role of citizens in social union governance as a way of responding to the shortcomings in executive federalism noted above, actual progress in implementing these provisions has been slow. A key consideration here is that the solutions entailed in SUFA involve an intense set of interdependent relationships among governments, as well as between governments and citizens. Therefore, if the governments of Canada are committed to pursuing this style of federalism, they will need to further develop the institutions of executive federalism and intergovernmental relations.

TRADITIONAL INSTITUTIONS OF THE FEDERATION

The traditional institutions include Parliament, Cabinet, political parties, and the Supreme Court. The historical failure of Parliament to provide a forum for inter-regional bargaining is the most conspicuous reason for the heavy reliance on executive interaction in Canadian federalism. Parliament continues to play a negligible role in intergovernmental relations, although it is possible that incremental reforms could enhance Parliament's stature in this area. Historically, political parties provided an institutional forum for inter-regional bargaining but, with the decline of brokerage politics over the past 30 years, they have been less able to fulfill this function. The Cabinet remains by far the most important of the traditional institution in Canadian federalism, but the shift toward prime ministerial government has been detrimental to federal-provincial relations. The Supreme Court can only react to the cases brought to its docket. Its impact is thus indirect. With its recent willingness to interpret intergovernmental agreements, however, the Supreme Court has provided governments and citizens an avenue of redress in the intergovernmental process. In sum, the traditional institutions of the federation, aside possibly from the Supreme Court, appear to have become even less effective in managing intergovernmental relations.

PARLIAMENT

In systems of responsible government, citizens should in principle be able to turn to Parliament either for political leadership, or at least oversight of the executive. In the world of Canadian intergovernmental relations, however, the political executive commandeers all of the initiative, while Parliament plays a negligible supporting role except in cases of large-scale constitutional reform. One major explanation for this state of affairs in Canada is the deficient role played by the Senate. It does not adequately represent regional interests, and it does not function as a chamber for the resolution of intergovernmental conflict. The House of Commons has also proven to be an ineffective institution in federal and intergovernmental matters. The first-past-the-post electoral system, adherence to strict party discipline, and the dominance of a powerful executive have all served to prevent the House from becoming an effective forum for inter-regional bargaining.

Proposals to reform Parliament are frequent and tend to be ignored by prime ministers. In his contribution to this volume C.E.S. Franks categorizes the reforms as either "incremental" in nature or "fundamental." Fundamental reforms would include the adoption of a proportional representation system, Senate reform and the introduction of a new level of "basic law" along the lines contemplated in the Charlottetown Accord.[19] Incremental reforms would include free votes in the House of Commons, the creation of new legislative committees in the Commons, including one on intergovernmental relations and another on human rights, as well as special provisions for double-majorities on language and cultural matters. (Intergovernmental legislative committees could also be established in the provinces.)

While Franks speculates that incremental reforms may not be sufficient to change Canada's executive-dominated Parliament, we lean to the view that the creation of legislative committees for intergovernmental relations could be beneficial, and relatively easy to adopt. The establishment of such committees would require the support of political executives. This, admittedly, could be a stumbling block to their realization, but it could also benefit the executive. The governments of Canada have made a commitment to the principle of citizen engagement, for example in the Social Union Framework Agreement, but it has proven difficult to realize in practice. We believe, however, that citizen participation could be effectively channelled through legislative committees in Ottawa and the provincial capitals. In this fashion, governments could realize their commitment to engage citizens, and citizens would have a transparent vehicle for ensuring that their views were taken into account by legislatures and governments in the processes of executive federalism. This was a suggestion that came up during the SUFA review and it is emphasized by David Cameron in this volume.[20] This modest proposal would address some of the concerns raised by Smiley more than 20 years ago, and it would be more consistent with the logic of Canada's parliamentary system of government.

PARTIES

In Canada, inter-regional accommodation was historically sought through the politics of "brokerage parties." For this model to work effectively, each of the major parties contesting federal elections was expected to aggregate demands in such a way as to satisfy the major regions of the country. Originally, the close working relationship between the federal and provincial wings of each party facilitated this inter-regional brokerage. The post-World War II version of the brokerage model, however, began to disintegrate in the 1960s. First, the federal and provincial wings of the Liberal and Conservative parties separated, except in Atlantic Canada.[21] Second, the federal Liberal and Progressive Conservative parties became less able or willing to engage in brokerage. This situation was exacerbated with the virtual collapse of the Progressive Conservatives in 1993 and the rise of the regionally based Reform Party and Bloc Québécois. In the process, the Canadian party system became regionalized, with no party having extensive roots in all regions.[22]

The brokerage model is not the only and perhaps not the best way for political parties to accommodate inter-regional differences. In contrast to the majoritarian winner-take-all character of the Anglo-American democracies (except New Zealand), Arend Lijphart has described the more consensual style of politics in the consociational democracies of western Europe.[23] In the consociational model, relatively segmented parties aggregate the interests and demands of their constituents. After the election — typically with a proportional representation electoral system — the various parties seek to reach accommodation in the legislature through coalition formation. In consociational democracies, as R. Kenneth Carty and Steven B. Wolinetz note in their chapter, inter-regional accommodation becomes the responsibility of the party system rather than individual parties.

With the decline of brokerage politics, there seems to have been an unstated assumption that parties no longer play a role in inter-regional and intergovernmental bargaining in Canada. Carty and Wolinetz argue, however, that a unique form of inter-party coalition politics occurs in the institutions of intergovernmental relations rather than in Parliament. This game of inter-party coalition politics differs from legislative coalition politics in some important respects, but the fact remains that in the peak institutions of intergovernmental relations, the primary actors are leaders of both a political party and a government. The leaders are thus presumably mindful of their party's interests, as well as governmental business. Carty and Wolinetz's coalitional metaphor provides a new way to understand the dynamic of intergovernmental negotiations. In the absence of brokerage parties and inter-party legislative coalitions, the party governments of Canada have of necessity played a game of intergovernmental coalition politics, but it is a game that does not appear to be as effective for managing the federation as either brokerage parties or coalition governments.

CABINET

As mentioned in the previous section, the structure and operation of the Cabinet are key variables influencing the processes of executive federalism. Donald Savoie has noted that "prime ministers are completely free to add, delete, and adjust the machinery of government at any time and as they see fit. In contrast, ministers, even the most powerful ones, do not have the authority to adjust even their own departmental mandate."[24] It would seem, however, that Canadian prime ministers have not designed their Cabinets to facilitate the processes of intergovernmental relations. Put another way, they have designed their Cabinets to attend to the demands of governing from the centre. Thus, changes to the mode of Cabinet operation over the past 30 years have done nothing to improve federal-provincial relations.

Since 1867, the federal Cabinet in Canada has not only constituted the political executive, it has played a special role in representing the federation's regional, linguistic, and cultural diversity. Historically, at least, regional interests were mediated by *regional ministers*. Herman Bakvis writes, "Regional ministers have at varying times been responsible for the party organization in their province or sub-region with a province; dispensing patronage; influencing expenditures affecting their region made by their own as well as by other departments; and injecting regional dimensions into the delivery of departmental programs."[25] While Bakvis believes that the roles of the historical regional minister have been exaggerated and the modern regional minister underestimated, he acknowledges that "contemporary regional ministers do have a lower profile than their predecessors."[26] The relative decline of the regional minister has served to diminish the autonomy of individual Cabinet ministers while further empowering the prime minister.

Savoie takes the argument a step further. Over the past 20 years, he argues, effective power has rested "with the prime minister and a small group of carefully selected courtiers," mainly in the Prime Minister's Office (PMO), but also with pollsters and select members of the Cabinet.[27] In short, he asserts, the "Cabinet has joined Parliament as an institution being bypassed."[28] For Savoie, the institutionalized Cabinet was a stepping stone from the departmentalized Cabinet to prime ministerial government.[29] In the process, Peter Aucoin declares, the Cabinet moved from a "conglomerate mode" of decision-making under Pierre Trudeau and Brian Mulroney to a "command mode" of decision-making under Jean Chrétien.[30]

When Chrétien took power he indicated that he would like to re-establish the departmentalized Cabinet,[31] but Savoie reports that Chrétien "left the machinery of government at the centre intact and as large and as powerful as it was under Trudeau and Mulroney."[32] It is not clear why Chrétien shifted from an apparent desire for independent ministers to a highly hierarchical Cabinet organization. He may have been compelled by the pressure of deficit politics to adopt a top-down management structure. Savoie has argued that the election of the Parti Québécois in 1976 served to concentrate power in the prime minister's office, and the close call of the 1995 referendum may also have prompted Chrétien to maintain a tight rein on his Cabinet.[33]

While ministers in the federal Cabinet were unable to stop the growing concentration of Cabinet power in the hands of the prime minister, provincial and territorial premiers have proven less pliable. In fact, they have used the vehicle of the Annual Premiers' Conference to attempt to assert a measure of national leadership of their own. An ongoing and unconstructive tension in relations among first ministers has thus emerged in recent years. Some of the tension is clearly related to clashes of personality (for example between Jean Chrétien and Ontario's former premier Mike Harris). Much of it was also a function of almost a quarter century of fiscal restraint and the financial hardships this created for all governments. We thus do not believe that the growing concentration of Cabinet power in the office of the prime minister is the only cause of the tense and often ineffectual relations among first ministers, or even its main cause. But the shift from departmental to institutional to prime ministerial Cabinet has doubtless exacerbated intergovernmental tension and served to weaken the Cabinet as a mirror of Canada's regional diversity.

THE SUPREME COURT

The Supreme Court of Canada has also been deeply involved in intergovernmental relations.[34] The Supreme Court was created by statute in 1875, but the

JCPC in London remained the court of final appeal until 1949. The Supreme Court's initial inclination to give wide latitude to federal powers was quickly curbed by the JCPC. John Saywell argues that when appeals to the JCPC ended, the Supreme Court again demonstrated a willingness to broaden the scope of federal jurisdiction.[35] In short, Saywell writes, the Supreme Court has been "innovative in finding new uses for the major sources of federal jurisdiction: the criminal law, trade and commerce, and the residual clause."[36] The Supreme Court also gave some credence to the federal spending power, although it has not made a definitive judgement on the subject.[37]

The Supreme Court's bias towards centralization in the 1950s and 1960s was troubling to francophone commentators in Quebec. "By the end of the century," Saywell writes, "the criticism had become more political and often focused on the legitimacy of the court itself."[38] The various reference cases surrounding patriation earned special condemnation from Quebec commentators. While sovereignists expressed a measure of satisfaction with the outcome of the secession reference case, the government of Quebec refused to participate in it, presumably because it believed the court was predisposed to supporting the federal government. The perception of bias has led Guy Laforest to state: "The Supreme Court of Canada should not have any authority on the territory of Quebec. Nor should Quebec accept the appointment procedures for justices of the Superior Court and the Court of Appeal provided for in the *British North America Act*."[39] While the vast majority of Quebecers support the values embedded in the *Charter of Rights and Freedoms*, many Quebecers also believed that its introduction would further consolidate the centralist bias of the Supreme Court. Their worst fears were perhaps realized when the Supreme Court struck down the infamous sign law just before the torturous conclusion of the Meech Lake process.

The centralizing potential of the Charter was recognized by English-Canadian commentators as well.[40] In *Canada: The State of the Federation 1994*, however, Janet Hiebert argued that those who posited the centralizing thesis overlooked the "potential for a federalist interpretation of the Charter,"[41] although she cautioned against coming to a definitive conclusion "in the absence of more jurisprudence."[42] In this volume of *Canada: The State of the Federation*, with the benefit of more jurisprudence, James Kelly provides empirical and theoretical support to Hiebert's counter-thesis. Kelly accepts Saywell's contention that the Supreme Court displayed a centralist bias in its interpretation of the division of powers, but he argues that "the trend towards centralization did not continue under the Charter, as the Supreme Court has guarded the federal character of Canada in its Charter jurisprudence and has developed an approach that advances provincial autonomy."

Unlike Parliament, the Supreme Court has been an active player in Canadian intergovernmental relations. In contrast to the proactive role played by the executive in shaping the game of intergovernmental relations, however, the court has been more reactive. It responds to the cases brought to its docket and, for better or worse, it usually provides a definitive answer to these conflicts. The reference cases on patriation and secession in effect established extra-constitutional parameters for the governance of the federation. Importantly, Johanne Poirier suggests in her chapter in this volume that the Supreme Court has demonstrated a willingness to interpret intergovernmental agreements. The *Canada Assistance Plan Reference* case in 1991 illustrates the potential and pitfalls of interpreting intergovernmental agreements. The court ruled that Parliament was free to alter its financial commitments to the provinces, but Poirier notes that "[t]he crucial financing clause was not contained in the intergovernmental agreement but in a federal Act." She maintains that the court did not make a general statement that no intergovernmental agreement could ever be legally binding. Instead, Poirier reminds us that intergovernmental agreements are generally concluded among political executives and that, depending on circumstances, they can be binding on executives unless altered by the legislative branch of government. Of course, executives have the considerable influence over the legislative branch of government, but the point is that executives may have to employ statutory means to overcome commitments made in intergovernmental agreements. Poirier also argues that it is open to the courts to make intergovernmental agreements legally more robust by giving more weight to one or more of the following: the federal principle; the idea of legitimate expectations; and/or the idea that constitutional conventions have emerged around intergovernmental agreements. To date, the court has indicated that only the division of powers and the Charter limits the sovereignty of parliament and legislatures. Nonetheless she also notes that the Supreme Court has admitted that citizens may also resort to the legal system to realize claims flowing from intergovernmental agreements.[43]

In effect, Poirier believes that intergovernmental agreements are not only an expedient instrument for intergovernmental collaboration but that they also assume a number of "para-constitutional functions." She writes, "[i]n an age of 'Charter citizens' who have learned to appeal to judges to protect their rights, it seems plausible that citizens and public interest groups are increasingly going to turn to courts as a means of controlling the ever-growing impact of executive federalism. Whether the parties to an agreement want it or not, and whether judges themselves welcome the trend or not, intergovernmental agreements are finding their way to court."

PEAK INTERGOVERNMENTAL INSTITUTIONS

As the traditional institutions of the federation — especially political parties and Parliament — have proven to be ineffective sites for intergovernmental relations, a number of non-constitutional institutions have arisen to manage the processes of intergovernmental affairs. Two intergovernmental institutions in particular stand out — the First Ministers' Conference (FMC) and the Annual Premiers' Conference (APC). As they are the drivers of intergovernmental relations in Canada, we describe the FMC and APC as *peak institutions*. The Western Premiers' Conference and the Council of Atlantic Premiers may be viewed as second-tier peak institutions. While the regional meetings of premiers and the APC have become regular and institutionalized, the FMC is irregular and non-institutionalized. In our view, the under-institutionalized character of the FMC has led to weak overarching coordination in Canadian intergovernmental affairs.

Neither the FMC nor the APC is provided for in the constitution or in legislation.[44] They thus lack the formal authority of a legislature or executive council (Cabinet). Their operating protocols and procedures are governed entirely by convention. Participation is not mandatory. They cannot force individual governments to abide by their decisions. Decisions are by consensus of the participants. Despite all of these limitations, the primary peak institutions have been central to determining the direction of Canadian federalism in a wide variety of policy areas, including federal-provincial financial relations, trade, health care and social policy. The FMC and the APC are in some respects organically linked as the decisions of each can affect the agenda of the other.

Martin Papillon and Richard Simeon view the FMC as "the weakest link" in the chain of intergovernmental institutions. By convention, the convening of an FMC is the prerogative of the prime minister. Under Prime Minister Jean Chrétien, the meetings became *ad hoc* events tending to focus on single policy issues, such as health care policy and its financing, as opposed to more wide-ranging discussions on the state of the economy or Canada's social policies. Part of the relationship also proceeded through informal discussion during Team Canada missions. When one considers an institution that is almost 100 years old, one would expect that its institutional framework would have become more fully developed or formalized. But this is not the case.

The APC's appearance on the intergovernmental scene is more recent. The first APC was convened in 1960, and premiers have met at least once a year since then. If the FMC has become less of a force in the intergovernmental relations arena over the last decade, the opposite is true of the APC. Initially the APC was primarily a social event with discussions focusing on matters of interprovincial concern. That has changed and, as Peter Meekison indicates elsewhere in this volume, the focus of the APC is now mainly on federal-provincial issues, with the provinces and territorial governments meeting to forge common positions. The preparation for the APC is considerable, with premiers receiving reports from a variety of ministerial committees. As a result of this extensive preparation by ministers and officials, there is continuity from one APC to the next. The same cannot be said for the FMC.

The Western and Atlantic Premiers' conferences are more recent institutions. The Western Premiers' Conference was a direct result of the 1973 Western Economic Opportunities Conference (WEOC) that brought the four western provinces together for a meeting with the federal government. The WPC has since become the principal intergovernmental mechanism for the western provinces to focus public attention on western concerns, and, with the addition of the three territories, northern concerns, and occasionally grievances in relation to the federal government. The WPC meets shortly before the APC each year. Its positions are often then incorporated into the APC agenda and supported in the APC outcomes.

The Council of Maritime Premiers was created in the early 1970s and the wider Council of Atlantic Premiers came into being in 2000. The latter council's objectives, structure and operating principles are set out in a Memorandum of Understanding on Atlantic Canada Co-operation.[45] The first objective in its mandate is the "development of common Atlantic Canada positions for Annual Premiers' Conferences and First Ministers' Conferences."[46] There are strong parallels between the Council of Atlantic Premiers and the Western Premiers' Conference, both in terms of objectives and processes. There are also some differences. The Council of Atlantic Premiers meets twice annually whereas the WPC meets only once. Each premier thus serves as chair for six months as opposed to a year for the WPC. The Atlantic council uses the Secretariat of the Council of Maritime Premiers for logistical support, whereas the secretariat function for the WPC is handled by the host province.

When considering the regional characteristics of the federation, the position of Ontario and Quebec are relevant because both can be viewed as regions as well as provinces. Jacques Bourgault's chapter gives an overview of Quebec's influence on intergovernmental relations since the 1960s. When the Parti Québécois was in power, Quebec's considerable influence was diminished by virtue of it secessionist agenda. The election of the Liberals in 2003 under federalist Premier Jean Charest has given Quebec the opportunity to again provide leadership in intergovernmental relations. This was demonstrated at the 2003 APC, when the premiers endorsed Quebec's proposal to establish a Council of the Federation. The October 2003 election of Dalton McGuinty's Liberals in Ontario also opens the door for stronger ties between Quebec and Ontario, a possibility underscored by the meeting between the two leaders before Premier McGuinty was sworn in.[47] Should the two provinces form their own "peak" institution, however informal, it could become a formidable force in intergovernmental relations.

In their efforts to ensure a strategic approach to managing domestic intergovernmental relations, first ministers are supported by intergovernmental affairs ministries, as detailed by Inwood *et al.* in their contribution to this volume. At the federal level, the intergovernmental ministry is located within the Privy Council Office, and in some provinces the intergovernmental ministers are similarly located within the premiers' or Cabinet office. It is not unusual for a first minister to retain the portfolio himself or herself. And even when the first minister does not do so, it is normal that he or she be very "hands on" with key files. Intergovernmental ministers and their deputies are typically the key players in helping to prepare first ministers for meetings of the peak intergovernmental institutions.

While the provinces are collectively coordinated by the APC, as well as regionally organized through the WPC and the Council of Atlantic Premiers, the FMC remains stubbornly resistant to institutionalization, notwithstanding numerous demands to the contrary. Simeon and Papillon note that calls for the regularization of First Ministers' Meetings, either in the constitution or as some kind of permanent institution complete with a secretariat, date to at least the report of the Rowell-Sirois Commission in 1940.[48] Since the mid-1970s, the APC has made repeated requests for a regular annual First Ministers' Conference, whether entrenched in the constitution or otherwise. The most recent example was the request made at the 2003 APC.

The APC, already much more institutionalized than the FMC, is in the process of undergoing what could turn out to be a considerable transformation. At the July 2003 APC, the premiers accepted the Government of Quebec's proposal to create a Council of the Federation composed of provincial and territorial leaders.[49] The council's objectives are to "address present and future challenges facing the federation in order to better meet the needs of Canadians."[50] It is to do this, *inter alia*, by "strengthening interprovincial-territorial co-operation" and "exercising leadership on national issues of importance to provinces and territories." The council is to meet at least twice annually. It is to be supported by a steering committee of deputy ministers and a secretariat. The Council of the Federation is in effect the institutionalization of the Annual Premiers' Conference.

As far as the premiers are concerned, the Council of the Federation is only the first part of a five-point plan "to revitalize the Canadian federation and to build a new era of constructive and co-operative federalism." The whole plan includes:

1.   Agreement in principle to create a Council of the Federation,

2.   Annual First Ministers' Meetings,

3.   Provincial/territorial consultation on federal appointments,

4.   Devolution of powers to the territories, and

5.   Establishment of federal-provincial-territorial protocols of conduct.[51]

As it stands, the Council of the Federation does not require any federal response. Implementation of the other four points, however, is dependent on the federal government's agreement and, without that agreement, intergovernmental relations in Canada will likely remain *ad hoc* and weakly coordinated from the top.

MANAGING INSTITUTIONS OF INTERGOVERNMENTAL RELATIONS

The day-to-day workings of the federation are managed by councils, conferences, and forums (the labels vary) of federal, provincial, and territorial line ministers and ministries. These intergovernmental relationships are not, however, free-standing. In principle, they are subject to the oversight of first ministers and, on occasion, intergovernmental ministers, although in practice this oversight is often difficult to achieve. They are also affected by the fiscal constraints imposed by finance ministers. As such, the relationship between federal and provincial (including territorial) finance ministers is critical. The bulk of intergovernmental collaboration, however, occurs between various line ministries. Over the last quarter century, interdependence among finance ministries has declined, partly as a result of fiscal retrenchment by Ottawa, but also due to the desire of some provincial finance ministries to enhance their autonomy. There does not, however, appear to be a similar trend among line ministries, which often display a fairly high degree of interdependence and collaboration. At this time, it is difficult to know if this co-operation between line ministries is sustainable given the increasing autonomy among finance ministries and the weak coordination in the peak institutions noted above.

FEDERAL-PROVINCIAL-TERRITORIAL FINANCE MINISTERS AND MINISTRIES

Apart from the constitutional distribution of legislative and revenue raising powers between orders of government, nothing is more basic to the functioning of the federation than the fiscal arrangements between governments, as Peter Leslie *et al.* make clear in their contribution to this volume. Like first ministers, finance ministers have no legally based institution that helps to guide their affairs. There is no constitutional provision that requires them to meet regularly. Nor are there formal rules for determining how decisions are to be taken, how disputes are to be settled, how agendas are to be determined, and decisions implemented. In contrast to first ministers, finance ministers work in relative secrecy. They do not announce their agendas in advance and they do not usually issue press communiqués when their meetings are over, although they typically do have some kind of media conference. Meetings are always chaired by the federal finance minister. Federal finance provides secretariat services for these meetings instead of relying on the Canadian Intergovernmental Conference Secretariat (which provides support for first ministers and line ministers).

Historically, Canadian finance ministers have addressed three areas of common concern: macro-economic management, revenue-raising, and expenditure control. The time devoted to macro-economic coordination has declined over the last couple of decades. This may be partly due to the reduced emphasis on counter-cyclical stabilization policy and partly because fiscal pressures simply took priority. The coordination of revenue-raising activities occupies a larger place in the work of finance ministries. Federal and provincial finance ministers have recognized that a lack of coordination raises the dangers of economically inefficient taxation. The result has been a set of formal and informal understandings among finance ministries, especially in relation to income tax collection, and to a much lesser degree, in relation to value added and sales taxes. There is little agreement, however, on the way revenues should be shared between federal and provincial governments, with provinces often arguing that Ottawa occupies too much tax room and that a larger share of government revenues should be in their hands. Some provinces demand that Ottawa transfer additional tax room, whereas others would prefer higher cash payments. Notwithstanding these differences, the level of revenue-raising coordination is significant, especially considering the constitutional autonomy of the two orders of government.

As for expenditure management, especially from the mid-1950s to the mid-1970s, there was considerable federal-provincial interdependence with the federal government frequently but not always demonstrating financial leadership through the spending power. Through intergovernmental agreements, Ottawa transferred cash or tax points to the provinces to launch new programs in a variety of areas from hospital and medical insurance to social assistance, post-secondary education, and social housing. For the most part, these agreements required the federal government to compensate provinces for half the operating costs of these new programs provided that certain conditions were met. In the years leading up to the federal Established Programs Financing legislation of 1977, federal cash transfers constituted around 25 percent of provincial revenues. Since 1977, there has been a trend away from conditional shared-cost programs to large block-funded programs. In relative terms, federal cash transfers to provinces have declined substantially and are now equal to around 15 percent of provincial revenues. The most controversial reductions have been associated with the previously large shared-cost programs. Equalization transfers have also fallen as a share of Gross Domestic Product (GDP).

From the 1960s to the 1990s, an informal but effective system of budget coordination developed between federal and provincial governments. Mechanically, it entailed federal, provincial, and territorial ministers of finance meeting in the autumn to discuss budgets for the next year, the federal government tabling its budget in February, with the provinces announcing their budgets in the weeks and months following Ottawa's. Since provincial revenues are affected by what is in the federal budget, this coordinated approach made it possible for provincial ministers to plan their budgets accordingly. Unfortunately, this useful if informal budget planning process has weakened in the last few years. Other elements of coordination have also weakened. In the quarter century following World War II, the fiscal arrangements established every five years tended to last the full time, but from 1982 forward the federal government has often reduced the level of fiscal transfers to the provinces before the end of the five-year framework. These unilateral actions reflected hard fiscal times at the federal level.

From this analysis the following picture emerges: little coordination in macro-economic planning and less than was the case in the 1960s and 1970s; reduced budget coordination; differing degrees of coordination in the taxation area, varying according to the tax base and province, with a trend toward greater provincial autonomy; ongoing and often acrimonious negotiation about the effective allocation of tax room; and a significantly reduced interdependence in expenditure programs. Thus, there remains a mix of autonomy and interdependence on financial and related program matters, but with a trend toward autonomy. If we are correct that the relationship among finance ministries is becoming more independent, then we would expect to see relatively little institutional development surrounding these ministers. That in fact is the case.

For those who consider that the autonomy of finance ministries is a good thing since it allows for tax competition and promotes fiscal responsibility, the recent trends in the relationship among finance ministers will be welcome. And the modest institutional support that accompanies this trend will also appear healthy. Conversely, for those who attach more weight to a substantial measure of joint planning and coordination, the opposite conclusion will emerge. Whatever one's view, however, the recent trend among finance ministries is to emphasize the autonomy of the two orders of government. In a world of growing economic and financial interdependence internationally, we wonder if this trend is sustainable domestically.

LINE MINISTRIES

Line ministries conduct the greatest part of the relationship between federal and provincial governments. There is a wide range of federal-provincial and interprovincial committees of ministers and officials, and the frequency of interactions is high. Intergovernmental relations are fairly continuous on such matters as health, social services and benefits, environment, transport, justice, trade and economic development, natural resources, and housing, to list but a few. The institutional support for these intergovernmental relationships has no basis in the constitution or even in statute law (with the rarest of exceptions).[52] In all cases, the institutional relationship is through some form of executive-to-executive interaction. The intergovernmental line institutions, in contrast to meetings of first ministers and finance ministers, are typically cochaired by a federal and provincial minister (with the choice of provincial minister rotating from year to year). In most cases, the decision rule is consensus. Similarly, there are no legally binding mechanisms for resolving disputes, although there are political understandings about how governments will resolve disputes relating to the *Canada Health Act*.[53] Whenever there are substantial federal cash transfers associated with the relationship among line ministries, however, the finance ministries become involved. And the relationship is then likely to exhibit an element of federal unilateralism. In general, there is little effective role for Members of Parliament or provincial legislatures before key decisions are taken.

Among the various line ministries, there is much diversity in the extent to which they publicize their work (for example, the nature and extent of the website they provide), the frequency of meetings (which can vary from several per year to one every three to five years), the resources they devote to a secretariat, and the range of activities that they deal with. These practices raise all the questions about accountability traditionally associated with executive federalism, although there are some recent cases of federal and provincial line ministries making efforts to clarifying who does what in complex intergovernmental relationships.[54] This diversity is reflected as well in Julie Simmons' chapter in this volume.

The nature of the relationship between federal and provincial governments has been analyzed using the independence-interdependence and hierarchical-parity criteria noted earlier for a sample of 19 programs and policies in the social policy area.[55] For this limited sample, there was an equal split between independent and interdependent relationships. Where there was interdependence, more often than not this was associated with the use of the federal spending power in areas of provincial legislative competence. Perhaps more surprising, the number of cases in which the federal government was seeing to be acting in a hierarchical (or unilateral) fashion was small — just three out of 19 programs. And two of the three hierarchical cases were related to fiscal arbitrariness by the federal government. The non-hierarchical relationships are, by and large, not controversial. No doubt for that reason they receive relatively little public debate and press or parliamentary coverage.

The fact that much of the federal-provincial relationship is conducted in an interdependent and non-hierarchical fashion does not, however, imply an absence of conflict. To the contrary, where there is considerable interdependence there is likely to be conflict as well as co-operation. Thus, we are not suggesting that non-hierarchical interdependent relations are warm and fuzzy. It is precisely because interdependence implies or often implies an intense relationship that it requires a lot of management. Differences cannot (by definition) be settled easily by one party imposing its will on the other. Moreover, the disagreements that do occur are not necessarily unhealthy for the state of the federation. To the contrary, they may represent an appropriate competition of ideas or interests. In any case, these are the kinds of situations where some measure of institutionalization in intergovernmental relations seems most necessary.

In sum, the relationships among line ministries may be moving in a different direction than those among finance ministries, especially with respect to the independence-interdependence axis. We suggested above that there is a trend for finance ministries to become more autonomous, whereas here we have observed that line ministries are often highly interdependent. In part, this difference may be because there is more scope for positive sum games in relations among line ministers than is the case among finance ministers. This tension between the way the institutions of line ministries and finance ministries operate has adverse implications for the effective workings of the federation.

GLOBALIZATION-URBANIZATION AND THE NEW INSTITUTIONS OF INTERGOVERNMENTAL RELATIONS IN CANADA

Intergovernmental relations in Canada have been dominated by the federal-provincial-territorial relationship. Under the constitution, the federal government was assigned responsibility for foreign relations, and provincial governments attend to municipal affairs. The twin processes of globalization and localization — what Tom Courchene terms *glocalization* — are blurring these jurisdictional boundaries.[56] Interdependence has not only thrust the federal and provincial governments together, it is compelling new relationships between the provinces and foreign governments (especially American states), as well as between federal and municipal governments.

The analytical framework used above for the discussion of federal-provincial relations can be applied to these emerging relationships. When these different orders of government operated independently of each other, there was little need for them to establish institutional decision-making forums. To the extent that they now wish to collaborate, especially as equal partners, it will become necessary to develop institutions to support their collaboration. One can only imagine that the sort of multi-centric collaboration that is now being contemplated, and that could involve federal, provincial, municipal, Aboriginal, and foreign governments, as well as transnational institutions, will be exponentially more complex than the relatively simple but nonetheless challenging federal-provincial interaction of the past 50 years.

At the sub-national level, the Government of Quebec engages in substantial international diplomacy, as detailed by Nelson Michaud in his contribution to this volume. Howard Leeson, also in this volume, outlines the ongoing transborder relationships between Saskatchewan and Alberta, on the one hand, and the neighbouring American states, on the other. Meekison notes that the WPC entered into an agreement with the Western Governors' Conference in 2000 which has led to annual meetings between representatives of the two organizations. The Eastern Canadian Premiers and New England Governors have held annual meetings since 1973, with the venue alternating between the two countries. The question of border security arising after 9-11 and the August 2003 power failure in the northeastern states and Ontario demonstrate the importance of and the need for effective transnational institutions and co-operation.

The general issue of federalism and international relations or the role and position of provinces in international relations is by no means a recent phenomenon. The 1937 decision of the JCPC in the *Labour Conventions Case* determined that the performance of treaties was subject to the distribution of legislative powers. The federal-provincial debate surrounding the Kyoto Accord indicates that the treaty process in Canada remains problematic. Additionally, continental economic integration has made provincial governments more conscious of economic competition from neighbouring US states, and possibly less concerned about economic ties among Canadian provinces.

This volume does not provide a definitive answer to the question of how international integration affects Canadian federalism. Two things, however, can be noted. The first is that it is increasingly accepted that there should be a provincial role in international negotiations that affect their jurisdictions. This is reflected in numerous ways, usually developed on *ad hoc* basis, but which nonetheless respond to functional requirements. This trend seems likely to continue. Second, the growing autonomy of provincial finance ministries may have some downsides for domestic intergovernmental relations, but it may enable the provinces to compete more effectively against neighbouring states. While there is evidence that transnational multi-level institutions are emerging, the challenge of multi-level governance is only just beginning to be addressed.[57]

As more than two-thirds of the Canadian population now lives in urban areas, the processes of urbanization might ultimately have a greater impact on intergovernmental relations than globalization. Under the constitution, municipal government is an area of exclusive provincial legislative jurisdiction. As a result, the provinces have consistently made it clear to the federal government that contacts with municipalities are to be made through the provincial governments, although some provinces hold to this position more strongly than others. At the 1978 APC the premiers argued that a federal presence in housing and urban affairs represented a duplication of government services.[58] The federal government subsequently closed its Ministry of State for Urban Affairs, and it has since had limited direct contact with municipalities, at least with respect to policy matters. In his contribution to this volume, Roger Gibbins thus describes the lack of formal relations between municipalities and the federal government as "the Missing Link." The federal government, however, is showing a renewed interest in municipal affairs, and municipalities seem receptive to a federal relationship.

Before becoming Prime Minister, Paul Martin indicated that cities would be one of his main priorities. In a speech to the Union of British Columbia Municipalities in the fall of 2003, Martin promised cities a share of the federal gasoline tax, and he indicated that he would like to meet annually with the Federation of Canadian Municipalities.[59] One need only reflect on the 1993 and subsequent federal infrastructure programs, federal responsibilities in the area of transportation and immigration, financial support for international sporting events, federal payments-in-lieu of municipal taxes, disposal of federal lands, economic development initiatives or public health concerns such as severe acute respiratory syndrome (SARS), to realize the very real role the federal government already plays in cities.

There are parallels between the federal interest in cities and the provincial interest in international affairs. The watertight compartment theory is increasingly difficult to use as a justification either for the exclusion of the provinces from the international arena or for the federal government from the municipal arena, if for no other reason than to recognize that jurisdictional boundaries are already blurred. Acknowledging this reality is one thing, but it is another to develop a set of rules where the different orders of government are comfortable with each other's presence and activities. Establishing these rules and creating the necessary institutions for managing these relationships will be one of the greatest challenges for Canadian intergovernmental relations in the coming decades.

IMPROVING EXECUTIVE FEDERALISM AND DEMOCRATIC ACCOUNTABILITY IN INTERGOVERNMENTAL RELATIONS

A number of conclusions emerge from this study. First, the realities of interdependence, which have grown more intense over the decades, create a high degree of intergovernmental interaction. Second, as the traditional institutions of the federation, especially political parties and Parliament, do not appear to be capable of handling intergovernmental relations, the burden of collaboration will continue to be borne by political executives. Third, the institutions and processes of executive federalism in Canada need to be more effective. In particular, there is a serious lack of coordination among first ministers at the peak of the intergovernmental hierarchy. This is reflected in what appears to be a structural tension between the high levels of interdependence among line ministries and growing independence among finance ministries, especially when fiscal wherewithal is often the lubricant greasing the relationship among line ministries. Fourth, globalization and urbanization are creating new pressures on governments, adding levels of governance to the interdependence that already exists. While the provinces would like to assume a greater role in Canada's external relations, the federal government is expressing a renewed interest in urban issues, which hitherto have been a provincial responsibility. Forging the appropriate institutions to accommodate these pressures will be one of the primary challenges for executive federalism in the

decades to come. Fifth, the creation of an intergovernmental affairs committee in Parliament and each legislature would hold the political executives more
accountable and facilitate a measure of citizen engagement in the world of
intergovernmental relations.[60] We also endorse David Cameron's proposal for
inter-legislative federalism. The Supreme Court's recent willingness to interpret intergovernmental agreements is a welcome development. We believe these
measures would rectify some of the more egregious pathologies of executive
federalism.

At this time, it is not possible to determine how fully the governments of
Canada are prepared to embrace collaborative federalism. The premiers often
talk the language of collaboration, but if we read between the lines, some of
them seem to be saying only that they need more fiscal resources from Ottawa. And the federal government at times appears to be seeking a level of
policy influence on provincial or joint programs that exceeds its fiscal contribution. With the collapse of the Meech Lake Accord, prime ministers became
reluctant to participate in regular annual meetings with the premiers. The government of Quebec opted not to endorse SUFA, which may be viewed as the
"constitution" of collaborative federalism. It is not necessary, nor even desirable, for governments to co-operate on everything. In practice, much of the
federation remains disentangled notwithstanding the rhetoric about interdependence. Independence is often a good thing — it keeps lines of accountability
simple and avoids the high transaction costs of intergovernmental relations,
and especially joint action. Our sense, however, is that interdependence is
growing simply because of the way the world is evolving. Whether we think
of financial flows, the spread of diseases, the World Wide Web, terrorism and
crime, internationally integrated production systems, popular culture, or a
myriad of other examples, connectedness across international borders is growing and spilling into domestic relationships. Thus, even if we adopt a healthy
dose of skepticism about the benefits of collaborative federalism, and the ease
with which it can be made to work, for better and worse, interdependence is
likely to remain with us, and will probably grow. But it would seem that the
various governments of Canada are almost as wary of institutionalizing collaborative federalism as they are of mega-constitutional change. Collaborative
federalism thus remains a work in progress.

As we complete this chapter in December 2003, we see encouraging signs.
The premiers have just put the finishing touches on their new Council of the
Federation, which they have projected "as part of their plan to play a leadership
role in revitalizing the Canadian federation and building a more constructive
and co-operative federal system."[61] Almost simultaneously, Paul Martin declared that "the federal government needs to work closely with provincial and
municipal governments," and he made it clear that "this cannot be done with
irregular or infrequent meetings that are treated more like ceasefire talks than
working sessions on Canadians' problems and aspirations. We need more

contact, more frequently, and less formally between all three orders of government in service of Canadians, who simply want to get things done."[62] He subsequently committed publicly "to hold annual First Ministers' Meetings."[63] It would seem that both orders of government recognize the need for collaboration, and in a way that at least begins to address the pathologies of executive federalism as practiced in the past. While these are positive signs, we should not assume that enhanced intergovernmental collaboration will lead automatically to a reduction in intergovernmental tension. Federal-provincial tension has been with us for a long time — a lot longer than any of us (including the senior editors of this volume) — and it will likely outlive us all (including the junior editor of this volume).

NOTES

1.   David Cameron and Richard Simeon, "Intergovernmental Relations in Canada: The Emergence of Collaborative Federalism," *Publius: The Journal of Federalism* 32, 2 (Spring 2002); Harvey Lazar, "The Federal Role in a New Social Union: Ottawa at a Crossroads," in *Canada: The State of the Federation 1997, Non-Constitutional Renewal* (Kingston: Institute of Intergovernmental Relations, 1998), p. 111.

2.   See, for example, the words of the preamble to the 1999 Social Union Framework Agreement, which reads: "The following agreement is based upon a mutual respect between orders of government and a willingness to work more closely together to meet the needs of Canadians."

3.   Richard Simeon, "Intergovernmental Relations in Canada Today: Summary of Discussion," in *Confrontation and Collaboration: Intergovernmental Relations in Canada Today*, ed. Richard Simeon (Toronto: Institute of Public Administration of Canada, 1979), p. 4.

4.   Ronald L. Watts, *Executive Federalism: A Comparative Analysis,* Research Paper No. 26 (Kingston: Institute of Intergovernmental Relations, 1989), p. 17.

5.   See the following works by Donald V. Smiley: *Constitutional Adaptation and Canadian Federalism Since 1945*, Documents of the Royal Commission on Bilingualism and Biculturalism # 4 (Ottawa: Queen's Printer, 1970); *Canada in Question: Federalism in the Seventies* (Toronto: McGraw Hill Ryerson, 1972); "An Outsider's Observations of Federal-Provincial Relations Among Consenting Adults," in *Confrontation and Collaboration: Intergovernmental Relations in Canada Today*, ed. Richard Simeon (Toronto: Institute of Public Administration of Canada, 1979).

6.   Watts, *Executive Federalism*, p. 4.

7.   Ibid., p. 4.

8.   Smiley, "An Outsider's Observations," pp.105-06.

9.   Simeon, "Intergovernmental Relations in Canada Today," p. 10ff.

10. See Donald V. Smiley and Ronald L. Watts, *Intrastate Federalism in Canada* (Toronto: University of Toronto Press, 1985), in co-operation with the Royal Commission on the Economic Union and Development Prospects for Canada. See also Alan Cairns, *From Interstate to Intrastate Federalism in Canada*, Institute Discussion Papers No. 5 (Kingston: Institute of Intergovernmental Relations, 1979).

11. Smiley and Watts, *Intrastate Federalism in Canada*, p. 63.

12. Watts, *Executive Federalism*, abstract.

13. J. Stephan Dupré, "Reflections on the Workability of Executive Federalism," in *Intergovernmental Relations,* ed. Richard Simeon (Toronto: University of Toronto Press in co-operation with the Royal Commission on the Economic Union and Development Prospects for Canada, 1985), p. 1.

14. Ibid., p. 4.

15. Ibid., p. 4.

16. Ibid., p. 23.

17. Federal/Provincial/Territorial Ministerial Council on Social Policy Renewal, "Introduction," *Three Year Review Social Union Framework Agreement,* June 2003, p. 3. See <www.sufa-review.ca>.

18. Ibid., p. 14.

19. According to Franks, basic law would be situated somewhere between an ordinary statute and constitutional entrenchment. Basic law would be easier to legislate than a constitutional amendment but would have more force and effect than an ordinary statute. A basic law to protect intergovernmental agreements from unilateral change was envisioned in the Charlottetown Accord (Section 26 of the Consensus Report).

20. See Federal/Provincial/Territorial Ministerial Council on Social Policy Renewal, "Social Union Framework Agreement Review, Web Site Submissions Summary," *Three Year Review Social Union Framework Agreement,* June 2003, pp. 8-9.

21. Rand Dyck, "Links Between Federal and Provincial Parties and Party Systems," in *Representation, Integration and Political Parties in Canada,* ed. H. Bakvis (Toronto: Dundurn, 1991).

22. It is much too soon to judge if the new Conservative Party is the beginning of a return to broader based brokerage-style parties.

23. Arend Lijphart, *Patterns of Democracy: Government Forms and Performance in Thirty-Six Countries* (New Haven: Yale University Press, 1999).

24. Donald Savoie, *Governing From the Centre: The Concentration of Power in Canadian Politics* (Toronto: University of Toronto Press, 1999), p. 43.

25. Herman Bakvis, *Regional Ministers: Power and Influence in the Canadian Cabinet* (Toronto: University of Toronto Press, 1991), p. 8.

26. Ibid., p. 285.

27. Donald Savoie, "The Rise of Court Government in Canada," *Canadian Journal of Political Science* 32, 4 (December 1999):635.

28. Ibid., p. 635.

29. Ibid., p. 636.

30. Peter Aucoin, "Prime Minister and Cabinet: Power at the Apex," in *Canadian Politics*, eds. James Bickerton and Alain-G. Gagnon, 3rd ed. (Peterborough: Broadview Press, 1999), pp. 119-126.

31. Savoie, *Governing from the Centre*, p. 325; and Aucoin, "Prime Minister and Cabinet," p. 126.

32. Savoie, *Governing from the Centre*, p. 325.

33. It is worth noting that, at the provincial level, power has also become very concentrated in premiers' offices.

34. The role of the Supreme Court in Canadian federalism has been vigorously debated. See Gerald Baier, "Judicial Review and Canadian Federalism," in *Canadian Federalism: Performance, Effectiveness, and Legitimacy*, eds. Herman Bakvis and Grace Skogstad (Toronto: Oxford University Press, 2002); John Saywell, *The Lawmakers: Judicial Power and the Shaping of Canadian Federalism* (Toronto: University of Toronto Press, 2002).

35. Saywell, *The Lawmakers*, p. 247.

36. Ibid. Both Peter Hogg and Peter Russell came to different conclusions when they examined this question. See Peter W. Hogg, "Is the Supreme Court of Canada Biased in Constitutional Cases?" *Canadian Bar Review* 67 (2001):721-39; Peter H. Russell, "The Supreme Court and Federal-Provincial Relations: The Political Use of Legal Resources," *Canadian Public Policy* 11 (1985):165-69.

37. Hamish Telford, "The Federal Spending Power in Canada: Nation-building or Nation-destroying?" *Publius: The Journal of Federalism* 33, 1 (Winter 2003).

38. Saywell, *The Lawmakers*, p. 301.

39. Guy Laforest, *Trudeau and the End of a Canadian Dream* (Montreal and Kingston: McGill-Queen's University Press, 1995), p. 191.

40. See Peter Russell, "Political Purposes of the Charter," *Canadian Bar Review* 6 (1983); Peter Hogg, "Federalism Fights the Charter," in *Federalism and Political Community: Essays in Honour of Donald Smiley*, eds. David P. Shugarman and Reg Whitaker (Toronto: Broadview Press, 1989); Alan C. Cairns, *The Charter Versus Federalism: The Dilemmas of Constitutional Reform* (Montreal: McGill-Queen's University Press, 1992).

41. Janet Hiebert, "The Charter and Federalism: Revisiting the Nation-Building Thesis," in *Canada: The State of the Federation 1994*, eds. Douglas M. Brown and Janet Hiebert (Kingston: Institute of Intergovernmental Relations, 1994), p. 156.

42. Ibid., p. 161.

43. See, *Finlay v. Canada (Minister of Finance)*, [1986] 2 S.C.R. 607, and *Finlay v. Canada (Minister of Finance)*, [1993] 1. S.C.R. 1080.

44. There are three exceptions to this comment, all to do with constitutional conferences. Section 37 of the *Constitution Act, 1982*, included a provision for a constitutional conference consisting of first ministers with respect to Aboriginal rights. Section 49 of the same Act provided for a constitutional conference to review the amending formula. Both provisions are now spent. A constitutional

amendment in 1983 includes a commitment to convene a constitutional conference to which Aboriginal representatives would be invited before an amendment
to Class 24 of Section 91 of the *Constitution Act, 1867,* or Sections 25, 35 and
35.1 of the *Constitution Act, 1982,* is made.

45. The Memorandum of Understanding on Atlantic Canada Co-operation was signed
    by all four premiers on 15 May 2000.

46. Ibid., p. 2.

47. Murray Campbell, "After years of trolling for attention, McGuinty's in the spot-
    light," *The Globe and Mail,* 21 October 2003, p. A13.

48. See *Report of the Royal Commission on Dominion-Provincial Relations* (Ot-
    tawa: Queen's Printer, Reprinted 1954), Book II, pp. 68-72, for the
    Commissioners' views. Among the numerous subsequent recommendations for
    the institutionalization of the FMC, the 1980 Lamontagne Report and the 1985
    Macdonald Royal Commission Report made particularly cogent proposals. See
    Standing Senate Committee on Legal and Constitutional Affairs, Report to the
    Senate of Canada, *Report on Certain Aspects of the Canadian Constitution* (Ot-
    tawa: Minister of Supply and Services Canada, November 1980); Royal Commission
    on the Economic Union and Development Prospects for Canada, *Report, Volume
    Three* (Ottawa: Minister of Supply and Services, 1985), p. 265. The section on the
    First Ministers' Conference is found in Volume Three, pp. 260-69.

49. Douglas Brown and France St-Hilaire, ed., *The Special Series on the Council of
    the Federation,* available at <www.iigr.ca>.

50. Foundation Agreement, 5 December 2003.

51. CICS News Release, "Premiers Announce Plan to Build a New Era of Construc-
    tive and Co-operative Federalism," 44th Annual Premiers' Conference,
    Charlottetown, 9-11 July 2003, Ref: 850-092/006. Note: the term for First Min-
    isters' Conference (FMC) was changed to First Ministers' Meetings (FMM).

52. One exception is the federal-provincial relationship for managing the Canada
    Pension Plan.

53. The dispute avoidance and dispute resolution commitments with respect to the
    Canada Health Act were spelled out in a letter dated 2 April 2002 from Anne
    McLellan, Minister of Health for Canada, to Gary Mar, Minister of Health and
    Wellness for Alberta. In this particular instance the other provinces and territo-
    ries had left the resolution of the issue to the federal and Alberta health ministers.
    Developing an effective dispute resolution mechanism was also one of the ob-
    jectives of the Social Union Framework Agreement.

54. This appears to be the case, for example, in relation to programs relative to
    children and in the area of labour market development.

55. Harvey Lazar, "Governance Aspects of the Social Union: A Sectoral Analysis,"
    June 2002. Available at <www.iigr.ca/publication_detail.php?publication=333>.

56. Thomas Courchene, "Glocalization: The Regional/International Interface," *Ca-
    nadian Journal of Regional Science* 18, 1 (Spring 1995); see also Hamish Telford,
    "Expanding the Partnership: The Proposed Council of the Federation and the

Challenge of Glocalization," in *Special Series on the Council of the Federation,* ed. Douglas Brown (Kingston: Institute of Intergovernmental Relations, 2003); <www.iigr.ca/pdf/publications/307_Expanding_the_Partnershi.pdf>.

57. For a broad comparative analysis of this issue, see Harvey Lazar, Hamish Telford, and Ronald L. Watts, eds., *The Impact of Global and Regional Integration on Federal Systems* (Kingston: Institute of Intergovernmental Relations, 2003).

58. The conference communiqué "Duplication of Government Services" can be found in Alberta Federal and Intergovernmental Affairs, *Sixth Annual Report to March 31, 1979* (Edmonton, 1979), p. 42.

59. Paul Martin, "Speech to the Union of British Columbia Municipalities," Vancouver, 25 September 2003. After becoming prime minister, he began to qualify that commitment.

60. Prime Minister Martin announced in late 2003 that there would be "an annual report to Parliament by the Minister of Intergovernmental Affairs on the state of federal/provincial/territorial relations, priorities, and initiatives." See <www.pm.gc.ca/eng/dem_reform.asp>.

61. Council of the Federation Founding Agreement, 5 December 2003, p. 1.

62. Paul Martin, "Making History: The Politics of Achievement," 14 November 2003, pp. 12-13. Available at <paulmartintimes.ca/the-campaign/politics-of-achievement_e.pdf>.

63. See <www.pm.gc.ca/eng/dem_reform.asp>.

II

Traditional Institutions

2

A Continuing Canadian Conundrum: The Role of Parliament in Questions of National Unity and the Processes of Amending the Constitution

C.E.S. Franks

Le rôle du Parlement canadien dans la plupart des domaines, incluant le processus législatif, les enquêtes de comités et les processus de responsabilité, n'a pas été particulièrement impressionnant ni important au cours de l'époque moderne. En effet, on peut argumenter de façon convaincante que malgré de nombreux efforts de réforme, ses pouvoirs et son influence ont diminué. La faiblesse qui limite son rôle et son influence dans d'autres domaines ont aussi limité son rôle en matière d'unité nationale et de réformes constitutionnelles. Des changements s'avèrent nécessaires pour qu'il puisse jouer un rôle plus efficace dans ces domaines importants et ailleurs. De petites réformes ont souvent été mises de l'avant, sans grand succès : vote libre accru, comités plus forts, influence supérieure sur le processus législatif, diminution du contrôle qu'ont les whips de parti et les leaders sur les membres. Des réformes plus fondamentales, comprenant un système de représentation proportionnel et une clarification du rôle du Sénat, offrent de meilleures chances de réussite. On peut faire davantage qu'on le croit généralement dans ces domaines sans s'aventurer dans le bourbier de l'amendement constitutionnel.

Discussing Parliament, national unity, and the constitution together highlights the fractured and complex nature of Canadian politics. At the national level the Canadian system blends, to the extent that oil and water can blend, two quite different and competing national forums for debate and decision-making: parliamentary government, and federal-provincial relations. The system of parliamentary government centralizes power in an executive, which is held responsible for the use of its immense powers by an elected House of Commons. The processes of federal-provincial relations diffuse power through, at a minimum, one national and ten provincial governments, with the possible addition of three territorial governments and other groups.

The constitutional amendments of 1981-82 were the product of federal-provincial negotiations, and especially meetings of the first ministers — that is the federal prime minister and the ten provincial premiers. The amending processes entrenched in the 1981-82 reforms are complex, and different amending procedures are required for different sections of the constitution. But all involve federal-provincial relations as a necessary part of the amending process. Amendments affecting some sections of the constitution such as the *Charter of Rights and Freedoms* must be agreed to by the prime minister and the first ministers of the provinces before the proposals can be approved by legislatures. It now appears that major constitutional changes require the consent of additional players, including the leaders of the three territories, Aboriginal leaders, and perhaps others before a final proposal is ready for ratification. A non-constitutional but apparently real requirement that major amendments must be consented to in a nationwide referendum further complicates the process. Parliament, in theory the central focus for national political debate and life, has only a small role in these constitution amending processes. The processes are so complex, and require the consent of so many diverse players, that comprehensive amendment does not appear to be a practical option for Canada at this time.

Most of the time, and for most issues, federal-provincial relations through executive federalism have worked well and produced important policies, coordination and consensus on a wide range of programs.[1] Modern Canadian social programs and economic development could not have been undertaken without this sort of instrument for intergovernmental relations. But in the crucial and highly symbolic area of constitutional reform, with the exception of 1981-82, executive federalism has not managed to create amendments acceptable to most players — and even the reforms of 1981-82 were not accepted by Quebec, the key player whose concerns reform was intended to assuage. Later efforts to win Quebec's acceptance of the constitution have not only been unsuccessful, but the failure of the two major efforts — Meech Lake in the 1980s and Charlottetown in the 1990s — created stresses that threatened national disintegration. Possibly the constitutional amending process has reached a dead end for the foreseeable future, at least for major revisions, those that P.H. Russell calls "mega constitutional politics ... concerned with reaching agreement on the identity and fundamental principles of the body politic."[2]

This impasse derives from many sources. Policies formulated and agreed to through executive federalism, including amendments to the constitution, come to Parliament like treaties to be ratified without the possibility of amendment, leaving Parliament in the role of bystander and kibitzer rather than lawmaker. Twenty-five years ago Donald Smiley observed that "the lack of Parliamentary involvement in federal-provincial relations is demonstrated not only in situations where it is restricted to the *post hoc* ratification of actions already agreed upon by the two levels of government, but also by governments bypassing their respective legislatures in announcing future policies."[3] If any-thing, the role of Parliament in federal-provincial relations has continued to diminish since then. Executive dominance in Parliament is closely related to the dominance of the executive in intergovernmental relations.[4] The one rein-forces the other, with the real opposition often being the other level of government, not the opposition within the federal or provincial legislatures themselves, thus reducing the importance of the assembly itself and debate within it. Executive federalism assumes that elite accommodation produces results acceptable to the electorate; in effect, that the agreement of political leaders equals the mobilization of consent. This no longer holds true in the area of constitutional amendment.

Many important players in Canadian politics seem to demand symbolic goods that they believe must be recognized through constitutional amend-ment and entrenchment. This has led to two problems: first, a devaluation of the legitimacy and importance of ordinary statute law as passed by Parliament as a protection and affirmation of rights and identity; and second, a sense of frustration and grievance because the constitutional amending process does not lead to the formal acceptance of their concerns. The importance of these symbolic statements, and demands by various groups for recognition in the constitution, have become underlying factors that make constitutional amend-ing so difficult.[5]

Constitutional entrenchment of the *Canadian Charter of Rights and Freedoms* in 1982 diminished the role of Parliament by shifting much of the responsibility for interpreting and defining human rights to the courts, mak-ing them a much more prominent player in national politics. While the executive took additional measures in pre-vetting to ensure that legislation met the new standards imposed by the Charter, Parliament did not add proce-dures or mechanisms for it to review bills from a rights perspective.

The challenge wrestled with in this chapter has been to identify ways to strengthen Parliament's role in questions of constitutional reform and national unity. The chapter focuses on Parliament, and not on whether or how the struc-tures and processes of federal-provincial relations and executive federalism might be improved. To explore Parliament's role, the chapter first examines the decline of Parliament as a national forum. Next it looks at what Parlia-ment has done in Canada's constitutional discussions, which helps to identify ways that Parliament, despite its apparent decline, has been influential in pro-moting constitutional reform and national unity. Finally, it looks at ways that the role of Parliament might be improved. In doing so, the chapter proposes a broad package of reforms that would serve to strengthen Parliament in all its functions and roles, and not just those relating to national unity, federal-pro-vincial relations, and constitutional matters. These reforms are proposed within the constraints of the present constitution. The chapter concludes that even accepting this formidable constraint, many valuable reforms can be made that would strengthen Parliament, and in so doing, strengthen its role in national unity and constitutional matters.

A PARLIAMENT IN DECLINE

Parliament's first and fundamental role is to make a government; that is, to enable a government to govern by enjoying the confidence of the House of Commons. Parliament also debates and votes on policies and legislation, holds the government accountable, creates an opposition or potential alternative government, recruits and trains political leaders, educates and informs the public, and mobilizes consent for the policies and programs of the government. The executive, in particular the Cabinet, has a central energizing and initiating responsibility in national life. Parliament holds the government accountable for its stewardship and handling of these immense powers and responsibilities in a continuing discussion, especially in the nationally elected House of Commons. The Senate, a body appointed by the prime minister, though its legislative powers are nearly equal to those of the Commons, is not a confidence chamber, and for most of Canada's history has played only a minor, though far from negligible, role in parliamentary government.

Compared with Britain's Parliament, the Canadian Parliament is government/executive dominated and highly partisan.[6] In Canada the government until recently decided who chaired committees. It still decides (as do the leaders of the other parties) who sits on committees and what goes into committee reports, and controls committee research budgets. Often no serious attempt is made to achieve consensus in committees and opposition parties frequently submit minority reports.[7] At both the federal and provincial levels political life has been dominated by long-lived governments and government parties, while the opposition has been weak and frequently fragmented.

The Canadian Parliament is also characterized by short-term, amateur members.[8] In most parliaments more than half the members will have served in the Commons for fewer than five years, while less than 10 percent will have served more than ten years. In comparison, in Britain, normally only 20 percent of members will have served fewer than five years, while over 50 percent will have served ten years or more. Tenure in the American Congress is even longer than in the British Commons. The brief tenure and short-term membership cause much of the weakness of the Canadian house.

The typical short-term member of Parliament in Canada contrasts with a typical long-term prime minister, which again illustrates the dominance of the executive in Canada, and the corresponding weakness of Parliament. Amateurism also leads to a large proportion of inexperienced ministers in the Cabinet, which in turn has its consequences for the distribution of power and the domination of Parliament and Cabinet by the prime minister.[9]

After most elections, 40 percent to 60 percent of members will be new to the house. The election of 1993 produced the highest turnover in Canadian history, with nearly 70 percent of the house new to Parliament, and the opposition in particular having few experienced members to serve as mentors. In contrast, the election of 2000 produced the lowest turnover, of only 13 percent.[10] Defeat in general elections causes most turnover. The Canadian electorate is notoriously volatile, and where in Britain at least three-quarters of the seats normally can be considered "safe," in the sense that the party of the sitting member is assured that its candidate, old or new, will be returned in the next election, in Canada, at best, only about 20 percent or so of seats meet this criterion. The causes of this volatility lie largely in the failure of political parties in Canada to gain the long-term allegiance of large parts of the electorate, though demographic change also plays a part.[11] With parties losing their strength and salience, citizens' concerns are increasingly being articulated and forwarded through non-party interest groups. This is especially true for issues on the "new" agenda: environmental concerns, identity issues including gender and ethnicity, etc.

Most members of the Canadian Parliament do not have a large "personal vote"; that is, support within the constituency for the sitting member independent of the electorate's feelings about party or party leader.[12] The success or failure of a candidate in Canada depends almost entirely upon party and party leader, with only about 3 percent depending upon the candidate.[13] This is much lower than in most advanced democracies.

Between 15 percent and 20 percent of serving Members of Parliament normally leave Parliament voluntarily from one election to another,[14] which is higher than the percentage leaving the British Parliament, or the American Congress, for all reasons, including death, defeat, and desire. In the United States voluntary retirements, though much rarer than in Canada, are "a cause for concern because they indicate a decline in the desire of able individuals to continue in politics."[15] Voluntary retirements are a much greater cause for concern in Canada where, among other things, they affect recruitment and training of political leaders, leading to a large proportion of politicians, including often even leaders of parties, being recruited from outside Parliament, and frequently with little experience in politics. Political careers in Canada, unlike the United States, do not normally involve a progression from local to provincial (state) to national levels.

A Parliament is only as good as its opposition. Judging by this standard, many Canadian Parliaments are not very good. For long periods the Canadian House of Commons has been dominated by a "Government Party" — a party which wins elections over a long period of time, occupies the centre of the political spectrum, and successfully renews itself, in part by adapting its policies and ideology to fit changes in the public. The federal Liberal Party has been such a dominant government party for most of the twentieth century.[16]

This creates a profound imbalance between the two sides of the house. The government side has experience and power, and the longer-serving politicians. The opposition side lacks experience, especially in office, and suffers from the habit of being opposition; that is, of opposing proposals placed before Parliament by the government, and of being critical of existing policies and administration. This, in turn, creates a negative and critical mindset in the opposition.[17]

The two factors of inexperience and negative attitude, when combined in a new government on the rare occasions when the opposition succeeds in defeating a government party in an election, make it difficult for the perennial opposition-turned-government to function effectively. Equally problematic, an opposition that is new to power, and perhaps to Parliament itself, has no investment in the programs or system of government, and can as a result be dangerously disruptive and ignorant of the problems facing those who govern rather than those who oppose. Such was the experience of the Progressive Conservative government under Prime Minister Brian Mulroney, first elected in 1984. Despite being the first government to succeed in winning back-to-back majorities in the house for the first time in more than 30 years, by the end of its second Parliament this government had lost so much electoral support that it lost all its seats but two in the election of 1993. The problem of governments composed of neophytes with little investment in or understanding of the system they inherit is at least as common at the provincial level as it is at the national, and has frequently led to difficulties in federal-provincial relations and attempts to amend the constitution.

Since 1921 the opposition not only has suffered from its perennially subordinate place in a system with one dominant party, but has also been split into two or more parties, often at opposite ends of the political spectrum. This makes it even less likely that any single opposition party will gain enough seats to form a government, or will be interested in forming a coalition with another opposition party in the event of a minority Parliament.[18] Canada's fractured opposition has been composed of up to four parties, some at one end of the ideological spectrum, some at the other, some expressing particular regional grievances, and with little in common except their hostility to the government. A successful government must accommodate and even integrate the competing desires of different regions and factions. Opposition parties in the Canadian Parliament have generally proven themselves unable to achieve this sort of interest aggregation in their policy proposals and electoral appeal. And while this might make life comfortable, easy, and secure for the government party, it does little to create the political dynamic and debate desirable for effective Parliamentary government.

While these features have characterized the opposition parties in Canada for decades, they have been exacerbated to an unprecedented extent following the general election of 1993, after which the opposition has been at its most fragmented, inexperienced, and weak. The Bloc Québécois, an exclusively Quebec Party whose raison d'être is breaking up the country through Quebec separation, became the official opposition in 1993. The Bloc had little interest in discussing many national issues, and the fact that its members address Parliament almost exclusively in French has meant that the English-speaking media have paid little attention to it. The second opposition party, the Reform Party (which became the official opposition after the election of 1997), was new to Parliament, and its members were even less experienced than those of the Bloc. Reform also was a regional party, representing western Canada, as is its successor, the Alliance Party. Its platform, a mixture of populist and radical sentiments, fits into the long Canadian tradition of agrarian radicalism and populism, though now this is combined with economic and social conservatism. The Alliance, under the leadership of Stockwell Day and his successor Stephen Harper, both new to Parliament, has not been an effective opposition. It has grabbed more attention for its internal rifts and struggles than for its policies or cogent criticisms of government.

Never before has the opposition been so regionally based or so fragmented. While this might make life easy for the Government, it has not, as yet, produced important and attention-grabbing debates, or impressive success in holding the government accountable. Parliament, if anything, has become a less interesting place, and less apparently vital to the well-being of the nation.

Over the past 40 years, when the increasing press of government business has made shortage of time a growing problem in the Canadian Parliament, oppositions have all too often wanted to obstruct government business — frequently for no better reason than simply to delay and embarrass the government. To counteract obstruction the government has restricted debate through closure and timetabling in advance. This process reached an historic extreme under the Mulroney Conservative government in the 1988-93 period, where closure and other time limiting devices were used more than they had been in the entire previous history of the Canadian Parliament. Even on important issues, debate on the floor of the house was limited to 20 hours.[19] The situation has, if anything, become worse since the Liberals came back into power in 1993.

This harsh timetabling prevents the Commons from having effective and newsworthy debates. It reduces the likelihood that the government can use Parliament to put its case to the people, to defeat the opposition's arguments, and to persuade the public that its measures were needed. Likely this abuse of parliamentary procedure helped to contribute to the Conservative government's crushing defeat in the 1993 election. Curiously enough it has not in any real sense made the Commons more efficient. The opposition has found ways of delaying and obstructing, frequently by spending even more time on the trivial bills than before because it is not allowed to spend this time debating the important issues. The total amount of time spent on government business did not become smaller. The opposition spent the time "saved" on major bills to debate minor ones; government and Parliament paid the cost of the illusory saving of time on debating crucial government policies.

In another peculiarly Canadian product, the normally moribund Senate took over where the Commons failed.[20] Between 1984 and 1993, the Canadian Senate, with its Liberal majority led by Allan MacEachen, was more active than it ever had been in its previous history. In many ways it, not the Commons, became the effective opposition to the government. The Senate transformed its role, and defied all previously understood norms and unwritten rules governing its behaviour. It precipitated an election by refusing to pass the free trade bill. It did not pass many other government bills. It engaged in protracted arguments with the Commons over others. Its obstruction of business from the Commons extended to supply, an area of legislation normally considered to be the purview of the Commons. It obstructed the important Goods and Services Tax (GST) legislation to the point that the prime minister resorted to a previously unused clause of the 1867 *British North America Act* to create a Senate majority of supporters. But activism did not win legitimacy for the Senate. Editorial opinion in newspapers continually questioned the right, or appropriateness, of a non-elected Senate confronting and defying a government in this manner. Activism, even when the Senate majority had public opinion on its side, as it did in the GST debate, had the paradoxical result of increasing demands for Senate reform.

The end result of this unhappy time of the Mulroney period was that the Commons was in disrepute because of its ineffectiveness, the government's ham-fisted controls had contributed to a lack of respect for it — and indeed, all government and parliamentary institutions — there were demands for reform that the government was unable to satisfy, the government failed to mobilize consent for its policies, and the Senate was no more highly regarded than before. Heavy-handed control over proceedings in the House of Commons was only one factor contributing to these dolorous results, but it was a far from negligible one. Parliamentary government is as much about accommodating minorities as allowing majorities to have their way. The Commons no longer works in a way that allows these slow processes of vision, revision, and accommodation to work. Parliament has indeed declined.

J.E. Crimmins and Paul W. Nesbitt-Larking,[21] replicating for Canada studies that had been done on the British Parliament,[22] found that during the post-World War II period there has been a substantial and continual decline in prime ministerial participation in Parliamentary debates. Parliament has become a less prominent place for major political announcements and debates. The growth of the media, particularly television, has provided political forums which compete with Parliament. In a prime ministerial speech or announcement outside Parliament the prime minister and his/her handlers can choose the venue, the group, and the time to make the most of the event: to have a favourable reception, to hit the national news at a time when the opposition cannot rebut, etc. In Parliament, where a ministerial statement or speech is followed by opposition comment, there is less opportunity to put a favourable spin on the occasion.

The bulk of media reportage of Parliament, particularly by television, is on question period. While question period itself is frequently dramatic, and on occasion has contributed powerfully to holding the government accountable or exposing flaws and weaknesses in administration and policies,[23] it also appears at times contrived, unconstructive, and overly confrontational.[24]

Parliamentary committees also suffer from lack of media attention. From 1993-95, a period of 156 weeks, major Canadian newspapers had only 54 articles of any sort about committee proceedings.[25] Considering that in an average year there will be more than 500 committee hearings, this does not suggest adequate coverage or public discussion. Furthermore, 26 of the 54 articles dealt with the finance and industry committees, indicating extreme media selectivity and lack of interest in most committees.

Neil Nevitte[26] concluded that Canadian experience of the decline of Parliament reflects what has happened elsewhere. Allegiance to traditional political parties has declined. Powerful new political movements, such as the environmental and women's movements, find themselves outside the party. The multiplicity of interest and pressure groups attempting to affect policies operates largely outside the parties, and outside traditional parliamentary institutions and processes. Interest groups use Parliament only as one out of many channels for influencing government. The attitudes of the post-World War II generation, in what is often termed the "post-materialist" era, are vastly different from those that preceded them. Politics of identity, aided by what Alan Cairns identified as "Charter Rights" groups[27] is taking the place of politics of class. The post-materialist generations have less concern (or fear) over economic issues, and are more concerned with quality of life issues. The traditional parties and politics do not reflect their agenda.

Many of these factors have, of course, affected executive federalism, and the processes for amending the constitution, as much as they have Parliament. The debacle of the attempt to make mega-amendments to the constitution through executive federalism in the Meech Lake Accord episode showed that the Canadian public no longer would accept decisions reached by first ministers as legitimate and binding; in the subsequent experience with the Charlottetown Accord, attempts to mobilize public support for broad amendments to the constitution through devices including executive federalism, parliamentary committee, public discussion by task force and widely reported constitutional conferences in the so-called peoples' round of discussions also failed to mobilize consent. Canadian politics has changed in the past 30 years, not least because attempts to amend the constitution and the quasi-successful amendments of 1981-82 (only "quasi" because Quebec did not then and has not since given its agreement to the amendments) themselves changed the processes and terms of reference of politics, and, through the introduction of the *Charter of Rights and Freedoms*, the relationship between citizens and government. Parliament is not the only institution of national politics to have had its prestige and influence decline during this period.

PARLIAMENT'S ROLE IN CANADA'S CONSTITUTIONAL DISCUSSIONS

The processes of constitutional amendment begin with a prime minister or provincial premier wanting a change in the constitution. Some minor amendments affecting only one province have had simple and specific goals, but for wider-ranging amendments, both motives and goals will be varied and often in conflict. The processes for amendment are themselves complex, with the written constitution containing at least three quite different processes, depending on the kinds of amendments desired and the actors involved. When large-scale mega-amendments are desired, the processes extend far beyond those found in the written constitution. Many provinces, for example, have legislated a requirement over and above the provisions of the written constitution that to be approved by the provincial legislature, constitutional amendments must first be approved by a majority of the electorate in a province-wide referendum. The failed efforts to ratify the Charlottetown Accord have made it most unlikely that any significant package of constitutional amendments can be made without support through a nationwide referendum.

This end result was not in anybody's mind when, after the failure of Quebec to support the amendments agreed to in the Victoria Charter by a First Ministers' Conference of 1971, Prime Minister Pierre Trudeau began once again the long, arduous, and slow process of actually amending the constitution. In 1972 a Special Joint Committee of the Senate and the House of Commons on the Constitution of Canada, chaired by Senator Gildas Molgat and Mark MacGuigan from the Commons, had held meetings in 47 cities and towns across the country, received 8,000 pages of evidence, and heard evidence from 1,486 witnesses at meetings attended by 13,000 Canadians. The committee concluded that the people wanted a new constitution and proposed detailed recommendations on what the new constitution should contain. This was the first effort to involve the people of Canada in discussion of constitutional amendment, and the first effort to use a parliamentary committee to stimulate such discussion.[28]

The election of the avowedly separatist Parti Québécois government in Quebec in 1976 stimulated a minor industry in constitutional reform. In 1979 the Trudeau-created Pepin-Robarts task force on Canadian unity submitted its report, *A Future Together: Observations and Recommendations*.[29] Trudeau's government made public its glossy booklet, *A Time for Action*, in 1978. In 1978 the Trudeau government proposed unilateral action to reform the constitution by the federal Parliament through a bill, C-60, which would, among other things, have created a "House of the Federation," constitutionally entrenched the Supreme Court and required provincial consultation in the appointment of its judges. Bill C-60, and along with it the possibility for unilateral federal action, was shot down by the Supreme Court in 1979 when it ruled that the federal Parliament could not by itself alter the Senate.

Trudeau, after losing the election of 1979, regained office in the election of 1980. The Parti Québécois government lost a referendum on independence in 1980. Trudeau needed to honour his referendum-time promise to amend the constitution and renew federalism. When the processes of executive federalism failed to reach agreement, Prime Minister Trudeau once again resorted to unilateral federal action. A special parliamentary committee in 1980-81, made up of ten senators and 15 Members of Parliament — 15 Liberals, eight Conservatives, and two from the New Democratic Party — had its hearings televised. It proposed many changes to the government's constitutional package, including women's and Aboriginal rights, and recognition of Canada's multicultural heritage. Many of the witnesses before the committee represented interest groups with a stake in amendments, and which later became mentioned in the constitution.

Executive federalism through First Ministers' Conferences on the constitution continued along with these parliamentary activities. An action brought in the Supreme Court of Canada by provinces hostile to Trudeau's approach resulted in the judges deciding that a "substantial degree" of provincial consent was required for amendments. In 1981-82 a revised package, supported by all provinces except Quebec (whose concerns the process was avowedly intended to mollify), after passing through the Canadian Parliament was passed by the British Parliament. Among their other provisions, these changes gave Canada the power to amend its own constitution without reference to the British Parliament. The only provincial legislature that voted on this 1981-82 amendment package was that of Quebec, and it not surprisingly voted against it. Russell concludes that, for the amendments of 1982, "the crucial instrument in the process of building legitimacy for the federal initiative was the special parliamentary committee that sat through the late fall of 1980 and early winter of 1981."[30]

The 1987 Meech Lake Accord of the Mulroney Conservative government attempted to rectify the problem of Quebec government's hostility to the 1981-82 constitutional amendments. The accord was reached through the processes of executive federalism and First Ministers Conferences with no involvement by the federal Parliament. In fact, Prime Minister Mulroney told the Commons that not one word of the document could be changed. Though the accord was subsequently approved by resolutions of the federal Parliament and the legislatures of nine of the ten provinces, its failure to gain approval of the tenth, Manitoba, in a cliff-hanger of last-minute efforts because of the opposition of an Aboriginal member of the assembly, and the reneging of Newfoundland after a new government came into power, plunged Canada once again into another constitutional crisis.

Many observers blamed Meech Lake's failure on the process. Decisions reached through executive federalism could no longer serve as a proxy for the consent of the people; so this argument went. A process which involved gaining the consent of Canada's citizens seemed to be needed. In late 1990 the Mulroney government tried most of tricks in the book, and some new ones, in its attempts to create a new consensus for constitutional amendments that would be supported by the government of Quebec. Under the chairmanship of Keith Spicer a "Citizens' Forum on Canada's Future" held hearings across the country. Despite the involvement of hundreds of thousands of Canadians in its work, the forum's report was more enthusiastic about constitutional reform than were Canadians as a whole, and the report not only overstated the desire for change, but understated Canadians' lack of enthusiasm for more destructive constitutional imbroglios.

A joint Senate-Commons committee established in late 1990, the Beaudoin-Edwards committee (named for its chairmen, Senator Gérald Beaudoin and Member of Parliament Jim Edwards), recommended in June 1991 that constitutional amendment should be preceded by hearings across the country by a parliamentary committee, and that regional vetoes similar to those proposed in the Victoria formula of 1971 should be adopted. The New Democrat members of this committee submitted a minority report recommending that constitutional change be preceded by a constituent assembly. In September 1991 the Mulroney government made its constitutional proposals public in its *Shaping the Future Together*. A second joint parliamentary committee, Castonguay-Dobbie, (named for its chairs, Senator Claude Castonguay and Member of Parliament Dorothy Dobbie) began hearings on these proposals, but early on it had to stop its work because of poor organization and badly attended meetings. Restarted as the Beaudoin-Dobbie committee, its committee's work was supplemented by five constitutional conferences held in different regions of the country. The committee's 131-page report, *A Renewed Canada*, again proposed comprehensive constitutional change. Intensive constitutional discussions between the first ministers followed, and in August 1992 the Charlottetown Accord was reached between the prime minister, the ten provincial premiers, two territorial leaders, and four Aboriginal leaders. In a nationwide referendum on 26 October 1992, this comprehensive series of proposals (the text of the Charlottetown Accord occupied 51 pages, not including two ancillary political accords), was defeated, gaining a majority in only three Maritime provinces, and (by a tiny margin) Ontario.

In 1993 the Conservative government suffered the worst electoral defeat of any government in Canadian history, with only two Conservative members — one, Jean Charest, a Cabinet minister in the Mulroney government, the other, Elsie Wayne, new to Parliament. The new Liberal government was headed by Jean Chrétien, an experienced politician. In a second Quebec referendum on sovereignty in October 1995, the pro-separation forces lost by a paper-thin margin. Prime Minister Chrétien promised during the referendum campaign that he would ensure that several key Quebec demands would be met if the referendum were defeated: a veto for Quebec over constitutional proposals, recognition of Quebec as a distinct society, and transfer of manpower training to Quebec.

The problem was how to honour these commitments. Comprehensive constitutional reform had proven not only close to impossible to achieve, but also to be an immensely destructive process for national unity. The official opposition returned in the 1993 election was the Bloc Québécois Party, which was not only exclusively based in Quebec, but was also dedicated to the separatist cause. Reform, the second largest opposition party, was exclusively based in the west, represented the voice of western alienation, and was not sympathetic to Quebec's concerns. Both Progressive Conservative and New Democratic parties had too few members to be recognized as parties in Parliament under the rules of the house. It would not have been possible for a parliamentary committee, whether of the Commons alone or a joint Senate-Commons one, to achieve a consensus on constitutional reform, let alone one satisfactory to the government. Neither constitutional reform nor extensive hearings by a parliamentary committee were attractive prospects.

The Chrétien government chose to honour its referendum-time commitments by using the parliamentary processes over which it had control. A bill establishing a veto over constitutional amendments for Ontario, Quebec, British Columbia, and two each of the Prairie and Maritime provinces was passed by the Commons on 13 December 1995, after the government limited debate at every stage and sent it to committee for less than two days of study. The Senate, which at that time was dominated by Mulroney-appointed Conservatives, vowed to take its time on the bill, but passed it in February 1996 after Prime Minister Chrétien had restored the upper chamber's Liberal majority through a hasty senatorial appointment. The government of Quebec, the Bloc, and the Reform Party had all opposed this bill. On 11 December 1995 the Commons passed a resolution recognizing Quebec as a distinct society, with both the Bloc and Reform voting against it. Unemployment insurance reforms introduced in December, and later passed, gave provinces control over manpower training. In June 2000, Parliament passed the "Clarity Bill," which gave the Commons the right to decide whether the question asked in a Quebec referendum met guidelines established by the Supreme Court in 1998. This bill met with a great deal of hostility both within Parliament and outside. Nevertheless, Prime Minister Chrétien again assured its passage through a flurry of Senate appointments.

This review of Canada's unhappy experience with mega-reforms to the constitution in the 1990s gives an impression that constitutional amendment is now impossible. But three constitutional amendments were made during the period: one to declare New Brunswick officially bilingual; the second and third to secularize the school systems of Quebec and Newfoundland. Each of these affected only one province, and each required only a resolution, not a statute, to be passed by Parliament. Mega-constitutional politics might well be as good as dead for the foreseeable future, but mini-constitutional politics were alive and kicking.

On several important occasions, and especially in 1981-82, a parliamentary committee proved to be a crucial part of the process of mobilizing consent for constitutional reform. This lesson was ignored at great cost in the unfortunate Meech Lake experience, and the problems engendered for these efforts by the processes of executive federalism proved to be insurmountable. Prime Minister Chrétien bypassed the constitution and used only the channels he could control within Parliament for honouring his 1995 referendum commitments. The blending of parliamentary processes and executive federalism in constitutional amending processes has not always been smooth or happy. Nevertheless, Parliament has proven to be a valuable part of the processes, and its committees have served as useful counterbalances to the conclusions reached by the first ministers.

THE QUESTION OF REFORM

Proposals to reform Parliament can be divided into two groups: those that tinker with the present system; and those that propose to change the system itself. The former offers a grab-bag list of incremental reforms; the latter, more profound revisions to the processes of representation and structure of power in the national government. In political science terms, the incremental reforms would not alter the "majoritarian" (I prefer the word "adversarial") nature of the Canadian parliamentary system, while the fundamental reforms would make the system less adversarial, and more consensual. These two kinds of reform are not mutually exclusive and in practice could complement each other, but they embrace fundamentally different approaches to reform.

More free votes and more effective committees top most lists of incremental parliamentary reforms. However, neither is so problem free nor so easy to make as is often supposed. Free votes, and greater independence for the individual MPs, have been proposed, and sometimes promised, by all parties and even governments;[31] as have more effective committees.[32] But the reality of the Canadian system is that parties and party leaders, not individual members, are what people vote for and how politics is perceived. The personal vote for MPs is minuscule and irrelevant to the outcomes of most elections. The media view any deviation from party discipline as a sign of weakness. Efforts to reform parliamentary committees have reached their limits, and these limits are dictated by the amateurism, rigid party lines, and government domination which characterize the Canadian parliamentary system.[33] A third reform, which was needed until members' pay was increased a few years ago, is to ensure that members are paid at an adequate level that they want to stay in Parliament. Other minor improvements could give Parliament a stronger role in intergovernmental relations and constitutional amendment, such as a standing committee on intergovernmental affairs, a committee on human rights, and special provisions of double majorities for language and cultural matters.

But making these incremental reforms would do little to change role of Parliament in Canada's executive dominated system. If the intention is to make serious change, then reform must go in a bolder and different direction and must deal with the roots of the problems, not the consequences. Major reforms would lead away from the present "majoritarian" system and towards a more "consensual" one, of the type most compatible with successful governance and unity in large, geographically and culturally diverse countries such as Canada.[34]

The first reform necessary for movement towards a more consensual system would be to introduce a system of proportional representation. This possibility has been discussed exhaustively by political scientists.[35] Its advantages include a House of Commons that would more accurately reflect the voting patterns of the electorate and the varieties of opinion within each province. It is also likely to lead to longer-serving members of Parliament. Its disadvantages include greater likelihood of more parties in the house and more minority parliaments, though these problems can be moderated by, for example, requiring a party to gain at least 5 percent of the national vote before it is entitled to representation in the house, and by creating an appropriate balance between MPs elected from geographical constituencies and MPs selected through party lists by proportional representation.

The second major reform towards a more consensual system would be to make the Senate more legitimate, and to define better its role in Canada's parliamentary processes.[36] A package for Senate reform would include clear procedural definitions of when and how the Senate can defeat and delay ordinary legislation, and a better way for appointing senators, such as from lists provided to the governor in council based on the results of province-wide elections.

Third, such important matters as the rights of minorities, provinces and regions, and agreements between levels of government could be made more secure through introduction of a level "basic law" intermediate between ordinary statute law and constitutional entrenchment. This basic law would be easier to legislate than constitutional entrenchment but would have higher symbolic value than ordinary statutes.[37] Something like this was proposed in section 26 of the Charlottetown Accord. The protection and symbolic legitimacy of basic law would give important semi-constitutional principles strong symbolic visibility and recognition. The process, for example, could require "basic law" to be approved, amended or repealed only after passage twice by Parliament, with a general election intervening between first and second passage. This very simple approach (compared with Canada's prohibitively complicated constitutional amending procedures) is used to amend the constitution of Sweden. Or an unusual majority, say two-thirds of the house, would be required to amend or repeal basic law.

For some years the federal government has been in a reactive and damage control mode. That seems to work well for periods of constitutional quiescence, and by 2003 the current tranquility has continued for nearly eight years; a long time in politics. But a reactive, damage control mode does not work in times of crisis. A move towards consensual government would be a positive action. It would create an alternative way of thinking about and resolving problems. It looks like a much bigger step than it actually is. Proportional representation and an elected upper chamber have been adopted by other major Westminster-style parliamentary democracies — New Zealand and Australia respectively. These "consensual" reforms would create a better climate for making incremental reforms — for loosening party discipline, and creating more independent and effective committees. All can be made without constitutional amendment.

A more consensual system would mean more defeats of government legislation in the house, and more dissent against party leadership by members. The role of the prime minister and Cabinet would be weakened, while other institutions would gain — the House of Commons, the individual member, committees, the reformed Senate, the variety of interests which want to influence government policy, to name a few. But this does not mean the end of responsible government. The conventions on confidence are much more flexible than are generally appreciated, and could certainly accommodate such a change.[38] The change would mean greater legitimacy for Parliament, government, elected representatives, and the legislative processes.

Incremental reform at best would not address fundamental problems. It would only reinforce the views of those who look on the present system with skepticism, if not despair, such as those who admire the American system, and the growing number of those who do not like the confrontational, adversarial nature of present parliamentary politics.

Movement toward a more consensual system has risks because it is an advance into the unknown. But elements of these reforms have been tried in other major parliamentary democracies, and Canada can learn and profit from their experience. The question that needs to be addressed is: What are the costs of not making such reforms? Is Canada going to sleepwalk into disintegration, with no attempt being made by the federal government to address the institutional and system problems that have led to recurring crises? Is no new initiative and vision going to come out of Ottawa? Can a bold effort at change have any worse effect than doing nothing? Changes toward a more consensual parliamentary system would be a journey into partly uncharted waters, but doing nothing or making incremental pseudo-reforms is riskier.

Reform to Parliament would not change the issues in the Canadian federal system. Quebec would still be predominantly French-speaking, the other nine provinces predominantly English-speaking. Quebec's resentment for the rest of Canada would still linger. The west would still feel alienated. Provincial and federal governments would still squabble over the distribution of powers and the appropriate role for the two (or three including municipal, or four adding in Aboriginal self-government) levels of government. Regional inequalities would not go away, any more than would Canada's continuing challenge of living with its powerful next-door neighbour. But even if the Meech Lake or Charlottetown processes had led to mega-constitutional change, these problems would still exist. A reformed Parliament would add something all too frequently missing from discussion of these issues. It would be a counterweight to the lopsided processes of executive federalism and First Ministers' Conferences. By contributing a stronger national forum and voice a strengthened Parliament could even lead to more interest in and support for the federal government and Parliament.

NOTES

This chapter is based on a study I prepared for the Privy Council Office in 1997. An expanded and revised version of it was published as *Parliament, Intergovernmental Relations, and National Unity* (Kingston: Institute of Intergovernmental Relations, Queen's University, 1999). My research on the Canadian Parliament was supported by a grant from the Social Sciences and Humanities Research Council.

1. J. Stephan Dupré, "Reflections on the Workability of Executive Federalism," in *Intergovernmental Relations*, ed. Richard Simeon (Toronto: University of Toronto Press, 1985), pp. 1-32; J. Stefan Dupré, "The Workability of Executive Federalism in Canada," in *Federalism and the Role of the State*, eds. Herman Bakvis and William M. Chandler (Toronto: University of Toronto Press, 1987).

2. P.H. Russell, *Constitutional Odyssey: Can Canadians Become a Sovereign People?* 2d ed. (Toronto: University of Toronto Press, 1993), p. 75; Jean Laponce and John Meisel, eds., *Debating the Constitution* (Ottawa: University of Ottawa Press, 1994); and C.E.S. Franks, "Representation and Policy-Making in Canada," in *Canada's Century: Governance in a Maturing Society*, ed. C.E.S. Franks, *et al.* (Montreal and Kingston: McGill-Queen's University Press, 1995).

3.   Donald V. Smiley, "Federalism and the Legislative Process in Canada," in *The Legislative Process in Canada: The Need for Reform*, eds. William A.W. Neilson and James C. MacPherson (Toronto: Butterworth, 1978), p. 74.

4.   Ronald L. Watts, *Executive Federalism: A Comparative Analysis*. Research Paper 26 (Kingston: Institute of Intergovernmental Relations, Queen's University, 1988).

5.   C.E.S. Franks, *The Myths and Symbols of the Constitutional Debate in Canada* (Kingston: Institute of Intergovernmental Relations, Queen's University, 1993).

6.   C.E.S. Franks, *The Parliament of Canada* (Toronto: University of Toronto Press, 1987).

7.   C.E.S. Franks, "Boxed in a Five-Cornered Circle: Accountability of the Public Service and Parliamentary Government in Canada." A study prepared for the Canadian Centre for Management Development, April 1995; Jacob S. Ziegel, "Was the parliamentary committee just a rubber stamp?" *The Globe and Mail*, 15 November 1996; and Jonathan Malloy, "Reconciling Expectations and Reality in House of Commons Committees: The Case of the 1989 GST Inquiry," *Canadian Public Administration* 39,3 (1996):314-35.

8.   Franks, *The Parliament of Canada*; Michael M. Atkinson and David Docherty, "Moving Right Along: The Roots of Amateurism in the Canadian House of Commons," *Canadian Journal of Political Science* 25,2 (1992):295-318; Doreen Barrie and Roger Gibbins, "Parliamentary Careers in the Canadian Federal State," *Canadian Journal of Political Science* 22,1 (1989):137-45; Jack Cramer, "Legislative Experience and Legislative Behaviour," in *Foundations of Political Culture*, eds. Jon H. Pammett and Michael Whittington (Toronto: Macmillan 1976); David Docherty, "Should I Stay or Should I Go? Career Decisions of Members of Parliament," in *Leaders and Leadership in Canada*, eds. Maureen Mancuso, Dick Price and Ron Wagenburg (Toronto: Oxford University Press, 1994); Gerhard Loewenberg and Samuel C. Patterson, *Comparing Legislatures* (Lanham: University Press of America, 1979); J.A.A. Lovink, "Is Canadian Politics too Competitive?" *Canadian Journal of Political Science* 6,3 (1973):341-79; and Sharon Sutherland, "The Consequences of Electoral Volatility: Inexperienced Ministers 1949-1990," in *Representation, Integration, and Political Parties in Canada*, ed. Herman Bakvis (Toronto: Dundurn Press, 1991).

9.   Sutherland, "The Consequences of Electoral Volatility"; Donald Savoie, *Governing From the Centre: The Concentration of Power in Canadian Politics* (Toronto: University of Toronto Press, 1999).

10.   As a result, in 2003 the Canadian House of Commons was in the anomalous position of having a higher proportion of members who had served nine years or more than at any time in its history.

11.   Harold D. Clarke, *et al.*, *Absent Mandate: Canadian Politics in an Age of Restructuring*, 3d ed. (Vancouver: Gage Publishing, 1996); and Laurence LeDuc, "The Changeable Canadian Voter," in *The Canadian General Election of 1988*, eds. Alan Frizzell, Jon H. Pammett, and Anthony Westell (Ottawa: Carleton University Press, 1989).

12. John A. Ferejohn and Brian Gaines, "The Personal Vote in Canada," in *Representation, Integration and Political Parties in Canada*, ed. Herman Bakvis (Toronto: Dundurn Press, 1991).

13. William Irvine, "A Review and Evaluation of Electoral System Reform Proposals," in *Institutional Reforms for Representative Government*, ed. Peter Aucoin (Toronto: University of Toronto Press, 1985), pp. 71-109; Michael Krashinsky and William J. Milne, "Some Evidence on the Effects of Incumbency in the 1988 Canadian General Election," in *Issues in Party and Election Finance in Canada*, ed. Leslie Seidle (Toronto: Dundurn Press, 1991); Richard Price and Maureen Mancuso, "The Ties That Bind: Parliamentary Members and Their Constituencies," in *Introductory Readings in Canadian Government*, eds. Robert Krause and R.H. Wagenberg (Mississauga: Copp Clark Pitman, 1991); and David M. Wood and Philip Norton, "Do Candidates Matter? Constituency-Specific Vote Changes for Incumbent MPs 1983-1987," *Political Studies* 40:227-38.

14. Franks, *The Parliament of Canada*; and Docherty, "Should I Stay or Should I Go? Career Decisions of Members of Parliament."

15. Steven G. Livingston and Sally Friedman, "Re-examining Theories of Congressional Retirement: Evidence from the 1980s," *Legislative Studies Quarterly* 18,2 (1993):231-53.

16. Reginald Whitaker, *The Government Party: Organizing and Financing the Liberal Party of Canada, 1930-58* (Toronto: University of Toronto Press, 1977).

17. Hugh Thorburn, "Interpretations of the Canadian Party System," in *Party Politics in Canada*, ed. H. Thorburn, 4th ed. (Scarborough: Prentice-Hall, 1979); and George Perlin, *The Tory Syndrome: Leadership Politics in the Progressive Conservative Party* (Montreal: McGill-Queen's University Press, 1980).

18. Ian Stewart, "Of Customs and Coalitions: The Formation of Canadian Federal Parliamentary Alliances," *Canadian Journal of Political Science* 13,3 (1980):451-79.

19. Ellen Sealey, *Mobilizing Legislation; Losing Consent: Treatment of the House of Commons Under the Mulroney Conservatives.* B.A. Honours thesis, 1995, Department of Political Studies, Queen's University.

20. C.E.S. Franks, "Constraints on the Operations and Reform of Parliamentary Committees in Canada," in *Working Papers on Comparative Legislative Studies II: The Changing Roles of Parliamentary Committees*, eds. Lawrence D. Langely and Attila Agh (Appleton, WN: Research Committee of Legislative Specialists, International Political Science Association, 1997), pp. 199-207.

21. J.E. Crimmins and Paul W. Nesbitt-Larking, "Canadian Prime Ministers in the House of Commons: Patterns of Intervention," *The Journal of Legislative Studies* 2,3 (1996).

22. Patrick Dunleavy, G.W. Jones and Brendan O'Leary, "Prime Ministers and the Commons: Patterns of Behaviour, 1868 to 1987," *Public Administration* 58,2 (1990):123-40; and Patrick Dunleavy and G.W. Jones with Jane Burnham, Robert Elgie, and Peter Fysh, "Leaders, Politics, and Institutional Change: The Decline of Prime Ministerial Accountability to the House of Commons, 1968-1990," *The British Journal of Political Science* 23,3 (Autumn 1993):267-89.

23. Franks, *The Parliament of Canada.*

24. Peter Dobell and Byron Berry, "Anger at the System," in *Parliamentary Government,* 39 (January 1993).

25. Franks, *The Parliament of Canada.*

26. Neil Nevitte, *The Decline of Deference: Canadian Value Change in a Cross-national Perspective* (Peterborough: Broadview, 1996).

27. Alan Cairns, "Constitutional Minoritarianism in Canada," in *Reconfigurations: Canadian Citizenship & Constitutional Change, Selected Essays by Alan C. Cairns,* ed. D.E. Williams (Toronto: McClelland and Stewart, 1995), pp. 119-41.

28. The constitutional events of 1972-93 are thoroughly discussed in Peter Russell's admirable *Constitutional Odyssey* (see Note 2).

29. Canada. The Task Force on Canadian Unity, *A Future Together: Observations and Recommendations* (Ottawa: The Queen's Printer, 1979).

30. P.H. Russell, *Constitutional Odyssey,* pp. 113-14.

31. Canada. House of Commons, *Report of the Special Committee on Reform of the House of Commons* (Ottawa: Queen's Printer, 1985); C.E.S. Franks, *Free Votes in the House of Commons,* a study prepared for the Honourable Harvie Andre, Government House Leader, 1991. Unpublished; and Andrew Heard, *Canadian Constitutional Conventions: The Marriage of Law and Politics* (Toronto: Oxford University Press, 1991).

32. Canada. The Task Force on Canadian Unity, *A Future Together: Observations and Recommendations* (Ottawa: Queen's Printer, 1979). Canada. House of Commons, *Report of the Special Committee on Reform of the House of Commons;* and Franks, "Constraints on the Operations and Reform of Parliamentary Committees in Canada."

33. Franks, "Constraints on the Operations and Reform of Parliamentary Committees in Canada"; Malloy, "Reconciling Expectations and Reality in House of Commons Committees"; and Ziegel, "Was the parliamentary committee just a rubber stamp?"

34. Arend Lijphart, *Democracies: Patterns of Majoritarian and Consensus Government in Twenty-One Countries* (New Haven: Yale University Press, 1984).

35. Alan Cairns, "The Electoral and the Party System, 1921-66," *Canadian Journal of Political Science* 1,1 (1968):55-80; Alan Cairns, "A Reply to J.A.A. Lovink, 'On Analyzing the Impact of the Electoral on the Party System in Canada'," *Canadian Journal of Political Science* 3,4 (1970):517-21; Michael Cassidy, "Fairness and Stability: How a New Electoral System Would Affect Canada," *Parliamentary Government* 42 (August 1992); William Irvine, "A Review and Evaluation of Electoral System Reform Proposals"; Donald Smiley, "Federalism and the Legislative Process in Canada"; Canada. The Task Force on Canadian Unity, *A Future Together: Observations and Recommendations;* David Elton and Peter McCormick, "Suppose your vote counted," *The Globe and Mail,* 14 March 1997, p. A17; *The Globe and Mail,* 25 March 1997. Skeptics: J.A.A. Lovink, "On Analyzing the Impact of the Electoral System," *Canadian Journal of Political Science* 3,4 (1970):497-516; and Franks, *The Parliament of Canada.*

36. Canada. The Task Force on Canadian Unity, *A Future Together: Observations and Recommendations*; Canada. *Consensus Report on the Constitution* (Ottawa: Supply and Services Canada, 1992); Campbell Sharman, "Second Chambers," in *Federalism and the Role of the State*, eds. Herman Bakvis and William M. Chandler (Toronto: University of Toronto Press, 1987), pp. 82-100.

37. Katherine Swinton, "Rebalancing the Canadian Confederation: The Constitutional Odyssey Continues," a paper presented at the conference to honour Peter Russell, University of Toronto, November 1996 (unpublished).

38. Andrew Heard, *Canadian Constitutional Conventions*.

3

Political Parties and the Canadian Federation's Coalition Politics

R. Kenneth Carty and Steven B. Wolinetz

La gestion de la fédération canadienne est généralement perçue comme un exercice intergouvernemental non partisan dont les partis politiques ont été systématiquement exclus. Ce chapitre remet en question cette perception de la dynamique du fédéralisme canadien. Les gouvernements de la fédération sont tous des gouvernements de parti, qui dépendent, en matière de survie et de pouvoir, d'engagements et de supporters partisans. Pour eux, la politique intergouvernementale est inévitablement une forme de coalition politique, mais une coalition nécessairement différente de celles mises en cause par les partis des autres systèmes fédéraux. Nous soulignons les caractéristiques fondamentales des coalitions fédérales des partis canadiens (au pouvoir) et explorons leurs conséquences sur le caractère et la santé des politiques fédérales et la capacité des citoyens d'utiliser les partis politiques à titre d'instruments démocratiques principaux.

Are political parties part of the problem or part of the solution for the better working of the Canadian federation? Most will instinctively say that they are both. After all, parties are the tools of conflict and political division, but they are also the instruments of compromise and governance. In Canada, parties have been especially important institutions because the very existence of the federation, and the constitutional arrangements that have defined its creation, expansion and reshaping, have been the product of party politicians working to resolve the political dilemmas of their day. This being so, it is striking how little attention has been paid to the role of parties, as primary political organizations of the society, in the managing of the Canadian federation.

In most democracies, political parties are instruments of distinctive social clienteles, articulating their respective interests and seeking power to advance their particular ambitions. And it is in the clash of electoral competition amongst parties that the competitive balances allowing for legitimate and necessary governing accommodations are struck. In Canada, however, this classic formulation has traditionally been turned on its head. Observers for over a century have argued that Canadian parties deliberately eschew homogeneous constituencies, coherent policies or distinctive programs, making them, in André Siegfried's words, "entirely harmless," preoccupied with "the pure and simple continuation of their own existence."[1] Analysts of the Canadian party system have claimed that this is a virtue, arguing that the very heterogeneity of the society threatened the survival of the political system. This meant that parties could not afford to represent sharply conflicting interests — of which primacy was given to two regionally based linguistic communities — for fear that party conflict would unleash forces that could escalate out of control. Thus, Canadian parties had to be masters of inter-group accommodation and, in the name of national integration, their primary latent function had to be that of interest aggregation. From this was derived the famous brokerage model of Canadian party politics, a model that charged each of the individual parties, rather than the party system as a whole, with brokering the principal political cleavages of the society. The favourite metaphor for the successful Canadian party was the famous omnibus, and the party system broke down whenever it stalled.

Notice that in this dominant account the federation worked when national parties were able, within themselves, to find a formula for accommodating the divergent demands of the regions and voters. The focus is almost exclusively on parties at the national level on the assumption that they are the most important partisan actors. The account pays little attention to the ways parties organize and operate in the provinces, or as more complex, multi-level institutions. Yet we know that party life in Canada is not simply a matter of national politics. Distinctive parties and party systems dominate provincial politics,[2] and the governments these parties control are central players in the life of the federation. If we are to come to grips with the role of parties in managing the federation, we need to turn our attention to the part they play across its system of multi-level governance. This is particularly important because relations between federal and provincial party organizations have changed dramatically over time. Once closely integrated, parties, and the party systems they constitute, are now largely disconnected.[3]

The study of political parties has been relatively silent on the question of how, and with what consequence, parties work in multi-level systems, largely because of the primacy given to national politics in most of the literature. As a result, there is little comparative or theoretical analysis of parties or party systems in federal polities. Steven B. Wolinetz has recently deduced a set of propositions about them,[4] and William Chandler, Lori Thorlakson and Wolfgang Renzsch[5] have all provided readings of federal party systems that contend that the cast of party organization, and the character of its competition, is shaped by the federal institutional setting. Thorlakson argues that cross-level party system incongruence is inversely related to the degree of decentralization — thus Canada's comparatively high levels of decentralization produce low levels of federal-provincial party congruence — while Renzsch claims that the differences between the German and Canadian party systems, in terms of party integration, "reflect different types of federal systems."[6] These arguments point to the institutional imperatives governing party structure and activity, though careful readings reveal that the dynamics in any federal system run in both directions: politicians and their parties do drive the workings of all democratic federations. In this chapter, we are not so concerned with the impact of a federal, multi-level system on the parties and their ability to perform the traditional functions demanded of them as with questioning the role of the parties on the operation of the federal system.

To help put the patterns of Canadian parties in perspective, we will begin by briefly noting the role of parties in managing the politics of several other western federations. The lessons of these polities confirm the importance of federal structures in shaping parties and party systems, but also remind us that each system inevitably takes on its own idiosyncratic dynamic. The next section of the chapter considers the role of parties in managing the federation in earlier periods of Canadian history, following Richard Simeon and Ian Robinson's mapping of the development of the federation to identify distinctive shifts in the very character of the country's federal processes.[7] Subsequent substantive sections then explore the character of federal party politics in the contemporary period, noting that successful parties must play two distinctive and often contradictory games. We identify several patterns of competition and co-operation played by the now disconnected parties across these two games, and conclude with reflections on their consequences for the politics of the country.

PARTY POLITICS IN FEDERATIONS

Federal political systems exist where unitary ones won't do. Inevitably, then, the multi-level political and administrative practices they engender and sustain are complex, often shifting to cope with the dynamics of a multi-layered society. The political parties in these federal systems find themselves adapting to the institutional imperatives that define the rules of the competitive games they must play. Consider the party systems of four Western democracies:

Germany: The German system is one of administrative federalism where policy is made at the centre and implemented in the Länder. That makes for high levels of institutional interdependence. The necessary intergovernmental accommodation is structured "by negotiation within the parties involved"[8] which puts a premium on national parties developing tightly integrated structures that can effectively integrate political competition and decision-making across the two levels. Parties organize from the bottom up, providing a recognizably hierarchical career ladder that allows politicians to make their way from local through state to national office. The result is a set of nationwide parties (although the Party of Democratic Socialism, descendent of the rulers of the old eastern German Democratic Republic, has yet to penetrate the area that made up the Bonn Republic) that operate across all levels of government and have powerful incentives to integrate their political policies across both levels and Länder. Coordination is reinforced by an important intra-state parliamentary mechanism — the state-based upper chamber, the Bundesrat — which can exercise a veto over federal legislation. This makes it crucial for parties to ensure that they are well represented in Länder legislatures and the governments that they control. The result is a system of integrated political parties, organized along a traditional left-right axis, that "exacerbate social conflict but integrate regional and federation-Länder institutional disputes."[9] These parties have emerged as vital instruments for managing the tensions of the German federation by providing internally consistent (both vertically and horizontally), alternate policy options and governing strategies across the system.

Australia: At first glance the Australian party system looks something like Germany's. Nationwide parties, aligned on a class-based left-right continuum, operate at both state and commonwealth levels and appear to stand for much the same policies in each forum. However, Australian national party organizations are centred in powerful state-level machines, each with distinctive regional interests, and so are not as hierarchical as in Germany. Individual parties themselves do not have the capacity or always the interest in being vehicles for managing the inevitable tensions of the federation. However, Canberra's bicameral parliament has produced a unique party dynamic that contributes to balancing interests by framing the partisan shape of the political system's accommodative practices. The House of Representatives, chosen by a majority electoral system, produces aggressive two-party competition; the Senate, with its proportional electoral system and equal state representation, produces multi-party competition. The country effectively now has two distinct national party systems made up of the same parties. In the competitive politics of the house system, parties play an aggressive winner-take-all game; in the accommodative Senate system, they are engaged in a more cooperative bargaining politics.[10] Much of the Australian parties' capacity to provide balance to national policy-making is to be found in the interaction of these two apparently contradictory party systems within the commonwealth parliament.

United Kingdom: The newly federalizing United Kingdom is quite a different kind of multi-level political system, for three of its four distinct regional units — Northern Ireland, Scotland and Wales — have unique sets of governing institutions and relationships to the central state, while the largest unit —

England — has no separate political institutions of its own at all. This is asymmetrical quasi-federalism writ large. The traditional national party system, looking superficially like that of Germany or Australia, plays little effective part in managing its multi-level politics. None of the major British parties has any presence in Northern Ireland, nor any role in bridging the politics of the province with the rest of the United Kingdom. For their part, the local parties in Northern Ireland are consumed with defending the particularistic claims of their parochial clienteles. Scotland and Wales have party systems that each pit different nationalist parties against Labour; the Conservatives are not a competitive presence in either. The third party, the Liberal Democrats, is positioned to play coalition games in Scotland and Wales but can do little more than operate as a "constructive opposition" at Westminster. Britain now has a party system in which Labour is the only major party with either an interest in or capacity to manage the divergent impulses of (most of) the "federation." Thus far, this highly centralized party has responded unevenly, providing for some decentralization, but not autonomy, for its Scottish and Welsh organizations. This is likely to prove difficult. The competitive balances are such that while Labour continues to play a traditional competitive game in general elections, it must play a coalitional game in Scotland, and an accommodative game in Wales.[11] How Labour will reorganize and reposition itself to do this is not clear. It is equally unclear how the Conservatives, who have little place in the Celtic provinces, will be able to manage the new federal system if and when they return to office.

Belgium: Over the past three decades Belgium has undergone a major decentralization and federalization of its governing institutions. This was driven by the politicization of the country's linguistic divisions, a process whose first victims were the political parties. In the aftermath, the parties split along linguistic lines leaving no single Belgian party system but rather two distinct ones — Flemish and Walloon. Despite the disappearance of federal parties, the national level remains the predominant focus for party activity and politicians' ambition.[12] The parties themselves have maintained their organizations and their control of both levels of government by retaining and exploiting immense patronage resources. However, managing this federation is increasingly complicated as the central state is being continually gutted, with authority being transferred up to higher levels (the European Union), or down to both regional and community authorities. To operate the political system, the regional parties that populate the parallel party systems have adopted "the norm and practice of double symmetry in composing coalitions."[13] This means parties from the same party family — across the whole system — move into government or opposition together, and that regional level coalition partnerships mirror those at the national level. Holding simultaneous elections at both levels facilitated that pattern, but the discontinuance of that practice after

1999 is likely to sharply increase the centrifugal pressures on Belgium's political life. The Belgian system now survives by combining the practice of segmented, patronage-driven competition with coalition politics.

These four examples illustrate that the role of individual parties and the shape of party systems vary considerably across multi-level political systems. There is no common or uniform role for political parties. In each case, the distinctive institutional arrangements of the particular political system govern the demands made on the parties and provide the framework within which they must manage the politics of federal governance. Though the basic structure of party competition is ordered by the underlying social cleavages of their respective societies, each of these polities has evolved a distinctive pattern of party organization and activity. In all, the parties must find a way to practice both *competitive* and *coalitional* politics, to structure electoral choice but then to accommodate the demands of governing. In Germany, this occurs both within and between parties. Parties build inter-Länder coalitions while each of their Land and federal organizations competes in discrete party systems with distinctive electoral cycles. The Australian parties manage by simultaneously operating in two national party systems, each of which is governed by unique electoral rules, and so have divergent competitive-coalitional imperatives. In Britain, the partisan management of the new federalizing constitutional arrangements present special challenges, for there is only one party positioned to operate in both the distinctive regional and national political arenas. Finally, Belgian parties continue to tie themselves to a pattern of two-level symmetrical coalitions despite having completely broken along regionally distinct linguistic lines.

Our understanding of Canadian parties has largely focused on their electoral role and on the individual federal and provincial governments that party system competition has produced. If we are to shift the focus to consider the role of the political parties in managing the Canadian federation, we need to start by exploring the way in which they practice coalitional as well as competitive politics, and how these two dimensions interact across the federal-provincial divide.

CANADIAN PARTIES AND THE SHIFTING FEDERATION

For all that Canadian politics and the patterns of party competition have changed since Confederation, the country's political parties have always been thin organizations. They are essentially nineteenth century cadre-style parties with comparatively modest organizational infrastructures and limited policy-making capacity.[14] From the beginning, they have been focused on their parliamentary wings and concentrated power in the hands of leaders seen to personify their claims and ambitions. Parties are not the instruments of an active and engaged citizenry. As Donald Savoie bluntly puts it, Canadian parties are not instruments of governing with a plan of action for when they come to office — they are little more than politicians' "election-day organizations."[15] Of course, it is in the creation and recreation of electoral alliances over the decades that these party politicians have struggled with the divergent pressures of the federation. And to be successful, or even to just survive, they have had to find ways to reflect the product of their electoral equations in meeting the challenges of governing an evolving and increasingly complex federal system.

In their sweeping account of the development of the Canadian federation, Richard Simeon and Ian Robinson are at pains to demonstrate that the very character of the federation, and so federal practice, has shifted dramatically over time. They argue that "federal form follows state function"[16] and suggest that large changes in the tasks demanded of the state — a dynamic they portray as being driven by societal accommodations and political alliances — have led to a succession of essentially different federal regimes in Canada. Their analysis is particularly helpful in identifying distinctive eras, each with characteristic political/governance formulae, and the periods of crisis interspersed between them. They suggest that, after a long period of "classic federalism," characterized by limited government with comparatively weak provincial states, the crisis of the 1930s and the mobilization imperatives of the war years stimulated the construction of a modern activist state whose politics were managed by "executive federalism." Writing in 1990, they saw that regime succumbing to a crisis of the post-war order which was, in turn, leading into a period of national reconciliation and collaborative federalism. We now know the latter to have been something of a false dawn. The defeat of the Meech Lake and Charlottetown constitutional accords, and the subsequent electoral earthquake of 1993 with its emergence of regional parties with radical agendas, has shaken the system — and we are left to ponder whether political parties are the instruments for managing or destroying the federation.

Simeon and Robinson give very little attention to the role of political parties as primary agents in operating the federal system. That being the case, it is useful to review briefly the ways in which the party systems have operated to manage the federal dimension of the political system in earlier periods, and the impact that changes in the federal arrangements have had on party organization and activity. That story provides the necessary context for understanding the parties' capacities for managing the contemporary system.

Politicians over the first half-century after Confederation, the classic period of Canadian federalism, were preoccupied with building a new state, growing the federation from four to nine provinces and slowly expanding the reach of party politics across the country and through the provinces. The parties of that era were tightly articulated networks that provided a common face to their supporters, who hardly distinguished between the worlds of federal and provincial politics. While Liberal governments in Toronto might fight with Conservative governments in Ottawa, together the two great parties tied the politics of the emerging political systems together. Thus Wilfrid Laurier's Liberals broke the Conservatives' hold on the national government in 1896 by riding to power on the backs of their strong provincial machines, only to have Robert Borden's Conservatives repeat the trick in 1911. In each case, important provincial party leaders joined the new administration to ensure its agenda incorporated their interests and issues. Escott Reid once claimed that "it is the give and take of patronage that binds together in an apparently indissoluble union federal and provincial politics."[17] If it did so, it was only by binding the federal and provincial parties together — when they came unstuck so too did the "indissoluble union." Nevertheless, for 50 years, these parties, offering competing approaches to the federal balance, provided a pattern of relatively homogeneous competition in the least regionalized party system in the country's history. The oscillation of the federal-provincial pendulum ultimately worked to the advantage of the provinces and the Liberals who were on that side of the swing, setting the stage for a transformation in the federation and a reconstruction of the party system that would be left to manage it.

That early party approach to managing the Canadian federation bears some of the marks of the contemporary German system. The parties of the day found a way to build political coalitions that at once reached both across the country and down into the provinces so that Conservatives or Liberals, wherever they were found, sang from the same page of the hymn book. Those competing alliances provided for a more integrated partisan approach to governance as the parties sought to stamp their preferences on the federation. In Canada, it may have been the imperatives of patronage rather than the appeals of ideology that cemented those coalitions together, but they were no less real for that. Inevitably, the introduction of a merit-based civil service led to the elimination of much of the patronage that had been necessary to maintain the parties, and in turn, it dissolved the organizational linkages that bound federal and provincial partisan interests together. That such reforms proceeded unevenly across the provinces only worked to fragment the national parties and contribute to the collapse of that first party system.

The story of the collapse of the party system in the years after the World War I is a familiar tale. It saw the failure of the Conservatives as a genuinely national party as well as the emergence of a number of small, regionally based parties, principally in western Canada. The result was the end of effective national party competition, and the beginnings of the separation of the national- and provincial-level party systems. Together these developments sapped the congruence of political interest between politicians in the two arenas of party life and so contributed to the erosion of an integrated federal politics. At the same time, the demands made on the governments that the parties were fighting over were themselves changing. First, the Great Depression generated demands for social and economic action from the central government that could not be met under the existing regime, and the very inability to alter significantly the political bargain codified in the constitution threw the long-standing system of classical federalism into crisis. Then, the subsequent wartime mobilization of the society over-rode existing federal-provincial balances with the enormous growth and concentration of the central government's place in the social and economic order.

Through this long period, the political management and direction of the federation was largely in the hands of the Liberal Party. It provided for this by maintaining the tradition of co-opting prominent regional figures into its national leadership cadre — the federal Cabinet. This was the ministerialist party, practicing the brokerage politics of the omnibus, which Reginald Whitaker[18] has so brilliantly chronicled. The big change was that much of the party system no longer spanned the federal-provincial divide, and even the Liberals in different regions were no longer always on the same page. When post-World War-II realities returned the agenda to contentious domestic issues, provincial parties pursuing their own distinctive agendas challenged the Liberals' claim to set the terms and direction of the federation. The party's long run, from 1935–57, was a function of the success and dominance of the central state. More importantly, it reflected the incapacity of the national party system to produce a credible alternative government given the Conservatives' organizational collapse and electoral failures in Quebec and on the Prairies. With little competition, the coalition-building brokerage demanded of Liberals was never so taxing as to threaten its electoral coalition.

Ultimately the Liberal Party's easy political hegemony proved its undoing. The ministerialism it practiced left the party little more than an extension of the Cabinet so that its political organization degenerated into Savoie's election-day front for the administration, what Whitaker was to label the "Government Party." Democratic party politics failed, leaving a political vacuum into which John Diefenbaker's Conservatives eventually exploded as they reshaped the political alignments of the country and weakened further the already fragile federal-provincial party linkages. At the same time, the federal system itself was undergoing major changes. The basis for a new, modern federalism had been laid through the development of a complex set of fiscal arrangements that were a second best response to the impossibility of constitutional reform to the federal order. These administrative responses laid the foundations for a federal politics of intergovernmental competition and co-operation.

MANAGING EXECUTIVE FEDERALISM

The politics of modern Canada have been the politics of executive federalism. With Ottawa holding the richest purse strings, and the provinces maintaining their pre-eminence over the expensive spending jurisdictions, the big issues of public policy have been settled in an elaborate system of intergovernmental accommodation presided over by the first ministers. Each of the governments involved is a party government, pursuing a distinctive electoral agenda in highly competitive, "winner-take-all" contests, and each is capable of generating the resources needed to secure its own re-election. No longer were the parties interested in, or capable of, integrating policies over both levels of government. Indeed, the very process of intergovernmental policy-making worked to fragment the parties as partisan organizations at each level sought to convince their electorate that they would aggressively defend their interest.

Bifurcating parties' electoral imperatives led to a pattern of disconnected competition, in which parties at each level had little need or desire for assistance from their namesakes at the other — indeed, relationships often oscillated between ambivalence and antagonism.[19] For instance, Joseph Wearing reports how, in the 1960s, the governing Saskatchewan Liberals no longer saw themselves as part of a larger Liberal cause but aggressively challenged the national Liberal government in order to woo Saskatchewan voters.[20] At the same time, the national party was seeking to distance itself from a Saskatchewan namesake that it feared was too right-wing for supporters in central Canada. The logic of this dynamic, repeated across the country, led to the separation of federal and provincial party organizations in all but the small Atlantic provinces and the ideologically more coherent New Democrats. With organizational fragmentation came financial independence and the development of distinctive and separate career paths for politicians. The upshot was a complex set of provincial and national political parties in which even members who came from the same political family, and bore the same name, no longer sang from the same page — indeed, they often appeared to be using quite different hymn books.[21] An important consequence of party fragmentation was a continuing divergence of the national and provincial party systems that had started in the inter-war west. Most Canadians faced different sets of choices in the "two political worlds"[22] in which they lived so that, even at the level of personal loyalty or activity, the parties lost their capacity to integrate the political life of the federation's citizens.

This standard interpretation of the parties' role in the system of executive federalism, and its impact on party politics, is primarily focused on competitive dynamics and their impact on the shape of the party systems. Unlike the brokerage model of the earlier period, it pays little heed to the parties as governors, and it emphasizes the extent to which electoral politics work to aggravate rather than ameliorate regional tensions. However, it is equally important to recognize that there is an accommodative dimension to the partisan management of federal-provincial issues. While Canadian parties, operating within their own sphere, appear to have an almost unnatural fear of coalition governments — preferring when necessary minority administrations — their leaders regularly actively engage in bargaining and accommodative coalition-style politics in the federal-provincial decision-making arena. While these political coalitions do not have the same formal shape as the coalition governments formed in many other parliamentary democracies, they do constitute much the same kind of inter-party issue management, decision-making and governing. Given its multi-level reality, several features of this distinctive Canadian coalition party politics mark it out from that in other systems — and have a considerable impact on how it structures the way parties must go about their business.

- Coalition members are party governments — not parties per se. The principal actors in managing the federation are governments, but they are almost always one-party governments. The politicians who speak for them owe their office to their party and must therefore be responsive to its partisan interests. However, they also need to be sensitive to the wider interests of the government they represent, and this has the consequence of drawing politicians away from a narrow interpretation of their party commitments.

- Coalition politics has no well-institutionalized structures. Coalition making in parliamentary systems normally focuses on Cabinet formation and maintenance processes, whose norms and procedures are clearly understood. Canada's coalition politics is played out in a range of under-institutionalized forums — for instance, the Annual Premiers' Conference, First Ministers Conferences, and a myriad of multi-level ministerial conferences (see the essays by Peter Meekison, Richard Simeon and Martin Papillon, and Julie Simmons in this volume) — which are poorly integrated and seek to obfuscate the partisan face of the interests involved. As a consequence, parties per se are estranged from the central task of political accommodation.

- Coalition activity emerges around issues, not programs. Intergovernmental bargaining and accommodation centres on specific issues or problems facing the governments. The participants' challenge is to develop the political will to make (or avoid) a decision, rather than a package of commitments that would constitute a wider political program. This makes for incremental decision-making in issue areas where consensus can be reached but continuing conflict or stalemate (maintenance of the status quo) in others. In this context, ongoing policy-making is not governed by consistent partisan orientations or coherent electoral mandates.

- Coalition formation does not involve creating minimum winning coalitions with policy-adjacent partners. In most democracies, party politicians seeking to build coalitions are sensitive to both the size and the policy coherence of their partnerships. The ideal coalition is no bigger than necessary and contains partners whose policy preferences are close to one another. Neither of these conditions holds in the world of Canadian federal-provincial coalition-making. With 11 governments (more if the territories are included) needed for major projects, coalitions must often reach from one end to the other of more than one spectrum. Thus, recent efforts to build constitution-mending coalitions required that Liberal, Conservative, New Democratic, Social Credit and Parti Québécois parties all be engaged. In such coalitions politicians lose their partisan anchors, and the electorate, much chance of holding them accountable. Even where smaller coalitions (involving fewer participants) are formed, the policy differences between the partners may be large.

- Coalition members cannot choose their partners. In typical coalitional politics, political parties can usually decide for themselves whether or not to enter a partnership with others. In those structured by the intergovernmental framework of the Canadian federation, the voters of the several distinct and disengaged party systems effectively choose coalition members when they elect a government. For instance, while most parties in the country might prefer to collaborate with a federalist party from Quebec, they do not always get that option; they have to take the party that the Quebec electorate sends. Thus, many parties come to office thinking that they will control the government they have just won. They do, but also soon discover that in many important area policy-making areas they have up to ten partners, none of whom they chose, and some who share few of their goals or priorities.

- Parties do not get to decide whether they will engage in coalition politics. It follows from the imperatives of federal-provincial policy-making that, if elected, parties must inevitably enter into a coalition game. Going it alone is difficult for governments with active agendas in areas of major social or economic policy except in the unusual circumstances where cost or externalities are not significant constraints. And parties that wish to forestall change, or shrink the very size and scope of government, will soon find that they are bound in a network of expectations and obligations that limit their autonomy.

- There is no transparent measure of the relative strength or value of coalition members. The genial fiction of Canadian federal-provincial relations is that all governments are equal, and in that all may be required for particular action, there is a sense in which this may be so. There is also little doubt that the big and rich governments generally have more manoeuvring room, but there are issues that may give a special claim to some (bilingualism to New Brunswick, agriculture to

Saskatchewan) or where particular parties have expertise or experience. Each of the participating parties is sensitive to its government's political base and that of its partners. Those with strong support at the beginning of a mandate will be freer than minority parties near the end, but none of these dimensions compare with the hard measures (e.g. seat shares) that partners can point to in traditional parliamentary coalition-building systems.

- Party labels are no guide to coalition partnership. With the fragmentation and separation of the national and provincial party organizations, party labels no longer provide any easy guide to the orientation or interest of coalition partners. For instance, Liberals occupy the left in some regions (Atlantic provinces) but the right in others (British Columbia) and coalition leadership must vary by issue to reflect these kinds of differences. The Trudeau Liberals' closest allies on the constitution were Conservatives in Ontario and New Brunswick, while the Mulroney Tories clung to the Quebec Liberals over free trade.

- The party coalitions are constantly changing. Members come and go in response to 11 unrelated electoral cycles that constantly produce partisan change and governmental turnovers. This means that there is no guarantee that those who begin a decision-making cycle will be around to see it through. The continuing change in the parties at the federal-provincial coalition table can have a significant effect on the conduct and outcome of its coalition politics. A dramatic instance of this occurred during the Meech Lake episode when the process was upset by important changes in the constitutional accord coalition that were forced, mid-game, by electoral turnovers in New Brunswick and then Newfoundland.

Beyond these specific features of the coalition process, the structural realities of the federation produce a set of competitive imperatives that shape the character of the parties engaged in this multi-level system. On the one hand, provinces have become the focus and instrument for the expression of regional interests and ambitions, and parties that fight to control them must work to define and reflect those impulses. Thus, successful provincial parties must *articulate* interests. By contrast, the national party system represents a complex layering of all these interests and the traditional role for national parties with a majoritarian bent has been to build electoral alliances that encompass competing interests. This is the model of the notorious omnibus party whose vocation is to *aggregate* interests.[23] This leaves the federation's decision-making coalitions made up of political parties whose fundamental approach to representation is at odds with one another. As interest aggregators, national parties are the natural coalition leaders but they cannot count on interest articulating provincial parties to approach problems, or represent the political world, from the same perspective or with the same ambitions. This fundamental difference in the very character of the parties forced to work together is a principal structural weakness in the coalition politics inherent in the Canadian practice of executive federalism.

THE PARTY POLITICS OF THE FEDERATION

Simeon and Robinson's portrait of the evolving character of Canadian feder-alism came to a close with the suggestion of a new phase — a renewed collaborative federalism characterized by increased harmony amongst the governments and promoted by the Mulroney Conservatives seeking to trans-form their party into a natural party of government. As it turned out, those efforts ultimately collapsed in the failures of the Meech Lake and then Charlottetown accords to amend the constitution, and the subsequent emer-gence of the populist western Reform Party and the revitalization of an aggressive Québécois nationalist movement in federal politics. Those events spilled into the national party system in the earthquake election of 1993. Not only did the political havoc it wrought mark it as the democratic election with the greatest partisan shift of any in the twentieth century, but it overturned the federal party system, which had been dominated by a set of national parties committed to a pan-Canadian approach to political leadership.[24] Strikingly, those events had no ripple effect on the provinces' parties and party systems (eschewed by Reform), which appeared unchanged by the transformation of federal politics. This was another clear confirmation of just how disconnected federal and provincial party politics have become in Canada.

Executive federalism, with its demands for coalition leadership from na-tional parties worked, in considerable part, because for three decades national politics was dominated by parties all prepared to preach and practice pan-Canadianism — that is, a commitment to building intra-party coalitions on the basis of agendas designed to attract nationwide support. The Liberals, Conservatives, and New Democrats constructed an oligopolistic national po-litical market rooted in a common understanding of the basis of the federation and the political norms governing it. Parliamentary majorities were no longer based on a marriage of the Prairies (Saskatchewan) and Quebec as they had been in the King-St. Laurent period. They came to turn on Ontario that had become the pivot of Canadian politics: the Liberals could prevail by marrying Quebec to Ontario; the Tories if a Prairie-Ontario partnership triumphed.[25] It was this precariously balanced pair of alternatives that the Conservative sweep of 1984 so upset. Through those years, government parties were less secure and had narrower caucuses than in earlier eras, but this simply strengthened the pan-Canadian electoral imperatives.

The revolt in the federal election of 1993 was a response by growing numbers of Canadians who felt shut out by the cozy philosophical and organizational hegemony that the three national parties had imposed upon the country's politics. Those parties' inability to deliver great constitutional reforms heralded their downfall, and all those who had not seen their interests represented in the dominant formula — Quebec nationalists, advocates of small government, believers in traditional social values, alienated westerners and populists — took the opportunity to flee to parties determined to advocate their interests rather than compromise their principles. When the dust settled, both the Conservatives and New Democrats had been devastated and, despite protestations to the contrary, reduced to little more than marginal actors from marginal regions. Their place in national politics was usurped by two new parties — Reform and the Bloc Québécois. These interlopers were fundamentally opposed to the old parties' definition and practices of pan-Canadian executive federalism, and committed to a politics of interest articulation. While the Liberals emerged from the election with a majority, it was one based on the lowest vote share of any majority government in the country's history. They managed this at the cost of making the party dangerously dependent upon Ontario — for the first time over half the caucus came from that province — and so hardly better placed to convince Canadians that it was capable of aggregating interests in the way traditionally expected of national parties. The passengers' problem was not that the omnibuses had stalled; it was that there were none left on the road.

Can Canadian executive federalism work without some pan-Canadian, interest-aggregating party to provide leadership to the coalition politics that are at its heart? That is the hard question raised by the collapse of the third (Diefenbaker through Mulroney) party system, for such a genuinely national party has yet to emerge from the post-1993 rubble. The Chrétien Liberal Party is often portrayed as unadventurous and risk-averse but, however wanting or not its ambition, it is limited by its very nature in its capacity to establish or lead the shifting federal coalitions. Its own shrunken position in the national party system, reduced to the voice of distinctive, increasingly regional, interests rather than the representative of an incipient national consensus, has deprived it of a claim to any special *primus inter pares* position in the management of the federation's political decision-making life. Neither of its principal opponents, the Bloc or the Alliance, provides a solution to the problem, for both seek to change the country's political dynamics by substantially reducing the place, and leadership, of the national government in the life of the federation.

Competition animates all of the country's parties and encourages them to take distinguishable positions on issues that fall into the federal-provincial arena. Though the parties and party systems at the two levels are disconnected, this does not mean that the operation or consequences of party competition are. The multi-level character of Canadian politics has a considerable influence on party fortunes, and through them, on the workings of the wider system. Most obvious is the ingrained habit of provincial governments taking an aggressive stance against Ottawa for local electoral advantage. Mobilizing against another government, whatever its partisan colour, rather than one's immediate opponents, can make it more difficult to reach intergovernmental accommodations than might otherwise be the case.

Governing parties may soon sense the limits to which they can push their federal-provincial partners. Opposition parties, whose political leadership often has no experience of the coalition imperatives of executive federalism, have a more limited appreciation and concern for their real manoeuvring room, and so the implications and consequences of the promises they make. In an attempt to defeat their local opponents, they may engage in an outbidding that is ultimately corrosive of the national system. The New Brunswick Liberals provide a classic example of this dysfunctional (for the system, but not their party) behaviour. By the mid-1980s, the party had suffered four successive defeats and it was desperate and determined to overthrow the long-running Richard Hatfield Conservatives. To do so required that they reclaim traditional bases in francophone areas of the province that the Conservatives had successfully usurped. In rebuilding those relationships, the opposition provincial Liberal party rejected provisions of the Meech Lake Accord and promised to have it changed to better reflect the concerns of the Acadian community. Once in office the party found itself trapped between that important electoral commitment, by which it had defined its interest, and the political realities of the federal-provincial world that made changes to the agreement impossible. This was an instance of an unanticipated shift in the wider coalition charged with managing the federation. It began the unravelling of Meech and all that eventually followed. While this is something of a dramatic case, it illustrates the ways in which the idiosyncrasies of domestic competition in one of the 11 party systems can spill over into the world of federal-provincial relations. And the very irregularity and disconnectedness of the electoral cycles involved makes managing a process that requires keeping 11 different governing parties onside particularly difficult.

Not surprisingly, the pressures of the game can also run in the other direction as parties build alliances and create obligations in the world of federal-provincial accommodation that are then called in under competitive pressure. This can happen within party families, as with Brian Mulroney's Conservatives when they came to the expensive aid of Grant Devine's government in Saskatchewan (though providing such help is a version of a game that is as old as the country). However, now that party organizations are truncated and disconnected, alliances forged in the federation's cause by parties in different families across levels have become a feature of the politics of the country.

One recent example of this was the Quebec Liberal Party's (government's) support for the national Progressive Conservatives' free trade program in the hard-fought general election of 1988. Quebec was only one of two provinces in which the Conservatives won a majority of seats that year, so that provincial Liberal support may well have been crucial to its re-election success. It would be rash to assume that the coalition partnerships built by governing parties, irrespective of the partisan labels they carry, do not make important subsequent differences to electoral outcomes at both levels, and so ultimately to the continuing management of the federation.

THE PLACE OF PARTY

Let us conclude by returning to our opening question — whether Canada's political parties are part of the problem or part of the solution to the challenges of managing the federation. Parties are first and foremost organizations engaged in political competition, but in the process of competing for power they can bridge differences by assembling broadly based electoral alliances, linking disparate interests and regions and, in multi-level systems of governance, drawing together politicians from the system's different levels. German parties do this through ideologically structured intra-party accommodations, the Australians' particular form of bicameralism leaves their national parties simultaneously engaging in separate competitive and accommodative party systems, while the Belgians use a complex system of matched post-election coalitions to structure patronage driven accommodations. The problem in Canada is that the structure of the federation leaves none of these options open to the political parties. Despite its regionalized multi-party politics, the single-member plurality electoral system, and the adversarial single-party executive-driven governments it produces, inhibit the opportunities or incentives for parties to engage in classic parliamentary-based coalition politics. Canada's accommodative coalition politics is thus pushed into the rather idiosyncratic form encountered, or avoided, in the federal-provincial intergovernmental dynamic that propels the federation. In this process, political interests are portrayed as governance issues and political parties — and the electorates that reward or punish them — are displaced from centre stage.

It is clear that the range and ability of national catch-all parties to aggregate interests and demands across the entire country has become increasingly narrow. For much of the twentieth century, the space consumed by government parties in assembling a brokerage-style omnibus or a pan-Canadian coalition left scant room for a second party to compete effectively against it. Since 1993, the regionally and ideologically fragmented party system has left the country without even one federal party able to generate significant support, and mobilize authoritative electoral coalitions, from all parts of the country. The result is that coalition making in the federal-provincial system is deprived of strong political (i.e. partisan) leadership.

In other federations, it is the parties' capacity to organize and integrate political life across levels that makes them primary instruments for political management. In Canada, the nearly complete disconnection between federal and provincial party organizations and competitive systems limits their ability to integrate the disparate elements of the federation. The newest federal party, the Canadian Alliance, has a truncated structure, deliberately disdaining direct provincial counterparts, while the older parties (outside of Atlantic Canada) operate, where they can, separate and largely autonomous party organizations dependent upon an ability to muster independent resources. This separation is reinforced by distinct federal and provincial career patterns, the comparatively short political careers of Canadian politicians, and the thin and intermittent cast of the parties' extra-parliamentary organizations. Disconnected party organizations, and the disconnected politics which they engender, may fit very well with a political system in which federal and provincial governments compete for scarce resources, but do very little to encourage common understandings or common solutions around which political — as opposed to governmental or bureaucratic — support might be mobilized.

The logic of contemporary Canadian party organization reflects the ways in which the Canadian confederation has evolved as well as broader trends in the party politics in liberal democracies. As such, contemporary parties appear to be neither part of the problem of Canadian politics — it might be more correct to say that they are a reflection of it — nor an obvious part of the solution. In the past Canadian parties used patronage, and then later regional brokerage, to mobilize electoral coalitions capable of supporting governments able to manage what was then a more centralized federation. The rise of active provincial governments and the emergence of distinctive party systems driving provincial agendas have stripped national parties of much of their ability to direct the federation. But the coalitions that parties, acting as governments, must now create to manage the federation are poor substitutes. Their very character — fleeting, shifting, and over-sized — makes them unresponsive, fragile and electorally unaccountable. Locked into this syndrome, Canadian parties hardly seem the instruments that a democratic citizenry can use for managing its federation.

NOTES

1.   André Siegfried, *The Race Question in Canada*, reprint (Toronto: McClelland and Stewart, 1966), pp. 112-14.

2.   R. Kenneth Carty and David Stewart, "Parties and Party Systems," in *Provinces: Canadian Provincial Politics*, ed. C. Dunn (Peterborough: Broadview Press, 1996).

3. Steven B. Wolinetz and R. Kenneth Carty, "Disconnected Competition in Canada." A paper prepared for the conference on Multi-Level Electoral Competition: Devolution in Comparative Context, Birmingham, 2001. Soon to be published under the same title in *Devolution and Electoral Politics: A Comparative Exploration*, eds. Dan Hough and Charlie Jeffery (Manchester: Manchester University Press).

4. Steven B. Wolinetz, "Parties in Multilevel Systems of Governance: A Working Paper on Parties and Party Systems in the European Union and Other Multilevel Systems of Governance and the Ways in Which they Might Develop." Prepared for the annual meeting of the Canadian Political Science Association, 1999.

5. William Chandler, "Federalism and Political Parties," in *Federalism and the Role of the State*, eds. H. Bakvis and W. Chandler (Toronto: University of Toronto Press, 1987); Lori Thorlakson, "Political Competition in Federal States: Measuring and Explaining Party System Congruence." A paper prepared for the conference on Multi-Level Electoral Competition: Devolution in Comparative Context, Birmingham, 2001; and Wolfgang Renzsch, "Bifurcated and Integrated Parties in Parliamentary Federations: The Canadian and German Cases," Working Paper 2001(4), Institute of Intergovernmental Relations, Queen's University, Kingston, at <qsilver.queensu.ca/iigr/publications/working_paper_series/renzsch.pdf>.

6. Renzsch, "Bifurcated and Integrated Parties in Parliamentary Federations," p. 23.

7. Richard Simeon and Ian Robinson, *State, Society and the Development of Canadian Federalism* (Toronto: University of Toronto Press, 1990).

8. Renzsch, "Bifurcated and Integrated Parties in Parliamentary Federations," p. 21.

9. Ibid., p. 24.

10. R. Kenneth Carty, "Australian Democrats in Comparative Perspective," in *Keeping the Bastards Honest: The Australian Democrats' First Twenty Years*, ed. John Warhurst (St. Leonards NSW: Allen & Unwin, 1997).

11. Anthony King, "Britain's Constitutional Revolution," in *Britain at the Polls, 2001*, ed. Anthony King (New York: Chatham House, 2002), pp. 61-65.

12. Lieven De Winter, "Multi-Level Party Competition and Co-ordination in Belgium." A paper prepared for the conference on Multi-Level Electoral Competition: Devolution in Comparative Context, Birmingham, 2001.

13. Ibid.

14. R. Kenneth Carty, "Canada's 19th Century Cadre Parties at the Millennium," in *Political Parties in Advanced Industrial Societies*, ed. P. Webb *et al.* (Oxford: Oxford University Press, 2002).

15. Donald Savoie, *Governing From the Centre: The Concentration of Power in Canadian Politics* (Toronto: University of Toronto Press, 1999), p. 344.

16. Simeon and Robinson, *State, Society and the Development of Canadian Federalism*, p. 339.

17. Escott Reid, "The Saskatchewan Liberal Machine before 1929," reprinted in *Party Politics in Canada* 4th ed., ed. H. G. Thorburn (Scarborough: Prentice-Hall, 1979), p. 31.

18. Reginald Whitaker, *The Government Party: Organizing and Financing the Liberal Party of Canada, 1930-1958* (Toronto: University of Toronto Press, 1977).

19. Wolinetz and Carty, "Parties in Multilevel Systems of Government."

20. Joseph Wearing, *The L-Shaped Party: The Liberal Party of Canada 1958-1980* (Toronto: McGraw-Hill Ryerson, 1981), pp. 28, 43.

21. Rand Dyck, "Links Between Federal and Provincial Parties and Party Systems," in *Representation, Integration and Political Parties in Canada*, ed. H. Bakvis (Toronto: Dundurn, 1991); Carty and Stewart, "Parties and Party Systems."

22. Donald E. Blake, *Two Political Worlds: Parties and Voting in British Columbia* (Vancouver: UBC Press, 1985).

23. John Meisel, "The Stalled Omnibus: Canadian Parties in the 1960s," *Social Research* 30,3 (1963).

24. R. Kenneth Carty, William Cross and Lisa Young, *Rebuilding Canadian Party Politics* (Vancouver: UBC Press, 2000).

25. R. Kenneth Carty, "On the Road Again: The 'Stalled Omnibus' Revisited," in *Canada's Century: Governance in a Maturing Society: Essays in Honour of John Meisel*, eds. C.E.S. Franks *et al.* (Montreal: McGill-Queen's University Press, 1995), pp. 197-98.

4

Guarding the Constitution: Parliamentary and Judicial Roles Under the Charter

James B. Kelly

Ce chapitre a pour but d'analyser l'effet de l'activisme judiciaire sur les institutions de la fédération canadienne et de critiquer l'analogie de «gardien de la constitution», employée tant par ceux qui défendent que ceux qui critiquent la Cour suprême du Canada. Même si la Cour est l'unique «gardien de la constitution» dans un sens purement juridique et formel, la réalité de gouverner avec la Charte et le fonctionnement informel de la constitution ont plutôt entraîné l'émergence de plusieurs gardiens de la constitution. En effet, l'émergence d'un activisme coordonné des droits, exercé par les institutions parlementaires et judiciaires, a assuré la protection des caractéristiques fondamentales de la constitution, soit le fédéralisme et la démocratie parlementaire. Le principe du fédéralisme, par exemple, a été protégé par une jurisprudence qui respecte l'autonomie des provinces ainsi que par un processus politique réformé qui relie les objectifs politiques aux valeurs de la Charte canadienne. L'émergence d'un tel processus politique constitue le résultat le plus important de l'enchâssement de la Charte et non pas de l'accroissement du pouvoir judiciaire.

The "guardian of the constitution" metaphor has been consistently used in *Charter of Rights and Freedoms* decisions by the Supreme Court, and first appeared during former Chief Justice Brian Dickson's judgement for the court in *Hunter v. Southam*.[1] Most recently, the court has reaffirmed this role in *United States v. Burns*, a case involving the issue of ministerial discretion and whether the Minister of Justice must seek assurances that the death penalty will not be sought for Canadian citizens requested for extradition to foreign jurisdictions. The ruling was that "the court is the guardian of the constitution and death penalty cases are uniquely bound up with basic constitutional values."[2] The guardian metaphor has been used by both the critics and supporters of judicial activism to demonstrate the significant impact that judicial decisions have had on Canadian democracy, with the critics suggesting that this activism has undermined Canadian democracy and resulted in a paradigm shift to judicial supremacy.[3] The supporters have embraced the guardian metaphor because it is claimed to advance the democratic dialogue between courts and legislatures that these scholars consider necessary for the maturing of Canadian democracy to a system based on constitutional supremacy.[4] Indeed, both positions contend that the guardian role is a fundamentally new function for the Supreme Court that is drastically different from its earlier responsibility as the "umpire" of Canadian federalism. Further, the critics have suggested that the Supreme Court has approached the guardian role in a way that has fundamentally weakened Canadian federalism, because the invalidation of provincial statutes as a violation of the Charter allows national values to trump provincial values and thus reduce the policy autonomy of provincial governments.[5]

This chapter assesses the guardian role as well as the impact of Charter review by the Supreme Court on provincial autonomy and policy diversity in Canada. In taking up this question, however, this chapter disputes that this role is a fundamentally different one for the Supreme Court, and contends that it is simply the modern manifestation of the "umpire of federalism" role now that the constitution has moved beyond its concern with the division of powers under the "old" constitution to explicitly protecting rights and freedoms under the "new" constitution. From the beginning, federalism has been a fundamental characteristic of the Canadian constitution and the Supreme Court has guarded this principle in its interpretation of both the division of powers and the Charter of Rights. Thus, I will challenge the position by judicial critics that the Supreme Court has undermined Canadian federalism by demonstrating the court's sensitivity to this principle in its Charter jurisprudence. Indeed, a case can be made that the court has re-emerged as the umpire of Canadian federalism during its Charter decisions, as the court's performance of this role was much in dispute before 1982,[6] and a balance does exist in the court's treatment of the two levels of government during its Charter and non-Charter jurisprudence involving rights and freedoms.[7] While this chapter contends that the Supreme Court has generally succeeded in protecting the fundamental characteristics of the constitution, either as the umpire or the guardian of the constitution, I do not agree with the supporters of judicial activism that the guardian role is solely performed by the Supreme Court, nor is judicially structured Charter dialogue essential to ensure the importance of Charter values in legislative schemes.[8] Thus, the guardianship of the constitution is not simply the result of judicial activism but also of legislative activism that has seen Parliament and the provincial legislatures act as guardians by reaching principled decisions that incorporate Charter values into the legislative process before judicial review occurs — if in fact it ever does.

This chapter is divided into three sections. In the first section, it will be contended that the Supreme Court's jurisprudence involving the division of powers and constitutional reform during the 1960s and 1970s served to discredit it as the umpire of Canadian federalism, as a bias in favour of the federal government clearly emerged on the part of the court. It will be argued that the trend towards centralization did not continue under the Charter, as the Supreme Court has guarded the federal character of Canada in its Charter jurisprudence and has developed an approach that advances provincial autonomy. Thus, it is suggested that the impact of judicial review on the "old" constitution, the *British North America Act, 1867,* and the division of powers, is fundamentally different than its effect on the "new" constitution. Because the centralization thesis has not made the distinction between the two constitutions, its proponents have, in my opinion, reached the questionable conclusion that the centralization of Canadian federalism that occurred during division of powers cases has continued under the Charter.

The second section will demonstrate the changing approach to the guardian role by the Supreme Court, where the initial outlook provided evidence for the theory of judicial supremacy. Indeed, the Supreme Court attempted to function as the guardian of the constitution in the legal sense and did not leave room for other political actors to participate in the protection of Charter values. However, this approach did not endure, and the reality of Charter interpretation and the limitations of the Supreme Court as a policy actor, where it must rely on parliamentary actors to implement judicial decisions, saw the court demonstrate a respect for the contributions made by other political institutions in a rights-based policy environment. In effect, the Supreme Court's approach to the guardian role changed from the singularity of the formal constitutional role, which proved to be unworkable, and came to recognize the reality of Charter politics, where the court must interpret the constitution in a manner respectful of the contributions of other political institutions. The emerging approach by the Supreme Court to remedies employed in Charter cases, where the court is more inclined to suspend decisions and allow legislative actors the chance to remedy unconstitutional legislation, is evidence of the shared responsibility for Charter protection between courts and legislatures that Janet Hiebert discusses.[9]

The final section will analyze how the federal and provincial governments have taken concrete steps to reform the policy process and how this has allowed principled decisions that respect Charter values to emerge from the parliamentary arena. This combination of judicial and parliamentary action has ensured that the constitution is the shared responsibility of legislative and judicial actors who guard the constitution and its fundamental characteristics.

JUDICIAL REVIEW AND TWO CONSTITUTIONS

Under the old constitution of the *BNA Act, 1867*, the Supreme Court was charged with protecting the fundamental features of the constitutional system, which included federalism and the division of powers. In performing this role, the Supreme Court was referred to as the umpire of federalism because it sought to balance the two levels of government and to protect the federal character of Canada. Under the new constitution, which includes the *Charter of Rights and Freedoms*, the Supreme Court continues to protect the fundamental characteristics of the constitution, which has now expanded to include entrenched rights within a federal system. Indeed, the shift in the court's language from the "umpire" of federalism to the "guardian" of the constitution has been taken as evidence that the Supreme Court views itself as the only guardian of rights, and thus, has been used to argue that Canada has suffered a shift to judicial supremacy. As Donna Greschner has noted, the umpire role "connotes moderation and humility, and implies another metaphor of moderation, that of balance."[10] Further, the umpire role "places the courts in an essential but not pre-eminent role, and would help dispel charges of an imperial judiciary."[11] The reality, however, is that the umpire and guardian roles are essentially the same in the political sense or the actual functioning of the constitution, though these roles have fundamentally different implications in the formal sense, thus creating the impression that the court has elevated itself — or has been elevated — to a position that compromises constitutional supremacy. The guardian role must be conceptualized as existing in two forms, the constitutional (formal), and the political (informal). As a matter of constitutional law, the Supreme Court is the guardian of the constitution, and much of the confusion regarding this role is the result of scholars equating the formal constitutional role with the reality of Charter politics and the informal functioning of the constitution within the political arena. Both the supporters and critics of judicial activism have applied the guardian metaphor solely as a matter of constitutional law and have neglected that, as a matter of constitutional practice, the Supreme Court shares this responsibility with the parliamentary arena.[12] This limitation is largely the result of the judicial-centred paradigm that has dominated the Charter debate, where the functioning of Canadian constitutionalism is determined by the impact of judicial activism on parliamentary institutions. If the Supreme Court is the only guardian of the constitution, then the constitution is not well protected, as very few statutes are reviewed for their constitutionality by the court. The forgotten legacy of the Charter project of former prime minister Pierre Trudeau is that it has not simply seen the emergence of rights-based decisions in the judicial arena, but has seen the emergence of principled decisions in the parliamentary arena as well.[13]

The emergence of legislative activism challenges the assumption that the net impact of the Charter has been simply to empower judicial actors. I suggest that legislative activism has two distinct components, parliamentary and bureaucratic activism, and further, that legislative activism allows a parliament-centred approach to the Charter to emerge. Perhaps more importantly, legislative activism ensures that multiple guardians of the constitution are present and illustrates that the informal functioning of the constitution has prevented the emergence of judicial supremacy. Indeed, the reformist potential of judicial activism for the parliamentary arena has been generally overlooked in the Charter debate and this is unfortunate, as Parliament and the provincial legislatures now explicitly articulate Charter values during the development of public policy, and this is designed to reduce the potential of judicial invalidation.[14] While legislative activism has prevented the emergence of judicial supremacy, Parliament, as an institution, has become further marginalized as a policy actor. Specifically, legislative activism is driven by its bureaucratic component, as much of the institutional reform of the policy process has been within the bureaucratic arena and has strengthened the coordinative capacity of the federal Department of Justice and the provincial departments of the Attorney General. Thus, the strengthening of executive-support agencies has allowed a parliament-centred approach to Charter review to emerge, but it is executive-dominated, and parliamentary activism, therefore, is generally under the direction of the Minister of Justice and not of Parliament and its committee system. This issue will be explored in the last section of this chapter.

The Supreme Court's successful performance as the guardian of constitutional principles, however, was much in dispute before the introduction of the Charter in 1982.[15] The consistent victories of the federal government in division of powers cases,[16] and perhaps more importantly, the serious defeats of provincial governments in economic and energy policy cases, challenge Peter Hogg and Peter Russell's conclusion that the Supreme Court did not demonstrate a bias in favour the federal government because the balance of the federation shifted decidedly in favour of Ottawa in division of powers cases.[17] This national bias continued beyond division of powers cases, and is illustrated by the fact that Parliament suffered relatively few significant losses in constitutional cases, and further, that many defeats were only partial and ultimately allowed the federal government to advance its constitutional agenda. For instance, the major federal defeat at the hands of the Supreme Court after 1949 occurred in *Reference re Legislative Authority of Parliament to Alter or Replace the Senate*, when the court decided that the federal government could not unilaterally change the essential characteristics of the Senate.[18] However, through a partial victory in *Attorney General of Manitoba et al v. Attorney General of Canada et al*, the Supreme Court decided that unilateral patriation of the constitution was legal but that convention required "substantial provincial consent" before Parliament could request changes to the Canadian constitution by Westminster.[19] This decision ultimately resulted in the patriation of the constitution largely along the lines desired by the federal government, with the notable additions of the Charter's notwithstanding clause and the natural resource amendment contained within section 92A of the *Constitution Act, 1982*.

It was within this context that the centralization thesis was developed and the court began to interpret the *Charter of Rights and Freedoms*.[20] Though the centralization thesis was the dominant interpretation of the impact of Charter review on provincial autonomy, the assessment of the evidence presented here suggests that the court has acted in an even-handed manner in Charter and non-Charter cases involving rights and freedoms, and has generally respected provincial autonomy.[21] This is a striking development, as the court's approach to constitutional questions and division of powers cases in the 1970s clearly suggested that the Supreme Court would continue to favour the federal government in its Charter jurisprudence, with serious consequences for Canadian federalism — as Alan Cairns argued, that judicial nullification of provincial statutes would validate national values and lead to the decline of policy autonomy at the provincial level.[22] The reconciliation between rights and federalism in the court's Charter jurisprudence is directly related to the changed nature of the umpire or guardian role after 1982, as well as the presence of a federalism discourse within the Supreme Court's interpretation of the Charter. The centralization thesis was generally accepted without criticism, illustrated by Peter Hogg's statement that the Charter's natural momentum is towards centralization because, "where guaranteed rights exist, there must be a single national rule,"[23] which resulted in the absence of a critical reassessment of the institutional role of the court in Canadian federalism, as it was widely accepted that the bias in favour of the federal government would continue after 1982. The failure to critically reassess the Supreme Court as the guardian of constitutional principles has allowed a number of assumptions to go unchallenged: first, that the impact of judicial review is fundamentally the same under the new constitution as it is in cases involving the old constitution; second, that this role continues to create a zero-sum relationship between the provinces and the federal government when it is performed in the context of Charter decisions and the new constitution; and finally, that the balance will be in favour of the federal government and will continue the trend towards centralization.

While the institutional role of the Supreme Court is the same under the Charter as it was under the *BNA Act, 1867*, there is an important difference in the impact of judicial review under the two constitutions that challenges the centralization thesis. Under the division of powers, the court determines which level of government has jurisdiction for specific policy areas. In effect, the court has to choose between governments, and this saw the court regularly favour the federal government. Under the Charter, however, a zero-sum relationship no longer characterizes the performance of the guardian role, as a Charter defeat for the provinces does not increase the jurisdictional responsibilities of the federal government. In this sense, the guardian role under the Charter has shifted from being a redistributive function that is zero-sum under the division of powers, to a responsibility that allows the court to rule that neither level of government may act in a manner that denies protected rights and freedoms, or conversely, that all governments may act in a certain manner. Thus, the role is fundamentally different under the Charter, as the court now attempts to defend the principles of federalism, such as diversity and provincial autonomy, when it attempts to guard the constitution. In effect, the role has shifted from being concerned with the governments of the federation to the values that structure the governments of the federation. These differences are important, as judicial review involving the new constitution, the Charter, challenges the centralist direction of the old constitution.

Table 1: Invalidated Statutes, 1982-2001[1]

	Upheld	*Invalidated*[2]	*Total*[3]
Federal Government			
Charter decisions	68 (67%)	34 (33%)	102
Non-Charter decisions	1 (100%)	0	1
Total decisions	69 (67%)	34 (33%)	103
Provincial Governments			
Charter decisions	34 (61%)	22 (39%)	56
Non-Charter decisions	9 (39%)	14 (61%)	23
Total decisions	43 (54%)	36 (46%)	79

Notes: [1]This table includes cases where the Supreme Court of Canada has used a number of remedies in addition to judicial nullification of statutes, such as suspended decisions, determining constitutional obligations, Aboriginal exemptions, and reading-in or reading-down definitions in legislative schemes.
[2]The total number of invalidations is 72, with federal (34) and provincial statutes (36) accounting for 70, and two invalidations involving municipal bylaws.
[3]This refers to the total number of statutes challenged, not the total number of cases, as many statutes have been challenged in multiple cases.

The empirical evidence demonstrates that the Supreme Court has acted in a balanced manner, as federal statutes have been found to violate protected rights and freedom in 47 percent (34/72) of cases where a constitutional violation has infringed either the Charter or the *Constitution Act, 1867* and provincial statutes represent 50 percent (36/72) of constitutionally invalid statutes remedied by the Supreme Court, with two invalidations affecting municipal bylaws. Peter Russell noted that prior to 1982, the Supreme Court of Canada demonstrated

an "uncanny balance" between the governments of Canadian federalism in its
constitutional jurisprudence, and attributed this to the court's recognition that
it had a "credibility problem because one side, the federal government, appoints them and constitutionally controls their institution."[24] However, there
is a notable imbalance between Charter and non-Charter cases, as a total of 58
statutes have been invalidated on Charter grounds, the federal government
accounting for 59 percent (34/58), and the provincial governments accounting for 38 percent (22/58) of statutes invalidated by the Supreme Court. The
real imbalance occurs in non-Charter invalidations, where provincial governments account for 100 percent of the invalidated statutes (14); which is not
surprising, as eight invalidations involve language and education rights protected in either section 93 and 133 of the *Constitution Act, 1867*, section 23 of
the *Manitoba Act, 1870*, or section 16 of the *Saskatchewan Act, 1905*. The
remaining six cases involve provincial statutes and regulations invalidated as
a violation of Aboriginal rights protected in section 35(1) of the *Constitution
Act, 1982*.

In the empirical analysis the Charter invalidations have been isolated, because to include the non-Charter invalidations would unfairly represent the
impact of judicial review on the respective governments. For instance, the
non-Charter challenges involve constitutional provisions that regulate the conduct of provincial governments and their treatment of language and education
minorities, and thus, the federal government could not be challenged on such
grounds. To include non-Charter invalidations would clearly demonstrate an
empirical trend that favours the federal government, but this would not be an
accurate account of the effect of judicial review on federal and provincial
statutes. For instance, the overall rates of invalidation demonstrate that provincial governments have suffered as a result of judicial review involving
constitutional protections, as 79 provincial statutes have been challenged as a
constitutional violation, and 46 percent (36/79) of challenged statutes have
been invalidated by the Supreme Court. In the case of the federal government,
the overall rate of invalidation is 33 percent (34/103), as a total of 103 federal
statutes have been challenged since 1982 — but only 34 statutes have been
invalidated by the Supreme Court. The empirical discrepancy lies in the non-
Charter challenges, which are exclusively directed at provincial governments.
Focusing on Charter challenges, a slight advantage is evident in favour of the
federal government, as 33 percent (34/102) of statutes are invalidated, whereas
provincial rates of invalidation on Charter grounds rise to 39 percent, as 56
statutes have been challenged and 22 have been invalidated by the Supreme
Court. While the rates of invalidation for Charter challenges suggest a slight
bias in favour of the federal government, this conclusion must be questioned,
given that the institutional responses to judicial activism have varied across
Canada, and the federal government clearly has the most developed Charter
vetting system within the parliamentary arena. Indeed, the differences in the

rates of invalidation may not be the result of judicial activism targeted against provincial statutes, but a reflection of the varied development of legislative activism at the provincial level.[25]

CHARTER INVALIDATION OF PROVINCIAL STATUTES

More than simply acting in a balanced manner toward the two levels of government in an empirical sense, the Supreme Court has also advanced provincial autonomy during the substantive component of its Charter jurisprudence. Indeed, the reconciliation between rights and federalism has been an enduring theme in the court's Charter jurisprudence, and serves to challenge the centralization thesis on a jurisprudential as well as an empirical level. The analysis in this section will proceed in two stages, and an important distinction will be made between Charter and non-Charter decisions by the Supreme Court. There is an assumption in the debate that the impact of judicial activism is largely negative, as it reduces provincial autonomy and establishes national standards in provincial areas of jurisdiction.[26] This assumption is more convincing in Charter decisions, as much of the Court's activism in non-Charter decisions involving language and education protections in the *Saskatchewan Act, 1905*, the *Manitoba Act, 1870*, and the *BNA Act, 1867*, simply require provincial governments to honour their original constitutional obligations towards linguistic and religious minorities. Provincial autonomy is constrained, but the impact has simply resulted in constitutional redress of political decisions that were inconsistent with constitutional requirements.

Turning first to activist decisions by the Supreme Court that identify Charter inconsistencies in provincial statutes, judicial review has led to a limitation on provincial autonomy, but it is difficult to characterize the invalidated statutes as substantively important policies, with the notable exceptions of Alberta's *Individual Rights Protection Act* in *Vriend* and section 29 of Ontario's *Family Law Act* in *M. v. H.* This is one of the limitations in the centralization thesis, as the proponents have failed to consider whether the court's decision to invalidate statutes undermines provincial autonomy in core or peripheral policy areas. Table 2 reveals that relatively few cases involving Charter review by the Supreme Court have resulted in the nullification of policies considered essential to the policy autonomy of provincial governments, though Quebec has experienced judicial invalidation of important language and cultural policies. Indeed, Peter Russell's insight that "with the exception of Quebec's language policy, social and economic policies of central importance to elected governments have not been significantly affected by the Charter," still remains the clearest analysis of the impact of Charter review by the Supreme Court.[27] For instance, judicial invalidation by the court has established national standards in the determination of judicial salaries in the trilogy of cases referred to as the *Judicial Independence Reference* and has

Table 2: Judicial Invalidations and Provincial Statutes, 1982-2001

Case	Government	Remedy
CHARTER DECISIONS		
Legal Rights (n=5)		
Reference Re Motor Vehicle Act	BC	Nullification
Corp. Professionelle des médicines v. Thibault	Quebec	Nullification
R. v. Campbell	Alberta	Suspended (1 year)
Judges of the Provincial Court of PEI	PEI	Suspended (1 year)
Manitoba Provincial Judges Association v. Manitoba	Manitoba	Read-down definition
Fundamental Freedoms (n=7)		
Ford v. Quebec	Quebec	Nullification
Devine v. Quebec	Quebec	Nullification
Edmonton Journal v. Alberta	Alberta	Nullification
Rocket v. Royal College of Dental Surgeons	Ontario	Nullification
Libman v. Quebec	Quebec	Nullification
UFCW, Local 1518 v. KMart Canada Ltd.	BC	Suspended (6 months)
Dunmore v. Ontario	Ontario	Suspended (18 months)
Equality Rights (n=5)		
Andrews v. Law Society (BC)	BC	Nullification
Miron v. Trudel	Ontario	Read-in definition
Eldridge v. British Columbia	BC	Read-in definition
Vriend v. Alberta	Alberta	Read-in definition
M. v. H.	Ontario	Suspended (6 months)
Minority Language Education Rights (n=4)		
Protestant School Boards v. Quebec	Quebec	Nullification
Mahé v. Alberta	Alberta	Declaration of rights
Reference Re Public Schools Act (Manitoba)	Manitoba	Declaration of rights
Arsenault-Cameron v. Prince Edward Island	PEI	Declaration of rights
Mobility Rights (n=1)		
Black v. Law Society (Alberta)	Alberta	Nullification
CONSTITUTIONAL DECISIONS		
Aboriginal Rights (n=6)		
R. v. Nikal	BC	Aboriginal exemption
R. v. Badger	Alberta	Aboriginal exemption
R. v. Adams; R. v. Côté	Quebec	Aboriginal exemption
R. v. Sundown	Saskatchewan	Aboriginal exemption
R. v. Marshall[1]	NB	Aboriginal exemption
R. v. Marshall	NB	Aboriginal exemption
Language and Education Rights (n=8)		
Quebec v. Greater Hull School Board	Quebec	Nullification
Reference Re Manitoba Language Rights (1985)	Manitoba	Suspended (5 years)
Reference Re Manitoba Language Rights (1992)	Manitoba	Suspension extended
Bilodeau v. Manitoba	Manitoba	Suspended (5 years)
R. v. Mercure	Sask.	Suspended (5 years)
Quebec v. Brunet[1]	Quebec	Nullification
Quebec v. Brunet	Quebec	Nullification
Sinclair v. Quebec	Quebec	Suspended (1 year)

[1]*Marshall* and *Brunet* involve multiple invalidations of statutes and regulations.

removed restrictions on interprovincial law firms in *Black v. Law Society of Alberta*.[28] This centralizing trend has also established national standards in appeal procedures in *Thibault* and removed publication restrictions in pre-trial civil procedures involving matrimonial disputes in *Edmonton Journal v. Alberta*.[29] Finally, the court lifted the advertising ban on dentists in *Rocket v. Royal College of Dental Surgeons*, and removed the citizenship requirement for admission to the British Columbia Bar in *Andrews v. Law Society (BC)*.[30]

Indeed, a case can be made that the substantive policy autonomy of the federal government has been compromised to a greater degree than that of provincial governments, and the financial implications of judicial invalidations have also been more onerous. In *Singh v. Canada* the Supreme Court invalidated the procedures established in the *Immigration Act* for determining "Convention Refugees," and in *Morgentaler* struck down section 251 of the Criminal Code that regulated the conditions under which legal abortions could be obtained.[31] More recently, the Supreme Court ruled that the discretionary authority of the Minister of Justice under the *Extradition Act* is subject to constitutional limitations, and decided in *United States v. Burns* that assurances must be sought that Canadians would not be subject to the death penalty in foreign jurisdictions.[32] Other notable federal statutes invalidated by the Supreme Court involve the *Tobacco Products Control Act* in *RJR-Macdonald* and sections of the *Canada Elections Act* dealing with restrictions on polling data that were invalidated in *Thompson Newspapers*.[33] Finally, the Supreme Court removed certain *Criminal Code* restrictions on the possession of child pornography in *Sharpe*.[34]

While invalidated provincial statutes do provide evidence for the centralization thesis, their precise impact on the policy autonomy of the provinces can be considered marginal at best, as the invalidated statutes represent peripheral jurisdictional responsibilities. Indeed, based on budget expenditures, health and education policy represent core provincial responsibilities and provide a truer test as to whether judicial review on Charter grounds has substantially limited the policy autonomy of provincial governments. On this point, there are a number of notable examples where the court has invalidated core provincial statutes as violating the Charter: for example, in such cases as *Ford v. Quebec* and *Devine v. Quebec*, where the Supreme Court ruled that sections of the *Charter of the French Language* violated freedom of expression.[35] Further, in *Eldridge v. British Columbia*, the Supreme Court ruled that the absence of services for the hearing impaired in the *Hospital Insurance Act* violated the Charter's equality rights protections, thus establishing a national standard in an important provincial responsibility.[36] Despite the invalidation of statutes in language and health policy, this has not significantly reduced the policy autonomy of provincial governments in core jurisdictional areas. For instance, the Quebec government quickly invoked the notwithstanding clause in response to the *Ford* and *Devine* decisions, illustrating how a judicial limitation on provincial autonomy can be a temporary state of affairs. While the *Eldridge* decision did result in the establishment of a national standard in health policy, as it requires provincial governments to provide translation services to the hearing impaired, this decision cannot be said to substantially interfere with the ability of the provinces to determine health policy or to significantly undermine diversity in the provision of health services by provincial governments.

The clearest examples of core provincial policies being invalidated by the court as inconsistent with the Charter occurred in *Protestant School Boards*, where sections of the *Charter of the French Language* that restricted access to education in English were found to violate section 23, and in *Libman*, where the spending restrictions on third parties in Quebec's *Referendum Act* were found to violate sections 2(b) and 2(d) of the Charter.[37] Both of these decisions received intense criticism as evidence of the centralization thesis, with Alan Cairns and Guy Laforest suggesting that *Protestant School Boards* established national standards in education policy,[38] and Joseé Legault concluding that *Libman* had "gutted our referendum law."[39] Both decisions, however, illustrate a fundamental weakness in the centralization thesis, as it is assumed that judicial decisions can fundamentally change public policy and that parliamentary actors simply accept the centralist implications of the court's Charter jurisprudence. *Libman* illustrates the latter point, with the court ruling that the maximum spending limitation of $600 for third parties not affiliated with either official committee was too low, and adopting the recommendation of the Lortie Commission that spending limits should be increased to $1,000 as a way to reconcile the offending sections of the *Referendum Act* with the Charter. While this decision did establish a national standard in third-party spending, *Libman* cannot be suggested to have undermined provincial autonomy, as Quebec still retains significant control over both the timing and structure of future referendum campaigns, despite the invalidation of minor sections of the *Referendum Act*. Further, *Libman* illustrates how the narrowing of provincial autonomy can be a temporary state of affairs, as the National Assembly quickly introduced amendments to the *Referendum Act* that addressed the inconsistencies between the Charter and spending restrictions in the *Referendum Act*.

In the case of *Protestant School Boards*, this decision illustrates the problematic assumption that a judicial decision, on its own, undermines provincial autonomy. My objection to the accepted interpretation of *Protestant School Boards* is the failure to recognize that the impact of a judicial decision declines in complex policy contexts, and thus, the impact must be evaluated on two levels: first, the constitutionality of the statute, and second, the functioning of a policy area. The constitutionality of a statute may be invalidated, but this may have little impact on the ability of a government to attain its policy objectives because of the important support structure provided by related policies that serve to offset the invalidation of one statute within a complex policy configuration. In the case of Quebec's restrictions on access to English education, the net effect on the province's ability to advance the broader policy objective of sustaining the linguistic dominance of francophones has not been undermined by the constitutional invalidation in this case. Peter Russell has advanced a similar conclusion, but in the context of section 23 of the Charter, suggesting it "even provides for Quebec's distinctiveness by leaving discretion over the language regime for the schooling of Quebec immigrants to the government and legislature of Quebec."[40] I would suggest that the functioning of this policy context, in addition to the structure of section 23, has offset the impact of judicial invalidation in *Protestant School Boards*, as the court's decision does not interfere with Quebec's control over education policy. Specifically, this policy context — and the attainment of its objectives — is directly related to domestic and international immigration patterns involving the province of Quebec. The court's decision to invalidate sections of Quebec's education policy only benefits English-speaking Canadian citizens that immigrate to Quebec, and thus, the reality of intraprovincial immigration patterns, where Quebec experiences a net outflow of anglophones, suggests that judicial review in *Protestant School Boards* does not undermine Quebec's ability to achieve its policy objective, given the linkages between language, education and immigration patterns in this complex policy environment. Indeed, the only way that *Protestant School Boards* could impact provincial autonomy would be indirectly, as it would require an inflow of anglophones to Quebec, and require the federal government to end the current practice of allowing Quebec to participate in national immigration policy that targets francophones and requires these new immigrants to initially reside in Quebec. In effect, the complexity of Quebec's education policy and its linkages to a web of interrelated programs has served to offset the impact of Charter review in a core provincial responsibility.

ADVANCING PROVINCIAL AUTONOMY

The effect of the Charter on provincial autonomy is not simply negative, with provincial statutes nullified by the Supreme Court and national standards imposed as a result. There is a positive aspect of Charter review for provincial autonomy, as the Supreme Court has articulated a federalism jurisprudence that has advanced policy diversity at the provincial level. I have previously referred to this as a three-part federalism jurisprudence that has allowed the court to reconcile rights and federalism during judicial review of the Charter.[41] This section will focus on the court's articulation of an explicit federalism jurisprudence, as it is in this context that the court has clearly advanced provincial autonomy by demonstrating a sensitivity to policy diversity. There are several notable examples where the Supreme Court has advanced provincial autonomy by articulating the importance of policy diversity in its Charter

jurisprudence, and this explicit federalism jurisprudence has generally occurred in cases involving core provincial responsibilities. For instance, *Jones*
involved education policy, *McKinney* and *Edwards Books* generally involved
labour relations, and *R. v. S.(S.)* involved provincial administration of the *Young
Offenders Act*.[42] In each case, the court recognized the importance of policy
variation in a federal state, and thus, allowed for diversity in the delivery of
core provincial responsibilities. For instance, in *Jones* the Supreme Court determined that the requirement of a provincial certificate for home instruction
under section 142(1) of the *Alberta School Act* violated freedom of religion
and the principles of fundamental justice advanced by section 7 of the Charter. However, the section 1 analysis by Justice Gérard Laforest is significant,
as the court recognized that the provinces must be provided with sufficient
manoeuvrability to achieve their policy preferences in education. As the
legislative scheme was determined to be administratively fair, the court found
that the limitations on freedom of religion and the principles of fundamental
justice were reasonable in a free and democratic society.[43]

The principle of policy diversity as a justification for establishing the rea-
sonableness of provincial statutes found to violate the Charter emerged in
Edwards Books and *McKinney*, where the court engaged in a comparative assessment of different provincial responses to the issue of mandatory Sunday
closings in *Edwards Books*, and mandatory retirement in *McKinney*. In both
cases, the court found that the provincial act in question violated the Charter:
freedom of religion was violated in *Edwards Books*, as the court decided that
a common day of rest compelled individuals to respect the Christian Sabbath;
and mandatory retirement policies were determined to have infringed on equality rights and the protection against discrimination on the basis of age in
McKinney. Similarly, in both cases the court found that the violations represented a reasonable limitation on entrenched rights and freedoms because of
the overriding importance of policy diversity in a federal system. Indeed, the
decisions by Justice Laforest in both cases are important for their comparative assessment of diverse provincial responses to the issue of mandatory
retirement and Sunday closing.

In *Edwards Books*, Justice Laforest accepted that Ontario's approach to
mandatory Sunday closing was a reasonable limitation despite its departure
from other provincial schemes because "the simple fact is that what may work
effectively in one province (or part of it) may simply not work in another
without unduly interfering with the legislative scheme."[44] Similarly, in
McKinney the court considered several provincial human rights codes and their
protections against age-based discrimination in its determination that Ontario's
mandatory retirement policy was a reasonable limitation on section 15(1). In
this case, the court decided that if the Charter applied, Ontario's *Human Rights
Code* would be a reasonable limitation because mandatory retirement policies
were a reasonable attempt to address youth unemployment. However, the court

recognized that several provinces had taken a different approach to the issue of mandatory retirement, with Justice Laforest reasoning that policy variation was necessary because of the complexity of interests affected by the policy: "The fact that other jurisdictions have taken a different view proves only that the legislature there adopted a different balance to a complex set of competing values."[45] By articulating the importance of provincial variation in public policies, as well as the court's decision to articulate diversity as an important value that can satisfy the reasonable limits test of the Charter, the Supreme Court clearly advanced provincial autonomy and recognized diversity as an important Charter value.

The importance of policy diversity is particularly evident in the administrative relationship that exists between the federal and provincial governments in the area of youth justice. While the federal government has jurisdictional responsibility for criminal law, many important federal statutes, such as the former *Young Offenders Act (YOA)*, provide the provincial governments with discretionary control over how to administer certain federal statutes. Ontario's decision not to exercise the discretion provided in the *YOA*, in which provinces were allowed to establish alternative sentencing procedures, was the basis of an equality rights challenge in *R. v. S.(S.)*, as it was contended that this failure had resulted in the unequal treatment of young offenders in Canada. The court rejected that provincial variation in the application of federal laws was inconsistent with equality rights protected in the Charter because of the overriding importance of the principle of diversity that structures all federations. It concluded: "The federal system of governance demands that the values underlying s.15 (1) cannot be given unlimited scope. The division of powers not only permits differential treatment based on province of residence, it mandates and encourages geographic distinction."[46] Justice Antonio Lamer expanded upon the importance of policy diversity later in his decision when he cautioned that "it is necessary to bear in mind that differential application of federal law can be a legitimate means of forwarding the values of a federal system."[47] The court's articulation of a federalism jurisprudence in *Jones, McKinney, Edwards Books* and *S.(S.)* is significant because it embodies the essential characteristics necessary for the court to function as the umpire of Canadian federalism. "A good umpire is impartial, aware of traditions and duty-bound to uphold the honour of the game; a bad umpire displays bias, indifference or conceit."[48] In this set of decisions, the Supreme Court clearly acted in a way that protected policy diversity, and did so in a manner that advanced provincial autonomy.

JUDICIAL ACTIVISM AND A DEEPENING OF DIVERSITY

The effect of judicial activism in non-Charter decisions suggests an irony for the centralization thesis. There is a belief that judicial invalidation of provincial statutes will undermine diversity and lead to a process of uniformity in public policy. Further, there is an assumption that provincial governments embody the essence of diversity that federalism is required to protect, as it was the presence of a provincial society that necessitated the adoption of a federal system in 1867.[49] But what if provincial statutes actually prevented diversity, and instead of leading to the homogenization of public policy, judicial activism required certain provincial governments to honour the original federal bargain that led to Confederation? The reality of judicial activism in non-Charter decisions involving Aboriginal rights and language and education rights is that provincial defeats have not lead to uniformity in public policy, but have deepened diversity in Canada. In the case of language and education rights protected outside the Charter, the impact of judicial activism has been to require provincial governments to respect the original federal bargain in these areas that were ignored by provincial governments soon after Confederation, or when individual provinces entered Confederation.[50]

Table 2 lists the instances in which the Supreme Court has invalidated provincial statutes as a violation of language and education protections within the *Constitution Act, 1867*, the *Manitoba Act, 1870*, and the *Saskatchewan Act, 1905*. With the exception of *Greater Hull School Board,* the court was asked to consider whether the decision by provincial governments to enact laws in either English or French violated several constitutional requirements that the records and journals of provincial legislative assemblies must be published in both English and French, and further, that either language may be used in court proceedings. This issue first emerged in *Reference re Manitoba Language Rights*, where the enactment of all statutes in English since 1890 was challenged as a violation of section 23 of the *Manitoba Act, 1870,* and section 133 of the *Constitution Act, 1867.*[51] Further, in *Bilodeau v. Manitoba* the court ruled that the *Summary Convictions Act* contravened section 23 of the *Manitoba Act, 1870*, because it provided only for a unilingual court summons, and a similar issue arose in *Mercure*, where unilingual court proceedings were challenged as a violation of section 16 of the *Saskatchewan Act, 1905.*[52] Finally, the court considered whether the unilingual enactment of statutes affecting the public service in *Quebec v. Brunet* violated section 133 of the *Constitution Act, 1867.*[53] In each case, the court had little difficulty in determining that the emergence of a unilingual system for the administration of justice and the unilingual enactment of provincial statutes and records clearly violated the respective provisions within the *Constitution Act, 1867*, the *Manitoba Act, 1870*, and the *Saskatchewan Act, 1905*. However, the significance of these cases is that they demonstrate the importance of the Supreme Court acting as the guardian of the constitution, as the provinces had clearly failed to respect the original federal bargain regarding linguistic duality in Canada. This is a common outcome in non-Charter cases involving language and education rights, as the lack of effective enforcement mechanisms before the

Charter ensured that the failure of the provinces to respect the original federal bargain in these areas was extremely difficult to remedy.

While judicial victories involving Aboriginal rights have interfered with provincial control over the fishery industry, these victories require the inclusion of an excluded community in the development of public policy. Indeed, the principle of inclusion as a way to deepen diversity was the basis of the *Vriend* decision and was an important aspect of the court's judgement in *M. v. H.*[54] At the very least, the court's approach to rights and freedoms has revealed the limitations in the centralization thesis and has exposed it as a theory not so much interested in protecting diversity, but simply a theory concerned with provincial autonomy. This reveals that the centralization thesis has not fully understood the changing nature of judicial review since the Charter's introduction, as this role has broadened from focusing on federalism as system of government to determining the effect of government action on the principle of diversity that is at the heart of Canadian federalism.

MULTIPLE GUARDIANS OF THE CONSTITUTION

The guardian of the constitution is a role that the Supreme Court performs simply in a legal sense, but the political reality is that this function is shared between courts and legislatures in the attempt to ensure that policy objectives are designed in a manner that advances Charter values. In effect, too much critical attention has been devoted to the court's use of this metaphor in the legal and constitutional sense, when in fact, the actual functioning of the constitution requires multiple guardians to ensure that Charter rights are adequately protected. While I do advance Charter dialogue as an important development that has facilitated multiple guardians of the constitution, I do not envision the metaphor in the same manner as Peter Hogg and Alison Bushell.[55] For Hogg and Bushell, Charter dialogue is initiated by the judiciary when it invalidates legislation because it "causes a public debate in which *Charter* values play a more prominent role than they would have if there had been no judicial decision."[56] In truth, this is simply Charter dialogue spoken with a judicial accent.[57] The reality is that Charter dialogue is not initiated by the courts through judicial activism, but begins in the political arena and is the result of legislative activism and the attempt by Parliament and the provincial legislatures to reach principled decisions that advance Charter values during the legislative process.[58]

There are two primary elements that demonstrate that the informal functioning of the constitution has seen the emergence of multiple guardians of the constitution, which perform complementary roles that advance Charter values in the legislative process. The first is the emerging approach to Charter review by the Supreme Court and the greater reliance on suspended decisions

in cases where the court determines that statutes infringe upon the Charter.[59]
By using a broad range of judicial remedies that invite legislative responses,
the Supreme Court clearly indicates that it does not envision itself as the sole
guardian of the constitution, and perhaps more importantly, that the court recognizes the constitution is a shared responsibility between courts and
legislatures.[60] The second element that has facilitated the emergence of multiple guardians is the reformed policy process within government, referred to
as legislative activism. This form of rights activism has two main components, bureaucratic and parliamentary activism, but legislative activism is
clearly driven by its bureaucratic component.[61] This is an important development, as the bureaucratic arena supports the Cabinet in the legislative process,
and thus, legislative activism has intensified the executive-dominance of the
parliamentary arena in Canada. What has emerged, therefore, is not a single
guardian of the constitution, but a complex relationship between the traditional institutions of the federation that share responsibility for the protection
of rights and freedoms in Canada. Thus, a parliament-centred approach to
Charter review has emerged, but it is clearly an executive-dominated process,
and the attempt to govern in a rights culture has further marginalized Parliament as an institution.

JUDICIAL REMEDIES AND CANADIAN DEMOCRACY

The complex approach to judicial remedies of statutes nullified by the Supreme Court as a constitutional violation illustrates that the informal
functioning of the constitution has facilitated the emergence of multiple guardians. Indeed, an important element of these remedies has been to provide
Parliament and the provincial legislatures with the opportunity to respond to
judicial invalidation of public policies. Table 3 has classified statutes found to
violate constitutional protections based on the nature of the remedy used by
the Supreme Court. The contention here is that different remedies allow the
court to either emerge as the guardian of the constitution in the legal sense, as
they ensure that judicial decisions are the final statement on rights and
freedoms, or prevent the court from solely performing this role, as the remedy
implicitly suggests that the court recognizes that it is part of a broader system
for protecting rights and freedoms. The judicial remedy of nullifying or altering a definition by reading-in or reading-down a legislative scheme would
serve to advance the court as the sole guardian of the constitution, whereas
suspended decisions and the declaration of a right would be judicial strategies
that allow Parliament, and the provincial legislatures with the ability, to respond to judicial decisions. On the surface, however, the nature of judicial
remedies would suggest that the court has functioned as the sole guardian, as
nullifications and judicially altered definitions of legislative schemes are a
common approach by the court when invalidating provincial statutes. The court

has employed the remedies of judicially altering definitions (eight cases) and nullifications (40 cases) in 67 percent (48/72) of statutes invalidated as a violation of a constitutional protection, thus suggesting the court has had the final word on the meaning of constitutional protections.

Table 3: Judicial Remedies, 1982-2001

Remedy	1982-1992	1992-2001	Total
Provincial[1]			
Read-in or down	0	4	4
Prequel	0	0	0
Nullification	12	1	13
Aboriginal exemption	0	6	6
Suspended	3	7	10
Declaration	1	2	3
Federal			
Read-in or down	1	3	4
Prequel	1	1	2
Nullification	15	10	25
Suspended	2	1	3
Declaration	0	0	0
Municipal			
Nullification	0	2	2
Total	35	37	72

Note: [1]Provincial statutes invalidated include non-Charter cases (14).

Due to space constraints, I will simply focus on the judicial remedies employed in cases involving provincial statutes invalidated by the court as a violation of the Charter (22 cases) or other constitutional protections (14 cases). However, the court's complex approach to judicial remedies is evident in its treatment of invalidated federal statutes, and thus, courts and governments at both levels attempt to protect the constitution in a complementary fashion. Indeed, the second decade of judicial remedies has seen the court less inclined to simply invalidate statues and more willing to suspend decisions or simply to declare constitutional rights, which does not impose a policy outcome but simply establishes the need for government action to satisfy a rights claim.[62] The court has nullified provincial statutes in 36 percent of cases (13/36), and has read-in or read-down definitions in 11 percent of decisions (4/36), which suggests that the court has viewed itself as the sole guardian, as 47 percent of invalidations (17/36) have seen judicial remedies that appear to prevent legislative responses. Indeed, this does characterize the court's approach to Aboriginal rights and the protection of linguistic and vulnerable groups, such as the gay and lesbian communities, as the court has exempted Aboriginal nations from the application of provincial laws in six cases, and the altered legislative schemes to include protection for gays and lesbians and the hearing impaired in two cases.[63]

A critical analysis of judicial remedies suggests that the court has approached the guardian role in an informal manner, as many remedies have invited provincial legislatures to respond to judicial invalidations. Hogg and Bushell have suggested that legislative responses to judicial invalidations demonstrate Charter dialogue and offset the negative implications of judicial activism.[64] While legislative sequels do demonstrate the emergence of multiple guardians of the constitution, along with Christopher Manfredi, I have taken issue with Hogg and Bushell's suggestion that all legislative sequels are evidence of Charter dialogue.[65] Indeed, a positive legislative sequel is required to constitute Charter dialogue because an equal relationship can only exist when minor legislative amendments are required to establish the constitutionality of a statute invalidated by the Supreme Court, as this suggests that the traditional institutions of the federation share responsibility for determining the meaning of rights and freedoms. Specifically, we were concerned that the legislative action of simply repealing sections identified by the Supreme Court as unconstitutional was not dialogue, as this negative act simply saw legislative compliance with judicial invalidation.

In the case of *Ford* and *Devine*, the National Assembly in Quebec City quickly invoked the notwithstanding clause in response to the invalidation of sections of the *Charter of the French Language*. Further, because of the narrow basis of the legislative invalidation in *Libman*, the National Assembly amended the *Referendum Act* to increase the spending restrictions on third parties to $1,000 as a way to reconcile the act with the Charter. Similarly, in *Royal College of Dental Surgeons,* the Ontario legislature removed the publication ban on dentists and introduced new guidelines to regulate advertising by this profession. The particular policy context in *Protestant School Boards* qualifies as a positive legislative response, as the complex policy configuration involving education, language and immigration policy has allowed Quebec to achieve its policy objectives despite the invalidation of sections of the education act. The significance of these positive legislative responses is that we see that the reversal of five nullifications in areas of provincial responsibility has tempered the force of judicial nullification: the use of judicial remedies that generally prevent legislative responses declines from 47 percent (17/36) to 33 percent (12/36) of cases.[66] Thus, the nullification of statutes may not prevent legislative responses, if the bases of invalidation are quite narrow or technical, and do not question the substantive elements of the act in question. As many nullifications are simply procedural in nature, the competent legislative body can introduce positive legislative sequels.

Former Deputy Minister of Justice John Tait remarked that "the wording, structure and application of the Charter suggest that all branches of government must work together in its evolution. At its highest level of principle, it is clear that all branches of government are responsible for carrying out the purposes of the Charter in every facet of government activity."[67] The narrow bases of several provincial invalidations illustrate the informal functioning of the constitution that facilitates multiple guardians, as the court does recognize that it is one actor responsible for protecting rights and freedoms. Indeed, the second largest category of judicial remedies for provincial statutes is the use of suspended decisions, where the declaration of unconstitutionality is suspended for a specified period to allow legislative reflection and responses to invalidated statutes. This remedy has been used in 28 percent (10/36) of cases. It clearly illustrates the limitations in viewing the use of the guardian metaphor in the legal senses because suspended decisions allow "the legislature to make the policy decisions involved in adapting their legislation to respect the Charter."[68] This occurred in *M. v. H.*, where the court suspended its decision that the *Family Law Act* violated section 15(1) of the Charter for six months in an effort to provide the Ontario legislature the opportunity to reflect on the definition of spouse and amend it accordingly. Further, the court suspended its decision for five years in *Manitoba Language Reference* to provide the legislature with some flexibility in its attempt to comply with section 23 of the *Manitoba Act*, which requires all records and acts of the Legislature to be printed in both English and French. More recently, the Supreme Court suspended the invalidation of section 3(b) of Ontario's *Labour Relations Act* for 18 months in *Dunmore v. Ontario*,[69] and suspended its ruling that the definition of picketing in section 1 of British Columbia's *Labour Relations Code* violated freedom of expression for six months.[70]

Aboriginal rights and the judicial remedy employed in these cases also challenge the notion that judicial invalidations undermine the policy autonomy of provincial governments. I have classified the remedy in section 35(1) cases as "Aboriginal exemption," to indicate the limited effect on provincial statutes and regulations regulating hunting and fishing that such invalidations produce. The precise impact of judicial activism in Aboriginal rights cases is complex, as the court's rulings have not nullified statutes and regulations, but have simply reduced the scope of these acts and their application to specific First Nations that demonstrate, in a court of law, that the regulations interfere with an Aboriginal right. Thus, the act stands but the application is simply narrowed. The judicial strategy of declaring the presence of a right has also limited the Supreme Court from functioning as the sole guardian of the constitution, as this judicial remedy has simply identified the rights of minority language education communities, and has left it to the discretion of provincial governments to provide adequate facilities to give effect to section 23. In *Mahé* the court refrained from nullifying the *Alberta School Act*, but simply determined that Alberta had failed to honour minority language education rights protected by section 23 of the Charter.[71] Further, this strategy categorized as "declaration of rights" also occurred in *Reference re Public Schools Act (Manitoba)* and *Arsenault-Cameron v. Prince Edward Island*, and represents 8 percent (3/36) of judicial remedies involving provincial statutes.[72] This strategy is significant because the court simply identifies a rights violation in provincial legislation, but leaves it to the discretion of the legislature to find a policy solution to in a very important area of provincial jurisdiction.

The complexity of the Supreme Court's approach to remedying constitutional violations in provincial statutes suggests that the legal dimension of the guardian role, where the Supreme Court is *the* guardian of the constitution, is really a limited component of constitutional review. Indeed, a total of 36 provincial statutes and regulations have been invalidated by the Supreme Court, but because provincial legislatures have been able to respond to judicial invalidation through the narrow basis of several nullified statutes (five cases), the use of suspended decisions (ten cases), the declaration of rights (three cases) and the complexity of Aboriginal rights cases, where the invalidation simply reduces the application of the act (six cases), the court can only be considered *the* guardian of the constitution in 33 percent (12/36) of provincial invalidations. Thus, the Charter has facilitated the emergence of multiple guardians of the constitution, as judicial decisions have generally allowed provincial governments to respond to questions of constitutionality in offending legislation.

LEGISLATIVE ACTIVISM CONFRONTS JUDICIAL ACTIVISM

The view of the Supreme Court as *the* guardian of the constitution, therefore, is not accurate, as the varied institutional responses by the parliamentary arena have seen the emergence of a rights culture within government.[73] In addition to this new policy process, political actors insisted that important textual instruments be included in the Charter to ensure that parliamentary actors could play a significant role in determining the Charter's meaning. As previously mentioned, the introduction of the notwithstanding and the reasonable limits clauses were designed as important parliamentary checks on judicial interpretation of the Charter. As well, the three-year delay involving the implementation of equality rights was designed to allow for a critical reflection by the parliamentary arena on the compatibility between existing policy and section 15(1) of the Charter. In response, Parliament and the provincial legislatures spent three years reviewing statutes to ensure that they properly reflected the new commitment to equality rights, and in those instances where existing policies were found to be in violation of section 15(1), amendments were introduced to reconcile the offending statute with the Charter's equality rights protection. In many jurisdictions in Canada, the three-year exercise in equality rights review culminated with the passage of omnibus legislation that amended all statutes identified to be inconsistent with section 15(1).[74]

The importance of this three-year delay is revealed in the fact that equality rights have had one of the lowest success rate before the Supreme Court (23 percent), and this suggests that the initial reform of the policy process in relation to equality rights served to prevent the loss of policy autonomy for the parliamentary arena.[75] In hindsight, a three-year delay should have been mandatory for the entire Charter, as this would have allowed for a significant reform of the machinery of government and prevented the emergence of intensive judicial activism that characterized the first years of the court's approach to Charter review. It appears that the British have learned from the Canadian experience, as the *Human Rights Act, 1998,* was delayed until October 2000 to allow the Lord Chancellor's Department time to reorganize and create a series of guidance documents to aid line departments in developing legislation in a new policy environment that emphasized rights and freedoms.[76] In Britain, legislative activism emerged first and allowed a parliament-centred approach to rights review to determine the political response to constitutional obligations. In Canada, a suspended declaration of the Charter would have reinforced the view that a shared responsibility for protecting rights and freedoms exists between courts and legislatures.[77] Indeed, this would have allowed the informal functioning of the constitution to determine the contours of the guardian metaphor and the present preoccupation with judicial activism may not have emerged in the Canadian debate.

While legislative activism has been very important in ensuring that policy decisions remain centred within the parliamentary arena, there is a notable imbalance between parliamentary and bureaucratic activism that has resulted in a further marginalization of Parliament and legislatures as policy actors. Specifically, parliamentary scrutiny of legislation for its relationship to the Charter is generally absent because this role is an informal and irregular practice of parliamentarians: no standing committee within Parliament or any provincial legislature has this scrutiny as part of its formal mandate. Indeed, parliamentary activism is notably lacking, and the review of legislation for its relationship to the Charter is the responsibility of the Department of Justice and provincial Departments of the Attorney General. Thus, legislative activism is driven by its bureaucratic component, and this has further intensified the emergence of an executive-dominated policy process. In the last 40 years, "parliamentary" reform has simply meant strengthening the decision-making capacity of the executive through the creation of central agencies.

The emergence of a rights culture within government has advanced this central agency rationale because the institutional response to the Charter has been to strengthen the Charter review capacity of the Department of Justice and provincial Departments of the Attorney General. Indeed, line departments at both the federal and provincial levels must, to varying degrees, consult with legal counsel to ensure the constitutionality of legislation. Thus, the central agency rationale has expanded from its former concern with offsetting bureaucratic power and allowing the Cabinet to achieve its policy agenda, to a concern with judicial power and the need to discipline the policy process to a rights culture. While legislative activism has facilitated the emergence of principle decisions that advance Charter values, Parliament and legislatures, as institutions, have become further marginalized as policy actors. Thus, a paler version of legislative activism occurs because of the dominance of the executive and the requirements of pre-judicial Charter review. The requirements of governing in a rights culture leads to the conclusion that the primary institutional outcome of the Charter has not been judicial supremacy but executive supremacy in the policy process. Indeed, executive supremacy is more a concern at the provincial level, where the cabinet is a more dominant entity, both in terms of a government caucus and its size in relation to the legislative assembly. In Quebec, the former Parti Québécois had a caucus of 64 in the 125-member National Assembly, and the cabinet was 34. In many jurisdictions, the provincial cabinet is roughly half of the governing caucus, the government controls two-thirds of the seats and the remaining seats are divided between two opposition parties. Given the level of executive dominance at the provincial level, parliamentary activism is virtually non-existent because of the limited development of parliamentary committees. Indeed, in British Columbia, Alberta and Prince Edward Island, the nearly total control of the legislative assembly by the government, where the opposition controls two seats, nine seats and one seat respectively, parliamentary committees have been replaced by government caucus committees, thus ensuring no effective parliamentary check on executive government.

The most advanced version of bureaucratic activism exists at the federal level, where the attempt to govern in a right culture was initially a reaction to judicial activism. In her capacity as Associate Deputy Minister of Justice (Public Law), Mary Dawson has stated that the initial activist approach to Charter review by the Supreme Court "served as a catalyst for some serious thinking about the handling of Charter issues."[78] In effect, judicial activism resulted in significant changes within the legislative process, reinforcing Janet Hiebert's position that a "relational approach to constitutional interpretation" exists between the parliamentary and judicial arenas. In the case of the federal government, a significant reform of the machinery of government was undertaken, and it was designed to ensure that new policy was developed in an environment that explicitly advanced the values entrenched in the Charter. For instance, the Department of Justice created the Human Rights Law Section to serve as a centre for Charter advice within the federal government, established the Charter Committee to provide leadership in the development of public policy, and created the Charter Litigation Committee to decide on litigation strategies involving federal statutes found to violate protected rights and freedoms.[79]

The emergence of bureaucratic activism in response to judicial activism underscores the important reform of the machinery of government at the federal level and how the parliamentary arena responded to the court's challenge to the policy process and the interpretation of the Charter. I have concluded in a previous work that this new policy process elevated the Department of Justice to the status of a central agency, as this new policy process is under the direction of the Department of Justice and has resulted in a significant decline in the nullification rate of statutes enacted by the Parliament of Canada.[80] Indeed, an important characteristic of invalidated statutes is the date of enactment, as a large number were enacted before the introduction of the Charter and before the policy process was reformed to include a vetting of legislation for its relationship to protected rights and freedoms.

At the provincial level, however, the highly institutionalized approach to Charter review introduced at the federal level has been rarely matched. Monahan and Finkelstein noted that only Ontario has introduced a Charter vetting system similar to Ottawa, and British Columbia and Saskatchewan have introduced Charter review to a lesser degree.[81] I have conducted research in the governments of Newfoundland, Ontario, Alberta and British Columbia and the findings by Patrick Monahan and Marie Finkelstein are generally accurate, though British Columbia has recently formalized the requirement that line departments consult legal counsel at the Ministry of the Attorney General for the Charter implications of policy from the earliest stages of a policy exercise.[82] Further, the Office of Legal Counsel has specified in its drafting guidelines for line departments that Crown lawyers must be engaged by policy-makers in the design of legislation to ensure that Charter issues are raised and properly addressed at the pre-legislative stage.[83] While important steps have been taken by provincial governments to redesign the policy process to engage in a pre-judicial review of legislation for its relationship to the Charter, a tremendous amount of variation exists in these responses, with a more informal review occurring in Newfoundland[84] and Alberta[85] and more institutionalized and mandatory reviews in place in Ontario[86] and British Columbia.[87] F.L. Morton has identified the stronger implications of Charter review for provincial governments and has concluded that this is directly attributable to the Supreme Court and its approach to interpreting rights and freedoms.[88] The institutional underdevelopment of Charter review at the provincial level challenges Morton's thesis, as the varied responses to Charter vetting within provincial governments suggests that institutional discretion within the parliamentary arena, not the discretionary choices of judges, explains the greater ability of federal statutes to survive Charter review by the Supreme Court.

What is lacking, therefore, is the institutionalization of parliamentary scrutiny of legislation that would complement bureaucratic review and the attempts by the executive to reconcile rights and legislative objectives.[89] Janet Hiebert has suggested that Canada should adopt Australia's model of parliamentary scrutiny of legislation for its consistency with rights and freedoms to ensure that the parliamentary arena fully considers the implications of legislation and its consistency with the Charter.[90] This is a very positive recommendation that would complement the Charter screening process that exists under the direction of the Department of Justice and would act as the public face of this important exercise.[91] The interviews that I have conducted with Crown lawyers who present section 1 defences for legislation found to violate the Charter indicate that the primary difficulty is not the test constructed by the court, but the difficulty in locating material within the parliamentary arena to mount a proper defence of a challenged statute.[92] For instance, many statutes that are defended as a reasonable limitation are generally quite old and no paper trail exists that allows Crown lawyers to demonstrate to the courts that the approach adopted represents a reasonable limitation on a protected Charter right. This parliamentary scrutiny committee would be particularly important in the case of litigation strategies involving the Department of Justice and section 1 of the Charter, as the legislative record of this committee would be vitally important in constructing a defence and convincing the court that an infringement constituted a reasonable limitation in a free and democratic society.

However, it was clear that Prime Minister Jean Chrétien was not willing to reinvigorate Parliament as a policy actor by reducing the executive-dominated policy process that exists. Regrettably, legislative activism will continue to be driven by its bureaucratic component because this approach to legislative scrutiny advances the ability of the executive to ensure that its legislative agenda will survive judicial review on Charter grounds. In truth, a simple procedural change could ensure the effectiveness of parliamentary scrutiny of legislation, and important lessons can be drawn from advanced Westminster democracies that have incorporated parliamentary scrutiny of legislation, such as Britain and Australia. In both counties, a parliamentary committee has an explicit mandate to perform this function, with Australia's Senate Scrutiny of Bills Committee responsible for ensuring that federal legislation advances Australia's domestic rights commitments, and the Joint Committee of Human Rights in Britain ensuring that legislation conforms to the *Human Rights Act, 1998*.[93] The effectiveness of these committees has not required major institutional reform of parliamentary government but a simple procedural change, where the committee membership is evenly divided between government and opposition, with the opposition parties controlling three seats on the six-person Scrutiny of Bills Committee in Australia, and the opposition parties holding six seats in the 12-member Joint Committee of Human Rights in Britain. Because of the composition of these two committees, the sponsoring ministers must respond to the potential rights violations identified by these committees to ensure that legislation can be presented before Parliament for a final vote. In Canada, the two committees that perform an informal scrutiny of legislation for its relationship to the Charter, the Standing Committee on Justice and Human Rights and the Standing Senate Committee on Legal and Constitutional Affairs, are dominated by the Liberal government. Total membership on each committee is 12, and the Liberal Party has 7 seats on each. While legislative activism exists in Canada, Britain and Australia, the Canadian version is clearly the most executive-dominated.

The different responses of provincial governments to the new policy environment introduced by the Charter speak to the federal character of Canada, as institutional variation in the machinery of government is a reflection of distinct approaches to public policy that occur in federal regimes. The significance of this development is that it suggests that democratic actors, and the administrative apparatus that supports the parliamentary arena, have taken concrete steps to ensure that the introduction of the Charter has not resulted in what Russell referred to as "a further flight from politics, a deepening disillusionment with the procedures of representative government and government by discussion as a means of resolving fundamental questions of political justice."[94] The emergence of a Charter screening process within the development of public policy is an important step that prevents the flight from politics that would surely transform the court into the only guardian of the constitution. While the Charter's introduction surely ended the parliamentary arena's monopoly over the development of public policy, this development has not facilitated the emergence of the court as the sole interpreter of rights and freedoms. The flexibility of the parliamentary arena and the ensuing reform of the machinery of government within the traditional institutions of the federation indicate that this loss of policy control has been a temporary state of affairs.

CONCLUSION

As an institutional actor in the Canadian federation, the Supreme Court has succeeded in developing an approach to Charter review that has seen a re-emergence of the umpire of federalism role that was much in dispute before the patriation of the constitution in 1982. This success is evident, both empirically and jurisprudentially, as the court has acted in an even-handed fashion in rights litigation, invalidating a nearly equal amount of federal and provincial statutes. In effect, the Supreme Court has succeeded in guarding the principles of the Canadian constitution, such as federalism and provincial autonomy, and has done so in a new policy environment that also requires the parliamentary arena to govern in a rights culture. Further, the court has developed a federalism jurisprudence in the context of rights litigation that has deepened diversity and allowed the provinces to approach complex issues in distinct ways. Indeed, the evolution of the limitations clause, where the court has accepted policy diversity as a justification for infringing protected rights and freedoms, clearly suggests the emergence of a federalism discourse within the court's Charter jurisprudence. This sensitivity to federal diversity has been an important, and unexpected, development in the Supreme Court's interpretation of the Charter, and has ensured the reconciliation between rights and federalism in Canada.

The introduction of the Charter has resulted in a complex approach to this document by both courts and legislatures. For instance, the emerging approach to judicial invalidation has seen the Supreme Court adopt the remedy of suspending declarations of unconstitutionality, which illustrates the presence of multiple guardians of the constitution and the limited utility of approaching the guardian role in the formal constitutional sense, where the Supreme Court is *the* guardian of the constitution. Indeed, the responsibility for judicial decisions that impact provincial autonomy is not simply borne by judicial actors, but by parliamentary actors, who control the machinery of government and can ensure that legislation is subjected to a Charter review that may limit the ability of courts to invalidate legislation as a violation of the Charter. Peter Russell has suggested that the court put "the brakes on the Charter express," but the analysis presented here suggests that legislative activism applied the brakes to the Charter express that threatened to derail constitutional supremacy in the first intensively activist years of Charter review by the Supreme Court.[95] In the final analysis, neither courts nor legislatures can function on their own as the guardian of the constitution, as this role requires collective action on the part of institutions and individuals committed to protecting the values enshrined in the Charter.

NOTES

I would like to thank Janet Hiebert for her excellent comments on an earlier version of this chapter, as well as Harvey Lazar, Peter Meekison, Hamish Telford, and anonymous reviewers who commented. I would also like to acknowledge the financial support provided by the Social Sciences and Humanities Research Council of Canada, Standard Research Grant (410-2001-0894), which made this research possible.

1.   *Hunter v. Southam Inc.,* [1984] 2 S.C.R. 145 at 155.

2. *United States v. Burns*, [2001] 1 S.C.R. 283, para. 35.

3. F.L. Morton and Rainer Knopff, *The Charter Revolution and the Court Party* (Peterborough: Broadview Press, 2000), pp. 57-58; Christopher P. Manfredi, *Judicial Power and the Charter: Canada and the Paradox of Liberal Constitutionalism*, 2d edition (Don Mills: Oxford University Press, 2001), pp. 21-24.

4. Lorraine Eisenstat Weinrib, "Canada's Constitutional Revolution: From Legislative to Constitutional State," *Israel Law Review* 33 (1999):37; Kent Roach, *The Supreme Court on Trial: Judicial Activism or Democratic Dialogue* (Toronto: Irwin Law, 2001), pp. 155-56; Peter Hogg and Allison Bushell, "The Charter Dialogue Between Courts and Legislatures (or Perhaps the Charter of Rights Isn't Such a Bad Thing After All)," *Osgoode Hall Law Journal* 35 (1997):75-124.

5. F.L. Morton, "The Effect of the Charter of Rights on Canadian Federalism," *Publius* 25 (1995):179-80.

6. Peter W. Hogg, "Is the Supreme Court of Canada Biased in Constitutional Cases?" *Canadian Bar Review* 67 (1979):721-39; Peter H. Russell, "The Supreme Court and Federal-Provincial Relations: The Political Use of Legal Resources," *Canadian Public Policy* 11 (1985):162; Paul Weiler, *In the Last Resort: A Critical Study of the Supreme Court of Canada* (Toronto: Carswell/Metheun, 1974), pp. 155-85.

7. Shannon Ishiyama Smithey, "The Effects of the Canadian Supreme Court's Charter Interpretation on Regional and Intergovernmental Tensions in Canada," *Publius* 26 (1996):83-100.

8. Hogg and Bushell, "The Charter Dialogue Between Courts and Legislatures (or Perhaps the Charter of Rights Isn't Such a Bad Thing After All)," p. 79.

9. Janet L. Hiebert, "A Relational Approach to Constitutional Interpretation: Shared Legislative and Judicial Responsibilities," *Journal of Canadian Studies* 35 (Winter 2001):161-81.

10. Donna Greschner, "The Supreme Court, Federalism and Metaphors of Moderation," *Canadian Bar Review* 79 (2001):48.

11. Ibid., p. 61.

12. Janet L. Hiebert, *Charter Conflicts: What is Parliament's Role?* (Montreal: McGill-Queen's University Press, 2002), pp. 52-72.

13. Interview with the Right Honourable Pierre Elliot Trudeau, P.C., Q.C., Montreal, 5 September 1997.

14. James B. Kelly, "Bureaucratic Activism and the *Charter of Rights and Freedoms*: The Department of Justice and Its Entry Into the Centre of Government," *Canadian Public Administration* 42 (1999):476-511; Patrick Monahan and Marie Finkelstein, "The Charter of Rights and Public Policy in Canada," *Osgoode Hall Law Journal* 30 (1992):510-16; Janet L. Hiebert, "Wrestling with Rights: Judges, Parliament and the Making of Social Policy," *Choices* 5 (1999):3-10.

15. For an analysis of the importance of the umpire of Canadian federalism role and its performance by the Supreme Court of Canada, see W. R. Lederman, "Unity

and Diversity in Canadian Federalism: Ideals and Methods of Moderation," *Canadian Bar Review* 63 (1975):597-620. For a thorough analysis of the Judicial Committee of the Privy Council and its impact on Canadian federalism, see Alan C. Cairns, "The Judicial Committee and Its Critics," *Canadian Journal of Political Science* 3 (1971):300-45.

16. *Reference re Offshore Mineral Rights of British Columbia,* [1967] S.C.R. 792; *Canadian Industrial Gas and Oil Ltd. v. Government of Saskatchewan,* [1978] 2 S.C.R. 545; *Central Canada Potash Co. Ltd. and Attorney General of Canada v. Government of Saskatchewan,* [1979] 1 S.C.R. 42.

17. Hogg, "Is the Supreme Court of Canada Biased in Constitutional Cases?" pp. 721-39; Russell, "The Supreme Court and Federal-Provincial Relations: The Political Use of Legal Resources," pp. 165-69.

18. *Reference re Legislative Authority of Parliament to Alter or Replace the Senate,* [1980] 1 S.C.R. 54.

19. Peter H. Russell, "Bold Statescraft, Questionable Jurisprudence," in *And No One Cheered,* eds. Keith Banting and Richard Simeon (Toronto: Metheun, 1983), pp. 225-26.

20. Guy Laforest, *Trudeau and the End of a Canadian Dream* (Montreal: McGill-Queen's University Press, 1995), p. 154; David Schneiderman, "Human Rights, Fundamental Differences? Multiple Charters in a Partnership Frame," in *Beyond the Impasse — Toward Reconciliation,* eds. Roger Gibbins and Guy Laforest (Montreal: Institute for Research on Public Policy, 1998), pp. 155-57; Yves de Montigny, "The Impact (Real or Apprehended) of the *Canadian Charter of Rights and Freedoms* on the Legislative Authority of Quebec," in *Charting the Consequences,* eds. David Schneiderman and Kate Sutherland (Toronto: University of Toronto Press, 1997), pp. 9-10.

21. James B. Kelly, "Reconciling Rights and Federalism During Review of the *Charter of Rights and Freedoms*: The Supreme Court of Canada and the Centralization Thesis, 1982 to 1999," *Canadian Journal of Political Science* 34 (1999):321-55.

22. Alan C. Cairns, "The Charter: A Political Science Perspective," *Osgoode Hall Law Journal* 30 (1992):618.

23. Peter Hogg, "Federalism Fights the Charter," in *Federalism and Political Community,* eds. David Shugarman and Reg Whitaker (Peterborough: Broadview Press, 1989), p. 250.

24. Russell, "The Supreme Court and Federal-Provincial Relations: The Political Use of Legal Resources," pp. 162-64.

25. Monahan and Finkelstein, "The Charter of Rights and Public Policy in Canada," pp. 501-44.

26. F. L. Morton, "The Effect of the Charter on Canadian Federalism," *Publius* 25 (1995):176-77.

27. Peter H. Russell, "Canadian Constraints on Judicialization from Without," *International Political Science Review* 15 (1994):173.

28. *Reference re Remuneration of Judges of the Provincial Court of P.E.I.,* [1997] 3 S.C.R. 4; *Black v. Law Society (Alberta),* [1989] 1 S.C.R. 591.

29. *Thibault v. Corp. Professionel Médicins du Québec,* [1988] 1 S.C.R. 1033; *Edmonton Journal v. Alberta,* [1989] 2 S.C.R. 1326.

30. *Rocket v. Royal College of Dental Surgeons,* [1990] 2 S.C.R. 232; *Andrews v. Law Society (B.C.),* [1989] 1 S.C.R. 143.

31. *Re Singh and Minister of Employment and Immigration,* [1985] 1 S.C.R. 177; *Morgentaler, Smoling and Scott v. the Queen,* [1988] 1 S.C.R. 30.

32. *United States v. Burns,* [2001] 1 S.C.R. 283.

33. *RJR-MacDonald Inc. v. Canada,* [1995] 3 S.C.R. 199; *Thompson Newspapers Co. v. Canada,* [1998] 1 S.C.R. 877.

34. *R. v. Sharpe,* [2001] 1 S.C.R. 45.

35. *Ford v. Quebec,* [1988] 2 S.C.R. 712; *Devine v. Quebec,* [1988] 2 S.C.R., 790.

36. *Eldridge v. British Columbia,* [1997] 3 S.C.R. 624.

37. *Protestant School Boards v. Quebec,* [1984] 2 S.C.R. 66.

38. Alan C. Cairns, *The Charter Versus Federalism* (Montreal: McGill-Queen's University Press, 1992), p. 85; Laforest, *Trudeau and the End of a Canadian Dream,* p. 134.

39. Joseé Legault, "How to deny Quebec's right to self-determination," *The Globe and Mail,* 21 August 1998.

40. Peter H. Russell, "The Political Purposes of the Charter: Have They Been Fulfilled?" in *Protecting Rights and Freedoms,* eds. P. Bryden, S. Davis and J. Russell (Toronto: University of Toronto Press, 1994), p. 37.

41. Kelly, "Reconciling Rights and Federalism During Review of the *Charter of Rights and Freedoms:* The Supreme Court of Canada and the Centralization Thesis, 1982-1999," pp. 321-55.

42. *R. v. Jones,* [1986] 2 S.C.R. 285; *R. v. Edwards Books and Art Ltd.,* [1986] 2 S.C.R. 713; *McKinney v. University of Guelph,* [1990] 3 S.C.R. 229; *R. v. S.(S.),* [1990] 2 S.C.R. 254.

43. *R. v. Jones,* [1986] 2 S.C.R. 285 at 304.

44. *R. v. Edwards Books and Art Ltd.,* [1986] 2 S.C.R. 713 at 802.

45. *McKinney v. University of Guelph,* [1990] 3 S.C.R. 229 at 314.

46. *R. v. S.(S.),* [1990] 2 S.C.R. 254 at 255-56.

47. *R. v. S.(S.),* [1990] 2 S.C.R. 254 at 289.

48. Greschner, "The Supreme Court, Federalism and Metaphors of Moderation," p. 48.

49. Samuel Laselva, *The Moral Foundations of Canadian Federalism* (Montreal: McGill-Queen's University Press, 1996), pp. 22-27.

50. Edmund A. Unger, "Justifying the End of Official Bilingualism: Canada's North-West Assembly and the Dual- Language Question, 1889-1892," *Canadian Journal of Political Science* 34 (2001):451-86.

51. *Reference re Manitoba Language Rights*, [1985] 1 S.C.R. 721.

52. *Bilodeau v. Manitoba*, [1986] 1 S.C.R. 449; *R. v. Mercure*, [1988] 1 S.C.R. 234.

53. *Quebec v. Brunet*, [1990] 1 S.C.R. 260.

54. *Vriend v. Alberta*, [1998] 1 S.C.R. 493; *M. v. H.*, [1999] 2 S.C.R. 3; Donna Greschner, "The Right to Belong: The Promise of *Vriend*," *National Journal of Constitutional Law* 9 (1999):417-40.

55. Christopher P. Manfredi and James B. Kelly, "Six Degrees of Dialogue: A Response to Hogg and Bushell," *Osgoode Hall Law Journal* 37 (1999):513-27.

56. Hogg and Bushell, "The Charter Dialogue Between Courts and Legislatures (or Perhaps the Charter of Rights Isn't Such a Bad Thing After All)," p. 79.

57. James B. Kelly, "The Supreme Court of Canada and the Complexity of Judicial Activism," in *The Myth of the Sacred: The Charter, the Courts, and the Politics of the Constitution in Canada*, eds. Patrick James, Donald E. Abelson and Michael Lusztig (Montreal: McGill-Queen's University Press, 2002), p. 114.

58. Monahan and Finkelstein, "The Charter and Public Policy in Canada," pp. 501-44.

59. Kent Roach, "Remedial Consensus and Dialogue under the Charter: General Declarations and Delayed Declarations of Invalidity," *University of British Columbia Law Review* 35 (2002):218.

60. Janet L. Hiebert, "Wrestling with Rights: Judges, Parliament and the Making of Social Policy," *Choices* 5 (1999):3-10.

61. Kelly, "Bureaucratic Activism and the *Charter of Rights and Freedoms*: The Department of Justice and Its Entry Into the Centre of Government," pp. 476-511.

62. Roach, "Remedial Consensus and Dialogue under the Charter: General Declarations and Delayed Declarations of Invalidity," pp. 218-21.

63. Miriam Smith, *Lesbian and Gay Rights in Canada* (Toronto: University of Toronto Press, 1999), p. 135.

64. Hogg and Bushell, "The Charter Dialogue Between Courts and Legislatures (or Perhaps the Charter of Rights Isn't Such a Bad Thing After All)," pp. 75-124.

65. Christopher P. Manfredi and James B. Kelly, "Six Degrees of Dialogue: A Response to Hogg and Bushell," *Osgoode Hall Law Journal* 37 (1999):513-27; Christopher P. Manfredi and James B. Kelly, "Dialogue, Deference and Restraint: Judicial Independence and Trial Procedures," *Saskatchewan Law Review* 64 (2001):323-46.

66. This figure includes the 11 percent (4/36) of cases where the remedy was reading-in or reading-down a definition in a legislative scheme.

67. John C. Tait, "Policy Development and the Charter," *Perspectives on Public Policy* 7 (1995):8. John Tait was Deputy Minister of Justice 1988-94.

68. John C. Tait, "Charter Remedies and Democracy," Presented at the Canadian Institute for the Administration of Justice (CIAJ) Annual Conference, Halifax, 19 October 1996, p. 6.

69. *Dunmore v. Ontario*, [2001] at <www.lexum.umontreal.ca/csc-scc/en/rec/html/dunmore.en.html>.

70. *U.F.C.W. v. Local 1518 v. KMart Canada Ltd.*, [1999] 2 S.C.R. 1083.

71. *Mahé v. Alberta*, [1990] 1 S.C.R. 342.

72. *Reference re Public Schools Act (Manitoba)*, [1993] 1 S.C.R. 839; *Aresenault-Cameron v. Prince Edward Island*, [2000] 1 S.C.R. 3.

73. Mary Dawson, "The Impact of the Charter on the Public Policy Process and the Department of Justice," *Osgoode Hall Law Journal* 30 (1992):597-600.

74. Monahan and Finkelstein, "The Charter of Rights and Public Policy in Canada," pp. 116, 510.

75. James B. Kelly, "The Supreme Court of Canada's Charter of Rights Decisions, 1982-1999: A Statistical Analysis," in *Law, Politics and the Judicial Process in Canada*, 3d edition, ed. F.L. Morton (Calgary: University of Calgary Press, 2002), p. 500.

76. Jeremy Croft, "Whitehall and the Human Rights Act 1998," *European Human Rights Law Review* 4 (2001):392-408.

77. Hiebert, "A Relational Approach to Constitutional Interpretation: Shared Legislative and Judicial Responsibilities," pp. 162-69; Janet L. Hiebert, "Why Must a Bill of Rights be a Contest of Political and Judicial Wills? The Canadian Alternative," *Public Law Review* 10 (1999):27-29.

78. Dawson, "The Impact of the Charter on the Public Policy Process and the Department of Justice," p. 596.

79. Kelly, "Bureaucratic Activism and the *Charter of Rights and Freedoms*: The Department of Justice and Its Entry Into the Centre of Government," p. 497.

80. Ibid., pp. 503-07.

81. Monahan and Finkelstein, "The Charter of Rights and Public Policy in Canada," pp. 506-09. For a thorough discussion of Ontario, see Julie Jai, "Policy, Politics and the Law: Changing Relationships in Light of the Charter," *National Journal of Constitutional Law* 9 (1996):1-25; Ian Scott, "Law, Policy and the Attorney General: Constancy and Change in the 1980s," *University of Toronto Law Journal* 39 (1989):109-26.

82. Interview with senior government official, Ministry of Attorney General, Government of British Columbia, Victoria, 11 December 2002.

83. Office of Legislative Counsel, *Guide to Preparing Drafting Instructions for Legislation*. Ministry of Attorney General, Province of British Columbia, August 2000.

84. Interview with senior government official, Department of Justice, Government of Newfoundland and Labrador, St. John's, 11-13 February 2002.

85. Interview with senior government officials, Ministry of Justice and Attorney General, Government of Alberta, Edmonton, 16-18 December 2002.

86. Interview with senior government official, Ministry of Attorney General, Government of Ontario, Toronto, 30 May, 8 November, 26 November 2002.

87. Interview with senior government official, Ministry of Attorney General, Government of British Columbia, Victoria, 9-11 December 2002.

88. F.L. Morton, "The Effect of the Charter of Rights on Canadian Federalism," *Publius* 25 (1995):173-88.

89. C.E.S. Franks, "Parliament, Intergovernmental Relations, and National Unity," Working Paper (Kingston: Institute of Intergovernmental Relations, Queen's University, 1999), pp. 21-22.

90. Janet L. Hiebert, "A Hybrid-Approach to Protect Rights? An Argument in Favour of Supplementing Canadian Judicial Review with Australia's Model of Parliamentary Scrutiny," *Federal Law Review* 26 (1998):115-38.

91. Janet L. Hiebert, "Legislative Scrutiny: An Alternative Approach to Protecting Rights," in *Ideas in Action: Essays on Politics and Law in Honour of Peter Russell*, ed. Joseph F. Fletcher (Toronto: University of Toronto Press, 1999), pp. 307-08.

92. Interview with senior government official, Department of Justice and Attorney General, Government of Alberta, Edmonton, 17 December 2002. Interview with senior government official, Ministry of Attorney General, Government of British Columbia, Victoria, 9 December 2002.

93. Senate Scrutiny of Bills Committee, at <www.aph.gov.au/senate/committee/scrutiny/cominfo.htm>; Joint Committee on Human Rights, at <www.parliament.uk/commons/selcom/hrhome.htm>.

94. Peter H. Russell, "The Effect of the Charter on the Policy-Making Role of Canadian Courts," *Canadian Public Administration* 25 (1982):32.

95. Russell, "The Supreme Court and the Charter: A Question of Legitimacy," p. 228.

III

Peak Institutions

5

The Weakest Link? First Ministers' Conferences in Canadian Intergovernmental Relations

Martin Papillon and Richard Simeon

Ce chapitre souligne la faiblesse institutionnelle des Conférences des premiers ministres (CPM) en tant que mécanismes de coopération au sein de la fédération canadienne. Malgré leurs rôle relativement important dans l'évolution du fédéralisme au Canada, les CPM demeurent un instrument utilisé de manière sporadique, obéissant à un minimum de règles et de procédures, servant plus souvent en période de crise ou pour des fins politiques ayant peu à voir avec la gestion de l'interdépendance entre les deux ordres de gouvernement. Cette faible institutionnalisation peut s'expliquer en partie par le contexte politique actuel mais surtout par des facteurs structurels, liés à la nature même des institutions politiques canadiennes. L'analyse débute par une revue historique des CPM, puis s'attarde à expliquer leur succès limité en tant que mécanismes de collaboration. Une revue des différentes propositions de réforme afin de donner un rôle plus important aux CPM est enfin proposée, en soulignant que les opinions sur le besoin de réforme varient selon la conception privilégiée du fédéralisme canadien. Si l'autonomie entre juridictions est la valeur principale à protéger, le modèle actuel peut sans doute suffire. Si la coordination et la coopération sont à privilégier comme le laisse entendre plusieurs études récentes, alors une réforme s'impose afin d'intégrer de façon systématique les CPM au régime intergouvernemental existant.

INTRODUCTION

The First Ministers' Conference (FMC) is often seen as the centrepiece or the pinnacle of the machinery of intergovernmental relations in Canada.[1] It is viewed as the capstone of a hierarchy of institutions, energizing and directing the work of ministerial councils and conferences, deputy ministers' meetings, and the host of officials' meetings below them. It is the forum at which the prime minister and premiers resolve fundamental differences and set policy directions for the country. The federal-provincial FMC, wrote Stuart

MacKinnon, long-time secretary of the Canadian Intergovernmental Conference Secretariat, is "the principal forum for the conduct of intergovernmental business in Canada today.... The FMC represents the concentration of executive and legislative powers in Canada."[2] In sum, FMCs are a central dimension of Canada's executive federalism.

This is certainly a justifiable view. On occasion, FMCs have indeed provided the arena for conducting profound debates on Canada's constitutional future and other matters. In a federal system characterized both by high levels of interdependence and by highly autonomous governments, the existence of a central point for managing their relationship is vital. And in a Westminster-based political system that concentrates enormous power in the hands of first ministers, clearly their meetings will be the most authoritative setting for the resolution of differences.

This view however, does not fully correspond to the history of intergovernmental relations in Canada. This chapter argues that — especially when compared with the Annual Premiers' Conference (APC), which brings together leaders of the provincial and territorial governments,[3] or with the numerous ministerial councils — the FMC remains a relatively underdeveloped institution. Meetings are ad hoc, sporadic, and often motivated by political ends only remotely tied to the management of interdependence between the two orders of governments. There are few agreed upon decision-making rules or procedures. There is often little organized bureaucratic preparation or follow-up compared with other intergovernmental forums. Nor are there clear links between the FMC and other intergovernmental institutions, or between it and federal and provincial legislatures.

This apparent lack of institutional strength is somewhat puzzling for such a central mechanism of intergovernmental relations. It is perhaps even more puzzling if situated in a discussion of what several analysts of federal-provincial relations have defined as a recent era of renewed intergovernmental collaboration after a period of intense and divisive constitutional conflicts.[4] Collaborative federalism, according to David Cameron and Richard Simeon, is "an intergovernmental process by which national goals are achieved, not by the federal government acting alone or ... moulding provincial behaviour through the exercise of its spending power, but by some or all of the 11 governments acting collectively."[5] If collaborative federalism is to be the template for the operation of the federal system, one would expect FMCs to emerge as a key forum of generating and extending collaboration.

Our analysis of the history of Canadian FMCs tells us, however, that after a steady growth from the 1950s onward and a quasi-institutionalization in the late 1980s, their role and significance changed dramatically in the aftermath of the Meech Lake and Charlottetown failures. The conferences were replaced by more flexible and somewhat more informal First Ministers' Meetings (FMMs) in the 1990s.[6] While such meetings have occurred with considerable frequency and have generally avoided the confrontations of the past, there seems to be little interest in further formalizing the process, or in making it a regular feature of federal-provincial relations, as the APCs have become. To the contrary, we will argue, despite the creation of an ever-growing array of ministerial councils and collaborative experiences at the departmental level, collaboration does not seem to be the guiding principle at the highest level of intergovernmental relations. The current structure of ad hoc meetings seems to confirm their status as a mechanism designed to deal with pressing issues on the political agenda rather than a forum for ongoing co-operation, as the logic of collaborative federalism would dictate.

If this description is accurate, then several questions arise. Why do FMCs and FMMs play such a limited role? Is this a problem for the operation of Canadian federalism? Does it matter? And if so, is it necessary or desirable to restructure and rejuvenate the FMC and give it a greater prominence and institutional status in the Canadian federal system?

The limited role of the FMC, we will suggest, is a result both of the changing political context, especially in post-Charlottetown Canada, and of the basic design of Canada's political institutions. In a Westminster-style parliamentary federal system, where governments are responsible to their respective legislature, executive summits are bound to have a limited decision-making role. In Canada, this is accentuated by a constitutional design that divides responsibilities into "watertight compartments" — in addition to the contemporary reality of broad areas of *de facto* concurrency, debate over where responsibility for different issues lies, and extensive fiscal transfers. This results in relatively few incentives for collaboration. Hence our conclusion that the FMC is a relatively weak, but essential, institution. Its role is explained by the tension between the need for co-operation to manage interdependence and the inherently competitive nature of the system. Its uncertain status lies in its omission from the original constitutional design.

Whether or not the weak institutionalization of the primary mechanism for collaboration at the summit is seen as a problem will depend on one's view of the basic principles that should guide the operation and management of the federation. If the autonomy of each government and its responsibility to its legislature and citizens are the dominant values of Canadian federalism, the current informal and unstructured mechanism for intergovernmental coordination is appropriate. In this model, rather than being a central institution in the operation of federalism, the FMC exists simply to serve the political needs of the constituent governments. From this perspective, greater institutionalization could perhaps even be a threat to the policy variation that defines federalism. But if coordination and co-operation along with common standards and policy harmonization are the goals to be emphasized, as suggested by the idea of collaborative federalism, then we should explore ways to build the FMC more fully into our intergovernmental regime.

The dilemma of what to do about the FMC is reflected in an old joke. Two people are leaving a restaurant. One says, "My, that food was terrible!" to which the other replies, "Yes, and the portions were so small!" Do we fix the FMC process, or just have less of it? We suggest there is perhaps room for improvement to the recipe, while keeping in mind not to expect too much of it.

We begin our analysis by tracing the history and development of the FMC, with particular reference to the experience of the last few years. We then step back to analyze the political dynamics that underpin the recent role of FMCs and explain their limited success in fostering collaboration at the highest level of executive federalism. We conclude with an assessment of the role FMCs should play in the future, and with a review of the major proposals for reform.

AN INSTITUTION IN THE MAKING? FMCs AND THE EVOLUTION OF CANADIAN FEDERALISM

THE EMERGENCE OF FMCs AS AN INTERGOVERNMENTAL MECHANISM

The need for a coordination and co-operation mechanism between the federal and provincial governments emerged soon after 1867. It nonetheless took 40 years after Confederation for a First Ministers' Conference to finally take place. At the time of Confederation, it was expected that each order of government would function within its own distinct areas of power,[7] and that unilateral federal powers such as disallowance (an instrument frequently deployed in the nineteenth century) would be sufficient to resolve any disputes. It rapidly became apparent, however, that some collaboration was necessary to adapt the original division of powers to the rapidly changing nature of Canadian society and economy.

The provinces, led by Honoré Mercier in Quebec and Oliver Mowat in Ontario, took the initiative. Elaborating the "compact theory" of Canadian federalism, they sought greater autonomy for the provinces and limits on federal powers to control them. Two interprovincial conferences took place, in 1887 and 1902, to discuss the provincial challenge to federal powers and its fiscal dominance. The conferences failed to reach a significant consensus and it became apparent that the direct involvement of the federal government was necessary to ensure further development in intergovernmental relations.[8]

The first official Dominion-Provincial Conference was called by Prime Minister Wilfrid Laurier in 1906 to discuss fiscal relations and the taxation proposals put forward by the provinces following their earlier meetings. Laurier was more sympathetic to provincial concerns than John A. Macdonald had been, and the conference agreed on a significant increase in federal transfers to the provinces in what was deemed, ironically, in retrospect, to be a "final revision" of the transfer system.[9] The next conference involving the federal government and the provinces did not take place until 1918, this time to discuss post-war reconstruction. It was followed in 1927 by a seven-day conference to discuss a broad array of issues ranging from economic policies to constitutional matters.[10]

The emergence of FMCs in the first part of the century was thus a slow and uncertain process. Provinces were wary of losing control of the intergovernmental agenda in a structure that could be dominated by the federal government; and the latter was less than enthusiastic about a process that could give more legitimacy to provincial claims. FMCs were ad hoc and exceptional in nature, focused on exchanging information and debating priorities rather than on decision-making or genuine negotiation.

The broad interpretation of provincial powers by the Judicial Committee of the Privy Council slowly changed the dynamic of Canadian federalism, giving more influence to the provinces. This, along with the progressive decline in the use of the federal government's powers of disallowance and reservation and the growth in the importance of policy areas under primarily provincial jurisdiction, led to an increased need for intergovernmental co-operation.[11]

Thus, after the 1927 conference, it was broadly understood that FMCs would be used by Ottawa as a mechanism through which to consult provinces on matters of common concern. Two sets of issues dominated in the 1930s and became the main questions to be debated in intergovernmental forums in the following decades. First was the constitution. With the Statute of Westminster in 1931, a glaring omission of the *1867 BNA Act* — the absence of a Canadian formula for amending the constitution — became more pressing.[12] The 1927 and 1931 conferences were the first of a series of attempts to address this question, which remained a central concern of intergovernmental relations until 1982.

The second fundamental concern was how to respond to the crisis of the Great Depression. Under prime ministers R.B. Bennett and William Lyon MacKenzie King, five federal-provincial conferences were organized between 1931 and 1935 to coordinate the governments' response. The conferences were constructive, as long as the discussions centred on how to deal with the economic crisis. Disagreement quickly emerged, however, when the division of powers was raised.[13]

The need to improve intergovernmental mechanisms as part of a more sweeping reform of the federation was thus becoming increasingly evident. Mackenzie King recognized this when he established a Royal Commission to explore the whole field of federal-provincial relations in 1937. The Rowell-Sirois Commission concluded that "Dominion-provincial conferences held at regular intervals, with a permanent secretariat, would conduce to the more efficient working of the federal system," the first of many such recommendations for greater institutionalization over the years.[14]

THE DEVELOPMENT OF SUMMIT FEDERALISM

It is only in the post-war period that FMCs became a central element in Canadian politics more broadly. The key domestic project was now to construct the welfare state. Most of the formal jurisdiction over related policy fields such as health, education and welfare lay in provincial hands — but most of the financial, political and bureaucratic resources were concentrated in Ottawa. Co-operation thus became essential if the goals of the welfare state were to be achieved. Two Dominion-Provincial Conferences on Reconstruction were held immediately after the war in 1945-1946, and starting in 1955, annual FMCs were convened to discuss taxation, transfer payments, the use of the federal spending power and the creation of national programs in areas of shared or provincial jurisdiction. Conferences of first ministers — still referred to as Dominion-Provincial Conferences — quickly became the main mechanism for negotiation, producing both co-operation and confrontation on the profound redesigning of the role of the state that was taking place at the time.[15]

As the stakes and the level of complexity of the issues discussed increased, the nature and frequency of the conferences also changed. Four conferences were held in 1950 and four more between 1955 and 1957. Under both prime ministers Louis St. Laurent and John Diefenbaker, they became more structured, with an agenda defined well in advance and increased preparatory work being undertaken by ministers and officials.[16]

This increase in frequency and importance reflected broader changes in the federal system that became even more prominent in the following decade. The conferences became an arena for the larger, wealthier provinces — Ontario, Quebec, and British Columbia — to oppose fundamental constitutional change or transfer of powers. FMCs were the only forum where provinces could be guaranteed direct representation and influence at the national level; at the same time, the federal government needed provincial co-operation for the implementation of its programs.

The development of a much more assertive Quebec government in the wake of the Quiet Revolution fundamentally changed the dynamic and the agenda of FMCs. Initially Quebec focused on questions within the existing constitution — a greater provincial share of tax revenues, the right to "opt-out" of shared cost programs, and establishment of a distinct Quebec Pension Plan, among others. After 1966, however, these demands came to be framed as calls for constitutional change, and the stakes correspondingly increased.

More generally, in this period, FMCs contributed greatly to two simultaneous trends which might otherwise have been contradictory. First, they facilitated considerable decentralization (including *de facto* asymmetry between Quebec and the other provinces), especially in fiscal federalism; and second, they facilitated the completion of the Canadian welfare state, with the adoption of medicare, the Canada Assistance Plan and other co-operative measures.

Given the absence of an alternative institutional forum for such fundamental discussions, First Ministers' Conferences were once again the logical arena to discuss proposals for fundamental redesigning of the country's basic law. The debate began with the Confederation of Tomorrow Conference in 1967 — called by Ontario Premier John Robarts. Miffed that a constitutional conference was called by a province, Prime Minister Lester Pearson declined to attend. Nevertheless, the conference mobilized Ottawa to act, and it was followed by seven constitutional conferences culminating in the failed Victoria Conference of 1971. By then FMCs had become became major political events, with increased media attention.[17]

A similar pattern persisted into the 1970s. The period between 1971 and 1983 saw the most intensive use of FMCs in Canadian experience, with the convening of 21 FMCs of various types. Social policy remained prominent, but the most contentious issues surrounded energy policy, pricing and revenues, issues that divided Canada starkly on regional grounds.[18] The constitution was back on the table in the late 1970s, following the election of the Parti Québécois in November 1976. Constitutional review conferences were held in 1978 and early 1979. During the 1980 Quebec referendum campaign on sovereignty, Prime Minister Pierre Trudeau promised a renewed effort at constitutional reform. At a meeting at 24 Sussex Drive in June 1980, the first ministers agreed on a new ministerial process co-chaired by Justice Minister Jean Chrétien and Saskatchewan Attorney-General Roy Romanow. Their efforts culminated in a dramatic Constitutional Conference of September 1980. At this conference, sharply polarized and competing views of the federation were paraded before the country as never before, showing the extent to which FMCs could as easily be a forum for confrontation as for consensus building.[19]

Thus, through the 1960s and 1970s, FMCs became a central part of Canada's institutional landscape. Most were held in the cavernous old Ottawa railway station, refurbished in 1969, and renamed the National Conference Centre. Conference agendas increasingly embraced all the major policy issues of the day. Meetings became more structured, with an agenda defined well in advance and greater follow-up. Preparatory work by ministers and officials grew in importance and delegation sizes increased significantly.[20]

The Canadian Intergovernmental Secretariat was created in 1973 to provide technical, logistical and communications support to the conferences. It built on the Secretariat of the Constitutional Conference, established in 1968. At the time there was some debate about whether it should be a vehicle for research, analysis and prescription — a kind of intergovernmental bureaucracy — or whether it should remain simply in a secretarial supporting role.[21] Reluctant to cede any autonomy, governments confined it to the latter function.

Nationwide, televised sessions contributed in raising the profile of constitutional reform, but they also transformed FMCs into much more than a forum where the heads of the executives of the Canadian federation exchanged views on current policy issues. They became important political platforms for political actors seeking to address a national audience; a political space where governments competed for legitimacy in the representation of citizens, and where fundamental questions about the very nature of Canadian federalism lay at the heart of the debate.

Provincial leaders increasingly used FMCs to claim a legitimate role in defending provincial and regional interests and in shaping national policy, especially in areas that were constitutionally defined as provincial jurisdictions. They questioned Ottawa's claim to represent "the whole nation." That led Trudeau to ask, in a famous confrontation with his provincial counterparts, "But who will speak for Canada?" Alberta Premier Peter Lougheed replied, "We all do." Increasingly, provinces saw themselves as equal partners in Canadian governance. Trudeau, in turn, vehemently rejected the image of Canada as a "community of communities," and scathingly rejected the idea that Ottawa should become "headwaiter to the provinces."[22] He developed a strong dislike for the conferences, which he saw as little more than a platform for posturing premiers to challenge the federal role. Trudeau's views appear to have had a strong influence on the attitude of another Liberal Prime Minister, Jean Chrétien.

These dynamics blended the differing material interests of Canada's regions, competition for public and media support, rival drives for power, status and recognition, the competition to win credit and avoid blame, and partisan and personal differences, into a highly charged and symbolic process. Conferences also often took on the character of what Robert Putnam defined as a "two-level game."[23] First ministers had to negotiate with each other to seek compromise; but they also had to appeal to their electorates back home — the only voters who could keep them in power.[24] Constitutional disputes were especially intense because stakes were higher and areas of possible compromise narrower, and because the participants often believed that the status quo was preferable to the alternatives put forward by their opponents.[25] In a sense, FMCs had both become more prominent in the Canadian system of government, but also more problematic. After the major compromises that had been made in the 1960s, now they appeared not to build trust, but to erode it; not to build consensus, but to display difference.

Despite the bitter taste for many participants left by the negotiation process leading to the 1982 constitutional package, FMCs continued to play an important role in intergovernmental relations in the 1980s. Section 37 of the *Constitution Act, 1982* required that another constitutional conference be convened within a year. The section also required that the conference agenda include the "identification and definition of the rights" of Aboriginal peoples, and that "the Prime Minister of Canada" invite both Aboriginal and territorial representatives to participate in that conference. It was duly held and resulted in amendments to Section 35 of the *Constitution Act, 1982* and a requirement to convene "at least two constitutional conferences."[26]

The election of a Conservative federal government led by Brian Mulroney in 1984 raised the possibility of a more harmonious federal-provincial relationship, especially as the impasse over energy and the National Energy Program (NEP) faded. Mulroney had built strong support across the country, not least among nationalists in Quebec, and promised to "replace the bias of confrontation with the bias of agreement." He promised that:

> To end parallel or incompatible planning once and for all between the two orders of government, we will set up a federal-provincial advisory and coordinating body which will operate at the highest level, namely with the 11 leaders themselves working together in an appropriate institutional framework advising as to the options envisaged and the directions to take.[27]

In that spirit, the federal government and all the provinces agreed in 1985 to hold an annual FMC to deal with economic and social policies.[28] Such annual conferences were indeed held until 1990. They covered a wide variety of topics. While little substantial policy development emerged from the process, they were successful in creating a positive atmosphere for collaboration and exchange of information on specific aspects of social and economic policies, and trade.[29]

But Mulroney's overriding goal was to resolve the constitutional impasse by bringing Quebec back into the "constitutional family with honour and enthusiasm." Constitutional talks were thus again on the agenda. But the strategy would be different this time. Rather than set-piece, high profile and formal FMCs, there would be careful and quiet diplomacy. After discreet soundings in provincial capitals, Mulroney decided to hold an informal meeting rather than a conference. The first ministers, no longer surrounded by phalanxes of ministers and advisers, met in the federal retreat at Meech Lake, and a few weeks later in the Langevin Block in Ottawa, to hammer out the Meech Lake Accord of 1987. Mulroney's objective in using a more informal process rather than the high profile constitutional conferences model of the past was to remove some of the media attention on the negotiations in order to avoid the two-level game described earlier and allow a more open discussion between first ministers. While an agreement was reached, the political costs of such a process became obvious in the following months. The well-known result was an unexpected popular mobilization against the accord that challenged as never before the legitimacy of the entire intergovernmental process, especially the FMC, now derided as those "11 men in suits," meeting behind closed doors to manipulate a constitution that, since 1982, had come to be seen as the "people's" constitution, not as the property of governments.[30]

THE POST-MEECH ERA: FMCs' DECLINE?

The establishment of FMCs as a core institutional feature of Canadian federalism was considered a *fait accompli* in the late 1980s. The 1987 Meech Lake

Constitutional Accord included a clause making mandatory at least two annual conferences on the constitution and on social and economic policies.[31] In 1988, Stuart MacKinnon, head of the Canadian Intergovernmental Secretariat, could plausibly conclude that FMCs had become "a firmly established forum for coordination and negotiation ... and in some key areas, it is clear that the initial, if not critical, focus of policy debate is now taking place at First Ministers' Conferences."[32]

This changed dramatically in the 1990s. With the Meech Lake Accord, the legitimacy and effectiveness of the FMC as the main forum to discuss constitutional reform was increasingly questioned. An FMC was held in June 1990 to rescue the failing Meech Lake Accord before the deadline for its ratification had passed. Perhaps this represented the nadir of the FMC as an institution that could foster an accommodative deliberation on constitutional matters. The constitutional discussions, initially called as an informal meeting over dinner one Friday night, became a marathon lasting a whole week, and concluding in the early hours of the following Saturday morning. The discussion went on behind closed doors, even as protesters gathered outside the National Conference Centre and public opinion rallied against the accord. The Annual Conference of First Ministers, as part of the 1985 agreement on such annual conferences, scheduled for Calgary in November 1990, was never held.

When constitutional debate was renewed in 1991, the federal government tried to create a more open process for constitutional renewal. After a long series of parliamentary hearings, published proposals, national conferences designed to involve citizens, and ministerial meetings involving representatives of Aboriginal peoples and the territories in high-level intergovernmental meetings, the Charlottetown Accord was hammered out, once again, in a series of informal First Ministers' Meetings.[33]

Despite this attempt to create a more open process, the Charlottetown agreement was still widely considered to be the product of executive federalism, with little democratic legitimacy. This was an important reason for its subsequent defeat in a national referendum. While much blame was put on the institution of the FMC itself, it is in fact the whole process of executive federalism that failed to answer demands for transparency and citizen participation. It would also be interesting to speculate how the Charlottetown Accord might have differed if the participating ministers had understood from the outset that their work was to be submitted to popular judgement.

Thus by 1992, FMCs, and especially the more informal constitutional meetings, had come to epitomize all the negative aspects of executive federalism: its lack of democratic legitimacy; its tendency to focus too much on regional differences and not enough on other dimensions of Canadian diversity; its competitiveness that was not conducive to compromise and workable solutions, and finally, its apparent role in transforming what should be a discussion about the best interests of the country into a power game between 11 first ministers (and, more recently, leaders of the three territories.). The Mulroney government did not renew the 1985 agreement to hold an annual FMC after the failure of Meech Lake.

In the new era there would be much less emphasis on FMCs as a kind of super-legislature. Indeed, the response to the widespread criticism was not to reform the institution, but to de-emphasize its role. FMCs had in a sense become victims of their success. Their size, the number of participants and the attention they received from the media had transformed them into an exercise of public relations where premiers and the prime minister were at least as much seeking national exposure to assert their legitimacy, in speaking in the name of their electorate, as they were discussing substantive issues. The effectiveness of such a heavy and politically charged process was questioned and new approaches to intergovernmental relations were sought.

The response to such critiques was the low-profile, small steps approach of the Chrétien government to renewal of the federation, and a new focus on collaboration on specific programs through contacts at the official and ministerial level rather than first ministers. Less formal and more private First Ministers' Meetings have now completely replaced the high-profile conferences of the 1980s.[34] No formally called FMC has been held since 1990. The commitment to hold an annual conference disappeared from the agenda, even though FMMs have in fact been held almost annually since 1993, as the following table shows.[35]

Table 1: First Ministers' Meetings From 1993 to 2003

Date	*Topics on the agenda*
Ottawa, 21 December 1993	Economic and fiscal environment, National Infrastructure Program, improving the efficiency of the federation
Ottawa, 18 July 1994	Internal Trade Agreement
Ottawa, 21 June 1996	The economy, constitutional obligation to review the amending formula (section 49), employment and social issues
Ottawa, 11-12 December 1997	The Canadian economy, social union, youth, health
Ottawa, 4 February 1999	Social Union Framework Agreement
Ottawa, 11 September 2000	Health Care Funding Agreement and Early Childhood Development
Ottawa, 4-5 February 2003	Accord on Health Care Renewal

How are the recent meetings different than previous conferences? The federal government has made a point of making such reunions as low-key as possible, appearing as meetings "among friends," rather than as political summits.[36] The focus, it says, is on collaboration and constructive exchange rather than disagreement and conflict. Public sessions, used in the past to voice dissent, have become an exchange of good will, with even the Quebec premier joining in.[37]

In that spirit, first ministers met in 1994 to sign the Agreement on Internal Trade (AIT), which had been negotiated by their ministers and officials. The meeting was celebrated more for its success in avoiding open conflict than for the substance of the agreement itself.[38] Similarly, in 1996, a meeting was required in order to fulfill the constitutional requirements under Section 49 of the *Constitution Act, 1982*. The prime minister and others sought to play down its significance, and little except agreement to pursue further discussion on various agenda items was accomplished.[39] The emphasis was now on lowering the temperature, and demonstrating to Canadians that federalism could function with a low-key, pragmatic approach. As Prime Minister Chrétien said at the meeting: "The FMM is not an occasion for high drama. We will not be rolling the dice on the future of Canada. The real work of nation-building is not glamorous."[40]

While Chrétien was largely successful in lowering the expectations and avoiding public displays of conflict during his first mandate, the lack of substantial discussion at the highest level of executive power became more problematic as time passed. The role of the state, and hence the structure and operation of the federal system, were undergoing a transformation in some ways as profound as that which had occurred after World War II. The struggle against deficits brought fundamental change in the structure of fiscal transfers to provinces. The redistribution of roles in managing the social union could not take place without substantial intergovernmental discussion. In the absence of other public forums for the representation of provincial and regional interests, FMMs regained some of their role as a central arena of political debate as discussions on the renewal of the social union took shape.

This was evident in a 1997 meeting focused on funding social programs, in the wake of drastic cuts in federal transfers. The meeting did produce an agreement to continue discussions related to the social union, but there were strong disagreements on its scope and even on the meaning of the final communiqué.[41] In 1999, provincially led negotiations on the social union were coming to a head. Ottawa responded by calling a meeting at very short notice in order to inject its own views. The result was the Social Union Framework Agreement (SUFA), signed by Ottawa and all provinces except Quebec.[42] During the last-minute negotiations, the federal government used its fiscal leverage — especially with the poorer provinces — to win a substantial protection of its role, blocking the more provincialist thrust of the early draft agreement drawn up by a provincial ministerial council, and provoking Quebec's refusal to sign.

Provinces were more successful at an FMM on health care funding in September 2000. They had begun calling for such a meeting, aimed at restoring some of the draconian cuts in the 1995 federal budget, the previous year.[43] Given widespread public fear about the future of medicare, Ottawa needed to demonstrate its financial commitment. Provinces, faced with rapidly escalating bills, desperately needed the federal financial assistance.[44] The success of the 2000 FMM can thus be attributed mostly to the pressure on all participants to reach an agreement. The political cost of disagreement would have been significant, not only for Quebec and the more combative provinces, but also for the federal government, which was preparing for an election at the time. In all these meetings, discussion was dominated by short-run political considerations.

A similar dynamic was at work when first ministers convened in February 2003. Now, two new reports on the future of health care in Canada were on the table, each calling for major change in the funding, organization, delivery and accountability of health policy. Both had received extensive publicity and fuelled calls for basic reform.[45] Again, Ottawa was prepared to inject additional funding, in return for greater visibility, more focused targeting of spending, more accountability, and a new council to monitor and assess health care outcomes. And again, provinces were desperate for increased resources, while remaining deeply resistant to increased constraints on their own freedom of action. The resulting 2003 First Ministers' Accord on Health Care Renewal[46] achieved the minimal goals of the parties, but fell well short of the system change envisioned in the Kirby and Romanow reports. Moreover, the accord had an ambiguous status — it was largely written by the federal government, and was not actually signed by the premiers, and was vague on crucial issues such as future funding, and the role of a monitoring council.

THE WEAKEST LINK?

This history demonstrates that the FMC has not emerged, despite numerous attempts in that direction, as an autonomous institution in its own right, in the sense of having a set of fixed rules and procedures, an established organization, and a set of distinct incentives, disincentives and constraints that are capable of influencing or shaping the behaviour and strategies of political actors. While evolution toward greater institutionalization seemed to be a logical expectation in the 1960s and again in the late 1980s, it is certainly not the case today.

Indeed, as we noted at the outset, the FMC process has no legal or constitutional existence; it exists solely at the whim of first ministers themselves.

Despite numerous proposals and attempts to do so, there is currently no requirement for meetings to be held annually, or at any other time. There is no independent bureaucratic backup, such as that provided by the European Commission in relation to the European Union Council of Ministers, that could give the institution a life of its own. There are no written rules of procedure. Normally FMCs, or FMMs, are called by the prime minister, usually when he or she feels it politically necessary or advantageous to do so. While premiers cannot ordain an FMC or an FMM, it is often pressure from them that leads to one being called. The 2000 meeting on health is an example. There are also no rules about the size or composition of delegations. While the prime minister normally chairs a meeting, and premiers speak in order of their province's entry into Confederation, few other procedures govern the debate. The implicit rule is that each government counts equally and the goal is consensus.

Most importantly, there are no decision-making rules, no voting procedures and no agreed standards with respect to public or media access. While conclusions are often set out in formal communiqués, and occasionally in more formal accords, these have no legal or constitutional status. Only in the broadest sense can they be considered binding. FMCs are also remarkably independent of the legislative process: there are no agreed norms for legislative discussion of the position a government will take into an upcoming meeting, or for regular reporting back to legislatures once meetings have been concluded. All this is a matter for decision by the first minister himself or herself, reflecting the dominance of first ministers in the Canadian system.

In sum, the FMC has failed to become an established forum where conflicts are solved and ongoing collaboration is established at the highest level of executive power. They have rather developed into a source of increased tension among leaders competing for legitimacy. FMCs are a national platform for competing political leaders, each claiming they talk in the name of Canadians, or at least of citizens of their provinces. FMCs and FMMs have also clearly suffered from their lack of transparency. They are perceived as reinforcing the dominance of the executive in the management of the federation and in Canada's version of parliamentary government more generally. The focus of the FMC seems to be more on reaching workable arrangements among elites than working toward the interest of Canadians as a whole. This has produced limited policy development and little effective collaboration in the implementation of the various agreements negotiated. It has also, as many authors have pointed out, created a backlash among Canadians against the traditional model of elite accommodation.

All this suggests that rather than being an "independent variable," the FMC appears to be largely a dependent variable. That is to say its role, character, and effectiveness at any given time reflect forces and pressures coming from outside the FMC process itself. Success, it seems, does not depend on the format of conferences, but rather on the nature of the debates taking place, on current political context, and on the nature of the Canadian federation itself.

A number of factors seem to shape the frequency and dynamic of FMCs at any given time. Given the focus on first ministers, a key factor is the preferences of the first ministers themselves, their personalities and their views about the operation of the federation. We have seen how prime ministers Pearson, Trudeau, Mulroney and Chrétien each saw the role of FMCs and FMMs differently. Similarly, the personalities of strong premiers, from William Davis to Mike Harris in Ontario, or from Peter Lougheed to Ralph Klein in Alberta, have strongly affected the intergovernmental relationship. So have the deeply ambivalent attitudes of Quebec premiers such as René Lévesque and Lucien Bouchard, torn between the need to make the system work for Quebecers and their desire to use the FMC as a platform of building support for sovereignty.

Closely linked to the interests and aspiration of individuals is a more general characteristic of first ministers that has sharply constrained a greater formalization and role for the FMC. It is in the nature of the constituent governments to wish to preserve as much autonomy and freedom of action for themselves as possible. Thus they will welcome FMCs when they appear to offer the opportunity to influence other governments, but they will be hostile to any development that might seem to lead to constraints on themselves.[47]

In general, it is provinces that have stressed the need for more, and more regular, FMCs. They provide a national platform from which their political status can be enhanced to bring pressure on the federal government. Ottawa has tended to be much less enthusiastic about FMCs. Why, federal officials ask, should we acquiesce to a greater provincial role? Why should we give premiers a national platform? This view was held especially strongly by Prime Minister Pierre Trudeau, who sought to defend national power against assertive provincialism and Quebec nationalism. Yet Ottawa has some advantages in the FMC arena. It has maintained much control over the timing of meetings and their agendas. The bureaucratic resources it can bring to a meeting far outweigh those that can be mobilized by any more than a few provinces. While it may be a disadvantage to be one against ten, it is potentially a big advantage to be a united one against a divided ten. In several cases we have reviewed, most notably the final conference leading to the 1982 constitutional settlement and the 1999 meeting that completed the SUFA, Ottawa has been able to use differences among provinces to its advantage.

Another contextual factor influencing the dynamics of FMCs is the play of electoral politics. FMCs are often used as an electoral platform; and newly elected prime ministers often declare their commitment to a new era of intergovernmental harmony, while later coming to see the need to co-operate with premiers as a constraint on their own freedom of action.

While context is important, it does not explain in itself the limited success of the FMC as a collaborative institution. The most important determinant of the ad hoc, unstructured and conflict-oriented nature of the FMC lies in the nature of the Canadian political system. First, the fundamental premise of a Westminster-style parliamentary system is that each government is responsible to its own legislature. This clashes fundamentally with the logic of the FMC as a decision-making body, which would imply that governments would become responsible and accountable to each other. This is not very problematic at lower levels of administrative and technical co-operation; it is much more so at the level of first ministers. Despite their many other differences, Canada and Australia share the Westminster model; thus it is no surprise that their patterns of FMCs are very similar.[48]

In addition, parliamentary government in Canada is a highly competitive, majoritarian, winner-take-all system, and it is no surprise that first ministers would take some of these styles of action into the forum of the FMC. This can help explain why, despite the fulsome commitment to building "mutual trust" in the SUFA and other agreements, recent FMMs remained heavily focused on mistrust and on competition for turf, blame avoiding and credit claiming. This is very different from the emphasis on consensus decision-making in German federalism, to take one example.

A final institutional factor explaining the unstructured form of the FMC lies in the basic federal design itself. The Canadian model of "separated" or "divided" federalism is predicated on the idea of watertight compartments and separate lists of powers. Of course the contemporary reality is one of interdependence and a broad swathe of *de facto* concurrency. This is why FMCs and the intergovernmental machinery are so important. But the logic remains, in the sense that FMCs and other intergovernmental bodies are an "add-on" to the basic design. They are necessary because of the overlapping responsibilities of governments, but in tension with the underlying logic of the system.

FROM FMC TO FMM: WHAT'S AT STAKE?

As noted earlier, after the debacles of Meech Lake and Charlottetown, governments appeared anxious to reduce tensions and to demonstrate the "workability" of the federal system. As a result, the federal government and the provinces wished to lower expectations about the importance of FMCs. In this they were largely successful. Much of the public criticism of intergovernmental relations has faded away. Most of the heavy lifting in intergovernmental relations now appears to be undertaken by the many ministerial councils that have evolved in recent years. Premiers, who used regularly to make an appeal for annual FMCs, no longer appear to do so, contenting themselves with calls for meetings on specific issues as they arise. Moreover, not only have FMMs replaced FMCs, but also informal discussions during private dinners or during "Team Canada" trade missions have come to epitomize this tendency.[49] First ministers try to spend time together in a positive and low-stress environment where media attention is not directly focused on intergovernmental tensions.

It could be argued that the distinction between FMCs and FMMs is more symbolic than substantial. Indeed, FMCs have no more legal status or political legitimacy as a decision-making instance than FMMs. As we saw, a few rules were established over time, which gave FMCs processes a more structured and formal nature FMMs don't have. FMCs were also attended by a great number of civil servants, political counsellors, as well as ministers with their own staff. They acquired with time a certain solemn nature and greater authority. FMMs are supposed to be dinners or less structured gatherings with a limited number of political aides. They are also called within short notice; the agenda is limited and generally known only a few days in advance. But even in terms of substance, the more recent FMMs have grown in size and media attention.

In a sense, the distinction is essentially symbolic. But symbolism is no less important. Given their informal nature, meetings are less demanding in terms of accountability. Reducing media expectations was admittedly an objective in lowering the profile of the meetings in the last decade. The distinction between FMCs and FMMs is significant in that it conveys a very specific message as to the nature of federalism at the summit: it is not an institutionalized part of our federal system. It reflects, in a certain way, the low level of legitimacy given to the process.

This begs the question of whether the current structure, with its emphasis on ad hoc and private meetings, is an effective response to the need for a legitimate forum for public discussion of broad policy directions at the highest level of governmental executives in the country. While more informal, key discussions and decisions are still taken behind closed doors, or in federal-provincial instances with limited citizens access.[50]

Recent experience has shown that FMCs or FMMs remain a core vehicle of intergovernmental relations in Canada even in the absence of any significant constitutional debates. The engagement of first ministers was central to completing the complex process of intergovernmental negotiations leading to the SUFA and the more recent agreement on health. As we saw, FMMs have been held intermittently since 1993. Moreover, the number of delegates in recent meetings has grown.[51] This is a clear indication of the importance of such meetings for their participants. Meetings are different and less structured, but no less important than the FMCs of previous eras.

The reliance on more informal mechanisms can be seen as a positive step in making the federation work. It is not, however, without consequences. FMMs have come to be seen as crisis management mechanisms rather than forums for broadly based collaboration among the partners of the federation. The gradual institutionalization of the FMC, until the late 1980s, served some purposes that remain relevant today. In a highly interdependent federal system where there is no effective representation of provinces at the centre, the FMC can play a key role as a visible forum for expressing and reconciling regional and national interests. In a governance system dominated by "the centre," agreement among first ministers is necessary to energize and direct co-operation at the level of ministers and officials. At a time when constitutional change is extremely difficult if not impossible, the FMC can be a valuable forum for a continuing debate about roles and responsibilities, in light of changing needs and circumstances. The current style and practice of FMMs is poorly designed to meet these broad objectives.

The increased institutionalization of FMCs in the late 1980s also meant less leverage for the federal government in setting the agenda, and for deciding on the timing and format of discussions. The retreat from a more structured and formalized process plays to the advantage of the federal government in strategic terms. As the 1999 SUFA and 2000 health meetings showed, provinces have little leverage in defining the timing and the agenda of FMMs, further alienating them from a process supposed to be collaborative. The current ad hoc pattern is not conducive to trust-building among participants. Nor is it well-designed to engage Canadians in considered debate about the evolution of the federation. The use of FMMs as a crisis management mechanism rather than a structured forum to voice and solve disagreements on a more routine basis provides a limited basis for constructive debate and ongoing collaboration.

OPTIONS FOR THE FUTURE

We have suggested in the previous section that the current model may be better at solving crisis than inducing ongoing collaboration among first ministers. But is this a problem? And if so, can it be improved? The answer to this question depends heavily on how one views the nature of the federation. On the one hand is the collaborative model that sees governance in Canada essentially as a partnership between two equal orders of government that collectively work together to serve the needs of Canadians. This model emphasizes the need for co-operation, harmonization, and mutual agreement on common values and standards. It follows that the FMC should play a crucial role in meeting these objectives and that it should be built more explicitly and formally into our institutional arrangements. This is, for example, the model proposed by André Bruelle in *Le mal canadien.* He proposes a model rooted in "partnership" and interdependence in which a permanent "Council of First Ministers" would establish common standards and make binding decisions much along the lines of the European Council of Ministers.[52] Tom Courchene similarly sees the need to bring the provinces "more fully and formally into the key societal goal of preserving and promoting social Canada," and suggests an enforceable interprovincial and federal-provincial accord that would set out an agreed set of standards and principles.[53]

There is, however, a more competitive view of Canadian federalism. It stresses the importance of autonomous governments, acting on their own within their jurisdictional limits, to meet the needs of their own electorates. This alternative view has been most forcefully expressed by Albert Breton, in his dissenting opinion to the *Report of the Royal Commission on the Economic Union* in 1985.[54] The virtues of federalism, he argues, lie in vigorous intergovernmental competition, and a wide diversity of policy responses. Where coordination is essential, he argues, it will be achieved — but by the independent responses of governments to political forces and the actions of other governments, not by painfully negotiated agreements that satisfy the political needs of the governmental elites while paying little attention to the wider society. In this model, co-operation is not the holy grail; it may even result in "lowest common denominator solutions" that please no one. In this conception of federalism, the FMC should play a limited role, and the current model may well be the most efficient.

Our analysis lies somewhere in between those two views. Intergovernmental accords such as SUFA and the AIT have indeed become important elements of the intergovernmental landscape. Most embody genuine commitments by all parties. But they are not formally binding or judicially enforceable.[55] Most of the recent agreements that have been signed have preambles to the effect that nothing in them should be interpreted as altering the distribution of power in the constitution.[56] In our view, that is as it should be in a parliamentary system of responsible government, in which each government must answer to its own legislature. Ideally, we should think of the FMC as a forum in which to argue, persuade, cajole, negotiate, share information, come to common understandings about overall policy directions, and so on — but not to legislate. A more binding and formalized decision-making process seems to be unnecessary. We do not suggest the FMC become a kind of super legislature. Even if that were desirable for policy reasons, the FMC has no legitimacy to play such a role, as recent history has shown. Hence, it is not necessary to build in formal voting procedures.

That being said, virtually every constitutional proposal of the past few decades — beginning with the Rowell-Sirois Report, and continuing with the Pepin-Robarts task force, the Macdonald Commission, and the Meech Lake and Charlottetown accords — has suggested that improvements to the current model are necessary. Such recommendations are based on several fundamental premises:

- First, despite the formal division of powers, Canadian governments are highly interdependent, hence a considerable degree of collaboration is needed to meet policy challenges effectively.

- Second is the realization that power is concentrated in first ministers; it is they who give direction and purpose to government. It follows that direction and purpose for the federation as a whole can come only from them acting together.

- Third is the realization that other Canadian institutions — notably the Senate and the party system — significantly fail to achieve the larger task of political accommodation in a divided society. That burden, then, falls largely on the processes of executive federalism, and on the FMC as its primary expression.

- Fourth is the perception that Canadian federalism is particularly competitive and adversarial compared with other federations with more elaborate and institutionalized mechanisms of intergovernmental relations. A more highly structured FMC might help build trust and co-operation and transform this culture of confrontation.

- Fifth, the need for greater transparency and accountability suggests that matters such as strengthening the social union should not be discussed behind closed doors, simply followed by a press conference. Citizens need to be more directly engaged in the development of the federation. So do federal and provincial legislators.[57]

The case for institutionalizing the FMC is thus a strong one. FMCs have had and will continue to play a significant role in Canadian intergovernmental relations. But what sort of reform could be undertaken, given the broader architecture of the federation?

A FEW MODEST PROPOSALS

- Require that FMCs be held annually, at fixed times, as with the Annual Premiers' Conference. This could be set out either in the constitution, in legislation or in an intergovernmental agreement. The relative success of the APC in producing ongoing exchanges and collaboration at the provincial level suggests the value of such a model.[58] The advantage might be that no longer would the holding of conferences be a political football, used to the advantage of particular government. If FMCs were built into the normal political calendar, officials and ministers could set their activities around them, the agenda could be developed more co-operatively, effective preparation could be carried out, and it would be much easier to develop regular delegation and reporting relationships with ministerial councils and others. The calling — or not — of meetings would be less politically contentious, and eventually the conferences might become less obviously visible as media events. Interest groups and parliamentary committees would also benefit from knowing well in advance when meetings would be held and what their agendas would be. The effect would be to make the FMC a more "normal" and routine fixture in the governmental landscape.

There is no guarantee that this would bring about greater intergovernmental trust and harmony. Indeed, to the extent that it would place the management of intergovernmental relations even more in the hands of first ministers and central agencies — the very groups now most concerned with turf, status, credit and blame — it might even exacerbate conflict. But the reality is that no institution can assure harmony; the same institution can be at one moment an arena for co-operation, at another moment an arena for bitter division and deadlock. Nevertheless, regularizing conferences could be a useful first step in making the process more neutral and thus more conducive to co-operation.

- Link the FMC more directly to the parliamentary and legislative process. This seeks to address the problem of accountability and the tension between the FMC and parliamentary government. At present the FMC is completely separated from the normal processes of parliament. It exists in a constitutional limbo. One consequence is that parliamentarians have no window on or access to the key intergovernmental institution. This should change. As we have noted, parliamentary committees should have the opportunity to scrutinize and comment on both the position a government will take to a conference, and to assess and debate the results. This could be facilitated if each legislature established a permanent standing committee on intergovernmental relations. In addition, opposition members should routinely be invited as observers at FMCs — as has happened in a few previous cases. Moreover, Canadian unity and intergovernmental relations might both be served in the long run by establishing an ongoing forum in which backbench members of parliament and provincial legislators can come together regularly to discuss common challenges. This could temper Canada's executive intergovernmentalism with a small measure of "legislative intergovernmentalism." The United States has both its Council of State Governors and its Council of State Legislators.

- A public window on the process. Despite the clamour for more intergovernmental relations following the Meech Lake Accord, the recent emphasis on informal FMMs has reinforced the closed character of first ministers' gatherings. While behind-the-scenes meetings are no doubt essential to hammering out agreements, any protocol establishing annual conferences should include the commitment to hold opening and closing sessions before the press. There may be some worry that this would produce grandstanding by first ministers, but it is more likely that open meetings would make them more accountable for their performance, and may encourage a stronger focus on the public interest than on concern for governmental status and turf.

CONCLUSION

First Ministers' Conferences have evolved toward greater institutionalization as their role in managing interdependence among the two constitutionally independent orders of government has increased. By the late 1980s, FMCs had become annual events with large delegations, and were often televised. FMCs were coming to be seen as the central element in intergovernmental relations. This changed in the aftermath of the often difficult and complex constitutional negotiations of the early 1990s. The character of FMCs, their lack of transparency and limited public input, were said to be directly responsible for the failure of constitutional renewal. The result was a retreat from institutionalization toward much more informal and ad hoc meetings and a renewed focus on creating collaboration channels at the ministerial and official levels, rather than at the highly politicized prime ministerial level. FMCs are, paradoxically, the least institutionalized and established of all intergovernmental mechanisms today.

The current status of FMCs, or FMMs, indicates the limits of collaborative federalism in an institutional and political context where confrontation and competition seems to be the rule. As J. Stephan Dupré argued in his essay on the workability of executive federalism, what is perhaps lacking at the highest level of the system is mutual trust.[59] Indeed, the extent of distrust seems to increase as intergovernmental relations moves from line officials, to central agency officials, to ministers, and then to first ministers. Institutional reform cannot create trust if the basic sense of common purpose or federal "comity" is missing. Modest reform to the structure and process of FMCs may, however, create at least some incentives to encourage co-operation.

As we have suggested, the current model can be seen as perfectly adequate if one views intergovernmental relations as a limited process for managing interdependence among competing governments. The reality is, however, that despite their constitutional independence, governments in Canada must collaborate, coordinate their action and discuss questions of fiscal distribution and shared jurisdiction.

First Ministers' Conferences are perhaps the weakest link in our intergovernmental system simply because too much is asked of a forum with such limited democratic legitimacy and autonomy. In a Parliamentary system, intergovernmental relations cannot replace the elected assembly as the source of executive powers and law-making. On the other hand, the absence of any other significant democratic space for the resolution of regional conflicts, a role normally played by the second chamber, creates a situation where FMCs are asked to play a double role: that of forum for necessary collaboration at the executive level and of forum for the expression and accommodation of regional differences. In a sense, this is why it is a weak but essential institution.

We cannot be sure that a more institutionalized process would reduce tensions or lead to more collaboration. But the establishment of annual meetings or conferences to manage the federation creates the potential for more routine discussion and greater follow-up on agreements. It could remove the tension inherent in crisis situation from most meetings, and allow a closer focus on substantive discussion. A greater involvement of legislatures in the process leading to and following the conferences could also remove some of the tension associated with the lack of legitimacy of such an executive-centred exercise.

NOTES

We are grateful to Senator Lowell Murray and to Peter Meekison, two veterans of the First Ministers' Conferences, for their very helpful comments and suggestions on this chapter.

1. See for, example, Richard Simeon, *Federal-Provincial Diplomacy: The Making of Recent Policy in Canada* (Toronto: University of Toronto Press, 1972), p. 125; James Ross Hurley, "Executive Federalism," in *Public Administration and Public Management Experiences in Canada*, eds. Jacques Bourgault *et al.* (Quebec: Les publications du Quebec, 1997), p. 114, Ch. 8.

2. Stuart Mackinnon, "First Ministers' Conferences," in *Proceedings of a Conference on Public Policy and Administrative Studies* (Guelph: University of Guelph, 1988), vol. 5.

3. See Peter Meekison's chapter in this volume for a detailed discussion of Annual Premiers' Conferences.

4. David Cameron and Richard Simeon, "Intergovernmental Relations and Democratic Citizenship," in *Governance in the Twenty-first Century: Revitalizing Public Service*, eds. B. Guy Peters and Donald Savoie (Montreal: McGill-Queen's University Press, 2000), pp. 58-118. See also Harvey Lazar, "Non-constitutional Renewal: Toward a New Equilibrium in the Federation," in *Canada: The State of the Federation 1997, Non-Constitutional Renewal*, ed. H. Lazar (Kingston: Institute of Intergovernmental Relations, Queen's University, 1998), p. 25.

5. Cameron and Simeon, "Intergovernmental Relations and Democratic Citizenship," p. 77.

6. As we will suggest, the distinction between FMCs and FMMs is perhaps more symbolic than substantial, although the change is significant inasmuch as it indicates an attempt to deinstitutionalize summit federalism as represented by the increasingly formalized and high-profile conferences of the 1970s and 1980s. Throughout the text, we will distinguish between FMCs and FMMs when referring to specific conferences or meetings, depending on their official title, but we will refer to the institution in general as the FMC.

7. The early years of the federation were characterized by a strong compartmentalization of powers and regular use, by the federal government, of its powers of reservation and disallowance. For a discussion of the original "compartmentalized federalism" see J. Stephan Dupré, "Reflections on the Workability of Executive Federalism," in *Intergovernmental Relations*, vol. 63 of the Royal Commission on the Economic Union and Development Prospects for Canada, ed. R. Simeon (Toronto: University of Toronto Press, 1990), p. 472.

8. For an analysis of early conferences, see Gérard Veilleux, *Les Relations Intergouvernementales au Canada, 1887-1967* (Montreal: Presse de l'Université du Québec, 1971), p. 33.

9. Richard Simeon and Ian Robinson, *State, Society and the Development of Canadian Federalism*, vol. 71 of the Royal Commission on the Economic Union and Development Prospects for Canada (Toronto: University of Toronto Press, 1990), p. 55.

10. The Canadian Intergovernmental Conference Secretariat compiled in 1988 a useful list of all First Ministers' Conferences since 1906.

11. For a discussion linking increased provincial influence to the establishment of regular federal-provincial collaboration, see for example *Report*, Royal Commission on Dominion-Provincial Relations (Ottawa: Queen's Printer, 1940), vol. 1, pp. 132-36. Hereinafter, the *Rowell-Sirois Commission*.

12. The Statute of Westminster established the independence of the British Dominions, by stating that they were no longer subject to UK law. The problem for Canada was that the *British North America Act* was a British statute, and it would have to remain so until Canada could agree on an amending formula.

13. *Rowell-Sirois Commission*, vol. 2, p. 69; as well as Gérard Veilleux, *Les Relations Intergouvernementales au Canada*, p. 58.

14. *Rowell-Sirois Commission,* vol. 2, p. 71. Similar proposals were regularly made later on, notably in the Victoria Charter of 1971, in the report of the Pepin-Robarts' Task Force on Canadian Unity in 1979, in the final report of the Royal Commission on the Economic Union and Development Prospects for Canada (the MacDonald Commission), as well as in the Meech Lake and Charlottetown agreements.

15. See Keith Banting, "The Past Speaks to the Future: Lessons from the Postwar Social Union," in *Canada: The State of the Federation 1997, Non-Constitutional Renewal*, ed. Harvey Lazar (Kingston: Institute of Intergovernmental Relations, Queen's University, 1998).

16. This led, among other things, to the establishment in 1955 of the Continuing Committee on Fiscal and Economic Matters, an intergovernmental group of officials mandated to exchange information and support the conferences and guarantee their follow-up. See Gérard Veilleux, *Les Relations Intergouvernementales au Canada*, p. 61, on the mandate of the secretariat.

17. The 1968 Constitutional Review Conference was televised for the first time.

18. Eleven FMCs took place in the decade the 1970s, of which at least four focused largely on energy and resource ownership and management. The economic

turmoil of the 1970s meant that the economy became much more prominent in conference agendas.

19. This failure triggered Ottawa's attempt to amend the constitution without substantial provincial support, and precipitated the dramatic chain of events taking place in Parliament, the courts and the UK, which led eventually to the late night negotiations of November 1981, the adoption of Canada's *Charter of Rights and Freedoms,* and a new formula for constitutional amendment.

20. At a conference in November 1963, 203 ministers and officials were present. At the December 1969 constitutional conference, there were 140 delegates — 51 ministers, 89 advisers, and 28 "observers." In Simeon, *Federal-Provincial Diplomacy,* p. 126.

21. The debate is summarized in Canadian Intergovernmental Conference Secretariat, *The Constitutional Review, 1968-71* (Ottawa: Information Canada, 1974).

22. See Simeon and Robinson, *State, Society and the Development of Canadian Federalism,* p. 274.

23. "Diplomacy and Domestic Politics: The Logic of Two-Level Games," *International Organization* 42 (1988):427-60.

24. See R. Kenneth Carty and Steven B. Wolinetz in this volume. The most dramatic example, perhaps, was Quebec Premier Bourassa's pencilled endorsement of the Victoria Charter, followed shortly by its repudiation after nationalist opposition arose in Quebec City.

25. Michael B. Stein suggested in an analysis of the constitutional negotiations from 1968 to 1981 that such process was not conducive to "integrative bargaining," a negotiation aimed at reaching a common compromise rather than focused on each participant's gains or losses. The "two-level game" of negotiations and public display of legitimacy is certainly less conducive to compromise in high stake constitutional negotiations. See M. Stein, "Canadian Constitutional Renewal, 1968-1981: A Case Study in Integrative Bargaining," Institute of Intergovernmental Relations, Working Paper No. 27 (Kingston: Queen's University, 1989).

26. Three such conferences were held in 1984, 1985, and 1987, but to little effect.

27. Mulroney's speech was given in Sept Isles, PQ, 6 August 1984; quoted in Simeon and Robinson, *State, Society and the Development of Canadian Federalism,* p. 302.

28. The Regina memorandum of understanding included the commitment to "review the state of federal-provincial relations; consult on major issues ... in particular the state of the economy; consider broad objectives for governments in Canada; and exchange information to facilitate planning for the operations of their government." The agreement was to be renewed after five years. The Regina agreement is discussed in MacKinnon, "First Ministers' Conferences," p. 8.

29. Indeed it can be argued that the trust and mutual understanding that was built up paved the way for the extensive consultations that were held during the negotiation of the Canada-US Free Trade Agreement. At an informal meeting in June 1986, Prime Minister Mulroney won approval of most premiers to enter negotiations. Over the course of negotiations, 11 more informal meetings of first ministers were held.

30. Alan Cairns, "The Constitutional World We Have Lost," in *Reconfigurations: Canadian Citizenship and Constitutional Change. Selected Essays by Alan C. Cairns*, eds. Alan C. Cairns and Douglas E. Williams (Toronto: McClelland and Stewart, 1995); Peter Russell, *Canada's Constitutional Odyssey*, 2d edition (Toronto: University of Toronto Press, 1992), p. 4.

31. Clause 8 of the Meech Lake Accord provided for an annual conference to "discuss the state of the Canadian economy and such other matters as may be appropriate," and clause 13 provided for an annual conference on the constitution.

32. MacKinnon, "First Ministers' Conferences," p. 25.

33. The accord was designed to retain the recognition of Quebec found in Meech Lake along with an equal recognition of others' aspirations, including Senate reform and Aboriginal self-government. In the subsequent referendum, the Charlottetown Agreement was rejected in most provinces.

34. Such meetings were held at least as far back as under Pearson and Trudeau in parallel to FMCs, mainly as a process of information sharing. As discussed earlier, under Mulroney, two meetings of first ministers were held to discuss the free trade negotiations. It is only with the Meech process, however, that FMMs came to replace FMCs.

35. For complete details, consult the web site of the Canadian Intergovernmental Conferences Secretariat at <www.scics.gc.ca>.

36. The news report on the 1996 meeting insisted on the low-key, non-confrontational, approach of the prime minister. See, for example, Paul Wells, "Don't expect much from first ministers' meeting — PM: There will be no 'rolling the dice' on Canada's future," *The Gazette*, 19 June 1996, Final Edition, p. A13.

37. In 1996, Prime Minster Jean Chrétien apparently warned his provincial counterparts of the importance of appearing united in public. The negative reaction following Glen Clark's public outburst against the federal government during the press conference after the same meeting suggests this view was shared by most participants. The newly elected Premier of British Columbia was censured as "inexperienced" and "still running an election" by Mike Harris of Ontario and Brian Tobin of Newfoundland. As reported in A. Wilson-Smith, "Mission Accomplished: Testiness Aside, the First Minister Reach Consensus," *Maclean's*, 1 July 1996, p. 17.

38. See "First Ministers Agreed on Trade," *The Gazette*, 19 July 1994, Final Edition, p. B1.

39. As for the constitutional requirement to evaluate the amending formula, when the question was raised, Quebec's Premier Lucien Bouchard excused himself (for three minutes) and the first ministers all agreed not to talk about it. See "Mission Accomplished: Testiness Aside, the First Minister Reach Consensus" *Maclean's*, p. 17.

40. As reported in Wells, "Don't expect much from first ministers' meeting — PM: There will be no 'rolling the dice' on Canada's future."

41. See the *Joint Communiqué*, First Ministers' Meeting, Ottawa, 12 December 1997. Virtually all points are followed by an asterisk referring to Quebec's disagreement. The communiqué is available at <www.scics.gc.ca/cinfo97>.

42. "A Framework to Improve the Social Union for Canadians: An Agreement between the Government of Canada and the Governments of the Provinces and Territories," 4 February 1999. Available at <www.scics.gc.ca/cinfo99>.

43. "Premiers call for first ministers meeting before Christmas," *The Canadian Press*, 26 November 1999; "First ministers meeting urgent, provinces say — Frustration mounts: Chrétien rules out date before summer," *National Post*, 6 March 2000.

44. Ottawa would have liked to attach more federal strings to its increased payments, but an Ontario-Quebec alliance prevented that, while allowing Quebec to sign the agreement.

45. Canada. Senate of Canada, Standing Committee on Social Affairs, Science and Technology. 2002. *The Health of Canadians — The Federal Role, Final Report.* The "Kirby Report" (Ottawa: Supply and Services Canada). Canada. Commission on the Future of Health Care in Canada. 2002. *Building on Values: The Future of Health Care in Canada.* The "Romanow Report" (Ottawa: Supply and Services Canada).

46. Available at <http://www.scics.gc.ca/pdf/800039004_e.pdf>.

47. This helps explain the reaction of premiers such as Alberta's Peter Lougheed for proposals to institutionalize the provincial presence in federal decision-making through creation of a council or house of the provinces. Lougheed objected to any new body that would interfere with his own ability as premier to speak for his province's interests. Lougheed did call for a house of the provinces representing provincial government, on the lines of the German Bundesrat in 1982, and later set up a provincial task force that called for an elected Senate. The same consideration helps account for the extreme reluctance to constitute the FMC as a binding decision-making body.

48. Ronald L. Watts, "Executive Federalism — A Comparative Analysis," prepared for the Federal-Provincial Relations Office of the Government of Canada, 30 April 1989.

49. But even these can be tripped up by the domestic rivalries — as when Alberta Premier Ralph Klein publicly handed the prime minister a letter challenging the federal commitment to ratify the Kyoto Accord on global warming during a Team Canada visit to Russia in February 2002.

50. See Julie Simmons' contribution to this volume on the increased role of ministerial councils.

51. According to the Canadian Intergovernmental Conferences Secretariat database, a total of 124 delegates were present in 1997, and 153 for the 2000 meeting on health. While this doesn't compare with the 236 delegates for the 1989 conference, it is still a large number that requires significant logistics and increases the complexity of negotiations. Most of the officials and ministers, however, remain in the background, not in the conference room itself.

52. André Burelle, *Le Mal canadien: essai de diagnostique et esquisse d'une thérapie* (St-Laurent, PQ: Fides, 1995), p. 162.

53. Thomas J. Courchene, "ACCESS: A Convention on the Canadian Economic and Social System," paper prepared for the Ministry of Intergovernmental Affairs,

Ontario. Reprinted in *Assessing ACCESS: Towards a New Social Union* (Kingston: Institute of Intergovernmental Relations, Queen's University, 1997).

54. Albert Breton, "Supplementary Statement," in *Final Report of the Royal Commission on the Economic Union and Development Prospects for Canada,* vol. 3 (Toronto: University of Toronto Press, 1985), p. 486.

55. On this, see the chapter by Johanne Poirier in this volume.

56. The 2000 agreement on health states: "Nothing in this document shall be construed to derogate from the respective governments' jurisdictions. The Vision, Principles, Action Plan for Health System Renewal, Clear Accountability, and Working Together shall be interpreted in full respect of each government's jurisdiction." See *First Ministers' Meeting Communiqué on Health,* 11 September 2000. Available at <www.cics.gc.ca/cinfo>.

57. See Cameron and Simeon, "Intergovernmental Relations and Democratic Citizenship," and also David Cameron's chapter in this volume.

58. As Peter Meekison suggests in this volume, Annual Premiers' Conferences are more effective as a tribune to collectively voice discontent toward the federal government than as a mechanism of interprovincial co-operation.

59. J. Stephan Dupré, "Reflections on the Workability of Executive Federalism."

6

The Annual Premiers' Conference:
Forging a Common Front

J. Peter Meekison

Ce chapitre soutient que la Conférence annuelle des Premiers ministres, depuis sa fondation en 1960, est devenue une force importante dans le domaine des relations intergouvernementales. On y trouve d'abord un retour sur les conférences initiales de 1887 à 1926. Le chapitre explore ensuite le développement de la Conférence et la transformation de son statut, qui est passé de rassemblement informel à celui d'institution beaucoup plus structurée. On fait alors l'examen de l'évolution de ses pratiques et conventions, dont le processus de prise de décision. De façon générale, la Conférence a eu tendance à se concentrer sur les questions fédérales-provinciales et, dans une proportion grandement moindre, sur les problèmes interprovinciaux. Le chapitre revient sur certains des principaux thèmes politiques sur lesquels la Conférence s'est penchée entre 1977 et 2001. Les trois thèmes relevés sont le fédéralisme fiscal, le renouvellement de la politique sociale et l'établissement de liens entre la Conférence des Premiers ministres et la Conférence annuelle des Premiers ministres. Cette dernière permet notamment aux provinces et territoires, de développer une prise de position commune à présenter aux discussions fédérales-provinciales ultérieures. La Conférence ne devrait pas être perçue comme un événement isolé mais bien comme une partie intégrante d'un processus continuel de dialogue et de consultation intergouvernementaux. Une raison du succès de la Conférence réside dans la préparation extensive consacrée au développement des positions politiques des Premiers ministres. La création du Conseil de la fédération lors de la Conférence de 2003 souligne son évolution et son institutionnalisation constantes.

At the 42nd Annual Premiers' Conference (APC) in Victoria, BC, in August 2001, the item that dominated the news before, during and after the conference was the provincial and territorial request that the federal government increase its spending on health care by \$7 billion and equalization by \$3 billion.[1] Stéphane Dion, Intergovernmental Affairs Minister for Canada, responded to the request on behalf of the federal government. He commented that this request "is not what Canadians want" and went on to call the request "unrealistic."[2] In a second communiqué, the premiers made it clear they wished to be "involved in international discussions respecting resources owned and managed by the provinces and territories."[3]

As a meeting of premiers, one would expect the agenda to consist primarily of issues of interprovincial concern.[4] The reality is far different, as the two communiqués from the 2001 APC indicate. The materials examined in this chapter suggest that the focus of the APC since its formation in 1960 has gradually shifted away from the discussion of interprovincial issues. The conference is now primarily concerned with policy issues that reflect the current state of federal-provincial relations. Given this federal-provincial focus, to some the APC is portrayed as an annual event whose principal objective is to have the provinces "gang up" on the federal government. The premiers, however, do not see these discussions as "hostile" to the federal government, but rather as an opportunity to address issues of mutual concern and to develop where possible a common interprovincial position. Invariably these mutual concerns have tended to focus on the federal-provincial dimension. As will be shown, the APC has become an integral component of the complex machinery of intergovernmental relations in Canada.

This chapter is divided into four parts. The first is an historical overview of the APC. The second is a comment on how it operates and the protocols associated with its functioning. The third is an analysis of communiqués from the 25 premiers' conferences, covering the years 1977-2001. The fourth part provides some concluding observations.

HISTORICAL OVERVIEW

THE INITIAL CONFERENCES, 1887-1926

The first premiers' conference — or as it was then referred to, interprovincial conference — took place 20 years after Confederation. The provinces had had two decades of experience with the new constitution and the evolution of the federal system. The conference was convened by Premier Honoré Mercier of Quebec and presided over by Premier Oliver Mowat of Ontario. Five of the seven provinces participated.[5] The federal government was invited but did not attend.

In his opening remarks to the delegates, Premier Mercier outlined his view of the conference's objective. He cautioned "that the Conference must not be considered in the light of a hostile move against the Federal Authorities."[6] He also stressed that the purpose of that meeting was to provide an opportunity for the provinces "to solve, in the general interest of the whole of Canada, such difficulties as experience has shown to exist in the relations between the General and the Provincial Governments."[7]

At the conclusion of the conference, the premiers proposed 17 constitutional amendments on a variety of subjects, including the process of selecting Senators, the declaratory power, disallowance and an enriched system of federal statutory subsidies provided for under section 118 of the *Constitution Act, 1867 (The British North America Act)*. In addition to the 17 constitutional resolutions, the conference also approved four others dealing with interprovincial matters. As Garth Stevenson notes, "The Interprovincial Conference itself was a major step in the direction of closer horizontal relations among the provinces."[8]

Fifteen years later, in 1902, the provinces met again to argue once more for an increase in federal statutory subsidies. In his letter of invitation to the other premiers, Premier Simon-Napoleon Parent of Quebec indicated that he had discussed the question of the meeting with Prime Minister Wilfrid Laurier. In his opening remarks to the conference he indicated that he "had every reason to believe" that the federal government would give "favourable attention" to provincial proposals. He also made it clear that "the persons convening it [the conference] do not intend to embarrass the Federal Authorities."[9]

Four years later, in 1906, the first Dominion-Provincial Conference, or what would eventually become known as the First Ministers' Conference (FMC), took place in Ottawa to discuss the resolutions from the 1902 Interprovincial Conference. The conference, which lasted for six days, included both a federal-provincial component and a series of interprovincial meetings to finalize the provincial position. The 1907 constitutional amendment regarding statutory subsidies was the result of the dual federal-provincial and interprovincial negotiations.

The final resolution of the last interprovincial session was a proposal for an annual premiers' conference "to consider matters of common interest."[10] It is of interest to note that these meetings were to be convened by the premiers of Ontario and Quebec, a clear indication of their pre-eminence among the provinces. Fifty-four years later when Quebec convened the first Annual Premiers' Conference, the resolution became a reality.

The next two interprovincial conferences were held in 1910 and 1913 respectively. They were convened by the premiers of Ontario and Quebec and held in the Railway Committee Room of the Senate of Canada. The 1910 meeting was convened at the request of the three Maritime provinces to discuss their representation in the House of Commons. After deliberating for one day, the "conference adjourned to a future day, to be fixed by the Premiers of Ontario and Quebec."[11]

While the 1913 meeting was to be the follow-up to the 1910 meeting, the conference agenda was expanded to include further discussion of federal subsidies and a few other matters. The premier of Nova Scotia, G.H. Murray, was elected as the conference chair. Prime Minister Robert Laird Borden welcomed the participants, and then withdrew. He was invited back the following day to receive the resolutions of the conference approved to that point, including one requesting an increase in federal subsidies to the provinces. Because of its relevance to the ongoing nature of federal-provincial fiscal relations, one of the resolution's recitals warrants repeating: "The financial arrangements made at the time and since Confederation have never been regarded as final by the Provinces."[12] After listening to the provincial position on the resolutions, the prime minister "saw no objection to the provinces coming at stated intervals — say, every ten years — to discuss and conclude any financial arrangements as between Canada and the provinces, if circumstances warranted it."[13] The final resolution of the conference was to the effect that the premiers should meet "from time to time to consider matters of common interest."[14] Considering the infrequency of interprovincial meetings up to this point, this proposal appeared more realistic than the one approved in 1906.

The conference minutes make it very clear that no consensus on Maritime representation in the House of Commons was possible. Judging from the number of withdrawn motions, one is left with the impression that little support existed for the Maritime position among the other six provinces. As a result, the premiers collectively did not take a position on the matter. The prime minister referred to this in the course of the debate the following year on the constitutional amendment that resulted in the Senate floor provision, Section 51A, being added to the *Constitution Act, 1867.*[15]

The last interprovincial conference of this period was held in June 1926. Among other things, the agenda included subsidies, corporate taxes and fuel production. In April 1926 the federal government had appointed the Duncan Commission to examine Maritime grievances. The conference supported the Maritime provinces by adopting the following motion: "This conference expresses its sympathy with those Provinces which, by reasons particular to them, have not progressed as anticipated, and urges upon the federal government that it favourably consider affording relief to each of such Provinces in a form that will ameliorate these conditions."[16] Thus the subject of regional disparities made its debut onto the premiers' conference agenda. The corporate tax item was intended to promote interprovincial co-operation in unifying the payment of corporate taxes. Alberta was concerned about energy policy and added the subject of fuel production, in this instance coal, to the agenda. The objective was to develop Canadian coal and reduce reliance on imports "thus aiding in the development of interprovincial trade." The premiers were invited to share their views on fuel production with a committee of the House of Commons at the end of their meeting.

Two matters concerning the logistics of the conference were addressed at the beginning of the 1926 conference. The first was the conference decision to exclude the press from their deliberations. Instead, the premiers agreed that "a press publicity committee should be appointed to give statements from time to time to the press."[17] The second was a decision not to invite federal representatives "as this was a purely provincial conference." At the conclusion of the conference, the premiers once again reiterated their idea that an annual gathering would be beneficial and that their next meeting should be in the west.[18]

These first six conferences, which span 40 years, highlight some of the recurring themes and practices of Canadian federalism at that time. Themes such as fiscal relations, regional disparities, and energy are also reflected in the 2001 premiers' conference communiqués. In this period the provinces met intermittently to discuss common concerns. The main reason for convening the meetings was federal-provincial relations, and only secondarily, interprovincial issues. The provinces did not shrink from proposing constitutional amendments when necessary to achieve their objectives. Furthering provincial autonomy was certainly one objective. Another was to redress the perceived vertical fiscal imbalance between the federal and provincial governments.[19] To this one must add the emerging horizontal fiscal imbalance.[20] The former is demonstrated in the recurring demand for an increase in constitutional subsidies, while the latter is reflected in the support for special treatment for the Maritime provinces. Ed Black suggests that the "concern [of premiers] was almost exclusively with concerting their complaints against the central government, and not with harmonizing their individual sets of administrative practices."[21] It is also worth noting the initiative by Quebec in using an interprovincial forum to further provincial interests. A final comment is the linkage between the interprovincial process and the gradual evolution of a federal-provincial process, the First Ministers' Conference. The emergence of FMCs in 1927, the onset of the Depression, and World War II and Reconstruction, delayed the institutionalization of the APC for several decades.

THE ANNUAL PREMIERS' CONFERENCE

The idea of convening an Annual Premiers' Conference was resurrected by Premier Jean Lesage of Quebec in 1960.[22] Although Premier Lesage convened the first meeting of premiers in 1960, he adopted Premier Mercier's strategy and asked Premier Leslie Frost of Ontario to chair it. Premier Frost, who had gone along with the idea of a conference, reportedly wanted to "restrict our meetings to provincial matters" and insisted "there must not be any ganging up on Ottawa."[23] Since then, premiers have held an annual meeting. As will be seen below, a number of conventions and practices have evolved with respect to the APC.

While the precedents for an annual meeting are readily available, the 1956 Tremblay Commission Report made the following recommendation:

> At present, there is no organization which ensures coordination of provincial policies. Yet the provinces should discuss among themselves, without the federal government's participation, the problems which are properly within their resort. That is the only means of working out a provincial policy, suited to each province but still Canadian in nature. Creation of a permanent Council of the Provinces on the model of the American Council of State Governments would fill a great need. Such an organization seems to us necessary for the preservation

of Canadian federalism. If the provinces do not agree to co-operate among themselves, the country's own interest will finally require the federal government to take over the supreme command.[24]

A review of a few texts on Canadian federalism published in the 1960s and 1970s indicates that, while scholars acknowledged the existence of the APC, they did not consider it to be a major influence within the federal system. In 1963, J. H. Aitchison stated "there is no reason why the premiers' conference should be so pure as to refuse to deal with some matters involving federal-provincial collaboration."[25] In 1965, in reference to Premier Jean Lesage's initiative, R. M. Burns wrote:

> As no official documents other than the usual official communiqués issue from these meetings it is not possible to form any worthwhile opinion as to their real value. However, what evidence we have would seem to show no great influence directly on the course of events even though they may well have served a useful purpose as a base for greater understanding — and indeed they are reputed to be very pleasant affairs.[26]

In 1972, Donald Smiley characterized the conferences as "informal meetings." To him the conferences provided the provinces with an opportunity "for sharing of views on matters of mutual concern and it is unusual for them for them to seek agreement on specific policies; there appears little disposition to arrive at a specifically provincial view or to gang up on Ottawa." He went on to assert, "In the past five years or so there appears to have been a declining interest among several of the premiers in these August conferences."[27]

That same year, Richard Simeon offered a different interpretation. He wrote that "the interprovincial conferences are becoming much more important in federal-provincial negotiations."[28] He noted the wide range of subject matters on the APC agenda such as medicare, equalization and fiscal relations.

By the 1980s a different perception of the APC had emerged. Donald Smiley had revised his earlier assessment. He noted that "the 1970s saw a resurgence of interprovincial collaboration involving both all the provinces and regional grouping of provinces. In particular, the provinces came to shed their former inhibitions about forming provincial united fronts against the federal government."[29] The Macdonald Royal Commission drew a similar conclusion. Commissioners noted: "These meetings at first concentrated primarily on coordinating approaches to issues of provincial concern. More recently their aim has been to unite provinces in their response to federal initiatives, especially in relation to fiscal and constitutional matters. On a few occasions, provinces have forged compromises among themselves in order to take up a common position."[30]

What caused this gradual transformation in the APC? A number of reasons come to mind. An obvious one was the protracted discussions on the constitution that dominated this period. Paralleling these negotiations was the ongoing debate on the subjects of fiscal federalism and federal spending power, one example being Established Programmes Financing (EPF). Another reason was individual provinces using the opportunity of the APC to solicit the support of other provinces on current federal-provincial disputes. For example, when provincial ownership of natural resources was threatened by emerging federal policies, Premier Peter Lougheed of Alberta made sure that the provincial interest was reflected in APC communiqués.[31] With President George Bush's 2001 proposal for a continental energy policy, it should not come as a surprise that premiers discussed energy at the 2001 APC. The shifting political landscape in Quebec has also influenced conference dynamics and deliberations. Regional groupings of provinces have pursued matters of particular interest to them. The efforts to forge a common front would suggest that, since the more limited purpose envisaged in 1960, the APC has evolved to reflect more closely the vision originally enunciated by Premier Mercier in 1887.

THE PRACTICES AND CONVENTIONS OF THE APC

The practices and conventions associated with the APC have evolved over the years. As an interprovincial meeting, it operates on the basis of provincial equality. Premiers are of equal status and share similar responsibilities in terms of their office. Conference dynamics are influenced by this reality. Some premiers may have more experience than others or a greater national profile but around the table they are equal. As a result, decisions are by consensus. There are no voting procedures. To facilitate the consensus building process the premiers will often meet privately to develop a common position or to finalize the communiqué.

For its first 21 years, the premiers' conference consisted of the ten premiers. In 1982, the two territorial leaders attended as observers. Over the next few years, the extent of the territorial leaders' involvement gradually increased. At the 1983 APC they participated in the general discussion of the agenda item on the economy. At the 1991 Conference in Whistler, BC, they were finally accorded full membership. With the creation of Nunavut, the three territories are represented.[32]

The conference sessions are closed to the media. An exception was the 1993 APC in Nova Scotia, the first such gathering after the public's rejection of the Charlottetown Accord the previous October.[33] Part of the conference was devoted to meetings with the five national Aboriginal organizations to discuss a new partnership. These sessions were open, and a verbatim transcript was made of the proceedings.

TURNOVER AND CONTINUITY OF PREMIERS

As a result of provincial elections and retirements the players and personalities at the APC are constantly changing. For the 25-year period covering the years 1977-2001, British Columbia was represented by seven different premiers, Quebec and Prince Edward Island by six, while Nova Scotia, Manitoba and Newfoundland each had five.[34] The province with the lowest turnover of premiers for the 25-year period was Alberta, with three. When one considers the matter of continuity from meeting to meeting, excluding 1977 as the base year, there were only seven conferences where the premiers attending included all of the participants from the previous year's conference. The longest period of continuity was the four APCs from 1982 to 1985. The 1982 APC, the conference following patriation of the constitution, had three new premiers in attendance, while the 1986 APC had four new participants.

Another factor to take into consideration is experience. For example, at the time of his electoral defeat in 1987, the "Dean" of the premiers was Richard Hatfield of New Brunswick. He had attended 18 premiers' conferences up to that point. In 1999, the year he was defeated, Gary Filmon of Manitoba was the "Dean," having participated in 12 APCs. What is clear from the foregoing figures is that the turnover of the premiers, either through voluntary or involuntary retirement, is now much more frequent. Although there is no indication that it has had an adverse effect on the APC, the institutional memory is reduced.

CONFERENCE LOCATION AND CHAIRING

While it is not chiseled in stone, the provinces have reached an understanding as to when and where they will host a conference. The conference is usually held in August. For the most part, the host province is known 10 years in advance, although occasionally a province will seek to change the order because of other commitments. For example, Manitoba has acted as host in years ending in zero because it wanted to host the 1970 conference, the year the province celebrated its 100th anniversary of entering Confederation. For similar reasons, British Columbia hosts the conferences in years ending in one. With the inclusion of the territories, this pattern of dates and locations may change over time.

Since 1963, the premier of the host province has chaired the APC. It is now understood and accepted that the premier of the host province becomes the "chair" of the premiers as a collectivity for the ensuing 12 months. This practice started in 1976 when Premier Lougheed continued to serve as chair when the APC reconvened in Toronto in October. In September 1997, Alberta hosted the meeting that resulted in the Calgary Declaration, but the chair was Premier Frank McKenna of New Brunswick.

The chair also acts as the main channel of communication between the prime minister and the provinces during this period. For example, in October 1976, Premier Lougheed sent Prime Minister Trudeau a letter on behalf of the premiers outlining the provinces' position on constitutional reform. The letter was initially drafted by Alberta and revised as necessary by the other provinces. For the most part, this communication link is relatively routine, consisting of forwarding the conference communiqués or working on the dates for a proposed First Ministers' Conference. At other times, the communication linkages may be particularly sensitive, a prime example being the weeks leading up to the November 1981 FMC on Patriation. It should be recalled that the provinces had split on this issue, with Ontario and New Brunswick siding with the federal government and the other eight provinces opposing the federal government's unilateral action. When Premier Bill Bennett of British Columbia needed to convene a conference call of the premiers, he had to make sure to distinguish between calls concerning all ten Premiers and calls of concern to those opposing unilateral patriation, the group of eight. On one occasion the wrong call was placed and Premier Hatfield had to be told to hang up! Another example was Premier Gordon Campbell of British Columbia as APC chair, canvassing the other premiers about the Canada-US border after the 11 September 2001 terrorist attack on the United States, and raising the matter with Prime Minister Chrétien in mid-October.[35]

In addition to the APC, the premiers have occasionally met at other times. They have convened these meetings either as a specific follow-up to their most recent annual meeting or to address a particularly urgent issue with respect to national unity or constitutional reform. Examples of follow-up conferences include February 1978 to receive a report on the state of minority language education, February 2000 to look at the funding of health care and social programs, and January 2002 to review progress on interprovincial discussions on health care. At the January 2002 meeting the premiers established the Premiers' Council on Canadian Health Care Awareness.[36] Conferences convened to discuss an urgent issue associated with national unity or constitutional reform include the 1967 Confederation of Tomorrow Conference, the October 1980 conference to assess provincial positions on the federal government's unilateral decision to proceed with patriation of the constitution, and the September 1997 conference that resulted in the Calgary Declaration.

THE CONFERENCE AGENDA

Conference planning begins well in advance of the actual event. While decisions on venue and dates are important, the main intergovernmental planning activity is setting the conference agenda and determining which province will assume, or be assigned, the responsibility for leading off the discussion on a particular topic. To a certain extent the formal agenda is only a guide. Agenda items such as "the economy," "the constitution," or "fiscal relations" are generic terms and serve only as a framework within which more detailed discussions can take place.

A number of factors influence the conference agenda and the ensuing discussion. Among the various factors there is an obvious degree of overlap. The current state of the economy is one of the principal factors that guides the agenda. It is not just the overall state of the national economy that is considered. The subtleties of regional and interprovincial differences are also addressed. To a considerable extent, the agenda item, the economy, serves as a valuable opportunity to exchange information and for premiers to learn more about the specific challenges faced by their colleagues. Specific aspects of the economy such as fisheries, transportation or internal trade that may be of particular interest to one or more provinces are often separately identified as sub-topics. The reality is that premiers are free to raise at the conference economic matters that are of pressing concern to their province and to convince their colleagues that they should be reflected in whatever conference communiqué is eventually produced.

The second factor that shapes the agenda is the identification of current federal-provincial policy issues and an assessment of the state of federal-provincial relations. The federal-provincial dimension is very significant in terms of influencing the agenda and the conference. This review may lead to inclusion of specific agenda items such as the constitution, social policy reform, intergovernmental co-operation, duplication of services or fiscal federalism.

The third factor that is taken into consideration is interprovincial co-operation. As noted above, in 1960 Premier Frost expected the APC to focus on "provincial matters." While such matters may have been the focus of the APC in its formative years, in the 1970s one can see that the agenda started to be dominated by federal-provincial issues. Since conference agendas are not normally released in advance of the APC, the conference communiqués have served as the record and they confirm this trend. That said, interprovincial co-operation continues to be an ongoing agenda item; just not the predominant one.

The fourth factor that has shaped the agenda and ensuing discussion is globalization. To a considerable extent the early premiers' conferences were primarily concerned with domestic matters. Even then international issues were addressed, such as the 200-mile limit and the management of fish on the continental shelf. In 1977 they specifically discussed Canada-US relations. Since then the bilateral trading relationship with the United States and specific trade disputes such as softwood lumber have generated discussion at several premiers' conferences. At the 2003 APC they stressed the importance of "an open and secure border with the United States" and emphasized that the "provinces and territories have unique relationships with states that can be used to further this objective...."[37] Because of the consequences on both provincial jurisdiction and economies and their involvement in the deliberations, international trade negotiations such as the Canada-US Free Trade Agreement (FTA), the North American Free Trade Agreement (NAFTA) and the Uruguay Round of Multilateral Trade Negotiations caused the premiers to examine international trade developments on a fairly regular basis at the APC. The premiers have also followed very closely the agriculture negotiations in the World Trade Organization (WTO). International discussions on the environment such as the Kyoto Protocol have also caught their attention. As indicated by the 2001 APC communiqué, the premiers also want be to be included in any international discussions pertaining to natural resources.

A fifth factor influencing the agenda is best characterized as conference continuity. As the APC agenda has evolved over the years, the nature of pre-conference preparation has also evolved extensively. In comparing conference communiqués from the mid-1990s with those of earlier conferences, it is evident that there has been a much greater degree of follow-up emanating from previous conferences. Put another way, the conference agenda is, to some extent, determined by whatever reports or follow-up the premiers requested at their previous meeting. The best example of this trend is the ongoing work of the Provincial/Territorial Council on Social Policy Renewal. It presented its fifth annual progress report to the 2000 APC. Other examples include a report from labour market ministers on a comprehensive youth employment strategy presented to the 1997 APC, a matter discussed at the 1996 APC. At the 2000 APC the premiers released their final report on the health care system, "Understanding Canada's Health Care Costs." At the 2001 Conference, they received a report from their finance ministers entitled, "Addressing Fiscal Imbalance." They called for the study at their 2000 meeting as a result of preliminary discussions on this subject at both the 1999 and 2000 conferences. What is also significant is that such reports are the product of an interprovincial effort. As a result, there is considerable continuity or overlap of portions of the agenda from one conference to the next.

With regard to conference planning, it should be realized that two planning activities occur simultaneously, the business agenda and the social agenda. It is this latter activity that distinguishes the APC from other intergovernmental meetings. Premiers and their delegations are encouraged to bring their spouses and children to the meeting. To a certain extent, the APC is a family affair. Through such activities the premiers and their spouses get to know each other on a personal level. They can and do form lasting friendships that are often reflected in the business meetings. These personal relationships transcend both party and region.

FEDERAL OBSERVERS AND THE CANADIAN INTERGOVERNMENTAL CONFERENCE SECRETARIAT

In 1970, the premiers invited federal observers to attend the conference, probably as a result of the constitutional discussions underway during that period. These observers were usually senior officials from the Privy Council Office (FPRO) and the Constitutional Conference Secretariat. Their presence helped to dispel the idea that the provinces were ganging up on the federal government. Taking prolific notes, they also acted as a conduit between the federal government and the provinces. At the 1974 conference, Premier William Davis encouraged the two federal observers to make sure "Pierre" or the "PM" was informed of this or that point. To Premier Lougheed, the federal presence and the not too subtle federal-provincial dialogue undermined the interprovincial dialogue and he, for one, wanted to bring an end to the federal presence. The issue was raised at the 1975 Conference in Newfoundland, with no formal decision being taken. As host of the 1976 APC, Premier Lougheed decided not to issue an invitation to the federal government to send observers. The practice ended with that meeting.

The 1975 conference saw a change in meeting administration — the inclusion of the Canadian Intergovernmental Conference Secretariat (CICS) to assist with the conference and to provide simultaneous translation. Until this conference the host province provided all secretariat services. The CICS has provided secretariat services since then, and conference documents can be found through their offices in Ottawa. Communiqués and other public information are posted on the CICS website.

INTERPROVINCIAL DIFFERENCES

As indicated at the beginning of this section, decision-making at the APC is by consensus, with that consensus being reflected in the conference communiqués. To this point it would appear that the objectives of the APC are to develop and to present a common front, thus portraying an image of provincial solidarity. While that may be the intention, the reality is that interprovincial disagreements are to be expected. Often they surface at the conference itself as the agenda items are addressed. Since the conferences are closed and provide ample opportunities for private sessions consisting of only the 13 leaders, the disputes that arise, for the most part, receive little publicity. The obvious solutions are to omit any reference to divisive issues in the communiqué, to issue no communiqué at all on those subjects, or to develop an acceptable compromise. All of these solutions have been used at one time or another. An alternative, but seldom-used approach, is to acknowledge the disagreement in the communiqué.

One example of the acknowledgement of differences approach occurred at the 1980 APC during the discussion on energy. Alberta and Ontario held very divergent views on crude oil pricing and export taxes on energy. The communiqué read: "The premiers, other than Ontario...."[38] Both provinces were satisfied with the result. It reflected broad provincial support for Alberta's position while Ontario was free to challenge policies it perceived as detrimental to its interests. The various references to the Quebec premier's non-participation in the discussion of the various progress reports from the

Provincial/Territorial Council on Social Policy Renewal are another example. The communiqués associated with these events typically included a note on Quebec's position that started with words like, "While sharing essentially the same concerns ...."[39]

The interprovincial differences identified above took place during the APC. In some instances disputes have surfaced shortly before or immediately after the APC. In these situations the disagreements became very public, and in some instances they strained relations between the warring premiers well after the event. One such dispute between Premier Lougheed of Alberta and Premier Davis of Ontario occurred just before the 1979 APC hosted by Quebec. At this time, Prime Minister Joe Clark was trying to develop his government's policy on energy. A few days before the APC convened, Premier Davis released the Government of Ontario's position paper on energy entitled "Oil Pricing and Security." When Premier Lougheed arrived at the conference he immediately convened a news conference, where he launched a blistering counterattack and completely rejected Ontario's position.[40] The conference communiqué reflected the different perspectives. The sharp division between the two provinces was also very much in evidence at the 12 November 1979 First Ministers' Conference on Energy.[41]

A second interprovincial dispute has emerged with respect to equalization. At the 1996 APC, the developing fault lines between the have and have-not provinces surfaced in a very public way. The point of contention at the 1996 conference was a study prepared for Ontario by Tom Courchene.[42] Although the communiqué made it clear that the Courchene report was not on the agenda, some of the participants disliked it and therefore were unlikely to ignore its content and recommendations.

In my opinion the genesis of the dispute can be traced back to the 1990 budget decision to place a cap on federal transfer payments under the Canada Assistance Plan (CAP) to the provinces of Alberta, British Columbia and Ontario.[43] These three provinces were then the so-called have or wealthy provinces because they were not in receipt of equalization payments. The other seven provinces that were receiving equalization payments were not affected by the budget policy. The three "have" provinces regarded the differential treatment as discriminatory and as an extension or enhancement of the overall equalization program. Where this perception and the divergence of provincial interests became readily apparent was during the discussions on the Charlottetown Accord.[44] When the federal government introduced the Canada Health and Social Transfer (CHST) in 1995, the formula for distributing the funds was based on the current method of allocating funds, which perpetuated the distortion caused by the cap on CAP. It was not until the 2001-02 fiscal year that equal per capita funding came into effect, finally ending the discriminatory treatment of the three "have" provinces.[45]

The fault lines between have and have-not provinces that became apparent at the 1996 APC were much more pronounced at the 1999, 2000 and 2001

APCs. To be sure, the conference communiqués reflect a degree of harmony, but the very public and continuing nature of the differences makes one ask about the degree of commitment to the consensus. At the 1999 APC, when discussing how the developing federal surplus should be spent, premiers divided over pressing for federal tax cuts, with Alberta, Ontario and Quebec supporting that position, and the other provinces pressing for more spending. Premier Gary Filmon thought the meeting was one of the most contentious in years. The compromise was to recommend tax cuts and the restoration of federal transfer payments, a position Premier Lucien Bouchard termed "balanced."[46] The premiers held a follow-up meeting in February 2000, the outcome being a letter sent to Prime Minister Jean Chrétien signed by the 13 leaders urging both tax cuts and an increase to the CHST.[47]

The 2000 APC was equally contentious, with a major dispute between Premier Ralph Klein and Premiers Bernard Lord and Brian Tobin over the calculation of federal transfers and equalization.[48] The split was also reflected in the discussions on health care, with Alberta, Ontario and Quebec not wanting further federal intrusions into provincial jurisdiction. The dispute flared up again a few days after the conference with Premier Tobin stating that Premier Klein was contributing to "a new kind of intolerance."[49] Premier Klein's response was to call these remarks "a crock" and to publish a letter in the *National Post* questioning the accuracy of that newspaper's accounts of the recent premiers' conference and indicating Alberta's support for equalization.[50] As the rhetoric escalated, Premier John Hamm of Nova Scotia weighed in and suggested the feuding stop because "the only person who benefits from premiers attacking each other in the weeks leading up to the first ministers' conference would be the prime minister."[51] Premier Hamm's intervention appears to be what was needed to settle things down.

In the days leading up to the 2001 APC the differences erupted again. This time Premier Mike Harris of Ontario was at the centre of the controversy. He rejected proposals from the Atlantic provinces for changes to the equalization formula. He chose a rather unfortunate analogy by commenting, "That's like somebody on welfare saying, 'Well I won the $1-million lottery and I have a $100,000 job, but I still want my welfare'."[52] In this instance the "lottery" was Premier Hamm's proposal that Nova Scotia's equalization payments should not be adversely affected by offshore oil and natural gas revenues. Premier Harris wanted the 2001 APC to push for additional federal funding for health care. The Atlantic provinces and Manitoba were not persuaded and wanted a review of the equalization formula.[53] To maintain a common front, the premiers adopted both positions.[54] The compromise was more of a truce and did not really come to grips with the tensions between the have and have-not provinces.

The net effect of the compromise was to ratchet up the amount of money the provinces were requesting from the federal government. Such a compromise may be politically expedient to get through the meeting but its staying power should be evaluated carefully. When the participants are forced to find a consensus in the time available, the options to accommodate differences on such fundamental questions as equalization, provincial autonomy or the federal spending power are very limited, particularly when some provinces have taken such strong positions in advance of the conference.

Personalizing the disputes, either through stereotyping or name-calling, makes it that much more difficult to work together and to develop compromise positions. Thus such clashes between premiers serve only to undermine their willingness and ability to develop common positions. In turn, the effectiveness of the APC as an interprovincial mechanism to find a common ground is greatly diminished.

The ongoing uncertainty related to the political status of Quebec and its willingness to endorse positions taken by the other provinces has also complicated the functioning of the APC. After the failure of Meech Lake, Quebec did not attend either the 1990 or 1991 conferences. At the 1994 APC, the premiers took the position of supporting the re-election of the Liberals under Premier Daniel Johnson. This position is best described as unusual. While provincial governments were not neutral during the 1980 referendum debate, they had not previously expressed a collective position on the outcome of Quebec elections. The Quebec electorate paid no attention to their declaration, and the following year they were joined by Premier Jacques Parizeau. He agreed to attend only if internal trade was placed on the agenda. In 1996 Premier Bouchard did not travel on the train from Edmonton to Jasper because he was concerned that the subject of national unity might be raised. At the 1999 APC, Premier Bouchard, as chair, became the spokesperson for the provinces. The press pointed out the obvious contradiction between his role as promoter of provincial interests including SUFA and his position on sovereignty and federal intrusions into areas of provincial jurisdiction.[55] As Premier Bernard Landry indicated on the eve of the 2001 APC: "I will not pretend that I want to rebuild the Canadian federation with them."[56] And herein was a dilemma for the APC as an institution.

Writing in 2001, Benoît Pelletier, then the official opposition critic on Canadian intergovernmental affairs, declared: "Quebec must once again play a leading role in Canada, especially with regard to the 'interprovincialism' that is becoming more apparent and is exemplified by the provinces' increasingly convergent interests and claims."[57] The election in 2003 of the Quebec Liberal Party with a strong and avowedly federalist leader appears to have had a profound effect on the dynamics of the 2003 APC. Comments reported by the press covering the 2003 APC emphasized the difference:

> Premier Ernie Eves said that Jean Charest's presence meant "quite a refreshing change in mood in the room" from earlier premiers' conferences.

"It kind of dawned on us how nice it was, finally, to have a province-of-Quebec representative at the table who wasn't coming up with 12 reasons why we couldn't do something," he said.

Alberta Premier Ralph Klein was even more outspoken.

"We were able to talk about federalism without having to apologize and without having to come to this news conference and say, 'with the exception of Quebec'," he said.

"It was music to our ears to hear a Quebec premier say, 'We want federalism, but we want federalism that works.' "[58]

THE ANNUAL PREMIERS' CONFERENCES: 1977-2001

This part of the chapter provides a summary of the main policy themes on which the APC has focused over the 25-year period from 1977-2001. The themes identified have been developed from an analysis of the conference communiqués. To some, these communiqués are self-serving, not too informative and not particularly riveting. While these criticisms may have some merit, they overlook the reasons for producing them in the first place. One clear purpose for having communiqués is to send a message to the federal government staking out the common provincial position. A second purpose is to serve as a record or minutes of the discussions and the consensus reached. A third purpose is to identify matters for follow-up to the meeting. The real question is what effect the premiers' conference has had on the federal system. A 25-year longitudinal survey is a useful tool to assist in answering that question.

The review of the communiqués made it clear that certain themes have tended to dominate the agenda over the years. From personal experience, a few that came immediately to mind were the constitution, fiscal federalism, energy, and the economy. After examining the communiqués, several others became more apparent. Their emergence reflects the constantly shifting intergovernmental policy interests throughout this period.

One of the most frequent agenda items has been the economy. While it can be considered a theme, it has primarily served as a kind of catch-all for a wide range of policy issues such as infrastructure, research and development, agriculture, employment insurance, interest rates, the deficit, and job creation. While the results of the discussions have been reflected in the conference communiqués, the specific issues addressed have not tended to be among the predominant themes.

The theme that has tended to dominate the APC agendas over the years is fiscal federalism. This theme includes Established Program Financing (EPF), the CHST, equalization, fiscal imbalance, deficits and the Goods and Services Tax (GST). A second theme that had a profound influence on the agenda for nearly 20 years was constitutional reform. Indeed, the 1992 APC was a very brief affair having been pre-empted by an FMC on the constitution that resulted in the Charlottetown Accord. With the rejection of the accord in 1992, that particular subject has not resurfaced, although premiers have addressed Aboriginal self-government since then. A third theme, and here there is an obvious degree of overlap and linkage with the fiscal federalism theme, is social policy renewal. A fourth theme is international trade and international agreements. A fifth is internal trade, frequently discussed in conjunction with trade in general. A sixth is energy, which includes discussions on natural resources. A seventh is environment. The eighth theme is federal-provincial relations. Under this heading is included the machinery of federal-provincial relations, such as requests for an FMC. This theme includes rebalancing, duplication and efforts to establish federal-provincial mechanisms such as the Federal/Provincial/Territorial Council on Social Policy Renewal and to conclude agreements such as the Social Union Framework Agreement (SUFA).

What I expected to find and did not was some kind of purely interprovincial policy theme or themes bundled together comparable to the agenda item on the economy. One subject that was on practically every APC agenda for a number of years was interprovincial trucking, but it was last discussed in 1981. A theme that does appear is internal free trade, but even here there is a federal-provincial dimension, as the Agreement on Internal Trade illustrates. The 1994 APC in Toronto included a separate agenda item on interprovincial cooperation. While there was a follow-up discussion at the 1995 APC, this agenda item does not appear as a recurring item in the conference communiqués and appears to have been superseded by other issues. Premier Gordon Campbell of British Columbia emphasized the interprovincial dimension at the 2001 conference. As noted above, at their January 2002 follow-up meeting, the premiers established the Premiers' Council on Canadian Health Care Awareness and some other interprovincial initiatives in health policy. Thus while the premiers have recently rediscovered the importance and benefits of interprovincial policy cooperation, the federal-provincial issues of the day have tended to take precedence over the interprovincial subjects. It is not that interprovincial issues are of lesser importance, but rather that they are not as pressing or as immediate as federal-provincial issues in terms of shaping the APC agenda, discussions and outcomes.

Space does not permit a detailed analysis of each theme. To give some indication of conference conclusions and undertakings I have focused on three of the themes identified. Because of its predominance and continuity, I have selected fiscal federalism, and because of the very obvious overlap included with it, the initiatives on social policy renewal. The third theme examined is the strong linkage between the APC and the FMC.

FISCAL FEDERALISM AND SOCIAL POLICY

Although the 1976 APC does not fall in the period under review, it is worth noting that at that conference, the premiers directed their provincial treasurers to develop a common position on Established Program Financing (EPF), the revenue guarantee and equalization.[59] As noted in the 1977 annual report of Alberta's Department of Federal and Intergovernmental Affairs, "One of the unique developments of the 1976 financial negotiations was that extensive discussions, for the first time in recent Canadian history, took place on an interprovincial level."[60] That the federal government did not embrace the common provincial position is beside the point; the provinces had embarked on the first of several initiatives to find common ground on this question. The common front continued through to the December 1976 FMC and influenced the shape of the final agreement.[61] As fate would have it, the December 1976 FMC was also the first intergovernmental meeting for the new Parti Québécois government of Quebec. Premier René Lévesque and Finance Minister Jacques Parizeau met with their provincial counterparts the evening before the conference began, and agreed to support the common provincial position.

As the time came to renegotiate the fiscal arrangements, both EPF and equalization received careful scrutiny at the 1981 conference. As the federal government considered restraint, the provinces contended that reductions in federal spending on either program would have negative effects on service delivery and increase regional disparities. The linkage between regional disparities and overall federal transfers is important because of the different interests around the table, particularly between those provinces that receive equalization and those that do not, a point examined earlier. This divergence of interests was readily apparent at both the 2000 and 2001 conferences.

The provincial position was based on a study of EPF prepared by finance ministers. Despite the provincial opposition, the growth rate of federal transfers was reduced when EPF was renewed in April 1982. At the 1982 APC, the premiers essentially reiterated the same position after the federal government had indicated further reductions in the growth rate were on the horizon. The federal government applied its "6 & 5" anti-inflation program to the post-secondary education transfer portion of EPF. The premiers criticized the unilateral nature of the federal actions, and characterized it as "disruptive to federal-provincial relations."[62] The May 1985 federal budget included an estimated $2 billion annual reduction in federal support to transfer payments by 1990, again through a reduction in the growth rate of the EPF cash transfer portion. At the 1985 APC the premiers stated that "offloading responsibilities and costs from one order to the other will not help in meeting service needs."[63] Further reductions in transfer payments followed in subsequent federal budgets including the cap on the Canada Assistance Plan in the 1990 budget. The provinces viewed these adjustments to the rate of growth of transfer payments as reductions. The federal government's position was that such adjustments were necessary to deal with the deficit and that planned transfers to the provinces had to shoulder some portion of the federal government's budget reductions. The adjustments and freezes to transfers and limits to equalization gave all provinces sufficient reason to develop a common front.

As governments began to tackle the fiscal challenges associated with these reductions in federal transfers, there was an important shift in the content of the APC agenda. At the 1991 APC, an agenda item on social issues was included. This item incorporated a range of social policy issues including health, education, training, children, and the financing of social programs. It was in the context of social policy that the "premiers unanimously deplored the federal action to break the Canada Assistance Plan through the unilateral imposition of a 5 percent ceiling on payments to Ontario, Alberta and British Columbia."[64] This conference marked the beginning of a major and ongoing effort to forge a common provincial front, not only with respect to challenging the reductions in federal transfers but also the unilateral nature of the federal decisions. Nowhere was the provincial concern over unilateral action more clearly demonstrated than in various provisions of the Charlottetown Accord, in particular the section on intergovernmental agreements and the proposed revisions to section 36, equalization and regional disparities.

At the 1993 APC, the beginning of a new interprovincial approach to social policy emerged. It should be recalled that this conference was held on the eve of the 1993 federal election. As a result, the message was directly aimed at the new government. Recognizing that social programs needed to be reformed, the premiers proposed "to renew the federal-provincial partnership within the following framework:

1.   preserve a reliable safety net while helping people get back to work;

2.   fair treatment of all provinces and territories by the federal government;

3.   restored federal commitment to Canada's social program and to adequate funding for those programs; and

4.   full consultation by the federal government in a multilateral forum with provinces and the territories on the social policy principles that will shape the renewal of Canada's major transfers."[65]

Subsequent premiers' conferences have built on this foundation.

The 1995 federal budget was of crucial significance in reinforcing the provinces' resolve to develop a common position. In the 1995 budget the federal government announced the establishment of the CHST. While EPF was a result of federal-provincial negotiations, the CHST was an example of unilateral federal action. As part of its efforts to reduce the deficit, Ottawa also announced a major reduction in the federal cash transfers to the provinces. Beginning in 1997-98, the federal cash transfer was set at $12.5 billion, a reduction of $6 billion from the 1995-96 payment.

Although there was no direct reference to the CHST in the 1995 APC communiqué, it is fairly obvious that the provinces were responding to the reductions. The conference communiqué reaffirmed that "provinces and territories are determined to speak with a common voice on the essential elements in the national debate on social policy reform."[66] In response to the new federal policies they stated that "it is unacceptable for the federal government to, on the one hand, reduce federal transfers to provinces and territories, and on the other prescribe the structure and standards of provincial and territorial social programs."[67]

To assist them in developing the common front the premiers established the Ministerial Council on Social Policy Reform and Renewal. The council's mandate was to:

- consult on federal reform initiatives and discuss common policy positions;

- formulate common positions on national social policy issues, and the means of ensuring consistency and greater flexibility in the design and the delivery of provincial and territorial programming; and

- draft a set of guiding principles and underlying values for social policy reform and renewal.[68]

In many respects, the 1995 APC was a watershed. It was the first APC for Premier Harris. It was the first and last APC for Premier Parizeau. It would also be the last conference for Premiers Harcourt and Wells. The CHST and related funding reductions were obviously of great importance and appear to have strengthened the resolve of the premiers to maintain their common front. The Agreement on Internal Trade had come into effect on 1 July 1995 and was the only subject on the agenda that interested Premier Parizeau. He was preoccupied with the 1995 Quebec referendum, which was only two months away.

As directed, the Ministerial Council prepared a report by the end of 1995 for the premiers' review. Quebec declined to participate in the process. The conference chair, by this time Brian Tobin, who had replaced Premier Clyde Wells, forwarded the report to the prime minister for inclusion on the agenda of the June 1996 FMC. At that FMC the first ministers agreed to initiate a federal-provincial process on social policy reform.

Two months later, at the 1996 APC in Alberta, the commitments made at the FMC were reviewed. The provinces continued to work on furthering the interprovincial position but without Quebec's participation. Thus one finds the emergence of both a federal-provincial and an interprovincial process operating in tandem. If the federal-provincial process did not lead to an agreement or agreements of some kind, the provinces would see if a purely interprovincial solution were possible. The premiers supported the idea of establishing a Federal/Provincial/Territorial Council on Social Policy Renewal. The 1999 Social Union Framework Agreement (SUFA), reinforced the role of this intergovernmental mechanism.

The premiers released their "Issues Paper on Social Policy Reform and Renewal: Next Steps," prepared for the 1996 conference.[69] They agreed with the paper's recommendations, one of which was to examine "options for intergovernmental mechanisms or processes to develop and promote adherence to national principles and standards." They also agreed to "create a forum of Ministers to co-ordinate an approach to overarching social policy issues of national importance." The ministerial council would "support and co-ordinate the work of sectoral ministries." Provincial finance ministers were directed "to work with their federal counterpart to ensure that an agenda for the redesign of financial arrangements proceeds and is coordinated with social policy renewal." Health ministers and social services ministers were requested to work with their federal counterparts to achieve certain policy objectives such as a joint administrative mechanism for interpreting the *Canada Health Act* and an integrated child benefit. The report established a systematic, comprehensive and continuing interprovincial approach to resolution of social policy issues. A new, and apparently permanent, ministerial committee in the form of the Provincial-Territorial Council on Social Policy Renewal was established.

At each premiers' conference since 1996, one can trace the continuing evolution of the interprovincial position on social policy renewal. The ministerial council has submitted a report on social policy to each premiers' conference since 1996. In 1997 the premiers agreed to develop "a broad provincial/territorial framework agreement to guide national social policy renewal." They confirmed again the need for their finance ministers to be involved and directed them "to work closely with the Provincial-Territorial Council on Social Policy Renewal to ensure that financial issues are coordinated with the work of the Council."[70] The premiers also wanted to see the role of the federal/provincial/territorial council strengthened and "its channels for communicating with First Ministers" clarified.

A few weeks later, the federalist premiers met in Calgary to discuss national unity and issued the Calgary Declaration. The seventh, and final, point in the declaration stated: "Canadians want their governments to work together particularly in the delivery of their social programs." Shortly after the 1997 federal election, Prime Minister Chrétien invited the premiers to an FMC in December. While national unity was not on the agenda, social policy reform was. The federal government agreed to negotiate a social union framework agreement. The SUFA became a reality at an FMC in February 1999. As part of the negotiations at the February meeting the federal government agreed to increase its funding for health care.

While a significant part of the agenda at the recent APCs was devoted to a review of the overall social policy renewal initiative, time was also spent on sectoral issues, such as health and children. At the 1998, 1999, 2000 and 2001 conferences, premiers pressed for restoration of CHST payments to their 1994-95 levels. At the 1999 conference, there were two references to the CHST plus a reference to the importance of equalization, once again reinforcing the linkage. In addition, in 1999, they sought "an appropriate escalator for the CHST cash transfer that keeps pace with cost and particular demand pressures."[71] At the 2000 APC they released a report entitled, "Understanding Canada's Health Care Costs." One of the report's recommendations was to restore the CHST. At the same time they released a document, "Premiers' Commitments to their Citizens." The commitments were in the areas of health care and its delivery. This was a prelude to the 11 September 2000 FMC. At the 2000 FMC the governments reached agreements on both health care and early childhood development. Additional federal funding was committed to both policy areas.

Another agenda item on the 2000 APC agenda that had emerged from the Western Premiers' Conference was the subject of fiscal imbalance. In this context there was further reference to the CHST and also a reference to equalization. Provincial finance ministers were asked to prepare a report on fiscal imbalance for the next APC. The report, "Addressing Fiscal Imbalance," was tabled at the 2001 conference. It focused on CHST and equalization and provided a series of options for consideration. It was this report that led to the request for additional federal funding, the request that was summarily dismissed by Minister Stéphane Dion.

The premiers followed up their August 2001 conference with a further meeting in January 2002 to continue their discussions on health care financing. Just before the meeting, Premier Klein announced that Alberta accepted all of the recommendations of a provincially sponsored task force on health care reform, chaired by Don Mazankowski, a former Deputy Prime Minister under Prime Minister Mulroney. The announcement help set the stage for the meeting. Among other things the Mazankowski report called for an increase in health care premiums and a greater private sector involvement in health care. The possible deleterious effects of this decision on the Romanow Royal Commission examining the medicare system were not lost on observers. Headlines in *The Globe and Mail* proclaimed, "'We cannot wait,' Alberta says" and "Premiers threaten to act alone on health."[72]

By the end of the conference the premiers had agreed to establish an interprovincially funded Premiers' Council on Canadian Health Awareness, with a mandate, budget and full-time staff to gather and disseminate information to Canadians on issues such as health care funding, health services innovation and best practices, human resource planning and management, drug effectiveness and assessment, and statistical comparisons provided by provinces and territories."[73] Interprovincial bodies of this kind are virtually unknown in Canada, one exception being the Council of Ministers of Education. The premiers' council became operational on 1 May 2002. While it is too soon to judge how effective the new organization will be, the very fact that the premiers created it reflected the growing gulf between the federal and provincial governments in health care.

The growing frustration with the federal government was particularly evident in the premiers' position on the need for a dispute resolution mechanism for the *Canada Health Act*. They made reference to the fact that the 1999 SUFA included a provision that such a mechanism would be developed for interpretation of the act. They delegated the task of working out an agreement to Premier Klein by 30 April 2002. They also issued an ultimatum: "Should discussions not be successful by April 30, Premiers agreed that the federal government will have essentially abandoned the Social Union Framework Agreement."[74] An agreement, the *Canada Health Act* Dispute Avoidance and Resolution process, was worked out between Alberta and the Minister of Health Anne McLellan.[75]

THE ANNUAL PREMIERS' CONFERENCE AND FIRST MINISTERS' CONFERENCES

The third theme selected for more detailed comment is the institutional linkage between the APC and the FMCs. This symbiosis or interdependence becomes readily apparent only after one examines the APC communiqués covering a number of years. Comparisons with the 1902, 1906, and 1913 conferences also suggest that this linkage is not a recent phenomenon. Before exploring the institutional linkages between the two institutions a brief comment on the development of the FMC is necessary in order to give a contextual basis for the analysis.

The FMC is a creature of invention and convention. It just happened and has now become an important part of the machinery of intergovernmental relations. Elsewhere in this volume Richard Simeon and Martin Papillon refer to the FMC as the "weakest link." Two aspects of the conventions of FMCs need to be taken into consideration. Firstly, they are convened at the prime minister's discretion.[76] Secondly, the subject matter of individual conferences varies considerably. For the purposes of this chapter the FMC's conferences can be divided into four broad subject categories: the economy, including fiscal relations; the constitution; social policy, including health; and other, such as energy.

After World War II, the practice of convening a periodic conference for a general discussion on the economy emerged, the first one being the 1945 Conference on Reconstruction. At first, such meetings were held approximately every five years. The five-year cycle tended to coincide with discussions on the renewal of the fiscal arrangements so it was not unusual for both matters to be discussed together. In 1968 with the commencement of intensive constitutional discussions by first ministers, the emerging practice of more frequent conferences on the economy was temporarily set aside. One of the conclusions of the December 1969 FMC on the constitution was for the first ministers to reconvene in February 1970 "to discuss non-constitutional matters, essentially the economic situation, pollution and the report of the Tax Structure Committee."[77] From that point on there was an apparent effort for the first ministers to meet more frequently to discuss the economy. One of the constitutional reforms included in 1971 Victoria Charter was a provision for an annual FMC. Thus one finds from this point on an expectation or understanding, at least on the part of the provinces, that an annual FMC would be held.

The APC has provided the occasion for the premiers to request that the prime minister convene an FMC. If an FMC is already scheduled or is on the horizon — as was the case when both the 1976 and 2000 APCs were held — the premiers used the opportunity to develop a common provincial position. However, given the sometimes rancorous nature of FMCs or the otherwise strained state of federal-provincial relations at the time of the request, the prime minister of the day has not automatically agreed to hold a conference because of the potential of the provinces "ganging up" on Ottawa.

The first APC I attended was in August 1974 in Toronto. One of my assigned tasks was to work on the conference communiqué. The very first paragraph in the communiqué called for "a private discussion [of first ministers] prior to the next federal budget." The purpose of the meeting was to examine "co-operative action on the major economic issues facing Canada today." It should also be remembered that Prime Minister Trudeau had just won a federal election the month before, in which wage and price controls were the main issue. In this instance the premiers were successful and the requested private meeting took place in October 1974.

Stressing the aggregate impact of provincial fiscal policies, at the 1976 APC, the premiers "agreed that they should meet annually with the prime minister to discuss and plan a national fiscal and economic policy."[78] Constitutional reform was also one of the agenda items at the 1976 meeting. In October, on the eve of the 1976 Quebec provincial election, Premier Lougheed, in his capacity as chair of the APC, sent Prime Minister Trudeau a letter outlining the results of the interprovincial constitutional discussions. One of the recommendations was a constitutional requirement for an annual FMC. In his detailed reply to the provincial proposal the prime minister agreed to the idea of an annual conference, something that he had agreed to previously in the 1971 Victoria Charter.[79]

When premiers met for the 1978 APC, they knew that a FMC on the constitution was scheduled for October. Accordingly, they set out a detailed provincial position on constitutional reform. The provincial position had an impact on the constitutional conference agenda. In addition to the planned constitutional conference, the premiers once again called for an annual FMC on the economy and suggested it be held at a fixed time, preferably in late November. The prime minister, now in the fifth year of his mandate, obliged. The November 1978 FMC on the economy was the second FMC on the economy to be held in 1978. One of the conference conclusions was that, "first ministers agreed that it is essential to continue to discuss and coordinate federal and provincial approaches to Canada's economic problems through an improved federal-provincial framework for consultations, discussions and concerted decisions."[80] They also agreed that First Ministers should meet "periodically," a less specific commitment than annually and that the next meeting would be late in 1979.

Despite the fact that Prime Minister Trudeau had been replaced by Prime Minister Clark, the premiers took as a given that the scheduled FMC would still be held in late 1979. Accordingly, the 1979 APC communiqués included several references to that meeting. In particular, the provinces wanted to discuss the economy, the completed Tokyo Round of trade negotiations and energy. They also made three suggestions to make "the conference's work more effective." They proposed:

1. the necessity of preparing a mutually acceptable agenda sufficiently in advance;

2. the establishment of an order of priority of the topics to be discussed; and

3. the distribution of briefing material for the Conference sufficiently in advance.

Although he did convene a meeting to discuss energy in the fall, Prime Minister Clark deferred the conference on the economy until January 1980. Fate intervened in the form of a lost confidence vote on the budget, however, and the conference on the economy was never held.

The 1980 APC was dominated by the state of the new round of constitutional negotiations. Despite their preoccupation with these negotiations, the premiers still spent time on an overview of the economy. By the 1980 APC, the Quebec referendum was history and the FMC on the constitution was only a few weeks away. The premiers noted that the last opportunity to discuss the economy had been two years earlier. They proposed that the policy coordination guidelines approved at the two 1978 FMCs on the economy be the starting point for the conference. In addition, they suggested eight other topics for inclusion on the agenda and stressed the need for conference planning. After the failure of the September 1980 constitutional conference and the decisions that fall by the federal government to proceed unilaterally with patriation of the constitution and to introduce the National Energy Program, one can understand why an FMC on the economy was not convened.

By the time of the 1981 APC, severe strains were evident within the federal system. The provinces had divided into two groups, those supporting the federal government's patriation initiative (Ontario and New Brunswick) and those opposed, "the group of eight." The conference had an air of tension as participants individually reflected on what the Supreme Court would decide on the patriation reference. The energy dispute between Alberta and Canada over the NEP had not been resolved. Despite their differences, the premiers made their recurring request for an FMC on the economy. They outlined a nine-point plan for economic recovery and once again referred to the 1978 understanding that there would be an annual conference. They directed Premier Bill Bennett, as the APC chair, to contact the prime minister and work out conference arrangements.

Once the Supreme Court released its decision at the end of September, attention immediately shifted to the resumption of constitutional negotiations. With a constitutional conference scheduled for November, the premiers met again in October to discuss that conference and to press Prime Minister Trudeau to convene a FMC on the economy. When the proposed FMC on the economy was the focus of their attention, all ten premiers participated. When the discussion turned to the constitution, the premiers of Ontario and New Brunswick withdrew and the group of eight met alone. As can be imagined there were issues of both logistics and protocol. The FMC on the economy was eventually scheduled for February 1982. By the time of the conference the patriation agreement had been reached, Quebec was challenging that decision in the courts and, with Quebec's rejection of the agreement, relationships within the federation continued to be strained. The February FMC was extremely acrimonious. After the conference, Prime Minister Trudeau declared the death of co-operative federalism.[81] Speaking a few days after the conference he said: "The old type of federalism — where we give money to the provinces, where they kick us in the teeth because they didn't get enough, and they go around and spend it and say 'It's all from us' — that type of federalism is finished."[82] He indicated he would no longer try to please the provinces.

At the 1982 APC, the premiers made what by this time one could call their traditional request for an FMC on the economy. Again the conference communiqué included a number of policy areas for consideration at the next, but yet-to-be-agreed-upon, FMC. Their message was clear: there is an ongoing need for the federal government to consult with the provinces on economic policies. The prime minister did not convene the conference. As one observer noted, "The federal government rejected a first ministers' conference as 'premature' and criticized the vagueness of the premiers' proposals." [83]

The premiers were not to be put off. At the 1983 APC one of the items on the agenda was a proposal for an annual FMC on the economy. Premier Davis of Ontario, the conference host, gave a prepared opening statement to the conference on the need for annual FMCs on the economy. He stated bluntly, "I believe that if we had convened regular, annual, conferences and succeeded in establishing coordinating mechanisms, our recent economic performance might have been better." He added, "No doubt based on what he viewed to be the unsatisfactory experience of the 1982 conference, the prime minister has expressed reservations about the likelihood of a positive outcome at any future First Ministers' Conference on the Economy. This has been a major factor in his failure to agree to holding such a conference." He concluded his remarks by stating that "the government of Canada has nothing to fear from such a conference."[84]

The conference communiqué referred to the need for a "co-operative atti-tude" between the federal and provincial governments. "In view, however, of the obvious reluctance of the prime minister to call a First Ministers' Confer-ence on the economy," the premiers suggested the prime minister meet with them individually as he done in the fall of 1977.[85] Prime Minister Trudeau turned down the request for an FMC but did meet individually with premiers Davis, Lougheed, Grant Devine and Howard Pawley. One reporter commented, "Mr. Trudeau's forays to confer individually with particular premiers on the economy appears to have produced as much contradiction and missed signals as the full-blown first ministers' conferences they seek to replace."[86] Another reporter observed that essentially what the prime minister wanted was "less posturing which means more in camera meetings and common statements" at FMCs.[87] The prime minister did not meet with the other premiers and the initiative simply disappeared as he began to contemplate his departure from politics.

The premiers persisted in trying to achieve their longstanding objective of having an annual FMC on the economy. The 1984 APC followed the pattern that had evolved over the previous few conferences. In this instance the APC was held shortly before the 1984 federal election. The premiers issued a communiqué on federal-provincial co-operation and approved a resolution "that a new era in federal-provincial relations begin with the objective of construct-ing a framework which would enable the provinces and the federal government to collectively work for the attainment of their mutually agreed economic pri-orities." Accordingly, they requested an FMC before the next federal budget "for the express purpose of setting priorities to ensure Canada's sustained economic recovery."[88]

Once again they were successful. Shortly after the election, Prime Minister Brian Mulroney convened a private meeting of first ministers in November 1984 where a federal document on economic renewal was discussed. At this meeting they agreed to hold a conference on the economy in February 1985.

In retrospect, the 1985 FMC represented a major breakthrough for the prov-inces because they had achieved their longstanding objective, a confirmed annual FMC on the economy. First ministers signed a Memorandum of Agree-ment to hold the annual conference each fall.[89] The agreement was good for five years and could be renewed. The purpose of the annual conference was to:

1. review the state of federal-provincial relations;

2. consult on major issues that concern both orders of government, in par-ticular the state of the economy;

3.   consider broad objectives for governments in Canada; and

4.   exchange information to facilitate planning for the operations of their governments.

In his closing remarks to the conference, Premier Lougheed expressed his pleasure that the agreement had been reached. In his opinion it demonstrated that "Confederation is working!"

The five-year commitment to annual FMCs had a major influence on the dynamics of the APC and the nature of its deliberations. To a considerable extent, the FMC could be viewed as a kind of extension of the APC. An alternative interpretation would be that the APC was the equivalent of an interprovincial dress rehearsal. The APC provided provinces with the opportunity to consider items to add to the FMC agenda, to identify common provincial positions and to determine areas where interprovincial preparation was necessary. One can see this pattern emerging at the 1985 APC. The premiers reviewed the Memorandum of Agreement and "felt strongly the primary focus of discussions at the First Ministers' Conference should be jobs and the economy."[90] Most of the individual communiqués included some reference to the forthcoming FMC. The premiers wanted regional economic development added to the FMC agenda. Provincial finance ministers were directed to report to premiers on tax reform, monetary policy and federal-provincial fiscal relations before the Halifax conference. As is readily apparent interprovincial preparation and coordination became of paramount importance.

In light of the agreement's provisions, at the 1986 APC one finds an agenda item on federal-provincial relations. It is under this heading that matters pertaining to fiscal federalism were addressed. Other items considered at their conference for inclusion at the 1986 FMC, scheduled for Vancouver, included agriculture, the Atlantic fishery, tax reform, agreements on fiscal arrangements and regional development. At the 1987 APC, fiscal relations, including equalization and EPF, health and education services, regional development and high technology were all items the premiers wanted placed on the FMC agenda. To assist them, they asked for a variety of reports from provincial ministers such as finance and health. One finds a similar approach to the agenda setting for the 1988 and 1989 First Ministers' Conferences.

In 1988, they reminded Prime Minister Mulroney of his 1985 commitment to the provinces that they would be involved as full participants in both the Canada-US FTA and General Agreement on Tariffs and Trade (GATT) negotiations. They also pushed for a provincial role in the dispute resolution mechanism in the FTA. Their objective was to negotiate a formal agreement with the federal government recognizing "the provinces' and territories' legitimate role in trade negotiations, agreement implementation and dispute settlement."[91] The provinces have continued to press for conclusion of such an agreement, so far without success.

The 1990 APC took place shortly after the failure of the Meech Lake Accord. For obvious reasons, Premier Bourassa did not attend. The premiers wanted the November 1990 FMC to proceed as planned. They also called "for a renewal of the accord on annual FMCs which was signed in Regina in 1985."[92] The day after the conference, Senator Lowell Murray responded for the federal government by stating that no conference was planned and, with the death of Meech Lake, these conferences needed to be re-evaluated.[93] It should be recalled that one of the provisions of the Meech Lake Accord was for an annual FMC on the economy. However, in the aftermath of the failure of Meech Lake and Quebec's subsequent withdrawal from major intergovernmental meetings such as the APC, renewal of the intergovernmental agreement was a non-starter.

At the 1991 APC meeting the premiers repeated their call for an annual conference and urged the prime minister to convene one before the end of the year. For the second year in a row the province of Quebec did not attend the APC. The request met with a considerable degree of success. Three FMCs on the economy were held between December 1991 and March 1992. At the third meeting, the communiqué focused on a variety of policy issues including social programs, internal trade and international trade.[94] It is a reasonable assumption that the federal government's willingness to hold this number of FMCs on the economy was directly linked to its constitutional initiative launched in September 1991. These conferences paralleled the activities of the Joint Parliamentary Committee on the Constitution (Beaudoin-Dobbie) and the six constitutional consultations held between January and March 1992. It was essential to show that federalism worked.

In the spring of 1992 constitutional negotiations began once more and became the focus of attention. The 1992 APC, scheduled for Charlottetown, was reconstituted as an FMC on the constitution. The Charlottetown Accord had several references to FMCs. It included a general provision for an annual meeting. The accord also included a provision identifying one of the agenda items for consideration at that annual conference. At Premier Bourassa's insistence, the accord incorporated a section to establish a framework governing the exercise of the federal spending power.[95] Each year there was to be an annual review of the progress in achieving the framework's objectives. The rejection of the Charlottetown Accord brought to a close the era of constitutional reform and with it the most recent attempt to entrench an annual FMC in the constitution.

The provinces shifted their attention away from the question of constitutional reform and back to other issues such as the economy, internal trade and, as discussed earlier in this chapter, social policy. The 1993 APC was the first meeting in several years where constitutional questions were no longer a consideration or preoccupation of the premiers. Once again the premiers made their annual request for an FMC on the economy. They suggested the issues they had addressed at their conference should form the agenda of such a conference. As was the case in 1984, the 1993 APC took place shortly before the federal general election, thus the communiqué was directed at the next government. In December 1993 the premiers met with Prime Minister Chrétien. Many of the issues reflected in the APC communiqués were discussed, including internal trade, social policy, infrastructure, and federal transfer payments.

The 1994 APC is the last conference where premiers proposed an FMC. They suggested the meeting be in the fall after the federal finance minister's economic statement. The premiers wanted to discuss "the federal fiscal plan and federal plans for social security." Given the focus on deficit reduction, the provinces argued that "predictability of federal fiscal arrangements and transfers is vital." They added, "There should be no surprises."[96] No conference was convened. In the February 1995 budget, they received a major surprise in the form of the Canada Health and Social Transfer. While Finance Minister Paul Martin had forewarned his provincial counterparts about reductions in federal transfers, the real surprise was the draconian nature of the reductions via the CHST. It was this "surprise" that caused the premiers to devote more attention to social policy and associated expenditures.

Unlike his predecessors, Prime Minister Chrétien, for whatever reason, appears indifferent to the practice of meeting with the premiers on a systematic basis to discuss broad policy issues. As a result, FMCs have tended to become sporadic, one-day negotiating sessions with a very specific agenda, and with participation usually restricted to first ministers. One could point to Team Canada missions as a kind of flying FMC but such missions are an unsatisfactory substitute for more structured and frequent meetings.

While a few FMCs have been held since 1993, other than the one in 1996 convened to discuss the federal government's evolving position on federalism, they have tended to focus on SUFA and the financing of health care. Given the very significant percentage health and social expenditures represent in provincial budgets, these policy issues have been a major preoccupation of the premiers at the APC, particularly since the 1995 federal budget. As was made clear in the previous section, premiers have continued to press the federal government to restore federal transfers to their pre CHST levels. They have also raised the issue of fiscal imbalance, a subject that the federal government appears unwilling to address, as indicated by Minister Dion's dismissal of the 2001 APC recommendations.

At the 2003 APC the premiers resurrected their request for an annual FMC. The proposal was included as one of five elements of a "plan to build a new era of constructive and co-operative federalism." The five point plan includes:

1.   Agreement in principle to create a Council of the Federation;

2.   Annual First Ministers' Meetings;

3.   Provincial/territorial consultation on federal appointments;

4.   Devolution of powers to the territories; and

5.   Establishment of federal-provincial-territorial protocols of conduct.[97]

A key difference between this proposal and earlier ones is that the provinces have now proposed that such meetings be co-chaired by the prime minister and the chair of the Council of the Federation. Agendas would "be jointly determined, with standing items on health, trade, finance, justice and the economy."[98] The premiers extended an invitation to the "next prime minister to meet with them at the earliest time possible."[99] This wording was a clear signal of their disenchantment with Prime Minister Chrétien's approach to intergovernmental relations.

   In 1956 the Tremblay Commission recommended the formation of a Council of Provinces, a Canadian equivalent of the Council of State Governments. The Council of the Federation, an idea proposed by Premier Charest of Quebec at the 2003 APC, is a very significant step towards achieving this recommendation. The premiers met in October and again in December 2003 when they signed a Foundation Agreement for an interprovincial/interterritorial body. The council is to "initially focus on areas of common interest (to the provinces) such as health care issues, internal trade, and the fiscal imbalance." Looking at the premiers' positions on co-chairing and agendas for FMCs and their objectives for the council, it is clear that they see the provincial and territorial governments collectively as the equal of the federal government. The very obvious overlap between the responsibilities assigned to the council and the matters identified for discussion at the annual FMC is a clear indication that the provinces intend to develop a common front for presentation to the FMC. Leaving aside the federal government's eventual response to these proposals, what is clear is that the council of the federation, assuming it becomes operational, will transform the APC from an annual meeting into a permanent organization with staff and budget. The Council of Ministers of Education could also be included under its umbrella.

CONCLUDING OBSERVATIONS

The Annual Premiers' Conference has evolved considerably since Premier Lesage convened the first gathering in 1960. Scholarly assessment of these early conferences suggested that their role in the federal system was not of any great significance. It was a loose organization, more of a social gathering of equals, meeting to address common interprovincial concerns. Over time it became evident that the common concerns had less to do with interprovincial issues and more to do with federal-provincial issues. By the early 1980s this transformation in the focus of the APC and its increasing influence of the course of intergovernmental relations had become apparent to observers of federal-provincial relations. The analysis of the APC communiqués for the 25 year period 1977-2001 supports this assessment.

The Annual Premiers' Conference communiqué was the message and the preferred medium for the premiers to deliver it was the First Ministers' Conference. To the premiers, the APC was one component of the machinery of intergovernmental relations. The communiqués reveal that a good part of the discussion at the APC was premised on the assumption or expectation that these same issues would be discussed at an FMC. Thus the APC should not seen as an isolated event but as part of an ongoing process of intergovernmental dialogue and consultation. The FMC was viewed as a kind of continuation of the APC. The APC conference communiqués following the 1985 Memorandum of Agreement to hold an annual FMC provide a good illustration of the interplay between the APC and the FMC. This five-year experience furthered the institutionalization of the APC and the willingness of the provinces to pursue a common front.

In 1976, the provinces made history with their collaboration in developing the provincial position on Established Program Financing. By 2001 such cooperation was commonplace. If one thing distinguishes conferences since 1995 from earlier ones, it is the degree of preparation for the APC by ministerial committees. Moreover, since some reports are now produced on an annual basis, there is considerable continuity from one conference to the next. In short, over the years the APC has become much more institutionalized than when it started in 1960. The APC should not be viewed as a stand-alone event but as part of an ongoing dialogue with each succeeding conference building on the foundation and consensus of previous gatherings. The extensive preparation of reports for the APC makes it more difficult for the federal government to reject out-of-hand APC proposals emanating from them. As the communiqués indicate, if the premiers are unsuccessful one year, at the next APC they will reaffirm their position until they finally get the federal government's attention.

What effect has the APC had on the federal system? Looking back over the years since 1960 it can be argued that the effect has been considerable. As a result of their APC deliberations and decisions, the premiers have been successful in engaging the federal government in a dialogue regarding a wide range of policy matters such as the economy, fiscal arrangements, and social policy. In some instances the discussions have led to federal-provincial agreements such as EPF, the 1985 Memorandum of Agreement on FMCs, the 1999 SUFA, and the 2000 Action Plan on Health. There were also successes in developing the agenda and framework for constitutional discussions.

With the focus on federal-provincial matters there is always the possibility that the federal government may simply ignore or dismiss the APC proposals, as was demonstrated after the 2001 meeting. Its unwillingness in 1990 to renew the 1985 Memorandum of Agreement on FMCs is another example. Put another way, with federal-provincial issues, other than its ability to forge a common front, the APC is not in the position to make the final decision. It can only recommend. While it can certainly influence the outcome and help to shape public opinion, the final decision must in some way include the federal government. How and in what manner the federal government chooses to respond is its responsibility. One option is to convene an FMC, with the final outcome being the result of the ensuing federal-provincial discussions. The APC may be institutionally strong but it is relatively weak in its capacity to make binding decisions on federal-provincial matters.

If the focus is on a purely interprovincial matter, the ability to reach a final agreement rests with the provinces and territories themselves. At the 1995 APC there was a pronounced shift in both emphasis and approach towards the federal government. The focus was on social policy including health care, and the preferred solution was to look for federal-provincial agreements. If an agreement was not achievable, the provinces were prepared to develop an alternative interprovincial position. Thus the provinces have established what in effect is a two-track strategy. The first track is the ongoing effort to develop a common provincial position to present to the federal government on social policy and health care. Although this is an interprovincial exercise, provinces are mindful of the very real federal-provincial dimension that casts a shadow over their discussions. The second track is the identification of an alternative, but strictly interprovincial, solution. The interprovincial position becomes the default position in the event of a federal-provincial impasse. The two-track strategy is very evident in the discussions leading up to the signing of the SUFA. The decisions on health care made at their January 2002 meeting is also a very clear signal that the premiers are willing to develop interprovincial solutions in this policy area, and to bypass the federal government.

Some individuals consider the development of a provincial/territorial common front as no more than "ganging up" on the federal government. That is certainly one perspective. It was a concern that Premier Mercier wanted to allay at the 1887 Interprovincial Conference. It was also an issue that Premier Frost wanted to avoid when the first APC convened in 1960. Prime Minister Trudeau's comments following the 1982 FMC are perhaps the strongest condemnation of this approach. One possible explanation for Prime Minister Chrétien's obvious reluctance to convene annual FMCs is that he does not want to give the premiers a platform or an opportunity to criticize the federal government.

While the idea of a common provincial front may have its critics, the premiers clearly believe that it serves a purpose. A justification for the common front is that it narrows down the issues and assists in focusing the federal-provincial policy agenda and priorities. Instead of a maximum of 14 different positions the common front reduces this down to two, the federal and the provincial/territorial. If a province, such as Quebec, chooses not to join the provincial consensus, the number of positions increases to three — the federal, the Quebec and the common provincial front. This tripartite division was very evident throughout much of the discussion on social policy renewal.

In assessing the effectiveness of the common front one cannot ignore the apparent reluctance of the Quebec government to participate fully in its development since the failure of the Meech Lake Accord and the election of the Parti Québécois in 1994. Over the decades, Quebec's voice at the APC and other intergovernmental gatherings has been significant. Its absence or muting means that an important perspective on the federal system is not at the table. Without Quebec being a full partner in APC discussions, the cohesion among the provinces suffers. In turn, the effectiveness of the APC as an institution is reduced.

To a considerable extent the common front represents the starting point for federal-provincial negotiations. It should not be construed as a "take it or leave it" approach. It is unrealistic to expect the federal government not to have a position of its own. The ultimate objective is to develop a federal-provincial consensus. As is evident from the analysis there are different outcomes depending on the subject at hand. If an FMC is requested, the prime minister may convene one, but the results of the conference are by no means predetermined. If an increase in federal funding is requested, additional money may be forthcoming, as was the case for health care at the 1999 and 2000 FMCs. The 2001 APC and the follow-up meeting in January 2002 reflect ongoing concerns with the level of federal financial support for health care.

The slightest indication that interprovincial differences exist gives the federal government several options by way of response. One is to dismiss the provincial position as "unrealistic" or too expensive, as Stéphane Dion did immediately after the 2001 APC. It is also an excellent opportunity for the federal government to develop a strategy of divide and conquer. Another option is to adopt a wait and see strategy, making the point that little is to be gained from a federal-provincial dialogue if the provinces cannot make up their own minds. If interprovincial policy differences are to be resolved, it must be done through the APC itself, not through premiers exchanging barbs with each other through the media. The recent effectiveness of the APC in achieving the SUFA and additional federal funding for health is a result of the extensive preparation of the provincial position over a number of conferences, and resolving interprovincial differences at these conferences. That has been a more proven and reliable path to success.

The temper of the times also appears to have an influence on the interplay between the APC and the FMC. The periods immediately after the patriation of the decision and the failure of the Meech Lake Accord were difficult for both interprovincial relations and federal-provincial relations. The stresses and strains precipitated by the constitutional reform negotiations spilled over into the general sphere of intergovernmental relations. While such low points exist, fortunately they do not persist indefinitely. One opportunity for the rebuilding or repairing the federal-provincial relationship occurs as a federal election approaches. At both the 1984 and 1993 Annual Premiers' Conferences, the premiers took full advantage of the opportunity to outline their concerns in anticipation of a change in government.

During the 1990s, as the APC became more institutionalized, while it appears the First Ministers' Conference became less so. Instead of the two conferences being on a continuum the two institutions now seem disconnected. The apparent reluctance on the part of Prime Minister Chrétien to support a more structured approach to intergovernmental relations resulted in fewer first ministers' meetings. APC communiqués make it clear that the premiers believe in federal-provincial consultation on a wide variety of subjects, including international issues. Given the growing interdependence with respect to legislative jurisdiction, consultation makes for better public policy. The absence of dialogue may produce the opposite effect and certainly contributes to strained relations, as was evident in the fall of 2002 when the federal government proceeded with ratification of the Kyoto Protocol.

As the institutions of Canadian federalism continue to evolve there is every reason to believe that the Annual Premiers' Conference will also continue to develop. As noted earlier, in 2001 the Quebec Liberal Party made it clear that it wants to "play a leading role with regard to 'interprovincialism'." With the 2003 election of a premier in Quebec with a strong predisposition to federalism, intergovernmental relations in Canada are certainly going to be affected. This became very evident at the 2003 APC.

Historically, the province of Quebec has played an important role in furthering interprovincial relations by convening both the 1887 Interprovincial Conference and the first Annual Premiers' Conference. Its proposal to establish a Council of the Federation is an idea that is fully consistent with these earlier initiatives. Moreover, formation of the council comes at a time when the provinces, often with the exception of Quebec, were already used to working together to forge common objectives. The recent creation of the Premiers' Council on Canadian Health Awareness was a small step in this direction. Now with the willing and enthusiastic participation of Quebec in formulating that common front, there is a fundamental change in the dynamics of interprovincial relations, a change that became readily apparent at the 2003 APC. With the very real possibility of the Council of the Federation transforming the Annual Premiers' Conference into a more structured and permanent organization, interprovincial collaboration appears to be on the verge of entering into new and as yet uncharted waters.

NOTES

1. 42nd Annual Premiers' Conference Communiqué, "Sustainable Health Care for Canadians," 2 August 2001.

2. Heather Scofield and Rick Mackie, "Premiers' wish list rejected," *The Globe and Mail*, 4 August 2001, pp. A1 & A5. The sub-headline was equally enlightening: "Bitter dispute erupts as Ottawa says $10-billion demand 'unrealistic'."

3. APC Communiqué, "Energy," 2 August 2001.

4. Today the premiers' conference participants include the ten premiers and three territorial leaders. For the sake of brevity the term premier will include both.

5. The participating provinces included Quebec (the host), Ontario (the conference chair), Nova Scotia, New Brunswick and Manitoba. British Columbia and Prince Edward Island did not attend.

6. Hon. H. Mercier, Premier of Quebec, "Opening Remarks to the 1887 Interprovincial Conference," *Dominion-Provincial and Interprovincial Conferences from 1887 to 1926* (Ottawa: King's Printer, 1951), p.11.

7. Ibid.

8. Garth Stevenson, *Ex Uno Plures: Federal-Provincial Relations in Canada 1867-1896* (Montreal and Kingston: McGill Queen's University Press, 1993), p. 187.

9. Hon. S. N. Parent, Premier of Quebec, "Opening Address to the 1902 Interprovincial Conference," *Dominion-Provincial and Interprovincial Conferences From 1887 to 1926* (Ottawa: King's Printer, 1951), p. 33.

10. Ibid., p. 63.

11. "Minutes of the Proceedings in Conference of the Representatives of the Provinces of the Dominion of Canada December, 1910," *Dominion-Provincial and Interprovincial Conferences from 1887 to 1926* (Ottawa: King's Printer, 1951), p. 67.

12. "Minutes of the Proceedings in Conference of the Representatives of the Provinces, October, 1913," *Dominion-Provincial and Interprovincial Conferences From 1887 to 1926* (Ottawa: King's Printer, 1951), p. 73.

13. Ibid., p. 76.

14. Ibid., p. 84.

15. See Paul Gérin-Lajoie, *Constitutional Amendment in Canada* (Toronto: University of Toronto Press, 1950), pp. 84-89.

16. "Proceedings of the Interprovincial Conference held at Ottawa, June 7th, 8th and 9th, 1926," *Dominion-Provincial and Interprovincial Conferences from 1887 to 1926* (Ottawa: King's Printer, 1951), p. 110. The same minutes also record the Maritime provinces' "appreciation of the sympathetic spirit manifested by the other provinces...." p. 114.

17. Ibid., p. 108.

18. Ibid., p. 114.

19. To fulfill their legislative obligations (fiscal needs), governments require revenues. Accordingly, one of the most fundamental decisions at the time of federating is the allocation of revenue sources (fiscal capacity). The reality is that fiscal needs and capacity are rarely in equilibrium. When there is a difference, a vertical fiscal imbalance is said to exist. In 1867 the vertical fiscal imbalance between the federal and provincial governments was addressed by a series of constitutionally guaranteed subsidies. Increasing these subsidies was the main agenda item at the 1902 and 1906 conferences.

20. Within the federation there are significant differences in fiscal capacity among the provinces. The reasons for the differences include demographic considerations such as the size and age profile of the population; uneven distribution of natural resources; geographic factors such as land area, climate, soil; and location within the federation. The differences among the constituent units in fiscal capacity reflect a horizontal fiscal imbalance. The equalization program addresses this difference.

21. Edwin R. Black, *Divided Loyalties: Canadian Concepts of Federalism* (Montreal and Kingston: McGill Queen's University Press, 1975), p. 101.

22. See Dale C. Thomson, *Jean Lesage & the Quiet Revolution* (Toronto: Macmillan of Canada, 1984), pp. 334-36.

23. Ibid., p. 335.

24. Quebec, *Report of the Royal Commission of Inquiry on Constitutional Problems* 3, Bk. 2 (1956):302.

25. J.H. Aitchison, "Interprovincial Co-operation in Canada," in J. H. Aitchison, *The Political Process in Canada* (Toronto: University of Toronto Press, 1963), pp. 153-70. Aitchison examined the Council of State Governments as a possible model for the Annual Premiers' Conference. See also, Richard H. Leach, "Intergovernmental Co-operation: Neglected Aspect of Canadian Federalism," *Canadian Public Administration* 2 (June 1959):83-99.

26. R.M. Burns, "The Machinery of Intergovernmental Relations: 2," reprinted in *Canadian Federalism; Myth or Reality*, ed. J. Peter Meekison (Toronto: Methuen, 1968), pp. 302-03.

27. D.V. Smiley, *Canada in Question: Federalism in the Seventies* (Toronto: McGraw-Hill Ryerson Ltd., 1972), pp. 63-64. The quote is found in the chapter on Executive Federalism.

28. Richard Simeon, *Federal-Provincial Diplomacy: The Making of Recent Policy in Canada* (Toronto: University of Toronto Press, 1972), p. 138.

29. D.V. Smiley, *Canada in Question: Federalism in the Eighties* (Toronto: McGraw-Hill Ryerson Ltd., 1980), p. 105.

30. Royal Commission on the Economic Union and Development Prospects for Canada, *Report* (Ottawa: Minister of Supply and Services, 1985), p. 269.

31. The first APC I attended was the one hosted by Ontario in 1974. I was assigned to the communiqué drafting team. My instructions from Premier Lougheed were

clear: the draft needed to reflect provincial ownership of resources. While individual governments may have had different views on crude oil pricing they were of one mind on the principle of provincial ownership of natural resources.

32. References to premiers after 1991 also include the territorial leaders.

33. The 1967 Confederation of Tomorrow Conference was the first televised intergovernmental meeting. It was a meeting of premiers convened by Premier John Robarts and was not an APC, but a special meeting of premiers to discuss national unity. It led to a series of federal-provincial negotiations on the constitution beginning in 1968.

34. The CICS published an excellent summary document in 2003 entitled *Premiers' Conferences: 1887–2002* (Ottawa: Canadian Intergovernmental Conference Secretariat, 2002). It serves as a very useful source, listing participants and subjects discussed. It should be noted that these numbers may not correspond to the number of premiers in a given province during the 25 year period. For example, Pierre Marc Johnson, who succeeded Réne Levesque as premier, did not attend an APC. While Dan Miller, who succeeded Glen Clark in BC, did not attend an APC, he did attend a premiers' meeting in February 2000 as a follow-up to the 1999 APC.

35. Chris Nuttall-Smith, "Campbell to urge PM to seal borders: BC Premier seeks role for provinces," *The Vancouver Sun*, 2 October 2001, p. A1.

36. See CICS News Release, "Provinces Pave the Way for the Future of Health Care." 25 January 2002, Ref: 850-085/004.

37. See CICS News Release, "Canada-United States Relations." 9-11 July 2003, Ref: 850-092/015.

38. See Alberta, Department of Federal and Intergovernmental Affairs, *Eighth Annual Report to March 31, 1981* (Edmonton, 1982). APC Communiqué Number 3, August 1980, p. 55.

39. See CICS News Release, "Fifth Progress Report On Social Policy Renewal Released to Canadians," August 2000, Ref: 850-080/015. One finds a similar disclaimer the year before, when Quebec hosted the APC.

40. For a copy of this news release, see Alberta, Department of Federal and Intergovernmental Affairs, *Seventh Annual Report to March 31, 1980* (Edmonton, 1981), p. 38.

41. Five weeks after the FMC the Clark government was defeated on a vote of confidence in the House of Commons on its first budget. A large part of the budget was devoted to energy policy. For a more detailed comment see David G. Wood, *The Lougheed Legacy* (Toronto: Key Porter Books, 1985), pp. 157-79.

42. The document in question was "ACCESS: A Convention on the Economic and Social Systems," a working paper prepared for Ontario. For a good discussion of the paper see *Assessing ACCESS: Towards a New Social Union* (Kingston: Institute of Intergovernmental Relations, Queen's University, 1997).

43. The 1990 federal budget placed a five percent cap on the increase in annual payments under the Canada Assistance Plan (CAP) to the provinces of Alberta, British Columbia and Ontario for two years. The 1991 budget extended this cap for an additional three years. The budget policy was known as the cap on CAP.

The three provinces were unsuccessful in their legal challenge. See *Re Canada Assistance Plan* (1991), [1991] 2 S.C.R. 525.

44. During the negotiations on the Charlottetown Accord I co-chaired the Committee of Officials looking at the division of powers and related matters such as equalization. The anxiety of the have-not provinces was reflected in the provisions on "Urban and Municipal Affairs, Tourism, Recreation, Housing, Mining and Forestry." See in particular subsection 4, which required the federal government to maintain its spending in these areas. The subsection was inserted at the request of the have-not provinces. During the discussion of amendments to section 36 of the *Constitution Act, 1982,* it was made clear on more than one occasion that, while support existed for equalization, federal policies which appeared to enhance equalization, such as the cap on CAP, were not welcome.

45. The 1995 federal budget terminated the EPF and CAP programs by combining them into a new block funding program called the Canada Health and Social Transfer, or CHST. The Canada Assistance Plan, introduced in 1966, was the last of the major shared-cost programs. It should be noted that the change to equal per capita funding also removed the pre-cap on CAP per capita benefit that provinces with more welfare recipients enjoyed. For example, pre-cap on CAP, Nova Scotia received more benefits per capita than Saskatchewan because it had a larger welfare bill. See note 48 for a description of EPF. British Columbia is now in receipt of equalization payments.

46. See Paul Adams and Richard Mackie, "Bickering ends with agreement on tax-cut call," *The Globe and Mail*, 11 August 1999, p. A4 for a commentary on the conference.

47. The 28 February 2000 Budget included an increase of $2.5 billion to the CHST.

48. John Ibbitson, "Tempers flare as premiers square off," *The Globe and Mail*, 11 August 2000, p. A1.

49. Justine Hunter, "Klein contributing to 'new kind of intolerance'," *National Post*, 17 August 2000, p. A1.

50. See Justine Hunter and James Cudmore, "Intolerance charge 'a crock': Klein," *National Post*, 18 August 2000, p. A1, and Ralph Klein, "Speaking for Alberta," *National Post*, 23 August 2000, p. A17.

51. Brian Laghi, "Premiers warned internal bickering could backfire," *The Globe and Mail*, 22 August 2000, p. A4. The FMC that Premier Hamm was referring to was the September 11 meeting on health care where additional funding was added to the CHST and for early childhood development.

52. Richard Mackie, "Harris compares Atlantic Canada to lottery winners on dole," *The Globe and Mail*, 19 July 2001, p. A1.

53. Richard Mackie and Kim Lunman, "Poorer provinces reject Harris's united front," *The Globe and Mail*, 2 August 2001, p. A1.

54. APC Communiqué "Sustainable Health Care for Canadians."

55. See Rhéal Séguin, "Bouchard's role as host riddled with contradictions," *The Globe and Mail*, 10 August 1999, p. A4.

56. Daniel Leblanc, "Landry vows he'll be blunt but friendly," *The Globe and Mail,* 30 July 2001, p. A4.

57. Benoît Pelletier, "Quebec's Choice: Affirmation, Autonomy and Leadership," *Policy Options,* April 2001:32. At the time he was also chair of the Special Committee of the Quebec Liberal Party on Political and Constitutional Future of Quebec Society.

58. Murray Campbell, "Premiers endorse Charest's national council: Quebec's leadership role heralds 'new era of constructive federalism'," *The Globe and Mail,* 11 July 2003, p. A1.

59. Established Program Financing (EPF) came into effect in 1977 and became part of the overall fiscal arrangements, which also included the tax collection agreements and equalization. The federal government terminated three existing shared-cost programs; the Hospital Insurance and Diagnostic Services Act, medicare and post-secondary education funding. They were replaced by a combination of tax point transfers and block (cash) grants distributed on an equal per capita basis to the provinces. For the background to the EPF see Pierre Elliot Trudeau, "Established Program Financing: A Proposal Regarding the Major Shared-Cost Programs in the Fields of Health and Post-Secondary Education," in *Canadian Federalism: Myth or Reality,* 3rd ed., ed. J. Peter Meekison (Toronto: Methuen Publications, 1977), pp. 246-58.

60. Alberta, Department of Federal and Intergovernmental Affairs, *Fourth Annual Report to March 31, 1977* (Edmonton, 1978).

61. See the Provincial Finance Ministers' Report prepared for the 1981 Premiers Conference contained in Alberta, Department of Federal and Intergovernmental Affairs, *Ninth Annual Report to March 31, 1982* (Edmonton, 1982), pp. 48-52.

62. For the Communiqué on federal-provincial relations see Alberta, Department of Federal and Intergovernmental Affairs, *Tenth Annual Report to March 31, 1983* (Edmonton, 1983), p. 31.

63. For the Communiqué on federal-provincial fiscal relations see Alberta, Department of Federal and Intergovernmental Affairs, *Thirteenth Annual Report to March 31, 1986* (Edmonton, 1983), p. 34.

64. For the Communiqué on social issues see Alberta, Department of Federal and Intergovernmental Affairs *Nineteenth Annual Report to March 31, 1992* (Edmonton, 1983), p. 53

65. APC "Final Communiqué," 27 August 1993, pp. 12-13.

66. APC "Final Communiqué," 25 August 1995, p. 1.

67. Ibid., p. 2.

68. Ibid., pp. 2-3.

69. APC Communiqué, "Social Policy Reform and Renewal," 23 August 1996. Prepared for the 1996 APC Provincial-Territorial Working Group on Social Policy Reform and Renewal.

70. APC Communiqué, "Social Policy Renewal," 8 August 1997.

71. APC Communiqué, "Priority Health Sector Issues," 11 August 1999.

72. See *The Globe and Mail*, 24 January 2002, p. A1, and *The Globe and Mail*, 25 January 2002, p. A1.

73. Canadian Intergovernmental Conference Secretariat, News Release, "Provinces Pave the Way for the Future of Health Care," 25 January 2002.

74. Ibid. See Ian Bailey, "Premiers give Ottawa health care ultimatum," *National Post*, 26 January 2002, p. A1.

75. The agreement is contained in a letter dated 2 April 2002 from Hon. A. Anne McLellan, Minister of Health, to Hon. Gary Mar, Minister of Health and Wellness, Province of Alberta. The process includes a third party panel and is patterned after the process found in the Agreement on Internal Trade.

76. An exception to this observation was the four constitutional conferences with Aboriginal peoples, which in turn were set out in the *Constitution Act, 1982*, and the 1984 amendment. One might also include conferences that are part of an agreed upon process such as the ones leading up to the 1971 Victoria Charter and the 1992 Charlottetown Accord, but it should be remembered that in both instances the process was initiated by the federal government.

77. *Constitutional Conference Proceedings, December 1969* (Ottawa: Queen's Printer, 1970), p. 246.

78. Alberta, Department of Federal and Intergovernmental Affairs, *Fourth Annual Report to March 31, 1977* (Edmonton, 1978), p. 52.

79. For copies of the correspondence, see ibid., Appendix VI, pp. 55-77.

80. Alberta, Department of Federal and Intergovernmental Affairs, *Sixth Annual Report to March 31, 1979* (Edmonton, 1979), p. 87.

81. A second FMC was held 30 June 1982 to discuss the 28 June federal budget. It was a private meeting at 24 Sussex Drive and lasted for five hours. The initiative for the meeting came from the federal government, not the provinces. That said, economic issues were addressed.

82. John Gray, "Generosity to provinces ends, bitter Prime Minister promises," *The Globe and Mail*, 27 February 1982, p. 1.

83. Sheilagh M. Dunn, *The Year in Review 1982: Intergovernmental Relations in Canada* (Kingston: Institute of Intergovernmental Relations, Queen's University, 1982), p. 96.

84. "Notes for a Statement by the Honourable William G. Davis, Premier of Ontario, on First Ministers' Conference on the Economy," Toronto, 9-11 August 1983.

85. APC Communiqué, "Meetings with the Prime Minister on the Economy," August 1983.

86. Robert Sheppard, "Political leaders lack the will to combat inflation," *The Globe and Mail*, 29 September 1983, p. 1.

87. Alan Christie, *The Toronto Star*, 28 September 1983, p. A1.

88. APC Communiqué, "Federal-Provincial Co-operation," 20-22 August 1984. (Emphasis in original.)

89. For a copy of the Memorandum of Agreement see Alberta, Department of Federal and Intergovernmental Affairs *Twelfth Annual Report to March 31, 1985* (Edmonton, 1985), p. 34.

90. APC "Communiqué," 21 August 1985.

91. APC "Final Communiqué," 27 August 1993, p. 5.

92. See Alberta, Department of Federal and Intergovernmental Affairs, *Eighteenth Annual Report to March 31, 1991*, p. 57.

93. Susan Delacourt, "Economic summit in limbo," *Globe and Mail*, 16 August 1990, p. A5.

94. See Alberta, Department of Federal and Intergovernmental Affairs, *Nineteenth Annual Report to March 31, 1992*, for a comment on the First Ministers' Conferences pp. 9-10 and for a copy of the communiqué from the third conference pp. 56-59. Quebec did not attend the 1991 APC.

95. See Draft Legal Text, 9 October 1992, Part IV, "Framework For Certain Expenditures By The Government Of Canada," p. 47. An FMC would also be convened to discuss the entry of new provinces.

96. APC "Final Communiqué," 1 September 1994, p. 2. The conference was held during the Quebec election. Eleven days later, September 12th, the PQ was returned to office.

97. CICS News Release, "Premiers Announce Plan to Build a New Era of Constructive and Cooperative Federalism," 9-11 July 2003, Ref: 850-092/006. Note: the term for First Ministers' Conference (FMC) was changed to First Ministers' Meeting (FMM).

98. Ibid.

99. Ibid, emphasis added.

7

The Western Premiers' Conference:
Intergovernmental Co-operation at the
Regional Level

J. Peter Meekison

La Conférence des premiers ministres de l'Ouest est une conséquence directe de la Conférence sur les perspectives économiques de l'Ouest de 1973; elle constitue l'une des plus récentes manifestations du fédéralisme exécutif. Elle est devenue le principal mécanisme de coordination de l'interaction des provinces de l'Ouest et, maintenant, des territoires, avec le gouvernement fédéral. Son programme est semblable à celui de la Conférence annuelle des Premiers ministres, que les Premiers ministres de l'Ouest utilisent pour obtenir des appuis pour leurs positions de principe. La Conférence des premiers ministres de l'Ouest n'a ni structure formelle ni secrétariat; elle fonctionne plutôt sur la base de la convention. Elle fait un usage étendu des comités ministériels pour créer ses positions de principe, amenant ainsi une continuité considérable d'une Conférence à l'autre. Bien que l'accent y soit surtout mis sur les questions fédérales-provinciales, on y traite aussi des problèmes interprovinciaux.

The Western Premiers' Conference (WPC) is a relatively recent arrival on the Canadian intergovernmental scene and owes its establishment to a federal initiative. After the 1972 federal election, the Liberal government was reduced to minority government status, due in part to the loss of 20 seats across the west. In order to improve its future political prospects in western Canada, the federal government announced in the 1973 Throne Speech its intention to convene a Western Economic Opportunities Conference. The conference participants consisted of the federal government and the four western provinces. While the WEOC was a one-time event, the WPC can trace its origins to that meeting and is now a well-established institution.

This chapter examines the evolution of the Western Premiers' Conference and its linkages to other components of the machinery of intergovernmental relations in Canada. As a regional grouping of provinces and territories, the WPC perspective is obviously influenced by that reality. While some of the matters discussed at the WPC concern only the region, other issues considered by the premiers transcend regional boundaries. Accordingly, the resolution of these broader policy issues is seen to be more effectively pursued at the national level. The possible avenues for national discussions include a meeting between the federal government and the WPC, a First Ministers' Conference and the Annual Premiers' Conference (APC). While all three avenues have been pursued, the more frequent linkages are with the APC. This is due to the practice of the WPC provincial and territorial premiers purposefully scheduling their yearly conferences to take place in the months leading up to the APCs and into which their work logically flows. Before discussing the WPC, a brief overview of the some of the demographic and economic characteristics of western Canada and the territories is necessary.

DEMOGRAPHIC AND ECONOMIC CHARACTERISTICS

Western Canada consists of the provinces of Manitoba, British Columbia, Saskatchewan and Alberta.[1] While some people view western Canada as a single region, others consider it as a combination of two regions, the Prairies and British Columbia.[2] Under the *Constitution Act, 1867*, the four western provinces form one of Canada's four Senate divisions, the only formal constitutional recognition of the region. The 1996 act regarding constitutional amendments, usually referred to as the *Regional Veto Act*, acknowledges British Columbia as one of five regions. With the inclusion of the three territories as members of the WPC, the conference was transformed from a purely western institution to a western and northern institution.

While the four western provinces share many common features, it would be a major error to assume that the west is a homogenous monolith. The Prairies were strongly shaped by the wheat economy. All four provinces are dependent upon the exploitation of natural resources. The three Prairie provinces were carved out of Rupert's Land and the North-western Territory and had to fight the federal government to gain ownership of the public lands and natural resources. In 1930, by means of a constitutional amendment, they were finally successful, placing them on the same footing as the other provinces. Alberta has the distinction of having the vast majority of Canada's onshore oil and natural gas reserves and the royalties that flow from these resources. Saskatchewan has an abundance of potash. Manitoba was the gateway to the west and was the first province added to Canada after Confederation. British Columbia, a separate Crown colony, became Canada's sixth province and is Canada's gateway to Asia.

Given the cyclical nature of prices for grain and natural resources, there has always been an element of boom or bust with regard to the four provincial economies. To offset the economic fluctuations, the four provinces have promoted economic diversification to lessen their dependence on agriculture, fishing and natural resources. Since their economic well-being depends to a considerable extent upon exports, the four western provinces have tended to favour free trade. As a result, they follow very closely all aspects of international trade negotiations.

Transportation is enormously important to the west because its commodities and resources are sold in international markets. Without the railways, wheat and coal cannot be shipped and potash is just another crumbly rock. Without pipelines, oil and natural gas remain in the ground. British Columbia entered Confederation because of the promise to build a railway to the Pacific coast. The railway came first to the Prairies and was linked to its economic development. Grain shipments, port facilities, freight rates, highways and interprovincial trucking are recurring themes in western Canadian politics and they are reflected in WPC agendas.

There are considerable differences in the demographics of the four provinces. In 2002 the population of the four provinces totalled 30 percent of the Canadian population.[3] Recent population growth in the west has taken place almost entirely in British Columbia and Alberta. In 2002 these two provinces had 44 percent and 33.1 percent of the west's population respectively. Over the 30-year period from 1971-2001, the population of Manitoba and Saskatchewan remained relatively constant at around one million for each province. Alberta led the country in terms of the rate of population growth, while Saskatchewan's population decreased. By 2025, BC's share of the western population is projected to be just under 50 percent of the total, driven largely by immigration. BC and Alberta have been net beneficiaries of interprovincial migration in Canada over the last 30 years, whereas Saskatchewan and Manitoba lost population to other provinces. One consequence is that their dependency ratio is slightly higher than that of the other two provinces.[4]

Based on the 2001 census, 62.1 percent of Canada's Aboriginal population lives in the four western provinces. With an Aboriginal population of 170,075, British Columbia has the largest total number of Aboriginal people of the four provinces. This figure represents 4.4 percent of the provincial population. The Aboriginal population of Manitoba and Saskatchewan is slightly smaller than that of BC. However, when viewed as a percentage of the total population for these two provinces, it is significantly higher, at 13.6 percent and 13.5 percent respectively. Thus in Manitoba and Saskatchewan the Aboriginal population can expect to have a greater influence both in provincial politics and in the provincial economy. While the Aboriginal population of Alberta is comparable to that of the other two Prairie provinces, it is only 5.3 percent of that province's population.

An examination of economic indicators also shows significant variation among the four western provinces. From 1961 to 2001 Alberta's share of the

Gross Domestic Product (GDP) of the four provinces increased from 30.1 percent to 43.2 percent. British Columbia's share remained approximately the same at 37.4 percent, while that of Saskatchewan and Manitoba decreased. Alberta and BC account for about 25.9 percent of Canada's GDP, with Saskatchewan and Manitoba accounting for about 6.3 percent. The services sector is more significant in BC and Manitoba than in Alberta and Saskatchewan, the difference arising from the larger share of GDP coming from the oil, gas and mining sectors.

As with the rest of Canada, trade with the United States is of major significance to the Western provinces. In 2002, 78.8 percent of Western Canada's exports, valued at $79 billion, went to the United States. The percentage of merchandise exports to the United States from the west is slightly lower than that from the other provinces. In 2002, 88.2 percent of Alberta's exports went to the United States, followed by Manitoba with 81.5 percent. Given the significance of this trade, transportation links and relations with the western United States are of importance to the western provinces, just as such links are to the rest of the other provinces. British Columbia and Saskatchewan at 68.7 percent and 61.7 percent respectively are less dependent on this trade pattern. Given the importance of trade with the United States it should come as no surprise that the Canada-US relationship is a recurring theme at the Western Premiers' Conferences. The softwood lumber dispute with the United States and the ban on the export of Canadian beef after the discovery of a single case of mad cow disease in 2003 serve as a reminder that this trading relationship is by no means conflict free.

While international exports represent a larger share of GDP to the west than do interprovincial exports, a comparison of interprovincial exports reveals differences in the importance of internal trade to the four western provinces. In 2001 Manitoba's interprovincial exports were 31.7 percent of GDP and were more important to Manitoba than international exports, which represented 30.3 percent of the province's GDP. In 2001 British Columbia was the least dependent on interprovincial exports, which were only 13.6 percent of GDP. Alberta and Saskatchewan, where interprovincial exports represented 21.6 percent and 25.6 percent of GDP respectively, were somewhere in the middle. The comparable figure for the rest of Canada was 18.9 percent. However, from 1981 to 2001 interprovincial exports increased in absolute terms for Saskatchewan, Manitoba and British Columbia. For Alberta they decreased, as they did elsewhere in Canada. The importance of internal exports, even with the decrease for Alberta, has been greater for the three Prairie provinces than for the other provinces in Canada.

As noted in a 2001 Canada West Foundation study on the state of the west, "Changes in interprovincial trade policy, such as the reduction of internal trade barriers through greater enforcement of the Agreement on Internal Trade, could be of particular importance to the Prairie provinces."[5] In the early years of the

WPC one finds continuing references to the need for an internal trade agreement, and in recent years, comments on the progress of negotiations on the AIT.[6]

This brief overview shows considerable variation among the four western provinces in terms of their economic circumstances and their relative position within western Canada today. What becomes clear is that the differences are greatest between British Columbia and Alberta on the one hand, and Saskatchewan and Manitoba on the other, particularly with regard to the rate of population growth and differences in their respective shares of the regional GDP. The population differences have implications for and an influence on the national stage, particularly the distribution of western seats in the House of Commons. After the readjustment of seats in the House of Commons following the 2001 decennial census, both British Columbia and Alberta will gain two additional members, beginning with the next federal general election, expected in 2004.

Before concluding this section some additional comments on Canada's North are necessary.[7] With the expansion of the WPC to include the Yukon, the Northwest Territories and Nunavut, which together constitute the North, some understanding of that region is necessary. There are four key considerations to bear in mind when considering the North. The first is the constitutional distinction between provinces and territories. While the federal government has devolved considerable authority from itself to the territorial governments and legislatures, the three territories do not have the same legal status under the constitution as do the provinces. With respect to the ownership of public lands and natural resources, their situation is similar to that of the Prairie provinces prior to 1930. Parliament still retains plenary authority over the territories. The second consideration is the size of the population. In 2002 the population of the territories was 100,000, or .3 percent of the total Canadian population. The third point is that the territories constitute 39.3 percent of Canada's land area, whereas the four western provinces constitute 29.1 percent of the land area. The fourth consideration is that Aboriginal peoples constitute the majority of the population in both the Northwest Territories and Nunavut. The percentage of the Aboriginal population of each territory, based on the 2001 census, is Nunavut with 82.5 percent, the Northwest Territories with 50.5 percent and the Yukon with 22.9 percent, respectively.

THE WESTERN ECONOMIC OPPORTUNITIES CONFERENCE (WEOC)

In 1973, three of the four western provinces had New Democratic Party (NDP) governments, while Alberta had a Progressive Conservative government. The senior premier, Ed Schreyer of Manitoba, had been in office for four years. The other three, premiers Peter Lougheed, Allan Blakeney and Dave Barrett had been in office since 1971, 1971 and 1972, respectively. In short, their collective political experience was modest but they were certainly cognizant of the historic importance of the WEOC that took place that year. Of equal importance, each premier considered himself the principal person to speak for and represent his province's interests.

At that time, interprovincial co-operation in western Canada was relatively new. Alberta, Saskatchewan and Manitoba had established the Prairie Economic Council (PEC) in 1965 and had met annually since then. The federal announcement provided them with the opportunity to join with British Columbia in forging a common western position to present to the Government of Canada. The three prairie premiers, meeting as the PEC, met in March 1973 in Winnipeg to discuss a common position. Premier Barrett was invited to attend the meeting. At that preparatory meeting the four premiers agreed to establish the Western Premiers' Council, later renamed the Western Premiers' Conference.[8]

Earlier efforts to develop intergovernmental linkages with British Columbia during Premier W.A.C. Bennett's time had been unsuccessful.[9] It should also be recalled that Premier Bennett was a strong and fervent proponent of the view that Canada was a country consisting of five regions, one of which was British Columbia. He surprised — or stunned may be a better word — the February 1969 constitutional conference with his five province plan.[10] In his opinion, his proposed new political configuration reflected the five economic regions of Canada. In support of his position, he noted the fact that both the Atlantic provinces and Prairie provinces had met immediately before the 1969 conference. To him their meetings demonstrated that each constituted "one region."[11] The demand for recognition as a distinct region was reflected in the wording of the 1971 Victoria amending formula.[12] Accordingly, one can see why his interest in western co-operation was limited.

The forerunner to the WPC was PEC. According to Blakeney, the PEC was formed with four objectives in mind: (i) to set out goals for regional progress; (ii) to co-ordinate economic development policies on a regional basis; (iii) to cut down areas of unnecessary conflict; and (iv) to discuss ways to resolve problems of mutual concern.[13] To Blakeney, the PEC "was focused primarily on specific technical questions rather than on broader issues of regional development strategy."[14] As Martin Westmacott and Phillip Dore observe, "No attempt was made to develop common policy positions nor to convey a "western Canadian" viewpoint to the federal government."[15] To Peter Lougheed, when he was opposition leader, the name of the organization was a "misnomer" and needed to be changed. In Lougheed's opinion PEC was not a success, "The concept is right, but it hasn't been successful by means of the existing vehicle ... it is time to reassess it."[16] He proposed an interprovincial secretariat with a policy research capacity "charged with examining proposed national policies and assessing them in terms of their Prairie implication."[17]

As one observer noted, "The narrow scope of the discussions at Prairie Economic Council meetings in the 1960s was due, in part, to the differing political and socio-economic interest and priorities which the provinces rigidly adhered to."[18] One is left with the general impression that the PEC was not a particularly effective organization.

The Western Economic Opportunities Conference was the catalyst that transformed PEC into the Western Premiers' Conference.[19] The conference agenda focused on economic opportunities, one of the four objectives of PEC. The four western provinces prepared four common position papers to present to the conference. The papers were on transportation, economic and development opportunities, agriculture and capital financing, and regional financial institutions. As Allan Blakeney noted:

> The four Premiers and the four governments struggled — and it was a struggle — to reach common positions to put to the federal government. That was a valuable exercise, though not always an easy one. It made us face realities. It encouraged us to cut down areas of competition and conflict amongst ourselves in the interests of the region as a whole. It forced us to consider our specific grievances within a broader framework for development of the region.[20]

When Peter Lougheed reflected on the conference his thinking was that the federal government would try to divide the provinces along partisan lines. His strategy "was to list all of the topics on which he felt the western provinces could agree — transportation, agriculture, some industrial areas — and to keep off the agenda the topics almost certain to cause friction among them, particularly energy."[21] According to Blakeney, differences were geographically based, primarily between British Columbia and the Prairies.[22]

The conference was televised. The opening exchange between the prime minister and the four premiers on a procedural point was particularly important. The provincial strategy was for the provinces to present their position papers and have the federal government respond. Prime Minister Trudeau was distinctly hostile to this suggestion. He said, "I am rather adamant in my position as the federal prime minister that federal-provincial conferences follow the usual pattern of the federal government not only chairing, but also leading off on the various items."[23] As Premier Ed Schreyer reminded him, "You are calling this conference because you wanted to solicit the views of those representatives of provincial governments in western Canada. So we put forward our views in the logical sequence that you respond to them."[24] The point having been made, a compromise was reached where the lead alternated between the provinces and the federal government. To the federal government, the conference was an opportunity to develop a new National Policy.

The conference ended with the premiers expressing varying degrees of disappointment with the federal positions and responses to their positions. The prime minister took note of their "disappointment," but added "there is probably no federal-provincial meeting from which the premiers didn't depart by saying that they were keenly disappointed, that their various demands have not been met."[25] While the prime minister referred to the conference as being "of possible historic importance to Canada as a nation" and "unprecedented," his final words perhaps reflected his real feelings. "Well, thus ends *the one and only* Western Economic Opportunities Conference."[26]

At the 1993 WPC in Canmore, Alberta, the premiers noted that "1993 marked the twentieth anniversary of the first and only Western Economic Opportunities Conference."[27] While the premiers emphasized their readiness to have another conference, the newly elected Prime Minister, Jean Chrétien, did not follow up on the suggestion.

There are two ways of viewing WEOC: either through a federal-provincial lens, or through an interprovincial lens. When viewed from the federal-provincial perspective, Gerry T. Gartner concluded, "Few concrete results can be attributed to the Western Economic Opportunities conference."[28] He also repeated a point made by Premier Blakeney at the close of the conference that little progress had been made toward the development of a new national policy. When viewed from an interprovincial perspective, the conference was very successful because it led to a lasting co-operative relationship among the four western provinces. The Western Premiers' Conference is WEOC's legacy. As stated by David Elton, "The creation of the Western Premiers' Conference, although a byproduct, was in retrospect the most noteworthy accomplishment of WEOC."[29]

Roger Gibbins notes that the Canada West Foundation is another legacy of WEOC. The Foundation's research agenda was influenced by "the feeling that at WEOC the western Canadian representatives had been outgunned by the research capacity, computer models and general expertise of the federal officials."[30] In the intervening years since WEOC, provincial officials have caught up to their federal counterparts.

THE WESTERN PREMIERS' CONFERENCE (WPC)

As already noted, WEOC was the catalyst that led to the formation of the Western Premiers' Conference. The influence of the WEOC experience, however, went far beyond that single event. For example, a comparison of the WEOC agenda with the agendas of subsequent WPCs shows a continuing emphasis on economic issues such as agriculture, transportation and economic development. However, in the mid-1990s, as part of the common provincial concern about the financing of health care and other social programs, one finds the inclusion on the WPC agenda of social policy issues. Another legacy is the extensive degree of preparatory work for each annual conference.

One of the main reasons for WEOC's success from an interprovincial perspective was the willingness of the provinces to concentrate on areas of common interest. To a considerable extent that practice continues to be observed. Its observance goes beyond developing a common front for federal-provincial questions and extends as well to matters of interprovincial co-operation, one example being internal trade. As Premier Blakeney remarked, "We have developed a common understanding of both the opportunities and constraints of joint action: we concentrate on those areas in which we agree, or where agreement seems possible, and de-emphasize areas of conflict."[31]

The conventions associated with the WPC are similar to those one finds with the Annual Premiers' Conference. The venue for the WPC rotates among the four provinces. A tradition of holding the meetings outside the capital city and in the smaller centres has evolved. As part of the conference activities the host province invites the community to a dinner to meet the visiting premiers, who add their words of welcome. With the expansion of the WPC to include the Yukon, Northwest Territories and now Nunavut, meetings have also been held in Dawson City and Yellowknife.

Although the conference that led to the formation of the WPC was televised, the WPC meetings themselves are not open to the public. In addition to the premiers, the other participants include ministers and officials. Interest groups do not participate. Unlike the APC, the WPC is considered to be more a working meeting with no social or spousal program other than the evening with the local community.

The host province acts as the conference coordinator and provides the secretariat services. The premier of the host province or territory acts as the spokesperson of the group. This role was underlined at the 2003 WPC in Kelowna, BC. During the meeting the premiers decided it was essential that they present their concerns with respect to the US embargo on beef immediately by means of a teleconference call to Prime Minister Chrétien. Their expectation was that they would all participate in the call. The prime minister agreed to hear their position, but only on the condition that it be a one-on-one conversation with the conference chair, Premier Gordon Campbell.

The WPC agenda is primarily developed by officials. The agenda is influenced by a number of factors including the state of the economy, the current state of federal-provincial relations, weather conditions, national unity, and international developments, including transboundary relations with the United States. In addition, there is a considerable degree of continuity between conferences, with ministerial committees being formed at one and reporting to the next. For example, since 1990, western finance ministers have prepared an annual report for the WPC reports on the state of fiscal federalism. The usual practice is to schedule the conference in spring, sufficiently far in advance of the APC to allow time for refinement of positions between the WPC and the APC. The timing of the WPC is not coincidental. When examining the WPC communiqués and those from the APC, it is readily apparent that one of the objectives of the WPC is to present the western policy positions to the APC to gain broader support for those positions.

As with so many other aspects of the operation of the federal system, personal relationships develop. A very obvious one was the very close relationship between premiers Blakeney and Lougheed, a working relationship that extended to their ministers and officials. Occasionally partisan politics and ideological difference surface, creating a certain degree of tension — and a very different relationship. A recent example was the 2000 WPC, where two New Democrat premiers, Saskatchewan's Roy Romanow and British Columbia's Ujjal Dosangh, criticized Alberta's Bill 11 regarding private health care facilities. The day before the conference, Premier Romanow was quoted as saying, "I don't intend to, in the interest of coming out with a united front, sacrifice any of the principles of publicly funded medicare." Premier Ralph Klein, in turn, "was 'angry' that Premier Romanow hadn't called him before publicly condemning the bill."[32] The dispute spilled over at the press conference the following day. Premier Klein said: "Basically, the long and short of it is I told these guys, 'You go home mind your own business, look at your own legislation and stay out of ours.'" Premier Romanow responded, "When it comes to medicare it's a national concern, everybody's concern. You have a right to comment on my legislation, I have a right to comment on your legislation if I think the birthright of Canadian citizenship like medicare is at issue."[33]

The conventions governing decision-making at the WPC are very straightforward. Decisions are reached through consensus which, in effect, means unanimity. The exchange between premiers Romanow and Klein referred to above is a good illustration of this convention. The comments from each premier make it clear that there were sharp differences of opinion regarding the provision of health care services among the premiers. Despite the very public nature of the dispute, these differences were not reflected in the conference communiqué. Indeed, Premier Romanow's reference to a "united front," underscores the conventional approach to decision making. Communiqués are prepared to show areas of agreement, not disagreement.

The WPC yields decisions on a wide variety of policy matters. These decisions frequently pertain to positions that the provincial governments wish to adopt or affirm concerning a particular federal-provincial policy issue, such as health. In other instances the agreement may be to co-operate interprovincially, for example by eliminating interprovincial trade barriers. Neither of these kinds of policy decisions, while important, imposes any legal obligations on the participants. Indeed, provincial sovereignty is never an issue. If there is a financial obligation incurred, it is subject to the usual provincial budgetary processes and scrutiny. Nevertheless, given the fact that individual premiers have agreed to do something, there is an implicit understanding or expectation that they will deliver on their commitment.

With the inclusion of the territories as full participants of the WPC, the number of participating governments has increased from the four to seven. The size of the group continues to be such that it is reasonably easy for working groups to meet, although it is more difficult for Nunavut delegates coming from Iqaluit. The relatively small number of participants also influences the meeting dynamics with greater opportunities for interventions and exchange of ideas.

With the addition of the territories, one finds much greater attention to the interests and concerns of the North. For example, since the 1996 WPC, the premiers have looked at the general issue of northern economic development. At their 1998 meeting in Yellowknife, NWT, they received a detailed report from ministers assigned to examine the matter. The conference communiqué stressed that "the territories need greater control of their resources in order to develop the North's economy in a way that is responsive to northern priorities."[34] At the 1999 meeting the premiers asked their economic development ministers to follow up on "co-operation in transportation corridor development, electronic highway infrastructure, and in trade and tourism promotion."[35] At the 2003 WPC the premiers supported the territories' request to "restore Northern Economic Development Agreements."[36]

As noted earlier, the constitutional status of the territories differs from that of the provinces. At the 2003 WPC, the western premiers released a communiqué "aimed at modernizing Confederation." Five matters were identified for reform "that do not involve changing the Canadian constitution." One of the proposed reforms was for the federal government to give the Northwest Territories and Nunavut more control over their natural resources, an arrangement reminiscent of the 1930 Natural Resources Transfer Agreement. Specifically, the western premiers recommended that:

> Northern devolution agreements with the Northwest Territories and Nunavut [be arranged] for the transfer of powers over northern lands, water and resources, including a fair share of resource revenues. Premiers agreed that the territories, *similar to provinces*, should manage and control the scope and pace of development of their resources and must benefit from this development, in order to create strong, self reliant territories that contribute to the benefit of all Canadians.[37]

The thrust of this proposal is similar to the 1930 Natural Resources Transfer Agreement through which the three Prairie provinces gained ownership and control over their lands and resources. Federal acceptance of this recommendation could be accomplished through legislation, as opposed to constitutional amendment. As these two examples illustrate, the WPC today serves as an important forum for the expression of territorial issues and concerns. It should also be noted that the same recommendation was included in the 2003 APC proposal to improve the functioning of the federal system.[38]

With the exception of British Columbia, during the WPC's existence the turnover of premiers has been relatively low. Alberta has had three; Saskatchewan, four; Manitoba, five; whereas British Columbia has had nine. The low turnover influences relationships and maintains a high degree of institutional memory and continuity.

POSITIONS OF THE WESTERN PREMIERS' CONFERENCE

The main source of information on the WPC for this part of the chapter is the conference communiqués. The policy issues that were addressed at WEOC, such as agriculture and transportation, continue to be prominent. For example, at the 1998 WPC, the premiers reviewed a major study on transportation. Among other things, the study, prepared by western transportation ministers, looked at a national highways program, interprovincial trucking regulations and transportation corridors.[39] Another theme one finds is national unity and constitutional reform. A recurring theme is the general subject of fiscal federalism. Since 1990, the western finance ministers have produced an annual report on this subject for consideration at the WPC. These reports have certainly influenced the discussions on this subject at the APC. The theme of trade, both internal and international, has been a constant from the very beginning. A number of ministerial reports on international trade have been prepared over the years. Interprovincial co-operation is also given a great deal of attention. As already noted, with the full participation of the territories, northern concerns are now reflected in the communiqués.

Space does not permit detailed comment on all of these themes. Three have been identified for more detailed comment: fiscal federalism, trade and interprovincial co-operation. Each of these reveals some of the unique characteristics of the WPC. Although reference is made to some of the early initiatives, the main focus here is on the period from 1990 to 2001.

To a considerable extent, the communiqués of the WPC focus on federalprovincial issues. While regional issues are addressed, such as the needs of the Port of Churchill, grain transportation and transboundary relations with neighbouring states in the United States, there is also recognition that many of these issues are of concern to the other provinces and consequently should be considered in a pan-Canadian context. Obvious examples are the discussions pertaining to fiscal federalism and social policy. In this regard, the premiers are of one mind: western positions are to be presented at either the next APC or First Ministers' Conference. An excellent example is the position taken at the 1996 WPC, held shortly before the June 1996 FMC. The communiqué stated that "Western premiers agreed that the Report of their Finance Ministers should form the basis of the national discussion."[40]

The communiqués reveal another fact, the extensive degree of preconference preparation in the form of ministerial committees and reports. While one can attribute this kind of preparation to the WEOC experience, the number of different working committees is significant. These reports and their recommendations add considerable depth and focus to the premiers' deliberations. Reports from western ministerial committees are frequently tabled at the following Annual Premiers' Conference and invariably influence the APC deliberations on the same topic. Thus, as they are being prepared, the authors are very conscious of the fact that these reports are likely to have a larger audience than just the western premiers.

An early example of a ministerial committee was the Task Force on Constitutional Trends, commonly referred to as "The Intrusions Task Force." Premiers established it in 1976 to examine federal intrusions into provincial jurisdiction. From 1977-79 the task force published three reports documenting instances where the four provinces believed that the federal government was intruding into their sphere of legislative jurisdiction. One reason for creating the task force was the belief that, all too often, provincial jurisdictional concerns tended to concentrate primarily on federal incursions resulting from the exercise of the federal spending power, and ignored other intrusions.

Armed with its provincial experiences in the area of natural resources, the task force looked at other policy areas such as consumer and corporate affairs, urban affairs, the environment and manpower and training. The task force examined federal legislation, regulations, the degree and adequacy of intergovernmental consultation and other policy instruments such as interventions before the Supreme Court of Canada. The premiers forwarded each report to the prime minister asking for both comment and an explanation of federal actions. These reports caused considerable grief in the Privy Council Office because they could not be ignored and required the preparation of detailed responses. After reviewing the task force's third report the premiers concluded the reports "had some positive results in sensitizing the federal government to legitimate western concerns." They added: "The lack of meaningful federal-provincial consultation, the main theme in the task force reports on constitutional trends, has also become the focus of many other federal-provincial discussions."[41] The premiers had achieved their objective.

FISCAL FEDERALISM

This theme was selected not only because it mirrors a similar theme found at the APC but also because it demonstrates the extensive degree of preparation at the ministerial level. The 1976 WPC addressed the renewal of fiscal arrangements including equalization, the tax collection agreements, and shared cost programs. The premiers forwarded the western provinces' position to the prime minister. It had an influence on the early negotiations of Established Programs Financing. The effectiveness of a common provincial position facilitated the creation of the interprovincial committee of finance ministers established at the 1976 Annual Premiers' Conference. The linkages between the WPC and the APC were very evident. The regional co-operation of the four western provinces facilitated the more broadly based co-operative approach taken by the 10 provinces. The fact that the APC was chaired by a western premier, Premier Lougheed, was also beneficial.

At the May 1990 WPC the premiers were very critical of the federal government's management of the economy, high interest rates, unilateral federal cutbacks on program spending and the introduction of the Goods and Services Tax (GST). They created a task force of their finance ministers to examine these issues and other questions associated with fiscal federalism. The ministers were required to work to a very tight deadline, as the premiers wanted their report in advance of the APC scheduled for mid-August in Winnipeg, Manitoba. The WPC reconvened in late July to review the western finance ministers' report. It should be noted that this meeting was convened in the weeks immediately after the failure of the Meech Lake Accord. After reviewing its content, the premiers released the report to the public. Among other things, the report recommended the western provinces set up their own tax collection system, legislated limits to government spending and federal withdrawal from certain shared cost programs such as medicare, with appropriate compensation to the provinces. One person compared the western provincial position to "the resolutions of the Stamp Act Congress in Boston in 1765."[42] Since Manitoba was the APC chair that year, it was not too difficult to have the western finance ministers' report tabled at the conference.

Since the first report in 1990, the WPC has received an annual report prepared by its finance ministers. While the specifics vary from year to year, the main theme — the state of federal-provincial financial relations — remains constant. The finance ministers have commented on the effects that federal budget deficits have had on provincial economies. They have highlighted the consequences to service levels caused by federal reductions in transfer payments and fiscal pressures caused by offloading. They have criticized the lack of federal-provincial consultation and unilateral federal decisions. They have commented on differential federal rates of tobacco taxation. They have proposed major changes to the tax collection agreements, arguing for a change from the "tax on tax" to a "tax on income." They have called for an independent revenue collection agency. They have supported equalization and have called for changes to the formula for calculating equalization payments. They have criticized reductions in federal funding for Aboriginal peoples, and emphasized the substantial Aboriginal population in western Canada. Considerable attention has been placed on the need for a review of social services. In short, nothing pertaining to fiscal federalism has escaped their critical assessment.

In their 1995 report, in response to cuts in federal transfer payments, the western finance ministers posed what to them was a fundamental question:

"What will the federal government's role in social policy be in the future as the federal financial contribution diminishes?"[43] They accused the federal government of "manipulating statistics in an attempt to downplay the significance of its action."[44] It is somewhat ironic that the 1995 WPC commenced the day after the 1995 Quebec referendum. The premiers "strongly endorsed" the report and "unanimously recommended that attempts to restructure and renew the country must include renewed fiscal arrangements as a first priority."[45]

The 1997 western finance ministers' report provided an assessment or report card on the current state of federal-provincial financial relations. It acknowledged areas where "the partnership" had been successful, examples being the National Child Benefit and the infrastructure program. Areas that they labeled as partially successful included Canada Pension Plan reform and labour market development. Areas where "the ideals of partnership" were not met included the harmonized sales tax and the Canada Health and Social Transfer (CHST). To them the CHST was "the most prominent example of a failure to follow a partnership approach to improving the federation."[46] Among other things, the ministers argued for equal per capita payments under CHST. They called the formula "flawed" and argued that it penalized BC and Alberta because of the cap on the Canada Assistance Plan (CAP) distortion.[47] In addition, they criticized the federal government for continuing to take credit for the 1977 tax point transfer under Established Programs Financing (EPF), calling it "misleading." They reinforced a point they had made in earlier reports and "called for a restoration of fiscal balance so that the order of government bearing the responsibility for growing expenditures has full access to commensurately growing tax sources."[48]

One can trace the rebalancing theme in subsequent reports. Vertical fiscal imbalance was the principal theme of the 1999 western finance ministers' report. The issue was emphasized again at the 2000 WPC. In this instance the premiers signaled their intention to raise the subject at the upcoming Annual Premiers' Conference. Fiscal imbalance was considered at the 2000 APC and the premiers took note of a background paper the western finance ministers commissioned to "to provide western premiers with an independent analysis."[49] This review in turn led to the preparation of a major paper on fiscal imbalance presented to the 2001 APC. This example illustrates the effectiveness on the part of the western premiers in furthering their concerns through the APC. At the 2003 APC the premiers established the Council of the Federation and a Secretariat for Information and Co-operation on Fiscal Imbalance, and placed the secretariat under the umbrella of the council.[50]

To a certain extent a seamless web exists in the area of fiscal federalism. The western premiers have made this subject a recurring agenda item at their annual conferences. To assist them they have had their finance ministers prepare a report on the current state of federal-provincial fiscal relations. Armed with this information they have been in a position to influence the proceedings at the APC, where today they represent the majority of the participants. As a general rule, the western finance ministers' reports do not present just a western perspective on fiscal relations but reflect concerns shared by the other provinces. Given the very different financial circumstances of the western provinces and the territories, the reports have to be sensitive to the different perspectives of have and have not provinces. There is strong support for equalization, which appears both in communiqués and the finance ministers' reports. The compromises and balance developed at the WPC appear to resonate with the other provinces. There are, as one might expect, exceptions to this general observation such as the ministers' May 2000 report, where they argued that the "western provinces and territories do not receive the same level of federal support for their academic, institutional infrastructure and economic development programs as central Canada."[51] Although the data tend to focus on western Canada, when viewed in terms of policy positions, there is little to distinguish between those advanced and adopted at the WPC and the APC. They reinforce and complement each other.

TRADE RELATIONS AND BORDER ISSUES

Trade, both internal and external, has been a policy issue that the western premiers have stressed since the WPC began. At the 1976 WPC the premiers called for western input into the General Agreement on Tariffs and Trade (GATT) negotiations and for a provincial participation of the federal negotiating team. At the 1984 WPC in Kelowna, BC, the premiers gave special attention to international trade as a policy area linking it to "furthering job creation, resource upgrading and the diversification of the western Canadian economy."[52] They encouraged the federal government to support the proposed new round of GATT negotiations and made the case for provincial participation. They also examined ways in which the western provinces individually and collectively could advance regional trade interests, examples being twinning relationships with provinces in China and provincial trade missions. The final theme in the communiqué was an acknowledgement of the "special trading relationships between Canada and the United States." To the premiers, "provinces have a unique role to play in promoting and furthering trade between the two countries."[53] These themes in one way or another continue to this day.

At the 1985 conference in Grand Prairie, Alberta, the premiers released a joint position paper, *Western Canadian Trade Objectives for the Next Decade.* The paper built on the foundation developed in 1984 and addressed a number of themes including trade objectives, such as pursuing multilateral trade negotiations and bilateral trade discussions with the United States. The paper went on to discuss the advantages of trade liberalization and emerging trade priorities. A key element of this discussion was the need for federal-provincial co-operation in developing and promoting international trade. In their communiqué on Canada-United States trade the premiers "proposed a comprehensive common market arrangement" between the two countries and "recommended this new direction to the prime minister." They were early advocates of the Free Trade Agreement (FTA)! In their communiqué on multilateral trade negotiations they stressed their concerns over constitutional jurisdiction. "Negotiations have been broadened to include consideration of many issues which, constitutionally, are either the responsibility of the provinces or are shared with the federal government."[54] These themes were essentially repeated at subsequent conferences. At the 1988 WPC they gave their "strong support to the Canada-US free trade agreement."

With the FTA agreed to, they concentrated on the Uruguay Round and the possible North American Free Trade Agreement (NAFTA) negotiations. They received reports from their ministerial working group on trade negotiations. If one message was clear, they wanted to be part of the negotiations to ensure western interests were reflected in the outcome. There has always been a degree of concern that western trade priorities would be subordinated or sacrificed to those of central Canada. This apprehension has led to the continued vigilance by the WPC on this subject, the high degree of preparation and the development of a common western position on trade.

At the 1990 WPC in Portage la Prairie, Manitoba, the western premiers met with the chairman of the Western Governors' Association; at that time, the governor of North Dakota. In many respects this was an historic event. The objective was to develop a relationship between the western premiers and western governors, one paralleling the relationship between the Eastern Canadian premiers and New England governors. The first of these meetings took place in Fargo, North Dakota, in July 1990. The main agenda item was "Extending State-Province Co-operation on a Western Regional Basis." Another topic for consideration was trade enhancement.[55]

Ten years later, following the WPC in Brandon, Manitoba, the premiers and governors formalized the arrangement. They agreed to a "Framework For WPC/WGA Linkage."[56] Symbolically, the ceremony took place at the International Peace Garden at the Manitoba/North Dakota border. The communiqué issued in 2000 "affirmed the need for open borders." In light of the events following the 11 September 2001 terrorist attacks, this long-standing relationship takes on a new significance. There is, as Premier Gordon Campbell has indicated, a role for provincial governments in addressing border issues.[57]

Among other things, the linkage agreement called for annual meetings between the two organizations alternating between the annual meetings of the WPC and the WGA. The first meeting took place in Idaho in August 2001, and the first meeting in Canada took place at the 2002 WPC. The US participants in

2002 included the governors of Alaska and Wyoming as well as Ambassador Paul Cellucci. The Canadian ambassador to the United States also attended the meeting. Matters discussed included energy and border issues such as security, transportation corridors and cross-border firefighting activities. One of the subjects discussed at the 2001 meeting was "agriculture, specifically animal health and safety regulations."

At the 1992 WPC at 108 Mile Ranch, BC, the seeds were sown for Team Canada trade missions. The premiers proposed "that the federal government join the western provinces and territories to examine cost-effective ways of taking advantage of these opportunities in trade promotion and economic development activities." The opportunities referred to were assessments of "market opportunities for western Canadians" resulting from the GATT and NAFTA agreements. The premiers also made reference to a proposed western premiers trade mission to the Asia Pacific region in 1993.

The "Team Canada" theme is reflected in the 1994 APC communiqué on trade. At the APC the premiers took note of the fact that "the prime minister and several premiers are planning a trade mission to Asia this fall." They went on to add that they "endorsed extending to all of Canada the western premiers' agreement to work together to build closer working relationships between business and governments to carry out an active Canadian trade strategy on the Pacific Rim."[58] Team Canada became a reality through this western initiative, a fact the western premiers noted at the 1997 WPC.

In the late fall of 2001 a "Team West" trade mission took place. Prime Minister Chrétien joined with the western premiers and territorial leaders in promoting US investment in Canada's energy sector. Among other things the prime minister emphasized the importance of security of supply and commented on the large reserves in the Alberta oil sands.[59] The premiers took advantage of their August 2001 meeting with western governors to discuss the trade mission.

In examining the communiqués from the 2001 WPC one is struck by the obvious importance the western provinces place on the bilateral relationship with the United States. As already noted, trade with the United States has a very significant effect on the west's economy. There are references to the United States in communiqués on trade, energy, climate change and western Canada-western US relations.

The premiers were very aware of the United States' energy policy document, *National Energy Policy,* released just before their 2001 meeting. They noted the discussions between the governments of Canada, the United States and Mexico with respect to a North American energy market. They stated, "It is essential that [all] provinces and territories be full participants in international discussions related to energy."[60] They also discussed "the vast potential of western and northern Canada to be a significant supplier of energy into the North American market."[61] They asked their energy ministers to meet in Calgary to discuss "priorities and objectives prior to the first meeting of the North American working group" and extended an invitation to both the federal minister and the other provincial ministers to join with them. The federal government and the other provinces accepted the invitation and the meeting was held three weeks later. While there was no agreement on a provincial role in the upcoming international discussions, the governments agreed to set up a committee of senior officials to "help develop Canada's position in energy talks with the United States and Mexico."[62] The WPC achieved part of its objective. To keep the pressure on the federal government, the position adopted by the WPC with respect to the continental energy policy was reinforced at the APC two months later.[63]

In addition to energy, they discussed the softwood lumber dispute and wanted to be fully involved both in developing Canada's position and in negotiations with the United States. While this round of negotiations in the softwood saga was ultimately a failure, the provinces were fully involved in them. They also took a strong position in opposition to "the bulk removal of water for export and any transfers of bulk water across provincial-territorial and/or international boundaries."[64]

One of the major items on the agenda of the June 2003 WPC was disaster relief for the cattle industry arising from the discovery of mad cow disease, including the reopening of the US border to trade in Canadian beef. A month later the more general issue of border relations with the US was discussed at the 2003 APC. A news release from the 2003 APC on Canada-US relations emphasized that "provinces and territories have unique relationships with states that can be used to further this objective [an open and secure border]...."[65] The language of the news release reflects and encourages the type of working relationship that exists between the WPC and the Western Governors' Association.

INTERPROVINCIAL CO-OPERATION

From the very beginning of the WPC, interprovincial co-operation has been stressed. For WEOC to succeed the four provinces had to co-operate in developing a common provincial position to present to the federal government. They were successful and this approach has characterized their efforts since 1973. The two previous issue areas illustrate one manifestation of interprovincial co-operation, the extensive use of ministerial working groups to prepare reports and recommend a western position for the premiers' consideration. To a considerable extent the focus of these efforts has been on federal-provincial policy questions. A Canada West Foundation research paper noted: "Arguably, this preoccupation with federal-provincial issues among both politicians and analysts has come at the expense of efforts to increase co-operation within the region in areas of provincial jurisdiction. At the same time it provides a valuable basis upon which to increase regional co-operation in other areas."[66]

Although there is a "preoccupation with federal-provincial issues," inter-provincial co-operation has also been pursued. An early example is the *Health Manpower Training* study commissioned in 1980 and coordinated by Alberta. The report was presented to the premiers at the 1983 WPC. The objective of the study was to rationalize the location and funding of training programs. A second objective was to look at health manpower planning. One eventual example of rationalization was the University of Alberta training a specified number of occupational therapy students from Saskatchewan. This activity was comparable to the program in veterinary medicine provided by the University of Saskatchewan on behalf of the western provinces. Another example was the study of a western electricity grid. At the 2001 conference the premiers "affirmed their willingness to continue to work together *on a western regional basis* to improve the management and delivery of health services."[67]

At the 1989 WPC in Camrose, Alberta, the premiers initiated a co-operative strategy for "sustainable economic and social development in the west." The strategy included a number of different elements such as trade and economic development, agriculture and food, environment, enhancing the quality of rural life, health, energy, education and training, and federal-provincial relations. Many of these themes had been addressed at previous conferences but this meeting attempted to package them together. The premiers released a series of communiqués on the various elements of the strategy and "pledged to have their governments work in close collaboration to implement the strategy."[68]

One can follow the evolution of these ideas in subsequent premiers' conferences. In 1993, they released a report entitled *Working Together — An Inventory of Intergovernmental Co-operation in Western Canada — 1980-1993*. One example given was the agreement to reduce interprovincial trade barriers in government procurement. At the same meeting they outlined a number of ways to co-operate in economic development, such as trade promotion and the development "of a 'code of conduct' to prevent destructive competition for investment." The following year they again emphasized the theme of western regional co-operation in a number of communiqués.

Western intergovernmental co-operation is now an integral part of the WPC agenda. Topics range from movement of bees to waste reduction, recycling, transportation of dangerous goods, pediatric cardiac surgery, public service renewal, and northern economic development, to a western health information collaborative. While there is not necessarily a specific agenda item devoted to this topic, the communiqués reflect the fact that the governments see significant advantages and benefits to regional co-operation. The challenge invariably is balancing the time available to consider the purely interprovincial subjects with the need to address the larger federal-provincial issues.[69]

CONCLUSIONS

There are several conclusions one can draw from the foregoing analysis. Perhaps the most obvious one relates to the amount of attention that's paid to federal-provincial issues. This should not come as a surprise as the WPC is the direct result of a regional federal-provincial conference, WEOC. As David Elton observed in 1988, "The most important function of the Western Premiers' Conference has been that of providing a mechanism and forum for coordinating the western provinces' interaction with the federal government."[70] In its 2003 study of interprovincial co-operation the Canada West Foundation stated that "regional co-operation in the area of federal-provincial negotiations has become a mainstay of intergovernmental relations in the west and tends to dominate formal mechanisms of co-operation."[71] The formal mechanisms are the WPC and its various ministerial committees.

In this regard the WPC has gone much further than the APC and, over the years, has developed a few instruments to gauge and comment on the current state of federal-provincial relations. An early example was the Intrusions Task Force. Today the finance ministers fill that role with their reports on fiscal federalism. These commentaries serve as a kind of report card and are not easily shrugged off by the federal government. Indeed the WPC has been instrumental in causing the federal government to change some of its policies, including the equal per capita CHST payment and the establishment of an independent revenue collection agency.

Despite their preoccupation with federal-provincial issues, the western provinces and territories recognize the importance of regional co-operation. In this respect they have been more effective and diligent in focusing on interprovincial relations than has the APC. Given the relatively small number of participants and their geographic propinquity, co-operation may be more readily achieved at the regional level.

For the most part, the modus operandi of concentrating on areas of agreement has served the WPC well. A virtual stream of ministerial reports and recommendations on a wide variety of subjects has reinforced this approach. The success of the WPC in framing western policy positions has been a result of the extensive use of ministerial meetings and reports to facilitate and focus the discussion at the annual WCP. The ministerial meetings provide an important mechanism to follow up on agreements reached. They also provide continuity of policy development from one conference to the next.

Although the WPC has been an effective advocate for western provinces and territories, one cannot ignore some of the potential problem areas. Chief among them is the growing disparities in wealth and population. While these differences are not a new phenomenon, recent trends appear to have generated a degree of tension among the participants. The tension arises when one province, in this case Alberta, acts as a magnet attracting skilled labour in a variety of areas or by providing services and salaries at levels with which other provinces cannot compete. While one expects some differences, at what point do these differences become impediments to co-operation?

A second problem, and it is probably related to the previous one mentioned, was the recent clash along party or ideological lines at the 2000 WPC on health care. One cannot simply dismiss such a public clash as an exception to the original approach of concentrating on areas of agreement and remaining silent on areas of difference. Given Saskatchewan's historic role in the development of medicare, it may well be an exception, but if they become too prevalent the spirit of co-operation may be jeopardized. Reports from the 2003 APC suggest that Premier Ralph Klein clashed with Premier Lorne Calvert of Saskatchewan over the proposal to establish a national health council.[72]

The day after the 2003 WPC adjourned the provinces of British Columbia and Alberta issued a news release that announced a new agreement, the Alberta/British Columbia Protocol, signed by the two provinces.[73] The two provincial governments share similar political values, a sentiment reflected in the news release, and which appears to be the raison d'être for the protocol's development. Premier Campbell was quoted as saying, "British Columbia and Alberta are both leading recognized initiatives to improve public service and value-for-money through public-private partnerships and other innovative approaches to service delivery and government procurement." Among other things the two premiers are "planning a joint marketing tour this fall [2003] across the United States to boost investment in tourism, technology and energy, and to build closer trade relationships with the most important customer for both of their provinces." The unknown in all of this is what effect, if any, this development will have on the WPC.

A final observation regards the lack of formal structure at the WPC. Through the ministerial committees and their reports and conventions associated with the WPC the annual conference comes together. To a considerable extent one conference builds on the other. As a result the agenda is fairly predictable, although the agenda is easily adjusted to reflect current issues, as was the case at the 2003 WPC with respect to discussions on mad cow disease.

It is clear from the conference communiqués since the mid-1980s that Canada-US trade relations are important to the western premiers. The agreement reached between the WPC and the WGA in 2000 is a significant departure from the less structured approach for purely domestic issues. The WPC has been effective to this point but the new linkages with the border states may lead to more formal structures and agreements.

The WPC has become a well-established part of the machinery of intergovernmental relations in Canada. In his analysis of executive federalism, Donald Smiley examined and assessed the interaction between federal and provincial executives.[74] Although the WPC is strictly an interprovincial organization, as demonstrated throughout this chapter, it acts as a "forum for coordinating the western provinces' interaction with the federal government." Thus the WPC should be considered as one of the newer elements of the continuously evolving system and processes of executive federalism. Ministerial reports prepared for the WPC, such as those from the western finance ministers, are a further manifestation of the processes of executive federalism. They are now a standard feature of the WPC. While such reports are made public they are not a product of public consultation or of legislative deliberations.

The WPC has become the principal mechanism for the western provinces, and now the territories, to focus attention on western and northern concerns and occasionally grievances with respect to federal-provincial policy differences. In order to strengthen its position and to assist it in achieving its objectives, the WPC has been very effective in ensuring that its perspectives are presented to the APC. With the WPC meeting shortly before the APC, the western premiers take full advantage of the sequencing of the two conferences. They use the APC to garner additional provincial support for their policy positions. The additional support makes it more difficult for the federal government to play one region off against another. It also increases the possibility of the federal government taking the position more seriously if it has national appeal. The premiers are well aware of these linkages.

The WPC was a direct result of a regional federal-provincial conference — the Western Economic Opportunities Conference. The WEOC agenda was devoted to economic matters and a discussion of federal economic policies as they affected the west. To a considerable degree that experience continues to influence the agenda and policy decisions of the WPC. Whereas the APC was established in 1960 to consider interprovincial matters, the opposite was true of the WPC. The raison d'être of the WPC was federal-provincial from the very outset. This preoccupation continues to this day. The emergence and development of the WPC has taken place as the APC's agenda has become more focused on federal-provincial issues. As a result, the two institutions have become mutually reinforcing. For this reason, it is fair to say that the Western Premiers' Conference can be seen, among other things, not only as an important institution in its own right but also as integral to the APC process.

NOTES

1. The four provinces are listed by their order of entry into Confederation: 1870, 1871, 1905, and 1905 respectively.

2. For a good overview of both regions see Gerald Friesen, *The Canadian Prairies* (Toronto: University of Toronto Press, 1984); and Philip Resnick, *The Politics*

of Resentment: British Columbia Regionalism and Canadian Unity (Vancouver: UBC Press, 2000).

3.   The data in this section are taken from Robert Roach, *State of the New West 2003: Western Canadian Demographic and Economic Trends* (Calgary: Canada West Foundation, May 2003).

4.   The dependency ratio is the number of people under 15 and 65+ per 100 people. Those between 15 and 64 are of "working age." The higher the ratio, the greater the tax burden per worker.

5.   Robert Roach, *State of the New West: Western Canadian Demographic and Economic Trends*, p. 69.

6.   See for example the communiqués from the 1998 and 1999 conferences.

7.   For the purposes of this paper the "North" is defined by the political boundaries of the three territories, which for the four western provinces is the region above the 60th parallel.

8.   See M. Westmacott and P. Dore, "Intergovernmental Co-operation in Western Canada: The Western Economic Opportunities Conference," in *Canadian Federalism: Myth or Reality*, 3rd ed., ed. J. Peter Meekison (Toronto: Methuen, 1977), pp. 340-52.

9.   Ibid., p. 346.

10.   See *Constitutional Conference: Ottawa, Second Meeting, 1969* (Ottawa: Queen's Printer, 1969), pp. 73-93, for Bennett's opening remarks to the conference.

11.   Ibid., p. 84.

12.   The Victoria formula took shape at a constitutional conference in February 1971. While BC was not recognized as a distinct region, the weight of its population within the west was factored into the formula: "any two provinces representing 50 percent of the population." BC was given a semi-veto. The fifth region argument was eventually recognized in the 1996 *Regional Veto Act*, Bill C-110.

13.   Allan Blakeney, "Western Provincial Co-operation," in *Canadian Federalism: Myth or Reality*, 3rd ed., ed. J. Peter Meekison (Toronto: Methuen, 1977), p. 241.

14.   Ibid.

15.   M. Westmacott and P. Dore, "Intergovernmental Co-operation in Western Canada," p. 343.

16.   See his remarks to the One Prairie Province Conference held in Lethbridge, AB, in 1970. David K. Elton, ed., *One Prairie Province? Conference Proceedings and Selected Papers* (Lethbridge: Lethbridge Herald, 1970), p. 399.

17.   Ibid. As premier, Lougheed did not pursue the idea of an interprovincial secretariat. The alternative he selected was to establish the Department of Federal and Intergovernmental Affairs.

18.   Gerry T. Gartner, "Co-operation Among the Western Provinces," *Canadian Public Administration*, 20 (1977): 177.

19.   The federal government published a verbatim record of the conference proceedings and the documents tabled at the meeting. See *Western Economic*

Opportunities Conference (Ottawa: Minister of Supply and Services Canada, 1977).

20. Blakeney, "Western Provincial Co-operation," pp. 242-43.

21. David G. Wood, *The Lougheed Legacy* (Toronto: Key Porter Books, 1985), p. 108. See pp. 106-10 for Lougheed's thoughts about WEOC.

22. Blakeney, p. 242.

23. *Western Economic Opportunities Conference*, p. 16.

24. Ibid., p. 17.

25. Ibid., p. 153.

26. Ibid., p. 154. Emphasis added. The first comment was in Trudeau's opening remarks and the last was in his closing remarks.

27. WPC News Release, "Western Economic Co-operation," 25 November 1993.

28. Gartner, "Co-operation Among the Weaker Provinces," p. 179.

29. David Elton, "Federalism and the Canadian West," in *Perspectives on Canadian Federalism*, eds. R.D. Olling and M.W. Westmacott (Scarborough: Prentice Hall Canada, 1988), p. 351.

30. Roger Gibbins, *Prairie Politics and Society: Regionalism in Decline* (Toronto: Butterworths, 1980), p. 205.

31. Blakeney, p. 243.

32. Adam Killick, "Western premiers butt heads over health legislation," *National Post*, 24 May 2000, p. A8.

33. David Roberts, "NDP premiers blast Alberta's Bill 11 as everyone's concern," *The Globe and Mail*, 25 May 2000, p. A8.

34. WPC Communiqué, "Northwestern Ministers' Report on Northern Economic Development," 3 July 1998.

35. WPC Communiqué, "Northern Economic Development," 21 May 1999, p. 4.

36. WPC Communiqué, "Western Premiers Support Territories' Requirement for Northern Economic Development Funding," 8-10 June 2003.

37. WPC Communiqué, "Western Premiers Pursue Canadian Reform," 8-10 June 2003. Emphasis added. The text has been edited from "to arrange" to "be arranged." The other four areas for reform included: regular First Ministers' Conferences, provincial participation in international discussions on natural resources and trade, new institutional arrangement to harmonize regulatory regimes and consultation by the federal government on certain federal appointments including Senatorial appointments.

38. CICS News Release, "Premiers Announce Plan to Build a New Era of Constructive and Cooperative Federalism," 9-11 July 2003, Ref: 850-092/006.

39. WPC Premier's Conference, *Western Transportation Initiatives*, a study prepared for the WPC by the western transportation ministers, 2-4 July 1998. For the position of the premiers, see WPC "Communiqué," 3 July 1998, pp. 2-4.

40. WPC Communiqué, 4 June 1996. See the "Seventh Annual Western Finance Ministers' Report."

41. The 1979 WPC communiqués are found in *Sixth Annual Report to March 31, 1979* (Edmonton: Department of Federal and Intergovernmental Affairs, 1979), pp. 61-62.

42. Link Byfield, "Finally, the premiers strike a decisive blow for the west," *B.C. Report*, 13 August 1990, p. 4.

43. "Sixth Annual Finance Ministers' Report," Saskatchewan, 1 November 1995, p. 1.

44. Ibid. p. 2.

45. See WPC Communiqué, 31 October-2 November 1995, p. 2. See the "Western Finance Ministers' Report."

46. *Towards a Better Financial Relationship between the Federal Government and the Provinces and Territories*, report of the western finance ministers, p. 10. Tabled at the 29-30 May 1997 Western Premiers' Conference, Campbell River.

47. The 1990 federal budget placed a 5 percent cap on the increase in annual payments under the Canada Assistance Plan (CAP) to the provinces of Alberta, British Columbia and Ontario for two years. The 1991 budget extended this cap for an additional three years. The budget policy was known as the cap on CAP. The three provinces were unsuccessful in the their legal challenge. See *Re Canada Assistance Plan* (1991), [1991] 2 S.C.R. 525.

48. Ibid. p. 14.

49. APC News Release, "Fiscal Imbalance in Canada," 9-11 August 2000, p. 1.

50. CICS News Release, "Premiers Announce Plan to Build a New Era of Constructive and Co-operative Federalism," 9-11 July 2003, Ref: 850-092/006.

51. *Toward Fiscal Balance: A Western Perspective*, report of the Western Finance Ministers, p. 11. Tabled at the 24 May 2000 Western Premiers' Conference.

52. See WPC Communiqué, 7-8 May 1984, p. 1.

53. Ibid., p. 6.

54. See WPC Communiqués #6 and #8, "Canada-United States Trade" and "Multilateral Trade Negotiations," May 1985.

55. See WPC Communiqué, "Meeting Between Western Premiers and Western Governors," 6-8 May 1990.

56. See WPC News Release, "Meeting Between Western Premiers and the Western Governors' Association," 25 May 2000.

57. See "Ottawa may draft second anti-terror bill," *National Post*, 20 October 2001, p. A6, for his comments.

58. APC, "Final Communiqué," 30-31 August and 1 September 1994, p. 6.

59. Doug Saunders, "PM offers Americans 'security' of oil and gas," *The Globe and Mail*, 29 November 2001, p. A15.

60. WPC News Release, "Energy," 30 May-1 June 2001. They also used this opportunity to "support [the territories'] continuing efforts to secure responsibility for natural resources from the federal government."

61. Ibid.

62. David Parkinson, "Steps taken to develop energy policy," *The Globe and Mail*, 22 June 2001, p. B3.

63. APC Communique, "Energy," 2 August 2001.

64. WPC Communiqué, "Trade: Current Issues and Recent Developments," 30 May-1 June 2001.

65. CICS News Release, "Canada-United States Relations," 9-11 July 2003, Ref: 850-092/015.

66. Robert Roach, *Common Ground: The Case for Interprovincial Co-operation in Western Canada* (Calgary: Canada West Foundation, January 2003), p. 11.

67. WPC Communiqué, "Health," 30 May-1 June 2001.

68. WPC Communiqué, "Overview: Co-operative Strategy for Sustainable Economic and Social Development in Western Canada," 27 June 1989. The other, specific communiqués, were included as part of the package.

69. The Canada West Foundation released a study by Lisa Fox and Robert Roach, *Good Neighbours: An Inventory of Interprovincial Cooperation in Western Canada, 1990-2002*, January 2003. The inventory of agreements gives one a good appreciation of the scope and nature of intergovernmental agreements. Some are bilateral, such as those between Alberta and Saskatchewan with respect to Lloydminster. Some involve the federal government. A few can trace their origins directly back to a WPC meeting.

70. Elton, "Federalism and the Canadian West," p. 356.

71. Roach, *Common Ground*, p. 11.

72. Richard Foot, "Premiers quarrel on health plan," *National Post*, 12 July 2003, p. A1.

73. British Columbia/Alberta News Release, "BC, Alberta Launch Ground-Breaking Agreement to Pursue Common Interests," 11 June 2003.

74. See for example his discussion on executive federalism in his book, *The Federal Condition in Canada* (Toronto: McGraw-Hill Ryerson, 1987), pp. 83-100.

IV

Managing Institutions

8

Managing Canadian Fiscal Federalism

Peter Leslie, Ronald H. Neumann and Russ Robinson

Dans la fédération canadienne, hautement décentralisée, existe un besoin d'un niveau considérable de cohérence, et de coordination en matière de politiques, conception de programme et pratiques administratives, particulièrement dans le domaine des finances publiques. Les mécanismes et pratiques qu'utilisent les ministres des Finances canadiens et leurs fonctionnaires ont un impact important non seulement sur l'efficacité de l'ensemble des finances nationales — d'où le «fédéralisme fiscal» — mais aussi sur l'efficacité des politiques et programmes sociaux, et, par conséquent, sur le développement socio-économique du Canada au sens large. Les zones centrales sur lesquelles l'attention intergouvernementale se porte constamment dans le domaine fiscal comprennent : les principaux programmes de transfert (la péréquation, le TCSPS, le financement des territoires et autres); la coordination des politiques fiscales ainsi que des systèmes et administrations en vue de minimiser les conflits, distorsions ou inefficacités; et le soutien aux préparatifs budgétaires visant une gestion fiscale efficace dans l'ensemble. Les fonctionnaires consacrent beaucoup d'efforts, à travers une hiérarchie de comités et sous-comités techniques et politiques, à préparer des discussions, négociations et décisions destinées aux ministres des Finances, qui, à leur tour, participent aux programmes des premiers ministres. Avec le temps, les défis auxquels doit faire face la «communauté» des Finances du gouvernement varient en termes de domaines nécessitant ses interventions — et d'urgence de ces dernières — et de degré de coopération ou de tension entre les gouvernements fédéraux, provinciaux et territoriaux. Ainsi, l'influence du travail continuel de préparation et de support des fonctionnaires des Finances fluctue selon les relations entre les ministres et la fréquence des rencontres. Les relations fiscales intergouvernementales ont connu une période creuse à cause des réductions budgétaires sévères des années 90, et bien que de récentes améliorations soient perceptibles, les modèles de comportement fédéraux et provinciaux ont aussi changé. Les défis actuels et futurs sont aussi complexes que ceux du passé; on pourrait même soutenir qu'ils le sont davantage. Il reste à déterminer si les mécanismes de coordination de longue date peuvent toujours répondre aux besoins, ou s'ils doivent eux-mêmes évoluer ou augmenter. Comme toujours, un leadership intergouvernemental soutenu et attentif ainsi qu'une motivation politique positive continueront d'être des éléments clés pour la réussite du système fiscal canadien.

INTRODUCTION

Among the institutions of the federation, mechanisms for federal-provincial-territorial (FPT) fiscal coordination are important, but almost invisible. What are those mechanisms? Why are they needed? What do they do? Do they work well? These are the questions addressed in this chapter.

Coordinating mechanisms are led by the finance ministers and various committees of officials. They meet in private, generally without public knowledge of what is being discussed, or even of the fact that meetings are taking place at all. Communiqués from finance ministers, when issued, and press conferences, when held, give only a brief glimpse into the activity underway. Also, of course, much of the preparatory work is done through private correspondence, or over the telephone. Thus there exists, away from the limelight, a "private world" of finance officials, within which personal relationships are formed, substantially influencing the functioning of the formal institutions and standardized procedures.

Fiscal coordination is needed because the federation is highly decentralized, both fiscally and constitutionally. Decentralization has the advantage of promoting flexibility or adaptability to regional differences in public attitudes, values, and policy preferences. These have been forged by our history and geography but are in constant change, reflecting regionally differentiated demographic, economic and other cultural trends. Despite regional differences, however, Canada is a country in which there appears to be broad public consensus on various social goals and on certain rights of citizenship; moreover, there is almost unanimous agreement, extending even to Quebec *indépendentistes*, on the desirability of preserving and strengthening the Canadian economic union. For these reasons a degree of policy coordination, including on the fiscal side, is needed to achieve coherence in economic and social policy. It may well be that closer economic integration on a continental scale, which in turn may be seen (at least in part) as a response to globalization, increases the need for policy coordination.

The tasks undertaken by finance ministers and their officials include (a) mutual consultation and/or negotiation regarding the "fiscal arrangements" — those policies and administrative practices regarding the allocation of tax room to federal, provincial, and territorial (FPT) governments, and redistribution of revenues through intergovernmental transfers; (b) avoidance of the market distortions and inefficiencies that can easily arise, and have arisen in the past, as a result of conflicting tax policies; and (c) coordination of federal and provincial budgets with a view to improving economic management. Necessary groundwork includes anticipation of future policy challenges as economic conditions and trade patterns change (a sort of collective "heads up" exercise), as well as attention to technical matters such as ensuring that federal and provincial officials are working with a common set of numbers, so policy consultation and negotiation are based on an agreed set of facts.

Whether or not the system works well must be judged on whether or not it functions effectively not only in good times but in difficult times as well: for example, when there are budget strains instead of projected surpluses, or when political divergence arises with respect to policy aims of the federal government and various provinces. Perceptions on the effectiveness of the system also depend on a variety of subjective factors such as public expectations, or changing perceptions of what the aims of policy should be; naturally, different individuals and different governments will assess the operation of the system on the basis of their specific interests or needs. No one should be surprised, then, to discover that the provinces and the federal government, rich provinces and poor ones, big ones and small ones, the provinces and the territories, each have their own views on how well the system works. In particular, Canadian nationalists on the one hand, and Quebec *indépendentistes* on the other, can scarcely be expected to appraise Canadian fiscal federalism by the same criteria, let alone to agree in their evaluations of it.

In what follows, we shall look first at the question of why a degree of fiscal coordination is needed, or what tasks need to be addressed, and are addressed, by the FPT finance ministers and their officials. In other words, what are the principal features and aims of Canadian intergovernmental finance? Then we will survey the mechanisms of coordination, and how they work. The final section evaluates the system in light of changing circumstances, taking account of subjective considerations. A major goal is to assess the seriousness of the challenges facing the intergovernmental finance system today, and to appraise the adequacy of institutional arrangements available to meet them.

CANADIAN FEDERATION AND FISCAL FEDERALISM

A basic challenge of federalism is to assign policy roles and fiscal resources among different orders of government in a desirable and effective way. That requires taking account of social and economic realities, including regional disparities and regional differences in public attitudes or policy preferences; it also requires a patterning of government activity that is reasonably efficient (i.e., is cost-efficient in terms of providing public services, and effective in terms of meeting a wide variety of other public objectives). In this context, a written constitution may be seen as facilitating or, potentially, limiting or constraining. Institutions of intergovernmental coordination are embedded within, or supplement, the constitutional framework in order to improve the assignment of policy roles and fiscal resources.

Intergovernmental mechanisms and processes thus have a variety of tasks to perform, even if one considers — as in this chapter — only the fiscal aspect of running a federal system. Primarily, finance ministers and their officials may help coordinate the provision of public services and investment in public infrastructure, and the financing of both. To realize these goals is the main objective of the fiscal arrangements that are a prominent feature of Canadian federalism. Relevant issues, discussed below, are the complementarity and coordination of policy roles, the sharing of jointly occupied tax fields or revenue sources, and the design and operation of a complex system of intergovernmental transfers. (In Canada, the transfers in question are those, both conditional and unconditional, from the federal government to provincial and territorial governments, and potentially also to municipalities.) A second dimension of fiscal federalism, as addressed in this chapter, has to do with the coordination of tax systems so as to remove internal fiscal barriers and artificial incentives, or at least prevent the emergence of new ones. At issue here are tax avoidance, the "double taxation" of individual or corporate incomes by competing jurisdictions, and the taxing, by provinces, of non-residents through indirect taxes. Finally, a third dimension of fiscal federalism concerns the coordination of federal and provincial budgetary policy in order to stabilize the economy against cycles of boom and bust, and to provide for sound or prudent financial management of the public household.

THE FISCAL ARRANGEMENTS

It is frequently argued, especially by provincial politicians, that certain policy roles are assigned by the constitution to the federal government, and others to the provinces, and that revenue shares ("tax room") should be allocated accordingly. When revenues match spending requirements, "fiscal balance" is said to have been achieved; it follows that the need for federal transfers to provincial governments is minimized, because most government programs will be financed out of own-source revenues. Of course, the need for intergovernmental transfers can never be eliminated altogether, as long as there is a federal commitment — as the *Constitution Act, 1982*, declares there is and shall be — to fiscal equalization. This is a federal program, the aim of which is to ensure that all provinces are able to provide reasonably comparable levels of public services at reasonably comparable levels of taxation. The minimal aim, then, of the fiscal arrangements — which in the circumstances outlined would be limited to revenue sharing, plus transfers for equalization purposes — is to see that governments have the money they need to fulfill their responsibilities for providing public services. In the fiscal federalism literature, and now increasingly in political debate, this is known mainly in negative terms as avoiding "fiscal imbalance," both vertical (i.e., between the federal government and the provinces and territories) and horizontal (i.e., among the provinces and territories, or across regions). If, as in Canada, the federal government is the agent of inter-regional redistribution — which is necessary, if horizontal fiscal imbalance is to be avoided — then Ottawa's revenue needs include the financing of the equalization program. In this "minimalist" view of fiscal federalism, if transfers for purposes other than equalization are made or are required, and they become a significant proportion of total transfers, that is a sign of vertical fiscal imbalance, which calls for a reallocation of taxing powers, or of the share of various revenue sources going to each of the major orders of government.

In practice, the fiscal arrangements have broader objectives than those just sketched out. That is because, in the view of the federal government, program responsibilities are not neatly divided, under the constitution, between itself and the provincial/territorial governments. On the contrary, policy roles are shared: from Ottawa's perspective, major objects of provincial expenditure such as health care, post-secondary education, and social security and income redistribution, as well as the provision of public infrastructure such as road networks and recreational amenities (parks, museums, concert halls, etc.), are not *exclusively* provincial. They are also, in the federal view, matters of broadly Canadian concern as public benefits are argued to flow beyond the boundaries of provinces delivering the service.

Accordingly, the federal government spends a lot of money in areas for which the provinces — some more emphatically or sweepingly than others — claim primary or even exclusive responsibility. Some of these expenditures are for programs both designed and administered by federal officials (for example, the child benefits program, "heritage" programs, national scholarships and research chairs in universities, research grants, and public health), while other such expenditures take the form of grants to provincial governments to help them fund a wide range of provincial programs, especially in health care, post-secondary education, and social services. Such special-purpose grants, notably the Canada Health and Social Transfer (CHST) that was introduced in 1995 — which soon, it appears, will again be split again into two major parts — are unquestionably an integral feature of the fiscal arrangements. Their legitimacy may be contested — indeed, for reasons that will be discussed below, that seems increasingly to be the case — but the transfers are in place, and their presence makes it impossible to present the fiscal arrangements as merely a set of measures to support a supposed constitutional allocation of policy roles. On the contrary, the fiscal arrangements have as much to do with the sharing of policy responsibilities as with their funding.

There are, then, two quite different understandings of what the fiscal arrangements are supposed to do. Or perhaps it would be more accurate to say that there is a continuum of attitudes, and that there has been a tendency over the past decade or so towards polarization. At one end of the spectrum are those who view the fiscal arrangements as, ideally, facilitating the separation of federal and provincial policy roles. For those holding to such a view, the aim of the fiscal arrangements is to ensure that governments have the funds they need to meet their responsibilities. The corollary of this position is that as certain matters constitutionally assigned to the provinces, such as health care, have become more costly, the provinces have needed more money, and the fiscal arrangements should ensure that they have added funds at their disposal. At the other end of the spectrum are those who see the fiscal arrangements as a means of enabling the federal government and the provinces to work together to achieve a set of substantive objectives of broadly Canadian concern, though policy design and delivery is adapted to regional needs and policy preferences. The underlying supposition here is that major public services (and again, health care is the most obvious example) are and should be a joint federal-provincial responsibility; policy roles are appropriately seen as complementary and mutually supportive, and the joint funding of those public services not only reflects this, but is instrumental in seeing to their coordination.

Different segments of this continuum are more heavily "populated" at different times. Thus, over the decades, there have been substantial shifts in mood and spirit on the question of whether it is better to separate policy roles or to facilitate co-responsibility and joint action. Real consequences flow from such shifts. At times when the concept of partnership is strongly at play, as during the 1960s and 1970s, there is likely to be a strong effort on the part of the federal and provincial governments to ensure consensus on revenue-sharing and transfers issues. On the other hand, the unilateralism practiced by the federal government from the early 1980s until and including the epoch-making federal budget of 1995 suggests that the concept of separation of responsibilities was more strongly held over that period. After 1995, the federal government tended to move back toward the co-operation or partnership idea, but the provinces had been burned, and have been more inclined toward the separation of policy roles. Whereas in the 1960s and 1970s only Quebec was really emphatic about protecting and enhancing provincial autonomy, since the mid-1990s, all the larger and wealthier provinces have tended toward a more autonomy enhancing policy stance on fiscal matters and governmental responsibilities.

In this atmosphere, it was not surprising that an attempt was made to develop some new "ground rules" for the federal participation in funding the programs delivered by the provinces. In 1999 the Social Union Framework Agreement (SUFA) was adopted by the federal government and all provinces except Quebec. Among other things, SUFA calls on the Government of Canada to consult with provincial and territorial governments at least one year prior to renewal of or significant funding changes in existing social transfers. With respect to any new Canada-wide initiatives in health care, post-secondary education, social assistance or social services that are funded at least in part through intergovernmental transfers, SUFA requires intergovernmental collaboration in setting priorities and objectives, and further specifies that no such initiative shall be introduced without the agreement of a majority (six) of provinces. Governments have just completed the three-year review of these arrangements called for in the agreement. While SUFA may have had some effects on the way Ottawa exercises its spending power (there are differences of view on this point), it is safe to say that SUFA has not as yet had a major impact on the broad thrust of the federal government's fiscal relations with the provinces and territories.

Federal-provincial conflict remained sharp throughout the 1990s. The FPT ministers of finance were at the centre of controversy, and their officials have had a difficult assignment to help their political masters with the important task of adapting the fiscal arrangements to changing public needs and expectations. Arguably, the temperature may have come down somewhat in recent years, although few would claim that a new equilibrium is in sight, or that there will be an easy return to quieter times.

Before proceeding further, it is essential to take note of two basic features of the Canadian constitution relating to fiscal matters. The first is that both the federal and the provincial governments have access, under the constitution, to most and perhaps all major revenue sources. In the case of income taxes, both personal and corporate, and payroll taxes, this is clear. However, this does not prevent sharp disagreement on the sharing of the tax base. For example, the federal government did not look kindly upon the introduction of payroll taxes by some provinces in the 1980s. This was matched from the provincial/territorial side with disapproval of the continuation through the 1990s of federal Unemployment/Employment Insurance premium rates far in excess of the levels required to fund the program.

In the case of consumption taxes, the situation is somewhat muddier, as the provincial legislatures have the power to levy neither tariffs nor indirect taxes. When, as in the early post-Confederation years, tariffs were the most important single source of government revenue, this was a significant limitation on provincial capacity to raise revenue, but it scarcely matters today. In addition, the provinces' inability to levy indirect taxes (taxes defined by the nineteenth century economist and political philosopher John Stuart Mill as those ultimately paid by persons other than those from whom the taxes are collected) would have been similarly restrictive, had not the courts permitted the levying of retail sales taxes. They did this by inventing a legal fiction that the retailer did not pay the tax, but only collected it for the Crown. Thus consumption taxes, in different forms, are available to both Ottawa and the provinces. Most controversial are revenues from resource production. Here the constitutional limitation is on Parliament, which cannot collect royalties from provincially owned resources. However, as the Trudeau government showed in enacting the National Energy Program in 1980, production taxes — levied on gross revenues from resource production — are within federal jurisdiction, and they are hard to distinguish, in practice, from royalties (in fact, that was one of the complaints of the oil-producing provinces, notably Alberta). Even with the clarification of provincial power over resources and resource production under the "resources clause" of the 1982 *Constitution Act*, production from natural resources remains in a variety of ways subject both to federal and to provincial revenue-raising measures. Finally, real estate taxes, although in practice levied mainly by municipal governments under authority from the provincial legislatures, are not constitutionally prohibited to the federal government. Thus, whether the focus is on income taxes, payroll taxes, consumption taxes, revenues from resource production, or real estate taxes, decisions on revenue shares are political. The constitution is limiting in some ways, but in the main its limitations can be circumvented by a variety of fiscal-legal stratagems. If revenue shares are allocated in any way, rather than being the subject of a governmental free-for-all, the constitution is not the instrument; the fiscal arrangements are.

A second point to make about the fiscal import of the constitution is that it imposes almost no limitations on what governments actually do with the monies they raise. As a result, the federal government may and does make grants to provincial governments on condition that the money be spent on approved programs or objects of expenditure. An exception, which is important, is that the conditions attached to such grants cannot be so precise as to amount to "a regulatory scheme." However, the burden of proof in such matters rests with persons who might claim interference with provincial legislative jurisdiction, and as a result, Ottawa possesses a far-reaching "spending power." In effect, it can induce provincial governments to alter their spending priorities and to design their programs in such a way as to make them eligible for federal subsidy. Unlike equalization grants, which are totally unconditional, such special-purpose transfers thus give the federal government an entrée into provincial policy decisions.

In some cases, but mainly prior to 1977, the grants were "conditional" in the sense that the amounts for which each province was eligible depended on its own budget commitment to the program. The simplest of several formulas that were devised, applying to specific programs, provided for a federal grant equal to 50 percent of the money spent by the province on approved objects of expenditure (e.g., care in hospitals but not in nursing homes, or drugs administered in hospitals but not those purchased from a pharmacy — two instances of restrictions that had the effect of skewing health care spending toward "high-end" services, because only such services were eligible for subsidy). Other formulas were more complex in design with a view to encouraging each province to keep its costs in line with those of the other provinces. After 1977, with the introduction of Established Programs Financing, or "block grants" covering the fields of health care and post-secondary education, the federal grants remained conditional in the sense that they had to be spent for certain broadly defined purposes, but were no longer related to levels of provincial spending. This removed a huge incentive to increase provincial spending, and to direct it only toward specified services. Of course, it also represented a shift from the concept of "partnership" to "separation" of responsibilities.

After 1977, in a series of steps culminating in draconian cuts in 1995, the formula for determining the size of federal specific-purpose transfers was made progressively less generous; the priority now was not to expand public services but to save money. What is important in the context of this chapter is to note three things: that specific-purpose transfers have been an integral and important feature of Canadian fiscal federalism over a period of more than five decades; that their legitimacy and underlying rationale have been subject to more or less constant assault from various quarters, especially in Quebec, but recently also from Ontario and Alberta and British Columbia; and that after 1995 — the year in which the federal minister of finance got most serious about eliminating the federal deficit, and did so in part by cutting transfers to provincial governments — the atmosphere deteriorated markedly. Vehement criticism of Ottawa's fiscal treatment of the provinces was voiced by, especially, the larger and wealthier provinces; and all provinces, with Quebec leading the charge, have been demanding redress of "fiscal imbalance." The federal response is to deny that any such imbalance exists, arguing that provinces have access to ample revenue sources, and that if they want to *both* control deficits *and* reduce taxes, they should not expect their choices to be financed by higher federal transfers (and concomitantly higher-than-otherwise federal tax levels).

Thus since the late 1980s, when fiscal "downsizing" began to be at the forefront of both the federal and the provincial policy agendas, there has arisen a new and particularly thorny question: which jurisdictions are able to claim political credit for tax reductions? Paradoxically, this question becomes more acute in times of buoyant revenues. It has been a source of confusion and irritation when, with surpluses looming for both federal and provincial governments, provinces have appealed to voters by cutting taxes — in itself, a welcome move even in Ottawa — but still demand increased transfers on the grounds that Ottawa has been running surpluses and has used them to reduce the national debt. Again, the provinces' rallying cry has been "fiscal imbalance." Adding to the force of provincial claims has been the fact that rising health care costs continue to absorb all available public cash, putting the squeeze on all other provincial programs. Health costs did shrink as a proportion of Gross Domestic Product (GDP) during the acute restraint years of the early to mid-1990s, but have resumed a relentlessly increasing path since then, with no end in sight.

Moreover, the provinces are aware that in an economic downturn, additional expenditures are always incurred for income security programs. In this area, with the abandonment of cost-sharing social assistance under the Canada Assistance Plan, the federal government now is less vulnerable than before, having transferred all that risk to the provinces. Such considerations sharpen the intensity of federal-provincial conflict over revenue shares. When the tax dollars roll in, which jurisdictions get to pay down debts? Which ones gain greater fiscal flexibility to pursue their policy goals, especially when such goals are not (any longer?) the subject of intergovernmental or cross-party consensus? Indeed, even in conditions — now more a historical memory than a present-day fact — where there is substantial coherence and agreement on broad directions for social, economic and fiscal policy, such agreement may reduce, but can scarcely eliminate, the potential for intergovernmental conflict over revenue shares.

In recent years, then, the fiscal arrangements have been under severe strain. The provinces and territories — along with the municipalities — now raise more than half of total public revenue in Canada, and account for about two-thirds of total public expenditure. The difference is made up of federal cash grants to the provinces, a combination of equalization and specific-purpose transfers. It is these two matters — revenue-sharing and intergovernmental transfers — that are at the heart of the fiscal arrangements. As the reliance on provinces, territories and local governments increases with respect to both program delivery and revenue raising, the fiscal arrangements and the mechanisms for their management obviously increase in importance.

In its broadest outlines, the system is a made-in-Ottawa one, but the provinces (and more recently also the territories) have traditionally had a hand, too, in its design. Inevitably, given the importance of the fiscal arrangements, meetings of First Ministers have been a locus for intergovernmental discussion of revenue-sharing and intergovernmental transfers of all kinds, but much of the background work and certainly the technical preparations have been the responsibility of the finance ministers and their officials. At the level of officials — the various committees described in the next section of this chapter — the agenda has been to a large extent set by signals of impending policy change sent by the federal government. Whether the policy outcomes, in the form of the fiscal arrangements, are in any real sense negotiated, is not a subject on which all participants will agree; the extent of provincial input or influence seems to have declined since the early 1980s. This worsened the climate, and provoked a response. More recently, the provinces and territories have been trying to expand their role, creating a political counterweight to federal dominance, by agreeing in July 2003 to create a Council of the Federation, led by premiers, with a secretariat for developing and presenting proposals for remedying fiscal imbalance. It is within this supercharged atmosphere that the finance ministers have the task of adapting the fiscal arrangements to changing economic, fiscal, and political conditions.

COORDINATION OF TAX SYSTEMS

A second dimension of fiscal federalism that is addressed in this chapter has to do with the coordination of tax systems so as to levy taxes efficiently and effectively and with minimal duplication of effort, to work against the proliferation of inefficient tax subsidies and tax avoidance schemes, and to prevent the erection of internal fiscal barriers. At issue here also is the avoidance of any "double taxation" of individual or corporate incomes by competing jurisdictions, as occurred when income taxes were first levied by provinces, and the taxing, by provinces, of non-residents through indirect taxes.

The federal government's approach to these issues during World War II and immediately afterward was to try to gain full control over the tax system, and to provide the provinces with a large part of the revenues they required. Thus was inaugurated a period of "tax rentals," under which the provinces, at Ottawa's request and pressure, gave up their right to levy personal income taxes, in return for federal grants. The tax rental agreements achieved, until Quebec introduced its own income tax in 1954, uniform rates of tax, and a single definition of "taxable income," which was contained in federal legislation. As noted below, the idea of maintaining a similar definition of corporate taxable income was a goal, despite Quebec, Ontario and Alberta operating outside of the Tax Collection Agreements and administering their own corporate income tax. At issue, then, has been the means of achieving tax coordination without a single tax system.

A large measure of coordination has been achieved, in fact, through the simple expedient of the federal government establishing the rules and the provinces agreeing to go along, with compatible legislation and regulations adopting the same or very similar definitions of taxable income, limiting the range of possibilities for the structure of progressivity and preferences, etc. This has been supported by the Tax Collection Agreements (TCAs) under which a single agency has collected personal income taxes for both the federal government and all provinces except Quebec and corporate income taxes for the federal government and all provinces except Quebec, Ontario and Alberta. At first the TCAs were administered by the Department of National Revenue, and latterly by the Canadian Customs and Revenue Agency (CCRA). The agreements are designed to support use of a "common tax base" and for ease of compliance. Importantly, the federal administration has also overseen the allocation of tax income within the TCAs among the provincial jurisdictions. The allocation formula has not been the subject of much concern, primarily because the provinces that stand to gain from allocation decisions are those who are outside of the Canadian Equalization Program (those within get equalized to a standard whether their shares are higher or lower), and those outside (principally Ontario and Alberta) levy their own corporate income taxes.

Usually federal leadership has been sufficient to achieve an adequate degree of coordination. This was backed up through the TCAs. The federal government simply set the rules for the boundaries of departures from the common system that they would be prepared to administer on behalf of provinces. Provinces administering income taxes outside the agreements and perhaps tempted to venture into new departures from the federal definitions were subject to pressure, not only from the federal government, but also from the corporate taxpayers who consider avoidance of a "tax jungle" to be of great importance. In fact, the Canadian system remains highly coordinated in comparison with the system in the United States.

Over the years, the tax collection agreements have become increasingly more permissive in terms of accommodating differences among the provinces in how they choose to tax their residents. At their core there has been, and remains, the principles that ease and efficiency of administration and compliance is important, that a tax jungle must be avoided, and that the same income flows should not be taxed by two or more provinces. This latter goal has been achieved by the simple expedient of allowing each province to claim 12 months' taxes from each resident at 31 December, even if the person concerned has moved to the province only late in the calendar year — a clear disadvantage to any province that experiences a net outflow of population.

Theoretically, the TCAs now allow for just about any provincial policy choices regarding tax structures. Earlier, a single rate of provincial tax, expressed as a percentage of tax payable to the federal government, provided provincial choice over their total income tax burden while maintaining common definitions and rate structures (thus common progressivity). Over time, provinces gained increasing latitude to define a system of exemptions and credits, adapting the provincial income tax system to the ideological or other preferences of the provincial government. Since 2000, the provinces have had first a choice and now a requirement within the tax collection agreements to stop expressing their tax rates as a percentage of "federal basic tax" (taxes owing to Ottawa, before factoring in various exemptions and surcharges) and instead, to levy a "tax on income" or a "tax on base." This allows provincial finance ministers even greater latitude than they had earlier gained, within the tax collection agreements, to set their own policies regarding the progressivity of the tax system — all the way from a flat tax (a single rate of tax no matter what a person's income), to a heavily graduated system. However, the CCRA retains the right to charge the "marginal cost" of administering measures that depart from federal definitions and practices. This could be used as a lever to restrict the range of options for provinces. But as administration costs are lowered due to new technology and practices, provinces (notably Alberta, British Columbia and Ontario) have mused about joining Quebec in withdrawing from the TCAs and collecting their own taxes. This then provides a counterbalance to any unreasonable "marginal cost" pricing by the CCRA. The fact that the Tax Collection Agreements have not been "modernized" to reflect the new flexibility, and to codify the restrictions and related administrative costs, attests to the complexity and potential for dissention that the new arrangements engender.

It should be noted that despite one piece of the rationale for establishment of the CCRA — that is, that it would be more "independent" of the federal government and could be more responsive as a collection agent for both orders of government — and despite provincial demands for a role in direction of the agency, the federal government still appoints the board members. While there is a requirement for representation from each province, provincial government nominees are not necessarily chosen.

The increasing latitude for provincial governments to design their own personal and corporate income taxes raises an important question: what actual or potential distorting effect as regards the location of economic activity and peoples' choices on where to live, does the variation in provincial policies create? This is clearly tied also to the question of achieving horizontal and vertical fiscal balance as discussed in the previous section of this chapter. There is no question that Canada now has a more diverse system of income taxes, personal and corporate, than was the case a few years ago. Does the machinery and practice of intergovernmental fiscal co-operation, while necessarily allowing for such diversity, still achieve a sufficient degree of co-ordination among the provinces — and indeed, between them and the federal government — to ensure that the Canadian economy is not splintered by conflicting and distorting policies?

There is also a second question of importance on this subject: are the tax collection agreements themselves in jeopardy? For several years, Ontario has wavered on the question whether to follow Quebec in imposing a personal income tax completely independently of the federal tax system. It continues to see potential advantages in levying a totally made-in-Ontario income tax. If it does so, would not other provinces, Alberta in the forefront, be tempted to do likewise? With Quebec, Ontario, and Alberta — and perhaps British Columbia as well — out of the tax collection agreements, they might apply to less than 20 percent of the tax base. With the flexibility inherent in the agreements, coordination would need to rest on less formal mechanisms.

Thus the FPT finance ministers and their officials already have a twofold challenge: as long as the present structure remains in place, to make it work well; and if it is broken up, to preserve whatever degree of tax coordination is considered necessary or desirable for the efficient functioning of the Canadian economy. The proliferation of trust activities and the growing ability of both persons and corporations to "move" financial activity and income from one provincial jurisdiction to the next simply through legal structuring and accounting methods also presents new challenges for tax coordination. In circumstances where the jurisdiction receiving the tax revenue is not the jurisdiction responsible for providing services to the taxpayer, the potential for tax havens arises.

A final, and rather different, question of coordination of tax systems arises regarding consumption taxes (Goods and Services Tax) and provincial sales taxes. Activity of the provincial and federal finance ministers again presents a pattern of mixed success. With the implementation of the federal GST, some provinces (Newfoundland, Nova Scotia, New Brunswick and Quebec) agreed to harmonization of consumption taxes (GST and provincial retail sales taxes). Interestingly, this was done in different ways. In the three Atlantic provinces, a harmonized sales tax is administered by the federal government. In Quebec, the provincial government collects the federal GST. Federal attempts to encourage other provinces to harmonize floundered on such matters as the rules for determining taxable and exempt goods and services, the appropriate tax rate, visibility of the tax (hidden in the price or added on), a process for making decisions on future amendments, and compensation for revenue shortfalls during transition.

Illustrative of the work of finance ministers and their officials is coordinated action with respect to tobacco taxes while retaining sensitivity to regional considerations. The federal government and provinces have been able to take harmonized action to lower tobacco tax rates in the effort to control smuggling activities and to raise them again when the smuggling threat subsided and health concerns were again asserted more strongly. Through an entire decade of action on this front, the actions were coordinated, though different in scope in individual provinces.

It is in working through such details that the role of finance ministers can work to the benefit of good governance, despite their policy differences. One factor working in favour of coordination is that most ministers are under similar pressures from their constituents with respect to the various tax measures.

COORDINATION OF BUDGETARY POLICY

Finally, a third dimension of fiscal federalism concerns the coordination of federal and provincial budgetary policy in order to stabilize the economy against cycles of boom and bust, and to provide for sound or prudent financial management of the public household.

The effectiveness of fiscal policy as an instrument for economic stabilization was a major federal objective between 1945, when the federal minister of reconstruction committed the government to Keynesian policies for achieving "a high and stable level of employment" without incurring undue inflationary pressures, and into the 1970s and early 1980. This, indeed, was a powerful reason for Ottawa's early postwar attempt to control the tax system through the tax rental agreements. However, there were always two major flaws in the attempt to make Keynesianism work in Canada, even if one assumes the validity and the practicality of the theory. One problem was that Canada was and is a federal state. As the size of the provincial public sector grew, both absolutely and relative to the size of federal spending and revenue-raising, federalism presented an increasing challenge for economic management or stabilization. The second problem was Canada's increasingly open economy, as several rounds of trade negotiations under the General Agreement on Tariffs and Trade (GATT), then the Canada-US "auto pact" of 1965, then the Free Trade Agreement (FTA) of 1989, and the North American Free Trade Agreement (NAFTA) in 1994 opened the borders to ever-heavier flows of trade and investment. Those agreements have led to ever-heavier trade dependency, particularly on the United States, and to an even more striking rise in inflows and outflows of investment funds. Along with those changes in basic economic conditions have come increasing constraints on economic and fiscal policy. In some cases those constraints result from commitments made under international agreements. But even more pervasively, they reflect market integration, which has made independent domestic management of the economy much more difficult, if not illusory and perhaps self-defeating.

In parallel with these changes in Canada's international position, and the increasing fiscal decentralization of the federation, both of which presented practical obstacles to counter-cyclical or stabilization policy, there occurred a shift in economic doctrine. With the "stagflation" that followed the Organization of Petroleum Exporting Countries-induced quadrupling of oil prices in 1973-74, Keynesianism fell out of fashion, first among a few "monetarist" economists, then among those governments (including Canada) that had taken Keynesian policy prescriptions seriously, then across almost the whole of the economics profession. In Canada, by the mid-1980s if not before, the primary aim of budgetary policy became, as in the 1930s, to curtail spending and adhere to a classical economic orthodoxy that stressed the importance of avoiding deficits and, where possible, of paying down accumulated debt. This was a shift in policy thrust that at first manifested itself most clearly among the more fiscally conservative, provincial governments, and took dramatic hold — after nearly a decade of half-measures — in Ottawa, with the 1995 budget. Already, 20 years earlier, the Bank of Canada had begun to take upon itself the main responsibility for controlling inflation; it pursued that policy single-mindedly (following the lead of the US "Fed") during the 1980s and early 1990s. Its policies increased the cost of borrowing for everyone, including governments, and contributed to the pressures toward cutting spending and avoiding deficits.

With the shifts in economic conditions and in prevailing economic orthodoxies that have briefly been alluded to, the tasks of coordinating budgetary policy — and thus the responsibilities of the intergovernmental machinery — have shifted focus in a dramatic way. At first (say, until the mid-1970s) the primary aim was to see that Ottawa and the provincial ministries of finance, especially in large provinces such as Ontario, did not work at cross-purposes, one trying to stimulate growth and augment employment, the other trying to curb inflationary pressures. This was the main purpose of holding pre-budget consultations, though their effectiveness in this respect was arguably never great.

Since the demise of Keynesianism for the variety of reasons identified here, it has been less clear why there should be much federal-provincial coordination of budgetary policy at all. That does not mean that the federal government and the provinces have no interest in the state of the economy or the vagaries of the business cycle or economic storms that may blow northward from the

United States, or across the oceans. All governments know that, at a minimum, they have to adapt their taxing and spending policies to changing economic conditions, and they have good reason to share the economic and fiscal forecasts they all make, and to receive briefings on the Bank of Canada's perspectives and expectations under alternative scenarios (not least because it is helpful to them to learn what they can about the bank's intentions on interest rates and the money supply). One reason for sharing information is that with the major exception of Alberta, the federal government and the majority of provinces are subject to similar fiscal forces.

However, for most jurisdictions, what matters today are the legislated or otherwise strongly held policy direction for program stability and balanced budgets. These objectives overrule stabilization considerations. Under the circumstances described, stabilization falls more heavily on the application of monetary policy and the actions of the Bank of Canada than on budgetary policy. Overall, budget coordination today appears to have more to do with structural issues (influencing the course of economic development at the provincial/territorial and Canada-wide levels) than with conjunctural (stabilization) ones.

FISCAL FEDERALISM AND INTERGOVERNMENTAL COORDINATION: CONCLUSION

In Canadian fiscal federalism, both the objectives aimed for through intergovernmental coordination and the circumstances under which governments have to work have changed substantially over the years. The three main aspects of fiscal federalism in Canada have been and remain: to design the fiscal arrangements (revenue sharing, allocation of policy roles, and fiscal transfers) and adapt them to changing conditions; to coordinate tax systems; and to achieve a degree of FPT budgetary coordination. In all three areas, over the decades, policy goals have been redefined, and governments' capacity for effective action has changed and perhaps diminished. Fiscal pressures have tightened, the federation has become increasingly decentralized in terms of spending responsibilities and revenue shares, and the integration of the global and especially the continental economies has proceeded apace.

These factors have significantly changed the policy challenges, or challenges of policy coordination, that governments face. It would be an exaggeration to suggest that there has ever been complete consensus between the federal government and the provinces, or among the provinces and territories, on substantive goals or objectives, but the partial consensus that earlier existed has tended to dissipate. Perhaps this is simply a reflection of the reality that provinces have become larger and less dependent on the federal government and its leadership. Alternatively, as provincial economies have become relatively more reliant on north-south trade and less on the Canadian market, there is less consensus on (and need for?) a "Canadian" strategy and more emphasis placed on regional strategies. Appraisals of what needs to be done have become more disparate as economic conditions and the public mood have evolved, as economic orthodoxies have been reshaped, and as the federal government has tended more toward unilateralism, while the provinces have increasingly adopted a go-it-alone position in relation to each other and, particularly, in relation to Ottawa.

Machinery of intergovernmental coordination tends to be more easily developed and to work better when consensus, or partial consensus, prevails. In the circumstances that exist today, finance ministers and their officials are at the centre of controversies that are to some extent of their own making, but mainly are presented to them as problems they have to cope with. The strains on the coordinating machinery that was put into place during the 1940s, 1950s, and 1960s have been considerable. Those strains have led to changes in the machinery and processes themselves — or at least in the ways they have been utilized — as described in the next section of this chapter. They have also led to a set of challenges, which it is the task of ministers and their officials to meet, as regards the constant adaptation of the fiscal arrangements, the design of tax systems, and budgetary policy. The capacity of the intergovernmental finance system to rise to those challenges will be reviewed and appraised in the concluding section.

FINANCE STRUCTURES, MECHANISMS, AND PROCESSES

Intergovernmental structures dealing with fiscal matters and involving finance ministers and their officials have a long and important history, consistent with the critical roles they have played in the nation's public finances. The issues of fiscal federalism they have had to cope with have led them to put into place a set of highly developed intergovernmental mechanisms and practices. Some have arguably been more technical and professionally oriented — and thus less overtly political — and also of longer standing than in some other areas of intergovernmental co-operation and conflict (policy sectors such as health care, environmental protection, or agriculture).

Whatever the policy areas or histories, one can discern several functions that officials, through intergovernmental processes and support structures, generally seek to perform in order to assist ministers and governments in fulfilling their mandates. These include:

- Identification of issues;
- Gathering of pertinent information;
- Development of policy options;
- Building consensus;
- Policy adoption and implementation;

- Administration and coordination;
- Monitoring, evaluation and accountability; and
- Issue resolution.

The work of officials and their various committees, working groups, task forces, etc. thus covers a range of tasks. The emphasis may change from time to time, and different groups may be assigned different responsibilities, or simply take them in hand. The various structures that make up the intergovernmental fiscal system — dealing, as has been outlined, with the design and working of the fiscal arrangements, and tax and budgetary coordination — are a mixture of the formal and the informal. At the apex of the system sit the finance ministers themselves, but the preparatory work and the routine are the daily preoccupation of what we have described as the "private world" of finance officials.

MINISTERS AND DEPUTY MINISTERS

The administration of Canada's major fiscal arrangements is generally the responsibility of the ministers of finance, who also deal with fiscal policy coordination and discuss monetary issues. Ministers are directly supported by their deputies in this work. Of course, with respect to major changes or new programs, first ministers (the prime minister and provincial/territorial premiers) may also be involved.

"First Ministers" and Their Intergovernmental Affairs Offices

First ministers maintain their own ongoing relationships and forums, supported by their own offices and staff. Each jurisdiction has an intergovernmental affairs office (in the provinces often within the office of the premier and in the federal government as part of the Privy Council Office, which serves the prime minister as well as a federal minister for Intergovernmental Affairs).

First Ministers' Meetings and the work of their intergovernmental affairs offices deal with all matters of coordination of activity between the orders of government and among the provinces. The agenda and the frequency depend highly on the political will and priorities of the federal prime minister of the day. Some recent Canadian prime ministers such as Brian Mulroney (1984-93) preferred intensive use of First Ministers' Conferences, while others, such as Jean Chrétien, prefer to meet premiers in more informal circumstances or bilaterally. (See the chapter by Richard Simeon and Martin Papillon in this volume for an elaboration on the role of first ministers.)

In addition to an irregular pattern of meetings involving all first ministers, there are Annual Premiers' Conferences and regional premiers' conferences, involving only the provinces and territories. (See the two chapters by Peter Meekison in this volume.)

In recent years, there has been a large measure of coordination between the work of the intergovernmental affairs (IGA) offices and Departments of Finance, with intergovernmental affairs officials often in attendance at major meetings of finance ministers or senior officials, and ministers of finance and their officials attending meetings of first ministers and the preparatory meetings. As well, reports emanating from the work of finance ministers and officials frequently are the subject of major portions of first minister/IGA meetings.

In 2000, improvements to funding for social programs (under the Canada Health and Social Transfer, or CHST) were offered to provinces by the prime minister at a First Ministers' Meeting, rather than by the federal finance minister (who had not met his colleagues except on a regional or bilateral basis for more than a year). The availability of both first minister and finance minister forums provides useful flexibility in handling major — sometimes contentious — issues of national importance.

Federal, Provincial and Territorial Ministers of Finance

Federal/provincial/territorial meetings of ministers of finance have traditionally been held twice a year, and more frequently if major changes to programs were under consideration. The convening of meetings is at the call of the federal minister, who sets the agenda (after seeking input from individual provincial and territorial ministers) and chairs the meetings. This is an increasingly contentious issue. Provincial and territorial ministers have advocated a system of co-chairs (with a P/T chair rotating amongst the P/T jurisdictions), as is the common practice in other F/P/T forums. While the federal ministers have refused to consider this alternative, the P/T chair (usually representing the jurisdiction which hosted the Annual Premiers' Conference) now has a role in presenting the consensus P/T positions on the agenda and substantive items, which the P/T ministers may have discussed prior to the F/P/T meeting.

Addressing the options and recommendations arising from the work of the technical, fiscal arrangements, taxation and Canada and Quebec pension plan committees is generally of considerable importance at these meetings. Finance ministers attempt to reach consensus, although in most instances the final decisions on transfer arrangements lies with the federal minister of finance and the national (federal) government. Thus the ministerial meetings serve for the most part to exchange information and to attempt to coordinate broad policy goals or persuade others of a course of action. However final fiscal decisions are almost always made by individual governments in the context of provincial budget statements made in their own legislatures, and in Parliament in the federal case.

In recent years, F/P/T Finance Ministers' Meetings have been less frequent. This may be related to the fact that the 1990s became a period of severe fiscal restraint by most governments, and this included significant reductions in federal transfers to provinces. Relationships became strained, and political posturing over these cutbacks created a more difficult environment for meetings at the ministerial (and thus also deputy ministerial) level.

Recent improvements in the federal budgetary situation have resulted in some recovery of transfers, although not to the extent demanded by provinces. Under these conditions, one might expect — or at least hope for — a return to more "normal" relations, with ministers and deputies resuming their former rhythm of more frequent and more collegial meetings. As noted earlier, many current issues in the federation have significant fiscal dimensions involving more than one order of government.

In the past budget coordination was an important focus for meetings. Ministerial meetings well in advance of the federal budget (normally put out annually in February) had been viewed as opportunities for provincial and territorial governments to influence federal budgetary decisions. Provincial budgets have usually followed the federal one, and were often influenced by the federal budget and any consultative meetings that preceded it. Similarly, meetings after all budgets have been brought down were regarded as opportunities to take stock of the aggregate set of decisions and the evolving state of the economy, in preparation for the next budget cycle.

The evolution of economic and fiscal policy discussed above has perhaps influenced the pattern of ministers' meetings. Beginning early in the post-war period, finance ministers met at least annually, and more regularly than any other federal-provincial forum. In the 1980s, federal Finance Minister Michael Wilson firmly established a regular pattern of pre-budget meetings in the fall or early winter, followed by a federal budget in February or March, then followed in turn by provincial budgets. There was usually a short post-budget meeting in June (after the last of the provincial budgets had been tabled). However, with the election of a new government, this pattern soon gave way to ad hoc schedules. Pre-budget meetings were not necessarily held. Some provinces began to schedule their budgets in advance of the federal budget. Indeed, even the pattern of having a regular annual federal budget was set aside after 2000. After presenting its budget on 28 February 2000, the federal government presented a mini-budget in the fall of that same year and then did not present another budget until 10 December 2001. And Ottawa did not present a budget in 2002. In 2003, it once again produced a February budget. Finance Ministers' Meetings became more sporadic and had less focus on budget coordination and more on other agenda items — fiscal transfers, the CPP, tax coordination issues, etc. Several provinces also moved from the former pattern of budget scheduling. In November 2001, the Province of Quebec presented a budget in November, with an update the following March. New Brunswick presented its budget in December 2002, and British Columbia presented its 2003 budget on the same day, February 18, as the federal budget. British Columbia has now legislated February dates for its budget presentations. There has been some conjecture that the federal government might move its annual budget presentation to October or November, which would allow provinces a period to reflect upon the impact of the federal budget on their budget outlooks. Thus each jurisdiction would operate more in a "responsive" than "coordinated" fashion on issues of fiscal policy.

Separate Provincial/Territorial Ministers Meetings

In recent years, provincial and territorial ministers of finance have begun to meet frequently among themselves. In the early 1990s, western finance ministers also began to meet separately and prepared a series of annual public reports on issues of common concern. These reports soon had an impact on the national agenda. After this development, the Atlantic provinces began to assert their interests as a block. More recently still, the provincial finance ministers have undertaken studies and arrived at consensus positions to be taken forward to the federal/provincial forum. Also, they have begun to take coordinated action independent of the federal government. Recent coordinated action with respect to major increases in tobacco taxes is one example.

The P/T finance ministers, in addition to setting their own agenda, usually operate under the general direction of the various premiers' conferences and report back them. This pattern is at play both at regional and national forums. The chairs of the Finance Ministers' Meetings are usually from the same jurisdiction as the host of the Premiers' conferences. Officials from the host province are generally expected to play a coordinating role in the production of reports, drawing on the expertise and work which is shared amongst all provincial officials. P/T reports from the finance ministers generally have a prominent place within the agenda of the premiers. The premiers may give direction for specific initiatives, or they may make room on their agenda to receive reports from the finance ministers. In addition, the P/T ministers of finance determine what items they wish to address as a group to the federal minister of finance.

"Continuing Committee of Officials" — The Deputy Ministers

The deputy ministers of finance from the federal, provincial and territorial governments form the Continuing Committee of Officials (CCO). It receives the reports and recommendations of the Economic and Fiscal Data Committee, the Fiscal Arrangements Committee, the Taxation Committee and the

Canada and Quebec Pension Plan Committee (reviewed below). In the past, the CCO has played a significant role in resolving issues arising in any of these committees of officials, sometimes meeting on its own, without reference to any particular ministerial meeting. However, in recent years, its primary role has been to prepare for meetings of ministers, establishing the agenda, rehearsing the positions to be taken into the meetings and providing ministers with necessary information with respect to options, recommendations and the positions of other jurisdictions. This work ensures that the limited time of ministerial meetings is used in the most productive fashion. As with the F/P/T Finance Ministers' Meetings, the federal deputy sets the agendas and chairs the meetings.

TECHNICAL AND POLICY COMMITTEES OF OFFICIALS

Federal and provincial Finance departments maintain a number of joint committees to produce technical analyses and policy options with respect to budget planning, the tax system and fiscal transfer arrangements. These include a Committee on Economic and Fiscal Data, a Taxation Committee, a Canada and Quebec Pension Plan Committee, and a Fiscal Arrangements Committee that in turn is supported by a Technical Committee on Transfers.

Committee on Economic and Fiscal Data

The federal-provincial-territorial Committee on Economic and Fiscal Data normally meets twice a year and plays a useful role in ensuring that the framework for collecting and analyzing data is applied on a consistent basis across Canada. For example, the financial management system of accounts provides a system that takes public accounts data of the federal and provincial governments and transforms them into a more comparable set of statistics. The committee also plays a role in projecting economic and fiscal results based on budgets and other information. In the latter case, it has performed a service to all jurisdictions as they begin to prepare their annual budgets.

Revenue Issues and the Taxation Committee

The Taxation Committee discusses issues of tax policy, administration and harmonization. As noted earlier, many tax fields are jointly occupied by the national and sub-national governments in Canada. Obviously, the imposition or withdrawal of one order of government into or from a shared tax field will affect the available tax room of the other. Furthermore, major tax changes of one jurisdiction can have significant impacts on another (e.g., an increase in a payroll tax that reduces the income tax base.) The combined burden of independently chosen tax rates is an obvious area of interest, but there are myriad more technical issues as well, such as varying definitions of tax bases, treat-ment of taxes or other levies paid to other jurisdictions, division of multi-jurisdiction income, fiscal year accounting practices, and co-operation in collection of similar taxes (income, sales, tobacco, fuel, etc.).

Under intergovernmental Tax Collection Agreements, the national Canada Customs and Revenue Agency collects personal and corporate income taxes on behalf of most provinces, although three large provinces administer their own corporate income tax, and Quebec administers its own personal income tax.

A major effort of the taxation committee in the 1990s was created by the transition of the federal manufacturers' sales tax into a value added tax named the Goods and Services Tax (GST). The federal government hoped that provinces would join them and have a Canada-wide harmonized sales tax, by integrating their provincial retail sales taxes into a more comprehensive GST. However, administrative and policy differences resulted in only three Atlantic provinces joining the federal government in a harmonized sales tax (HST). This HST is administered by the federal government. In the province of Que-bec, the harmonized (combined) sales tax is administered by the provincial government. Ontario and the three western provinces levying general sales taxes — neither Alberta nor the three northern territories have such a tax — continue to collect their own sales tax, while the federal government collects its GST.

As noted earlier, effective tax administration requires some coordinated action among governments. Matters arising from joint occupancy of tax fields, and issues such as tax evasion though loopholes and smuggling are addressed by the Taxation Committee, with the objective of taking coordinated action. Recommendations of the Taxation Committee are generally taken directly to ministers for decision, with the deputy ministers' committee (see above) par-ticipating somewhat more actively in the tax area than with the Fiscal Arrangements Committee issues.

Canada/Quebec Pension Plan Committee

Constitutional changes in 1951 and 1964 had the effect of transferring much of the financial responsibility for, and the administration of, old age security programs to the federal government. However, under section 94A there is an important qualification on Parliament's legislative powers relating to old age pensions and supplementary benefits. The qualification is that no federal law "shall affect the operation of any law present or future of a provincial legisla-ture" in this field. In practice, the significance of this limitation on federal legislative power is that a province that chooses to exercise control over con-tributory pensions (as distinct from the old age pensions funded out of general federal tax revenues) may do so. Quebec has chosen this option. Thus, when the Canada Pension Plan (CPP) was brought into being in 1965, it applied to all provinces except Quebec, the residents of which were covered — and remain so — by the Quebec Pension Plan (QPP). The two plans were coordinated through extensive federal-provincial negotiation, in which Quebec played a uniquely important role. The federal legislation establishing the CPP provides for joint policy oversight by the two orders of government; amendments to the law require a measure of provincial consent. Specifically, federal legislation amending the CPP requires the concurrence of the legislatures of seven provinces, which together make up at least one-half of the Canadian population. (This is the only program that has this kind of formal decision rule.) In this respect Quebec is on an equal footing with other provinces. It is thus an open question, when policy changes (contribution levels and benefits) are required, whether Quebec is to maintain a policy of harmonization with the CPP, or Ottawa has to adjust its policies in order to harmonize with the QPP. In practice, both have to evolve together, and this requires federal-provincial machinery in which Quebec, among the provinces, plays a an obviously key role.

The CPP/QPP Committee, in consultation with the administrators of the program in Human Resources Development Canada and *la régie des rentes du Quebec*, discuss and propose any changes to benefits and premiums. This committee is the main formal forum for the exchange of views, and it is where indications are provided as to how each government might vote on any proposed changes. It does not, however, have continuing administrative responsibilities, for example as regards to investment policy. This is a role that in 1998 was assigned to an arm's-length CPP Investment Board (CPPIB). It is federally appointed, but the provinces have input into the appointment process. Policy recommendations of the CPP/QPP Committee and of the CPPIB are directed to the federal/provincial meetings of ministers.

The Fiscal Arrangements Committee

The Fiscal Arrangements Committee (FAC) is composed of assistant deputy ministers from the federal government and all provinces and territories, and generally meets twice a year. Most participants enjoy direct access to their ministers and deputy ministers and therefore can present their government's positions during discussions. Their task is to develop policy options for ministerial decision with respect to major issues involved in the equalization program, the Canada Health and Social Transfer (CHST) and other major transfer programs. The FAC may also discuss the Territorial Financing Formula (TFF), although the review and renewal processes for that major transfer are often handled through what is essentially a sub-group, involving the territorial and federal officials.

The FAC draws on the expertise of the Technical Committee (see below), some members of which also attend and participate in the FAC meetings.

Issues that are dealt with in the FAC include basic methodologies to be used for distribution of transfers, adequacy and affordability issues which translate into standards, floors, ceilings and other parameters, and contentious technical issues that have not been resolved in the Technical Committee. The options developed by the FAC are usually considered directly by ministers, although some vetting by deputy ministers might occur as well.

Technical Committee on Transfers

The Technical Committee's primary responsibility is to consider the detailed operation of the Canadian Equalization Program. It meets approximately four times a year and circulates documents between meetings. In this capacity, members discuss the methodology for the equalization program and, in particular, the modeling of the Representative Tax System (RTS). Therefore, they must bring to the forum an indepth knowledge of the provincial tax bases and techniques for developing proxy or melded bases, necessary when provincial tax regimes have different profiles.

The national government has the largest staff involved in this work and generally prepares initial discussion papers. However, the provincial members frequently prepare alternative discussion papers or work with their federal counterparts in working groups to develop the material. All committee members participate in the consideration of these papers. Their specialized knowledge and expertise is concentrated within the committee. Therefore its decisions with respect to these technical aspects are rarely challenged.

The committee also addresses administrative issues, such as calculation and payment schedules, when necessary. The Technical Committee will provide guidance and advice to the (more senior) Fiscal Arrangements Committee with respect to the effects or impacts of adopting different methodologies and standards and other issues requiring policy decisions.

These committees typically carry out their work "behind closed doors." In contrast to the more open American Congressional committee processes, they are not part of the public policy dialogue among citizens, outside organizations, the media and the government. While they report to the CCO and ministers meetings, and these bodies may direct additional work to be undertaken, the FAC and the Technical Committee most often set their own agendas. These decisions are based on their unique understanding of the technical issues arising with respect to the transfer programs, often deriving from longstanding membership in the committees. While the federal government chairs the meetings and officially sets the agenda, there are few instances when an issue raised by any participant is not aired. Most commonly, the atmosphere is more collegial than adversarial.

The FAC and the Technical Committee can and do gain access to outside expertise, such as from academics, private agencies and "think-tanks." The committees obtain information from such sources in a variety of ways: by reviewing published work, by participating in public workshops and conferences, and sometimes by engaging in private consultations on specific issues.

A recent development in the transfers area has been the holding of one-day workshops involving both officials and invited academic experts, who present and discuss papers relating to the policy interest of the officials' committee. The committee then holds its regular meeting, without the outside academics or other guests present, perhaps on the next day. This allows government officials to hear from the experts and debate issues "without prejudice" to the positions they might adopt inside their committee, while the academics on the other hand gain a better appreciation of the current issues and priorities being examined inside government.

OTHER MECHANISMS

Fiscal Program Administration

The amounts and flows of funds resulting from intergovernmental fiscal arrangements in Canada are primarily formula driven. The formulae, especially with respect to the Canadian Fiscal Equalization Program, are complex and involve hundreds of different data series. With reliable data from Statistics Canada, administrative issues have related more to estimations and timing.

Advance payments for the equalization program, for example, are made based on federal and provincial estimates of revenue that are expected to be raised in the year ahead, linked to the latest official demographic and economic data from Statistics Canada, as well as Finance Canada's economic and fiscal forecasts. However, often there are large lag periods before actual data is available from Statistics Canada, stretching out well past the end of any particular fiscal year. Adjustments are made over a three-year period as revised fiscal, economic and demographic data become available. These retroactive adjustments — perhaps triggered by census data or changes to economic variables may be unpredictable and can be quite large, with a somewhat destabilizing impact (due to either positive or negative "surprises" for provincial government financing). This has been an issue for intergovernmental discussion from time to time. The same process of advance payments based on preliminary federal estimates, with subsequent adjustments to reflect the sums actually collected, applies to the revenues from personal and corporate income taxes administered on behalf of provinces by the federal government. These adjustments can also be quite large. For equalization-recipient provinces, the feedback of this data into the formula may provide an offsetting and stabilizing effect.

Another issue which may fall into the administration category is the treatment of tax room ceded by the federal government to provinces 25 years ago.

Both orders of government claim credit for these revenues as part of their support to health care, post-secondary education and other social programs. This lack of clarity — and conflicting political claims — creates some confusion, so that public understanding of "who is responsible and accountable for what" is sometimes blurred. This provides a reminder that in any federation, clear information and public understanding is a challenge. The potential for ambiguity is always present, underlining the importance of nurturing an informed electorate.

The Canada Revenue and Customs Agency (CCRA)

Tax Collection Agreements (TCAs) were mentioned earlier, in connection with work of the Taxation Committee. Traditionally the federal Department of National Revenue had administered income taxes of those provinces that participated in the TCAs, at no cost or at marginal costs associated with province-specific tax provisions (e.g., specialized tax credits or benefits).

In the 1990s National Revenue was transformed into an independent corporation. This Canada Customs and Revenue Agency (CCRA) has more flexibility (than under the previous federal departmental structure) to collect revenues for both provincial and federal governments, in accordance with provinces' increasingly independent tax policies and preferences.

An example of the latter increase in provincial independence was the advent, for the 2001 tax year, of separate provincial tax rate schedules and tax forms, replacing the previous practice of province's "piggybacking" on the federal structure by choosing a simple multiple of the federal tax calculations. This conversion from a so-called "tax-on-tax" to a new "tax-on-income" (TONI) regime was preceded by more than ten years of discussion and negotiation between governments, and its administration is arguably better accommodated by the CCRA, whose practices and policies are more explicitly influenced by all participating governments.

ASSESSMENT AND PROSPECTS

TENSIONS AND ISSUES

The previous sections have outlined the nature and (some recent) history of intergovernmental objectives and challenges faced by finance ministers, and have provided a summary of the structures used by ministers and officials for addressing those challenges and fulfilling their mandates. A key issue is whether or to what extent these mechanisms and processes of intergovernmental fiscal coordination are capable of handling the tasks that a well-functioning intergovernmental system should perform, in light of recent developments and prospective challenges.

Certainly the system has been in motion, and there have been many tensions, including:

- the "cap" on the Canada Assistance Plan, with the consequent divergence of federal shares of provincial social assistance costs;
- the need to fund the CPP/QPP through increased premiums, or to face the bankruptcy of the programs sometime before 2020;
- increasing disputes over "fair shares" and "fiscal imbalances";
- redesigns of equalization and adjustments to territorial financing arrangements;
- evolution to the CHST, with sharp federal cuts, partial restoration and now an intent to divide it in two new federal programs to replace block grant transfers to provincial governments;
- the provinces' increasingly strident demands for more tax room (the wealthier ones) or more generous transfers (all provinces); and
- the provincial pressures to achieve greater tax flexibility and independence from federal tax policy, through discarding the "tax on basic federal tax," and the advent of the "tax on income" regime.

The past decade has been one of the more contentious ones in terms of fiscal federalism. However, to judge whether our institutions serve us well or are deficient, they must be judged in difficult times as well as in times of relative affluence. The post war period from the 1950s through the 1970s can be seen in retrospect as a time when the federal government and the provinces were enjoying a solid fiscal position and were building new social programs. Few would argue that the finance ministers did not play a key role during those halcyon days.

In the late 1970s, fiscal pressures began to build and by the 1990s there was a consensus from most governments and the public that restraint and restructuring were needed in order to restore the fiscal health of both orders of government and of the nation as a whole. Service costs needed to be restrained and taxes needed to be reduced. Again, the finance ministers were central, but there was dissention and more unilateralism than in the past. Agreements, such as the CPP/QPP restructuring and the change from "tax-on-tax" to "tax-on-income," were less "newsworthy" than the unilateral action on the CHST, disagreements on the fiscal imbalance issue, and especially on the appropriateness of federal or provincial tax cuts at a time when health care and other social programs were underfunded. Occasionally, as with the restoration of CHST funding late in the decade, the finance ministers appeared to be less in charge of the process than they had been at any time in the modern era.

However, by the end of the century, deficits had been tamed, tax rates were lower and restoration of funding to social programs had begun. Canada appeared to have succeeded in these tasks, while many industrial nations had not yet turned their fortunes around to the same degree.

If it appeared that the country just managed to muddle through, was it because the institutions were deficient? Or had they proven capable of surviving through a very tough spell? Had the work of finance ministers and their officials contributed to the successes, despite the tensions which were apparent for all to see? Or could the conflict and disruption have been less if there had been better intergovernmental mechanisms for analysis and discussion, for the setting of national goals, and for dispute settlement? Perhaps the best judge of that is the public at large.

Though most issues of this kind receive attention from the media and the public, public scrutiny and debate on issues of intergovernmental fiscal relations is less robust than one might anticipate given the material available. Yet financing health care and post-secondary education, tax competitiveness and harmonization, and even more abstract concepts such as fiscal imbalance can be "newsworthy" on virtually a day-by-day basis. Informed opinion is important, because it will probably remain true that the nitty-gritty, highly political and highly technical aspects of intergovernmental fiscal initiatives and negotiations will be hammered out largely out of public view, with finance ministers relying on support and expertise from their officials, who in turn will continue to strive for mutual understanding and compatible positions across governments. Some of the issues they currently face are outlined below, many being left over from the tumultuous past decade.

Revenue-Related Issues

One of the key developments of the past 25 years, beginning with the "tax transfer" as EPF was introduced, has been the replacement of federal government support with provincial own-source revenues. This greater provincial "fiscal independence" has nevertheless created tensions. Relevant perspectives and opinions include:

- The federal government has little practical or moral authority to propose national initiatives or prescribe national standards, when it is contributing much less of the revenue;

- Toward the end of the 1990s, the growing disparities between Alberta and the rest of Canada had begun to engender an unhealthy form of tax competition. Lower tax rates in Alberta may provide adequate funding for social programs. However, some provinces had been unable both to meet the competition and to maintain the social safety net. As a result, provinces have called for a strengthening of the Fiscal Equalization Program.

- The move by provinces to levy personal income tax on income (TONI), rather than on basic federal tax, has wiped out one automatic element of tax harmonization. Furthermore, the inability to conclude new tax agreements to reflect the new TONI arrangements raises the threat that more provinces may withdraw from the CCRA. Greater co-operative effort will be needed to avoid a "tax jungle" with different rules for establishing taxable income, different tax credits and a potential for different treatment of the same income when it is allocated to different jurisdictions.

While some federal and provincial players have begun to question the reduced role for the federal government, others press for further decentralization and disentanglement of the federal government from the financing of provincial programs. In 2002, the Séguin Commission recommended to the Government of Quebec that the federal government cede the GST to provinces in order to enable them to fund health care pressures, citing the imbalance between the revenue sources available to the two orders of government and their responsibilities.

Alternatives to the proposal of the Séguin Commission are increases by provinces in existing taxes and fees (coincident with federal tax reductions), a further retrenchment of provincial programs and greater reliance on the private sector to provide "social insurance," particularly for the rapidly growing costs for health care, and/or higher transfer payments (equalization, the CHST or new transfer instruments).

Equalization

As noted earlier, with growing reliance on provincial own-source revenue, the maintenance of equity relies increasingly on the equalization program and all provinces, including non-recipients, have proposed that the program be strengthened. Fortunately, fiscal capacity disparities among provinces, with the exception of disparities caused by resource wealth in Alberta, have been narrowing over the 45-year history of the program, though this progress stalled during the period of protracted restraint in the 1990s. Thus the program in its current form (similar in most parameters since 1981) costs one-third less when measured against GDP, 20 percent less as a proportion of federal revenue and 11 percent less against total public sector expenditure than it did 22 years ago, and this despite the fact that provincial own-source revenues have grown strongly and there are now eight recipients, including British Columbia. Some would take this as strong evidence that the program works to create equity without creating disincentives against efficient economic development or fiscal policy.

Affordability with respect to strengthening the current equalization program would appear to rest as much on which provinces are recipients (British

Columbia now in, Saskatchewan moving out), than the cost of changing its design. Recently proposed changes include removal of the ceiling on growth in payout levels, tax base measurement changes, and improving revenue coverage. Of course, this is not a new phenomenon. In the late 1970s, concern that Ontario could become a recipient and thus dramatically increase the program's cost led to the introduction of a five-province standard. At the present time, only a change to include Alberta's resource revenue in the standard would be likely to raise the relative cost of the program to its 1980s level. Major technical changes such as moving to a "macro approach" from the current Representative Tax System could have major impacts on the sum and distribution of entitlements, and seem unlikely to be pursued in the next renewal, scheduled for 2004.

Health Care and the CHST

Health care funding continues as the number one public policy issue. It is also one of the two major issues in fiscal federalism in Canada, with equalization being the other. Therefore, it is surprising, and perhaps an indication that the institutional structures of the finance ministers are inadequate or have been so weakened by the strains of the past decade, that finance ministers have not been "centre stage" in the debate, at least at the federal/provincial/territorial level. They have been more active in preparing the stage with studies and options presented to the premiers.

The Romanow Royal Commission, the Senate Committee study (the "Kirby Report") and many other initiatives have come along since mid-2002. Negotiations to address the funding issues have resulted in "arrangements" (as opposed to "agreements") hammered out at First Ministers' Conferences in 1999 and 2002. In what provinces call "good first steps," the federal government has begun to provide increased support to health care. However, there has been no signal that the federal government will adhere to the requests of provinces and territories that further major funding be provided in an unconditional manner through the CHST. And health care funding is not the only issue involved here. Some would like to see the CHST block fund abandoned in favour of transfer payments applied to specific program areas and goals. Clearly, such a plan would come under considerable attack from defenders of provincial authority, particularly in Quebec and parts of western Canada.

It is not at all clear whether the finance ministers will reassert their once-dominant position with respect to the fiscal arrangements. If they do so, this will still leave matters of program direction, setting national standards, inducements and penalties, etc., to other ministers, but they will operate within a fiscal framework established by first ministers, largely under the influence of their respective ministers of finance.

Fiscal Stabilization

Arising more recently on the provincial/territorial agenda has been the issue of restoring a role for the federal government in providing fiscal stabilization. There are at least two major aspects to this issue. The first is a matter of ensuring that counter-cyclical fiscal policy remains an option available to Canadian governments and that the social safety net programs provided by provinces are not subject to unnecessary restraint and expansion cycles. This could require the federal government to shoulder more of the costs in a downturn (essentially reversing the policy course adopted when the federal government abandoned social service cost-sharing under the Canada Assistance Plan). Alternatively or additionally, it could require providing meaningful revenue guarantees, a policy also virtually abandoned with the restructuring of the fiscal stabilization program in 1991.

The other aspect is to provide protection against the unpredictable swings in provincial entitlements under the tax collection and transfer programs. As noted earlier, the system of advance payments and subsequent adjustments can result in large revenue "shocks." Balanced budget legislation in several provinces provides increasing pressure to ensure that the instability of provincial revenues as occurred in the 1990s is not repeated in the current decade.

Initiatives Outside of the Traditional Fiscal Arrangements

A new perspective on the potential role of the "third order of government," i.e., the municipal sector and large city governments in particular, is creating issues and debates regarding urban governments. Some provinces rearranged both responsibility and funding roles vis-à-vis municipalities, causing significant controversy and uncertainty. These changes are still being debated even while being implemented: tensions, protests, frustration and frayed relationships are still the order of the day between many municipal governments and boards (health, education) and their provincial "paymasters."

There is a large backlog of public capital at all levels, including:

- Defense
- Public housing
- National road transportation system
- Post-secondary institutions, including research facilities and equipment
- Health care — equipment, seniors' facilities
- Urban infrastructure — road, mass transit, water and sewage.

As a result of the above configuration of issues and pressures, the federal government seems to be (once again as in many periods in the past) seeking creative ways to play a role in educational, infrastructure and related municipal concerns. In the background is a growing belief in the powerful role to be played by cities ("urban agglomerations") in the changing global economic order, adding to a myriad of already familiar concerns: aging facilities, new transportation and communications requirements, and, in general, pressures of rapid urban growth.

Some of the significant recent federal budget surpluses that have not been "deployed" to tax or debt reductions have been channelled into special funds to promote innovation research and programs, university scholarships, senior academic appointments ("Chairs"), research "centres of excellence," health research institutes, and others. Such initiatives provide more direct federal linkages to and participation in priority areas that otherwise — and at other times — might have been pursued more indirectly through cost-shared transfer programs or broader fiscal transfers.

Some of these initiatives and funds can be seen as creative inventions whereby multi-year investment activities have been financed in advance in a form of "endowments." However, they have been attracting accountability concerns and complaints from the auditor general, since they are structured so that their management, and thus also the deployment of funds, are removed from direct parliamentary scrutiny. Debate is currently active respecting the appropriateness of such mechanisms, and more stringent accountability requirements are being implemented.

PROSPECTS AND CHALLENGES

This chapter has examined the functioning of finance ministers and the institutions supporting fiscal federalism. It has been noted that there have been agreements and successes in conduct of fiscal policy. However, during the past two decades, there has been more unilateral action and more public dissention among ministers. More issues seem to be in a perpetual state of review and irresolution than in the previous two decades.

What are the reasons for the apparent weakening in the role of the joint federal/provincial finance "machinery"? Has the strengthening of the P/T consensus completely changed the dynamics of these meetings? Was the behaviour of the separatist Quebec government a major factor? Are these "shifts" simply a function of the period of acute restraint which now appears to be behind us? Or, have the personalities of the day played a determining role, both at finance and at the first ministers' level? While it is difficult to be definitive, some impressions emerge from the material in this chapter.

Arguably there has been a decline, over the past ten years in particular, in the ability of F/P/T finance ministers to be a galvanizing force in the nation, exercising collective stewardship of the nation's public finances.

- With respect to the coordination of budget policy, the seemingly coordinated tax reductions and attacks on deficits were actually, in the main, a result of both orders of government reacting to similar pressures and opportunities. Indeed, the similar approaches to tax reductions taken by the Ontario and federal governments appear to have been the root of much mutual animosity, with both orders of government claiming credit for tax reductions but blaming the other for deteriorating health care, urban decay and other issues.

- The agreement on tax on income and the partial harmonization of sales taxes (Quebec and east) suggest a minor degree of success with respect to tax harmonization, though with potential for future difficulties and challenges as provinces move to take greater control of their respective tax structures.

- Finance ministers have not come to any recent, significant agreements, either on specifics or on broad frameworks, with respect to federal government transfer payments. There have been extensions of the equalization arrangements, but with dissent on many technical issues.

- Considerable action has moved to the First Ministers Forum, as with the 1999 pre-election CHST deal and the 2002 First Ministers Health Arrangement.

In terms of process, F/P/T finance ministers have been meeting infrequently, with as little media attention as possible. On the other hand, the CCO (deputy ministers) and various sub-committees, while almost irrelevant to the ministers' sporadic meetings, remain functional and prepared to support any new joint initiatives of finance ministers. They have played a role as support to the intergovernmental affairs offices and first ministers. They are heavily involved in renewal of the equalization program. Behind the scenes, they were instrumental in developing a coordinated response to a major federal accounting error, which resulted in overpayments of income tax and equalization entitlements to provinces.

Importantly, the provinces have grown less dependent on the federal government. Federal transfers are a much less significant part of the provincial budgets, especially in the larger, more affluent provinces. The dynamics at play in the federation, not the least of which is to improve relations with the Province of Quebec, are such that the federal government is far more judicious than in the past in using its "spending power" to leverage provincial government expenditures. Furthermore, on the one hand, provinces are more cognizant of the need to have regional policies which respond to the realities of their economies and their reliance on north-south trade, rather than on the Canadian market. On the other, they are more prepared to engage with each other (without the federal government at the table) on economic and social issues and in balancing policies which respect different regional emphases.

In conclusion, Canadians should not become complacent about the ability of their governments to "muddle through" the challenges ahead. The challenges are not becoming easier or simpler. There are serious horizontal and vertical imbalances which arguably will threaten Canada's ability to continue the social safety net programs built up in the post-war period. Coordination of tax systems in the manner achieved 50 years ago (tax harmonization with federal rules, etc.) is not acceptable to the provincial governments in an era when provinces and municipalities raise most of the revenue and there is the potential for huge interprovincial differences in tax rates. Reallocation of tax room (together with a strengthened equalization effort), will become a source of even greater pressure, not only in light of Quebec's fiscal agenda, but also in dealing with the fiscal imbalance created by Alberta's growing fiscal superiority. If there are to be national standards in areas of provincial jurisdiction, they may have to be negotiated among the provinces, with the federal government perhaps playing mediating or even policing roles. The federal government might be able to apply some leverage, but provinces have little patience or even ability to accept tied funding which increases costs without matching revenue increases.

As noted earlier there are other major issues with fiscal dimensions on the horizon — a new deal for urban governments, infrastructure renewal, agricultural support, environmental initiatives in response to the Kyoto Accord, and our response to trade disputes. In short, the future looks to be as challenging as the past two decades and quite unlike the period of the relatively benign 1950s and 1960s, when the main game was to agree on new programs financed by the rapidly growing bounty from taxes already in place.

If disputes arise, it appears quite clear that Canada cannot look toward two avenues for dispute resolution that have proven useful in other federations. First, there is a lack of cohesion of political parties at the federal and provincial level, and second, we have little practice or tradition of seeking and receiving judicial resolution of intergovernmental conflicts.

In the past, Canadians have been quite well served by ongoing intergovernmental mechanisms and practices, and have been creative in developing new structures to meet new or changing needs. It may be that the structures now in place, in particular those of the finance ministers and their officials as discussed in this chapter, including the new and strengthening provincial/territorial forums, will be up to the challenge of establishing collaborative action based on greater unity of purpose and common goals. Or perhaps provincial-territorial forums might at least be able to broker acceptable compromises with respect to fiscal arrangements, reflecting diverse goals.

Some might argue, as insurance, that we should consider evolving new institutional structures to guide and assist finance ministers in this role. For example, consideration could be given to:

- Establishing more firm rules for federal funding in areas of provincial jurisdiction, such as those provided for in the SUFA agreement;
- Developing some dispute resolution mechanism(s). Their structure might take different forms. For example, they might be binding or reliant on moral suasion, independent or appointed by governments, etc.; and
- Developing new forums with a broader spectrum of players: for example, including municipal representatives.

Examining our system of intergovernmental fiscal relations (writ large and encompassing non-governmental institutions and the public) suggests that Canada has the flexibility and the tools to address the challenges ahead. We have a base of existing structures that has evolved over time and continues to evolve. We can rely on these or add to them, with necessity playing its usual role as the mother of invention. However, no machinery, no matter how well designed, can of itself resolve fundamental conflict when intractable issues come to the fore. They may do so as a result of major changes in the Canadian, North American, and global economies, or of intensified conflict within the federation at the political level, or both factors together. This elementary observation merely underscores an obvious fact: that enlightened leadership and marshalling toward unity of purpose can ease the path we follow. Well-designed institutions and coordinating mechanisms may make it easier to grapple with difficult policy problems and challenges, but are no panacea, nor a substitute for political will and sustained, attentive intergovernmental leadership.

9

Intergovernmental Officials in Canada

Gregory J. Inwood, Carolyn M. Johns and Patricia L. O'Reilly

Comme c'est le cas dans tous les domaines de la gouvernance contemporaine, le fédéralisme a dû faire face à un paysage en transformation rapide. Ce chapitre évalue la gestion des relations intergouvernementales en examinant le profil et le travail des représentants intergouvernementaux à la lumière des récentes réformes administratives. Pour ce faire, il combine les résultats d'un sondage et ceux d'entrevues menées avec de hauts fonctionnaires d'organismes centraux provinciaux et fédéraux et des ministères de la Santé, de l'Environnement et du Commerce, dans le but de mettre à jour et de réévaluer la littérature didactique sur leurs rôles et fonctions. Il donne aussi la perspective de ces fonctionnaires sur l'avenir des relations intergouvernementales. Le chapitre en vient à la conclusion que le monde des fonctionnaires intergouvernementaux a été relativement épargné face à l'impact considérable de la réforme du secteur public, plusieurs pratiques anciennes continuant de modeler les relations intergouvernementales au Canada.

INTRODUCTION

Emerson wrote that "an institution is the lengthened shadow of one man." This chapter examines the shadows cast by the men and women who work within the intergovernmental senior public service in Canada.[1] There have been some significant shifts in federalism generally, and calls more specifically for a new co-operative federalism in the name of reinventing government. The current climate of administrative reform in Canada raises interesting questions about the changing (or unchanging) nature of this group of actors in the Canadian federation. What is the nature of the contemporary intergovernmental public service? Is it evolving or has it remained essentially the same after a decade or more of public sector reform? Have the character and roles of the intergovernmental public service been affected by recent attempts at reform? Or have they remained largely sheltered from it?

The study of federalism and its administration attracted attention in the 1970s and 1980s at a time of growth in intergovernmental institutions and interactions.[2] Scholarly analysis of intergovernmental machinery, fiscal federalism, and non-elected intergovernmental officials appeared.[3] Empirical and theoretical advances were made regarding the nature and management of intergovernmental affairs, partly in response to the growth in intergovernmental activities and the emergence of intergovernmental specialists as a distinct cohort of public service professionals.[4] Although research continued on the constitutional, fiscal and policy aspects of federalism through the 1980s, 1990s and beyond,[5] the study of intergovernmental administrative machinery and personnel witnessed a decline. This is particularly evident in contrast to research which has blossomed in the United States and elsewhere in the past two decades.[6]

The past decade has witnessed a new era of administrative reform of the public service, for example under the rubric of managerialism and New Public Management (NPM), which itself has been the object of considerable study in Canada.[7] "Managing across levels of government," "intergovernmental partnerships," "joining up government," and building "vertical and horizontal capacity"[8] have become important components of public sector reform to varying degrees at all levels of government. What little academic research there is regarding the implications of administrative reform on intergovernmental relations has just begun to examine the rationale and factors associated with rethinking government and federalism.[9] There has been some analysis of the fit between administrative reform and the emerging "collaborative model" of federalism as defined through administrative and financial arrangements.[10] But overall the development of this new work is hindered by a lack of knowledge of the character and developments of intergovernmental administrative relations in Canada today. Are contemporary reforms changing, or likely to change, the character, composition or roles of the Canadian intergovernmental public service? What do intergovernmental officials themselves see as the most significant changes to date, and what do they prophesy for the future of their work?

METHODOLOGY

Although we have approached this study without preconceived hypotheses,[11] the methodological challenges of assessing the roles of intergovernmental officials within executive federalism are many and help to explain the lack of research in this area. The challenges begin with simply defining the universe of intergovernmental officials. For the purposes of this research, we used an operational definition adopted from John Warhurst: intergovernmental relations specialists are public servants who work solely or primarily on intergovernmental business. They are located either in line departments or in separate units within central agencies, and are responsible for the coordination of relations with other governments and of intergovernmental activities within their own government.[12] Information on these public service professionals and their world has been obtained from secondary sources, interviews and survey data, but each has its limitations.

Where the existing secondary literature is concerned, there is a lack of recent research in this area, as well as a lack of comparability to previous research. Where elite interviews are concerned, there is the issue of the reliability of the respondents' recollections, as well as the question of whether the right people are captured in the interview net. Where the survey instrument is concerned, difficulties arise in terms of response rate, uneven distribution of responses across governments, policy sectors and occupational ranks. Moreover, it is difficult to discern the level of change over time for the simple reason that there is virtually no baseline data against which to measure and compare the results. In short, each approach individually has limitations.

Our solution is to combine the three approaches in a synthesis, which hopefully overcomes some of these liabilities while drawing from the best contribution each method makes to our understanding of the roles of intergovernmental officials. To this end, a strategy for constructing an information base was developed. This involved a literature review of both secondary documents and government publications. As well, approximately 50 elite interviews were conducted in 2002 with senior intergovernmental officials. And a survey was administered in 2001 to 296 federal and provincial intergovernmental officials in both intergovernmental central agencies and intergovernmental departmental units in three policy sectors: health, trade and environment.[13] The response rate of 24 percent presents some limitations in terms of generalizing about the findings. The ability to determine the statistical significance of the survey is limited as the total population of intergovernmental officials is unknown. In addition, the limitations of the sampling method used must be taken into account in interpreting the findings from the survey. For this reason, the results of the mail survey are interpreted in the context of the interviews and the secondary literature on intergovernmental officials in Canada. Each component of the methodology is discussed briefly in Appendix I.

We turn now to the survey and interview findings.[14] This section includes a discussion of the findings in the context of the changing nature of intergovernmental officials' roles in the broad climate of administrative reform and the contemporary world of Canadian intergovernmental relations.

FINDINGS AND ANALYSIS

DEMOGRAPHIC PROFILE, EDUCATIONAL BACKGROUND AND CAREER EXPERIENCE

The demographic profile and career background of intergovernmental officials in Canada is remarkably homogeneous (see Table 1). The officials range

Table 1: Demographic Profile of Intergovernmental Officials in Canada

Age		Ethnicity	
Range	26-57	White	81%
Mean	46	Black	1%
Median	46.5	Korean	1%
		Other	13%
		No response	3%
Gender			
Female	29%		
Male	71%		

Note: Numbers may not add up to 100% due to rounding.

in age from 26 to 57, with a median age of 47. By way of comparison, the average age in the federal public service overall in the 1990s was 41.[15] Intergovernmental officials are overwhelmingly male and white (although one respondent reported his ethnicity as "Albertan") a fact that is inconsistent with the gender profile of the public service as a whole, although closer to its ethnic composition. By way of comparison, in 1997, 50 percent of the federal public service were women, while 5 percent were visible minorities, 2 percent were Aboriginal, and 3 percent were persons with disabilities.[16]

Although it is impossible to trace causal links between demographics and job behaviour or policy outcomes, it might be postulated that the general homogeneity of generation, ethnicity, and gender of intergovernmental officials could have some bearing on their understanding and appreciation of the "shared concepts" that exist within the overall *esprit de corps* of the field. In considering the potential influence of administrative reform in intergovernmental relations, one might also look for congruity between the dominant ideas therein such as adopting certain practices and values from the private sector to the public sector,[17] and the educational background of intergovernmental officials.

Intergovernmental officials are well educated (see Table 2). All but one of the respondents reported having a Bachelor's degree or higher. Most hold a Master's degree (58 percent), while fewer have a PhD (7 percent) or LLB (3 percent). Over 50 percent of intergovernmental officials have training in

Table 2: Educational Background of Intergovernmental Officials in Canada

Highest Level of Education Reported		Disciplines/Areas of Study (for highest level completed)	
High School Diploma	1%	Political Science/Public Administration	22%
CGEP	0%	Geography/Planning/Environmental Studies	14%
College	0%	Administration/Commerce	13%
Bachelor's Degree	33%	Science/Engineering	9%
Master's Degree	58%	Psychology/Sociology	7%
PhD	7%	History	7%
Other: LLB	3%	Law	4%
		English/Philosophy	4%
		Economics	4%
		Education	3%
		Not indicated	12%

Note: Numbers do not add up to 100% due to rounding.

the social sciences and humanities. Twenty-two percent have a background in political science and public administration, while 14 percent come from geography/urban planning/environmental studies. Administration/commerce backgrounds were the next highest at 13 percent. Other areas of study, all below 10 percent (in descending order), were science and engineering, law, economics and education.

Officials were also asked about their career background prior to working in intergovernmental relations (see Table 3). Policy analysis and program management and evaluation made up 63 percent of the prior career experience of the intergovernmental officials surveyed. With regard to the longevity of their work experience in the public service, the duration ranges from six months to 31.5 years in government in general, and from six months to 28 years in intergovernmental relations specifically (see Table 4). While mean years in government is 16.8, the mean in intergovernmental positions is only 6.6 years. The majority, 57 percent, have been in intergovernmental relations for fewer than five years.

It is interesting to note how few economists and business-educated officials there are in intergovernmental relations given the emphasis in many recent reforms on private sector principles and practices. Economists make up only 4 percent of those who serve in intergovernmental relations units — notwithstanding the observation that historically the public service has been

Table 3: Career Background of Intergovernmental Officials

Policy analysis	37%
Program management	23%
Private sector	13%
Political aide	8%
Non-profit sector	4%
Program evaluation	3%
PS management	
General	11%
HR	1%
Information management	0%
Finance	2%
Other	
Law	1%
Foreign service	2%
Academe	1%
Journalism/publishing	2%
Education	2%
Self-employed	1%
Municipal affairs	2%
Scientist	3%

Note: Some respondents checked more than one category.

Table 4: Years in Government and Intergovernmental Work

Years in Government		Years in Intergovernmental Relations	
<1-5	9%	<1-5	56%
5-10	21%	5-10	25%
10-15	13%	10-15	12%
15-20	23%	15-20	3%
20-25	11%	20-25	3%
25-30+	23%	25-30+ 0%	
Mean: 16.8 years		Mean: 6.6 years	
Range: 6 months - 31.5 years		Range: 6 months - 28 years	

Note: Numbers do not add up to 100% due to rounding.

disproportionately dominated by economists[18] If Frank Underhill was right and economists are the "intellectual garage mechanics of Canadian capitalism,"[19] they appear to be less involved in keeping the engine of intergovernmental affairs tuned up than might be expected. It is very possible, however, that the economists, who may theoretically be more sympathetic to the economic theory which underpins administrative reform, may gravitate to departments of Finance and have intergovernmental roles within finance ministries. With regard to the shared concepts of the business world, only 13 percent of intergovernmental officials have business administration and commerce degrees, so the vast majority of intergovernmental officials were at least not originally trained in private sector economics, practices and values central to contemporary precepts of administrative reform.

RESOURCES: IMPLICATIONS OF PUBLIC SECTOR REFORM FOR PERSONNEL
AND MONEY

Under the restructuring and reinventing of government in the past ten or more years across Canada, the public service has experienced considerable cuts to resources. But it is notable that the importance of intergovernmental relations was so deeply inculcated in the federal government's public service reform agenda that among the six key questions of the wide-ranging Program Review exercise was the "Federalism Test," which asked: "Is the current role of the federal government appropriate, or is the program a candidate for realignment with the provinces?"[20] Between 1994 and 1998, after the federal Program Review had been instituted, the Department of Foreign Affairs and International Trade (DFAIT) was required to reduce its spending by about 20 percent, Environment by about 35 percent, and Health by close to 10 percent.[21] Given the overall cutbacks to the federal public service, it is not unreasonable to expect that intergovernmental officials have had to wrestle with declining resources as part of the "do more with less" mantra of contemporary administrative reform. A similar claim can be made in regard to most provincial governments as well.

In the survey, officials were asked to reveal whether they had witnessed a change in either the number of intergovernmental specialists in their units or their overall budget from 1990 to 2002. What is most striking is that in the 12-year period under consideration, the predominant perception of intergovernmental officials across the country was that there was either no change or an increase in staffing at a time when cutbacks were conventionally regarded as the norm (although 21 percent thought there had been a decrease in staff between 1990 and 1995). (See Table 5).

Budget estimates over this same time period reveal a similar set of perceptions (see Table 6). Less than 23 percent of respondents reported the 1990s as an era of restraint or "cutbacks," while half (in the 1990-1995 period) to 75

Table 5: *Perceived Change in Number of Intergovernmental Specialists*

1990-1995		1995-Present	
Significant decrease	6%	Significant decrease	7%
Decrease	16%	Decrease	6%
No change	33%	No change	37%
Increase	19%	Increase	37%
Significant increase	4%	Significant increase	9%
N/A – no response	23%	N/A – no response	4%

Note: Numbers do not add up to 100% due to rounding.

Table 6: *Perceived Changes in Budgets of Intergovernmental Units*

1990-1995		1995-Present	
Significant decrease	4%	Significant decrease	9%
Decrease	19%	Decrease	9%
No change	24%	No change	37%
Increase	20%	Increase	29%
Significant increase	4%	Significant increase	9%
N/A – no response	29%	N/A – no response	9%

percent (in the 1995-2002 period) experienced this time period as one of either no change or an increase in budget over the 12-year period. The evidence suggests that intergovernmental relations were at least partially spared the contemporary "roll-back" of the state.[22]

How do we account for the fact that intergovernmental units were not targeted for reduction of either personnel or budgets? The "hot politics" over the Quebec referendum in the early to mid-1990s, and key intergovernmental issues such as health care in the late 1990s, may have contributed to a climate of maintaining and even expanding intergovernmental units. And perhaps the centrality of intergovernmental relations to the workings of the Canadian political system has sheltered this area of the public service at the federal and provincial levels. Even in British Columbia under the new Gordon Campbell government, the intergovernmental unit was spared from the dramatic downsizing which hit other government departments.

At the same time, though, officials articulated the concern that although personnel and budgets were generally spared, workload still increased tremendously in some cases. Some officials, for instance, decried the fact that although they were ostensibly policy analysts and advisors, additional communications functions had been added to their already taxing workload. Also, there was often concern expressed that the rapid turnover of officials, particularly at the deputy minister level, impedes the operation of the system overall. The attendant lack of experienced leadership and corporate memory was seen as problematic. But experience, of course, is a two-edged sword. While it permits the capacity to become an "expert" in a given field, it also, according to some officials interviewed, inculcates patterns and habits which may make an official less adaptable to rapid or far-reaching change. As one former senior federal public servant commented, "Central agency intergovernmental officials are old in their thinking. They are stuck in executive federalism. They are the keepers of the 'have to' of the mechanics of federal-provincial relations." A culture of professional protocol predominates and overshadows the need to adapt to changing policy needs.

THE ROLE OF THE INTERGOVERNMENTAL SPECIALIST

Intergovernmental officials were asked what they considered to be their most important functions and responsibilities. Not surprisingly, the list they produced was long and varied, but the process-related items that were mentioned most frequently greatly outnumbered the more policy-related items (accounting for the fact that some might be found in either category).

The process-related items included:
- Giving support and advice to their political leader(s) (first ministers, ministers, cabinet);
- Improving the management of the federation and contributing to national unity;
- Contributing to economic and social progress;
- Promoting local/provincial/regional/national interests;
- Liaising and developing inter- and intra-government/department networks;
- Managing human resources and dispute avoidance and resolution;
- Strategic communications planning, negotiating, coordinating and building consensus;
- Receiving input from stakeholders and creating partnerships; and
- Improving service to Canadians and eliminating duplication.

The policy-related categories included:

• Engaging in horizontal policy work and ensuring integration of policy issues; and

• Giving strategic policy advice and monitoring issues.

When asked about the priority of their various roles, officials frequently expressed the view that "we are here to serve the minister," and clearly with a field of work referred to as intergovernmental *relations*; there is considerable emphasis on maintaining good relations — or working relations among various actors (between and within governments, as well as with stakeholders and citizens). Indeed, nearly three-quarters of officials surveyed reported increased interactions with other ministries or agencies within their own government.

The considerable emphasis on process and relationship management indicates there has not been significant change since the early 1980s when John Warhurst noted intergovernmental officials were "concerned with process rather than particular policies or programs."[23] But it also points to an important distinction between intergovernmental officials working in central agencies and those working in intergovernmental units within line departments. While the former are strongly process-oriented, the latter come from more policy-oriented positions within their respective sectors. In times of strong intergovernmental focus on policy issues (for example, health policy in the last few years) this distinction results in the potential for increased tension between the process-related officials in the central agencies and the policy-related focus of the departmental intergovernmental officials.[24] As Bruce Pollard revealed some years ago, this tension is not a new one.[25] If the past is any indication of who might carry the most weight (the central agency intergovernmental officials or the department intergovernmental officials), it is the central agency officials who have typically played a key role in executive federalism, especially those in the Privy Council Office (PCO).[26] Donald Savoie's study of the executive dominance of the Canadian political system also sheds some light on the degree of influence of the public servants in the PCO responsible for intergovernmental relations (and the corresponding relationship within their provincial equivalents). In Savoie's analysis, the growing influence of federal intergovernmental officials parallels the growing influence of the centre in recent years.[27] One former deputy minister of Intergovernmental Affairs in the PCO points to the importance of the policy-making and implementation roles of these non-elected officials who function at an important nexus between policy and administration.[28]

One might expect administrative reform to have influenced the ongoing relationship between the process function and the policy function in intergovernmental relations. On the one hand, given the management and results-based focus of much recent administrative reform,[29] it might be expected to enhance the dominance of the central agency approach to intergovernmental relations and shift the focus of intergovernmental officials from policy to management.

Savoie suggests, for example, that the NPM "has very little to offer on policy." Instead, with its emphasis on private sector management techniques, it speaks to the need for more "doers" and fewer "thinkers."[30] On the other hand, as Jacques Bourgault and Barbara Wake Carroll suggest, as the new managerialist perspective is brought to bear, and the making of policy is separated from its execution, more power is given to agencies and operational staff through empowerment of employees in relation to their bureaucratic superiors. Thus, the grip of central agencies is loosened by giving departments more autonomy, and corporate-style contracts focusing on performance are used to oversee the relationship between ministers and their departments.[31]

So far, intergovernmental officials seem less affected by contemporary managerial changes than might be expected. This is consistent with the conjecture that central agencies as the managers of such reforms have been spared the impact of those reforms.[32] Performance measures, for instance, were only occasionally mentioned as significant innovations affecting intergovernmental officials. Despite some provinces such as Alberta and Ontario embracing them enthusiastically from the early and mid-1990s onward, performance measures are extremely difficult to apply to intergovernmental relations. Thus, measures tend to focus on process outputs rather than the performance outcomes that proponents of administrative reform argue are essential to enhancing accountability and promoting a continuous improvement culture in the public service. Still, elements of contemporary administrative reform appeared at least tangentially in some officials' comments; for instance regarding partnerships, collaboration, strategic analysis, and a more results-based focus to federal-provincial relations.

In terms of the implications of administrative reform, one official reported, "We have gone from a postal box kind of service to greater emphasis on working in partnerships and collaboration, with a focus on improving results for Canadians." Another official talked about the emerging results-based focus of intergovernmental work. The "current period is more focused on demonstrating results of improved federal-provincial relations," he/she claimed, "whereas the mid-1990s was a period of intense negotiations."

Officials also commented in the survey and interviews on the ways in which their roles and responsibilities had changed in the time they had worked in intergovernmental relations. Consistent with the view that the focus on formal constitutional reform has given way to non-constitutional bargaining and negotiation, about one-third of respondents regard constitutional reform as insignificant for the foreseeable future (see Table 8). Yet one-quarter still think formal constitutional reform remains a significant tool for intergovernmental relations. But overall, officials reported a decline in time spent on the constitutional file, while fiscal matters continued to be important. One official reported "more emphasis on co-operative decision-making, less on confrontational jurisdictional issues."

Resources and workload issues were also related to shifts in the roles of intergovernmental officials. For some, the move to a more strategic and analytical role was important. Said one western observer, "Due to cuts followed by no growth, [we] need to be more strategic in terms of involvement of staff in process undertakings. We can no longer be 'on' every issue." Another official reported "a more strategic approach as opposed to ad hoc, issue-by-issue approach" as a noticeable change. Another pointed to an "increase in strategic analysis (for example, scenario building), and an increase in comparative analysis (in comparison with other federal countries)," while another commented that these shifts also were related to rank, saying, "As I moved to positions of increasing responsibility, my role changed from communicating positions to helping determine the strategic/policy positions of government."

Many officials complained of the increased bureaucratization of intergovernmental relations. As one official said, "The number of intergovernmental committees has risen exponentially. In fact, if we were to spend all of our time at IG meetings, we would rarely be in the office." Others at the more senior level of the public service noted more frequent and sustained contacts and negotiations with other governments, and more time spent on multilateral as opposed to bilateral relations. One official reported that "intergovernmental relations started with just myself in 1986, doing everything from filing clerk to deputy minister." Today, that official's roles are greatly expanded.

Trends in executive federalism reveal a steady increase in the number of ministerial, and especially officials', meetings.[33] Through the 1970s and 1980s the frequency of officials' meetings consistently outnumbered ministerial meetings.[34] There is some evidence, however, that the meetings of administrative officials dropped after the early 1990s, when governments were focusing on public sector reform under conditions of fiscal constraint. But it is difficult to attribute this decline in meetings of officials to public sector reform as significant events such as the constitutional negotiations were occurring simultaneously. Also during this period the *ministerial* meetings were more numerous than *senior officials'* meetings.[35] Part of the impetus behind administrative reform in the 1990s was the feeling that public servants had become too powerful in relation to the politicians. In other words, the relationship had strayed too far from the precepts of the politics-administration dichotomy, and the imbalance had to be righted.

Between April 1999 and March 2000 there were 61 federal-provincial-territorial meetings covering almost all fields of governmental activity: 26 of these meetings were among senior officials and 35 among ministers.[36] However, there is some evidence from our interviews that meetings and more informal communications of intergovernmental officials are increasing.

One relative constant in comparing the roles of officials under current conditions of administrative reform to those of 20 and 30 years ago is the politicized role of officials. Ken Kernaghan and David Siegel suggest that intergovernmental officials are unlike other public servants in the extent to which they are required and expected to assimilate political decision-making into their roles. "Both scholars and practitioners of intergovernmental relations have perceived a tendency among intergovernmental officials to become somewhat more politicized than other public servants," they argue, since "in the course of intergovernmental negotiations, the line between explanation and defence becomes blurred. As a result, intergovernmental officials tend to be more involved in politics in the broad sense of that term."[37]

When asked in interviews where the site of decision-making rests in the system, senior intergovernmental officials began their answer by affirming the authority of their minister or government, but then went on to ascribe a considerable degree of decision-making *in practice* to the intergovernmental bureaucracy. The sheer volume of federal-provincial interactions within the context of executive federalism underlines the necessity of officials' prominent place. As with other portfolios, the physical and mental limitations preclude the ability of any single minister to master all the briefs before her or him. Heavy reliance on officials is a requisite of the job for ministers, and this reliance opens the door for the public servant to engage in actual decision-making, rather than just the tendering of advice. Yet even the officials themselves often cannot keep up with the volume of work. As several senior officials lamented in interviews, the high turnover rate of deputy ministers meant that expertise was lost that might otherwise be brought to bear on policy questions, although this is not an issue restricted just to intergovernmental ministries.

Another notable change in the roles of intergovernmental officials relates to the increasing importance of negotiating and administering intergovernmental agreements. One official drew a link between the new demands of multilateral and bilateral agreements, such as the Canada-Wide Accord on Environmental Harmonization, and the intensification of officials' responsibilities "including strategic advice, policy research, coordination of departmental positions, timing/ priority setting, senior briefings, [and the] federal Cabinet process." Another noted that this has had implications for the work of intergovernmental specialists in intergovernmental ministries and central agencies, in contrast to their counterparts in intergovernmental units in line departments, and stated that "the policy analytical work has shifted from the IGR department to the line departments." Another official noted that this has resulted in "a general downloading of administrative responsibilities as department budgets are squeezed for efficiencies."

In interviews officials also reported a more regional focus in their work, with "regional" implying interprovincial and international as well as federal-provincial. Said one, "We have worked to stretch our engagement from national committees working on harmonization issues to Canada-US [interactions, and] federal-provincial-municipal interactions in areas outside our basic mandate. We are attempting to influence broad public policy developments to achieve better results." A few commented on increased interactions with First Nations, with some provincial governments such as Alberta and Saskatchewan integrating intergovernmental and Aboriginal Affairs departments. As well, some mentioned "more frequent and sustained contacts and negotiations with other governments." One official reported spending "more time on multilateral as opposed to bilateral (province-federal) relations. [There is] more political interest and attention to intergovernmental matters." Another said he/she spends more time on "international relations, and more interdepartmental relations." This broader focus also meant that "communications functions have increased," particularly "contact with the public."

OTHER SIGNIFICANT ACTORS IN INTERGOVERNMENTAL RELATIONS

Officials were asked who they felt would be the most significant actors in intergovernmental relations in the next decade (see Table 7). First ministers were regarded as significant by four-fifths of respondents, while ministers were seen as significant by nearly as many. But almost four-fifths of officials also felt that senior public servants would continue to be a significant cohort over the next decade. Sixty percent of respondents saw central agencies as likely significant intergovernmental actors in the next decade, while a small number (12 percent) felt they would be insignificant.

Table 7: Significant Intergovernmental Actors in the Next Decade

	% Very Insignificant	% Insignificant	% Don't Know	% Significant	% Very Significant
First ministers (PM and premiers)	3	6	7	51	29
Ministers	1	4	9	66	13
Members of the Legislature	11	54	19	4	1
Members of the Senate	42	37	10	1	0
Central agencies	3	9	21	51	9
Senior public servants	1	4	9	61	17
Courts/judiciary	0	13	26	43	8
Other: – Auditor General					2
– First Nations governments				2	

Note: Where numbers do not add to total sample size, respondents did not answer the question.

Asked about the influence of our political institutions, not surprisingly, officials saw parliamentarians as peripheral players in the next decade of intergovernmental relations. Seventy-five percent of intergovernmental officials said members of the legislature were insignificant in the conduct of intergovernmental relations, a point which reflects a concern raised by Donald Smiley over 20 years ago about executive dominance of intergovernmental relations,[38] an issue discussed separately in this volume by David Cameron. Seventy-nine percent saw senators as insignificant actors, while the remainder of officials did not know if they were significant. Not one respondent replied that the Senate would become a significant actor in the next ten years. The courts and the judiciary were seen as significant by 49 percent. A few respondents indicated (in the "other" category) that First Nations governments and the Office of the Auditor General would be significant actors in the next decade. Where the Office of the Auditor General is concerned, intergovernmental relations has been flagged as an area of concern in several reports between 1994 and 2002.[39]

These findings tend to confirm the continuing strength and resilience of executive federalism. Notwithstanding its delegitimation through the era of the Meech Lake and Charlottetown accords, first ministers and their senior officials are still seen as the predominate actors in intergovernmental relations; parliamentarians are seen as quite tangential to the process; and the courts are seen to play an important but residual role as arbiters of disputes, even though they were quite prominent in particular cases in the 1980s and 1990s, such as the patriation and secession references. In this sense, traditions are proving to be fairly resistant to change.

INTERGOVERNMENTAL MECHANISMS AND INTERACTIONS

A variety of mechanisms, old and new, have been utilized over the years to facilitate intergovernmental relations. Formal mechanisms for intergovernmental business include separate, central agency intergovernmental units and departmental intergovernmental units within both levels of government, as well as intergovernmental secretariats and committees.[40] Quasi-formal conferences and meetings such as first ministers' and premiers' meetings have also become part of the existing mechanisms of intergovernmental activity. In addition, there has been restructuring of agencies with intergovernmental functions, the incorporation of new information and communications technologies into service delivery functions,[41] the facilitation of citizen participation and consultation,[42] and development of intergovernmental forums and machinery at the departmental and project level,[43] to name a few innovations.

In terms of the influence of formal mechanisms of intergovernmental relations, 80 percent of survey respondents see first ministers as the most important actors (see Table 7) and there was concern expressed about the infrequency of

First Ministers' Conferences (FMCs). Provincial officials also expressed some discontent with the federal control of both the frequency and the agendas of the First Ministers' Meetings (FMMs). Some are calling for regularly scheduled, co-chaired (federal and provincial/territorial) meetings. Ironically, while some officials complained about the informal, even social, nature of Annual Premiers' Conferences (APCs) of the past, several, particularly eastern officials, lamented the loss of social contact among the actors in recent years. They see these "social" relations as important to the building of networks of ongoing personal relations, and the trust-ties essential to intergovernmental co-operation and collaboration. (It may also be a helpful condition for smaller provinces to have more voice in discussions, given their lower numerical political weight.)

Some concern was expressed about the value of the FMCs/meetings and APCs with regard to substantive rather than issue-specific or crisis-driven agendas. One key federal official commented that while the FMCs had been "good in the past, [they are] now irregular, brief and focused on a few issues." (See also Richard Simeon and Martin Papillon in this volume.) And as Peter Meekison demonstrates, also in this volume, since the APCs have tended to follow the latest federal-provincial developments and disputes rather than inter-provincial issues, this would mean they too have been prone to focus on the major federal-provincial issues of the day. Likewise, Patricia O'Reilly found the federal-provincial-territorial health conference system and subsequent FMMs dominated in the early 1990s by crisis issues and hot politics such as blood-Hepatitis C at a time when larger, long-term health care restructuring problems were reaching major proportions.[44]

Simeon and Papillon also comment, as did several officials interviewed, on the highly political rather than "substantive" nature of the FMMs where the political leaders are competing, under intense media scrutiny, both among themselves and with their electoral opponents back home. And while it is, of course, the role of the politicians to be "political" in any of these forums, it does call into question the value of these forums as problem-solving mechanisms, particularly for long-term policy issues of concern to the electorate.

Having said this, however, many officials commented on the considerable background work of the public servants done in preparation for these meetings — all within the given agenda of the political leaders, of course. Officials engage in months of work in the pre- and post-conference activities of setting the agendas, arranging the meeting places, dates and times, meeting with counterparts from other governments to draft the official communiqué, briefing the ministers on the outcome of the meeting, doing the research for the policy issues under consideration, and drafting the resulting policy documents. And while first ministers, quite rightly, have the final say on proposals their officials have developed, in reality, their interest and input varies considerably. In some cases where the politicians take little interest or are lacking in knowledge, the officials can greatly inform the process and outcome. In other cases the politicians make the decisions regardless of the work of their officials. One former deputy minister told the story of how he and his officials had worked very hard to produce a meticulously researched and thoroughly argued briefing for their premier recommending on unassailable grounds that their province not join a particular federal-provincial trade agreement. Confident that their premier was convinced of the merits of the argument, the deputy minister watched in consternation as the prime minister approached this premier at the conference to discuss the issue, slapped him on the back and proclaimed "Premier, we have been old friends for 30 years. We can do a deal on this." Notwithstanding the objections of the officials, the deal was done.

One interesting issue raised by a former bureaucratic participant is "how officials react to the very public spats over policy between the different premiers or between federal ministers and provincial premiers." There is some evidence to suggest that strained relations at the political level do sometimes spill over into the bureaucratic realm. It is well known, for instance, that Prime Minister Jean Chrétien had difficult relations with former Ontario Premier Mike Harris, former Quebec premiers Lucien Bouchard and Bernard Landry, and Alberta Premier Ralph Klein. But interviews confirmed that intergovernmental officials' relations were not necessarily hindered by these "surface" relationships. In two of the four relationships at least, officials said they worked very well together despite the antipathy of the politicians.

When asked about the more particular mechanisms for intergovernmental activity, over four-fifths of officials saw fiscal arrangements as continuing to be significant for intergovernmental relations in the next decade (see Table 8). Bilateral and multilateral intergovernmental agreements were also ranked as important, particularly the Social Union Framework Agreement (SUFA), the Agreement on Internal Trade, and the Canada-Wide Accord on Environmental Harmonization. When asked if interactions with other ministries/agencies in their governments had increased, decreased or not changed, 73 percent reported an increase and 19 percent reported no change. None of the respondents indicated a decrease.

With regard to interactions with the public, mechanisms to enhance citizen participation in intergovernmental relations were seen as likely to be significant in the near future by about one-half of officials, while one-quarter saw them as likely insignificant. Interview responses were mixed. Those who regarded public participation as having been hijacked by powerful interest groups expressed some cynicism. As several officials commented, "Interest groups are not *the public*." From the provincial standpoint, the problem of "national" groups that act as Trojan horses for federal government interests was referred to more than once. Several provinces have mobilized their own "publics" according to officials.

Table 8: Significance of Intergovernmental Mechanisms in the Next Decade

	% Very Insignificant	% Insignificant	% Don't Know	% Significant	% Very Significant
Formal constitutional reform	10	29	29	21	4
Social Union Framework Agreement	6	26	24	28	10
Fiscal arrangements	1	1	6	47	39
Bilateral agreements	0	14	12	58	11
Multilateral agreements	0	4	14	54	21
Informal administrative arrangements	0	14	21	43	13
Intergovernmental agencies	3	19	41	26	4
Citizen participation	4	20	19	33	19
Dispute avoidance mechanisms	1	17	24	40	11
Dispute resolution mechanisms	1	16	17	46	13
Third-party involvement	6	21	39	20	9

Note: Where numbers do not add up to 100%, respondents did not answer the question.

The very definition of "the public interest" in intergovernmental relations is problematic for officials. Ottawa speaks of the national "public interest," to back the *Canada Health Act*, for example, but the provinces have no recourse to this type of discourse and become worried that this is just a cypher for justifying federal intrusions into provincial jurisdiction "without [spending] any money." The very definition of "the public" itself is problematic. Officials at both levels in interviews expressed concern about the domination by powerful interest groups of public consultations. Moreover, provincial officials expressed the added concern that many interest groups appear to be predisposed to favour the federal government on many issues.

The propensity of the federal government to go straight to "the people" with programs such as the Canada Millennium Scholarship Foundation is evidence for some provincial officials of a regrettable turn in intergovernmental relations, though it was highlighted as a point of pride by a federal official. The provinces are concerned that such initiatives bypass jurisdictional niceties. Federal officials, on the other hand, see mechanisms through which direct responsibility and accountability (and votes) can be realized as increasingly important.

Responses with regard to public participation show it as both positive and problematic. Officials reported positive results of public consultation in the work on the National Child Benefit and the homelessness files, for example. But there were also several examples of less successful attempts. One western provincial official noted that public fatigue with the "endless meetings" regarding land use policy resulted in some disaffection for the process by the officials. Perhaps the ultimate symbol of the unresolved ambiguities around public participation is SUFA.[45] While the document itself contains provisions promoting public participation, the process leading to its creation, as well as its review, have been strikingly lacking in public input.

The relatively recent calls for more public participation and public accountability have generally foundered on the traditionally closed and secretive nature of executive federalism wherein a certain schizophrenia toward public participation seems to exist.[46] For instance, on some "hot ticket" items such as health, politicians have found reason to bring in the public, particularly during election campaigns. But there has also been an apparent shift away from an emphasis on public participation as evident in the public consultation approach surrounding the proposed Environmental Management Framework Agreement (EMFA) in 1995 compared with the negotiations in 1997-98 surrounding the Canada-Wide Accord on Environmental Harmonization. Patrick Fafard and Kathryn Harrison[47] argue that public consultations were scaled back and less ambitious to avoid the fate of the EMFA.

When asked about new dispute avoidance and dispute resolution mechanisms (as set out in SUFA), about one-half of officials surveyed saw dispute *avoidance* mechanisms as increasingly significant, while one-fifth saw them as insignificant (see Table 8). As for dispute *resolution* mechanisms, roughly the same numbers prevail. But where third-party involvement is concerned, most officials responded by saying that they did not know if this was a significant or insignificant development, while about one-quarter said it was significant, and just over one-quarter said it was insignificant. As for SUFA itself, the verdict is mixed. Just over one-third regarded it as significant, while almost exactly one-third felt it was insignificant. However, the *spirit* of SUFA, if not SUFA itself, was often seen in the survey, but especially in the interviews, as signifying important values and principles in intergovernmental relations.

More generally, both the survey and interviews showed that intergovernmental officials have felt pressures to expand their interactions beyond the federal-provincial framework. They have reported increased interactions with departments both within their governments and with other orders of government, and to a much lesser degree, increased interactions with municipal and

international actors and the public. One official commented on the importance of the "development of [provincial] intergovernmental affairs
bureaucracies" in this regard. These trends are consistent with the changing
role of public servants in general as "greater proportions of public managers'
time are caught up in handling the interdependencies between their organizations and others."[48] Not only do managers now operate within their home
agency and jurisdiction, they also perform numerous activities within the vertical realm and the horizontal realm.[49] One respondent stated that an increase
in horizontal interactions with other departments stemmed from a "responsibility to ensure a corporate approach to intergovernmental relations."

Strikingly, a large number of officials responded "don't know" when asked
questions about new mechanisms of intergovernmental relations (see Table 8).
This is suggestive of a number of possibilities. It may imply the reluctance
with which officials view change to the status quo of intergovernmental relations, preferring to manage affairs through traditional mechanisms. It may
also reflect the uneven emphasis on each of these mechanisms in each province and Ottawa. For example, interviews revealed that officials across the
country hold quite contrary views about the importance of SUFA. Some regarded it as a vital framework for future intergovernmental social
policy-making. Others seemed barely cognizant of its existence. This difference in perceptions may also be related to the functional duties of individual
respondents, as well as their policy orientation (general intergovernmental,
trade, environment or health). Interestingly, for a survey focused on *intergovernmental* officials, less than one-third felt that intergovernmental agencies
were likely to be significant in the next decade. Many officials (though less
than a majority) expressed the view that they did not know if they would be
important. In any event, it suggests further investigation may yield fruitful
insights into the prospects for success of the adoption of new mechanisms for
intergovernmental relations generally.[50]

One aspect of intergovernmental relations that remains under-researched is
that of informal mechanisms of interaction. Intergovernmental business in the
federation is conducted not just formally through structures but also through
informal "pre-structural" relations which vary in degrees of institutionalization, emphasis on decision-making versus implementation, and transparency.[51]
Informal administrative arrangements were regarded as significant by almost
two-thirds of officials, while only a small percentage regarded them as insignificant (see Table 8). This speaks to the enduring characteristic of executive
federalism wherein networks of officials still conduct business and share information through their own private networks.[52] Several officials commented
on the importance of being able to connect with their counterparts in other
governments on the phone or via email, sometimes on an almost daily basis.
The tendency for networks of officials to constellate for the purposes of conducting business through informal channels which are closed to external scrutiny,

public participation and accountability stands in contrast to many of the account-ability and empowerment principles espoused by proponents of contemporary administrative reform.

SIGNIFICANT DEVELOPMENTS IN INTERGOVERNMENTAL RELATIONS

Given the opportunity to elaborate in the survey and interviews on the most significant developments in intergovernmental relations in the past decade, officials focused on several main themes in which the traditional fault lines of Canadian federalism were apparent. One official pointed to the ongoing pres-sures of "territoriality and ego." Provincial officials tended to decry federal unilateralism as understood in a variety of manifestations, and officials at both levels commented on the decline in the Quebec-constitutional file. One said future relations would revolve around "Quebec's status, Alberta's wealth and Ontario's attitude."

Certain federal actions and attitudes drew criticism from provincial offi-cials. Several provincial officials cited the Canada Health and Social Transfer (CHST) as a major irritant. The "fiscal imbalance (vertical and horizontal) and health/social costs on provincial funding capacity" coupled with "federal unilateralism" as well as "provincial downloading on municipalities" were all seen as problematic. One official commented that "deficit-cutting by the fed-eral government has a severe impact on the provinces' ability to act and set their own agendas." Another official referred to the "shift by the federal gov-ernment from transfers-to-governments to transfers-to-individuals." One provincial official commented on the "greater attempt by the federal govern-ment to direct provincial policy decisions (without providing adequate funding) through the alleged need for greater public accountability." Another official labeled this the "one size fits all approach" and another, the "emergence of the federal 'visibility and relevance' agenda." Overall, there was considerable reference (not only from the provinces) to federal government "intransigence" and "unilateralism," coupled with "an attitude of superiority." A general "decline in trust levels" and lack of genuine interest in co-operative approaches were cited as problems for the future.

Not surprisingly, then, the "politics of parsimony" was blamed for strain-ing federal-provincial relations. However, one provincial official commented on the positive effect this had had on "greater provincial cohesiveness." He/she noted the "continuation and even acceleration of a longstanding trend to-ward fiscal decentralization and greater (if almost complete) autonomy of the provinces."

Officials seemed divided over whether the overall pattern of relationships was more or less confrontational, and many cited examples of increased attempts at co-operative behaviour: for example, the National Child Benefit and the Canada-Wide Accord on Environmental Harmonization were seen as "models for co-operative action," a matter discussed in more detail by Julie Simmons in this volume. Note was also made of the increased incidence of regionalized relationships such as "the development of PT meetings without the federal government." These developments were fostered by what several officials cited as the new "focus on partnerships" and "solidarity" for which SUFA and the NCB were often cited. One western official observed that there was a "less confrontational attitude by the regional representatives of the federal government towards provincial officials." Another Atlantic official referred to "regular formal dialogues with the feds" where all were "supposedly equal at the table."

In contrast, interprovincial competition between the have and have-not provinces was cited as an ongoing problem. One official noted the "development of coordinated interprovincial responses, though the outcomes have generally tended to favour the richer provinces," and this official also noted "greater assertions of Ontario's interests at the expense of those in other provinces (and the expense of national unity)." One official complained, more generally, of "continuing regionalization and lack of interprovincial co-operation" in intergovernmental relations.

Officials at both levels commented on the decline in the Quebec-constitutional file saying the "cresting of the Quebec sovereignty movement in 1995-1996 and its subsequent decline have fundamentally altered Quebec's influence and the responses of other governments." (See Jacques Bourgault in this volume). A Quebec official noted the lack of interest in addressing Quebec's ongoing concerns, lamenting over "the rest of Canada's incapacity to propose an acceptable compromise for the reintegration of Quebec in the Canadian constitution." Another official from outside Quebec said there is "less attention paid [now] to national unity and the concerns of Quebec and more attention to provincial-US relations." Said another from the west, there is also "a shift in Ontario towards a more aggressive stance vis-a-vis Ottawa, and continued distancing by Quebec."

Finally, a grab bag of other issues was mentioned frequently enough to warrant mention. A handful of officials, particularly those from western Canada and the territories, cited the "establishing of First Nations governments" as important. Several officials talked about the impact of globalization, the free trade agreements and other supranational developments affecting intergovernmental relations in a variety of ways. Lastly, the issue of public participation and "the growth and importance of NGOs in the formation of public policy" was also considered by some officials to be a significant development in contemporary intergovernmental relations.

CONCLUSIONS

Intergovernmental relations has been defined as "the workhorse of any federal system, operating at the interface between what the constitution provides and what the practical reality of the country requires."[53] James Q. Wilson suggested that public administration "is a world of settled institutions designed to allow imperfect people to use flawed procedures to cope with insoluble problems."[54] Both remind us of the constraints under which officials labour.

This chapter considered a number of factors in its exploration of the role of intergovernmental relations officials. These included the demographic profile, educational background and career experience of officials; the role of the intergovernmental specialist; significant actors in intergovernmental relations; mechanisms of intergovernmental relations; and its significant developments.

The chapter first asked, "What is the nature of the contemporary intergovernmental public service?" As far as the demographic profile, educational background and career experience of officials is concerned, there is a striking homogeneity which may contribute to a set of "shared concepts" infusing the work of officials. As for the role of the intergovernmental relations specialist, process-related roles predominate over policy-related roles. Central agency officials who tend to be more process-oriented than line department officials continue to carry considerable weight.

Is the contemporary intergovernmental public service evolving or has it remained essentially the same for the past several decades? Perceptions about significant actors in intergovernmental relations reveal that executive federalism still predominates. First ministers and senior intergovernmental officials in intergovernmental agencies and ministries with central agency functions remain key. The significance of intergovernmental specialists in finance departments, however, is an under-researched area of importance currently being investigated by the authors.

When asked about intergovernmental mechanisms and interactions, officials noted that First Ministers' Conferences, Annual Premiers' Conferences and ministerial conferences, while important, were generally driven more by the hot issues or intergovernmental crises of the day than by more long-term substantive concerns. This is consistent with recent academic analysis. However, despite the criticism, officials tend to support these forums of intergovernmental interaction. In fact, they call for more meetings; with provincial officials, not surprisingly, calling for more provincial influence in their timing and agendas.

In addition, the domination of powerful interest groups which do not really represent "the people" was cited as problematic. Differences over the definition of the "public interest" also continue to serve as an irritant in intergovernmental relations. Mechanisms for avoiding and resolving disputes were seen as important. And recent developments in this area with regard to disputes over health care issues may lead to a greater focus on such mechanisms in the future. Still, officials revealed that they feel pressures to extend their interactions beyond traditional forums of federal-provincial intergovernmental relations common to executive federalism toward more horizontal and multilateral relations. This would include, for example, other departments within their own governments and other orders of government, some municipal and international actors, and the public. In other words, they anticipate greater responsibilities in the vertical and horizontal realms. Informal mechanisms continue to be important in intergovernmental relations. But these tend to be under-researched given the difficulty of identifying and accessing them.

Has the current climate of administrative reform in Canada affected this group? Have the character and roles of the intergovernmental public service been affected by recent attempts at reform? Or have they remained largely sheltered from it? The impact of administrative reform is considerably less evident than might be expected given its impact across the public service in general in most governments in Canada. The evidence suggests that when looking at the implications of these changes for intergovernmental officials, the impact on their roles and interactions have been subtle. Their educational background suggests that relatively few are academically conversant with the precepts of managerialism, which is one fact which may help explain the relatively weaker impact of this managerial approach. There is little to suggest that intergovernmental officials are much focused on restructuring roles and institutional arrangements for performance and service delivery goals associated with contemporary administrative reform. There is also little evidence to suggest these officials, particularly in the central agencies, are focused on outcomes or citizen participation.

The implications for administrative reform of the fact that intergovernmental units have apparently experienced fewer cutbacks, or indeed, actual increases in staff and budgets, help explain this finding. Intergovernmental relations was at least partially spared wholesale restructuring and its attendant effects possibly due to "hot politics," and the centrality of intergovernmental relations to the workings of government in general. But this relative stasis in resources means that the old culture, patterns and habits of intergovernmental relations have been able to persist while change was happening all around in the general public service. The relative lack of impact of administrative reform on the relationship between process and policy functions is striking. Intergovernmental officials seem less affected by contemporary managerial changes, although some impact is present at the margins. Moreover, some of the traditional formal and informal mechanisms of executive federalism do appear to militate against administrative reform and may help to explain the slow acceptance of its new managerial practices in this field. These include, for example, the centralized nature of decision-making in intergovernmental relations, the dominant role of elites, the closed nature of the system, and its highly political nature. Given the impact of public sector reform agendas in other federal countries (for example Australia and the United States), it is notable that administrative reform has not been as central to the agendas of intergovernmental relations in Canada.

What do intergovernmental officials themselves see as the most significant changes to date, and what do they prophesy for the future of their work? Officials noted a more regional focus to intergovernmental work, implying federal-provincial, interprovincial and international regional work. In addition, they reported less time spent on the constitution, and more on non-constitutional bargaining and negotiation, though many think constitutional reform remains a significant tool for the future. But overall, fiscal matters continue to be the most important issue for intergovernmental officials. Increased bureaucratization and the intensification of their roles in areas such as strategic advice and analytical work were remarked upon by officials. Some see an important shift from central agencies to line departments in this regard. One constant from the past is that considerable policy influence and decision-making authority remains in the hands of non-elected officials, reflecting the politicized role of intergovernmental officials first noticed 20 to 30 years ago in the academic literature.

Finally, it is apparent that many of the traditional fault lines of federalism are still present, although in contemporary manifestations. For instance, there is considerable provincial anger about downloading deficits by the federal government, and there are continuing tensions between the have and have-not provinces. In addition, there are differing views as to whether the overall pattern of relations between the federal and provincial governments, and even between provincial governments, is more or less confrontational than in the past. Several examples were given of co-operation despite considerable ongoing conflict. Overall, if indeed institutions are "the lengthened shadow of one man" (or woman), it seems clear that the long shadows cast by the actors who forged the system of executive federalism still filter the light by which officials today go about their work.

APPENDIX 1
Methodological Note

A: Defining and Capturing the Sample. Using the operational definition as the basis for finding intergovernmental specialists for the survey and interviews, a sample was generated to include those working in intergovernmental relations ministries, units in central agencies, and in line departments. As part of a larger research project on intergovernmental policy capacity, intergovernmental officials from three policy areas were targeted for sampling at the federal and provincial levels: health, environment and trade. The sampling covered deputy ministers and assistant deputy ministers in intergovernmental units or with intergovernmental responsibilities in line departments. The sample also included officials in lower ranks who fit the definition above including directors, senior and junior policy analysts in intergovernmental units and intergovernmental officials with communication and coordination titles.

The sample of intergovernmental specialists was generated from three sources. A broad search of officials with "intergovernmental" in their position title was conducted at the federal and provincial levels. The *Scott's Government Index 2000* (formerly the *Corpus Government Index*, 1984-1999) was used as the first source to generate a listing of federal and provincial officials who worked in intergovernmental units or had "intergovernmental" in their position titles. The second source was an online and manual search of government telephone directories. This search rounded out the sample of intergovernmental generalists and increased the sample of intergovernmental specialists who worked in intergovernmental units in health, environment and trade. The third source was interviews and conference networking. The total sample of intergovernmental generalists who work in intergovernmental ministries and units in central agencies was 91. The totals in each of the specialized policy areas was 72 in environment, 54 in health and 79 in trade at both levels of government. The total sample size was 296.

Arguably, given its prominence in intergovernmental and other affairs, departments of Finance could have been included in our sample. However, because of resource and time limitations, we decided to rely on questions *about* the role of finance rather than *to* finance. Additional SSHRC funding has allowed us to expand our interview sample (discussed below in Section D) to target officials in Finance departments with intergovernmental work as their primary role.

B: Analysis of Secondary Literature. Analysis of secondary sources was undertaken, which updates previous research[55] on the structures, functions and resources of intergovernmental ministries and units. Systematic analysis of the roles of officials has not been undertaken in about 15 or 20 years, particularly in the era of dynamic and widespread reform in the public sector and intergovernmental relations.[56] The literature is thereby deficient in contributing to our understanding of this aspect of the institutional features of intergovernmental administrative relations.

C: The Survey. The survey was designed around four core research questions about intergovernmental officials. Who are these people and what do they do? How have their roles changed in the past decade? What are their current perspectives on recent intergovernmental innovations? What are their perspectives on the future challenges in intergovernmental policy-making and "managing across levels of government"? The survey collected baseline data on the demographic profile of intergovernmental officials, their perceptions on recent and future developments in intergovernmental relations, and intergovernmental challenges and directions in general and in specific policy areas.

The survey was pretested for methodological soundness by two researchers and two PhD students not associated with the project, and was reviewed by the Ryerson University Ethics Review Board. Pretesting of the survey design, though limited, did allow for modifications that improved the validity of the results. The survey was distributed by mail to the sample in March 2001. Due to a low response rate of 14 percent, a follow-up distribution of the survey took place in September 2001. This raised the overall response rate to 24 percent.

Several methodological problems emerged in the survey research. Since we do not know the universe, we cannot assess the optimum sample size, degree of accuracy (that is, margin of error) or confidence level of our results. The response rate of 24 percent is problematic in that non-respondents may differ from respondents in significant ways. However, it can be said that the response rate is acceptable for a survey of this type given the closed nature of the respondents' working world. The fact that there may be an uneven distribution of responses across governments, policy sectors and occupational ranks means that qualifications need to be attached to conclusions. In any event, as Barbara Wake Carroll and David Siegel point out, quantitative research "is based upon statistical assumptions about the distribution of the sample and the inclusion of the sampling which are rarely met."[57]

Despite these methodological limitations, we believe that the survey generates useful data from which to draw inferences about the roles of intergovernmental officials. Rather than attempt to employ statistical exactitude, we opted to adopt the idea of "logical generalizations." Carroll and Siegel describe this methodological approach this way:

> In logical generalization one can generalize if three questions can be answered. Is there any logical reason to think, if my 20, or 50, or 200 respondents have told me this, that it is not true? (Alternatively, would they tell me this if it was not true?) Is there any other logical explanation for this behaviour, pattern,

phenomena, or observation? Finally, is there any reason to think that if I have been consistently told this by 200 people, the next 200 might tell me something different?[58]

Combining the quantitative research conducted through the survey with qualitative approaches of elite interviews (described in Section D) and analysis using secondary sources overcomes the liabilities of each individual approach. One final note is that to date, the data have not been disaggregated by level of government of by policy area for this study. More sophisticated analysis of the data will be conducted as part of the larger research project on a comparative analysis of intergovernmental policy capacity in trade, environment and health.

D: Elite Interviews. Research questions related to the changing nature of accountability in the new intergovernmental context, and the degree to which intergovernmental officials have been directly involved in new directions and innovations in the intergovernmental context, were explored in the interview stage of the research agenda. Questions about the policy capacity of the federal system were explored in the broader context of recent developments in federalism and public sector reforms.

To this end, first, a significant number of subjects from governments across the country were selected based initially on the survey sample database. Subsequently a snowball sample was generated and we solicited officials' views about who else ought to be interviewed. Interviews were conducted with over 50 senior officials in Ottawa and provincial capitals. The interviews began in 2001 and are ongoing. The interviews consisted of a series of open-ended questions and ranged in length from 45 minutes to two hours. Some telephone interviews have also been conducted.

The difficulties of elite interviews in intergovernmental relations can be generalized from those of almost any interviews with public servants. For instance, over 20 years ago David Good noted the challenges for researchers of delving into the closed and secretive world of officialdom. He wrote:

> Information flows through private circuits — personal telephone conversations, confidential memoranda, closely guarded briefing notes, or selective dinner parties. Decisions are taken in private — over intimate lunch-time chats, in the sanctity of a departmental office, or behind the closed doors of a cabinet committee room. Civil servants are, quite understandably, sworn to their oaths of secrecy, politicians maintain their mutually accepted pledges of confidentiality to their fellow colleagues, and outsiders, the few who have links to the inside, protect their sources to maintain their access.[59]

Moreover, the workaday world of senior civil servants is packed. They generally are focused on the next items in their Daytimers, and have little opportunity for reflection or re-examination of past initiatives. The challenges for the researcher are daunting, especially when considering the complexity, traditional secrecy and sensitivity of intergovernmental relations. The competition for scarce resources that characterizes normal departmental intrigue is magnified and multiplied by virtue of the involvement of ten provincial governments, three territories, and Native groups as well as Ottawa. Knowing something of the interests involved in this labyrinth is daunting enough. With a constantly shifting constellation of government-to-government alliances and enmities overlaid with a system of heavily invested personal networks and trust ties, it is hard to get people to reveal frankly their positions and insights. The literature on field officials provides some help in this regard, though it is slim.[60]

But as Good also points out, insiders, like everybody else, enjoy talking about what they do. And given the relatively small community of interested outsiders in intergovernmental relations, finding kindred spirits with shared interests in the esoteric worlds of federalism can be a bit cathartic. Still, "In their tightly knit community, participants play by the norms of reciprocity," Good argues. "Acquiring crucial information from someone now, implies an obligation to be forthcoming later. Reciprocity takes its shape, not in direct bilateral trading, but through indirect, multi-lateral community exchanges."[61] The task of the researcher, then, is to be aware and sensitive to the norms of the community, know what questions to ask, and to be prepared to exchange information. How to "appear to be bright in the beginning while being ignorant at the outset," is, nonetheless, an anxiety-inducing conundrum.

Another problem, as Carroll and Siegel point out, is that elite interviews are "dependent upon the participant's accurate recollection of events and motivations."[62] Moreover, officials understandably want to be perceived in the best possible light and may massage their responses to reflect this. Nonetheless, there is great value to elite interviews if they are conducted and analyzed properly.

A standard set of open-ended questions was devised, although officials were permitted wide latitude if they seemed determined to focus on some particular aspect of the issues we raised. Most were very forthcoming with this information, and after a while word spread in the intergovernmental community that we were doing this work, and many doors opened to us. No government refused to talk to us.

NOTES

The authors would like to gratefully acknowledge the financial support of the Social Sciences and Humanities Research Council Federalism and Federations Research Grant Program (Research Grant # 832-2000-0036), as well as the Ryerson University Scholarly, Research and Creativity Faculty of Arts Research Grant Program. In addition we would like to thank our editors, Peter Meekison, Harvey Lazar and Hamish Telford; Alan Noel for his comments on an early draft; the anonymous reviewers who provided us with invaluable feedback; and our research assistants, Darren Cooney, Yolanda Tse, Jay Jastrebski, and Rosie Kogan. We are grateful as well to the many intergovernmental officials who gave their time to us for interviews and who answered our survey. Their contribution to our understanding of their roles was immense. Errors of fact and interpretation in this chapter, however, are ours alone.

1. For the sake of brevity throughout the text, references to federalism and federal-provincial relations will be deemed to include territorial governments and officials as well.

2. Donald V. Smiley, "Public Administration and Canadian Federalism," *Canadian Public Administration*, 7 (1964):371-388; Donald V. Smiley, "Federal-Provincial Conflict in Canada," *Publius* (1974):7-24; Donald V. Smiley, "An Outsider's Observations of Federal-Provincial Relations Among Consenting Adults," in *Confrontation and Collaboration: Intergovernmental Relations in Canada Today*, ed. Richard Simeon (Toronto: Institute of Public Administration, 1979), pp. 105-11; J. Peter Meekison, ed., *Canadian Federalism: Myth or Reality?* 2d ed. (Toronto: Methuen, 1971); Richard Simeon, *Federal-Provincial Diplomacy: The Making of Recent Policy in Canada* (Toronto: University of Toronto Press, 1972); Richard Schultz, *Federalism, Bureaucracy and Public Policy* (Montreal: McGill-Queen's University Press, 1980); Audrey Doerr, "Public Administration: Federalism and Intergovernmental Relations," *Canadian Public Administration*, 25 (1982):564-79; Richard Simeon, ed., *Division of Powers and Public Policy* (Toronto: University of Toronto Press, 1985); Donald V. Smiley and Ronald L. Watts, "Intra-state Federalism in Canada," *Research Study for the Royal Commission on the Economic Union and Development Prospects for Canada*, volume 39 (Toronto: University of Toronto Press, 1985).

3. Audrey D. Doerr, *The Machinery of Government in Canada* (Toronto: Methuen, 1981); Audrey Doerr, "Public Administration: Federalism and Intergovernmental Relations"; Timothy B. Woolstencroft, *Organizing Intergovernmental Relations* (Kingston: Queen's University, Institute of Intergovernmental Relations, 1982); Bruce G. Pollard, *Managing the Interface: Intergovernmental Affairs Agencies in Canada* (Kingston: Queen's University, Institute of Intergovernmental Relations, 1986); Donald V. Smiley, *Canada in Question: Federalism in the Eighties*, 2d ed. (Toronto: McGraw-Hill Ryerson, 1980); Garth Stevenson, *Unfulfilled Union: Canadian Federalism and National Unity* (Toronto: MacMillan of Canada, 1979).

4. John Warhust, "Canada's Intergovernmental Relations Specialists," *Australian Journal of Public Administration* 42, 4 (1983):459-85.

5. David Milne, *Tug of War: Ottawa and the Provinces Under Trudeau and Mulroney* (Toronto: Lorimer, 1986); Herman Bakvis and William M. Chandler, eds., *Federalism and the Role of the State* (Toronto: University of Toronto Press, 1987); R.D. Olling and M.W. Westmacott, eds., *Perspectives on Canadian Federalism* (Scarborough: Prentice Hall, 1988); Carolyn J. Tuohy, *Policy and Politics in Canada: Institutionalized Ambivalence* (Philadelphia: Temple University Press, 1992); Peter H. Russell, *Constitutional Odyssey: Can Canadians Become a Sovereign People?* 2d ed. (Toronto: University of Toronto Press, 1993); Francois Rocher and Miriam Smith, *New Trends in Canadian Federalism* (Peterborough: Broadview Press, 1995); Ronald L. Watts, *The Spending Power in Federal Systems: A Comparative Study* (Kingston: Queen's University, Institute of Intergovernmental Relations, 1999); Gregory J. Inwood, "Federalism, Globalization and the (Anti) Social Union," in *Restructuring and Resistance: Canadian Public Policy in an Age of Global Capitalism*, eds. Mike Burke, Colin Mooers and John Shields (Halifax: Fernwood Press, 2000); Herman Bakvis and Grace Skogstad, eds., *Canadian Federalism: Performance, Effectiveness and Legitimacy* (Toronto: Oxford University Press, 2002).

6. M. Painter, "After Managerialism — Rediscoveries and Redirections: The Case of Intergovernmental Relations," *Australian Journal of Public Administration*, 54, 4 (1998):44-54; Organization for Economic Co-operation and Development, Public Management Committee, *Managing Accountability in Intergovernmental Partnerships* (Paris: OECD, 1999); Robert Agranoff and Michael McGuire, "American Federalism and the Search for Models of Management," *Public Administration Review* (November/December 2001):352-59.

7. Peter Aucoin, *The New Public Management: Canada in Comparative Perspective* (Montreal: Institute for Research on Public Policy, 1995); Jacques Bourgault and Barbara Wake Carroll, "The Canadian Senior Public Service: The Last Vestiges of the Whitehall Model?" in *Public Administration and Public Management: Experiences in Canada*, eds. Jacques Bourgault, Maurice Demers and Cynthia William (Quebec City: Les Publications du Quebec, 1997), pp. 91-100; B. Guy Peters and Donald J. Savoie, eds., *Taking Stock: Assessing Public Sector Reforms* (Montreal: McGill-Queens University Press, 1998); B. Guy Peters and Donald J. Savoie, eds., *Governance in the Twenty-First Century: Revitalizing the Public Service* (Montreal: McGill-Queen's University Press, 2000); O.P. Dwivedi and James Iain Gow, *From Bureaucracy to Public Management: The Administrative Culture of the Government of Canada* (Peterborough: Broadview Press, 1999).

8. Organization for Economic Cooperation and Development, *Managing Accountability in Intergovernmental Partnerships* (Paris: OECD, 1997 and 1999). United Kingdom. Cabinet Office, *Modernizing Government*. White Paper, (March 1999); Carolyn M. Johns, *Non-Point Source Water Pollution Management in Canada and the United States*. PhD. Dissertation, McMaster University, 2000; Canada. *Using Horizontal Tools to Work Across Boundaries: Lessons Learned and Signposts for Success* (Ottawa: Canadian Centre for Management Development, 2002).

9. Carolyn M. Johns, Patricia L. O'Reilly and Gregory J. Inwood, "Intergovernmental Relations, Intergovernmental Management and Intergovernmental

Officials in Canada: A Research Agenda," paper presented to the Annual Meeting of the Canadian Political Science Association, Laval University, Quebec City, in 2001; Carolyn M. Johns, Patricia L. O'Reilly and Gregory J. Inwood, "Public Sector Reform, Intergovernmental Administrative Machinery and Intergovernmental Officials in Canada," paper presented to the Annual Meeting of the Institute of Public Administration of Canada, Halifax, in 2002.

10. Gregory Marchildon, "Constructive Entanglement: Intergovernmental Collaboration in Canadian Social Policy," in *Collaborative Government: Is There a Canadian Way?* eds. Susan Delacourt and Donald G. Lenihan (Toronto: Institute of Public Administration of Canada, 1999), pp. 72-80; Richard Simeon, "Rethinking Government, Rethinking Federalism," in *New Public Management and Public Administration in Canada*, eds. Mohamed Charih and Arthur Daniels (Toronto: Institute of Public Administration of Canada, 1997), pp. 69-72. Susan Delacourt and Donald Lenihan, eds., *Collaborative Government: Is There a Canadian Way?* (Toronto: Institute of Public Administration of Canada, 1999); Organization for Economic Cooperation and Development, *Managing Accountability*; Rod Dobell and Luc Bernier, *Citizen-Centred Governance: Intergovernmental and Inter-institutional Dimensions of Alternative Service Delivery* (Toronto: IPAC-KPMG, 1996); Rod Dobell and Luc Bernier, "Citizen Centred Governance: Implications for Intergovernmental Canada," in *Alternative Service Delivery: Sharing Governance in Canada*, eds. Robin Ford and David Zussman (Toronto: IPAC-KPMG, 1997). For example, Richard Simeon and others have concluded that overall, new approaches to "making federalism work" are consistent with many elements of NPM. Both value decentralization, place less emphasis on formal rules and arrangements, and more emphasis on flexible agreements and informal approaches in the context of greater fiscal restraint and efficiency. Simeon, "Rethinking Government, Rethinking Federalism," p. 86.

11. See the discussion of methodology in Barbara Wake Carroll and David Siegel, *Service in the Field: The World of Front-Line Public Servants* (Montreal: McGill-Queen's University Press, 1999), chapter 2.

12. At the time of writing, the authors had begun to examine the role of officials in Finance departments, but the findings are too preliminary to incorporate in this study. John Warhurst, "Canada's Intergovernmental Relations Specialists," p. 459.

13. Carolyn M. Johns, Patricia L. O'Reilly and Gregory J. Inwood, "Intergovernmental Relations."

14. For readability we have conflated the categories of "significant" and "very significant," as well as "not significant" and "not very significant." For more detailed variation please see the tables. Where direct quotes are used, they are the exact words of a single official, but reflect opinions which were indicated by several officials.

15. Canada. Treasury Board Secretariat, "Employment Statistics for the Federal Public Service," in *Report of the Auditor General of Canada* (Ottawa: Minister of Supply and Services, 1998).

16. Ken Kernaghan and David Siegel, *Public Administration in Canada*, 4th ed. (Toronto: Nelson, 1999), p. 583.

17. See Peter Aucoin, *The New Public Management: Canada in Comparative Perspective*; Gregory J. Inwood, *Understanding Canadian Public Administration: An Introduction to Theory and Practice*, 2d ed. (Scarborough: Prentice Hall, 2004); Ken Kernaghan and David Siegel, *Public Administration in Canada*; and B. Guy Peters and Donald J. Savoie, *Governance in the Twenty-First Century*.

18. Gregory J. Inwood, *Continentalizing Canada: The Politics and Legacy of the Macdonald Royal Commission* (Toronto: University of Toronto Press, forthcoming); Alain-G. Gagnon, "The Influence of Social Scientists on Public Policy." in *Social Scientists, Policy, and the State*, eds. Stephen Brooks and Alain-G. Gagnon (New York: Praeger, 1990), pp. 1-18; R.B. Bryce, "Public Servants as Economic Advisors," in *Economic Policy Advising in Canada: Essays in Honour of John Deutsch*, ed. David C. Smith (CD Howe Institute, 1981); Harold Adams Innis, "The Rowell Sirois Report," *Canadian Journal of Economics and Political Science*, 6 (1940):565.

19. Frank Underhill, *In Search of Canadian Liberalism* (Toronto: MacMillan, 1996), p. 180.

20. Canada. Privy Council Office, *Program Review and Getting Government Right* (Ottawa: Public Works and Government Services, 1994); Allan Tupper, "Intergovernmental Canada: Towards a Redefinition," in *Hard Choices or No Choices: Assessing Program Review*, ed. Amelita Armit and Jacques Bourgault (Toronto: Institute of Public Administration of Canada, 1996), pp. 121-27.

21. Canada. Minister of Finance, *Budget in Brief*, p. 9.

22. Quantitative data related to this preliminary finding is currently being collected as part of further data collection on intergovernmental budgets at the federal and provincial level.

23. John Warhurst, "Canada's Intergovernmental Relations Specialists," p. 460.

24. Gregory J. Inwood, Patricia L. O'Reilly and Carolyn M. Johns, "A Comparative Analysis of Intergovernmental Policy Capacity in Trade, Environment and Health," paper presented to the Canadian Political Science Association General Meeting, Laval University, Quebec City, in 2001.

25. Bruce G. Pollard, *Managing the Interface: Intergovernmental Affairs Agencies in Canada*.

26. Donald J. Savoie, *Governing From the Centre: The Concentration of Power in Canadian Politics* (Toronto: University of Toronto Press, 1999).

27. Ibid.

28. George Anderson, "The New Focus on the Policy Capacity of the Federal Government," *Canadian Public Administration*, 39, 4 (1996):469-88.

29. B. Guy Peters, *The Policy Capacity of Government* (Ottawa: Canadian Centre for Management Development, 1996); Donald Savoie, *Thatcher, Reagan and Mulroney: In Search of a New Bureaucracy* (Toronto: University of Toronto Press, 1994).

30. Donald J. Savoie, "What is Wrong with the New Public Management?" *Canadian Public Administration* 38, 1 (1995):118.

31. Jacques Bourgault and Barbara Wake Carroll, "The Canadian Senior Public Service: The Last Vestiges of the Whitehall Model?"

32. Andy Tamas, "The Manager and the New Public Service," *Canadian Public Administration*, 38, 4 (1995):613-21; Donald J. Savoie, *Governing from the Centre.*

33. On the frequency of intergovernmental meetings, see also the chapter in this volume by Julie Simmons.

34. Herman Bakvis and Grace Skogstad, eds., *Canadian Federalism: Performance, Effectiveness and Legitimacy*, p. 9.

35. Ibid.

36. Stéphane Dion, "Governmental Interdependence in Canada," notes for an address when he was president of the Privy Council and minister of intergovernmental affairs to the Canadian Study of Parliament Group Conference, Ottawa, Ontario, 11 June 2000.

37. Ken Kernaghan and David Siegel, *Public Administration in Canada*, p. 477; George Anderson, "The New Focus on the Policy Capacity of the Federal Government"; "Politicization refers to the process by which officials become increasingly involved in politics, either in the partisan sense or in the broader sense of the authoritative allocation of values for society." (Kernaghan and Siegel, *Public Administration in Canada*, p. 476.)

38. Donald V. Smiley, *Canada in Question: Federalism in the Eighties.*

39. In 1994, the Auditor General identified intergovernmental issues as a matter of special importance. In the 1999 report, issues related to collaborative arrangements were a central theme. And in several reports during this period, the AG highlighted intergovernmental concerns related to financial management and accountability in specific policy areas and in relation to administrative reforms: for example, in 1998 related to the creation of the Canadian Food Inspection Agency, in 2000 related to regulatory reform, and in 2000, as a central theme of the Report of the Commissioner of the Environment and Sustainable Development. See Canada. Office of the Auditor General, Report of the Auditor General of Canada (Ottawa: Minister of Supply and Services, 1994-2002).

40. Timothy B. Woolstencroft, *Organizing Intergovernmental Relations*; Ken Kernaghan and David Siegel, *Public Administration in Canada.*

41. Roger Gibbins, "Federalism in a Digital World," *Canadian Journal of Political Science*, 33, 4 (2000):667-90; Canada. *Intergovernmental Study of Online Access to Government Information and Services in Canada*, Executive Summary (April 1996).

42. F. Leslie Seidle, "Executive Federalism and Public Involvement: Integrating Citizens' Voices," paper presented to the conference on the Changing Nature of Democracy, University of Manitoba, Winnipeg, 2000; Susan D. Phillips, "SUFA and Citizen Engagement: Fake or Genuine Masterpiece?" *Policy Matters* (Montreal: Institute for Research on Public Policy, 2001); Matthew Mendelsohn and John McLean, "Getting Engaged: Strengthening SUFA Through Citizen Engagement," paper presented to the Forum on the Social Union Framework Agreement, Regina, 2000; Miriam Wyman, David Shulman and Laurie Ham, *Learning to*

Engage: Experiences With Civic Engagement in Canada (Ottawa: Canadian Policy Research Network, 1999); David Cameron and Richard Simeon, "Intergovernmental Relations and Democratic Citizenship," in *Governance in the Twenty-First Century: Revitalizing the Public Service*, eds. B. Guy Peters and Donald J. Savoie (Montreal: McGill-Queen's University Press, 2000).

43. Canada. *Using Horizontal Tools to Work Across Boundaries.*

44. Patricia L. O'Reilly, "The Federal/Provincial/Territorial Health Conference System," in *Federalism, Democracy and Health Policy in Canada: Social Union Series*, ed. Duane Adams (Montreal and Kingston: Institute of Intergovernmental Relations and McGill-Queen's University Press, 2001), pp. 107-30.

45. Patricia O'Reilly and Gregory J. Inwood, "Social Union Partnership Feasibility: Existing Health Sector Collaborative and Governance Mechanisms," paper presented to the Canadian Political Science Association, Quebec City, 2000.

46. Patricia O'Reilly, Gregory J. Inwood and Carolyn M. Johns, "Intergovernmental Policy Capacity in Canada," paper presented to the Canadian Political Science Association (Toronto, University of Toronto, 2002).

47. Patrick C. Fafard and Kathryn Harrison, eds., *Managing the Environmental Union: Intergovernmental Relations and Environmental Policy in Canada* (Montreal and Kingston: Institute of Intergovernmental Relations and McGill Queen's University Press, 2000).

48. Donald F. Kettle, "Governing at the Millennium," in *Handbook of Public Administration*, 2d ed., ed. James L. Perry (San Francisco: Jossey-Bass, 1996), pp. 5-18.

49. Canada. *Using Horizontal Tools to Work Across Boundaries*; Robert Agranoff and Michael McGuire, "American Federalism and the Search for Models of Management," p. 672.

50. Some efforts have been initiated by the federal and provincial governments to explore the implications of new intergovernmental mechanisms on the roles of officials. For instance, in 2002, the Canadian Centre for Management Development published the results of a Roundtable on Horizontal Mechanisms. See Canada. *Using Horizontal Tools To Work Across Boundaries: Lessons Learned and Signposts for Success.* In 2000, the centre established an Action Research Roundtable on the Implementation of the Social Union Framework Agreement. Members of both roundtables included federal, provincial, territorial and First Nations public servants, non-governmental organizations, private sector actors, academics and members from Canadian think tanks. Although the SUFA roundtable recognized that SUFA applies specifically to social policies and programs, the spirit of the agreement and implications for intergovernmental relations and management resulted in a report that was designed for all federal public servants, with specific case studies drawn from social policy and program areas. See Canada. *Implementing the Social Union Framework Agreement: A Learning and Reference Tool* (Ottawa: Canadian Centre for Management Development, 2001). Provincial governments have also been advocating re-definitions of federalism, intergovernmental relations and management. See Ontario, Ministry of Intergovernmental Affairs, *Common Sense Federalism:*

Ontario's Intergovernmental Approach in the "Single-Taxpayer Nation," speech by Minister Norm Sterling at the Institute of Intergovernmental Relations Symposium, Queen's University, Kingston, 9 June 2000.

51. David M. Cameron, *Structures of Intergovernmental Relations* (Ottawa: Forum of Federations, 2000).

52. David Good, *The Politics of Anticipation: Making Canadian Federal Tax Policy* (Ottawa: Carleton University, 1980), p. 200.

53. David M. Cameron, *Structures of Intergovernmental Relations.*

53. James Q. Wilson, "Can the Bureaucracy be Deregulated? Lessons From Government Agencies," in *Deregulating the Public Service: Can Government be Improved?* ed. John J. Dilulio Jr. (Washington: The Brookings Institute, 1954). Cited in Donald J. Savoie, "What is Wrong with the New Public Management?" *Canadian Public Administration*, 38,1 (1995):112-21.

55. See, for example, Bruce G. Pollard, *Managing the Interface: Intergovernmental Affairs Agencies in Canada*; John Warhurst, "Canada's Intergovernmental Relations Specialists"; Timothy B. Woolstencroft, *Organizing Intergovernmental Relations*; Donald V. Smiley, *Canada in Question: Federalism in the Eighties*; Richard Simeon, *Federal-Provincial Diplomacy: The Making of Recent Policy in Canada*; Edgar Gallant, "The Machinery of Federal-Provincial Relations," in *Canadian Federalism: Myth or Reality?* 2d ed. (Toronto: Methuen, 1971), pp. 254-64.

56. Carolyn M. Johns, Patricia L. O'Reilly and Gregory J. Inwood, "Public Sector Reform, Intergovernmental Administrative Machinery and Intergovernmental Officials in Canada."

57. Barbara Wake Carroll and David Siegel, *Service in the Field: The World of Front-Line Public Servants* (Montreal: McGill-Queen's University Press, 1999), p. 28.

58. Ibid., pp. 28-29.

59. David Good, *The Politics of Anticipation: Making Canadian Federal Tax Policy,* p. 199.

60. See Barbara Wake Carroll and David Siegel, *Service in the Field: The World of Front-Line Public Servants;* and David Good, *The Politics of Anticipation: Making Canadian Federal Tax Policy.*

61. David Good, *The Politics of Anticipation: Making Canadian Federal Tax Policy,* p. 200.

62. Wake Carroll and Siegel, *Service in the Field,* p. 28.

10

Securing the Threads of Co-operation in the Tapestry of Intergovernmental Relations: Does the Institutionalization of Ministerial Conferences Matter?

Julie M. Simmons

Ce chapitre a deux buts : d'une part, dégager, à travers le temps, des tendances de l'activité intergouvernementale ministérielle et sous-ministérielle; d'autre part, en s'appuyant sur trois récents cas de collaboration intergouvernementale, évaluer l'idée selon laquelle l'augmentation du nombre de forums ministériels institutionnalisés entraînera une collaboration et un consensus accrus au sein des gouvernements. Il analyse d'abord des données de rencontres, aux niveaux provincial/territorial (PT) et fédéral/provincial/ territorial (FPT), de ministres et/ou sous-ministre, rencontres ayant reçu le soutien du Secrétariat des conférences intergouvernementales canadiennes. Il montre alors que la fréquence des conférences ministérielles intergouvernementales varie selon le temps et que le nombre de rencontres a, dans l'ensemble, augmenté depuis 1974. On a observé une tendance vers l'activité de niveau FPT aux dépens du niveau PT, mais elle s'est estompée à la fin des années 90. On évoque alors la possibilité que les rencontres PT deviennent peu à peu une composante essentielle du dialogue FPT en cours. Le chapitre examine ensuite la variation des caractéristiques structurelles ou du degré d'institutionnalisation de trois forums de discussion entre ministres, forums issus de trois secteurs différents. Par l'examen des processus récents et des créations politiques de ces trois forums, il fait voir qu'il n'existe aucune corrélation entre l'institutionnalisation des forums ministériels et la nature des compromis et consensus adoptés par les ministres en faisant partie. Ces constatations suggèrent que la poursuite de l'institutionnalisation en question ne produira pas nécessairement une plus grande collaboration. Le chapitre conclut en proposant des facteurs alternatifs qui peuvent expliquer la variation de la collaboration ministérielle intergouvernementale.

INTRODUCTION

At the ninth national seminar of the Institute of Public Administration of Canada (IPAC), held in 1978, contributors gave their impressions of "intergovernmental relations in Canada today," recording their observations in a volume similar in some ways to this one.[1] At that time, participants noted that the number of intergovernmental meetings of first ministers and ministers had doubled over the previous decade, establishing an "industry" of intergovernmental relations. With governments establishing intergovernmental central agency style units, there was little reason to believe that a decline in the growth of intergovernmental relations lay over the horizon. A second key theme emerging from the conference was conflict in intergovernmental relations. In contrast to the generally co-operative intergovernmental relations of the earlier period, the process was thought to have become a "cockpit for mutual recrimination" rather than mutual accommodation. In the words of Gérard Veilleux, *"Les gouvernements se parlent de plus en plus. Pourtant, certains pourraient croire que plus ils se parlent, moins ils semblent s'entendre."*[2]

This chapter has two aims. The first is to determine how intergovernmental relations have evolved since the 1978 conference, examining the patterns of ministerial and deputy ministerial conferences over time. The second is to revisit a suggestion put forward at the conference about how to reduce conflict in intergovernmental relations. It was then argued that "fixed meeting dates, firm agendas and the continuity to serve the required ongoing negotiating," possibly brought about by the creation of a permanent secretariat independent of both levels of government, might provide "incentives for the achievement of compromise and consensus."[3] As Richard Simeon and Martin Papillon reveal in their analysis of first ministers' conferences (FMCs) in this volume, however, "summit federalism" has not become regularized or formalized in this sense. Nonetheless, intergovernmental developments in the late 1990s do suggest that, in several specific policy sectors, intergovernmental co-operation has become more fully established.

Such federal- provincial-territorial forums — in some cases known as ministerial councils — have become institutionalized as sites for the negotiation of accords, agreements and communiqués across a broad number of policy areas. Some of these agreements codify the mandate of these forums, and put in place commitments to transparency — reporting policy developments and their effects to the public through intergovernmental publications and reports. Some ministerial forums establish regular meeting schedules and a handful have permanent intergovernmental secretariats to provide administrative support. These developments provide the opportunity to assess whether there is a link between the degree of "institutionalization" or "formalization" of ministerial conferences and ministers' ability to develop compromise and consensus.

Drawing upon data maintained by the Canadian Intergovernmental Conference Secretariat (CICS), I demonstrate that intergovernmental meetings of ministers and deputy ministers have not grown steadily in number since the late 1970s, but rather have risen and declined over time. Second, intergovernmental relations among ministers have become more formalized over time with the CICS supporting more intergovernmental activity taking place among elected representatives.

This chapter then turns to the development of three specific intergovernmental agreements, each of which is part of the post 1995 non-constitutional rebalancing era.[4] These are the National Child Benefit (NCB), developed by the Ministers Responsible for Social Services; the Canada-Wide Accord on Environmental Harmonization, developed by the Canadian Council of Ministers of the Environment; and the Canada Forest Accord and National Forest Strategy (1998-2003), developed by the Canadian Council of Forest Ministers. I first establish criteria for measuring the degree of institutionalization of each council. I then assess the degree of institutionalization in each of the three ministerial forums and the extent to which their processes and agreements reflect compromise and consensus, according to specific indicators. The conclusion is surprising: greater institutionalization does not appear to result in compromise and consensus in ministerial decision-making either in terms of the process leading to the agreements or the effects of the agreements on policy development in the policy sectors examined here. Rather, compromise and consensus are contingent on other factors, such as the will of governments; the personalities of the intergovernmental actors; and the developments and pressures external to the intergovernmental deliberations, some of which are specific to the policy sector and problem, the others apparent in policy-making more generally.

MINISTERIAL COUNCIL MEETINGS, CONFERENCES, FORUMS AND COUNCILS

Intergovernmental meetings of ministers or senior officials of various sectors are not a new phenomenon. The great majority of formal intergovernmental meetings of ministers involve "sectoral" or "line" ministers responsible for specific areas of public policy, and the majority of intergovernmental meetings of officials involve "sectoral" or "line" ministry officials.[5] But despite the prominence of these conferences, it is not easy to determine exactly how many of them occur. The Canadian Intergovernmental Conference Secretariat provides conference support and information services to the "majority of high-level intergovernmental conferences," and has maintained the most comprehensive public record of intergovernmental activity since its inception in 1974. These data capture the ebb and flow of interprovincial (or provincial-territorial — PT) and federal-provincial (or federal-provincial-territorial — FPT) meetings of ministers and deputy ministers — a task much more difficult at the time of the IPAC conference in 1978.[6] However, the CICS does not attend every meeting of this kind, and its records are based on fiscal years,

beginning April 1 and continuing to March 31 of the following year. Thus, we
cannot be as confident that more precise analysis based on this data reflects
the reality of the intergovernmental landscape.

Nevertheless, Figure 1 indicates that there was a dramatic drop in the intergovernmental meetings of ministers and deputy ministers following the 1978
conference, and this drop would be the first of many reflected in the CICS
records. It will come as no surprise even to the most casual observer of intergovernmental relations that the sharp peaks in the number of conferences
attended by the CICS loosely correspond to the years during which governments were involved in the high politics of constitutional change.[8] While First
Ministers' Conferences are not included in the data, the peaks may also reflect that some prime ministers are willing to host regular FMCs, which tends
to generate intergovernmental agendas for line ministers to pursue. It is also
interesting to note that these sharp peaks and gradual troughs amount to an
overall increase in intergovernmental activity over three decades. Table 1 indicates that there was a 9.4 percent increase in the average number of
conferences annually in the second half of the period covered (1987-2000) as

**Figure 1: *Summary of Federal-Provincial-Territorial Meetings of
Ministers and Deputy Ministers Served by the Canadian
Intergovernmental Conference Secretariat*[7]**

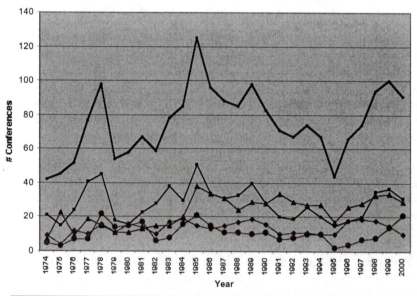

**Table 1: Summary of Average Number of FPT and PT Ministerial
and Deputy Ministerial Meetings Served by the Canadian
Intergovernmental Conference Secretariat**

Meeting Participants	A 1974-2000 Yearly Average	B 1974-1986 Yearly Average	C 1987-2000 Yearly Average	D Change in Yearly Average of C to B (%)	E 1990-1994 Yearly Average	F 1996-2000 Yearly Average	G Change in Yearly Average of F to E (%)
FPT Ministers	23.2	17.7	28.3	59.9	29.0	30.0	3.4
PT Ministers	13.5	12.8	14.3	11.7	11.6	16.0	37.9
FPT Deputy Ministers	28.0	29.6	26.7	–9.8	22.6	28.2	24.8
PT Deputy Ministers	10.7	12.0	9.6	–20.0	9.2	10.8	17.4
Total	75.5	72.0	78.8	9.4	72.4	85.0	17.4

compared with the first (1974-86). This lends credence to the claim that the intergovernmental conference is the "most Canadian of institutions."[9]

However, Table 1 also indicates that this increase is not equally attributable to the activity of deputy ministers and ministers. These data reveal that ministers have met more often each year on average from 1987-2000 than they did from 1974-1986, whereas deputy ministers have met less often each year on average (column D). Also important is the distinction between FPT and PT activity. Table 1 reveals that the yearly average of FPT ministers meetings from 1987-2000 rose almost 60 percent over the yearly average of FPT ministers meetings from 1974-1986.

These data also support the perception that the introduction of the 1995 Canada Health and Social Transfer (CHST) and the referendum in Quebec correspond with a lull in intergovernmental interaction, followed by an increase. The average number of CICS-supported conferences per year in the post-referendum era reflects a 17.4 percent increase over the average number of CICS-supported conferences in the pre-referendum 1990s (Column G). Curiously, however, if one separates this outlier year from the others during this decade, there has only been a 3.4 percent increase in the average number of CICS-supported FPT ministers conferences per year in the years 1990-94 and 1996-2000. This minimal increase is apparent in the more or less horizontal line of FPT ministerial meetings in the

1990s in Figure 1, with a sharp dip evident at the time of the referendum. In contrast, there were much larger increases in PT ministers' meetings.

Several conclusions can be drawn from these observations. First, the frequency of intergovernmental ministerial conferences undulates over time. However, unlike previous crests reflected in the CICS data, the surge in intergovernmental conferences at the sectoral level of the late 1990s corresponds to non-constitutional rather than constitutional negotiations. Second, over time there has been an increase in ministerial meetings, and a decline in CICS-supported deputy ministerial meetings. This decline in meetings of deputy ministers supported by the CICS does not necessarily mean that there is less contact among deputies. Indeed, it is likely that the increase in intergovernmental ministerial meetings leads to more, not less deputy minister contact as the deputy ministers prepare ministers for these intergovernmental meetings. Perhaps then, the decline in CICS-supported deputy minister activity reflects a shift away from formalized meetings and an increase in more informal deputy minister contact through conference calls and the like. While this more informal contact may be out of necessity, it may also reflect a greater level of comfort and familiarity with engaging one's colleagues in other provinces brought about by the overall increase in intergovernmental meetings of ministers. Third, there has been a notable shift towards FPT intergovernmental activity rather than PT intergovernmental activity over time, but the late 1990s do not follow this trend. Even if one excludes the "trough" of intergovernmental meetings in 1995, the yearly average number of FPT ministers meetings in the second half of the 1990s and the first half of the 1990s is virtually the same, whereas PT activity has increased notably. In his consideration of Annual Premiers' Conferences (APCs) in this volume, Peter Meekison puts forward a hypothesis that might explain the recent upswing in PT activity. As in his analysis of the changing role of the APC vis-à-vis the FMC, the role of PT ministers meetings may be shifting from forums for the discussion of interprovincial issues to essential components of an ongoing dialogue with the federal government where provinces have an opportunity to establish a common front vis-à-vis the federal government prior to FPT ministers' meetings.

These data show that contact among ministers of various sectors has become more formalized in that relying on the CICS for conference support and information services signifies more formal interaction. More specific indicators of formalization or institutionalization are discussed below as I now consider whether there is a link between compromise, consensus and institutionalization.

THE INSTITUTIONALIZATION OF MINISTERIAL COUNCILS

FPT ministerial conferences vary from sector to sector based on a number of characteristics including:

- substance of interaction (information exchange or substantive policy development);
- the nature of the participants (non-elected government officials and/ or elected ministers; central agency actors and/or line ministry actors; actors from several line ministries or specific to one policy area)
- decision-making styles (adversarial bargaining or team-oriented problem solving, for example); and
- the tasks attended to at these meetings, and the relationship between the substance of intergovernmental negotiations and the policy objectives of individual ministers within their own jurisdictions.

Perhaps the most obvious difference is in their titles. Many ministerial conferences are simply referred to as meetings of "ministers responsible for" a specific sector. Social services, justice, housing, agriculture, and local government are some of the areas that follow this pattern. Still others are referred to as councils, such as the Wildlife Ministers Council of Canada, the Council of Ministers of Transportation and Highway Safety, and the Council of Education Ministers. Still other groupings of ministers are labelled "forums," such as the Forum for Labour Market Ministers, or "conferences," such as the Annual Conference of the Federal-Provincial-Territorial Ministers of Health. But while a "council" may suggest a greater degree of institutionalization than mere "meetings" of ministers, this is not always the case.

There are also a number of *structural* features that distinguish each forum and influence the degree of institutionalization. Indicators of institutionalized forums include an established mandate, and organizational features such as a network of bureaucratic support reflected in a structure of subcommittees with clearly defined terms of reference and a shared understanding of how they are linked to each other. They may even have a secretariat that serves an administrative function, or proposes new policy directions and options to the forum. An institutionalized forum would likely have a clearly articulated process by which the chair of the council is determined. Along with these structural features, an institutionalized forum would have an established history of consistent interaction among its ministers.

THE CANADIAN COUNCIL OF MINISTERS OF THE ENVIRONMENT, THE CANADIAN COUNCIL OF FOREST MINISTERS, AND MINISTERS RESPONSIBLE FOR SOCIAL SERVICES

The most institutionalized forum examined here is the Canadian Council of Ministers of the Environment (CCME), the site for the development of the Canada-Wide Accord on Environmental Harmonization. Its history dates from 1964, when the Canadian Council of Resource Ministers was incorporated.

This forum had a clearly defined membership (all federal and provincial ministers with natural resource-related duties), structure and purpose. Its successor, the Canadian Council of Resource and Environment Ministers (CCREM), was well instituted at the time of the 1978 conference on intergovernmental relations.[10] In fact, it was one of the few intergovernmental forums with an established secretariat at that time. In 1989 the CCREM was renamed the CCME, and in 1991, its purpose was redefined. Unlike intergovernmental forums where the interaction between governments is limited to an exchange of information, the council's 1991 revised purpose formalized a commitment to joint action on environmental issues, the harmonization of "the development and implementation of environmental legislation, policies, procedures and programs," and the development of "nationally consistent environmental objectives, [and] standards." At this time the CCME also introduced new organizational instruments, including a full-time secretariat (currently located in Winnipeg, and supported by the governments through an established funding formula), a Deputy Ministers' Committee (which is required to meet at least once per year), a series of steering committees, and a management committee. The CCME also set a precedent by defining and embedding consensus decision-making in its constitution (Canadian Council of Ministers of the Environment Secretariat).[11] The chair of the CCME, referred to as the president, rotates annually among the ministers. The ministers meet regularly at least once a year, but usually more often.

While some other forums of ministers such as the Canadian Council of Forest Ministers or the Forum of Labour Market Ministers maintain web sites, none is more developed than that of the CCME. This web site has traditionally provided information on CCME priorities, access to its publications, drafts of initiatives, and reports on implementation of initiatives. The current web site provides information on how CCME priorities are set, an organizational chart, and the vision statement. The vision statement clearly illustrates the CCME's institutionalization and its orientation towards co-operation. It describes the CCME as providing "Federal, Provincial and Territorial Ministers a forum for discussion of the harmonization of laws, policies and actions; and the development of co-operative action by the member governments to address issues of national and international concern."[12]

Like the CCME, the Canadian Council of Forest Ministers (CCFM), the forum which acts as the trustee for the National Forest Strategy, has an established history, network of officials supporting the council, a secretariat, regular meetings, and a system whereby the chair of the council rotates among the ministers. While reflective of a significant degree of institutionalization, these supports are not as robust as those of the CCME. The CCFM was established in 1985 and meets annually (with other meetings scheduled as necessary). The secretariat "resides with the chair" and, while it is assisted by the Canadian Forest Service, it does not have the resources or permanency of the secretariat of the CCME. The CCFM has an established structure of committees and a web site that provides information on 14 initiatives of the CCFM as well as copies of publications and reports pertaining to these initiatives. But this information is not as comprehensive as that available on the CCME web site. The CCFM has, however, established rules about decision-making and guidelines for co-operation. In 1995 it endorsed a Framework for Federal Provincial Territorial Co-operation in Forestry that establishes principles of co-operation among governments, areas of priority for co-operation, and examples where effective coordination between the two levels of government has been achieved through the CCFM. Nevertheless, this document is less specific than the vision statement of the CCME in terms of identifying how to achieve compromise and consensus within the CCFM itself.

Of the three forums examined here, the Ministers Responsible for Social Services is least institutionalized. While the provincial and territorial ministers of social services have a longstanding tradition of consistent interaction, and defined purposes for the meetings of ministers and deputy ministers, the federal-provincial-territorial ministers' forum does not. According to CICS records, with the exception of a Federal-Provincial-Territorial Conference of Ministers Responsible for Social Services and Income Security in 1992, the social services ministers did not meet with their federal counterpart in the ten years prior to the National Child Benefit negotiations.[13] Even after these negotiations began, the FPT social service ministers did not have a regular meeting schedule, a codified mandate, explicit decision-making rules, or a collective funding arrangement for a secretariat, web site and so on. The administrative support for the forum fell primarily to the province that was chair of the ministers' table for the year. However, the PT social services ministers did begin regularly reporting to the Provincial Territorial Council on Social Policy Renewal after the latter was created in 1996, and its activity is documented in the PT council's annual progress reports. The focus of the FPT deliberations and the results of these deliberations were indirectly linked to this reporting process.

Since the development of the NCB, additional institutional supports have been put in place. For example, there are now established terms of reference for several federal-provincial-territorial committees of officials, and there is an NCB web site that outlines the initiative, and provides annual progress reports and other related information. But at the time that the NCB was developed, FPT ministers and officials were largely without institutionalized intergovernmental supports, with the exception of the existing PT structures.

It appears, then, that if institutionalization of ministerial forums and compromise and consensus are correlated, we would expect to see the greater coordination and collaboration among ministers of the environment and forestry than among social services, both in terms of the process leading to intergovernmental agreements and the impact of the agreements on each government's policies. However, as the following consideration of three major intergovernmental agreements affiliated with the three forums suggests, this pattern is not at all clear.

CHARACTERIZING COMPROMISE AND CONSENSUS

Some have labelled the non-constitutional renewal of the federation as collaborative federalism, which by its name suggests consensus and compromise. For example, in the Institute of Intergovernmental Relations' 1997 volume of *Canada: The State of the Federation*, editor Harvey Lazar defined collaboration as "governments working together on a *non-hierarchical* basis in a way that reflects their *interdependence*," and suggested that intergovernmental developments in social, environmental, internal trade, and First Nations policy between 1993 and 1997 reflected this kind of interaction.[14] In 1999, the Auditor General of Canada also noted an increase in what he termed "collaborative arrangements" or arrangements where "planning and decision-making is shared between the federal government and one or more non-federal partners."[15] While in some cases the result was to "rationalize" and "disentangle," in others it was to pursue joint action. In both cases, however, governments were seeking joint solutions to common problems.

Not all observers agree that these developments reflect a partnership of equals. It has been argued that the federal government has defined the parameters of the debate, established the limits of compromise, and sometimes virtually unilaterally defined the outcome of intergovernmental relations, demonstrating a pattern of federal-provincial relations that is more hierarchical than collaborative.[16] There is no doubt that the absence of Quebec from many of the compromises reached by other governments in many intergovernmental policy developments of the rebalancing era is more consequential than the footnote attached to each of these intergovernmental agreements implies. Moreover, not all federal-provincial agreements are the result of shared processes of decision-making with participating governments collectively holding the pen. For example, the Social Union Framework Agreement, signed by all governments but Quebec, is a formal agreement to work together, but both levels of government were unable or unwilling to agree to a federal-provincial process where they both shared in writing its text.

We need a more nuanced and fine-grained analysis of similarity and difference, success and failure. Kathryn Harrison has made an important advance in this regard, moving beyond the co-operation/conflict dichotomy.[17] She distinguishes between the rules of engagement, or the structure of intergovernmental relations as reflected in formal arrangements, and these relationships in practice, reflected in federal and provincial policy developments in the aftermath of these formal arrangements. While governments may formally agree to work together to develop shared policies or to minimize overlap of their policies, their subsequent policy objectives may be incompatible with the other level of government, and their relations in practice may reflect patterns of independence, conflict, or competition rather than collaboration. These concepts are well-suited to help clarify the role and importance of formal arrangements. Here we take a closer look at the *negotiating process* leading to the formal arrangements.

Similarly, assessments of the success of intergovernmental interactions are open to different interpretations. For some "success" is seen largely in terms of process: we talked; we avoided a big fight; we got an agreement that everyone can live with; we ensured that the lines would be open for future communication and co-operation. For others success is less a matter of how much harmony there is than what kind of policies arise: to what extent were the agreements substantial, enforceable, etc., and to what degree did they better equip governments individually and collectively to respond to the policy challenges that confronted them? Again, it is a matter for research whether the substantive implications of co-operative activity are preferable to the outcomes that result from competition and independent action.

This suggests the need to explore two levels of analysis. The first is to explain how and why co-operation develops, and, in particular why it tends to vary across policy sectors. Here co-operation is the dependent variable. The second level is to ask how and why the extent of intergovernmental collaboration matters. This is a contested question. On the one hand is the view that co-operation is essential to permit government collectively to meet the policy challenges that face Canada, and that excessive intergovernmental competition is a threat to unity in a fragile country. The alternative view, most closely associated with the work of Albert Breton and Fritz Scharpf,[18] is that co-operation and harmony should not be seen as ends in themselves; the collaboration can become government by a "cartel" of federal-provincial elites; and that subordinating policy content to the imperative of consensus results in decisions that are vague, lowest common denominators. In this chapter, we focus on the first set of questions.

Co-operative relations are difficult to identify because the existence of an agreement signed by representatives of most governments reveals little about the extent of the concessions the various parties had to make to reach it. For example, one agreement may have greater substantive impact on existing government policies, but have taken very little effort and required little compromise on the part of the signatories, while others may have less substantive impact on existing government policies but have taken great effort to reach carefully negotiated compromise. These assessments are made all the more difficult because agreements can also appear to have great policy consequences, but in practice lead to little, if any change. In this chapter, co-operation, or consensus and compromise, is disaggregated to take into account different stages in the negotiating process. We ask: i) was there an intergovernmental agreement, ii) did both levels of government agree to a process for collectively formulating the agreement, and iii) did the agreement — regardless of whether it is characterized as "disentangling" or "harmonizing" — have tangible effects on the policy development within the jurisdiction of each of the participating governments?

COMPROMISE AND CONSENSUS – AN EVALUATION

CANADA-WIDE ACCORD ON ENVIRONMENTAL HARMONIZATION

The Canada-Wide Accord on Environmental Harmonization, approved in January of 1998 by all participants in the CCME except Quebec, is a framework for the negotiation and implementation of future sub-agreements (bilateral, regional or multilateral) intended to harmonize environmental management.[19] This framework articulates a common vision, objectives, and principles to govern the partnership between jurisdictions. When ministers approved the accord, they also announced three sub-agreements on environmental inspections, environmental standards, and environmental assessment. The ministers' collective endorsement of the accord reflects a measure of compromise and consensus among participating governments. As the guide to the accord states, "The accord reflects the willingness of governments to come together as partners, and their commitment to meet their legal obligations for environmental protection."[20] The process leading to the accord reflects a significant degree of federal-provincial determination. Even after the federal minister walked away from an earlier attempt at an intergovernmental agreement in 1996, officials at both levels of government worked to rescue the agreement, engaging in an exercise leading to consensus among all governments but Quebec. The accord has been examined at length elsewhere,[21] but for the purpose of this study it is useful to examine the language of co-operation and compromise in the agreement. The Canada-Wide Environmental Standards sub-agreement provides "a co-operative, coordinated federal provincial and territorial approach" for identifying priorities requiring standards, developing these standards, and agreeing on government actions and obligations to attain these standards.[22] While the accord recognizes that governments are "committed to achieving a consistent level of environmental quality across Canada," implying consensus and compromise, it also recognizes the need for local, regional, provincial and territorial flexibility. Accordingly, the sub-agreement encourages governments to devise work plans to achieve the standards. But how each jurisdiction meets this goal is "at the discretion of the responsible government." That is, there is consensus to rationalize or disentangle the implementation of collectively devised targets.[23]

There has been significant momentum behind the harmonization initiative since the announcement of the accord and the initial three sub-agreements. Along with the development of an inspections and enforcement sub-agreement, and the creation of an annex to the accord on accountability and stakeholder participation, there have been Canada-wide (as opposed to federal) standards developed for several substances, and these standards have been set at a surprisingly high level.[24] However, public reporting on standards implementation within the CCME will not take place for years to come.[25] Thus, in many respects the greatest tests of strength of momentum behind the co-operative dynamic are yet to be confronted by the CCME. Furthermore, the accord emphasizes governments' retention of their legislative authorities, highlighting the agreement's lack of legal status, as well as the ability of any government to act within its existing authority if it chooses not to participate in a consensus. Thus, one should interpret the significance of these early signs of compromise and consensus with caution. Had governments successfully agreed to an earlier more specific proposal to harmonize environment management in 1996, the ensuing policy change may have been more readily apparent.[26]

NATIONAL FOREST STRATEGY

Unlike the Canada-Wide Accord on Environmental Harmonization, The National Forest Strategy (1998-2003) and the Canada Forest Accord do not establish groundrules for developing national (as opposed to federal) standards or principles for disentangling roles and responsibilities. Instead, the Canada Forest Accord reaffirms the commitment of the members of the Canadian Council of Forest Ministers (along with 30 non-governmental signatory organizations) "to maintain and enhance the long-term health of our forest ecosystems, for the benefit of all living things both nationally and globally, while providing environmental, economic, social and cultural opportunities for the benefit of present and future generations."[27] The National Forest Strategy is the companion to the accord, and delineates nine strategic directions intended to guide Canada's approach to sustainable forest management. These strategic directions define 43 principles, 31 objectives and 121 specific commitments. The accord, which does not make reference to the strategy, takes the form of a poster with the signatures of representatives of the 43 partners appearing at the base.

By signing the accord, governments, industry and professional associations, conservation, and Aboriginal organizations agree to each provide a "public and measurable action plan ... appropriate to [their] respective circumstances and capabilities."[28] In practice, these action plans are designed with reference to the commitments in the National Forest Strategy. These signatories are members of the National Forest Strategy Coalition, which oversees the planning, implementation, and evaluation of the strategy, and reports to the CCFM, the trustee of the strategy.

The strategy and the forest accord are significant examples of collaboration. They reflect principles to which the forestry community is currently committed as well as the guidelines and goalposts for advancing sustainable forest management. They are the result of an extensive consultative process involving multiple strategy drafts written by a federal-provincial and non-government writing team; regional and national forums; summaries of feedback from these forums; and opportunities for written comments by government and non-governmental actors. Since the accord and strategy were made public, new signatories to the accord have been added, and the secretariat for the strategy has analyzed the gaps in achieving the strategy's objectives based on the action plans of the signatories. The coalition has also published a record of accomplishments entitled *Our Evolving Journey Toward Sustainable Forests*.[29]

However, there are several indications that the consensus among the signatories is hollower in substance than the strategy and the accord imply. Unlike the standards sub-agreement negotiated by the CCME that commits *governments* to "ensur[ing] that standards are met through the application of their respective environmental management programs," in this case there are no specific actors identified as responsible for working towards each of the commitments identified in the National Forest Strategy. It is up to individual signatories to determine what aspects of the strategy pertain to them. Both agreements commit governments to action plans, but the strategy does not include any associated timelines.

In contrast, the CCME's standards sub-agreement states that where environmental issues "are transboundary or have interprovincial/interterritorial effects, or where an integrated Canada-wide approach is required, governments will seek agreement on a timeframe and how to attain the standard endorsed by Ministers." While the National Forest Strategy Coalition secretariat has prepared a "gap analysis" to establish if any of the 121 commitments of the strategy have been neglected in the development of action plans, there is no systematic way of linking the efforts of any one of the signatories active in achieving any of the 121 commitments. And although the standards sub-agreement of the CCME permits governments to withdraw from an implementation agreement if they give six months notice, this "way out" could end up as a political "stick" that encourages a greater degree of co-operation and consensus when compared with the "carrot" of being a National Forest Strategy Coalition member. In the case of the former, the formal absence of one government from the implementation of a standard will be more visible to other governments, environmental groups, and citizens than the lack of compliance in the case of the latter.

With the National Forest Strategy, the goal of the mid-term and final evaluations (conducted by an independent panel of experts) is to measure *collective* progress toward sustainable forest management. This provides much less incentive for any one government to comply, as no one signatory will be singled out for lack of action. A skeptic may be inclined to conclude that without identifying who is responsible for what, and without timelines and clearly defined targets, the Canada Forest Accord and National Forest Strategy are effective as public relations tools, but have limited capacity to motivate coalition members to coordinate their efforts, or even modify each government's existing policy trajectory.

Early observations of coalition activity also suggest that the co-operation and compromise implied in the accord and strategy are more difficult to achieve in practice. According to the 2000 *Report of the Commissioner of the Environment and Sustainable Development*, not one signatory had completed their action plan by the deadline of December 1998. There was no systematic follow-up with the organizations that had not submitted an action plan before the end of 1999, and by January 2000, only 17 of the 42 governments and organizations had achieved this task.[30] The mid-term evaluation of the strategy has now been completed and it indicates that "the signatories to the Forest Accord ... continue to demonstrate a commitment to sustainable forest management across the country."[31] But it also notes that there has been progress to date on only 39 of the 121 commitments.

It would be unfair to argue that governments are not enthusiastic about the strategy or that they are unwilling to implement it, especially since the life cycle of the strategy is not complete. Also, the collective approach to evaluation could be interpreted not as a weakness of the consensus and compromise among the signatories, but as a reflection of the holistic approach of the coalition to the concept of sustainable forest management. And many of the ways in which this concept is expressed in the individual commitments are not amenable to measurement, resembling commitments to an ongoing approach to issues more than goals to be achieved. But the consequence is that it is difficult to envision what a fully implemented strategy would look like. A separate initiative of the CCFM to develop criteria and indicators of sustainable forest management will likely result in more clearly defined ways of measuring the practice of sustainable development. But while the process leading to National Forest Strategy and accord were exercises in compromise and consensus, the reporting procedure attached to these agreements leaves little incentive for governments to modify their existing approaches and priorities in this policy area.

NATIONAL CHILD BENEFIT

First ministers have referred to the development of the NCB as the "model of co-operation that commits all governments to action."[32] Under this commitment, the federal government, which announced its first investment in the

1997 budget, provides a supplement to low-income families receiving the Canada Child Tax Benefit. The provinces may then reduce social assistance payments for families with children by this same amount, and reinvest these "savings" in programs and benefits for children that reflect each province's preferences and priorities. These "reinvestments" must fall within broad parameters of reducing the depth of child poverty and assisting low-income families with children in finding and keeping work, or promoting attachment to the workforce. These reinvestments include such programs as early childhood services and children-at-risk services; provincial child benefits and earned income supplements; childcare; and supplementary health benefits.[33] The Quebec government agrees with the basic principles of the National Child Benefit, but did not partake in its development.[34]

While there have been many debates over the appropriateness of this response to child poverty,[35] there is no doubt that this is a significant accomplishment in terms of compromise and consensus among the participating governments. It is in strong contrast to the limited interaction between the federal and provincial governments in matters of social policy during the early 1990s. In addition to the absence of federal-provincial-territorial meetings of ministers, the federal government unilaterally reduced transfers to the provinces with the introduction of the Canada Health and Social Transfer in 1995. The provinces found themselves excluded from this profound reshaping of circumstances under which social policy initiatives had to be sustained.

Banding together in this context, provincial and territorial social service ministers worked to devise a new model for the delivery of social services, proposing a detailed redefinition of social services roles and responsibilities of federal and provincial-territorial governments. Premiers created the Ministerial Council on Social Policy Reform and Renewal, and its first report carried a similar theme, seeking to clarify federal-provincial responsibilities for social programs. Key to both was a model that provided for a strong federal role in the provision of income supports, and a strong role for provinces in the delivery of services. This translated into a proposal for the "consolidation of income support for children into a single national program, jointly managed by both orders of government, with options for either federal or provincial-territorial delivery of benefits."[36]

With the lack of institutional structure supporting FPT negotiations, the absence of the federal government from the provincial process, and the provinces' shared experience with the introduction of the CHST, one might have been inclined to conclude that a co-operative process with the federal minister of social services was more remote than ever. Yet, the federal government joined with the provinces in creating the FPT version of the Ministerial Council on Social Policy Renewal, and its members made the development of an integrated child benefit one of their first priorities. While the social services ministers' reunion with their federal counterpart, Doug Young, was particularly rocky, Pierre Pettigrew, his successor, helped nurture a new spirit of camaraderie among the ministers. In 1996, 1997, and 1998, federal, provincial and territorial social services ministers directed the newly created NCB working group of officials, co-chaired by a provincial and a federal representative, to work on the details of the new program. At its largest, the working group involved health, finance, social services/human resources and intergovernmental officials, and it continues to stand out among social policy working groups as benefiting from a particularly co-operative dynamic.

While the NCB is perhaps the most significant of the three agreements in terms of its effect on existing government programs and policies of the participating governments, it is ironic that the NCB is not codified in a public intergovernmental agreement. Rather, the federal government paved the way for the new benefit system with its announcement in the 1997 budget to consolidate the Working Income Supplement and the Canada Child Tax Benefit, and the social services ministers outlined the new benefit system in public pamphlets thereafter.[37]

Of the three intergovernmental initiatives examined here, the NCB is the most advanced in its implementation. The commitments of the federal government to index the NCB and the ongoing expansion of the NCB supplement to the Canada Child Tax Benefit have fortified the financial backbone of the initiative. The governance and accountability framework, together with the Statement by Federal-Provincial-Territorial Ministers Responsible for Social Services on future directions for the NCB, confirm the ministers' apparent commitment to working together. The governance and accountability framework entrenches a role for FPT Ministers Responsible for Social Services by designating this forum as "the principal mechanism for governance of the National Child Benefit." Furthermore, it sets in place some broad guidelines for resolving disputes, and identifies the FPT NCB working group of officials, the FPT social services deputy ministers, and the ministers responsible for social services as the possible sites for problem-solving.

While the devising of specific "outcome indicators" to gauge the impact of the NCB on reducing promoting attachment to the workforce is in the nascent stages, the reporting scheme remains one of the most advanced among recent intergovernmental agreements. However, as new governments are elected, the foundation of the model of "recovery reinvestment" appears to be shifting slightly. Initially, New Brunswick and Newfoundland were the only two governments who chose not to "adjust" their social assistance benefits. They are now joined by Manitoba.[38] This is not to say that these governments are not committed to the NCB model, as the NCB model was designed to accommodate provincial governments that choose to pass onto social assistance recipients the full NCB supplement. Indeed, one of the key characteristics of the model was that it provided for reinvestments "reflective of each jurisdiction's special needs and priorities." However, the model is demonstrating some frailties. As new governments are elected with new perspectives on the relative importance of reducing public expenditures versus sustaining publicly funded programs, some ministries may find it difficult to spare reinvestment initiatives from possible cuts to their overall budgets. These dynamics, together with the lack of public awareness of the division of responsibilities for new supports and services, may cause social services ministers to consider modifications to the model in the future.

The concept of the "welfare wall," and the view that child poverty is best tackled by adjusting social assistance benefits so that parents on social assistance do not necessarily see a net increase in government financial support as a result of the NCB supplement, are two key pillars of this initiative. Yet, with the possibility that newly elected governments will choose not to recover the supplement from parents on social assistance, it appears that the NCB, through its broad discretion accorded to provinces, does not bind future governments to these characteristics.

TAKING A STEP BACK — COMPARING THE THREE CASES

The intergovernmental conferences of deputy ministers and ministers over the last two decades provide us with a rich source of information about general trends and a wealth of developments for specific case-study-based research. This allows us to reconsider some of the assumptions and ideas expressed during the 1978 conference, "Intergovernmental Relations in Canada Today." The "industry" of intergovernmental relations and the officials that work within it have not set us on a steady trajectory of more intergovernmental activity. Based on data collected by the CICS, we now know that while intergovernmental conferences have increased over time, ministerial conferences follow a cyclical pattern, likely reflecting the prerogatives of specific first ministers, and the issues (constitutional or non-constitutional) of the day.

The surge in overall intergovernmental activity in the second half of the 1990s reflects an increase in meetings of government officials and ministers of specific sectors, rather than an increase in summit or first minister relations. But this trend by itself does not confirm a shift to collaborative relations among governments. David Cameron and Richard Simeon have written of collaborative federalism that it "is very much a work in progress, a project in the making, more advanced in some policy areas than others."[39] The consideration of three key intergovernmental initiatives of three sectoral federal-provincial ministerial forums lends credibility to this claim. In every case, consensus and compromise were demonstrated in as much as participating governments collectively experienced a process leading to each agreement and publicly endorsed the resulting agreement. Each case also reflected a commitment to principles, more specific in some cases than in others. But they differ significantly in other ways. The Canada Forest Accord and National Forest Strategy represent a broad-based consensus, but the spectrum of signatories is vast in part because the 121 commitments are binding on no one in particular. The Canada-Wide Accord on Environmental Harmonization represents a different kind of consensus. Rather than a statement of commitments, it outlines the framework and process for arriving at future sub-agreements. In the case of the standards sub-agreement it also outlines a framework and process for arriving at jointly devised standards to be implemented as each jurisdiction sees fit. On the one hand, this "agreement to agree" may appear less substantive than the commitments in the National Forest Strategy. On the other hand, the articulation of steps to achieve agreement coupled with the commitment to demonstrate how jointly devised standards will be achieved in each jurisdiction implies a commitment to future joint decision-making.

Based on these observations one could argue that compromise and consensus appear to be more secure in more institutionalized decision-making environments. Recall that the CCME was more established than the CCFM as a decision-making forum. However, the NCB commitment does not follow this pattern. Like the Canada-Wide Accord, the NCB reflects a combination of collaboration and rationalization. Yet it is remarkable that what is described by some observers as one of the most significant social policy developments in years was devised within an intergovernmental forum that not only lacked the institutional fortification of the CCME or even the CCFM, but also had a recent history of relatively fractious federal-provincial relations.

This is not to suggest that the CCME or the CCFM have fallen short of their goals — indeed they may not have sought a greater degree of consensus and collaboration than that which was realized in the Canada-Wide Accord and Forest Strategy. But these cases do make clear that policy co-ordination and consensus decision-making among governments do not require institutionalized intergovernmental forums for deliberation. It may even be the case that the lack of established supports, traditions, and procedures in the federal-provincial-territorial ministers of social services forum and within the NCB working group created flexibility that encouraged rather than inhibited policy innovation. Cameron and Simeon have observed that ministerial councils "have become the workhorses of the (intergovernmental) system, and are gradually assuming a solidity and continuity that they have not typically had before."[40] But the cases examined here suggest that solidity and continuity do not determine which ministerial forums will be the workhorses or where compromises and consensus will be achieved. The NCB, the most complex arrangement examined here, was devised within the ministerial forum with the least solidity and continuity.[41]

In terms of whether the agreements have tangible effects on the subsequent policy developments of each government, again there is no clear link with institutionalization. In the case of the Canada-Wide Accord on Environmental

Harmonization it is too early to tell, whereas with the National Forest Strategy governments have been slow to respond. With the National Child Benefit, the broad discretion accorded to provinces for redirected funds makes non-compliance virtually undetectable.

If not the institutionalization of federal-provincial-territorial ministerial forums, what does account for the instances of consensus and compromise reflected in the processes of these three forums and the impact of the agreements they negotiate? Several alternative explanations can be culled from studies of previous intergovernmental developments in Canada. One institutional change thought to have contributed to more conflictual relations over time is the creation of intergovernmental specialists, located in ministries or agencies close to the centre, and focused on a government's broad strategy for intergovernmental relations. Relations that are "factored," or in other words conducted at the sectoral level, rather than at or near the level of summit relations, will likely be more successful.[42] This is because program specialists are more likely to share common norms and values associated with the policy field, and to face similar constituencies and clienteles.[43] Still others stress the importance of departmentalized, rather than centralized, Cabinet decision-making models which grant to sectoral ministers and officials the discretion necessary to reach intergovernmental agreement,[44] or that the emergence of complex policy objectives of elected governments, increasingly common during the establishment of the welfare state, reduces the discretion of intergovernmental actors,[45] and mitigates incremental sectorally specific ad hoc agreements.[46] But as levels of conflict and collaboration rise and fall over time, and the presence of intergovernmental specialists and centralized decision-making remain, the power of these explanations declines. These explanations are also not well-suited to understanding variation in patterns of co-operation across sectors apparent at one point in time.

An alternative set of actor-centred explanations emphasizes individual approaches of intergovernmental participants, rather than institutional developments. In 1970 D.V. Smiley argued that the "personalized fabric" of intergovernmental relations, or the attitudes of intergovernmental officials and the self-imposed restraints on their behaviour, were particularly beneficial for the establishment of federal-provincial co-operation. This was most likely to exist when the turnover of intergovernmental participants in a specific issue area was infrequent.[47] Constant communication between federal and provincial participants is also thought to enhance the accuracy of the perceptions of the objectives and interests of other governments, which is considered key to establishing intergovernmental co-operation.[48]

A third set of explanations focuses on characteristics of the issue itself, and environmental constraints surrounding it rather than actors or institutional settings. "Conflicting partisan objectives," economic strains, or other broad changes may give rise to "genuine intractable differences,"[49] potentially overwhelming the strength of personal ties among intergovernmental officials or the institutional settings thought to be more likely to facilitate cooperation. Several have also concluded that conflict is more likely during periods when governments or regions hold deeply divergent views of the essence of the political community and citizenship.[50] The nature of the issue at hand also appears to play a significant role in determining whether co-operation or conflict among governments will arise.[51] In some cases the issue allows for the use of the instrument of the federal spending power, which tends to grease the wheels of co-operation.[52] In others, where the status or identity of particular communities or regions is at the heart of the issue, or where governments are united along regional or linguistic lines, cooperation is thought to be less likely.[53]

The instances of co-operative processes and intergovernmental agreements examined here are best understood as the result of environmental factors, some of which are broad, affecting an array of policy areas, others specific to each policy problem. For example, the desire for the federal government to demonstrate that it was possible to renew the federation through non-constitutional means as part of their "plan A" approach to national unity provided momentum in the CCME deliberations and social services ministers' consideration of an integrated child benefit. The desire of some provinces to streamline environmental assessment procedures, and the low salience of environmental concern among the public are part of the sectorally specific web of pressures that nudged governments toward a harmonized approach to environmental management.[54] In the case of the National Child Benefit one can point to the impending 1997 federal election, the increasingly visible scar of child poverty in Canada, the limited popularity in neo-liberal times of increasing social assistance rates, and the appeal in an era of fiscal restraint of designing a supplement delivered through the tax system rather than a more visible social entitlement, as some the environmental factors which accounted for the commitment of governments to the NCB. In the case of the National Forest Strategy, we have argued elsewhere that more important than the degree of institutionalization of the coalition or CCFM was the international scrutiny of Canada's forest community, the desire of the federal government to establish a common approach in the absence of jurisdictional authority or cash to finance federal transfers to provincial forestry coffers, and the decision of the federal government to step back from forestry commitments in the aftermath of the failed Charlottetown Accord.[55] Also, the presence of non-governmental actors in the deliberations leading to the National Forest Strategy diminished the likelihood that this process would be clearly linked to substantive policy changes.

But it also appears that intergovernmental actors do not merely react to environmental circumstances. The agency of individuals was a factor contributing to compromise and consensus in the case of the NCB, where the approach of Minister Pettigrew, and the personalities and ideas of key federal and provincial officials, helped establish a sense of trust and camaraderie at the ministers' table and within the working group, which is not apparent in other aspects of intergovernmental social policy, or in other ministerial councils and their working groups.

More generally, it can also be argued that the extent of consensus and compromise in these three cases reflects the extent of compatibility between the objectives of both levels of government, greatly defined by jurisdictional authority, and the enduring rationale of ministerial responsibility. With an agreement such as the NCB, provincial governments gained access to additional funding without giving up policy autonomy, while the federal government gained visibility as a provider of assistance while maintaining control over the reins of its spending power. In the case of the National Forest Strategy, the federal government, lacking the jurisdictional capacity to impose national standards, and the provinces, which have traditionally guarded their authority over their forestry practices, found the strategy format and the collective approach to evaluation mutually agreeable. In both cases, the behaviour of both levels of governments suggests adherence to the core assumption that extra-parliamentary bodies and decisions made therein ought not to compromise the legislative discretion of individual governments.

It is also interesting to note that in at least one case examined here, collaborative intergovernmental activity corresponds with an increase in post-agreement institutionalization of the ministerial forum. Social services ministers have collectively established an NCB web site, and there are now terms of reference for joint committees of officials supporting the federal-provincial-territorial social services ministers. This suggests that in some cases institutionalization is perhaps the outcome of co-operation rather than a precursor to it.

At the 1979 seminar on confrontation and collaboration in intergovernmental relations, participants ultimately agreed that "no amount of manipulation of the mechanisms of intergovernmental relations could remove the difficulties" contributing to conflictual intergovernmental relations.[56] The three cases considered here hint that this claim resonates beyond shifts in general patterns of intergovernmental relations across time to sectorally specific intergovernmental developments.

NOTES

Information gleaned from a number of interviews with federal and provincial officials informs this chapter. Because these interviews were conducted on the basis that views shared would not be attributed to specific individuals, I have incorporated this information in the body of the text without attribution. I wish to thank Richard Simeon, Linda White, Luc Turgeon, Martin Papillon, the two anonymous reviewers and the editors of this volume for their constructive criticism and useful comments on an earlier version of this chapter. This research was funded in part by the Social Sciences and Humanities Research Council of Canada.

1.   R. Simeon, "Intergovernmental Relations in Canada Today — Summary of Discussions," in *Confrontation and Collaboration — Intergovernmental Relations in Canada Today*, ed. R. Simeon (Toronto: Institute of Public Administration of Canada, 1979).

2.   Gérard Veilleux, "L'évolution des mechanismes de liaison intergouvernementale," in *Confrontation and Collaboration — Intergovernmental Relations in Canada Today*, ed. R. Simeon (Toronto: Institute of Public Administration of Canada, 1979).

3.   D. Stevenson, "The Role of Intergovernmental Conferences in the Decision-Making Process," in *Confrontation and Collaboration — Intergovernmental Relations in Canada Today*, ed. R. Simeon (Toronto: Institute of Public Administration of Canada, 1979).

4.   This is one characteristic attributed to collaborative federalism in D. Cameron and R. Simeon, "Intergovernmental Relations and Democratic Citizenship," in *Governance in the Twenty-first Century: Revitalizing the Public Service*, eds. B. Guy Peters and Donald J. Savoie (Kingston and Montreal: McGill-Queen's University Press, 2000), p. 77.

5.   These ministers and officials are not always affiliated with the same ministries (for example there may be formal intergovernmental meetings involving representatives of health and social services ministers together); and there are often "central agency" intergovernmental officials present.

6.   Territorial ministers have come to participate in ministerial meetings. The data presented here do not distinguish between those meetings where they are in attendance and those where they are not.

7.   Figure 1 and Table 1 exclude meetings and conferences conducted at the level of first ministers (such as the Annual Premiers' Conferences). Data for the fiscal year 2000 are based on an unofficial tally of Canadian Intergovernmental Conference Secretariat-sponsored ministerial conferences.

8.   It should be noted that the data do not include other forms of intergovernmental interaction that are less formal, such as telephone conversations, email correspondence and the increasingly utilized "conference call." Nor do they capture the interaction below the deputy ministerial level, which in every sector is no doubt a routine occurrence. It does not incorporate bilateral and regional meetings either.

9.   Canadian Intergovernmental Conference Secretariat (2002), *Our Role*, available at <www.scics.gc.ca/role_e.html>.

10. Indeed, the concept of secretariats is not new. In fact, at the time of the 1979 conference, Council of Ministers of Education, Canada (CMEC), and the then-Canadian Council of Resource and Environment Ministers (CCREM) as well as the Canadian Council of Transport Ministers each had its own secretariat. See G. Robertson, "The Role of Interministerial Conferences in the Decision-Making Process," in *Confrontation and Collaboration — Intergovernmental Relations*

in Canada Today, ed. R. Simeon (Toronto: Institute of Public Administration of Canada, 1979).

11. Canadian Council of Ministers of the Environment Secretariat, *CCME History*, unpublished document.

12. Canadian Council of Ministers of the Environment (1998), *A New Vision for the Canadian Council of Ministers of the Environment*, available at <www.ccme.ca/1e_about/1ed.html>.

13. There were, however, occasional FPT deputy ministers meetings, and meetings of lower-level, non-elected officials. The first meeting of the FPT ministers was 13 January 1997.

14. H. Lazar, "Non-Constitutional Renewal: Toward a New Equilibrium in the Federation," in *Canada the State of the Federation 1997*, ed. H. Lazar (Kingston: Institute of Intergovernmental Relations, Queen's University, 1998). Emphasis in original.

15. L.D. Desautels, "Accountability for Alternative Service-Delivery Arrangements in the Federal Government: Some Consequences of Sharing the Business of Government," in *Collaborative Government: Is there a Canadian Way? New Directions*, no. 6, eds. S. Delacourt and D.G. Lenihan (Toronto: Institute of Public Administration of Canada, 1999), p. 24.

16. A. Noel, "Canada: Love It or Don't Leave It!" *Policy Options* (January-February 2000):34-36; A. Noel, "Power and Purpose in Intergovernmental Relations," *Policy Matters* 2,6 (2001).

17. K. Harrison, "Intergovernmental Relations and Environmental Policy: Concepts and Context," in *Managing the Environmental Union: Intergovernmental Relations and Environmental Policy in Canada*, eds. P.C. Fafard and K. Harrison (Kingston: School of Policy Studies, Queen's University, 2000).

18. A. Breton, "Supplementary Statement," in Royal Commission on the Economic Union and Development Prospects for Canada, *Report*, Vol. 3 (Ottawa: Supply and Services Canada, 1985); and F.W. Scharpf, "The Joint Decision Trap: Lessons from German Federalism and European Integration," *Public Administration* 66, 3(1988):239-78.

19. However, Quebec did participate in parts of the negotiations leading to both the first and second attempts to reach an intergovernmental agreement in this policy area. All references to the consensus among governments reached in the accord do not include Quebec.

20. Canadian Council of Ministers of the Environment (1998), *Guide to the Canada-Wide Accord on Environmental Harmonization*, available at <www.ccme.ca/3e_priorities/3ea_harmonization/3ea1_accord/3ea1a.html>.

21. M.S. Winfield, "Environmental Politics and Federalism," in *Canadian Federalism: Performance, Effectiveness and Legitimacy*, eds. H. Bakvis and G. Skogstad (Toronto: Oxford University Press, 2002); P.C. Fafard, "Groups, Governments and the Environment: Some Evidence from the Harmonization Initiative," in *Managing the Environmental Union: Intergovernmental Relations and Environ-*

mental Policy in Canada, eds. P.C. Fafard and K. Harrison (Kingston: School of Policy Studies, Queen's University, 2000); K. Harrison, "Federal-Provincial Relations and the Environment; Unilateralism, Collaboration, and Rationalization," in *Canadian Environmental Policy: Context and Cases*, 2d ed., eds. D.L. VanNijnatten and R. Boardman (Toronto: Oxford University Press, 2002); and P.C. Fafard, "Green Harmonization: The Success and Failure of Recent Environmental Intergovernmental Relations," in *Canada the State of the Federation 1997*, ed. H. Lazar (Kingston: Institute of Intergovernmental Relations, Queen's University, 1998).

22. Canadian Council of Ministers of the Environment (1998), *Canada-Wide Environmental Standards Sub-agreement*, available at <www.ccme.ca/3e_priorities/ 3ea_harmonization/3ea2_cws/3ea2a.html>.

23. Canadian Council of Ministers of the Environment (1998), *Guide to the Canada-Wide Accord on Environmental Harmonization*.

24. Harrison, "Federal-Provincial Relations and the Environment: Unilateralism, Collaboration, and Rationalization."

25. For example, in the case of particulate matter and ozone, the first report on progress toward meeting the standard will be issued in 2005. There will also be annual reports on achievement of the standard, beginning in 2011, one year after the target date of 2010. In the case of dioxins and furans, the CCME will receive jurisdictional reports on achieving the standard in spring 2004 and spring 2008, with existing facilities required to meet the standards in 2005 or 2006 depending on the nature of the facility. See Canadian Council of Ministers of the Environment (2001), *Canada-Wide Standards for Dioxins and Furans*, available at <www.ccme.ca/pdfs/com_meetings_04_e/d_amd_f_standard_e.pdf>.

26. Fafard, "Green Harmonization: The Success and Failure of Recent Environmental Intergovernmental Relations."

27. Canadian Council of Forest Ministers, Canada Forest Accord (Ottawa: Canadian Council of Forest Ministers, 1998).

28. Canadian Council of Forest Ministers, National Forest Strategy (1998-2000), *Sustainable Forests: A Canadian Commitment* (Ottawa: Canadian Council of Forest Ministers, 1998).

29. Canadian Council of Forest Ministers, National Forest Strategy Coalition, *Canadian Accomplishments: Our Evolving Journey Toward Sustainable Forests 1997-2000* (Ottawa: National Forest Strategy Coalition, n.d.).

30. This number includes the federal government and eight of the nine provinces. In addition, Quebec had also prepared an action plan. See "Co-operation Between Federal, Provincial and Territorial Governments," *2000 Report of the Commissioner of the Environment and Sustainable Development* (Ottawa: Department of Public Works and Government Services Canada, 2000), ch. 7, p. 4.

31. Gardner Pinfold Consulting, *A Mid-Term Evaluation of the National Forest Strategy 1998-2003, Sustainable Forests: A Canadian Commitment* (Ottawa: National Forest Strategy Coalition, 2001).

32. Federal/Provincial/Territorial Council on Social Policy Renewal, News Release, "Council on Social Policy Renewal Launches Work on Framework Agreement for Canada's Social Union," 13 March 1998.

33. Canada. *The National Child Benefit Progress Report: 2000*, available at <http://www.nationalchildbenefit.ca/ncb/NCB-2000/toceng-reinvest2.html>.

34. Any references to provinces or provincial governments and social services ministers' positions in this case do not include the government of Quebec.

35. D. Durst, ed., *Canada's National Child Benefit: Phoenix or Fizzle?* (Halifax, NS: Fernwood, 1999); and K. Battle and M. Mendelson, eds., *Benefits for Children: A Four Country Study* (Ottawa: Caledon Institute of Social Policy, 2001).

36. Ministerial Council on Social Policy Reform and Renewal, *Report to Premiers* (1995), p. 14.

37. Social services ministers have since added to public intergovernmental records through a statement by Federal Provincial and Territorial Ministers, and the development of an NCB Governance and Accountability Framework. See Federal/Provincial/Territorial Ministers Responsible for Social Services, *NCB Governance and Accountability Framework*, 12 March 1998.

38. New Brunswick has never adjusted social assistance payments to recover the NCB supplement. After Premier Camille Theriault replaced Premier Frank McKenna it became clear that New Brunswick would not "recover and reinvest." Newfoundland and Labrador chose not to adjust in 1998-99, and in 2000-2001. Manitoba has not recovered the NCB supplement increase in 2000-2001. See the *National Child Benefit Progress Report: 2000*. It appears that actions of these governments are somewhat parallel to Quebec as it too does not recover the Canada Child Tax Benefit from social assistance recipients. However these three governments continue to take part in the initiative in that they report their NCB "initiatives" in the annual NCB progress reports.

39. Cameron and Simeon, "Intergovernmental Relations and Democratic Citizenship," p. 102.

40. Ibid., p. 82.

41. This is not to say that the NCB is representative of other initiatives that fall under the rubric of the social services ministers' intergovernmental forum. Indeed, not all have benefited from the same co-operative dynamic. Nevertheless, the NCB case exemplifies that institutionalization is not a prerequisite to co-operation among governments.

42. D.V. Smiley, "An Outsider's Observations of Federal-Provincial Relations Among Consenting Adults," in *Confrontation and Collaboration — Intergovernmental Relations in Canada Today*, ed. R. Simeon (Toronto: Institute of Public Administration of Canada, 1979); D.V. Smiley, *Canada in Question: Federalism in the Eighties*, 3rd ed. (Toronto: McGraw-Hill Ryerson Limited, 1980); D.V. Smiley, *The Federal Condition in Canada* (Toronto: McGraw-Hill Ryerson Limited, 1987).

43. R. Dyck, "The Canada Assistance Plan: The Ultimate in Cooperative Federalism," *Canadian Public Administration* 19,4 (1976):587-602; D.V. Smiley, "Public

Administration and Canadian Federalism," *Canadian Public Administration* 7 (1964):371-88; D.V. Smiley, "Cooperative Federalism: An Evaluation," from *Constitutional Adaptation and Canadian Federalism Since 1945.* Vol. 4 of the Documents of the Royal Commission on Bilingualism and Biculturalism (Ottawa: Queen's Printer, 1970). Reprinted in *Canadian Federalism: Myth or Reality,* ed. J.P. Meekison (Toronto: Methuen, 1977); and Smiley, *Canada in Question.*

44. J.S. Dupré, "Reflection on the Workability of Executive Federalism," in *Intergovernmental Relations,* ed. R. Simeon (Toronto: University of Toronto Press, 1985).

45. D.V. Smiley, "Cooperative Federalism."

46. D.V. Smiley, "Federal-Provincial Conflict in Canada," *Publius* 4 (1974):7-24; reprinted in *Canadian Federalism: Myth or Reality,* ed. J. P. Meekison (Toronto: Methuen, 1977); Smiley, *The Federal Condition in Canada.*

47. Smiley, "Cooperative Federalism," p. 263. See also Smiley, "Federal-Provincial Conflict in Canada."

48. Smiley, "Federal-Provincial Conflict in Canada"; Smiley, *The Federal Condition in Canada.*

49. D.V. Smiley, *Canada in Question: Federalism in the Seventies* (Toronto: McGraw-Hill Ryerson, 1976), p. 75; see also Smiley, "Federal-Provincial Conflict in Canada"; K. Norrie, R. Simeon and M. Krasnick, *Federalism and Economic Union in Canada,* Vol. 59 of the Royal Commission on the Economic Union and Development Prospects for Canada (Toronto: University of Toronto Press, 1986); and J. Warhurst, "Canada's Intergovernmental Relations Specialists," *Australian Journal of Public Administration* 42, 4 (1983):459-85.

50. Norrie, *et al., Federalism and Economic Union in Canada*; and Smiley, *The Federal Condition in Canada.*

51. D.V. Smiley, "The Structural Problem of Canadian Federalism," *Canadian Public Administration* 14 (1971):326-34; Smiley, *Canada in Question*; Dupré, "Reflection on the Workability of Executive Federalism"; and Norrie, *et al., Federalism and Economic Union in Canada.*

52. Norrie, *et al., Federalism and Economic Union in Canada.*

53. Cameron and Simeon, "Intergovernmental Relations and Democratic Citizenship."

54. Harrison, "Federal-Provincial Relations."

55. J.M. Simmons, "Patterns of Process: Understanding the Role of Non-Governmental Actors in the Development of the Canada Forest Accord and the National Forest Strategy 1998-2003," paper presented at the annual meeting of the Canadian Political Science Association, Quebec City, 2001.

56. Simeon, "Intergovernmental Relations in Canada Today."

V

Regional Institutions and Relations

11

Alberta/Saskatchewan Transborder Contacts with US States: A Survey and Analysis Revisited

Howard Leeson

En 1975, on a tenu à Ottawa une conférence sur la dimension fédérale des relations extérieures. Bien que la plupart des articles se soient concentrés sur le rôle du Québec, ou sur l'interface fédérale-provinciale dans les affaires mondiales, certains se sont penchés sur ce qu'on pourrait appeler des microcontacts entre les sous-groupes des états fédéraux du monde. Plus particulièrement, l'un d'entre eux s'est intéressé aux contacts transfrontaliers entre les provinces de l'ouest canadien et des états américains. Cet article présentait les données selon un cadre de travail analytique et arrivait à des conclusions sur la direction de ces contacts. Ce chapitre poursuit le travail ainsi entamé, y ajoutant une comparaison entre les contacts de l'époque et ceux de 2001, 26 ans plus tard.

INTRODUCTION

In 1975 a conference on the federal dimension in external relations was held in Ottawa. While most of the papers concentrated on the role of Quebec, or the interface of federal and provincial governments in world affairs, a few looked at what could be called micro-contacts between the subunits of federal states in the world. In particular, one looked at transborder contacts between western Canadian provinces and US states. That paper organized the data in a framework of analysis and came to some conclusions about the direction of those contacts. This chapter builds on that work, providing a comparison of those contacts with similar contacts in 2001, 26 years later.

The events of 11 September 2001 in the United States have fixed in everyone's mind the importance of the "global village" and "globalization." No longer is a state immune to events elsewhere on earth, and while the new interdependence may bring economic benefits, ignoring others and their interests can be fatal. Although security issues involving terrorism and Iraq will probably continue to dominate the international agenda for some time, most matters involving globalization and international interdependence will be sorted out in a less dramatic fashion. Increasingly, easy transportation and communication, and the economic consequences of this new milieu, mean that virtually all activities in the world will become to some degree interrelated.

How will political decision-makers take account of this change? What political structures are needed to keep order and facilitate life in the global world? More importantly, what will be the impact of globalizing forces on domestic political structures, especially in federal states like Canada? Will globalization mean a more centralized federation as most political decisions become internationalized, or will it mean, as some have said, that national governments will become increasingly irrelevant?

In the conference that generated this chapter these broad questions were addressed by proposing several hypotheses, most of which were based on two important assumptions. The first assumption was that the world is indeed integrating, globally and regionally, and that this integration is globally pervasive. The second assumption is that the resulting interdependence and integration would require a political response. That is, institutions and political decision-makers must respond to the external pressures and demands of globalization by modifying political institutions and behaviour. These responses, it was assumed, would be more difficult to generate and sustain in federal states such as Canada.

As a result of the above assumptions a specific hypothesis was put forward by the conference. "Political integration between Canada and the United States will increase — including provincial-state linkages and perhaps community cross-border linkages — in response to escalating trade and other cross-border interaction."[1]

This chapter tests one part of this hypothesis. It compares data on transborder contacts between the provinces of Saskatchewan and Alberta on one side, and several US states on the other. The data result from studies done by the author in 1975 and 2001.

It is apparent from the comparison of data in the chapter that the above hypothesis could not be fully sustained. That is, the integration of social and economic activities in North America has not led to a concomitant increase in subunit contacts between states and provinces in the US and Canada. However, as we will see, it has led to a deepening of the "quality" of the contacts involved.

GLOBALIZATION AND INTERNATIONAL INTEGRATION

Much is being made of the impact of globalization on the role of the nation state in the world. However, there is little consensus on what is meant by the term globalization. Daniel Madar says in his book on international relations:

"Globalization has been used in so many contexts that it can refer to almost anything that is international and widespread."[2] He restricts his own generalizations to matters that are mainly economic, made possible primarily by changes in the technologies associated with communication and transportation, the growth of the General Agreement on Tariffs and Trade after World War II, and the removal of restrictions on monetary policy in the last several decades. He readily concedes, however, that the implications of these changes go far beyond the economic world:

> The pervasiveness of these changes and the industrial advantages of scale and efficiency have raised questions about sovereign statehood's future. Will it turn out to have been a transitional form of human organization? Will functions that have been regarded as sovereign prerogatives, such as regulating the transborder movement of capital and goods and managing national economies, pass into the hands of the private sector or international institutions?[3]

In other words, will globalization force important political changes in the world system, as we know it? Further, will these changes be restricted only to the external political relations of states, or will internal political arrangements also be changed?

INTERNATIONAL INTEGRATION THEORY

Globalization is not new. The globe has been "shrinking" for some time. The forces of technology and social organization have been at work for centuries, but have become most apparent in the last several decades. Academics began to look at this phenomenon with more interest in the 1960s. It was proposed then that there was a causal link between social and economic processes and political institutions; that is, that increasing economic integration in the world was forcing political integration also. Writers such as Amitai Etzioni outlined the rationale for this assumption.

> The central variable for the "take-off" of supranational authority is the amount of international decision-making required. This in turn is determined largely by the amounts and kinds of flows that cross international borders.... Moreover, the relationship seems not to be linear; that is, some increases in a particular flow (or shared activity) can be handled by the old decision-making system, but once a certain threshold is passed some supranational authority is almost inevitable.[4]

Thus, for Etzioni, political structure was perceived to be the outcome of other social processes, especially economic activity, and the volume of these contacts could be used to predict the likelihood of the creation of new international political structures and entities. Such an approach conceives of politics as the dependent variable. Later theorists, such as Michael Haas, Joseph S. Nye, and James N. Rosenau began to question the usefulness of this blunt approach. They began to talk in terms of cascading interdependence, complex governance, subsidiarity, and a positive role for the state.[5] All, however, noted the nexus between liberal institutions and the development of supra-national governing bodies.

However, international integration has not proceeded in a homogeneous manner in the world. Most clear examples of international integration seem to be occurring at the regional level. The European Economic Union is the best-known example of regional integration, and consequently the one most often used by those studying in this area. As noted above, the fact that international integration is occurring at the regional level has not changed the theoretical approach of those who propose pluralist theories to explain increasing political integration. A belief in pluralism has dominated both those in academe and in the emerging institutions of the EU. Most firmly believe in the inevitability of the process, that it is "good" for Europeans, and that it will be achieved by democratic means. Put another way, the process will succeed because most people in the EU want political integration to take place in order to maximize economic and social benefits.

It has come as a shock therefore to many "Europeanists" to find out that there is increasing resistance to the project. Political integration is not inevitable, and indeed may be failing. This situation is addressed in the white paper just released by the Commission of the European Communities in July 2001.

> European integration has delivered 50 years of stability, peace, and economic prosperity. It has helped to raise standards of living, built an internal market and strengthened the Union's voice in the world. It has achieved results which would not have been possible by individual Member States acting on their own.

> These results have been achieved by democratic means. The Union is built on the rule of law; it can draw on the Charter of Fundamental Rights, and it has a double democratic mandate through a parliament representing EU citizens, and a Council representing the elected governments of member states.

> Yet, despite its achievements, many Europeans feel alienated from the Union's work.[6]

Alienation from the new political structures of the EU was forecast by many observers. They worried that such arrangements, while nominally democratic, were actually created and sustained by economic and political elites who did little to ensure that allegiances to the new political structures would be strengthened in the several states. European integration, to use a cliché, is only "skin deep."

Such a discussion is important for our purposes since it suggests that even when using democratic means, such supranational integration can be problematic, and may not be inevitable, especially for federal states where jurisdiction is divided. If it is imposed without consultation, or participation, it probably further decreases the chance of permanent acceptance. In other words, it is possible to challenge the assumption that political integration is the simple product of economic and social integration, and that it will proceed inevitably in a linear manner.

THE IMPACT OF GLOBALIZATION ON FEDERALISM

Much of the above discussion will be familiar to students of Canadian federalism. It represents the first attempts to explain political integration and disintegration, attempts that were rooted in a crude socio-economic determinism. The decade of the 1970s saw the development of more sophisticated hypotheses about the linkages between political power, the state, and evolving economic and social structures in Canada. These hypotheses began to accentuate the role and power of governments and their relationship with each other.

Previous frameworks of analysis dealing with federalism had concentrated on formal legal arrangements and how these arrangements changed over the decades following Confederation. In particular much was made of the reversal of the "constitutional intentions" of the founding fathers. Federal-provincial conflict in the early years was ascribed to the natural "jostling" that came from attempts to sort out the proper roles of the federal and provincial governments. The forces that drove these changes were governments and the courts. Federalism was a "balance" between two orders of government, a balance that could be described in terms of a legal equilibrium. That equilibrium could be upset by any of the players, thus disturbing the intended relationships. The two orders of government might be in conflict with each other, but conflict was not the intended or acceptable outcome. Indeed, a federal arrangement became "more perfect" if there was less overlap and conflict.

Later conceptions of the roots and arrangements of federal states took issue with assumptions that federal systems were solely political or legal. Writing in 1952, W.S. Livingston had this to say: "The essence of federalism lies not in the institutional or constitutional structure but in the society itself. Federal government is a device by which the federal qualities of the society are articulated and protected."[7]

Implicit in this analysis was the premise that regional interests might be articulated through provincial governments. This put them in competition with each other and the federal government, at least some of the time. In other words, pluralist assumptions about liberalism, and thus competition, were fundamental to federalism. A federal system was one in which competing regional interests sought to articulate and legitimize their claims in the whole society.

This view of Canadian federalism was further strengthened in the next decade by analysis of the activities of certain provincial governments as they sought to strengthen their role in the federation through the use of natural resource revenue. It was loosely referred to as "province-building," a term that came to be associated with any activity that sought to build the economic, social, or political community at the provincial level. Again, the federal system was pictured as one in which there was intense competition for power, not only to represent regional interests, but also to build the power of the provincial state. By the 1980s then, it was not only accepted that both competition and conflict characterized the Canadian federal system, but more importantly, competition and conflict for the sake of power itself had come to be important. As Donald Smiley said in 1979: "It seems impossible to escape the conclusion that for both orders of government jurisdictional autonomy has become an important independent value."[8]

The conception that the state had interests of its own, and that these interests were primarily about enlarging its "market share" in the world of politics, was not universally accepted by students of federalism. While most were willing to concede that competition had some influence on the goals of government, they also remained convinced that the governments were primarily influenced by outside interests. This included not only pluralists, but also some, such as Anne Legare, writing from a Marxist perspective.[9] Indeed, others such as Albert Breton despaired that there was not more competition in the system.[10]

By the 1990s it was clear to most observers that integration and disintegration of political units was a complex process in which political behaviour was important, if not decisive. This was especially true in federal systems, where sovereignty is divided and the political structures respond to both external and internal centrifugal and centripetal forces.

A FEDERALISM OF RESTRAINT

The last decades of the twentieth century brought with them not only the globalization of economic and social activity, but the globalization of ideas and ideologies as well. Critical to earlier analyses had been the assumption that the state would continue to have a large and expanding role in society. This assumption remained unchallenged by most students of federalism then. Writing in 1993, Richard Simeon succinctly summarized the changes that took place in the 1990s:

> We are only just becoming familiar with the federalism of restraint, the federalism of hard times. It is likely to be very different from the competition and conflict associated with the federalism of growth, which characterized the period between the 1960s and the 1980s. Then the governmental competition was over the expansion of government activities and the competition for credit. Today it is about downsizing, restructuring, and the avoidance of blame.[11]

While Simeon emphasized the importance of the fiscal crisis (although at the time no one knew how short-lived that it would be), others such as Paul Barker emphasized the conjunction of this with external influences.

> Since the mid-1970s, the federal government had been experiencing sizable budget deficits, but in the 1980s the problem assumed much larger dimensions.... A second force was globalization and the internationalization of economic activity. To remain competitive in this new environment, Canada had to restructure its social programs.[12]

Thus, in the 1990s Canadian governments were "downsized," and the role of each order of government redefined by the fiscal crisis and the economic imperatives generated by the new globalizing world. The result was a "leaner and meaner" version of what went before. This necessitated new arrangements that maximized transparency, accountability, efficiency, disentanglement, and the removal of overlap and duplication.

It was no longer acceptable for governments to use scarce resources, or squander comparative advantage, in competition with each other. Conflict, overlap, and duplication were out, and constructive co-operation was in. Terms like "reinventing government," "re-balancing," "cross-system initiatives," and others became common in the effort to redesign institutions or devolve responsibilities.

In other words, to further the analysis of Simeon, we adjusted not only to the federalism of restraint in the early 1990s, but the federalism of the right, a federalism in which the downsizing of government at all levels became not only necessary but desirable. Federal-provincial co-operation was cast in terms of the removal of government from many activities, or where that was not possible, in limiting the scope of government involvement and intervention. In terms of our international relations it meant the adoption of the Free Trade Agreement and then the North American Free Trade Agreement in order that economic relations could be freed from the shackles of government intervention, federal or provincial. The Agreement on International Trade is the complementary domestic agreement to NAFTA.

In this new federalism the role of all governments was reduced, and the role of some new international agencies, such as NAFTA dispute panels, was introduced. A premium was placed on co-operation in some areas, and competition in others. Herman Bakvis and Grace Skogstad put it very well in their new book on Canadian federalism:

> Thus, the emerging portrait ... reveals both the competitive and cooperative faces of Canadian federalism at work.... Competitive federalism is fully evident in social programs.... The cooperative dimension is also fully displayed, most notably in governments' responses to the challenges of internationalization and the need to coordinate their actions to promote mutual trade liberalization goals.[13]

Co-operation and competition are not so neatly divided into external and internal dimensions, however. Most provincial governments are prepared to compete with each other internationally for economic reasons, just as they do domestically. They weigh the advantages of international participation in both competitive and co-operative terms, seeking to maximize advantages for local businesses or other groups. Thus, they may co-operate with the federal government and other provinces on some initiatives, such as Team Canada missions, while competing with them in other situations. All of this activity has a long and honourable history in Canada. Canadian provincial governments have participated internationally for most of the life of this nation.[14]

THE ROLE OF PROVINCES IN INTERNATIONAL INTEGRATION

What then is the role of provincial governments in the "New World Order" of North America? We are left with contradictory possibilities. As we have seen there are powerful influences pushing political integration. The first is the continued economic integration of the region, together with formal arrangements such as NAFTA. The second is the ideological convergence about the role of government. That is, at least in the economic sphere, we are governed by the maxim that the government that governs least governs best. Third, there is the perception that governments must adopt policies where needed that will enhance our competitive position in the world. These are generally located in the areas of taxation and social spending. The buzzword associated with this process is "convergence." Governments are converging toward policies that will provide maximum flexibility to the private sector in order that they can compete and create wealth in the marketplace. This trio of forces would seem to dictate that provincial governments are to be marginalized in a globalizing world. However, not all authors agree. Some point out that provinces in Canada have been increasingly involved in trade negotiations because of the need to ensure provincial implementation of international trade treaties. Others point out that regional needs in both the US and Canada have prompted states and provinces to seek regional arrangements with each other meant to redress unacceptable national government policy. While the former is true, and certainly interesting, it is the latter point that is the focus of this chapter.

Douglas Brown and Earl Fry have the following to say about why transborder subunit contacts might increase in the globalizing world.

> The incongruous result [of national policies] is that the continentalist options that have limited appeal at the national level frequently enjoy considerable allure at the regional level. These opportunities for regional alliances [of states and provinces] signal greater strains for national integration but will induce higher degrees of north-south integration.

> Precisely how influential provincial cross-border activity will be in determining the degree of north-south integration is difficult to gauge.... [However] this cross border integration will likely be accompanied by a corresponding decentralization within each federation.[15]

Brown and company conclude that provincial governments will increasingly seek direct contacts with their US state counterparts for economic reasons. They also conclude that these contacts will not imperil Canadian federalism. Indeed, they propose that these contacts can be positive if properly handled: "However, if the political advantages inherent to federal states are to be realized, more effective internal collaborative structures should be established between the levels of government in both nations."[16] Thus, for Brown, Fry, and Groen, increasing economic integration in North America, and more subunit contact between state and provincial governments, will force governments in Canada to seek new structures of collaboration in our federal system. It remains for us to determine if their conclusion, which is in agreement with most of the theorists we examined above in relation to European integration, about greater subunit contact is true.

TRANSBORDER CONTACT IN NORTH AMERICA, 1975

Transborder contact in North America has been the subject of sporadic study during the past three decades. Much of the initial work, generated in the 1970s, concentrated on determining the amount, type, and origin of such contact. It assumed that transborder contacts would be shaped by several variables. These included economic contact and integration, geographical proximity, historical contact, immigration patterns and transportation co-operation. Economic contacts were assumed to be the most important of these variables.

An early study of transborder contacts was undertaken by Frank Swanson.[17] His study was done for the US State Department and concentrated on the role of American states. It was most useful for its early classificatory scheme. Others (including this author) have built upon this work. In a 1975 paper I outlined the difficulty of developing a useful classificatory scheme.

> One of the problems involved in analyzing transnational interactions has been developing a classificatory system which identifies the contacts involved in such a way as to allow the surveyor to draw some meaningful conclusions. Early studies tended to catalogue provincial transnational activities as if they were unique, needing no systematic scrutiny. Only when Professors Leach, Walker and Levy undertook to survey the provincial governments in Canada did the first attempts at classification start. In a joint study they catalogued these contacts by function, type and method. The functional categories appeared incomplete, probably because most contacts revolved about a few issue areas. State/provincial interactions were divided into formal/informal according to the type of agreement. Those that were signed were considered formal, those reached by telephone, personal contact, or some other method were considered informal. Finally, interactions we considered bilateral if they did not involve the national government, and third party if they did. Professor Swanson's study used the same basic classificatory model, expanding the number of functional categories to 11, dividing the types of interactions into agreements, understandings, and arrangements, in order of declining formality, and identified other government multilateral or general.[18]

In that paper I decided to develop a new classification scheme to better identify contacts. This included four classifications: type of interaction, function, frequency of contact, and method of contact. Definitions of these categories included the following characteristics.

TYPES OF INTERACTIONS

- Agreements: Any interaction undertaken in writing and either signed jointly, or agreed to by correspondence
- Arrangements: Any interactive procedure not necessarily involving signed documents or correspondence which has the agreement of all parties.

These two categories incorporated the salient characteristics of both the Leach and Swanson studies. However, they did not assume that a formal agreement necessarily requires some future interaction between governments.

FUNCTIONAL CATEGORIES

This dimension contained six categories. These were: economic, environmental, cultural, human services, political and general.

- Economic: Any agreement that was essentially economic in nature, including those involving energy and other natural resources
- Environmental: Any arrangements that involved matters like air quality, water apportionment or flooding, etc.
- Cultural: Interactions that had as their basis cultural contacts with other states
- Human Services: Contacts which facilitated private or public contacts in categories such as transportation and social welfare
- Political: Trips, visits, and other executive or legislative contacts between officials of provincial and state governments
- General: All classification of contacts not included above.

FREQUENCY OF INTERACTION

Previous classificatory systems attempted to link formality and the need for future interactive procedures. The fact that the two need not always be connected is at least partially substantiated by this study. Accordingly, three categories of frequency of interaction were established.

- Regular: Any interaction that occurred with regularity, such as annual conferences or regular committee meetings, or an agreement or arrangement which necessitated a continual high level of interaction, such as licensing understandings.
- Occasional: Interactions that happened more than once, but which had not fixed pattern of occurrence.
- Unique: An interaction necessitated by a particular event that did not carry with it the necessity of future transnational contact.

ACTOR ROLE

- Province-State: Interactions that were undertaken by the provincial and state governments without involving the federal government of Canada. This did not preclude the US national government from being involved.

- Province-Canadian Government-State: Interactions that included a provincial government, the Canadian government, and a state government. The US national government or its agencies might have been involved.

Since the intent of the study was to determine both the type and extent of Alberta/Saskatchewan interactions with state governments, no attempt was made to evaluate the independence of US state government interaction. Therefore the role of the US federal government was held constant.

The data involved in this first study are displayed in Table 1. Some general observations about the data were made at the time. First, that there were almost as many agreements as arrangements was not consistent with previous studies; the Swanson study in particular. In the Swanson examination there were almost twice as many arrangements as agreements. Closer examination of the data revealed, however, that most of the agreements were about licensing of motor vehicles. Formal agreements did not cover a wide range of subunit contact.

The arrangement category revealed a broad distribution of interactions. This indicated that Alberta/Saskatchewan and state governments were more willing to enter into informal arrangements on a wide variety of subjects than they were to formalize such arrangements. This is understandable given their position as sub-national actors. It is unclear whether the reluctance to formalize arrangements originated mainly with the state or provincial governments. That Alberta and British Columbia joined the interstate compact on reciprocal licensing arrangements without the apparent involvement of the Canadian federal government would indicate the provincial governments were likely to be bolder in formalizing arrangements than US state governments.

Functional classifications were dominated by two categories: economic, and human services. Most economic interactions revolved about natural resources, (75 percent), with energy arrangements (18 percent) accounting for most of the rest. The natural resource interactions generally revolved about fish and game, game birds, border waters, and co-ordination of resource protection activities such as control of forest fires. Energy agreements concerned energy exploration and geological activity near the border, and exchange of technical information. Surprisingly, there was only one agricultural interaction, an arrangement between Oregon and Alberta to advise each other of new plant diseases.

Most of the human services interactions involved transportation; in particular, licensing agreements on license fees, and other regulatory aspects of motor vehicle transportation. Other interactions included agreements of civil defense and mutual aid arrangements in case of disaster.

Table 1: Alberta/Saskatchewan Interactions by Type, Function, Frequency and Method

| | Agreement | | | | | | Arrangement | | | | | |
| | Regular | | Occasional | | Unique | | Regular | | Occasional | | Unique | |
	Province-State	Prov.-Fed.-Gov.-State	Province-State	Prov.-Fed.-Gov.-State	Province-State	Prov.-Fed.-Gov.-State	Province-State	Prov.-Fed.-Gov.-State	Province-State	Prov.-Fed.-Gov.-State	Province-State	Prov.-Fed.-Gov.-State
Economic			2		2		9		18	6	4	3
Environmental							3	1	1	1		
Cultural												
Human services	43		1	2			4	1	7			
Political									2		2	1
General												

Notes: Agreements = 50
Arrangements = 63
Total interactions = 113

Environmental interactions were generally of an information exchange nature. This usually meant meetings involving the US Environmental Protection Agency.

Political interactions included reciprocal visits by governors, premiers, or legislators. They were generally not associated with any particular objective.

When the interactions were broken into frequency of contact categories some surprising results were obtained. Over half (54 percent) of the interactions were of a regular nature, about 31 percent of the interactions were classified occasional, and only 11 percent were unique.

Unique interactions tended to be either economic or political in nature. Such things as negotiations on the future of the potash industry in Saskatchewan, the Montana-Alberta pipeline discussions, the Poplar River Power Plant in Saskatchewan, and exchange legislative visits dominated the unique category.

Perhaps the most startling result arose when the interactions were categorized according to involvement or non-involvement of the Canadian national government. Of the one 113 interactions, only 15 (13 percent) involved the Canadian federal government.

When the interactions were broken into Alberta and Saskatchewan categories (see Table 2), it was evident that Alberta had slightly more interactions than Saskatchewan. The bulk of the extra contacts for Alberta were in transportation. This is understandable since Alberta became a member in 1975 of the interstate compact on "uniform vehicle registration," while Saskatchewan did not. Saskatchewan had a larger number of economic interactions. Other categories were essentially the same. Thus, the data did not reveal any startling differences.

Finally, the interactions that involved border states were separated. Of the total contacts (113) only 26 (23 percent) involved border states. The comparable figure in the Swanson report was 62 percent, although the mid-west figure was only 31 percent, not too different from this initial study.

Table 2: Transborder Contacts by Province and Functional Classification

	Alberta	Saskatchewan	Total
Economic	18	24	42
Environment	5	3	8
Cultural	0	0	0
Human services	38	20	58
Political	3	2	5
General	0	0	0
Total	64	49	113

Some general observations were made. First, when transportation agreements were excluded, the provinces were not heavily involved in interactions requiring signed agreements. By contrast, they appear to have been quite prepared to enter into informal arrangements on a wide variety of subjects. Second, interactions tended to cluster about two major functions: economic, and human services. Third, when transportation agreements were removed the majority of the remaining contacts were predominantly of an occasional economic nature. Fourth, the Canadian national government was not involved in most interactions. Fifth, most interactions of a political nature were at a low level of importance. Sixth, most interactions were of a recent nature, (post-1960), indicating a growing propensity to interact. Seventh, subjects of Alberta/Saskatchewan interactions tended to follow the major system level concerns of the provinces. For example, the cultural category is empty. (A similar study of Quebec would probably find some interactions in this category). Eighth, most transnational interactions of a bilateral nature were not of political importance.

The first study tried to grapple with some interesting questions. What were the causes of interaction between Alberta/Saskatchewan and American states? How were the provincial governments organized to handle these interactions? Was the importance of provincial-state interactions changing and how did the provinces perceive their position in these contacts? What were the constitutional implications, if any, of these interactions, and were there any other general implications that should have been noted?

The 1975 paper provided no complete answer to the first question as to motivation for transborder contacts. It seemed that provinces collaborated with states on policy in their area of legislative competence, and because jurisdictional parameters appeared unclear. This was certainly the case with Alberta/Saskatchewan. The paper concluded that:

> None of the causes noted above are sufficient to cause province-state interactions which exclude the Canadian national government. Something more is involved, the perception of the provincial government of its role in a particular situation. It may, for a variety of reasons including time parameters, availability of federal assistance, direct contact from state officials, past legislative contacts, domestic political considerations, economic pressure, or even department empire building, decide to interact in a direct manner with an American state government.[19]

Most importantly, the paper did not conclude that general continental integration was sufficient to impel states and provinces toward greater contact. Indeed, the paper was careful to note that political roles were very important.

> Valuable insights can be gained from refining and cataloguing present data as well as determining future interactions. Such insights can still be used to analyze the impact of trans-border contacts in all jurisdictions involved. However ... given

the fact that the governments of Alberta/Saskatchewan appear to be more concerned with establishing new roles within the Canadian confederation than with seeking new or stronger ties with foreign governments we should not look for any dramatic changes in the trans-border activities of these two Canadian provinces.[20]

The 1975 study was most important in establishing some baseline data and comparing them with data from other studies at the time. It was, understandably, inconclusive with regard to trends of contacts. This awaited future studies such as the one done for the 2001 conference.

TRANSBORDER CONTACT IN NORTH AMERICA, 2001

The data categorization scheme developed in 1975 has been modified somewhat for the presentation of the 2001 data. In particular, the categories dealing with agreement and arrangement have been excluded. More will be said about this below. We begin in Table 3 by displaying the interactions of each province.

Table 3: Alberta Interactions by Type, Function and Frequency

	Regular		*Occasional*		*Unique*	
	Province-State	*Prov.-Fed. Gov.-State*	*Province-State*	*Prov.-Fed. Gov.-State*	*Province-State*	*Prov.-Fed. Gov.-State*
Economic	15	0	0	0	1	0
Environmental	0	0	0	0	0	0
Human services	5	0	0	0	0	0
Political	0	0	0	0	0	0
General	3	0	0	0	1	0

Transborder contacts totalled 25 for the province of Alberta. They are predominantly economic, regular, and made directly with US states. These include bilateral contacts with border states such as Montana and Idaho on matters of agriculture, business relationships and tourism. They also include multilateral economic contacts at the multilateral regional level such as the Pacific Northwest Regional Economic Conference, Rocky Mountain Trade Corridor, and the Western Association of State Departments of Agriculture. Finally, Alberta is involved with national and international economic bodies such as the Canadian/American Border Trade Alliance.

Some other observations include the following:

- Within the largest category, economic contacts, there is the following distribution:
  - 16 percent of all interactions involved trade (other than agriculture)
  - 16 percent involved energy
  - 16 percent involved natural resources
  - 12 percent involved agriculture
- 40 percent of human services interactions involved transportation.
- The general category includes conferences and other interactions which deal with a wide variety of issues.
- In five instances interactions involved Alberta as an observer; that is, a non-voting associate member only (e.g., The Interstate Oil and Gas Compact Commission).

Finally, it should be noted that 20 percent of the interactions could be classified as agreements, and 80 percent as arrangements.

Table 4: Saskatchewan Interactions by Type, Function and Frequency

	Regular		Occasional		Unique	
	Province-State	Prov.-Fed. Gov.-State	Province-State	Prov.-Fed. Gov.-State	Province-State	Prov.-Fed. Gov.-State
Economic	8	3	0	0	0	0
Environmental	0	0	0	0	0	0
Human services	4	0	2	0	0	0
Political	0	0	0	0	1	0
General	5	0	1	0	0	0

Once again the transborder contacts (24 in total) are predominantly of a regular economic nature, between the province of Saskatchewan and the various US states. Surprisingly, the contacts look much like those of Alberta. For example, agricultural contacts were 13 percent for Saskatchewan, compared with 12 percent for Alberta. As you might expect the bilateral contacts included North Dakota, which is contiguous with Saskatchewan. Some other observations are:

- The economic category contained the following breakdown:
  - 17 percent of all interactions involved natural resources
  - 13 percent involved agriculture

- − 8 percent involved trade
- − 8 percent involved energy
- • 17 percent of human services interactions involved transportation.
- • The general category includes conferences, councils and associations that deal with social issues, federalism, transportation, etc.
- • In three instances Saskatchewan is involved as a non-voting member of an organization.

Once again, the overwhelming number of interactions involve arrangements (79 percent) compared with agreements (21 percent).

There are some differences between Alberta and Saskatchewan that should be noted. First, Saskatchewan has several economic contacts that include the federal government on a regular basis, while Alberta has none. This is because Saskatchewan has ongoing obligations regarding water and air quality in the Souris Basin, as well as issues surrounding water apportionment that include the province, the state of North Dakota, and the federal governments of both countries. Second, a higher percentage of Alberta's transborder contacts are of a regular economic nature, while Saskatchewan has more contacts in the general and human service categories. Finally, although not shown on the tables, several of the Saskatchewan contacts involve Manitoba. Again, this is because of water arrangements and transboundary issues that involve these two provinces with adjacent US states.

TRANSBOUNDARY CONTACTS, 1975 TO 2001 — A COMPARISON

Table 5 consolidates the data for Alberta and Saskatchewan from both the 1975 and 2001 studies. It excludes the agreement and arrangements categories. Several things are obvious from the comparison.

First, the total number of contacts has decreased dramatically. There were 113 in the 1975 study, while there are only 49 in the 2001 study. One explanation for this decrease involves the way in which transportation contacts are handled. In 1975 there were a number of individual agreements with different states designed to accommodate reciprocal treatment of vehicle licensing. Shortly after data was compiled in 1975, Alberta joined the US interstate compact on reciprocal licensing arrangements. Saskatchewan joined in 1993, and BC in 1996. All other provinces joined this year, making this a uniform arrangement for all of Canada and the United States. As explained on the International Registration Plan (IRP) web site:

> In 1968, an [American Association of Motor Vehicle Administrators] subcommittee was formed to develop a plan that would incorporate all theories of reciprocity, and attract all jurisdictions of the United States and Canada into one uniform agreement. The subcommittee, which was made up of motor vehicle

Table 5: Alberta/Saskatchewan Participation in Transborder/US Bodies – Comparison 1975, 2001

	1975 Regular		1975 Occasional		1975 Unique		1975 Total	2001 Regular		2001 Occasional		2001 Unique		2001 Total
	Province-State	Prov.-Fed. Gov.-State	Province-State	Prov.-Fed. Gov.-State	Province-State	Prov.-Fed. Gov.-State		Province-State	Prov.-Fed. Gov.-State	Province-State	Prov.-Fed. Gov.-State	Province-State	Prov.-Fed. Gov.-State	
Economic	9	0	20	6	6	3	44	23	3	0	0	1	0	27
Environmental	3	1	1	1	0	0	6	0	0	0	0	0	0	0
Human services	47	1	8	2	0	0	58	9	0	2	0	0	0	11
Political	0	0	2	0	2	1	5	0	0	0	0	1	0	1
General	0	0	0	0	0	0	0	8	0	1	0	1	0	10
Total	59	2	31	9	8	4	113	40	3	3	0	3	0	49

administrators and transportation industry representatives, set out to draft a suitable agreement.

The report by the subcommittee was examined at the 1971 AAMVA Vehicle Reciprocity Workshop and was referred to the subcommittee for further development. The draft agreement, "Standard Reciprocal Agreement Governing the Operation of Vehicles Between Jurisdictions," was considered at the AAMVA Annual International Conference in Wichita, Kansas, in September 1972. AAMVA went on record as endorsing the concept of proportional distribution of registration fees of interjurisdictional vehicles.

As the final draft of the plan was being prepared in July 1973, the name was changed to the International Registration Plan. The project was presented to the AAMVA Annual International Conference in September 1973. A resolution passed at the conference making the IRP a reality, with the hope of creating the first national uniform interjurisdictional registration plan.

Today, the 48 contiguous US states, the District of Columbia and ten Canadian provinces — Alberta, British Columbia, Manitoba, New Brunswick, Ontario, Prince Edward Island, Newfoundland and Labrador, Nova Scotia, Quebec and Saskatchewan — are all members of IRP and participate in the plan, which authorizes registration of over 2.0 million commercial vehicles. In addition, the repository continues to have an open dialogue with Mexico on entering the IRP.[21]

The IRP is a most interesting organization. It is incorporated in Virginia, and has its head office there. There is now a 12-member board. Two of those members are from Canada. However, members are organized into four geographical regions that do not take account of the international border. It is a true transborder organization in that it is not authorized by international treaty. The result of this agreement is that the individual agreements on licensing have all disappeared, decreasing dramatically the overall number of transborder agreements.

There may be one other explanation for the decrease in contacts. The 1975 study involved interviews with various departments and central government officials. The 2001 study relies on consolidated data from departments of intergovernmental affairs. It is possible that the inventories in 2001 are not as complete as in 1975. However, it is unlikely that IGA officials would be unaware of 50 percent of the transborder contacts of their government. It is more likely that the total number of contacts has decreased.

It should be noted that Mexican states, though not yet a members of the IRP, are now involved with US states and Canadian provinces in several ways. For example they are members of the States-Provinces Agricultural Accord, and the North American Agricultural Marketing Officials forum. Many of the contacts now involve participation by Canadian provinces in annual meetings of organizations. Examples for Alberta are Pacific Northwest Economic Region, Rocky Mountain Trade Corridor, Western Governors Association, Canadian/American Border Trade Alliance, as well as several energy organizations. Saskatchewan does not participate in as many of these associations as does Alberta, but some examples include the Western Association of State Departments of Agriculture, and the Western Interstate Energy Board, as well as several agencies associated with the Poplar River and Souris Basin. This means that longer-term, north-south relationships are involved, something quite different from 1975. Finally, it should be noted that one agreement flows out of the NAFTA accord.

If there are far fewer transborder contacts than in 1975, those that exist are far more regular. In 1975 approximately 80 percent of overall economic contacts were of an occasional or unique nature. In 2001 that figure is reversed completely. All but one contact is regular. The same is largely true in the other categories. Interestingly, the role of the Canadian federal government has diminished. In 1975 it was involved about 13 percent of the contacts, while in 2001 that number has slipped to about 6 percent.

Finally, it should be noted that there are far fewer agreements than arrangements in 2001. Arrangements account for 78 percent of the contacts, leaving only 22 percent as agreements. The comparable figures in 1975 were 56 percent arrangements and 44 percent agreements. This reflects, in large part, the removal of the individual licensing agreements that have been replaced by the IRP. However, it is also obvious that many of the current contacts involve membership or observer status in regional or sector specific organizations. While these may be useful for provinces, and regular, they do not incur any lasting legal obligations.

CONCLUSIONS ABOUT THE MERGED DATA

Several specific conclusions can be noted about the comparison between 1975 and 2001 data. First, and perhaps most important, it is apparent that transborder contact between these two provinces and American states remains largely underdeveloped. Neither province has made it a priority to engage the US states in transborder development. Put another way, there has been no political commitment to increasing and solidifying transborder relationships by either Alberta or Saskatchewan. The fact that two provincial governments, operating independently on this matter, have come to the same policy conclusion indicates that neither province perceives any major political or economic advantage to increasing these contacts.

Second, and in some ways contrary to what has just been concluded, the quality of remaining contacts has changed since 1975. As mentioned above, contacts are more regular and consistent. Provincial governments now feel more at home in US state organizations. By contrast, American states still do not participate in interprovincial organizations in Canada.

Third, the remaining transborder contacts are increasingly economic and specialized. This includes membership in organizations such as the IRP.

Fourth, federal government involvement in transborder contacts is now minimal. This probably reflects the increasing specialization of contacts in the economic sector. It would be interesting to know what if any information is passed on to Ottawa about these meetings. The lack of involvement by Ottawa in these contacts may also reflect the fact that the federal government is now more at ease with provincial international affairs, especially where it involves the United States.

GENERAL CONCLUSIONS

We began this chapter seeking to test one general hypothesis. That hypothesis was: "Political integration between Canada and the United States will increase — including provincial-state linkages and perhaps community cross-border linkages — in response to escalating trade and other cross-border interaction."[22]

This hypothesis was based on a number of assumptions. These were, first, that political integration follows economic integration insofar as administrative arrangements become necessary to facilitate "business"; second, that governments may be instrumental in encouraging or delaying this integration; and third, that special kinds of integrative institutions may need to be established in a federal state such as Canada in order to deal with this kind of integration. Of specific importance to this hypothesis were some unarticulated assumptions. The most important was that transborder contacts would develop because states and provinces share economic activity that is conducted in contiguous states and provinces. We also assumed that globalization would "routinize" many previously unique kinds of contacts, ensuring that they are dealt with as "non-political" matters by states and provinces. Finally, even where states and provinces were not geographically contiguous, if they had similar economic bases or markets for goods or services, we assumed that routine economic contacts might require political contacts between the provinces and states.

Out of this, then, one would expect that the hypothesis would be interpreted to mean that transborder contacts would be increasing in numbers, that the increase in contacts would be primarily in the economic area with states that have common economic interests, and that these contacts would now be of a more regular and administrative nature than in the past. Finally, it should be interpreted to mean that these contacts would be increasingly undertaken without the involvement of the federal government.

A review of the data indicates that our hypothesis, as explained above, is only partially supported. First, and most important, the absolute number of contacts between Alberta/Saskatchewan and US states is lower in 2001 than in 1975. This is explained in part by the growth in involvement of Canadian provinces in the IRP. However, this mitigating factor is insufficient to explain why there is not growth in other areas. One explanation lies in the geography of the situation. Unlike the southern area of Ontario, or southern BC, there has traditionally been little contact between these two provinces and contiguous US states. This has not changed in the past 25 years. There are still minimal transportation links, and little flow of goods and services north and south. While large amounts of oil and natural gas flow through contiguous states from Saskatchewan and Alberta, it has not altered the overall situation. In other words, the economic growth and contact in other areas, such as between southern Ontario and the North Eastern states, has no parallel on the Great Plains. Therefore we need to modify the general hypothesis about Canada/US contacts to take account of regional differences.

The second part of the hypothesis, that contacts have increasingly become economic, regular, and administrative is supported by the data. Contacts are concentrated in the economic area, on a regular basis. The inclusion of the Canadian provinces in the IRP provides some proof for the proposition that globalization and North American economic integration is forcing political integration. As well, the two provinces in this study now routinely participate in annual and other regular meetings of organizations that involve US states.

The third part of the hypothesis, that these contacts will increasingly be conducted without the federal government, is also supported by the data. The role of the federal government has diminished considerably since 1975.

We are left with an hypothesis which is only partially supported. However, as the vernacular goes, "two out of three ain't bad." This is especially true when you consider the type of contacts and the involvement of provinces in organizations such as the IRP. There is little doubt that some integration is taking place at the subunit level.

Two other matters need to be considered. The first is the impact of this change on the Canadian federation. This study tells us that transborder contact has very little impact on federal-provincial relations or interprovincial relations. None of the involvement is of a "high political" nature. Nor is there anything that would require federal oversight. We should hasten to add that this may not be true in other areas of Canada.

The second matter relates to democracy. That is, is there a democratic deficit being created by transborder contact? Again, from this study, the answer is no. Nothing in this contact has diminished the ability of provincial legislatures to act when needed. There are no agreements that parallel some of the provisions of NAFTA, for example. One could argue that we have abdicated decision-making on matters such as automobile licensing and regulation to a US dominated body, but this argument is in my opinion weak at best. Involvement is voluntary, and can be terminated immediately.

We are left, therefore, with an inconclusive result. That in itself, however, is just as important a result as any. It will be interesting to compare these data with data from other regions bordering the US. It may be that for historical, geographical, and other reasons the results from this study are not consistent with results from other regions.

OVERALL ASSESSMENT

As we can see from the analysis above, the results of this study are somewhat counter-intuitive. The assumptions of international integrationists, and of North American scholars such as Brown and Fry, are not entirely borne out by this study. However, there is evidence that the results might be regional-specific, and more research is needed in order to refine the general hypothesis to take account of these regional differences. In one sense, this is what makes specific research most interesting. General assumptions about globalization need to be tested for specific accuracy. We may indeed be moving toward the "global village," but we may also find that the "neighbourhoods" of that village differ dramatically.

POSTSCRIPT

Since this chapter was initially completed some matters have emerged which may give us pause to reflect on its conclusions. The first is that the US desire to implement more stringent security arrangements in their country and in North America as a whole as a result of the September 11 events has proved to be more than a little vexing for some of the provinces. In an attempt to deal with these problems provincial governments have become more involved with their counterparts across the border.

The second matter has to do with the increased number of trade irritants that have emerged between the US and Canada, some with an important impact in western Canada. The most significant is the softwood lumber controversy, which has an impact on all western provinces, but most particularly, on British Columbia. Efforts to deal with this matter have been led by the federal government, but provincial governments have been very involved in the preliminary negotiations that shape the Canadian position. Sometimes this has led to discussion between provincial and state governments on specific issues.

A third matter that has arisen is the further institutionalization of relationships between the western premiers and the western governors. In the year 2000 the premiers and governors agreed to a framework for Western Premiers' Conference/Western Governors Association linkage. This agreement called for annual meetings between the two organizations, which were held in 2001 and 2002. Such contact undoubtedly raises the likelihood that the provinces and the states will engage in more individual interaction. We will have to wait and see if this is the case. (For more on this see Peter Meekison's chapter on Western Premiers' Conferences in this volume.)

Finally, the closing of the US border to Canadian cattle and beef as a result of the discovery of a single cow with bovine spongiform encephalopathy in May 2003 has led to the substantial involvement of provincial governments in efforts to get the border reopened to Canadian beef. In particular the visit of Premier Ralph Klein with Vice President Dick Cheney in the US in the summer of 2003 raises the possibility that there will be more provincial government interaction with both the federal and state governments south of the border. Whether or not this results in more specific and fundamental change to the kind of contact reviewed in this chapter remains to be seen.

NOTES

1. Managing Tensions: Evaluating the Institutions of the Federation Conference, Kingston, 2-3 November, 2001.

2. Daniel Madar, *Canadian International Relations* (Scarborough: Prentice Hall-Canada, 2000), p. 157.

3. Ibid.

4. Amatai Etzioni, "The Epigenisis of Political Communities at the International Level," in *International Politics and Foreign Policy*, ed. James N. Rosenau (New York: The Free Press, 1969), p. 351.

5. Barry B. Hughes, "Evolving Patterns of European Integration and Governance: Implications for Theories of World Politics," in *Controversies in International Relations Theory*, ed. Charles W. Kegley, Jr. (New York: St. Martin's Press, 1996), pp. 223-43.

6. Commission of the European Communities, "European Governance: A White Paper." White Paper #7, #428 (Brussels, 25 July 2001).

7. W.S. Livingston, "A Note on the Nature of Federalism," in *Canadian Federalism: Myth or Reality*, 2d ed., ed. J. Peter Meekison (Toronto: Methuen, 1971), p. 22.

8. D.V. Smiley, *Canada in Question: Federalism in the Eighties* (Toronto: McGraw-Hill Ryerson, 1980), p. 114.

9. Anne Legare, "Canadian Federalism and the State," in *Federalism in Canada*, ed. Garth Stevenson (Toronto: McClelland and Stewart, 1989), p. 249.

10. Albert Breton, "The Theory of Competitive Federalism," in *Federalism in Canada* (Toronto: McClelland and Stewart, 1989), p. 457.

11. Richard Simeon, "Fiscal Federalism," in *The Future of Fiscal Federalism*, eds. Keith G. Banting, Douglas M. Brown and Thomas J. Courchene (Kingston: The Institute of Intergovernmental Relations, Queen's University, 1993), pp. 136-37.

12. Paul Barker, "Disentangling the Federation: Social Policy and Fiscal Federalism," in *Challenges to Canadian Federalism*, eds. Martin Westmacott and Hugh Mellon (Scarborough: Prentice-Hall Canada, 1998).

13. Herman Bakvis and Grace Skogstad, "Canadian Federalism: Performance, Effectiveness, and Legitimacy," in *Canadian Federalism: Performance, Effectiveness, and Legitimacy* (Don Mills: Oxford University Press, 2002), p. 10.

14. Howard Leeson and Vanderelst Wilf, *External Affairs and Canadian Federalism: The History of a Dilemma* (Toronto: Holt Rinehart and Winston, 1975).

15. Douglas M. Brown, Earl Fry and James Groen, "States and Provinces in the International Economy Project," in *States and Provinces in the International Economy* (Berkeley, CA: University of California Press, 1993), p. 10.

16. Ibid., p. 17.

17. Roger Frank Swanson, *State/Provincial Interaction* (Washington, DC: The Canus Research Institute, 1974), p. 290.

18. Howard Leeson, "Alberta/Saskatchewan Transborder Contacts with US States — A Survey and Analysis," p. 10. Unpublished paper.

19. Ibid., p. 24.

20. Ibid., p. 25.

21. Available at the International Registration Plan web site, <www.aamva.org/IRP/about/mnu_abthistory.asp>.

22. Managing Tensions Conference, November 2001.

12

Quebec's Role in Canadian Federal-Provincial Relations

Jacques Bourgault

Ce chapitre veut évaluer l'influence du gouvernement du Québec dans les relations fédérales provinciales au Canada depuis la Révolution tranquille. Après avoir examiné les ressources de l'influence, les enjeux de la spécificité du Québec, il analyse l'exercice de cette influence jusqu'en 2001 dans les mécanismes coordination fédérale provinciale. Le chapitre veut expliquer le fonctionnement de ces facteurs d'influence dans les relations fédérales provinciales, interprovinciales et dans les relations avec le gouvernement fédéral.

The mandate of this chapter is to deal with Quebec's role in the development of federal-provincial relations in Canada since 1960. Few studies of federalism have been conducted on the influence exerted on the central state by its federated units (states, provinces, Länder), and those that do exist tend to be institutionalist in orientation.[1] This chapter takes a different approach by focusing instead on the role of power and influence. Quebec counts for an important part of the Canadian population, and contributes to Canada's specific character as compared with the United States. The more influential Quebec's distinct character is in Canada, the more distinct Canada's own character will appear. From another perspective, arguments concerning Quebec's real influence in Canada are used to either justify or combat the idea that the province should become independent. Quebec does not, of course, create the Canadian identity on its own; nevertheless, its contribution to that identity is undeniable.[2]

I begin by defining the concept of influence, and follow up with an examination of the context and goals of federal-provincial relations since 1960. I then consider some particular events where influence was exercised; namely, federal-provincial conferences. The methodology used to gather useful data for this text included a press review of material covering 30 major federal-provincial conferences, along with biographical analysis and testimony by the principal players. Once this material had been gathered, a reference text was submitted for commentary to a group of Quebec and federal negotiators who had worked on these agreements. These methodological choices, the only ones available apart from direct observation, were intended to clarify the role played by Quebec. This has been done with the recognition that, if the observations of other provincial negotiators and media from other Canadian regions had been included in the study, they may have helped produce slightly different conclusions.

This chapter will attempt to verify the hypothesis that Quebec has, for some time, played a leading role in the evolution of executive federalism. It will also seek to analyze what, from Quebec's point of view, has contributed to or limited the exercise of this influence.

Forty-one years of federal-provincial relations include a very long list of conferences, initiatives and meetings.[3] Within the framework available, I selected several of the larger or more important events. Different choices, of course, might have led to different conclusions.

ROLES: POWER OR INFLUENCE?

Robert A. Dahl has defined "power" using the following formula: the power of A over B is the capacity of A to make B do something that B would not otherwise have done had A not intervened. Henry Mintzberg finds this definition too narrow, since it is limited to a single transaction. He uses a broader approach, inspired by Bertrand Russell, for whom power consists of "producing the desired effects."[4] Nigel Nicholson explains the concept differently again,[5] referring to Max Weber, for whom power is the probability that one actor within a social relationship will be able to control resources, events and other people to carry out his own will despite resistance, regardless of the basis on which this probability rests. Michel Foucault, in Dominique Colas' summary,[6] also places power in the context of a transactional relationship. Power comes from multiple sources and is exercised from innumerable standpoints in a context of unequal relations situated in a framework larger than the observed transaction. These relations are initiated by the inferior party in a process of resistance. They are intentional, yet they are also subjective. Michel Crozier conceives of a transactional power strategy for any organization, which turns on behavioural predictability and is based on the assessment of interests and the control of information.[7]

These authors have noticed the resemblances between power and influence, which are terms that are often treated synonymously, especially since, in English, "influence" and "control" can appear to be the verbal equivalents of "power."[8] The literature also concurs that we can distinguish three modes of power. First, "injunctive" power is effectively exercised only by the proper symbolic authority.[9] Second, "dynamic" power[10] is expressed as repression or the threat of repression. Finally, power to "influence"[11] is a broad form of voluntary or involuntary authority exercised by one person over another: this is the effect an individual's use of power has on others. An influential person has authority over the person being influenced, of course, but not necessarily "dynamic" power over them. Jacques Bourgault has already noted the bi-directional nature of the relationship between power and influence:[12] the corollary of power being exercised through influence is that using influence may grant an actor power over others.

In federal-provincial relations, power to influence comes from moral authority or from duress, mutual agreement or firm belief, which comes from an ideological or rational commitment. The role of a subordinate actor such as a province is based more on the capacity to influence one's peers or federal negotiating partner than on duress or injunction. André Bernard writes that influence is a form of political participation and that power is shared, in the case of federal-provincial relations, through an interplay of degrees of influence.[13] For example, Roger Gibbins writes that Quebec's presence is useful to Alberta, notably because it balances the political influence of Ontario.[14]

Influence is all the more important in the context of federal-provincial institutions because there is no clearly established jurisprudence setting out the division of authority. Some powers are shared,[15] others are implicit, residual, or exercised as discriminatory powers, as in the case of the spending power, the power to act in the national interest, or emergency powers.[16] Richard Simeon clearly explains the extent to which federal-provincial relations are based on interdependence between the levels of government.[17]

This chapter will study the types of influence Quebec has been able to exert by playing various roles in the recent evolution of Canadian federalism. It will also examine the extent to which other provinces have been able to take advantage of the opportunities created by Quebec's demands. Quebec has had a particular interest in encouraging interprovincial co-operation, since without unity among the provinces, it would not only have been less able to confront Ottawa, but it would possibly also have had to contend with provinces that were envious of its special treatment, insistent on a "ten standardized provinces" view of Canada, or worried that their own demands might fail for lack of funding.

STAKES AND HAZARDS OF INFLUENCE

In federal-provincial relations, influence plays a role in setting agendas, organizing the sequence of events before and after meetings, shaping the positions of the other provinces and especially, in satisfying one's own goals. For Quebec, this involves guiding the agenda-setting process, influencing the level of demands, generating arguments the other provinces will find useful, encouraging partners to maintain their positions, and helping to develop acceptable compromises. The influence of Quebec has been felt in terms of its capacity to mediate, to be the focus of a common front, to lead the assault (to use a military image), to research, improve upon and act as the conscience of federal positions (in particular the "final offer"), etc.

Quebec's difficulty in influencing the other provinces is not insignificant: each province has its own demands, based on its history, values, political trends of the moment and in particular, its geographical circumstances, economic structure and diversity. Over the decades, the provinces have responded in varying ways to issues raised by Quebec. In the 1960s, they sought accommodation with Quebec. They then adopted a more calculating approach, before settling, after 1980, on a position much more like a centralizing form of federalism.

They have also varied in their responses to demands based on the Quebec "cause." In the 1960s, the provinces tried to procrastinate in order to "find an amicable solution" and were then stupefied to see that Quebec's aspirations had grown. Finally, they declared themselves exasperated at the rise of the independence movement. The debate on asymmetrical federalism that followed the failure of the Meech Lake Accord was an illustration of this impatience: most provinces rejected asymmetry and many even denied that it had ever existed in Canada, despite the obvious circumstances of Quebec and certain other provinces or groups of provinces.

We must also take provincial public opinion into account. Each province has its own electoral calendar, and every year we find provincial governments at different stages of the election cycle. This affects their behaviour: they might be preparing for elections and urgently in need of funds[18] or becoming more protective of their jurisdictions. They might be in the second year of a mandate and seeking additional revenues through more or less transparent agreements. Or they might be new governments just arriving on the scene, hoping to make a name for themselves on the national stage or to affirm their presence locally, but still more or less naive and inexperienced, and lacking commitment to past agreements. This stance was evident, for example, in the initial reactions of Frank McKenna, the Meech Lake Accord's first gravedigger.

Pressure in the House of Commons can also play a role. This can come from the agendas of parties holding the balance of power in minority governments — the New Democratic Party (NDP) was for a long time a centralizing party, in order to protect the inter-regional redistribution imbedded in Canada-wide health care and other social programs — or from regional sensitivities that must be protected with the next election in mind (Progressive Conservatives and the Canadian Alliance, typically presented by Quebec media as defending the interests of western Canada). My reading of Canadian public opinion during this period is that, aside from a group of English Canadian intellectuals, it neither understood nor supported Quebec's demands. Often, provinces were more "provincialist" than supporters of Quebec's special status. As the political processes in Canada became more enriched, and as information began circulating more effectively in the media, it became progressively more difficult for provincial governments to show too much support for Quebec's demands without irritating their own public opinion. We see this in the very reserved support given the Meech Lake Accord as well as in the willingness of Canadians not to try to accommodate Quebec's needs. We also see it in the fact that most provinces rejected the rather timid Charlottetown Accord.

There are also difficulties in evaluating Quebec's "inadequate" influence. Some say that Quebec had too much influence in 1963-64, and that its current level of influence is "normal" given its demographic weight. Others say that Quebec's influence is insufficient given its historical place and its contribution to Canada's uniqueness. Another standard position is that over the last 42 years, Quebec has had more than its fair share of influence, given the fact that four of the eight prime ministers came from the west and combined, spent five years in office; that one came from Ontario and spent five years in office; and three came from Quebec, and combined, spent 32 years in office. However, such mathematical formalism is not the soundest basis for judging Quebec's influence, since these formulas do not capture the character and convictions of the prime ministers in question. Indeed, two of the three Quebecers mentioned took the hardest lines against Quebec's demands! Influence measurement is surely not a matter of linguistic fit and not always of mathematics and legal arrangements.

THE STAKES FOR QUEBEC

Why would Quebec seek leadership in federal-provincial relations? What are the stakes for Quebec? The answer has both defensive and offensive dimensions, both of which relate to Quebec's socio-political uniqueness in Canada.

Of all the provinces, Quebec is the most sensitive about its powers. This is because, on the one hand, it considers itself the province most unlike the others and, on the other hand, it believes that the agreement of 1867 gave it vast areas of jurisdiction that have been limited by the agenda of a "centralizing" federal power in Ottawa. Of course, the arrival of the independence movement and the election of a Parti Québécois majority to the legislature exacerbated this sensitivity, but it had already existed well before 1976. As Joe Clark writes:

> Quebecers know they are a minority and need to act together to protect their destiny. The government is the expression of the community. That is why constitutional powers assigned to that government are seen as so important in Quebec.[19]

From a sociological standpoint, language, culture, social practices, values and history make Quebec the province whose inhabitants consider themselves the most different from those living in the capital of Canada, where decisions are taken. Proud of their uniqueness, they seek to maintain it and fear they might lose it through overly uniform national arrangements. More than the other provinces, Quebec fears that its special character might be diluted or ignored were it to allow another level of government to replace it by making decisions in areas falling within its jurisdiction.

From a financial standpoint, provincial areas of jurisdiction have expanded considerably and become more expensive since World War II, and especially since 1960:

> The growing needs in the 1960s were not in areas of federal jurisdiction but in those of the provinces.

> More of the social programs were in areas that were, constitutionally, provincial: most of the initiative and financial capacity was federal.[20]

Quebec believes that it must both protect its jurisdiction and recover the taxation powers (or some of their product) that were given up to the federal government during wartime, or that have become more lucrative over time.

During the Quiet Revolution, Quebec francophones turned to an enlarged role of the state to achieve their collective aspirations. To begin with, the state provided individuals with indispensable services that almost no francophone in Quebec could pay for privately. In addition, during that period the Quebec public sector provided privileged access to francophone Quebecers seeking careers in management. Protecting and extending Quebec's areas of jurisdiction, then, contributed to satisfying these needs and justified this strong sensitivity to what Quebec governments would come to call "federal intrusions into provincial jurisdictions."

In 1960, Quebecers had the impression that the century-long economic shift toward Ontario had occurred at their expense, thanks to a central state power from which they had been excluded. If we believe the French-speaking politicians of the period, Canadian decision-makers were "managing" Canada without considering Quebec's interests. The quasi-exclusion of francophones from upper management positions in the Canadian public service between 1867 and 1968 is also widely recognized.[21] Several other historical episodes, both distant (the Test Act) and more recent (both Conscriptions), helped solidify the conviction among Quebecers that their progress as a society could come about only if they managed their own affairs. You could not trust "the outsiders" (*les autres*)! Quebecers needed additional powers to manage their own interests independently.

Even in French speaking society in the 1960s, there were many motives for increasing the powers of the Quebec state. Public opinion perceived a power struggle between anglophones and francophones; the French-speaking financial class was emerging and wanted more room and resources to manoeuvre;

and the intellectuals and technocrats wanted wider jurisdiction to advance their own agendas.

In addition, the French-speaking population was becoming proud of its ability to (finally) advance an authentically *québécois* social project and hoped to prove that it could manage it successfully. This Quiet Revolution saw several new programs emerge, as well as the expansion of Hydro-Quebec. It made possible educational reform, and provided collective financial levers such as the *Caisse de dépôt*. In this context people in Quebec feared that federal interventions might, deliberately or not, harm the development of an authentically *québécois* social project. This explains why all Quebec governments, sovereignist or not, have treated federal-provincial relations as being of the highest importance, and why they have also consistently mounted the battlements in defense of Quebec's interests.

Connections among money, autonomy, identity and political capital have progressively led Quebec and Ottawa to systematize their struggle for sources of financing to guarantee their ability to intervene, accomplish their programs and perhaps be perceived as useful to the population they claim to serve. This might be the same for other provinces, except that their perceptions of history, collective identity and the stakes are very different.[22]

For Quebec, the stakes vary with the purposes of influence. Claude Morin distinguishes between three distinct objectives of influence:

1. To modify, prevent or accelerate *current or future government projects* (social, economic, etc). Influence is exercised in a way that respects the overall framework and the ongoing rules of the game. The English Canadian provinces are almost always limited to this type of influence.

2. *Modification of the system through correctives or reforms of a constitutional or structural nature.* The goal here is to produce a more or less major transformation of political approaches or the rules of the game. Only Quebec has attempted to use this kind of influence. It is the only province to have called the system into question — something no other province has had historical or cultural reasons to do.

3. *Replacing the current system with another one*; that is, special status for Quebec or sovereignty-association. No other province has ever had such a goal. As Morin says: "But Quebec's efforts in this direction have forced Ottawa and the rest of Canada to make various 'concessions'."[23]

The degree of a player's ambition to be influential depends on the stakes involved in the power relations. These stakes have been greater for Quebec than for any other province. They were also quite different since Quebec, regardless of the party in power since 1936, has been the province least attached to a strong central government in Canada. An important observation in this context is that the Quebec government tends to misread the interventions of other provinces that challenge the authority of Ottawa, and in particular tends to overestimate their desire to contribute to the "balkanization of Canada." These sorts of miscalculations have had an important impact on Quebec's own strategy and positions in its struggles against centralization.

THE CONTEXT OF FEDERAL-PROVINCIAL RELATIONS

Putting Duplessis aside, the atmosphere of federal-provincial relations was positive during the years prior to 1960.[24] During World War II, jurisdiction over income tax was ceded to Ottawa. In addition, governments had not yet professionalized their interrelational apparatus, something Alberta prided itself at being the first to do, in 1972.[25] On the other hand, the federal government had already proposed an ambitious, pan-Canadian plan at the Reconstruction Conference of 1945:

> After the Dominion Federal-Provincial Conference on Reconstruction in 1945-46, the federal government presented a bold series of proposals, drafted by its ambitious new public service experts, which included a wide range of social programs.... The federal government continued to pursue their vision of social reform and Keynesian economic management over the ensuing decades.[26]

A number of decisions by the Judicial Committee of the Privy Council during the 1930s, then by the Supreme Court of Canada after 1951, involving a sweeping interpretation of several concepts, expanded federal jurisdictions at provincial expense. Such was the case with the residual power, spending power, emergency powers, the general theory of peace, order and good government, and the theory of unassigned areas. This seemed to give judicial sanction to a project perceived as politically legitimate:

> Keynesianism: after the war it was obvious the federal division of powers ... would reassert itself.... The courts largely abandoned the notion of a watertight division of legislative power, which would have imposed a crippling burden on the very much enlarged sphere of government, and recognized a much larger area of concurrent jurisdiction, as well as sanctioning co-operative arrangements. This was largely initiated by a dominant and much more sophisticated federal bureaucracy, and significantly funded by the much more ample treasury of the federal government.[27]

Once the bureaucrats had been put in place and the ministers were enjoying recognized areas of jurisdiction, it was very hard to get them to work together, even in the name of co-operative federalism. The former Clerk of the Privy Council, Gordon Robertson, explains this in his memoirs:

> It was especially difficult to give substance to it [co-operative federalism] when ministers and departments with programs and 'turf' to defend were reluctant to see concessions of function or of funds to the provinces, and when there was no focal point to advance the application of the policy itself.[28]

It was also unsurprising that Pierre Trudeau's centralizing agenda was well received by senior federal public servants. Indeed, a former Conservative Cabinet minister who later became a senior bureaucrat under the Parti Québécois has declared that "roadblocks in federal-provincial relations and federal encroachments are mainly due to the senior federal public service trying to protect its turf and simplify its task by retaining as many powers as possible!"[29] Jean-François Lisée also reports a similar attitude toward manpower negotiations, but puts it down to a sense of knowing better or, perhaps, national obligation.[30] Senator Roch Bolduc, a former Quebec deputy minister, denounced to Lisée the overreaching ambition of bureaucrats involved in preparing federal proposals for the Charlottetown conference. "The federal bureaucrats simply tried to expand their field of activity as much as possible to the detriment of the provinces, with no concern for the mess they were going to cause."[31] Another ex-deputy minister from Quebec confirms this observation but sees no conspiracy:

> They have a nationalist view of their country, not in an ethnic sense but in the imperialistic sense of the term: they believe in their country and in their role at the centre of its development. They see themselves as on a proud mission to implement this vision, for which they deliberately go outside of the formal constitutional framework. They have a lot of trouble with the constitution and use their spending power outrageously to get around it. They want national standards everywhere![32]

On Quebec's side, the premier's office has had technical counselors since 1960, charged with overseeing federal-provincial relations. Then, in 1961, a very influential Ministry of Federal-Provincial Relations was formed — a post originally held by the premier.[33] In 1967 it became an Intergovernmental Department that also embraced international relations. This was a powerful and prestigious ministry, led by senior bureaucrats who, in many cases, actively participated in all Cabinet meetings.

Quebec was the very first province to create such a department, a model for those later established by most of the Canadian provinces. All of Quebec's positions were channeled through that department, which had the exclusive power to "shepherd" all interprovincial and federal-provincial negotiations in all domains, to sign agreements (or delegate signing authority) following from those negotiations. This ministry's authority over international relations ended when the Parti Québécois took power in 1976, establishing a separate ministry for those functions. The creation of this department resulted from the consciousness, in the early 1960s, that most of the instruments needed to modernize Quebec had to be negotiated with Ottawa, including fiscal and administrative arrangements, major national programs and constitutional agreements.

OPPORTUNITIES FOR INFLUENCE

CONFERENCES AS INSTITUTIONS AND CHESSBOARDS

The Annual Premiers' Conference (APC) is a grouping of all the provincial and territorial premiers from Canada. The federal prime minister is not invited to participate.[34] The Quebec City Interprovincial Conference on 1-2 December 1960 was of particular symbolic importance. Called at Quebec's initiative, this was the first such conference in modern times,[35] and all the provincial first ministers attended. Pressure was brought to bear to create a permanent secretariat for the provinces. Before the creation of the Department of Federal-Provincial Affairs (DFPA), it was the Premier's Office that coordinated the preparation, along with the involved departments. This function was taken over by the DFPA starting in 1963.

The First Ministers' Conference (FMC) appeared as a regular meeting in the 1960s. The most spectacular of these was the televised 1968 meeting involving the Johnson-Trudeau clash, which raised Pierre Trudeau's popularity across Canada and left Quebec's Premier Daniel Johnson flatfooted on the issue of cultural protection. It was the first time a federal official publicly challenged the social and cultural pretensions of Quebec.

These conferences provided the opportunity for Quebec to use a multilateral approach when a bilateral approach was not productive. Lots of federal-provincial relations were bilateral in the John Diefenbaker era, while Lester Pearson, Joe Clark and Brian Mulroney, due to differences in personal styles, would use bilateral conversations with Quebec to prepare multilateral conferences. With Trudeau and Jean Chrétien, given their opposition to any special status for Quebec, bilateral agreements were frowned upon as a means of dealing with national issues. Therefore, the multilateral approach used in these conferences offered Quebec the opportunity to participate in more or less flexible "national agreements" that could accommodate Quebec's specificity, without seeming to engage in any form of asymmetrical federalism. In this sense the APC permitted Quebec to plead its case before the other premiers and try to build a consensus that would avoid isolating the province as the "only opponent to central power." The FMC served much more as a platform from which Quebec could alert Canadian public opinion as to its specificity.

SECRETARIATS

Quebec seems to have played a role, albeit marginal, in the creation of the Canadian Council of Ministers of the Environment in 1964. This nonprofit organization exists to promote a common federal-provincial environmental agenda.[36] At the time, no government in Canada had a ministry dedicated exclusively to this problem.

In 1967, Quebec, which had been mobilized around this issue since 1961, played a major though not exclusive role in the creation of a Council of Ministers of Education of Canada, intended to promote co-operation among the provinces on subjects of mutual interest.[37] This topic had dominated the agendas of Quebec governments since 1960, no matter what their degree of nationalism. It is an area of clearly provincial jurisdiction and therefore an important domain within which to establish a strongly activist provincial agenda.

SPECIAL ARRANGEMENTS

Quebec has put forward numerous demands regarding its constitutional powers throughout the evolution of its project of national self-affirmation, and, regardless of which party held power, has continually denounced what it has seen as federal encroachments on its jurisdiction. This sensitivity has been liveliest in areas affecting individuals, such as immigration and manpower. The former is significant because it can contribute to either the survival or the assimilation of francophones; the second matters because of its connections with training and the provincial field of education. As well, irrespective of which parties were in power, Quebec and Ottawa have signed several agreements concerning immigration since 1967, mainly regarding immigrant selection and integration (the Lang-Cloutier, Andras-Bienvenue, Couture-Cullen, and Gagnon-Tremblay-McDougall agreements). Quebec thus finds itself in a unique trailblazing position in Canada, while Canada's willingness to make these administrative arrangements shows openness to a kind of asymmetrical federalism. The administrative nature of such arrangements brings with it a certain jurisprudential fragility; nevertheless, it is hard to see how Ottawa could repudiate these agreements without the party in power paying a political price, as long as Quebec retains a large francophone population.

Regarding manpower, the 1997 administrative agreement, which transferred management of funding and programs to Quebec along with employee positions, shows Quebec's influence, since it was the first and most insistent province to demand that these powers be transferred. Nevertheless, insofar as such an agreement was offered to all provinces and concluded with most of them, we should not see this as evidence of a power relation, but rather as an example of intellectual influence in Ottawa. The fact that federal elections were coming soon may have also helped Ottawa expedite the process of arriving at an agreement with Quebec, since it was the most demanding province.

One final point: the agreements regarding provincial collection of the Goods and Services Tax show that Ottawa had sufficient confidence in Quebec's administrative ability under the Robert Bourassa government to let it collect its new tax on goods and services.

OCCASIONS OF INFLUENCE

The number and frequency of the various federal-provincial conferences has grown spectacularly over the last 40 years.[38] These offer the provinces four different ways to play the game. First, they can turn to Ottawa to influence national policies with short-term effects (for example, through equalization or the Canadian position on international accords such as the General Agreement on Tariffs and Trade). Second, there are situations where a province must negotiate in the face of federal power (to obtain tax points, transfers and areas of jurisdiction; to limit the application of federal areas of jurisdiction; to gain co-operation agreements between Ottawa and one or more provinces). Third, there are situations where finite resources must be divided among provinces (fishing quotas, agricultural production quotas, subsidies, and so on). Finally, some conferences, no less important, are about issues not of a specifically provincial nature (women's rights, Aboriginal affairs, and so on).

QUEBEC'S INFLUENCE AT CONFERENCES

Let us now examine some of the main interprovincial and federal-provincial conferences to observe the kind of influence Quebec has been able to exercise, and on what basis it has done so. I have chosen a thematic as opposed to a chronological approach, with the recognition that individual conferences may have crunched more than one issue and that in most cases constitutional, fiscal and social issues are interdependent.

FISCAL ISSUES

1. The Federal-Provincial Conference, July 1960. Jean Lesage had proposed to put an end to the joint programs that had been negotiated over the previous 25 years. In their place, he sought compensation corresponding to the amounts of the conditional grants given by Ottawa.

Ottawa accepted this proposal at the conference of March-April 1964, replacing hospital insurance, old-age assistance, blind and disabled persons allowances, vocational education assistance and public health programs with a 20-point abatement on personal income tax. Quebec made its proposal under a system that could apply to all provinces. A transition period was proposed, lasting from 1965 to 1970.[39] A definitive withdrawal from joint programs was proposed at the premiers' conference of November 1971, at which time the federal government tried to extend the transition period beyond 1972. Quebec argued against this, but Ottawa maintained its position. Ontario wanted to acquire the same deal that Quebec had obtained in 1964, but Ottawa opposed it.[40]

2. The Conference on Tax Sharing and Joint Programs, 14 September 1966.
Mitchell Sharp, the federal finance minister, announced an end to bargaining
with the provinces over powers and federal transfers. According to Louis
Bernard, "such doves as Al Johnson were being squeezed, because Ottawa
had blocked the system."[41] A federal withdrawal from certain joint programs
in exchange for tax points occurred for the last time, and a new openness to
double taxation and overlapping fiscal jurisdictions emerged. For Parizeau,
this was the end of the Pearson era and the beginning of the federal establishment of its spending power. The conference continued at the end of October,
when the Quebec and federal delegations confronted one another and ended
without an agreement. Seeing the sourness of this debate, the Ontario premier
called a provincial First Ministers' Conference on the constitution.

3. The Finance Ministers' Conference, 12 July 1971. While preparing for the
Federal-Provincial Fiscal Arrangements Act of 1972-76, the provinces used this
conference to demand a net transfer of fiscal resources to cover the growth of
their expenses and debts, which were proportionately higher than those of the
federal government. Quebec suggested that the formula establishing equalization
payments should consider the tax effort index and overall revenue, which would
have included municipal revenues, school taxes and borrowing revenues. The formula was not significantly modified. However, transfers were slightly increased.

*4. The Finance Ministers' Conference, 6-7 December 1976 (followed by the
First Ministers' Conference of 13-14 December).* The federal government
wanted to consult with the provinces in order to review the principle of tax
revenue guarantees before presenting the next five-year law on fiscal arrangements. In the first case, the federal government refused to continue financing
50 percent of costs whose growth it could not control; by way of compensation, it offered two income tax points (in fact, one point and its cash equivalent),
while the provinces were demanding four. During the conference the other
provinces softened their demands to three points, while Quebec maintained
the hard line of four. In the end, Ottawa left the provinces with only two points.

The provinces thought that equalization payments, estimated by the provinces to be worth the equivalent of 12.5 new income tax points, should be
based on the average revenues of the two richest provinces. The federal side
held to its position that they should be based on the national average revenues
for all ten provinces, but raised its contribution to the equivalent of 13.5 points
on the last day of the conference.

Quebec did not force the agenda of this conference, nor did it have any
special influence on the debates, especially since the recent election of a PQ
government reduced its legitimacy in federal eyes. Quebec found itself isolated over its demand for four points in compensation. At best, its firmness
contributed to improving the federal offer.

5. Transfer Payments, 28-29 November 1985. At this conference Quebec rallied the other provinces: despite the deficit, they would not accept cuts to the Established Programs Financing (EPF). Quebec played the role of conscience at this meeting. In the end there were EPF cuts, but they were not as high as the Mulroney government had envisaged.

SOCIAL ISSUES

1. The Quebec City Conference, 31 March to 2 April 1964 — Pension Plans, Student Loans and Family Allowances. At the conference of July 1963, Jean Lesage put forward his theory of constitutional supremacy over pension funds. In March 1964, Canada announced a pension plan for all of Canada, whereas Quebec wanted its own public retirement program. When Judy Lamarsh presented her plan for a public retirement fund during the conference, she thought it would be more refined than Quebec's, not realizing that Quebec City had finished the detailed preparation of its own program. Immediately after her speech, Premier Lesage explained the project envisioned by Quebec and placed "before her the Dupont Committee's two immense volumes."[42] Quebec's plan included establishing a cumulative fund for contributions to be invested in the provincial economy. He "had even had the rate of increase calculated for each of the provinces" according to the Quebec model. Joey Smallwood of Newfoundland and John Robarts of Ontario spoke out in favor of the Quebec model, a fact Lester B. Pearson seemed to find quite amusing.[43] Several senior federal public servants also thought the Quebec plan was superior. Gordon Robertson, for example, judged it "clearly more attractive."[44] Moreover, Pearson's counselors, in particular Bryce and Kent, wanted to give more content to the vague concept of cooperative federalism that Kent had set out in 1961,[45] and they did all they could to allow the two regimes to coexist. Their principle has been described as follows:

> The irony is that there has been so little recognition that a "different" treatment for Quebec, when there is good reason for it, need not be something "more" and need not be discriminatory; it can simply be "different" for a society that in many respects has characteristics and priorities that can be accommodated without injury to other provinces if there is a will to do so.[46]

The fiscal sharing arrangements were also raised in March of 1964: in the 25-25-100 formula, Quebec demanded point transfers on personal, corporate and inheritance taxes. The provinces contested the fiscal arrangements of 1962-67 at this conference. Ottawa had proposed that the provincial share of federal individual income tax should increase from 16 percent in 1962 to 20 percent in 1967. Under pressure from Quebec,[47] the federal government increased its offer by two points for 1965 and by four points for 1966.

Aside from announcing a review committee on taxation whose aim was merely "to permit the conference to end on a note of hope rather than of disaster,"[48] this conference ended in a conflict between Quebec and Ottawa. Quebec refused to adhere to the student loan program, rejected a family allowance extension to cover children 13-16 years old, and demanded that the federal government withdraw from 29 joint programs while still insisting on receiving more tax points. Quebec objected to the program guaranteeing student loans (education is a provincial jurisdiction), but the other provinces accepted federal intervention in this program. In fact, Quebec wanted to withdraw, with full financial compensation, from all the "mixed" programs but three: the Trans-Canada highway, the Confederation Centennial, and the *Aménagement rural et développement agricole* (ARDA).

This crisis ended on April 20, when bilateral negotiations resulted in a federal withdrawal from nine joint programs with $218 million in compensation, allowing Quebec to launch its own student grants and loans program.[49] Among other things, Quebec finally accepted that Ottawa could administer a national family allowance program if Quebec could have its own system, for which Ottawa gave Quebec three tax points. Quebec had thus already succeeded in "opting-out" with full financial compensation.

Quebec's influence in this case was so strong, and the federal concessions so significant, that Morin[50] claims there was a later attempt, by the federal government, to regain the initiative at the federal-provincial conference of 1970.

Gordon Robertson attributes the concessions Ottawa had to make at the 1963 and 1964 conferences to a lack of preparation by the federal bureaucracy and to Pearson's sympathy for the Quiet Revolution.[51] One result of this experience was the immediate formation of the Federal-Provincial Relations Office of the Privy Council!

2. *The Federal-Provincial First Ministers' Conference in Ottawa, 19 to 22 July 1965.* Each province had its own demands. The Maritimes wanted a larger part of federal education subsidies; Ontario and British Columbia were more preoccupied by economic development; whereas Quebec wanted to create its own health insurance system. The provinces were receptive to Quebec's position, insofar as they saw it serving their interests. This mirrored their practice in the dispute concerning mining resources, when they formed a common front around mining resources on the ocean floor, a domain over which Ottawa wanted its jurisdiction recognized. The conference agenda was not influenced by Quebec, but Quebec spearheaded the provincial charge on health insurance.

Quebec influenced the level of provincial demands, especially on the issue of mining. Quebec helped shore up the demands of the other provinces by maintaining its position on mining, as well as regional development, throughout. Ottawa compromised by agreeing to consult Quebec when it came time to develop a region that concerned it. More than just this, faced with Lesage's anger and the provincial common front, Ottawa agreed to consider a joint memorandum on maritime borders from Quebec, Manitoba and Ontario.

Quebec took issue with federal regional development policy and the concept of "designated regions," to which it opposed the notion of development hubs. For sociological and administrative reasons, Quebec considered itself the principal policy-maker in this area. Morin notes that the federal government ended up using Quebec's approach by adopting measures adapted to local circumstances.[52]

3. The Conference on Social Programs, January 1966. Quebec wanted to convince Ottawa to modify the system of family allowances by increasing payments and extending coverage to age 18, and offered to pay half of this increase itself. The federal government was willing to look at increasing its payments but reminded the provinces that there would be no question of giving them this jurisdiction, which it had occupied since World War II. The federal government considered it the cornerstone of the whole social security structure. Several provinces (Ontario, Newfoundland and Manitoba) supported Quebec's position and were ready to pay half of the cost increase. Quebec exercised genuine influence here, by demonstrating that the system of family allowances was obsolete.

An agreement was also reached on cost sharing between the two levels of government for the Canada Assistance Plan, but Quebec was less visible in this process.

4. The Constitutional Conference, 5-7 February 1968. Pearson proposed an initiative to reform the constitution through an ongoing series of constitutional conferences. Among other things, the conferences were to focus on individual rights, official languages, reforming central institutions, the division of powers and the amending formula. Quebec wanted to start by negotiating the division of powers, but denied seeking special status while demanding greater decentralization. The other provinces accepted the bilingualism principle (Ontario and New Brunswick) and the respect of francophones' rights in general, but they did not aspire to an indepth constitutional revision. Alberta, Saskatchewan and Newfoundland were mistrustful of agreements that could grant special status to Quebec or characterize the negotiations as being between two linguistic communities. Ontario and Nova Scotia left the door open to revising the division of powers and were nervously sympathetic to Quebec's demands.

Quebec had a significant influence on the agenda of this conference. It also influenced the level of the demands being made, since the other provinces were rather reactive in this regard. The conference made progress on the linguistic front in particular, but this was not due to the efforts of Quebec so much as the federal delegation's activism and the quality of its preparation.

5. *Social Union, 4 February 1999.* The discussions leading to the social union agreement extended over three conferences: in Saskatoon (August 1998), Victoria (28-29 January 1999) and Ottawa (4 February 1999). They were an initiative of the provinces intended to limit Ottawa's spending power. In August 1998, Lucien Bouchard agreed to join the other provinces in banding together to demand a stop to the country's "profound dysfunction," a reference to the fact that the federal government was using its spending power to intervene more and more in areas of provincial jurisdiction (for example, the Millennium Scholarships). To limit the extent of Ottawa's spending power, the provinces hoped to sign an agreement on a social union with the federal government.

Alain Noël writes critically about the support given by the other provinces, saying that their approach was very different from Quebec's. The other provinces were not pursuing their own policies so much as participating in the construction of a pan-Canadian national policy. The smaller provinces were ready to sacrifice everything for more money, while the others wanted a pan-Canadian vision, and none considered Quebec a trustworthy ally. Some provinces (Saskatchewan, Manitoba, and Nova Scotia) stated that they would not imperil their values for an alliance with Quebec.[53]

The provinces demanded that Ottawa seek the support of a majority of provinces before being permitted to launch any new program, and that it recognize the right of any province to opt out with full financial compensation, on the condition that that this money be invested in the same sector. Ottawa rejected this element, which was a deal-breaker for Quebec, because it hoped to restrict its application and because it wanted a side agreement with the provinces on health care. The provinces formed a common front, insisting that no deal would be struck outside of the social union.

With the support of several other provinces, Quebec actually became the most fervent supporter of this condition. The challenge was to maintain the consensus reached in Saskatoon. As Bouchard stated, "Nothing is settled if everything isn't settled."

Quebec did not believe it had to give anything away on health care, since it is a strictly provincial jurisdiction. To this the federal minister Stéphane Dion replied that the federal government had every right to exercise its power to spend in this area.

Seeing the provincial determination to have cash transfers restored for health care, Ottawa negotiated a provincial commitment to reinvest these funds in health services, to respect the principles of the *Canada Health Act*, and, moreover, to exchange information so that their performance could be compared and citizens better informed. According to this three-year administrative agreement, Ottawa would not, at least in principle, be permitted unilaterally to start up new social programs in such areas as health and social services if these were to be financed or co-financed by cash transfers to the provinces. It could only do so with the support of a majority of provinces. The provinces would decide what kind of program to start up, but would nonetheless have to submit to Ottawa's objectives in order to obtain federal funding.

The provinces ended up settling for less than their demands, indicating that their influence, and that of Quebec, was weak.[54] While Ottawa wanted its spending power recognized, the provinces wanted it curtailed — and this agreement did not limit the federal spending power. Quebec wanted full financial compensation for opting out of a program, and in this it upheld the provincial consensus reached six days prior to the conference. However, during the conference this consensus exploded, and the provinces agreed with Ottawa on a minimalist framework. Quebec, isolated, refused to sign on. Harvey Lazar notes here the limits of collaborationist federalism, even in the context of the federal machinery,[55] and Noël considers this approach to federalism to be hierarchical.[56] And indeed, it does appear that money creates de facto hierarchies! Noël even describes this approach to federalism, following Lazar, as "unilateralist."[57]

On 4 February 1999, Quebec alone rejected the social union, claiming that to ratify such an agreement would be an historical step backward, both on the federal spending power and on the right to act in areas of provincial jurisdiction. This refusal was due to the absence of an opting out clause with full financial compensation and the fact that Ottawa was maintaining its right to create new social programs in the form of fiscal transfers to individuals, as in the case of the infamous Millennium Scholarships.

Quebec also rejected the notion that "only six provinces could impose their views on the others." This reduced the influence of the so-called rich and powerful provinces, including Quebec, Ontario, Alberta and British Columbia, while the six poorest provinces could have found themselves susceptible to financial blackmail meant to persuade them to accept federal intrusions that would otherwise be unacceptable.

Quebec was confident up to the end that the provincial consensus would win out over Ottawa's proposals, and tried to convince the provinces of the merit of holding firm to the position they had reiterated just a few days earlier in Victoria. But faced with the progress this agreement represented for the other provinces, not to mention a large sum of money for health care, the provincial premiers preferred to ratify the social union. This left Quebec once again on its own on social policy, as in Victoria in 1971.

The initiative in this debate did not originate in Quebec. However, Quebec played a leading role throughout the discussion and the fact that pressure was maintained on Ottawa up to the very end had a great deal to do with Quebec's determination to see that provincial rights were respected. The provinces were susceptible to Quebec's arguments right up to the moment of rupture.

Quebec received no compromise, though Ottawa did state that Quebec would be permitted to benefit from the accord despite not signing it. However, like other provinces, in order to receive federal monies Quebec would have to accede to national standards.

6. Health Care Conferences, 2000. At the 30-31 March Conference, the federal government wanted a national policy and programs. Quebec wanted automatic increases in federal transfers, according to demographic changes, and demanded a five-year guarantee on the amount to be transferred ($23.4 billion). The other provinces, following Quebec, said that they wanted to return to the 1994-95 funding level. In the end, there was no federal commitment but the provinces had found a platform for establishing a common front. In this case Quebec seems to have been pivotal in the formation of the common front and the setting of the agenda.

The 11 September conference discussed the federal role in health care. The federal government wanted to create three distinct funds, a public accountability system and better public recognition of its financial contribution. Quebec rejected any encroachment on its jurisdictions, demanded a return to the historical bases of financing and refused to be accountable to the federal level for the exercise of its own jurisdiction. The other provinces were divided on the question. Saskatchewan and British Columbia accepted an increased federal role in return for supplementary funding, while Alberta and Ontario were opposed.

The conference ended with an agreement on increased federal funding of health care that turned around the Ontario-Quebec axis. Growth would be slow but genuine, and there would be no additional accountability. Quebec even had the accord adorned with a preamble reiterating the constitutional status quo. Mike Harris had persuaded Bouchard to accept a compromise here, but the main discussions had turned on Quebec's concerns. As usual, Quebec was the guardian of provincial jurisdictions.

CONSTITUTIONAL ISSUES

1. The Charlottetown Conference, 1 September 1964. This conference was primarily about the constitutional amending formula and, secondarily, the fusion of the Maritime provinces (proposed by Louis Robichaud). Quebec favored the Fulton formula of September 1961, with technical reservations concerning article 91.1. Its agreement, alongside that of Saskatchewan (in 1961, Ross Thatcher had rejected the provincial veto — in fact, Quebec's veto — on language, property rights and civil law) was interpreted as opening the door for a constitutional repatriation agenda.

2. The Finance Ministers' and Attorneys General Conference on the Fulton-Favreau Formula, 13-14 October 1964. The finance ministers laid out the mandate for an intergovernmental commission on the tax system and a constitutional amendment formula was adopted thanks to an amendment to the Fulton proposal (unanimity for structural provisions; veto for provinces affected by amendments; 7/50 rule for other provisions). In 1966, Quebec finally rejected this "Fulton-Favreau" mechanism following opposition in Quebec public opinion, which saw it as "binding the province to the good will of the other provinces and the central government."[58] In fact, Quebec believed it was possible to interpret this formula so that any province could veto any proposal that increased the legislative capacity of any other province. Quebec's influence manifested itself here in the form of a veto on any formula that did not receive its approval.

3. The First Ministers' Conference, 1967. At the instigation of Quebec, the premiers' conference in Toronto in November 1967 maintained a focus on constitutional reform. Several federal-provincial conferences would follow between 1968 and 1971, culminating in the Victoria conference.

4. The Victoria Conference, 14 to 16 June 1971. The fact that a permanent mechanism for constitutional review was considered at this conference was largely due to Quebec's request and a federal initiative. Quebec had less influence on sensitizing other provinces to its decentralization demands.

Quebec hoped to have the province's constitutional paramountcy recognized on matters of social policy through a modification of article 94A (family allowances, workforce training, guaranteed income supplements, youth allowances, social allowances, unemployment insurance, old-age pensions, and additional contributions). According to direct observers such as Peter Meekison, an advisor to the Alberta government at that time, "Bourassa won his request for an amendment to the existing 94A by including the words family, youth and occupational training allowances. But he also wanted a clause guaranteeing financial compensation if a province opted out of existing programs. Trudeau flatly refused ... just as he had refused to give guarantees on equalization. My sense is that this latter concern was the reason why Quebec used its veto."[59]

The federal government expressed its fear that federal social programs would be eroded. It wanted to keep the upper hand in income security because of the large sums it invested there, and saw the need for a national policy. The other provinces wanted to debate the economy and were looking for federal cash transfers above all. They had diverse positions on social policy: in particular, Nova Scotia, New Brunswick and Saskatchewan opposed provincial paramountcy, whereas Ontario and Manitoba were sympathetic in principle with Quebec's position.

After having refused a first time to modify the constitution, Ottawa made a counter-proposal, the "Canadian constitutional charter" whose ten sections foreshadowed the *Constitution Act of 1982*. This document offered paramountcy to the provinces, notably for old-age pensions and family allowances, but maintained federal prerogatives in health care and unemployment insurance. The provinces accepted the federal position, but Quebec, which had seemed to accept it, ended up turning it down because the Victoria Charter made no mention of provincial paramountcy in social policy. This was despite the fact that this charter had been carefully constructed to guarantee a veto to Quebec on any constitutional amendment to federal institutions, though without explicitly naming the province or giving the appearance of granting special status.[60]

As I understand it, Quebec was extremely influential during this conference, both in terms of setting the main agenda and in terms of how the dossiers were addressed. As with Fulton-Favreau, Quebec's influence took the form of a veto that kept the talks from evolving, a fact that disappointed and irritated several premiers. Joey Smallwood concluded, prophetically, that Canada would survive Quebec's abstention and would do fine without its agreement.[61]

5. Constitutional Negotiations, 1980-81. These 1980-81 constitutional negotiations, held from 2-5 November in Ottawa, were pushed forward by two primary forces. On the one hand, there was Pierre Elliott Trudeau's agenda, already set forth in Victoria and whose urgency was apparent from the attempt at unilateral repatriation in 1980.[62] On the other hand, Quebec had become embroiled in the negotiations since the failure of its referendum initiative. Pressure was also felt from the push for Aboriginal rights and for the rights of provinces to their natural wealth. In this respect, Quebec's role in fixing the agenda of the negotiations was not negligible, but also far from exclusive. The common front of eight provinces, called the Group of Eight and formed in April 1981, had not only broken up, but had left Quebec alone and isolated. Quebec had organized and led the GOE at the price of effectively abandoning its veto on constitutional amendments, since it was demanding total opting out with full financial compensation.

Interpretations surrounding the conclusion of that historical conference are controversial, as the Peter Lougheed-René Lévesque correspondence, aptly illustrates. Lévesque and his minister Claude Morin argued that they were deceived and left alone,[63] while Lougheed replied that the GOE's agreement was intended only to stop Trudeau's unilateral action and was not binding on the final position any province would take.[64] The GOE later developed a formula for amendment and some basic principles on power sharing (such as the opting out formula). Lougheed noted that Quebec was the first to breach the agreement on 3 November, in supporting Trudeau's position on a national referendum without consulting with the seven other provinces. Quebec, in turn, complained that Saskatchewan and later Newfoundland had breached the agreement first. The bottom line is that last minute negotiations took place during the very last evening and night of this conference, without the presence, the consultation or the input of Quebec. The basis for an agreement was found on that night, and at the daily 8 a.m. breakfast meeting, to which Quebec came late (and that had in any case begun before 8 a.m.), a final deal was reached. Quebec had little or no time to change the resultant *fait accompli*. This was the result of the longstanding mistrust between provincial officials and Quebec. Meekison's account of the Winnipeg strategy meeting of May 1981 between the provincial partners is instructive in this regard. At the meeting, Quebec's Minister Morin argued for putting the case against unilateral patriation before the tribunals: "If we win in the UK we win, if we lose in the UK, we win." As a result, "the cohesiveness of the Group of Eight was further undermined," Meekison wrote, since representatives of "other provinces" felt the only objective Quebec had in mind was to prove that federalism was unworkable.[65] Lougheed recalls also that on the 4 November late afternoon meeting of the GOE, Quebec was ready to write the final press release acknowledging the failure of the conference, while some provinces preferred to wait until the last morning to write it. Was this a sign of Quebec's eagerness to announce the failure of the talks? Or was it proof of the provinces' secret intention to proceed with "last minute talks"? In the end, it is possible that both of these positions reflected the truth.

Lougheed's reply to Levesque on the substance of Morin's complaints is not very convincing: "I would have thought that every Premier would have expected a great deal of lobbying and exchanges of views over the evening of November 4th ... You made no attempt to discuss the future course of events with any of the other premiers."[66] Lougheed did not address the fact that neither did officials from any province attempt to get in touch with any Quebec officials on that evening, while significant talks were going on with federal officials and while talks were going on between many provincials officials. In fact many provinces did not believe in the PQ government's sincerity in this process, so, in all probability, they concluded that the deal they wanted was easier to draft without Quebec's presence.

The fact that an accord was signed without Quebec, based on an agreement reached at a time when Quebec's absence had been planned, showed how limited Quebec's influence had become after the Supreme Court judgement denying that its historic right of veto was legally binding.[67] Ironically, Quebec's influence at this conference served only to undermine its own goals, in that it motivated the other provinces to conclude a deal that would demonstrate that Canadian federalism was not, in fact, an impossible dream. Despite unanimous opposition from the National Assembly, including the federalist opposition that had been fighting only 18 months earlier to preserve and renew Canada, the accord was signed by the other provinces and the federal government.

6. Meech Lake Accord, 1987. The goal of this accord was to amend the 1982 *Constitution Act* so that Quebec would be able to sign it. A great deal of attention was thus paid to the Robert Bourassa government's expectations (the five conditions to agree to the *Constitution Act*, issued in 1985 by Minister Gil Rémillard), and Quebec had a great deal of influence over both the agenda and the process. To the extent that the head of Quebec's government agreed with it, it could be said that the accord was acceptable to him and that Quebec believed it had had sufficient influence over its content.

After a series of bilateral and multilateral meetings between Quebec officials and officials from other provinces, Quebec set the agenda and the 1986 APC agreed to it. The initial Meech Lake Accord was modified during a last conference in the Langevin Block. This was not due not to further requests from Quebec but because other provinces had demanded that certain matters be clarified. Some believe that the Meech agreement was watered down at this meeting, becoming the Meech-Langevin Accord, a sign of Quebec's weakening position and influence. Indeed, these people say it testified to Quebec's willingness to share its influence. Others, when interviewed, held that the only changes were restricted to minor details.

In the end, the Conservative ministers and the provincial First Ministers did not really "sell" the accord to English-Canadian public opinion. Fearing the public's reaction, they hoped the usual process of negotiation would satisfy the population. Instead, they were sharply accused of concocting agreements "behind closed doors" — though curiously, this argument had not been raised over an agreement reached behind closed doors, without Quebec, only five years earlier! Quebec nationalists also had serious trouble accepting the accord.

Premier McKenna, newly risen to power in New Brunswick, was the first to dare turn against Meech, saying he did not feel bound by the word of his predecessor, Premier Richard Hatfield. Clyde Wells and Gary Filmon followed. The procedural pretext used by Manitoba Member of the Legislative Assembly Elijah Harper allowed Filmon to say he regretted the "unintentional delay" that permitted Wells to avoid committing himself before the deadline. In fact, a convergence around Trudeau's vision of Canada (Trudeau himself was personally active in the blockade campaign), including the traditional rejection of Quebec's special status, prevented the accord from being adopted by two provincial legislatures before the self-imposed three-year deadline. Some argue that Bourassa's decisions on linguistic rights in Quebec (the use of the notwithstanding clause in the sign law case), and its negative impact on many members of Canada's anglo intellectual community, was the cause of the accord's failure. But this argument neglects the criticisms relating to "a behind closed doors agreement" that were voiced across Canada as a reason for opposing the accord. In this case, Quebec's influence had been greater in the negotiating hall than in the forum of Canadian public opinion.

7. The Charlottetown Accord, September 1992. Once more an attempt was made to produce a federal-provincial agreement modifying the constitution, thereby opening the door for the signature of Quebec. This time, however, Quebec was no longer the central province setting the agenda and directing the process. In fact Quebec, frustrated after the Meech Lake agreement failure, initially decided to stay on the outside and joined the talks only long after their beginning. Quebec's strategy appeared to be something like the following: "We will join the group after they agree on a package and then we will negotiate one on one with the group of ten plus the Aboriginal peoples." According to one participant, lots of issues were already closed by the time Quebec joined the talks, hence it was too late to radically change the package. The western provinces wanted concessions on resources, equality of the provinces in the Senate, and more representative judicial appointments; Aboriginal peoples wanted their rights more fully recognized; and several provinces wanted to restrict the reach of any concessions they had to make to bring Quebec into the constitutional fold.

The scope of the Charlottetown Accord of 28 August 1992 was larger than Meech. In addition, it defined the distinct society less specifically and did not make Quebecers feel as secure about using this concept in the process of constitutional interpretation. One participant feels Quebec's success was demonstrated by the insertion of the final section on the spending power. During these negotiations, the Quebec question preoccupied the rest of Canada, while Quebec's influence was less important than during the Meech Lake process. There are three reasons for this: first, Bourassa never clearly formulated his demands, whether during the preparatory discussions or at the conference itself;[68] moreover, Quebec's apparent claims were less well received by the provincial premiers; and finally, Quebec had no influence on the agenda. Certain new clauses were added that weakened Quebec's position relative to the rest of Canada (regarding, for example, the spending power and the Senate). Premier Bourassa centralized negotiations around himself and paid no attention to his advisors or the files that had been carefully prepared by the senior public service. For this reason, he has been accused of improvising his performance.[69]

This accord would later be rejected in a referendum in a majority of the provinces, including Quebec, where it was thought to offer insufficient autonomy. The other provinces considered the share given to Quebec and the provinces in general to be too large. When Trudeau publicly denounced the accord as too decentralizing, he influenced a part of the anglophone electorate, as well as a particular school of federalist thought in Quebec.

VARIOUS IMPORTANT CONFERENCES ON SPECIFIC ISSUES

At the National Security Conference of August 1967 Quebec exercised no particular influence since the federal side was open to satisfying all provinces. At the Aboriginal Affairs Conference in 1998, following the Erasmus-Dussault report, Quebec adopted the same position as the other provinces. At the Environment Conference in 1998 Quebec played some role in awakening national sensitivity to greenhouse gas emissions and for the need to devise a mutually acceptable solution. At the 2000 Agricultural Conference the positions of Quebec and Ontario were satisfied by Ottawa, which expanded its budget to satisfy also Manitoba and Saskatchewan. Quebec was not able to exert a positive influence on Ottawa and its competitors at the 2001 Fisheries Conference, and lost quotas on three species of fish and crustacean. Outside of the conference scene Quebec was also influential, leading the support for the North America Free Trade Agreement (NAFTA) in the late 1980s.

ANALYSIS

ROLES PLAYED

An analysis of these conferences/events produces the following observations:

- Quebec instigated the events of 1960;
- It organized provincial common fronts in 1960, 1965, 1966 (social assistance programs), 1980-81, 1985, 1999, and 2000 (the Toronto-Quebec axis on health care);
- It instigated new ideas or proposals in 1960, 1965, 1966 (fiscal sharing) and 2000 (agriculture and health care);
- It significantly contributed to the content of the agenda in 1960, 1965 (Fulton-Favreau), 1967, 1968, 1971, 1985, 1987 (Meech) and 1992;
- It improved upon federal proposals in 1964 (Charlottetown), 1965, 1976, 1980-81, 1985 and 1999;
- It significantly influenced the outcome of the conferences of 1960, 1964 (pensions and Charlottetown), 1970-71 (Victoria), 1980-81 and 1987 (Meech);
- It blocked the proposals of 1964 (Fulton-Favreau) and 1971 (Victoria);
- It exercised a mitigated degree of influence while seeking its objectives in 1980-81, 1992, 1999, 2000 (agriculture) and 2001 (fishing quotas); and
- It withdrew from the debate in 1998, leaving an empty chair and exerting no direct influence.

Quebec's influence seems to have declined over the years, despite such concrete developments as secretariats for education and the environment and administrative agreements on important matters such as immigration (Andras Bienvenue 1968), GST collection (1993), social assistance and employment (1998), and other more minor agreements that more or less arose out of conflict (the Millennium Scholarships in 2000). Quebec's influence here appears non-negligible, but a net diminution is observable between 1960 and 2001 in its degree (regarding agendas and options), nature (the influence is considered legitimate for technical reasons, not historical or moral ones), and product (the degree of satisfaction it brings).

QUEBEC'S INFLUENCE: IMPORTANT FROM 1960-70

The period in which Quebec had the greatest influence is unquestionably 1960-70. The province went into negotiations extremely well-prepared, and its senior public service already had a very good reputation in Canada.[70]

At the beginning of the 1960s, the other provinces did not take these talks as seriously as Quebec did, and in general did not prepare for them very well. Claude Morin, then a deputy minister, writes that only Quebec, Ontario and Saskatchewan seemed professionally prepared at these conferences, while other provinces, lacking either the interest or the financial resources, were represented by an old Ottawa lawyer or an accounting firm. "We prepared papers for them. We told them, 'Now, this is what we're discussing, and this is what you'll get it if works.'"[71] During the Charlottetown Accord, Quebec's senior public service appeared to have just as well prepared, but Bourassa appears not to have made use of the work his group produced. "Their influence [with Bourassa] equaled absolute zero."[72]

A clear willingness to reach a consensus existed among the English Canadian elites from 1963-1970. The federal public service showed signs of guilt regarding the treatment of francophones outside Quebec, and witnesses to the Laurendeau-Dunton Commission, as well as its report, were more or less open to bilingualism. Lester B. Pearson, the diplomat who became prime minister, sought to establish a more harmonious form of federalism and was willing to take risks to make it happen.

Apart from the prime minister's agenda and the great influence of some of his political and administrative counsellors, such as Tom Kent and Al Johnson or his predecessor, Bob Bryce, other cyclical factors reinforced Quebec's influence during this period. For example, if Ontario's deputy finance minister had been a less insightful individual than Ian MacDonald, who knows how Quebec's initiatives might have been received? Gérard Bergeron[73] suggests more prosaically that the fact that four of the previous six federal governments had been minority governments encouraged a greater desire at the federal level to please Quebec public opinion; especially since its interlocutor from 1960-66, the government of Jean Lesage, seemed to have popular support in Quebec. Proximity to the federal elections of 1963 and 1965 would also have made the imperative to accommodate Quebec's electorate that much more pressing.

DIRECT INFLUENCE BECAME MARGINAL UP TO 2001

Quebec's successive retractions (Fulton-Favreau and Victoria) exasperated the national capital and political leaders in the other provinces. The question became, "What does Quebec want?" When Pierre Trudeau arrived on the scene with his more centralizing vision of Canada and an approach to Quebec that claimed it had no need of special status in Canada, Ottawa's attitude changed radically, starting at the conference of 1967. The Supreme Court decision affirming that Quebec's constitutional veto was a not a legally binding convention whittled down Quebec's arsenal and caused the other premiers to feel they no longer had to deal with Quebec.

In general, Quebec's influence in the agenda-setting process and over the final results of the conferences has diminished. Moreover, agreements have more frequently been reached without Quebec's assent and even against its will (repatriation, the National Youth Benefits Program, the *Clarity Act*, the social union): "On a series of questions, Canada now marches on as if Quebec did not exist or did not matter."[74] Outside of the Mulroney period, we have also seen little federal willingness to accommodate Quebec. The approach seems rather to be to interact both with the Quebec government and directly with its public, rather than treating the Quebec government as its people's sole representative. This seems to exasperate the political scientist Alain Noël, who writes in the conclusion of his analysis of the social union negotiations: "Quebec has never been so marginalized in the Canadian Federation."[75]

In an interview in 2001, Claude Morin places Quebec's reduced position in context:

1. It is often said these days, notably by Jean Charest, Leader of the Liberal Opposition in Quebec City, that Quebec has lost influence in Canada. The truth is that under Jean Chrétien and for the time being, all the provinces have lost influence. At least half of them put up with this, while the others sporadically criticize and make demands. Quebec does this more intensely than the others, since its political integrity matters more to it.... That's why Quebec sees implications in every file connected to its jurisdiction as having ramifications for its integrity. The other provinces are much less preoccupied by this side of things because their citizens are members of the Canadian nation, of which the federal government is the political center and the main instrument.

2. Quebec's lack of tangible influence — and thus lack of results — regarding its status should not obscure the fact that the Quebec-Canada problem has dominated Canadian politics for most of the period since 1960 and that while this issue is currently 'dormant' it has not disappeared. Thus, Quebec's influence on the political agenda has always been either directly in the forefront or potentially resurgent ... Unless Ottawa

wins its wager for transferred loyalty, the Quebec question can return at any time. The problem is thus to evaluate how likely this transfer is, and whether it will be confirmed over time. Personally, I believe that this possibility is nonexistent ... We can see this in Europe, where people are willing to make all sorts of arrangements, as long as the 'motherland' remains intact.[76]

CONTEXT

Over the last 40 years, Quebec's political clout has declined overall in Canada. Its share of the population has fallen from 31 percent to 22 percent; the percentage of francophones in Canada has fallen from 33 percent to 23 percent; the percentage of Quebec Members of Parliament has fallen from 28 percent to 25 percent; Quebec's participation in the Cabinet has declined from 33 percent to 21 percent; and its relative contribution to the Gross National Product has declined. All these are factors explaining the relative decline in the hearing it receives.

In this period, the idea of Canada has also changed, and this has detracted from the legitimacy of some of Quebec's demands. From the idea of two founding peoples we have turned to the notion of multiculturalism, while we have also been witness to slow improvements in the recognition of Aboriginal rights. From a historical and sociological perspective, Quebec's claim to special status is no longer rooted in the firmest of soils.

Federal political leaders now express a clear, radical agenda on these matters, which is based on a more centralized view of Canada. While it is difficult to publicly explain a dogmatic approach to collaborative, asymmetrical or cooperative federalism, the more basic idea of a strong central Canada is easier to express, and here Chrétien has followed the agenda of his spiritual father, Trudeau, who "tested the limits of federal powers in field after field."[77] In this way, Chrétien has transformed the country.[78] One of the bases for this approach is an extension of the spending power and, implicitly, a theory of auxiliary jurisdiction. From this point of view, the provincial role has become more fragile on any subject matter with national repercussions (standards, mobility, identity, and so on). Another contributing factor is the argument that pan-Canadian equality is needed to deal in concert with globalization and to improve technical and regional political interaction at various levels.

Public opinion in other provinces is now better informed concerning the stakes and the negotiations process. Because it is rather hostile to any proposals that would give Quebec special status, provincial leaders cannot be too conciliatory, especially when an election is coming. Federal proposals now also tend to be much better prepared by the bureaucracy, which has become increasingly better organized around these subjects. The development of an institutionalized Cabinet with specialized committees and highly structured decision procedures reinforces the conformity of ministerial decisions and prevents ministers from making ad hoc agreements with provinces.[79] This argument also applies to provinces with institutionalized Cabinets[80] and structured ministerial relationships. The role of bureaucratization in reinforcing dogmatism at the expense of pragmatism thus works at two levels.

Jean-François Lisée promotes the thesis that Quebec loses influence when two discordant voices claim to speak for the province and the French Canadians who live there.[81] This was the case during the Trudeau years and during his intrusion into the debate on the Charlottetown Accord, but it was not the case in 1991, when Mulroney's Quebec ministers held back their opinions during the long period in which Robert Bourassa seemed incapable of making himself clear.

We might further explain the dilution of Quebec's influence by the fact that the other provinces now appear better prepared while negotiating agreements, which means Quebec no longer enjoys the standing with them that it once did. This was especially true during the 1980s, while Quebec was playing its "empty seat" gambit, having withdrawn from the conference table under both Levesque and Bourassa. "They gradually developed a model without us!" said a retired senior bureaucrat, who added that the Quebec public service's poor grasp of English reduced the effective influence of the Quebec team. "Everything happened in English, and at that level one must be excellent, not merely functional. Remember Bourassa in Charlottetown!"[82]

The failed referendums on sovereignty, combined with the absence of alternative courses of action for Quebec, diminished the sense of urgency and danger felt by other Canadian provinces. It is possible to detect a certain disillusionment in English Canada regarding the effectiveness of offering concessions to Quebec, and this appears to be a structural effect extending into Canada's future. Concessions to Quebec are seen as encouraging the sovereignist movement. Is it, then, possible that the push for independence has contributed to reducing Quebec's influence? At first sight, this argument seems tenable, since the movement might have frightened or disillusioned potential allies. However this loss of influence was already in evidence under the Liberals in 1970, beginning as it did with Trudeau's plan for a strong central Canada. For that matter, we might also think of Quebec's political activism from 1970 to 2001 as a means of compensating for its loss of alternative avenues of influence in Canada, providing it with a status it might not otherwise have enjoyed. In other words, Quebec's interests may ultimately have been better served by a combative stance rather than an accommodationist stance, given that the intergovernmental climate in this period frequently became trapped in the logic of a zero-sum game.

Alternatively, we might explain this phenomenon by the rise of a new kind of thinking in Canada, where legalism and perpetual quarrels over jurisdiction with uncertain outcomes has given way to a pragmatism more suited to short-term, concrete arrangements. Furthermore, the reduction in growth of federal spending since 1977, followed by the cutbacks of 1985 and 1995, have starved the provinces and made them more ready to accept encroachments in return for cash.

SOME INFLUENCE, EVEN SO

Quebec's influence did not vanish between 1970 and 2001, but its appearance and impact were altered. Quebec is still influential in defining the issues, establishing power relations that create provincial unity, and defending provincial jurisdiction. In essence, it remains "the only government that would challenge federal hegemony in a fundamental way."[83] In this sense, Quebec has been effectively playing the "Canada card," helping to preserve Canada's specific form of federalism, in opposition to the American model. Quebec has also influenced the themes and trajectories of negotiations, since social thinking developed in Quebec often affects policy development during federal-provincial meetings. Finally, Quebec is opening doors: it demands or hopes that its field of operation will be preserved. This is generally refused at first, and then granted to all provinces in order to avoid granting special status or seeming to create an asymmetrical form of federalism (as for example, in the agreement on professional training and the case of the Millennium Scholarships). This makes the federal position on Quebec more difficult to maintain, according to an ex-bureaucrat, since whatever Quebec gets must also be offered to the other provinces sooner or later!

However, Quebec's capacity to defend its own powers has sharply declined, as was illustrated by the debate relating to the modification of the *Young Offenders Act*. Quebec still claims, in vain, not only that its successful experience has not been taken into account in this 2001 federal law, but that the legislation has interfered with Quebec policy.

ELEMENTS OF INFLUENCE

My initial hypothesis was that the sources of influence would include elements of moral authority, mutual agreement and credibility. This moral authority is grounded in history, cultural duality, and conviction. With regards to the Quebec case, after 1970, the role of moral authority based in history and cultural duality has diminished in the face of multiculturalism, the equality of provinces perspective, and symmetrical federalism. Agreements mutually reached between provinces have not always held. Credibility seems to have played a certain role, but this has varied during the period under study.

My analysis of the proposed chronology has uncovered six influential resources or conditions for wielding influence:

- Vision: having clear objectives and an ability to translate them rapidly and effectively into stances and negotiating tactics. "You score points by being the first to stake out the territory."[84] This was the case in 1964 (transfers) and in 1999, for example. When Quebec's position was ambiguous and uncertain, as in 1964, 1971 and to some extent in 1980, its influence was diminished.

- Having the ability to conceptualize, analyze, stimulate, calculate and project.[85] The high quality of Quebec's public service gave it some influence up to the beginning of the 1980s. Bourassa illustrated the perils of ignoring this resource, when he failed to listen to the opinions of his public servants during negotiations on the Charlottetown Accord in 1992.

- Being the only one with this ability. The federal government established a precursor of the Office of Federal-Provincial Relations in the mid-1960s. Once this office had reached a certain level of competence, Quebec's influence declined.

- The credibility and leadership of the political or bureaucratic interveners (the degree to which the spokesperson is taken seriously, placing discourse in the context of a vision, respect for previous commitments, the ability to have one's adversaries recognize one's contributions). As a former federal minister who was considered a man "with his act together," Jean Lesage could reassure his partners in this regard. This was not the case with Bourassa, who was considered to be unpredictable after the 1971 Victoria Conference. Nor was it the case for leaders of PQ governments, who were burdened, in the eyes of their partners, with the desire to break up Canada.

- Mastery over the discourse, beginning with mastery of the language spoken by one's partners and adversaries. This means properly understanding their arguments, being able to effectively respond and present one's own thesis, and to be better received than the others. In the 1960s, Quebec's political and upper-level bureaucratic negotiators had an excellent mastery of the English language and culture because they had already worked in Ottawa or studied in Great Britain or the United States. In 1992, the media reported confidential sources who revealed that Bourassa, his health failing, was finding it difficult to fully understand the other premiers or make himself understood by them. Several Quebec deputy ministers have recalled how important it is for Quebec's senior bureaucrats and ministers to have a perfect mastery of English. They regret that his has not always been the case over the last 25 years.

- Internal cohesiveness and the degree of one's support in civil society both contribute to a speaker's credibility. It is certain that Quebecers' indecision about whether to follow the PQ on independence weakened their negotiators' positions, since in negotiation, the question that continually arises is, "What happens if I refuse?" When the reply is, "Nothing tragic," one's tendency is not to cede ground. Moreover, the referendums broke the cohesion of Quebec civil society, an effect to which several groups financed by the Government of Canada also contributed.

The challenge of wielding influence is also a function of its multifaceted reception by one's partner or adversary in discussions: a degree of openness and a will to establish long-term co-operation extend influence, whereas a perception of hostility and threat reduce it. It is certain that the mental and political attitudes taken by Prime Minister Pearson and the senior bureaucrats of his day both at the federal level (Johnson, Robertson) and in Ontario made it easier for Quebec to wield influence, than did Pierre Trudeau's more centralizing agenda and the approach of the ministers and senior clerks charged with implementing it. The visions of federal prime ministers play an ongoing role in this respect. Whereas Pearson, Clark and Mulroney were more open, Trudeau and Chrétien proposed a more centralizing vision.

CONCLUSION

The elements affecting influence gathered in this study are as follows: the nature of the federal plan (the Pearson plan and the Mulroney era gave Quebec more influence than the Trudeau doctrine); the political cycle (the stability of federal governments that constructed the analyses opposing sovereignty); real or alleged perceptions of one's discussion partners (with centralizing or sovereigntist agendas), which can be used as a pretext to set aside the other's concerns; provincial fiscal vulnerability; and the quality of administrative preparation.

Over the years, Quebec has seen its influence decline quite visibly. This has not been the case with the other large Canadian provinces, often because they had none or did not seek it as ardently. Federalist expectations vary strongly across Canada, and despite short-term readings of the polls it is not obvious that a centralizing agenda such as Trudeau's, which Jean Chrétien is pursuing, will increase federalism's popularity in Quebec. The fact is that since 1968, these centralizing agendas have been accompanied by a constant rise in support for sovereignty in Quebec. Lacking a clear sense of their influence in Canadian institutions, the people of the province of Quebec might end up creating their own field of influence — unless, that is, they first disappear as a significant political community, which is, perhaps, somebody's cynical goal.

NOTES

The author wishes to thank Fatou Touré and Patrick Dubois for their work as research assistants, the former public servants for their counsel, and Queen's University for its support. A special thanks to Harvey Lazar and Peter Meekison, as well as the many colleagues who commented on this chapter. Carole Garand must also be thanked for her work supervising the editing. The opinions and errors remain the author's sole responsibility.

1. Rollin Bennet Posey, *American Government*, 11th ed. (NJ: Rowman & Allanheld, Helix Books, 1983), pp. 231-34.

2. Kenneth McRoberts, *Un pays à refaire : l'échec des politiques constitutionnelles canadiennes* (Montreal : Éditions du Boréal, 1999), pp. 377-79.

3. James Ross Hurley, "Executive Federalism," in *Public Administration and Public Management: Experiences in Canada*, eds. J. Bourgault, M. Demers and C. Williams (Quebec: Les Publications du Québec, 1997), p. 112.

4. Henry Mintzberg, *Power In and Around Organizations* (Englewood Cliffs, NJ: Prentice-Hall, 1983), p. 5.

5. Nigel Nicholson, *The Blackwell Encyclopedic Dictionary of Organizational Behaviour* (Cambridge, MA: Blackwell Business, 1995), p. 437.

6. Dominique Colas, *Dictionnaire de la pensée politique* (Paris: Larousse, 1997), pp. 209-10.

7. M. Crozier and E. Friedberg, *L'acteur et le système* (Paris: Éditions du Seuil, 1997).

8. Henry Mintzberg, *Power In and Around Organizations*, p. 5.

9. Guy Hermet *et al.*, *Dictionnaire de la science politique et des institutions politiques*, 4th ed. (Paris: Armand Colin, 2000), p. 249.

10. Vincent Lemieux, *Les chemins de l'influence* (Quebec: P.U.L., 1979), p. 55.

11. John R. Schermerhorn *et al.*, *Comportement humain et organisation*, French adaptation by Claire de Billy, 2d ed. (Montreal: Éditions du Renouveau pédagogique, 2002), p. 398.

12. Jacques Bourgault, "Paramètres synergiques du pouvoir des hauts fonctionnaires," *Revue canadienne de science politique* 26, 2 (1982):220.

13. André Bernard, *La vie politique au Québec et au Canada*, 2d ed. (Quebec: PUQ, 2000), p. 6.

14. Roger Gibbins and Guy Laforest, *Sortir de l'impasse: les voies de la réconciliation* (Montreal: Institut de recherche en politiques publique, 1998).

15. Edmond Orban, *Le fédéralisme?* super État fédéral? Association d'États souverains? (Quebec: Hurtubise HMH, 1992), p. 65.

16. Claude Morin, "Le problème Canada-Québec: origine, évolution, perspectives" (Montreal: *L'action nationale*, 1996), pp. 190-95.

17. Richard Simeon, "Changing Patterns of Intergovernmental Relations in the Canadian Federation," draft paper, 2001, p. 44.

18. Jean-François Lisée, "Avec des amis comme ça," *La Presse*, 23 October 2001, p. A17.

19. Joe Clark, *A Nation Too Good to Lose* (Toronto: Key Porter, 1994), p. 93.

20. Gordon Robertson, *Memoirs of a Very Civil Servant* (Toronto: University of Toronto Press, 2000), p. 303.

21. Jack Lawrence Granatstein, *The Ottawa Men: The Civil Service Mandarins: 1935-1957* (Toronto: University of Toronto Press, 1982), p. 16.

22. Louis Sabourin, Passion d'être, désir d'avoir: le dilemme Canada-Québec dans un univers en mutation (Montreal: Éditions du Boréal, 1992), p. 67.

23. Author's interview with Claude Morin, 2001.

24. Christian Dufour, "Quebec's Intergovernmental Relations," in *Public Administration and Public Management: Experiences in Canada*, eds. J. Bourgault, M. Demers and C. Williams (Quebec: Les Publications du Québec, 1997), p. 322.

25. David Elton and Peter McCormick, "The Alberta Case: Intergovernmental Relations," in *Public Administration and Public Management: Experiences in Canada*, eds. J. Bourgault, M. Demers and C. Williams (Quebec: Les Publications du Québec, 1997), p. 222.

26. Ralph Heintzmann, "Canada and Public Administration," in *Public Administration and Public Management: Experiences in Canada*, eds. J. Bourgault, M. Demers and C. Williams (Quebec: Les Publications du Québec, 1997), pp. 8-9.

27. James Mallory, "Particularities and Systems of Government," in *Public Administration and Public Management: Experiences in Canada*, eds. J. Bourgault, M. Demers and C. Williams (Quebec: Les Publications du Québec, 1997), p. 17.

28. Robertson, *Memoirs of a Very Civil Servant*, p. 219.

29. Marcel Masse, Seminar given to the UQAM Political Science department, February 1998.

30. Jean-François Lisée, *Le Naufrageur, Robert Bourassa et les Québécois 1991-1992* (Montreal: Éditions du Boréal, 1994), pp. 31, 33.

31. Ibid., p: 61.

32. Anonymous interview, 2001.

33. James Iain Gow, *Histoire de l'administration publique québécoise*: 1867-1970 (Montreal: Presses de l'Université de Montréal, 1986), p. 184.

34. Honorier Mercier held the very first one in 1887 in Quebec City, according to Gow, *Histoire de l'administration publique québécoise*, p. 49.

35. The previous one was held in 1926, according to Gow, *Histoire de l'administration publique québécoise*, p. 184.

36. James Hurley, "Executive Federalism," p. 117.

37. Ibid.

38. Ibid., p. 112.

39. Claude Morin, *Le pouvoir québécois ... en négociation* (Montreal: Éditions du Boréal, 1972), p. 36.

40. Ibid., p. 41.

41. Pierre Duchesne, *Jacques Parizeau: Le Croisé 1930-1970,* vol. 1 (Montreal: Éditions Québec-Amérique, 2001), p. 413.

42. Ibid., p. 348.

43. Ibid., p. 349.

44. Robertson, *Memoirs of a Very Civil Servant,* p. 220.

45. Ibid., p. 219.

46. Ibid., p. 221.

47. Claude Morin, *Le pouvoir québécois ... en négociation,* p. 56.

48. Robertson, *Memoirs of a Very Civil Servant,* p. 220.

49. Pierre Duchesne, *Jacques Parizeau: Le Croisé 1930-1970,* p. 350.

50. Author's interview with Claude Morin, 2001.

51. Robertson, *Memoirs of a Very Civil Servant,* pp. 243-45.

52. Claude Morin, *Le pouvoir québécois ... en négociation,* pp. 122-23.

53. Alain Noël, "Without Quebec: Collaborative Federalism with a Footnote?" Working paper (Montreal: Institut de recherche en politiques publiques, 2000), p. 6.

54. Ibid., p. 5.

55. Harvey Lazar, "The Federal Role in a New Social Union: Ottawa at a Crossroads," in *Canada, the State of the Federation 1997,* ed. H. Lazar (Kingston: McGill-Queen's University Press, 1998), p. 131.

56. Alain Noël, "Without Quebec," p. 18.

57. Ibid., p. 4.

58. Claude Morin, *Le pouvoir québécois ... en négociation,* p. 137.

59. J. Peter Meekison, *Constitutional Patriation: The Lougheed-Levesque Correspondence* (Kingston: Institute of Intergovernmental Relations, Queen's University, 1999), pp. 9-10.

60. The language in article 49.1 is a good example: "Every province that at any time before the issue of the proclamation had ... a population of at least 25 percent of the population of Canada."

61. Joey Smallwood, *Le Devoir,* 19 June 1971, p. 9.

62. Meekison, *Constitutional Patriation,* pp. 9-10.

63. Ibid., pp. 14, 30.

64. Ibid., p. 22.

65. Ibid., p. 7.

66. Ibid., p. 25.

67. [1982] 2 RCS. *In the Matter of a Reference to the Court of Appeal of Quebec Concerning the Constitution of Canada*, 793-816.

68. Jean-François Lisée, *Le Naufrageur*, p. 365.

69. Ibid.

70. Robertson, *Memoirs of a Very Civil Servant*, p. 320.

71. Duchesne, *Jacques Parizeau*, p. 410.

72. Jean-François Lisée, *Le Naufrageur*, pp. 80-81.

73. Gérard Bergeron, "Le Canada en régression historique," *Le Devoir*, 9 May 1990, p. 7; 10 May 1990, p. 9.

74. Alain Noël, *Without Quebec*, p. 13.

75. Ibid., p. 12.

76. Author's interview with Claude Morin, 2001.

77. Alain Noël, *Without Quebec*, p. 823, citing Richard Simeon and Ian Robinson.

78. Ibid., p. 298.

79. Ibid., p. 9.

80. Christopher J.C. Dunn, *The Institutionalized Cabinet* (Toronto: McGill-Queen's University Press, 1995).

81. Jean-François Lisée, *Le Naufrageur*.

82. Anonymous interview, 2001.

83. Alain Noël, *Without Quebec*, p. 11.

84. Joseph Facal, *Le déclin du fédéralisme canadien* (Montreal: VLB éditeur, 2001), p. 60.

85. George Anderson, "The New Focus on the Policy Capacity of the Federal Government," *Canadian Public Administration* 39, 4(Winter 2002):478.

13

Quebec and North American Integration: Making Room for a Sub-National Actor?

Nelson Michaud

Depuis la fin des années 1980, le Canada semble s'être commis envers un engagement de plus en plus important dans les affaires hémisphériques. Pour les provinces canadiennes, et plus particulièrement pour le Québec, un engagement de ce genre présente des défis particuliers puisqu'il interpelle plusieurs champs de compétence provinciale. Il est donc fort important de voir ce que cet engagement signifie pour les relations internationales du Québec. Quel en sera le résultat? Comment seront-elles affectées? Comment est-ce que le nouveau contexte favorise une nouvelle orientation, voire une nouvelle approche des relations internationales? Ce chapitre cherche à répondre à ces questions. Pour ce faire, il propose l'analyse de deux dimensions des relations internationales du Québec telles qu'exprimées dans les déclarations des trois principaux partis politiques et dans des lois récemment adoptées par l'Assemblée nationale. Ces dimensions permettront de voir si les institutions politiques du Québec sont sensibles au phénomène de la continentalisation et si des mécanismes de coordination des efforts des provinces canadiennes sont déployés afin de faire front commun devant ces nouveaux défis. À la lumière de l'élection d'un parti fédéraliste à la tête du Québec en avril 2003, cette analyse est fort pertinente pour nous permettre de mieux cerner les orientations de politique possibles que ce gouvernement pourrait envisager.

Since the mid-seventeenth century, international relations have traditionally been the preserve of sovereign states. However, the realities of the contemporary world are undermining this established order and leading both practitioners and researchers to consider what changes will have to be made to adjust to these new realities, which are found at two levels.

At a first level, we have to consider the nature of the state, indeed of states that are constructing networks, mechanisms, and institutions to facilitate their exchanges, whether from the politico-diplomatic, economic, or cultural point of view. When, in the mid-nineteenth century, Canada adopted a federal form of state, it was one of the first countries to have done so. This occurred 200 years after the founding of an international relations system based on the unitary state. The early 1990s, and particularly the implosion of the Union of Soviet Socialist Republics and Yugoslavia, caused theorists of federalism to worry about the "survival of the species." This historical convulsion, although likely experienced by the peoples involved more as a political, indeed human, cataclysm, nevertheless quickly gave way to a resurgence of the spirit of federalism. This phenomenon even reached some unitary states, such as Great Britain and China, that were quick to borrow some elements of federalism by implementing a degree of regional political devolution, or through the establishment of autonomous economic regions. In the summer of 2001, Italy also embraced this trend when its citizens voted by referendum in favour of adopting a federal system to replace the unitary state that had existed since the country's unification in the nineteenth century. Although there are currently more unitary than federal states, many of the world's great powers — the United States, Russia, and Germany — and middle powers — Canada, Brazil, Australia, and India — are today living and evolving under a federal regime. In fact, almost half the world's population lives in a federal system.

At a second level, federalism entails, by definition, a separation of fields of jurisdiction. Theoretically and practically, this means that some international interactions can happen in one or several of the fields that come within the exclusive jurisdiction of the federated state, and not of the federal state to which it belongs. Although for 100 years international activity essentially took place in fields in which the federal state could legitimately intervene, federated states have been led to try to intervene in their own names for a host of reasons, including the growing complexity of many issues, the ease with which information flows, and the development of state intervention in sectors devolved to federated states. Most of these changes surfaced in the last third of the twentieth century and are increasingly evident today.

In response to this new international context, a number of federal states have chosen to develop mechanisms that provide their federated units with a voice in these matters, as demonstrated by a recent study of Germany, Australia, Belgium, Brazil, and Canada.[1] Clearly, the responses to this situation vary greatly from one state to another, and it is virtually impossible to identify a unique or even predominant way of handling the question.[2] In any event, it is evident that federal states are increasingly recognizing the autonomy of federated entities in economic and cultural matters — areas that are of considerable interest to the federated states — though their scope of autonomy is wider in the former than in the latter. To a certain extent, such a conclusion is only natural, since economic and cultural disparities within a state are among the factors that lead to the adoption of a federal regime instead of a unitary regime. Moreover, the study also demonstrated that globalization does not threaten the survival of federal states insofar as they have the mechanisms needed to allow their federated units to adapt and to develop appropriate responses to needs generated by the pressures of globalization. This last point is in agreement with Kim Richard Nossal's assessment[3] and offers a fine illustration of the argument developed by Ronald L. Watts when after W.S. Livingston, he refers to "the importance of social forces in moulding federal political institutions and their operation."[4]

However, these general conclusions leave open a very important issue in the particular case of Canada — the dynamics of continental integration. Indeed, since the late 1980s, Canada has been on a seemingly irreversible path that is leading it toward growing participation in hemispheric affairs. In this respect, Canada has been highly active in economic matters, including the signing of a free trade agreement with the United States, its extension to include Mexico (the North American Free Trade Agreement), the negotiation of a similar agreement with Chile, and its participation in the negotiations to establish the Free Trade Area of the Americas (FTAA). This latter involvement has become so important that Canada matched its participation in hemispheric economic affairs with political participation by becoming a full member of the Organization of American States (OAS) after having sat as an observer for nearly 20 years.[5]

For Canadian federated entities, this kind of involvement can have important consequences, especially for Quebec. As Luc Bernier has convincingly demonstrated, Quebec's international relations developed in a haphazard fashion and principally along the axes linking Quebec City to France and the United States.[6] The opening up to the Americas and continental integration therefore constitute much more than a mere strand of globalization, though they are most visible because of geographic proximity. Moreover, it is important to ask what this integration implies for Quebec's international relations. What will be its result? Do Bernier's conclusions still hold, or is the context forcing Quebec, as an autonomous infra-national actor,[7] to change its approach?

This chapter seeks to answer these questions. To this end, I will draw on the programmatic-pragmatic dialectic suggested by Vincent Lemieux[8] in order to explore two dimensions of Quebec's international activities. The first dimension is an analysis of the positions expressed in the policy statements of the principal political actors. These positions are found in the policies of the Parti Québécois (PQ) government, as well as in the platforms of the Quebec Liberal Party (QLP), which served as the official opposition in the National Assembly before forming the government on 29 April 2003, and of the Action démocratique du Québec (ADQ), a political party that, for a time, appeared to be an emerging political force. The second dimension deals more concretely with Quebec's actions in the field of international relations. Here, we will explore recent legislative initiatives by the Quebec government.

Within the wider framework of this volume, these research themes provide the opportunity to explore more particularly a number of specific aspects of federative mechanisms in the Canadian context, which in turn will make it possible to test certain hypotheses. First, it will be interesting to determine whether political institutions are highly sensitive to the external pressures and demands that are multiplying in the context of continentalization. Second, it will be useful to explore whether new mechanisms of internal coordination might emerge as a means of coordinating the efforts of the Canadian federated entities on the international stage. And, third, in view of its longstanding involvement in the sphere of international relations and its history of establishing institutions that reflect the specificity of its social composition, it will be worthwhile to consider whether Quebec will oppose the establishment of such interdependent institutions, whether existing or proposed, in its conduct of international affairs. First, however, Quebec's international involvements need to be put into historical perspective.

QUEBEC'S INTERNATIONAL RELATIONS: A PATTERN OF AUTONOMOUS DEVELOPMENT

Although this is hardly the place to provide a thorough history of the administration of Quebec's international relations,[9] it is nevertheless important to have a good understanding of its roots in order to explain and understand Quebec's contemporary international activities. To this end, I shall pay particular attention to the focus of these international activities and to the dimension of institutional interdependence. Clearly, from the beginning of the contemporary history of its international relations, Quebec has always defined its position in spite of any federal discomfort about the place that a federated entity wants to occupy in the world, discomforts that have frequently been fuelled by the presence of political forces (partisan, parliamentary, and popular) that clearly express their longing to acquire the status of international actors recognized since the Treaty of Westphalia.

The analysis of Quebec's international relations frequently looks back only on its recent history, beginning in the 1960s. However, to limit their history to the last 40 years cuts short a much longer tradition. In fact, two phases need to be distinguished. The first phase, which was characterized by discontinuity over time, dates back to before Confederation, to 1816, when Lower Canada opened an office in London. In 1881, Quebec appointed an Agent General in Paris and later, opened an economic office in New York in 1941.[10] During the 1940s and 1950s, not much was done because the Maurice Duplessis government was in fact more concerned with domestic affairs than with external relations. The New York exception was justified by the potential of markets in the US northeast to help revive a Quebec economy that, having been severely shaken by the Depression of the 1930s, wanted to make the most of the burgeoning war economy. The existence of these foreign offices did not conflict with Canadian institutions. A degree of autonomy that allowed provincial activity in foreign countries for the purposes of essentially commercial representation was tolerated.[11] The level of coordination was not an issue of debate, since the essentials of foreign policy remained at the time under the control of the central government.

The second phase began with the Quiet Revolution, initiated by Liberal Premier Jean Lesage's team when he came to power in 1960. At that time, Quebec opened up to the world in a variety of ways. First, Quebec saw in the possibility of hosting the 1967 World's Fair an opportunity that it could not afford to miss. In addition, flowing from the government restructuring that was a characteristic of the Quiet Revolution, it became apparent that there were fundamental needs for expertise to help create certain Quebec institutions; notably in the field of education, an area that fell within provincial jurisdiction pursuant to Section 93 of the *British North America Act*. In striking contrast with the preceding era, Quebec established international partnerships that made it possible to seek out this expertise and that, at the same time, threw wide open the doors to intergovernmental relations with sovereign state bodies.

These activities, despite their sometimes improvised appearance, were nevertheless conducted within a modest framework. This framework was set out in a speech by Quebec's Minister of Education, Paul Gérin-Lajoie, to the members of the consular corps in Montreal in 1965. In that speech, he declared that Quebec intended to extend the administration of issues coming under provincial jurisdiction to the international arena. The question of federal-provincial institutions, and still less interprovincial institutions, was therefore essentially irrelevant. Quebec intended to act alone in the spheres that had been devolved to it by the Canadian constitution.

However, the constitution was silent on the question of the international role of the federated entities. Whereas other federations, such as Belgium and Germany, had explicitly addressed the question of the fields and mechanisms of international involvement by their federated entities, the Canadian constitution provided no guidance in this respect. Section 132 of the *Constitution Act, 1867*, clearly gave the Canadian government and parliament "all Powers necessary or Proper for performing the Obligations of Canada or of any Province thereof, as Part of the British Empire, towards Foreign Countries, arising under Treaties between the Empire and such Foreign Countries." However, its scope, even in terms of the coordination of diplomatic activities, remained limited. First, it should be noted that this provision did not address the powers of each level of government, but instead the onus on the Canadian government to honour the obligations entered into in its name by the Empire. In a 1937 decision, the Judicial Committee of the Privy Council in London, the highest court with jurisdiction in Canada at the time, freed the provinces from this obligation, declaring that they were not bound by treaties concerning matters lying within jurisdictional spheres. Second, although such measures were understandable in 1867, they clearly became obsolete when Quebec was "emancipated" internationally; indeed, they had become outmoded at the point when Canada won its own *de jure* independence in international affairs with the adoption in 1931 of the Statute of Westminister.[12] In the absence of constitutional restrictions or authority, Quebec instead intended to establish a practice that would be to its advantage, with a view to eventually having it recognized as such. This was the objective of the "Gérin-Lajoie doctrine" to which I referred above.

This statement of intent was not warmly welcomed by federal actors, and most Canadian governments have since tried to limit Quebec's role in the international arena. There was, however, one well-known exception to this iron law — the openness demonstrated by Prime Minister Brian Mulroney's Conservative government, which proved much more flexible than its predecessors, even reaching an agreement that gave Quebec a say in La Francophonie.[13] The intransigence that was otherwise demonstrated towards Quebec's international ambitions was justified by the view that it was necessary to maintain the integrity of the federation. For those holding this view, a more flexible posture would run the risk of supporting the initiatives of actors who wanted to advance the cause of independence by giving Quebec international recognition before the fact. The supreme historical paradox, however, was that federalist Liberal governments in Quebec committed more resources to Quebec's foreign presence than did Parti Québécois governments, since economic conditions often forced the PQ to make significant spending cutbacks, including cutbacks in spending on Quebec's representation abroad.[14]

The 1960s were thus marked by a revival in Quebec government's international activities after an hiatus. And for analytical purposes, the Quiet Revolution marks the beginning of a distinct and coherent period. Although Quebec is not the only province to have been active on the international stage, its approach over the last 40 years sets it dramatically apart from the others. The other provinces, at least those that have an international presence, have taken advantage of the powerful leverage offered by the federal government through trade missions, not to mention renting space in Canadian embassies, to promote their interests. Quebec is also distinct in having a Department of International Relations, whereas in the other provinces, international relations are handled within departments responsible for other matters, such as intergovernmental relations (Alberta and New Brunswick) or trade (Ontario and British Columbia). In addition, the Quebec department publishes policy statements that are to all intents and purposes white papers.[15] The department possesses branches in the form of a network of government houses, government offices, government bureaus, and trade branches, most of which function as quasi-diplomatic missions through which the Quebec government reaches outward and monitors key foreign trends. Fundamentally, these are tools recognized and used by all Quebec governments to ensure that the province's interests are protected abroad. Any attempt to revert to the previous structures would be unanimously[16] interpreted as a backward step in the defence of these specific interests. However, as we shall see, some actors might consider changing this practice, which would contradict the hypothesis that Quebec is reticent about getting involved in institutions aimed at managing interdependence. Here we are dealing with *how* Quebec's international relations are managed. A different conclusion might be reached as regards *what* its international relations concern, since its foci have evolved over time.

The geographic foci of Quebec's international relations have generally been determined according to priorities dictated by short-term operational needs. Although the United States easily takes first place in economic terms, France wins hands down in the cultural and institutional realms. However, these two countries have not been the only ones to attract Quebec's attention. From an economic point of view, Germany, and more traditionally, England, are strong runners-up. Quebec also maintains ties with the Walloon community and with Bavaria, two federated entities that share common dynamics and challenges with Quebec. However, the axes running to Paris and Washington (the latter via New York for reasons of domestic diplomacy) have traditionally seen by far the highest density traffic. Ivo D. Duchackek's characterization of this pattern is quite interesting. Duchackek portrays Quebec as having two privileged relationships: the first, which is explicit, is comprised of the close affective, cultural, and political ties that it maintains with France; the second, tacit in nature, is the relationship that it has with its only foreign neighbour, the United States. This latter relationship is distinct in that it is largely lacking in sentiment and is instead essentially pragmatic and commercial.[17] The haphazardness and relative lack of coordination of Quebec's initiatives alluded to by Ivan Bernier do not diminish the relative importance of the relationship. As we shall see, it is at this level that we are able to identify changes that reveal new priorities.

THE PROGRAMMATIC DIMENSION: STATEMENTS THAT REVEAL DIFFERENCES

As a consequence of the historical evolution outlined above, one of the distinctive features of Quebec is that political and policy discourses contain proposals about the management of international relations in the strict sense. In this respect, the more established parties — the Parti Québécois and the Quebec Liberal Party — set out better articulated and developed positions than does the Action démocratique du Québec, the third party that, for a moment, was thrust into the political limelight as a result of its brief leap in popularity in public opinion polls and its spring 2002 byelection victories.[18] It will therefore be interesting to analyze the positions of each party, and to determine whether these positions confirm each of the hypotheses identified above.

THE PARTI QUÉBÉCOIS' PROPOSALS

Until April 2003, the Parti Québécois held the reins of government in Quebec. Statements about international relations can therefore come from three sources: departmental policies, the minister's public pronouncements, and the party's platform. In the spring of 2003, the National Assembly had not yet reconvened and the PQ, as the official opposition, had not yet brought forward new international policy stances. I will therefore explore in turn each of the available elements to determine whether globalization has had any noticeable impact on the evolution of Quebec's geographic priorities, either through a change or diversification of focus.

The first document is the strategic plan of the Department of International Relations.[19] This plan might be viewed as a pragmatic rather than programmatic output; however, if we consider its nature, it is clearly a program that is guiding the activities of the department during the years 2001-04. The strategic plan was originally meant to be a white paper like those published by previous governments, but the provisions of the new *Public Administration Act* requires each Quebec government department to publish such plans. Although the 67-page document deals with all aspects of policy, we shall focus on the two dimensions that we have identified as research parameters.

Let us begin by analyzing the focus of the major thrusts of international relations policy in Quebec. In this respect, the strategic plan sets out the government's priorities in the field of international relations in an innovative way, in terms of functions and axes. This has to be seen as the result of purely administrative demands placed on the department. It is by looking at the section on the policy function that we can discern, divided into bilateral and multilateral relations, the axes or geographic areas on which Quebec's activities will focus. Right away, the addition of a multilateral dimension puts La Francophonie in a different niche than Paris-Quebec City relations. With respect to bilateral relations, a key place continues to be reserved for the United States and France (the latter still enjoying a "privileged status among European countries"[20]); but an opening is also made to more numerous regions in the Americas and Europe, relegating the other continents to a third level. We can therefore see a widening of the department's priorities as regards the focus of Quebec's international relations. This widening takes Quebec's traditional focus as its starting point, although the United States and the Americas supplant France and Europe in the order in which the priorities are presented. The force underlying the shift towards continentalization can therefore be seen. However, the unique character of each of the traditional relationships, as described by Ivo D. Duchacek, has not changed: the interest in the United States is essentially economic,[21] whereas in the case of France the accent is more on political and cultural affairs, with economics following behind.[22]

Quebec's international relations policies within the context of Canada as a whole are also considered. The document provides a brief historical overview of this issue and analyzes Quebec's reaction to contemporary Canadian foreign policy.[23] Although the strategic plan pledges Quebec's support of the first pillar of Canadian foreign policy (promoting prosperity and employment), as well as its full respect of Ottawa's jurisdiction[24] as regards the second pillar (the protection of Canadian security in a stable world), it is asserted that Quebec has "no other choice but to dissociate itself from the third"[25] pillar (to project Canadian values and culture abroad), since the "formulation of this objective ... was not in any way agreed with the government of Quebec, even though its subjects [education, culture and identity] are first and foremost within its jurisdiction. This objective continues to ignore that Quebec is a society forged by both a unique culture as well as by values and institutions that express the deep-rooted character of that society."[26] Although the document refers to the need for "energetic mobilization by all governments,"[27] it does not go so far as to call for the establishment of coordinating organizations. Mobilization is therefore not a synonym for concerted action. Quite to the contrary, it is concluded that "the international activities of the Quebec government, in those areas over which it has jurisdiction, cannot, without undermining their effectiveness, be satisfied with such ad hoc arrangements because their haphazard nature, basically a backward step, sharply reduces its scope."[28]

For their part, statements by the minister of the former PQ government also reflect a reordering of priorities as regards the focus of Quebec's international relations. Thus, Minister of International Relations, Louise Beaudoin's speeches concerning some aspect of continentalization were becoming increasingly frequent.[29] At Porto Alegre, Brazil, the minister herself clearly summed up this diversification of "targets" in the following way: "Far from turning their backs on this reality, Quebecers, while strengthening their ties with France and Europe, are easily accepting their American-ness."[30] This means, quite obviously, that a certain degree of attention is paid to the powerful southern neighbour,[31] a discourse that was reflected in the opening of a number of delegations or other Quebec bureaus, notably in Los Angeles, Chicago, Boston, and Miami.[32] However, it is interesting to note that there was no mention of any perceived need to coordinate Quebec's activities. The declarations were so clear that this silence is tantamount to a tacit yet unequivocal affirmation of Quebec's desire to go it alone.

Let us turn, finally, to the party's platform. Within the organizational structure of the PQ, there is an "International Relations Committee" that has the mandate of proposing strategic directions and policies, "to establish and maintain informational and collaborative relations with political parties in other countries or other organizations interested in the development of a sovereign Quebec," as well as "to participate in animating Party life and the training of activists in the international dimension of the exercise of sovereignty, and to exercise, in co-operation with the leadership of the Party, any of the functions of information, training, foreign representation, or in response to requests from the local diplomatic corps, to make the point of view of the Party known and to defend its interests."[33] The close link established between the international dimension of policies and Article 1 of the party program is clear. The chairperson of the committee, Daniel Turp,[34] took part in the round table on Quebec's international relations. His interventions provide us with very well-outlined statements on the issue.

In his remarks, Turp defines Quebec's international relations policies as "a way to extend its societal project abroad and to choose partners who share its values and its major objectives."[35] His principal innovation, to which he refers throughout the discussion, is the broadening of the doctrine of international extension of Quebec's internal jurisdiction to include the "appropriation of the international jurisdiction of Canada." This means that "Quebec ... should say to the federal government that the federal government can never again ratify a treaty unless Quebec has assented to a treaty dealing with the matters that fall within its jurisdiction."[36] In addition, the recognition of Quebec on the international stage will be achieved by means of its representation in international organizations "that deal with questions that fall within the constitutional jurisdiction of Quebec ... even if it is not a member of these organizations."[37] Turp does not deny the importance of the traditional foci of Quebec's international relations, but he considerably widens their scope,[38] beyond even a continentalization perspective that he nevertheless recognizes. In fact, he even goes so far as to set out the reciprocal effect of globalization on Quebec's international relations: globalization and continentalization are not only forcing a redefinition of the foci of Quebec's international relations, their impact is also forcing the recognition of the non-sovereign state as a legitimate interlocutor.[39]

In this context, it is clearly the relationship with the federal government that is being called into question. Turp recognizes the need to try to convince the central government to accept Quebec's position (as he redefines it), but he is openly skeptical about the prospects because he says that he has observed a "withering of consultation": "We live in a federation that was supposed to be a federation in which we co-operate, in which the federated states have an important place, and in which they co-operate with the federal government, [but] the current reality is that the federal government represents everyone ... and the federal government does not consult." This leads him to offer his solution: "I don't need the federal government any more."[40] For the PQ, therefore, there is no reason to participate in the creation of mechanisms for coordinating the international activities of Canada's federated entities.

To complement these stances, it is possible to consider resolutions voted at a policy meeting held by the Parti Québécois the weekend before the election was called.[41] Resolutions then agreed on allow a more direct reading of what the PQ team was aiming for than do the statements contained in the electoral platform per se.

PQ militants adopted 14 resolutions covering wide aspects of Quebec's international actions. Some address more traditional elements of Quebec's international relations (for instance, reinforcing international relations with French-speaking states), but many others are characteristics of a new mood. Several elements refer to international treaties related to the FTAA, cultural diversity, or poverty. Moreover, these proposals are framed within a more general resolution that "requires that Quebec be associated with the negotiation and the writing of any international treaty that deals with questions of its interest and that Quebec may be admitted to directly participate in the proceedings of any international organization responsible for the application and the interpretation of such treaties."[42] Elements that characterize an international doctrine that seeks to influence an international context characterized by globalization are clearly present and are repeated in other resolutions that, for instance, bear upon the establishment of missions of observers over international institutions or the plea in favour of a greater accountability for international institutions. The attribution of a specific role to Quebec's delegations is signalling an allocation of resources aimed at implementing the doctrine favoured by the PQ government. None of these resources, though, is devoted to a higher level of coordination among Canadian federal entities' international initiatives.

The sources consulted to gather a sample of PQ statements about international relations have the advantage of covering all of the possible origins of the policies of a governing party: departmental, governmental, and partisan. On the basis of these sources, we can clearly see a recognition of the influence of globalization and continentalization on the geographic focus of international policy, even though the traditional policy foci are explicitly reiterated and reaffirmed. On the other hand, as regards the need for a coordinating agency, it is not surprising to learn that the reaction of a party whose primary objective is the rejection of federalism is unanimously negative, running from a critique of their effectiveness (by the party), to an implicit rejection (by the minister) all the way to an explicit rejection (by the department).

THE QUEBEC LIBERAL PARTY'S PROPOSALS

As the official Opposition, the QLP had to demonstrate its ability to be "a government in waiting," as is the established tradition in a parliamentary system. This demonstration is achieved particularly through programmatic statements on various topics. As regards Quebec's international relations, the most important source is undoubtedly the strategy document prepared by Benoît Pelletier, a constitutional law professor and Member of the National Assembly

(MNA) for Chapleau, a riding in the Outaouais.[43] The proposals contained in the document were adopted by all of the party's delegates at a convention in November 2001, and they therefore constitute the clearest programmatic position that the party offers in the field. In addition, Pelletier had the opportunity to set out his party's position at the round table organized by the *Cercle québécois des relations internationales*. He also added to his proposals in an op-ed published less than two weeks before the spring 2003 general election was called.[44]

These proposals outlined in the QLP constitutional paper are part of a wider set of statements regarding "the political and constitutional future of Quebec society" within the Canadian federation. In this light, it is not surprising that the recommended approach is grounded essentially in legal and constitutional considerations, as is clearly suggested by the title of this section of the report: "Quebec's International Activities Within the Framework of Canada's Constitution."[45]

For the QLP, "the affirmation of Quebec at the international level ... is, ultimately, an expression of the originality of Quebec."[46] Thus, its spokesperson argues that "most local issues, which are covered in subsection 92(16) of the *Constitution Act, 1867*, have a transborder, or even external, dimension,"[47] not to mention that international treaties deal increasingly with subjects that the Canadian constitution assigns, exclusively or on a shared basis, to the provinces. This analysis provides a new underpinning for the Gérin-Lajoie doctrine of the extension of Quebec's internal jurisdiction outside its borders. In fact, the tone that emerges from the Liberal position as a whole suggests a resolute program: "Quebec has to become a leader again, a pioneer as regards the international role"[48]; "Quebec has scored points on the international stage by showing considerable audacity, by proving itself to be perseverant, and by being rebellious. Quebec's international aspirations could be much higher than they currently are,"[49] says Pelletier.

That said, it must be remembered that the QLP, although its platform is to some degree autonomist, remains a federalist party. As a result, the unequivocal direction that Quebec's international relations should go in is clearly marked: "to strengthen Quebec's place, but in the context of the Canadian federation," and "to move Quebec forward while respecting the Canadian constitution"[50] are clearly enunciated objectives. In addition, "Quebec can be more active to the extent that it doesn't engage in activities that are incompatible with the major Canadian external affairs policies, which is the reason why there is a need to reconcile federal activity ... with Quebec's activity."[51] It is interesting to note here the meaning attached to the relationship. In the framework of our study, this might lead us to expect to find traces of mechanisms for coordinating interdependence.

This sort of nuance might be perceived as the roaring of a toothless tiger. However, the strategic directions recommended in both the QLP's policy document and Pelletier's public remarks and writings offer a number of subtle distinctions. The need for a stronger affirmation of Quebec's international role is corroborated by the existence of numerous grey areas in the international role of the provinces as a result of constitutional imprecision. According to the authors of the policy, there is therefore no incompatibility between the activities that they believe Quebec could undertake and respect for constitutional parameters, because these activities can be slotted into the many gaps that the present framework leaves open.[52]

Finally, the QLP draws a clear distinction between foreign affairs in the federal jurisdiction and the international relations that Quebec can legitimately pursue, and believes that the latter should go beyond political affirmation, indeed beyond economic matters, and cover a wide range of issues. The terms used to express this position leave no room for doubt: "Quebec's affirmation on the international scene must focus not only on the province's specificity, but also on all the other issues that are under its jurisdiction."[53]

The first factor that we are analyzing, i.e., the impact of globalization and continentalization on policy statements, is echoed in the programmatic statements of the QLP, which contain sections specifically devoted to these topics. In the first place, globalization creates the dual challenge to Quebec of becoming more open to the world while at the same time preserving its distinct identity — challenges met in particular by a defence of cultural diversity. In addition, continentalization is viewed not only from an economic point of view, but also from the angle of social rights and cultural and legal diversity, since, like Quebec, many Latin American societies are part of the civil law tradition.[54] There is absolutely no doubt that continentalization has influenced the statements of international policy made by the QLP. They stress that the new continental agreements touch on many of the areas over which Quebec has legislative jurisdiction and that Quebec therefore should make its voice heard in international forums, either directly (it is "essential for Quebec to occupy the place it deserves in international organizations, and for the respective roles and responsibilities of Quebec and the federal government at the external level to be defined more clearly"[55]) or through the Canadian voice, essentially, it seems, for strategic reasons. This position is close to that advocated by the PQ, although it is advanced in a less peremptory manner. The example of the defence of the French language — although disputed by PQ spokespersons[56] — is given to illustrate this strategic support of action that makes use of Canada's voice: according to the Liberals, Canada's weight is more likely to influence policies that favour linguistic diversity than Quebec alone could achieve, since French is spoken by barely 1 percent of people in the Americas.

The QLP therefore links two elements on which this study focuses: meeting the challenges of continentalization will be much more effective if there are adequate mechanisms to coordinate the activities of the federal and Quebec governments. Here, the dual federalist/autonomist orientation of the QLP is reflected in the approach it advocates. Pelletier believes that Quebec should "not only be informed and consulted, but also actively involved"[57] in a range of activities, including economic promotion programs. The QLP therefore recognizes the role that Quebec should play on the international scene, but because this role covers areas in which a number of actors are involved, it advocates a reconciliation of "Quebec's international affirmation with the fundamental need for Canada to retain the authority it requires to conduct a coherent foreign policy." The actions of each of the governments must therefore be seen as "compatible and complementary."[58] Pelletier clarifies this idea by adding that "we can agree to speak with a single voice ... but it must not be forgotten that [Canada] is a federal state, not a unitary one. In other words, the provinces must also have a say, be consulted, and be fully involved in the negotiation process."[59]

In concrete terms, this means that it should be possible for Quebec to intervene, on its own initiative, in matters devolved to it by the constitution, that it should be able to rely on Canada's influence and diplomatic weight for the same purposes, and that it should also be able to influence Canadian foreign policy proposals that concern areas in which Quebec society has irons in the fire. To achieve this, two paths are identified. One is explicitly mentioned in relation to the proposals concerning the affirmation of Quebec: the formalization, through administrative agreements, of the international role devolved to Quebec.[60] (Interestingly, the QLP's proposal does not limit this procedure to Quebec and explicitly extends it to the other provinces.)

In another section of the document, the second path is presented in the context of a discussion of the integration of provincial interests through some sort of institution for managing the interdependence of the provinces on international questions. The justification of this option is undoubtedly based on the recognition of the existence of "almost permanent frictions between the federal and Quebec governments in the area of Foreign Affairs and International Relations."[61] The Liberal spokesperson advocates the establishment of a Council of the Federation, "a special forum for intergovernmental co-operation and discussion on macro-economic issues," the mandate of which would also cover "social issues."[62] The structure of this council would include, in particular, an International Relations Secretariat, which would have the task of "reviewing the international treaties Canada is considering signing in order to identify those that would have an impact on the powers of the provinces and examine the conditions under which the provinces could participate in the negotiations," as well as to carry out "in-depth analyses of international conventions, agreements, protocols and treaties [so as to arrive at] a detailed examination of the economic, political and constitutional implications...."[63] Such a mechanism is reminiscent of those analyzed by Chris Kukucha.[64] Indeed, this would involve enriching and integrating, within a clearly defined structure, the mandate of the system of federal-provincial committees that already have as their main task the monitoring of issues related to international trade.

The most recent Liberal policy statement does not deviate from these positions. In the short text published in *La Presse*,[65] the MNA for Chapleau brings forward five objectives that include a genuine international doctrine that calls for the reinforcement of Quebec's presence "in all meetings and international forums dealing with education, language, culture, and identity," as well as in various capitals and international organizations. This call for action is framed within what Pelletier identifies as being an "international complement [and no more the external extension of] to Quebec's constitutional jurisdiction." The fifth objective reflects a genuine international doctrine and here, the influence of globalization is incontestable: the author asks for Quebec's involvement in the process leading to the adoption of a treaty or convention on cultural diversity. No doubt we are in presence of a direct call to exercise influence on the international scene. For the PLQ, the allowance of resources is also a necessary complement, notably — and in it, the party differentiates itself from the PQ — toward Canadian intra-national coordination.

A few days after the Quebec Liberal Party achieved power, the new government had already sent clear signals about the importance it would give to Quebec's international relations. In his swearing-in speech, the new premier declared: "Societies such as Québec, which do not benefit from the advantage of the numbers, have a duty of daring. Our economy and our culture depend on our skillfulness to make us being recognized on all continents."[66] Moreover, Quebec's deputy premier — without a doubt the member of Cabinet closest to the premier — has been given the International Relations portfolio; the then premier-to-be hastened to confirm official visits of the Minister-President of Bavaria, Edmund Stoiber, and of the French Prime Minister, Jean-Pierre Raffarin; and he has himself seized the first opportunity of an official visit to the American metropolis (New York City) to meet briefly with American Secretary of State Colin Powell, and for a longer period with the governor of the state of New York, George Pataki.[67]

Overall, the Quebec Liberal Party's proposals can be summed up as follows: building on Quebec's tradition of autonomy in international relations, the party seeks a still more active involvement, not only in the cultural field, but also in economic, political, and legal matters. This involvement would take place within the Canadian constitutional frameworks that the party would seek to clarify, particularly by means of a coordinating body, the International Relations Secretariat of the Council of the Federation. This secretariat would make it possible for Quebec and the rest of the provinces to play a more active role in determining those aspects of Canadian foreign policy that affect them. Lastly, it is clear that Liberal policies all reflect concerns related to the characteristic issues of continentalization.

THE PROPOSALS OF THE ACTION DÉMOCRATIQUE DU QUÉBEC

The sudden rise of the ADQ in the spring and summer of 2002 as a political force and the scarce resources that it had prior to that point may explain, in part, the scanty references in its platform to Quebec's international relations. Moreover, the party sees itself as populist, as is clear from the highly publicized positions it has taken. Ideas about international relations do not fit easily into this sort of discourse.[68] Thus, the party's program neither mentions nor alludes to Quebec's international relations.[69] In fact, the substantive or the qualifier "international" and their derivatives only appear three times in the document: in reference to Quebec's "internationally recognized" economic expertise (p. 8), to "international competitiveness" (p. 11), and to Québécois "internationally recognized" artists (p. 100).

The round table on Quebec's international relations is therefore our best point of reference. Marie Grégoire, one of the party's early architects, who was to briefly sit in the National Assembly as the MNA for Berthier, represented the ADQ at the conference. Her contribution to the round table also reflected the relative lack of attention paid to the issue of Quebec's international relations. For example, in her opening remarks, she made reference to "Gérin-Lajoie who came here,"[70] as if he had been a foreign emissary rather than a Quebec government minister.

Grégoire set out the ADQ's position on Quebec's international relations in terms of the party's three strategic pillars, what the ADQ's spokespersons identify as the "three axes of Quebec's development": developing a culture of innovation, creating accountability, and rebuilding confidence in the political and administrative institutions of government. Applied to the field of international relations, these three axes highlight a major, essentially economic, priority; "to create a brand image" as a means to foster prosperity. "We advocate that international relations be focused more on contributing to the prosperity of Quebec than on the debate surrounding its political status,"[71] and centred on "marketing Quebec's attributes."[72] In concrete terms, this means that "the mission of Quebec diplomats would be to alter their approach and become decision-makers, networkers, and developers in order to do a better job for Quebec."[73]

As regards the foci of Quebec's international relations, the ADQ does not seem to have been influenced by the trend toward continentalization. At the very most, its representative tried to clarify how the existing axes ranked by first seeking to "strengthen Quebec's presence south of the border."[74] She also said that "the fact that our focus is the development of linkages with America in no way prevents Quebec from playing a leading role in La Francophonie."[75]

As for a structure to manage interdependence in the face of international pressures impacting on the federated units, the ADQ gives no hint of whether such a structure is needed or should be opposed. In fact, we have to look elsewhere in the party's political program to shed light on this issue: the ADQ is committed to drastically reducing the number of state institutions. It would therefore be surprising if it were to add here a structure dedicated to the coordination of policies that it in fact intends to manage autonomously.

This analysis is, however, only circumstantial. Indeed, it is difficult to infer the party's position as regards a structure for managing interdependence from the ADQ statements since some of them are flatly contradictory. For example, if the "policy of the outstretched hand" toward the federal government is applied to international relations, as it is elsewhere in the ADQ's platform, and if the party wants to act in areas that fall under Quebec's jurisdiction "without being in opposition to federal institutions," the need for coordination seems minimal. On the other hand, when Marie Grégoire declares that "we also want Quebec to exercise its full sovereignty in fields not specifically mentioned in the constitution, that is, the residual powers," we find ourselves at an impasse. Indeed, since these powers are constitutionally assigned to the federal government (section 91), the position taken here by the ADQ implies either the need for a major constitutional amendment as suggested in its "plan for constitutional peace"[76] (a 180-degree turn for the spirit of the present constitution) that could not be accommodated in the current political climate; or the establishment of an organization to manage the probable results of such a policy, a solution that appears to run counter to the ADQ's whole approach vis-à-vis the state apparatus; or a lack of knowledge of the fundamental facts that are needed to understand the issue. In the face of so many inconsistencies, it has to be concluded that the proposal put forward here by Grégoire cannot be implemented and should therefore be disregarded. Nevertheless, her statements allow us to conclude that the ADQ is not attached to the traditional foci of Quebec's international relations and that it tacitly rejects the need for a mechanism to manage the interdependence of the component parts of the Canadian federation in the area of international relations.

The spring 2003 electoral campaign could have brought some new elements to be considered, but such was not the case. The ADQ platform did not add to what was already in the public domain. And, following the elections, in which only the party leader Mario Dumont held his seat, it will be interesting to see how this four-member caucus with a 75 percent turnover rate will deal with international relations questions.

THE PRAGMATIC DIMENSION: AN OPEN AWARENESS

Since the programmatic dimension of any political action cannot, in itself, lead to the electoral successes that are needed to put it into effect, it will therefore be interesting to complete our study with an analysis of its inevitable complement, the pragmatic dimension.[77] To this end, we will analyze two pieces of legislation dealt with by the Quebec National Assembly. The first is the *Act to amend the Act respecting the Ministère des Relations internationales*. This Act gives legislators a role in ratifying important treaties that have an impact on questions falling within Quebec's constitutional jurisdiction. The Act was adopted by the National Assembly in May 2002. It will therefore be possible not only to analyze the content of the Act but also the positions that the various political parties espoused when it was being studied.[78] The second piece of legislation is the bill establishing the *Observatoire québécois sur la mondialisation*, a research body that had a mandate to provide Quebec with points of reference and analysis to better position its activities in the context of globalization. In this second case, the bill was adopted in November 2002, thereby also providing us with a complete record upon which to base our analysis.

AN *ACT TO AMEND THE ACT RESPECTING THE MINISTÈRE DES RELATIONS INTERNATIONALES*

Despite its brevity (just 13 sections), this bill is far-reaching in its effect. Its principal objective is to establish a "mechanism enabling the National Assembly to approve any important international commitment the Government intends to make either in respect of a Québec international agreement or an international accord pertaining to a matter within the constitutional jurisdiction of Québec."[79] In a way, this is a first implementation of what Daniel Turp identified above as the internal re-appropriation of Canada's jurisdiction over international matters.[80] In addition, the legislation sets out the functions of the minister of international relations in this area and indicates the manner in which the Quebec government may be bound, or give its assent to the federal government's expressing its consent to be bound, by an international accord. Lastly, the Act confers on the minister of health and social services the power to enter into international agreements in areas falling within his or her jurisdiction.

During the debate in the National Assembly, Minister of International Relations Beaudoin took the lead in presenting the government's position. She underscored the democratization of the process, which changes the responsibility for approving international agreements from a governmental to a legislative function, including parliamentary committees where citizens will be able to make their views known regarding the agreement being considered. Here, the minister referred explicitly to the possible treaty concerning the Free Trade Area of the Americas, although she did not identify this feature of continentalization as the reason why the government had introduced the Act.[81] She used the same example during the hearings of the parliamentary committee.[82] For his part, her parliamentary assistant, Guy Lelièvre, member for Gaspé, referred to the Multilateral Agreement on Investment.[83] In this case, the dimension of globalization was present, although it was not in the forefront of the government's arguments. The second dimension guiding our analysis, the presence or rejection of an institution for managing interdependence, was not raised. At the very most, we can conclude that such institutions were tacitly rejected, since the Act gives the National Assembly complete authority to act in this matter — the first time a legislative assembly on the British model has given itself such powers. Confirmation of this may be found in the minister's statement that she saw "a very powerful signal to Ottawa regarding ratification."[84] Even in Australia, where globalization seems to reverse a trend favouring the central government, a trend sanctioned by the country's High Court, there are no such provisions. As Brian Galligan puts it, "Politics remains the key forum where the Commonwealth [Australia's federal government] has to legitimate any incursions into state jurisdictional areas, with the state remaining vigilant about their interests and politically adept to defend them."[85]

The bill did not give rise to lengthy debate and it was adopted unanimously by the members present for the final vote. The PQ government team kept the number of its participants in the debate to a minimum. For the Liberal official Opposition, two members were the main speakers: Margaret Delisle, member for Jean-Talon and Opposition spokesperson on international relations; and Benoît Pelletier, the author of the report that was analyzed in the preceding part of this chapter. The ADQ did not see fit to speak out on the bill, even though its leader supported it at the end of the day.

Since the government's views have already been examined, it only remains to analyze the position of the official Opposition. First and foremost, taking support from the recognition in Quebec of the legitimacy of ratifying treaties and its capacity to sign agreements, the Opposition congratulated the government for its initiative to allow members of the National Assembly to take part in a process that, it stressed, would consider treaties that concerned Quebec's jurisdiction. Pelletier insisted that "this is not an issue on which it is necessary to show partisanship. Quebec's higher interests have to be put first."[86] In addition, Pelletier returned to the arguments that he had made at the round table on Quebec's international relations: "This bill is part and parcel of Quebec's wish to take on a larger role on the international scene and we can only salute such a move," adding that "of course, the exercise of this role should respect the federative principle."[87] His colleague, Delisle, emphasized as well that the QLP "considers international relations to be enormously important."[88] Although Pelletier raised a question about the implications of the process, that is, how the content of agreements and treaties ratified in this way would be integrated into Quebec law, the assurance he received on this point allowed him to support the bill without any other reservations.[89] The issue of continentalization was explicitly brought up by two members, Henri-François Gautrin (Verdun) and Fatima Houda-Pépin (La Pinière). These members referred to the treaty concerning the FTAA,[90] but, as it was the case with the government, this was not a fundamental argument made in support of the bill. As regards the question of interdependence, other than Pelletier's passing reference to the federal jurisdiction, the Liberals made no more of the issue than had the PQ government.

As important as this legislative measure was, particularly because of its innovativeness, it provides us with a quite paradoxical portrait: the unanimity that it elicited leaves us without any debates that can be used to bring the core arguments up to date. As a result, we are left with a bill that appears to be marginally linked to the issue of continentalization and which, because of the mechanisms it creates, remains completely silent about, indeed brushes away, the need to coordinate the international relations activities of the federated units in Canada.

AN *ACT RESPECTING THE OBSERVATOIRE QUÉBÉCOIS DE LA MONDIALISATION*

To begin with, the very title of this Act evokes one of the dimensions explored in this study. Its origins are clearly associated with the public's interest in, as well as certain of its fears about, globalization "for some years now and especially since the Third Summit of the Americas held in Québec City."[91] In fact, throughout the debates, both in the chamber and committee, it was clearly established that the need for the *Observatoire* was related to the FTAA negotiations and the World Trade Organization's Doha round. Globalization and continentalization were therefore clearly identified as the initiating factors.

The bill describes the mission of the *Observatoire* as being "to further the understanding of the phenomenon of globalization and provide dependable information enabling Quebecers to fully appreciate the issues at stake."[92] This is to be accomplished by the dissemination of the results of its work, monitoring the conditions related to globalization, the organization of activities aimed at raising public awareness and education, and the annual publication of a "status report on globalization viewed from the standpoint of the interests of Québec."[93] In the press release announcing the introduction of the bill, it was stated that the minister "believes that it is so important to promote controlled and balanced globalization that she made it the subject of one of the sections of the bill."[94] The *Observatoire* was not conceived as a government agency, but rather as an autonomous institution.

This assurance about the nature of the institution unravelled somewhat during the debates leading to the adoption of the bill. The Liberal Opposition certainly raised repeated doubts about the independence that the *Observatoire* would have vis-à-vis the government, but it was particularly in the objectives that the *Observatoire* was set up to achieve — indeed, in the nature of its activities — where things got hopelessly tangled up.[95] On the one hand, the minister frequently reiterated that the *Observatoire* would be neither a research organization, nor a consultative body, nor a permanent socio-economic summit, but rather "a genuine round table"[96] where those interested in globalization would meet in order to discuss and exchange available information on continentalization and globalization. She also saw it as a means of "citizenship participation"[97] in the debate, stressing that it would provide a forum in which people "can make their voices heard" regarding the major issues associated with globalization[98] as well as providing, through the *Observatoire's* web site, an important means of disseminating information to the public and of democratization,[99] an overture with a populist flavour that was also lauded by her colleague from the riding of Frontenac.[100] For the minister, in a nutshell, "the first and ultimate objective of the *Observatoire* is to see to it that Quebec citizens are as well informed as possible about the issues of globalization."[101] She affirmed, moreover, that it would serve as a means of better understanding what was presently going on behind closed doors,[102] a claim called into question by the official Opposition's critique.[103]

On the other hand, despite objectives that appeared clear on their face, the picture became a little blurry when the member from Saint-Jean, a member of the minister's own party, spoke highly of the research that would be conducted at the *Observatoire*, even drawing a parallel with a European institution that he saw as being similar, and vaunted the usefulness of the data to be produced to help the work of members of the National Assembly in every respect.[104] The minister avoided contradicting either herself or her colleague when she made a clear and precise link — calling it "a necessary complement,"[105] "a piece of legislation complementary to and logically related to the democratic structure established by Bill 52,"[106] — between the *Observatoire's* output and the use to which legislators would put this output in the framework of the new powers that had been conferred on them by Bill 52 (discussed above).[107] This question concerning research also surfaced in relation to another issue that created some problems of consistency: despite the fact that the *Observatoire* was supposed to be more like an agora than a research centre, it would have an academic advisory committee.[108] Would the *Observatoire* be dedicated to research or not? The answer was not clear. At best, it could be concluded that some research might be conducted at the request of those who would come together at the *Observatoire*, the overlap with university research being sometimes denied, sometimes criticized. Finally, the minister didn't make matters any clearer when, in trying to define the *Observatoire's* activities, she lumped together the following: "stimulate thinking ... stimulate discussion ...via a program of public activities, animation, physical [*sic*] education activities, publication activities."[109] Mention was even made of the role that the *Observatoire* would play as a francophone disseminator of information.[110] As can be seen, an effort was being made to cover a great many angles, even though these issues were logically a matter for future decisions by its board of directors.

Despite these differences of opinion exploited by the Liberal Opposition, which linked them to the multiple perceptions expressed during the public hearings on the bill,[111] it nevertheless remains that the *Observatoire* was undoubtedly conceived to promote autonomous action by Quebec rather than as an integrating organization within the Canadian federation. Indeed, this is reflected as much in the text of the law as in the documents that accompanied its introduction. These documents do not mention the federated nature of Quebec, but, a little like the legislation studied above, the purpose of the Act — to "give Quebec ... a useful tool ... to more fully understand as a society the issues and impact of the phenomenon"[112] — makes an appeal to autonomous action, in the tradition of Quebec's place and role on the international scene.

The only mention of the federal dimension was made by the spokesperson of the official opposition. Although she recognized the importance of the issue and the interest in creating a tool to deal with it, she criticized the structure favoured by the government and made reference to the Pelletier report discussed earlier, citing as needed lengthy excerpts.[113] Her remarks were not heeded by the government.

The QLP therefore voted against the bill at all stages of its adoption, evoking the heaviness of the *Observatoire's* structure (comparing it to a "clumsy and blind elephant"[114]), the vagueness of its objectives, and the inadequate distinction between its political and administrative dimensions.[115] As for the ADQ, its surfeit of discretion made the minister's blood boil:[116] the party took part in neither the preliminary consultations nor in the parliamentary committee that did the clause-by-clause study of the bill. During the debates on second and third readings, their spokesperson, the member for Saguenay, contented himself with, first, a three- or four-minute speech, and then with a five-sentence speech to oppose the Act on the grounds "that it looks big, that it looks complicated .... It isn't necessary to create an additional structure ... that we're going to have to get rid of later on."[117]

Even though the debates were quite brief, and riddled with needless repetition and some incongruities,[118] it can be concluded that the bill was strongly inspired by the phenomena of continentalization and globalization and that it did not take into account the federated dimension of Quebec. This dimension might nonetheless be studied by the *Observatoire*, even though the bill does not provide for a coordinating mechanism to deal with interdependence. In fact, the minister's own words affirm the dual nature of the exercise, i.e., the influence of continentalization and globalization and the pursuit of an essentially Quebec objective: what she was seeking through the adoption of the Act "is transparency and democracy through knowledge ... [it is] to confront the culture of secrecy surrounding the current trade negotiations by means of a resolutely democratic project in the service of the Quebec people."[119]

In the end, the two bills analyzed here offer us a similar picture. In both cases, concerns about continentalization and globalization played a role, although more in the second case than in the first. However, the tradition of autonomous behaviour by Quebec in the field of international relations appears to have been maintained, which significantly reduces the perceived need to coordinate activities with the other federated entities in Canada. Only the Quebec Liberal Party brought up, in passing, the federal framework during debate on the bills, though in so doing it did not weaken its commitment to autonomous action by Quebec in this area.

CONCLUSION

This analysis has made it possible for us to explore the programmatic and pragmatic dimensions of Quebec's international activities as proposed by the various political protagonists of this federated state. We turn now to the results we have obtained.

Table 1: The Programmatic Dimension

Party/ Dimension	Subjects Treated by International Relations	Focus	Coordination within the Federation
PQ	Political, cultural, economic	Influenced by continentalization and globalization, as much due to their impact as to the possibilities of a federated state being recognized as a legitimate international actor	Quebec's autonomy reaffirmed; unanimously negative reaction, ranging from a critique of its effectiveness (the partisan position) to implicit rejection (the minister's position), all the way to explicit rejection (the departmental position).
QLP	Economic, cultural, legal, political	Conscious of continentalization and globalization; open to new foci	Formalization through administrative agreements; clarification of Canada's constitutional framework, notably by means of the International Relations Secretariat of the Council of the Federation, which would allow Quebec and the other provinces to play a more active role in the determination of those aspects of Canadian foreign policy that affect them.
ADQ	Economic promotion	Traditional: France and the United States	Reaffirmation and increase of Quebec's autonomy through an appropriation of residual powers in order to extend the field of Quebec's international jurisdiction; no mechanism.

It is of considerable interest to note the large number of differences that exist between the parties. In fact, by charting the positions of Quebec's political parties according to the influence of continentalization/globalization on the focus of international relations on the one hand, and on the basis of the coordination of the activities of the federated states on the other, we obtain a distribution that clearly shows these differences (see Figure 1).

Figure 1: Position of Quebec political parties concerning:
            1) the weight they attach to continentalization/globalization
            (c/g) in international relations; and
            2) the need for Quebec-federal (Q-f) coordination

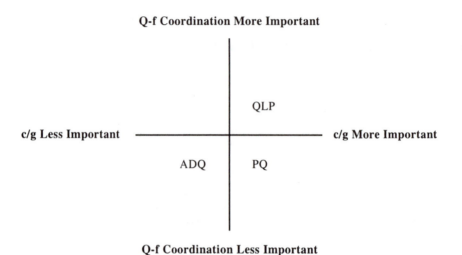

As regards the hypotheses that we sought to test, it seems clear that the PQ and QLP are more sensitive to the external pressures generated by continentalization and globalization than is the ADQ, as evidenced by the redefinition of the focus of international relations policy by the first two and the maintenance of the status quo by the latter. However, only the PLQ advocates a mechanism for coordinating the activities of the federated entities with the federal government, although it nevertheless affirms Quebec's autonomy in the management of its international affairs. The other two parties reject new mechanisms of internal coordination of the activities of the Canadian federated entities on the international scene. Lastly, all three parties, although to different degrees, defend Quebec's autonomy in the management of its international relations. It will therefore be interesting to see, in the long term, whether Quebec, if led by a PQ or ADQ government, would be able to fight off the establishment of such interdependent institutions, existing or proposed, in the conduct of its international affairs, which would not necessarily be the case for a QLP government.[120] The results of the 2003 provincial general elections will provide the first grounds to test the validity of this prediction.

Of particular interest is that none of Quebec's political parties are located in the upper left quadrant, which combines a stronger integration of the activities of the federated entities with a lesser sensitivity to the vectors resulting from continentalization and globalization. From this it can be concluded that, although to different degrees and with different levels of sensitivity, all of Quebec's political parties demonstrate a desire for international activity managed in an autonomous fashion by the federated entity. It would therefore be utopian to predict that, in the foreseeable future, Quebec will alter the course on which its international activities have been headed in the last 40 years.

From the point of view of the pragmatic analysis, these findings do not change much. As demonstrated in Table 2, although a slight variation can be observed in the level of influence of continentalization and globalization on the focus of the two bills analyzed here, the question of Quebec's autonomy is not in any doubt.

However, the differences observed raise several issues. First, the fact that these were government-sponsored bills may provide a reading closer to the PQ's position. In addition, the small sample means that it would be dangerous to generalize the conclusions that we have drawn, which suggests that further research is needed to test their validity. Finally, if one thing stands out from these bills, it is the reaffirmation of the wish for autonomy rather than the resort to coordinating bodies, a position also supported by the QLP as shown by the first bill being adopted unanimously. The results that we reached in the first part of this study regarding our hypotheses are therefore simply further reinforced.

Obviously, then, this study is only a partial analysis of the subject. To claim that the phenomenon depends only on political will, or on the focus or the mechanisms advocated in the area of international relations, would be a distortion

Table 2: The Pragmatic Dimension

Action/Dimension	Focus	Coordination within the Federation
Act respecting the MRI	Continentalization and globalization are raised, though not as the principal reason for the bill	No mechanism; promotes autonomous action by Quebec
Act respecting the Observatoire québécois de la mondialisation	To respond to globalization	No mechanism; purpose is to promote autonomous action/activity by Quebec

of reality. Thus, Stephen Krasner,[121] in examining the concept of sovereignty — a particularly important parameter in international relations — highlights two dimensions: power and authority, the latter being the recognition of one actor's power by another actor. Authority is necessary in order to engage in genuine action on the international level, a factor that is, moreover, recognized in the department's strategic plan, which underscores it in an eloquent way, since it rests on the fact that "numerous states have recognized *de facto* [Quebec's] capacity to act"[122] on the international scene. Far more than any other issue, this question cannot be neglected and constitutes an interesting area of future research in order to develop a better understanding of the subject.

NOTES

1.   Nelson Michaud, "Federalism and Foreign Policy: Comparative Answers to Globalization," in *Handbook of Federal Countries 2002*, ed. Ann Griffiths (Montreal and Kingston: McGill-Queen's University Press, 2002), pp. 389-415.

2.   A number of studies have analyzed this phenomenon in the Canadian context, including: Ivan Bernier and André Binette, *Les provinces canadiennes et le commerce international* (Quebec City: CQRI, 1988); Douglas M. Brown and Murray G. Smith, eds., *Canadian Federalism: Meeting Global Economic Challenges* (Kingston: Institute of Intergovernmental Relations, Queen's University, 1991); Tom Keating and Don Munton, *The Provinces and Canadian Foreign Policy* (Toronto: Canadian Institute of International Affairs, 1985); *Études internationales* (special issue), 25, 3(September 1994). For more general treatments, see Ivan Bernier, *International Legal Aspects of Federalism* (New York: Longman, 1973); Douglas M. Brown and Earl H. Fry, eds., *States and Provinces in the International Economy* (Berkeley: Institute of Governmental Studies, University of California Press, 1993); Renaud Dehousse, *Fédéralisme et relations internationales: une réflexion comparative* (Brussels: Bruylant, 1991); Brian Hocking, *Foreign Relations and Federal States* (London: Leicester University Press, 1993); Hans J. Michelmann and Panayotis Soldatos, *Federalism and International Relations* (Oxford: Clarendon Press, 1990).

3.   Kim Richard Nossal, *The Politics of Canadian Foreign Policy* (Toronto: Prentice Hall, 1995), p. 294.

4.   Ronald L. Watts, *Comparing Federal Systems*, 2d ed. (Kingston: Institute of Intergovernmental Relations, Queen's University, 2000), p. 15.

5.   For an astute analysis of the factors that led Canada to join the OAS, see Gordon Mace, "Explaining Canada's Decision to Join the OAS: An Interpretation," in *Diplomatic Departures: The Conservative Era in Canadian Foreign Policy, 1984-1993*, eds. Nelson Michaud and Kim Richard Nossal (Vancouver: UBC Press, 2001), pp. 142-59.

6.   Luc Bernier, *De Paris à Washington: La politique internationale du Québec* (Quebec: Presses de l'Université du Québec, 1996).

7. This term might take some readers aback, while delighting others. Its use here does not imply either the endorsement or rejection of any particular political credo, but should instead be interpreted as reflecting the recognition that Quebec enjoys internationally.

8. Vincent Lemieux, 1977, "Esquisse d'une théorie d'évolution des parties," *Canadian Journal of Political Science* 10, 4(1977):841-56.

9. A good overview of this history can be developed by consulting a number of studies. In addition to the analysis by Bernier cited earlier, see Louis Balthazar, Louis Bélanger and Gordon Mace, *Trente ans de politique extérieure du Québec 1960-1990* (Sillery: Septentrion and CQRI, 1993); Louis Bélanger, *Deux analyses sur l'évolution de la politique internationale du Québec (1989-1992)* (Quebec City: Institut québécois des hautes études internationales, 1996); "Les espaces internationaux de l'État québécois," paper presented to the Canadian Political Science Association, 1993); Marcel Bergeron, *Évaluation du réseau de représentation du Québec à l'étranger* (Quebec City: ministère des Affaires internationales, 1988); *Évaluation du réseau de représentation du Québec à l'étranger: la représentation du Québec en Amérique latine et aux Antilles, rapport synthèse présenté au ministre des Affaires internationales* (Quebec City: ministère des Affaires internationales, 1989); Georges Cartier and Lucie Rouillard, *Les relations culturelles internationales du Québec* (Sainte-Foy: ENAP, 1984); Gérard Hervouet and Hélène Galarneau, eds., *Présence internationale du Québec: Chronique des années 1978-1983* (Quebec City: Centre québécois des relations internationales, 1984); Christopher Malone, *La politique québécoise en matière de relations internationales: changements et continuité (1960-1972)*, 1974. Master's thesis, Ottawa University; Shiro Noda, *Les relations extérieures du Québec de 1970 à 1980: comparaison des gouvernements Bourassa et Lévesque*, 1989. Doctoral thesis, Université de Montréal, Département d'histoire; Paul Painchaud, "L'État du Québec et le système international," in *L'État du Québec en devenir*, eds. Gérard Bergeron and Réjean Pelletier (Montreal: Boréal, 1980); François Poulin and Guy Trudeau, *Les conditions de la productivité des délégations du Québec à l'étranger* (Sainte-Foy: ENAP, 1982); Louis Sabourin, *Canadian Federalism and International Organization: A Focus on Quebec*, 1971. Doctoral thesis, Columbia University; Jean-Philippe Thérien, Louis Bélanger and Guy Gosselin, "La politique étrangère québécoise," in *Québec, État et société*, ed. Alain G. Gagnon (Montreal: Québec/ Amérique, 1994), pp. 255-78. For relations between Quebec and the United States, see Louis Balthazar and Alfred O. Hero Jr., *Le Québec dans l'espace américain* (Montreal: Québec-Amérique, 1999); Jean-François Lisée, *Dans l'œil de l'aigle: Washington face au Québec* (Montreal: Boréal, 1990; Claude Savary, ed., *Les rapports culturels entre le Québec et les États-Unis* (Quebec City: Institut québécois de recherche sur la culture, 1984). The early relationship between Quebec and France is analyzed in Frédéric Bastien, *Relations particulières: La France au Québec après de Gaulle* (Montreal: Boréal, 1999); J.F Bosher, *The Gaullist Attack on Canada, 1967-1997* (Montreal and Kingston: McGill-Queen's University Press, 1999); Jean-Marc Léger, *La Francophonie: grand dessein, grande ambiguïté* (Montreal: Hurtubise HMH, 1987); Alain Peyrefitte, *De Gaulle et le Québec*. Montreal: Stanké, 2000); Dale Thomson, *De Gaulle et le Québec*

(Saint-Laurent: Éditions du Trécarré, 1990). Finally, some of the actors who were present when these policies were developed have written analyses or memoirs: Robert Comeau, ed., *Jean Lesage et l'éveil d'une nation*, Quebec City: Presses de l'Université du Québec, 1989); Robert Comeau, Michel Lévesque and Yves Bélanger, eds., *Daniel Johnson: Rêve d'égalité et projet d'indépendance* (Quebec City: Presses de l'université du Québec, 1991); Paul Gérin-Lajoie, 1990, *Combats d'un révolutionnaire tranquille* (Montreal: Centre éducatif et culturel, 1990); Pierre Godin, *Daniel Johnson*, volume II: *La difficile recherche de l'égalité* (Montreal: Éditions de l'homme, 1980); Paul Gros d'Aillon, *Daniel Johnson: l'égalité avant l'indépendance* (Montreal: Stanké, 1979); Jean-Marc Léger, *Le Temps dissipé* (Montreal: Hurtubise HMH, 2000); Jean Loiselle, *Daniel Johnson: Le Québec d'abord* (Montreal: VLB éditeur, 1999); Paul Martin, *Fédéralisme et relations internationales* (Ottawa: Queen's Printer, 1968); Claude Morin, *L'art de l'impossible: la diplomatie québécoise depuis 1960* (Montreal: Boréal, 1987); Claude Morin, *Mes premiers ministres* (Montreal: Boréal, 1991); Jacques-Yvan Morin, *Nécessité d'une politique extérieure pour le Québec; allocution devant l'Association des économistes du Québec* (Montreal, 6 May 1983); Dale C. Thomson, *Jean Lesage et la Révolution tranquille* (Saint-Laurent: Éditions du Trécarré, 1984).

10. Which makes it the oldest Quebec foreign institution in uninterrupted existence.

11. Kim Richard Nossal — "An Ambassador by Any Other Name? Provincial Representatives Abroad" in *Diplomatic Missions: The Ambassador in Canadian Foreign Policy*, ed. Robert Wolfe (Kingston: School of Policy Studies, Queen's University and Ottawa: Canadian Centre for Foreign Policy Development, 1998), p. 161 — refers to section 92.4 of the constitution, in English, to justify the establishment of foreign offices since the law allows "The Establishment and Tenure of Provincial Offices." Such reading is interesting as long as you stay with the original English text, but loses its strength when one relies on the French translation, which more restrictively refers to "La création et la tenure des charges provinciales."

12. Canada had already begun to exercise *de facto* influence at the time of World War I, at the time of the Treaty of Versailles and, especially, during the 1922 Chanak crisis (on which, see Nelson Michaud, *L'énigme du Sphinx* (Quebec City: Les Presses de l'Université Laval, 1998), pp. 185-86 — and the signing of the 1923 Halibut Treaty with the United States when the British emissary, who had come to sign the treaty, was relegated to the rank of a silent witness.

13. Indeed, this openness played an indispensable role in the establishment of La Francophonie. On this, see Luc Bernier, "Mulroney's International Beau Risque: The Golden Age of Québec's Foreign Policy," in *Diplomatic Departures: The Conservative Era in Canadian Foreign Policy, 1984-1993*, eds. Nelson Michaud and Kim Richard Nossal (Vancouver: UBC Press, 2001), pp. 128-41.

14. The reopening of several Quebec missions over the last years of the PQ government is an exception to this otherwise established pattern.

15. For example: *Le Québec et l'interdépendance; le monde pour horizon* (1991), published under the Liberal government of Robert Bourassa; and *Le Québec dans un ensemble international en mutation* (2001), by the Parti Québécois government.

16. The desire to build upon past advances was evident in the presentations made by representatives of the PQ, the QLP, and the ADQ during a debate organized by the Cercle québécois des affaires internationales in March 2002. Available at <www.lecercle.qc.ca/eve_affiche.php?no=13)>.

17. Ivo D. Duchacek, *The Territorial Dimension of Politics Within, Among, and Across Nations* (Boulder: Westview, 1986), p. 270.

18. The importance of these victories was heightened by the fact that they came in ridings that had been "orphaned" following the dramatic resignation of several Cabinet ministers.

19. Ministère des Relations internationales, *Le Québec dans un ensemble international en mutation: Plan Stratégique 2001-2004* (Quebec City: Ministère des Relations internationales, 2001).

20 Ibid., p. 40. [translation]

21. Ibid., p. 37.

22. Ibid., p. 41.

23. For a summary of this policy, see *Canada in the World*, available at <www.dfait-maeci.gc.ca/foreign_policy/cnd-world/menu-en.asp>.

24. Ministère des Relations internationales, *Le Québec dans un ensemble international en mutation*, p. 23.

25. Ibid. [translation]

26. Ibid. [translation]

27. Ibid., p. 24. [translation]

28. Ibid. [translation]

29. In 2002, the minister's speeches have addressed many subjects, including the FTAA (see <www.mri.gouv.qc.ca/francais/ministere/allocutions/2002/discours_20020126_fr.html> and <www.mri.gouv.qc.ca/francais/ministere/communiques/2002/20020610_fr.html>); cultural industries and cultural diversity in the Americas (see <www.mri.gouv.qc.ca/francais/ministere/allocutions/2002/discours_20020422_fr.html> and <www.mri.gouv.qc.ca/english/ministere/speeches/2002/discours_20020515_an.html>); and economic issues (see <www.mri.gouv.qc.ca/english/ministere/speeches/2002/discours_20020516_an.html> and <www.mri.gouv.qc.ca/francais/ministere/communiques/2001/20010607_fr.html>).

30. See <www.mri.gouv.qc.ca/francais/ministere/allocutions/2002/discours_20020201_fr.html>. [translation]

31. For example, see <www.mri.gouv.qc.ca/francais/ministere/allocutions/2002/discours_20020603_fr.html> and <www.mri.gouv.qc.ca/francais/ministere/allocutions/2002/discours_20020521_fr.html>.

32. See <www.mri.gouv.qc.ca/francais/ministere/communiques/2002/20020430_fr.html>, <www.mri.gouv.qc.ca/francais/ministere/communiques/2001/20011015_fr.html>, and <www.mri.gouv.qc.ca/francais/ministere/communiques/2000/20000921_fr.html>.

33. See <partiquebecois.org/zones/www/index.php?pg=25>. [translation]

34. He was elected MNA for Mercier, a downtown Montreal riding, on 18 April 2003.

35. See <www.lecercle.qc.ca/doc/extraits-debat-partie-2.mp3>. [translation]

36. See <www.lecercle.qc.ca/doc/daniel-turp-pq.mp3>. [translation]

37. Ibid. [translation]

38. See <www.lecercle.qc.ca/doc/extraits-debat-partie-1.mp3>.

39. Ibid.

40. See <www.lecercle.qc.ca/doc/extraits-debat-partie-2.mp3>. [translation]

41. Parti québécois, *Propositions adoptées au Congrès d'orientation du parti québécois 2003.* See <www.partiquebecois.org/temp/20030309_pleniere.pdf>.

42. Idem, p. 11.

43. Benoît Pelletier, ed., *A Project for Quebec: Affirmation, Autonomy and Leadership* (Quebec City: Quebec Liberal Party, 2001). On 29 April 2003, Pelletier has been sworn in as associate minister for Canadian Intergovernmental Relations and for Native Affairs.

44. Benoît Pelletier, "Un rôle accru: Le rôle du Québec sur la scènes internationale lui est essentiel afin de prolonger sa personnalité singulière," *La Presse*, 25 February 2003, p. A-15.

45. Pelletier, *A Project for Quebec*, p. 101.

46. See <www.lecercle.qc.ca/doc/extraits-debat-partie-2.mp3>. [translation]

47. Pelletier, *A Project for Quebec*, p. 102.

48. See <www.lecercle.qc.ca/doc/benoit-pelletier-plq.mp3>. [translation]

49. See <www.lecercle.qc.ca/doc/extraits-debat-partie-1.mp3>. [translation]

50. See <www.lecercle.qc.ca/doc/benoit-pelletier-plq.mp3>. [translation]

51. Ibid.

52. Ibid.

53. Pelletier, *A Project for Quebec*, p. 102.

54. Ibid., 107.

55. Ibid., 101.

56. See <www.lecercle.qc.ca/doc/extraits-debat-partie-1.mp3>.

57. Pelletier, *A Project for Quebec*, p. 103.

58. Ibid., 102.

59. See <www.lecercle.qc.ca/doc/extraits-debat-partie-1.mp3>. [translation]

60. Pelletier, *A Project for Quebec*, p. 103.

61. See <www.lecercle.qc.ca/doc/extraits-debat-partie-1.mp3>. [translation]

62. Pelletier, *A Project for Quebec*, p. 92.

63. Ibid., p. 95.

64. Chris Kukucha, research results presented at the "The Administration of Canadian Foreign Policy: A Renewed Challenge?" conference, Hull, QC, November 2001.

65. Pelletier, "Un rôle accru, " *La Presse.*

66. See <www.premier.gouv.qc.ca/general/communiques/2003/nominations_29_04/discour_1.htm>.

67. For a more complete analysis of these first signals, see Nelson Michaud, "Charest annonce ses couleurs," *Le Soleil*, 15 May 2003, p. A-17.

68. As Marie Grégoire stressed, in answer to a question at the round table on Quebec's international relations: on election day, the Quebec voter "is not going to ask himself or herself a question about the type of power, but 'what's in it for me?'" See <www.lecercle.qc.ca/doc/extraits-debat-partie-2.mp3>.

69. See <http://www.adq.qc.ca/programme/index.html; consulted in autumn 2002>.

70. See <www.lecercle.qc.ca/doc/marie-gregoire-adq.mp3>.

71. Ibid. [translation]

72. See <www.lecercle.qc.ca/doc/extraits-debat-partie-2.mp3>. [translation]

73. See <www.lecercle.qc.ca/doc/marie-gregoire-adq.mp3>. [translation]

74. Ibid. [translation]

75. Ibid. [translation

76. See <www.adq.qc.ca/programme/index.html, p. 109>. [translation]

77. In the Quebec political system, characterized by *brokerage politics* — the inevitable result of the first-past-the-post voting system — a party that sticks rigidly to a programmatic approach could not garner enough votes to win power. A certain measure of pragmatism is therefore necessary.

78. At that time the PQ formed the government, the QLP sat in the capacity of the official opposition, and the ADQ was the third party, also in opposition.

79. Bill 52, *An Act to amend the Act respecting the Ministère des Relations internationales and other legislative provision*, 2002.

80. See <www.lecercle.qc.ca/doc/extraits-debat-partie-1.mp3>.

81. National Assembly of Quebec, Parliamentary Proceedings, 36th Legislature, 2nd Session, *Journal des débats* (Hansard), 20 March 2002.

82. National Assembly of Quebec, Parliamentary Proceedings, 36th Legislature, 2nd Session, *Débats de la Commission des institutions*, 30 April 2002, 16:30.

83. National Assembly of Quebec, Parliamentary Proceedings, 36th Legislature, 2nd Session, *Journal des débats* (Hansard), 20 March 2002.

84. National Assembly of Quebec, Parliamentary Proceedings, 36th Legislature, 2nd Session, *Débats de la Commission des institutions*, 1 March 2002, 16:00. [translation]

85. Brian Galligan "Globalization and Australian Federalism," in *Impact of Global and Regional Integration on Federal Systems*, eds. Harvey Lazar, Hamish Telford and Ron Watts (Montreal: McGill-Queen's University Press, forthcoming).

86. National Assembly of Quebec, Parliamentary Proceedings, 36th Legislature, 2nd Session, *Journal des débats* (Hansard), 20 March 2002. [translation]

87. National Assembly of Quebec, Parliamentary Proceedings, 36th Legislature, 2nd Session, *Journal des débats* (Hansard), 9 May 2002. [translation]

88. National Assembly of Quebec, Parliamentary Proceedings, 36th Legislature, 2nd Session, *Journal des débats* (Hansard), 8 May 2002. [translation]

89. National Assembly of Quebec, Parliamentary Proceedings, 36th Legislature, 2nd Session, *Débats de la Commission des institutions*, 30 April 2002, 16:30.

90. National Assembly of Quebec, Parliamentary Proceedings, 36th Legislature, 2nd Session, *Journal des débats* (Hansard), 20 March 2002.

91. Ministère des Relations internationales, Québec@Monde, 28 August 2002. See <www.mri.gouv.qc.ca/quebec_monde/en/mot_ministre.html#mission>.

92. Bill 109, *An Act respecting the Observatoire québécois de la mondialisation*.

93. Ibid.

94. Ministère des Relations internationales, Media Release, 4 June 2002. See <www.mri.gouv.qc.ca/francais/ministere/communiques/2002/20020604_fr.html>. [translation]

95. This was a problem succinctly raised by the Liberal member from Viger. See <www.assnat.qc.ca/fra/Publications/debats/journal/ch/021106.htm>.

96. See <www.assnat.qc.ca/fra/Publications/debats/journal/ch/021106.htm>. [translation]

97. See <www.assnat.qc.ca/fra/Publications/debats/epreuve/ci/021105/0930.htm>.

98. See <www.assnat.qc.ca/fra/Publications/debats/journal/ch/021023.htm>.

99. See <www.assnat.qc.ca/fra/Publications/debats/epreuve/ci/o21105/1000.htm>.

100. See http://www.assnat.qc.ca/fra/Publications/debats/journal/ch/021023.htm>.

101. See <www.assnat.qc.ca/fra/Publications/debats/journal/ch/021106.htm>. [translation]

102. See <www.assnat.qc.ca/fra/Publications/debats/epreuve/ci/021105/0930.htm>.

103. The minister frequently made allusions to this point, but particularly stressed its importance at the committee hearings: <www.assnat.qc.ca/fra/Publications/debats/epreuve/ci/o21105/1100.htm>.

104. See <www.assnat.qc.ca/fra/Publications/debats/epreuve/ci/o21105/1000.htm>.

105. See <www.assnat.qc.ca/fra/Publications/debats/epreuve/ci/021105/0930.htm>.

106. See <www.assnat.qc.ca/fra/Publications/debats/journal/ch/021106.htm>.

107. See also <www.assnat.qc.ca/fra/Publications/debats/journal/ch/021023.htm>.

108. The ambiguity arose from the fact that although the *Observatoire* is not at all a research centre, this committee "is going to be mandated to evaluate the relevance and adequacy of the work of the *Observatoire* when a research project is involved. It will not conduct research itself, but will be able to have it done and it will be able to have the right to initiate suggestions to the board of directors," as the PQ member from the riding of Saint-Jean summarized it. His Liberal colleague from the riding of Outremont added that it was a "review committee

like those found in institutes" (read "research institutes"). To which the minister responded: "That's an excellent summary .... That's it. That's it. Yes, that's it." See <www.assnat.qc.ca/fra/Publications/debats/epreuve/ci/o21105/1200.htm>. [translation]

109. See <www.assnat.qc.ca/fra/Publications/debats/journal/ch/021107.htm>. [translation]

110. Ibid.

111. See <www.assnat.qc.ca/fra/Publications/debats/journal/ch/021023.htm>.

112. Ministère des Relations internationales, *Québec@Monde*, 28 August 2002. See <www.mri.gouv.qc.ca/quebec_monde/en/mot_ministre.html#mission>.

113. See <www.assnat.qc.ca/fra/Publications/debats/journal/ch/021023.htm> and <www.assnat.qc.ca/fra/Publications/debats/journal/ch/021106.htm>.

114. See <www.assnat.qc.ca/fra/Publications/debats/epreuve/ci/o21105/1000.htm>. [translation]

115. See <www.assnat.qc.ca/fra/Publications/debats/journal/ch/021107.htm>.

116. See <www.assnat.qc.ca/fra/Publications/debats/epreuve/ci/021105/0930.htm>.

117. See <www.assnat.qc.ca/fra/Publications/debats/journal/ch/021023.htm>. [translation]

118. Each of the parties contributed to this: the Parti Québécois by the vagueness that arose around the question of the mandates and the objectives to be assigned to the *Observatoire*; l'Action démocratique du Québec by its minimal and insubstantial participation; and the Liberal Party by its vote against the principle of the bill, even though, according to the party's spokesperson, the official opposition agreed with this principle. (See <www.assnat.qc.ca/fra/Publications/debats/journal/ch/021023.htm> and <www.assnat.qc.ca/fra/Publications/debats/journal/ch/021106.htm>.) In addition, the same spokesperson, after having suggested an amendment that was accepted by the minister (section 23 of the Act), ended up voting against her own idea. See <www.assnat.qc.ca/fra/Publications/debats/epreuve/ci/021105/1200.htm>

119. See <www.assnat.qc.ca/fra/Publications/debats/epreuve/ci/021105/0930.htm>. [translation]

120. This hypothesis is based on established practice of Quebec in the field of international relations; that is, its history of establishing institutions that reflect the specificity of its social composition and the willingness of political actors to continue along this path.

121. Stephen Krasner, *Sovereignty: Organized Hypocrisy* (Princeton: Princeton University Press, 1999).

122. Ministère des Relations internationales, *Le Québec dans un ensemble international en mutation*, (2001), p. 21.

14

The Missing Link: Policy Options for Engaging Ottawa in Canada's Urban Centres

Roger Gibbins

Le manque d'engagement direct et explicite dans les affaires municipales de son gouvernement national rend le Canada unique parmi les fédérations développées. Cette particularité est curieuse compte tenu de l'importance des régions urbaines dans l'économie du savoir et du niveau très élevé d'urbanisation dans l'ensemble du pays. Cependant, reconnaître le problème — car le manque de politique urbaine fédérale est un problème croissant — ne revient en rien à le solutionner. Le gouvernement fédéral dispose d'un certain nombre d'options d'engagement stratégiques comprenant les transferts fiscaux, les programmes d'infrastructures, les conventions tripartites et l'usage accru des organismes bénévoles. Un examen attentif de ces options est nécessaire avant que des mesures précipitées ne soient prises.

Canada is increasingly unique among Western democratic states in that the national government lacks any explicit engagement in urban affairs, in those policy arenas that shape the economic prosperity and quality of life for the country's urban centres. A superficial look at an organizational chart for the Government of Canada, or for that matter a detailed search, would lead to the conclusion that Canada is still a rural community. Although federal officials are required to look at new policy proposals through a "rural lens" in order to ensure that rural concerns are accommodated, there is no comparable urban lens. This lack of engagement with urban affairs is puzzling for a number of reasons:

- Canada is a heavily urbanized country, and urbanization has steadily increased since the end of World War II.
- At the time of the 2001 Census, 64.3 percent of the Canadian population lived in metropolitan regions with populations larger than 500,000.

- Urbanization is not confined to any one region of the country. Western Canada, for example, long the rural heartland, is now as heavy urbanized as other regions. Even the Yukon and Northwest Territories are marked by the urban dominance of Whitehorse and Yellowknife.

- There is growing evidence that large metropolitan regions are the motors of the new, knowledge-based economy, the primary links to the global economy, and the principal sites of creativity, immigration settlement and research-intensive universities.

- Canada's international competitors, including the European Community, Australia and the United States, have been investing heavily in urban infrastructure and transportation connections, and in the creative capacity of urban communities.

Canada therefore stands apart with respect to the federal government's neglect — and it is not benign neglect — of urban affairs.

How do we account for this neglect? One commonly encountered explanation is that urban affairs fall within the constitutional domain of the provincial governments, and therefore Ottawa faces a constitutional prohibition. More specifically, it is pointed out that section 92.8 of the *Constitution Act* assigns "municipal institutions" to the provinces, rendering urban affairs a no-go area for the federal government. However, section 92.7 of the *Constitution Act* assigns "the establishment, maintenance and management of hospitals" to the provinces. Yet this constitutional provision has not precluded a massive federal presence with respect to health policy: Health Canada, the *Canada Health Act*, support for medical research and large fiscal transfers to the provinces all speak to the irrelevancy of section 92.7. The assignment of municipal institutions to the provinces is no more a constraint on the federal government's engagement in urban affairs than is the assignment of hospitals to the provinces a constraint on the federal government's engagement in health policy.

Thus the constitutional constraint argument is bogus, and should not be taken seriously by Canadians trying to come to grips with contemporary urban issues. While the federal government lacks the capacity to restructure municipal institutions, there are no constitutional constraints on its use of the spending power (sections 91.1A and 91.3) in urban affairs, or on its programmatic engagement. This conclusion is supported by comparative analysis of other federal states.[1] The national governments of Australia and the United States, for example, have no greater constitutional beachhead in urban affairs than does the Government of Canada, but in neither case has this precluded an active engagement.

Are there other reasons for the lack of federal engagement? Part of the explanation may lie with the general institutional inertia that grips Canadian political life: we are a very conservative people when it comes to parliamentary institutions and traditions. Municipal governments, moreover, have not made a consistently strong public case for federal engagement, and although they were certainly vocal in the early 1970s,[2] it has only been in recent years that their voice has been reinvigorated. Provincial governments have been wary of further federal intrusions onto provincial turf. Citizens have also tended to lodge their political identities with provincial rather than local communities, although this situation may be changing. For example, a 2001 survey asked over 3,200 western Canadian respondents about their primary identity: 26.6 percent gave a *local identity* compared with 27 percent who mentioned their province, 12.1 percent who mentioned western Canada, 28 percent who mentioned Canada, 2.4 percent who mentioned North America, and 4.4 percent who selected an identity with the world at large.[3] Finally, the explanation for the lack of engagement may lie with the simple absence of political will or creativity; the federal government is not explicitly engaged in urban affairs because it chooses not to be engaged.

However, the failure of the federal government to develop and support a national urban strategy goes beyond the absence of political will. *There is also genuine uncertainty about the instruments through which a national urban strategy might be brought into play.* In short, even if there was the *will*, there is no consensus on the *way*. If the potential policy tools were clear, political will might be easier to mobilize. Unfortunately, this is far from the case. The present analysis, therefore, considers a number of ways in which a national urban strategy might be brought into play. Hopefully this analysis will feed into a growing debate on the role of cities within the Canadian federal state. This debate has been finding expression in editorial pages, position papers by the Federation of Canadian Municipalities (FCM), and private sector actors (most notably the Toronto Dominion Bank), as well as at the Winnipeg and Vancouver gatherings of the C5 mayors (the mayors of Montreal, Toronto, Winnipeg, Calgary and Vancouver meeting under the inspirational leadership of Jane Jacobs), the February 2002 meeting of FCM's Big City Mayors caucus, internal deliberations within the federal government, the Prime Minister's Task Force on Urban Affairs and its final report authored by Member of Parliament Judy Sgro, and in the policy musings of federal Liberal leadership candidates. It is clearly a debate whose time has come.

STRATEGIC OPTIONS FOR FEDERAL ENGAGEMENT

A number of strategic options can be put on the table for federal engagement in urban affairs. Some of these come with considerable historical experience relating directly to urban affairs or in analogous public policy areas, while others are more speculative in character.

WAITING FOR THE NEXT OLYMPICS

Many of the most notable federal impacts on the urban landscape have come through major Canadian-hosted international events such as Expo 67 in Montreal, the Montreal Summer Olympics, Expo 86 in Vancouver, and the 1988 Calgary Winter Olympics. The federal urban strategy in this respect has been one of "seizing the day." The most recent examples have come in connection with Toronto's bid to host the 2008 Summer Olympics, and with the Vancouver/Whistler bid to host the 2010 Winter Games. As part of the bid to the International Olympic Committee, the governments of Canada, Ontario and Toronto agreed to a cost-shared, multi-billion dollar redevelopment of the Toronto waterfront. (When the bid failed, redevelopment also stalled.) Similar although likely more modest agreements in principle have been generated by the Vancouver/Whistler bid. This form of opportunistic federal intervention can have a major and positive impact. There is no question, moreover, that future Canadian bids for world sporting events or expositions will necessarily entail financial support from the Canadian government; this is a given in the nature of the competition. However, a coherent federal urban engagement strategy cannot be patched together from such opportunistic and episodic events, ones that will leave many urban centres untouched. Engagements such as the proposed waterfront redevelopment should be seen as no more than the icing on a much larger and more comprehensive urban engagement cake, a cake that is not yet in the mixing bowl, much less the oven.

FISCAL TRANSFERS

Canadian federalism has been characterized from the get-go by fiscal transfers from Ottawa to the provincial governments, transfers designed in large part to support programs nominally falling within the provincial field of responsibility. Fiscal transfers spring from a fundamental structural imbalance in the federation: parliament has greater taxation capacity relative to its jurisdictional responsibilities than do the provinces, hence the systematic transfer of tax revenue from the federal government to provincial treasuries.

In many respects, a similar structural imbalance argument *could* be developed for city governments, although to date, this has not been made with sufficient rigour. If those governments are now facing a set of responsibilities in excess of their fiscal capacity,[4] then a case for transfer payments could be made. (The case would be strengthened to the extent that off-loading has occurred, although here again the rhetorical argument is stronger than the empirical evidence.) However, this case may not necessarily entail a federal role. If the responsibilities the cities are shouldering fall primarily within the legislative jurisdiction of the provinces, then the transfer argument applies first and foremost to municipal-provincial fiscal relations. The case with respect to provincial governments need not apply to the federal government. To date, the major transfer issues relate to provincial government support for municipal governments, and whether such transfers are sufficient and predictable enough to facilitate effective planning at the municipal level.

For a number of reasons, the introduction of a *federal-municipal* fiscal transfer analogous to the now-departed Canadian Health and Social Transfer is unlikely in the foreseeable future:

- A stronger short-term case can be made for enhanced provincial-municipal transfers, or for the transfer of some provincial tax capacity to city governments.

- If there is still a need for financial infusions from the federal government, it is not clear if such infusions should be federal-municipal in character, or should be routed through the provincial governments. In short, the problem may rest with federal-provincial fiscal relations. Solving the ongoing federal-provincial fiscal imbalance in Canadian federalism *might* give provincial governments the financial wherewithal to address municipal concerns.

- The federal government is unenthusiastic about unconditional transfers whereby it picks up the bill but has difficulty claiming a proportionate amount of political credit. Given Ottawa's wariness and its preference for conditional over unconditional transfers, it will be hard to generate political support for federal-municipal fiscal transfers.

- The Auditor General has begun to flag fiscal transfers as a problem, arguing that they reduce Parliament's accountability for the funds it raises.[5] The AG's concerns may be expressed with even greater vigour should federal-municipal transfers be considered.

Thus, while one could argue that municipal governments face a structural shortfall analogous to that faced by provincial governments, it is less clear that federal-municipal fiscal transfers are the solution. Even if they are a part of the solution, there is no glimmer of political will in this respect.

DEDICATED TAXES

A variant of fiscal transfers can be found in a strategic approach based on dedicated taxes. Admittedly, governments in Canada have generally shied away from dedicated taxes of the kind used to finance the interstate highway system in the United States. Instead, they have preferred to aggregate all tax revenues within a consolidated revenue fund, and thus not to link particular programs with specific tax sources. Although this may be a laudable approach to public finance, Canadians still face taxes that appear to be dedicated. Examples include Employment Insurance premiums (even though the size of the EI surplus makes it clear that EI premiums go well beyond a dedicated tax), provincial health care premiums, and the airport security tax. A more specific example, and one that is being highlighted increasingly by big city mayors, is the federal fuel tax on gasoline. The mayors make a telling political argument: Ottawa is extracting literally billions of dollars in tax revenues from cities through the fuel tax but is contributing next to nothing in return to the transportation infrastructure generating the tax revenues. A more appropriate approach, they argue, would be for the federal government to rebate some or all of the fuel tax to municipal governments who, in turn, would use the revenues to support transportation infrastructure. Such a system is currently in place in Alberta, where the provincial government rebates four and a half cents per litre back to the major cities for infrastructure support. If the federal government maintains the high-profile fuel tax, it can expect to receive ever more strident arguments that it should contribute to infrastructure support.

It should be noted that there is no necessary link between a dedicated tax and unconditional transfers to city governments. The proceeds from a dedicated tax could flow first into a new federal department or agency charged with responsibility for urban infrastructure. With this mechanism in place, appropriate political credit for federal financial participation would be assured. It would also be possible to adjust the level of the fuel tax in response to public transportation needs or the potential impact of the Kyoto Accord.

MINISTRY OF STATE FOR URBAN AFFAIRS

In the early 1970s, Pierre Trudeau's Liberal government established the Ministry of State for Urban Affairs (MSUA). The ministry struggled on with little impact until it was abolished at the end of the first Trudeau regime. The public administration consensus is that MSUA was a failure, that it was unable to promote or support an urban agenda. MSUA was a horizontal organization without sufficient funds or ministerial clout to influence the more powerful line departments. As such, its capacity to coordinate line departments, and to bring urban affairs into focus, was very limited. Unfortunately, this perception of failure has had a paralytic effect when it comes to new proposals for federal engagement with urban affairs. In this case, we may be learning the wrong historical lessons. The cross-silo nature of MSUA may be more in line with contemporary public administration philosophies than it was with the temper of the times in the 1970s, and therefore it seems premature to dismiss MSUA as a potential model for the early 2000s.

The MSUA experience does raise an important issue, and that is how best to organizationally spearhead a federal engagement strategy. A Secretary of State position would not carry Cabinet weight proportionate to the economic and demographic weight of Canadian cities; such an appointment today might be seen more as a slight than as a progressive step. Should there then be a full ministry analogous to the US Department of Housing and Urban Development (HUD) in the United States or the Minister for London in the United Kingdom? A Cabinet committee charged with responsibility for the urban agenda? Or, as William Thorsell has suggested, should the responsibility be lodged within the Prime Minister's Office?[6] If the arguments about the importance of cities in the knowledge-based economy are correct, then a full place for urban affairs at the Cabinet table makes sense, as half measures would postpone rather than facilitate an effective federal strategy. In any event, whatever the best organizational vehicle might be, it would make little sense to launch an urban engagement strategy and then neuter it within the bureaucratic and ministerial worlds of the federal government.

THE VOLUNTARY SECTOR AS A PROXY

Much of the federal government's engagement to date with urban affairs has come through financial support for non-profit organizations active in large metropolitan communities. Examples include financial support for Native Friendship Centres, multicultural organizations, and homeless shelters. In many respects, this has been a laudable form of urban intervention, one that meets real social concerns while at the same time sustaining a vibrant non-profit sector. To use a term coined by Peter Leslie, the federal government's Voluntary Sector Initiative can be seen as an urban strategy by stealth. However, it is not a substitute for a more comprehensive urban strategy that would also address transportation infrastructure, the tax capacity of city governments, and global competitiveness. While there is no need for direct federal delivery agencies in areas presently occupied by non-profit organizations, there is a need to go further with a federal strategy. There is also a need to give higher public and political profile to the federal government's engagement with urban issues, a need that cannot be met through federal engagement mediated through the voluntary sector.

SIGNAGE

It is sometimes suggested that an urban strategy of sorts does exist, but that it lacks visibility. It is argued that when all of the existing federal activities within urban centres are taken into account, the sum total amounts to a very considerable federal effort to address urban issues and concerns. All that is needed, therefore, is better signage to inform Canadian citizens that the federal government is indeed on the job. While this argument should not be dismissed out of hand, it fails to come to grips with the reality that the sum total of federal activities on the urban scene may not amount to a coherent federal strategy. The total may be much less than the sum of its parts. Signage alone is not the answer; there has to be some mechanism to weave existing and future federal activities into a coherent strategic position.

INFRASTRUCTURE PROGRAMS

In 1993, the new Liberal government in Ottawa launched the $6 billion Infrastructure Works Program as a partnership among the federal, provincial, territorial and municipal governments. The program's objective was to accelerate economic recovery by creating short and long-term jobs in local communities, and to renew and enhance their physical infrastructure. The Canada Infrastructure Works Program did indeed stimulate local economies by generating direct and indirect jobs, particularly in the construction sector, with estimates running as high as 100,000 new jobs.[7] The program served the federal government's overall strategy of using infrastructure improvement to enhance the competitiveness of Canada's communities. Projects included road and transportation system improvements, water and sewer improvements, and upgrades to community and recreational facilities to enhance the quality of life and create new employment opportunities. The overall success of the project led to its renewal in 1997, and its ongoing status within federal government program priorities.

The tripartite infrastructure initiatives should not be understated as innovations in Canadian federalism, ones that will have considerable staying power. They have built an established track record of intergovernmental collaboration that embraces all three levels/orders of government, although in some cases municipalities have definitely played second or third fiddle to their provincial governments. Province-specific management committees have been put into place. The Infrastructure Canada program in Manitoba (ICM), for example, provides for the establishment of a joint management committee to administer the program and to recommend projects for funding. Western Diversification takes responsibility for the federal government, with the program being managed provincially by Manitoba Intergovernmental Affairs. A similar structure has been put in place in Saskatchewan. The Alberta management committee for the Infrastructure Canada-Alberta (ICA) Program is slightly different in that urban and rural representation is included at the management table. The Alberta Association of Municipal Districts and Counties (AAMDC) and the Alberta Urban Municipalities Association (AUMA) have been consulted in the development of the new program. Representatives of the two organizations sit on the joint federal-provincial Management Committee to ensure municipal input continues through the life of the program. In other provinces, these representatives are not at the table, yet they are consulted throughout the process.

Infrastructure Canada, the municipal component of the new physical infrastructure program, builds on the success of the previous Canada Infrastructure

Works Program. However, it has a more strategic focus, with a view toward the long-term benefits of building a twenty-first century infrastructure, improving the quality of life for all Canadians, and enhancing the quality of our environment. There is, for example, an explicit focus on green infrastructure projects. Other key components of the new program include a more flexible cost-sharing formula and improved openness to private sector partnerships in order to promote new ways of financing and delivering public services.

At the same time, the infrastructure programs provide at best a start for a coherent federal urban engagement strategy. Their focus to this point has not been explicitly or exclusively urban: municipalities big and small have been brought under the tent. In addition, the focus on infrastructure, while important, is still too narrow. Urban affairs reach far beyond roads and sewers. It is also important that any federal strategy has greater continuity and predictability. A contra-cyclical program based on stimulating employment is not enough — we cannot afford to address the concerns of cities only when the economy is in the tank, or for that matter only when surpluses are readily at hand. Finally, the infrastructure programs are driven to a significant degree by political considerations. Note, for example, the recent decision by the federal government to have infrastructure decisions made within Cabinet and caucus rather than by an arms-length agency. This decision may make sense in terms of accountability, but it does not provide city governments with the predictability they need for effective planning. In short, while the infrastructure programs may make sense on many levels, they are not to be confused with a coherent and comprehensive urban engagement strategy on the part of the Government of Canada.

TRIPARTITE URBAN DEVELOPMENT AGREEMENTS

Western Canada has been the site of some innovative urban development agreements designed to bring the federal, provincial and municipal governments into play within jointly managed programs. The focus of these agreements has been explicitly urban, and their design is flexible. The Winnipeg Development Agreement (WDA), for example, was put into place in March 1995. It was a $75 million agreement, cost-shared equally among the three levels of government. The WDA provides useful evidence that the three levels of government can work together, within their respective mandates and jurisdictions, and with the communities and businesses of Winnipeg to support the long-term sustainable economic development. The three key foci have been community development and security, labour force development, and strategic and sectoral investments. Although the initial five-year agreement expired in March 2002, it has recently been renewed.

The Vancouver Agreement (VA) is an unfunded agreement signed by the federal (Western Economic Diversification), provincial and city governments in March 2000. The three key themes are community health and safety, economic and social development, and community capacity building. Funding has come from a pooling of existing departmental funds, although collaborative mechanisms are in place to allocate new funding should it materialize in the future. The VA is meant to cover the whole of Vancouver, but its focus to date has been on the Downtown Eastside (DTES). Its priority has been the development of the Downtown Eastside Agreement to tackle severe drug problems. From the perspective of the City of Vancouver, the agreement provides the city and its citizens with a framework for action that compels the provincial and federal governments to take responsibility for issues within their jurisdiction. It is also meant to show which levels of government are responsible for each action, and to highlight the severity of Vancouver's drug problem. The overarching goal of the framework is to develop a "regional" approach to the development of services and to convince the provincial and federal governments of the wide-reaching implications of Vancouver's drug problem.

It is difficult to determine whether the urban development agreements in western Canada provide a suitable model for a more comprehensive strategy of federal engagement with urban affairs. While there are some promising signs, the ground for a larger federal strategy has been more dented than broken in western Canada. On the plus side, the agreements demonstrate a limited willingness and capacity of the federal, provincial and municipal governments to work together. The underlying principles and operating procedures seem to provide a sound tripartite model. However, Western Diversification's considerable creativity with respect to urban development agreements was not matched with sufficient resources. The Edmonton Agreement has folded, and agreements have not been struck in Saskatchewan. (A stumbling block in Regina is how best to roll First Nation communities and governments into the tripartite framework without implying that First Nation governments are on a constitutional par with municipal governments.) The most promising agreement appears to be the Vancouver Agreement, with its relatively tight focus on the DTES initiative. It is still too early, however, to know if the Vancouver Agreement will be effective or sustained.

CONCLUSIONS

We are left with a complex dilemma. The instrumentalities currently open to the federal government may not be sufficient or appropriate to support an effective strategy of federal engagement in urban affairs. At the same time, there are a number of additional concerns that inhibit federal engagement. As noted above, the federal government is appropriately concerned about offending the sensitivities of provincial governments, and about public perceptions that it may be reopening the constitutional debate. The price tag of an effective federal strategy is unclear, although there is no question that it will be substantial if any such strategy is to have effective leverage on the prosperity of urban centres. This lack of clarity is a significant obstacle as economic uncertainty grows. Perhaps of greatest importance is the politically difficult task of creating boundaries for a federal urban strategy. If it were to apply to all 4,500 local governments across the country, the federal effort would be severely diluted — the urban strategy would be little more than a strategy for Canadians wherever they might chose to live. However, drawing a line in the sand and thereby restricting an urban strategy to only a handful of urban centres, even a large handful, would be a tough task indeed. The realities of Canadian federalism would dictate that at the very least the federal strategy would have to be relevant for all ten, thus setting up Charlottetown as the benchmark. The primal drive in Canadian political life for inclusive programming runs counter to an urban strategy that would be truly urban.

However, if the arguments about cities as motors of the new, knowledge-based economy are correct, Canadians will not be well served by inertia on the part of the federal government. The competitive position of Canadian cities in the continental and global economies will suffer. It simply makes less and less sense for the federal government to continue to ignore Canada's urban face. More attention is being paid to broadband connections for rural communities than is being paid to the connectivity of large cities to the global economy. It is not clear, however, that federal programs on topics such as innovation can work effectively without explicit connection to the health and vitality of Canada's major urban regions. More importantly, the continued unwillingness of the federal government to come to grips with Canada's urban face will leave the country poorly prepared for intensifying global competitiveness. A prosperity agenda, or an innovation agenda, that fails to recognize this urban face will not serve Canadians well.

None of the above should be taken as a call for the Government of Canada to bypass the provincial governments as it seeks to construct an urban agenda, and as it seeks to create policy instruments for engagement in urban affairs. Such an approach would be unnecessarily confrontational. However, neither should wariness of provincial governments pose an insurmountable obstacle to federal engagement. There are tripartite mechanisms with both demonstrated success and potential.

In the short term at least, the greatest constraint is money. Greater federal engagement with Canada's major metropolitan regions will inevitably come with a price tag attached. In the unsettled economic environment, this may seem like an inappropriate time to urge the federal government to consider a policy of engagement. And yet, if we simply sit and wait for the good times to return, and only then begin to discuss the possible instrumentalities of federal engagement, Canada may be outflanked by her international competitors. The health of our cities is not something to consider only when the times are good;

it may be even more important to consider when the times are, if not bad, then at least uncertain.

NOTES

This chapter was first presented to the State of the Federation 2001-2002 Conference held in Kingston in November 2001, which was funded and hosted by the Institute of Intergovernmental Relations at Queen's University. I would like to acknowledge the research assistance of Melissa Dickey.

1.   Loleen Berdahl and Sophie Sapergia, *Urban Nation, Federal State: Rethinking Relationships* (Calgary: Canada West Foundation, 2001).

2.   Lionel D. Feldman and Katherine A. Graham, *Bargaining for Cities: Municipalities and Intergovernmental Relations* (Montreal: Institute for Research on Public Policy, 1979).

3.   Loleen Berdahl, *Looking West: A Survey of Western Canadians* (Calgary: Canada West Foundation, 2001).

4.   Casey Vander Ploeg, *Dollars and Sense: Big City Finances in the West, 1990-2000* (Calgary: Canada West Foundation, 2001).

5.   Roger Gibbins, Loleen Berdahl and Katherine Harmsworth, *Following the Cash: Exploring the Expanding Role of Canada's Auditor General* (Calgary: Canada West Foundation, 2000).

6.   William Thorsell, "Paul Martin's cities slip is showing," *The Globe and Mail*, 22 October 2001, A15.

7.   Canada/Nova Scotia Infrastructure Works Program Extension, Backgrounder, at <www.tbs-sct.gc.ca/news97/nr2802be.html>.

VI

Enhancing Legitimacy and Accountability in Intergovernmental Relations

15

Intergovernmental Agreements in Canada:
At the Crossroads Between Law and Politics

Johanne Poirier

Les ententes intergouvernementales (EIG) sont omniprésentes dans la pratique du fédéralisme canadien. Ce chapitre vise trois objectifs. La 1ᵉʳᵉ partie fait état de la pratique des EIG : qui les négocie ? où les trouve-t-on ? quel rôle est dévolu au législateur face à ces instruments par excellence du fédéralisme coopératif ? La 2ᵉ partie aborde la question de la «justiciabilité» des ententes. Produits indéniables de tractations politiques, les EIG n'échappent cependant pas au droit. Elles peuvent générer des obligations de nature juridique entre exécutifs, bien que le pouvoir législatif puisse légiférer à l'encontre d'une EIG. Par ailleurs, les citoyens peuvent saisir les tribunaux pour s'opposer à la conclusion d' EIG ou en exiger l'application. Ces scénarios soulèvent des questions d'identification du tribunal compétent et d'éventuelles réparations. Enfin, la 3ᵉ partie examine les fonctions «para-constitutionnelles» des EIG. Malgré leur potentiel d'efficacité sur le plan de l'administration publique, les EIG peuvent brouiller la ligne de partage des compétences, ce qui entraîne des conséquences pour les tiers, et modifie les équilibres au sein de la fédération. Les EIG ne permettent donc pas de renouveller le fédéralisme «en dehors» de la Constitution, mais parfois à l'encontre de celle-ci.

INTRODUCTION

Intergovernmental agreements (IGAs) represent omnipresent instruments of policy-making, relation-building and constitutional engineering in federal systems. Literally hundreds of IGAs have been concluded over the years between provinces, and mostly between provinces and the federal government in a wide spectrum of policy areas. Yet the contractual arrangements between orders of government have received surprisingly limited academic attention in Canada.[1]

The objective of this chapter is threefold. The first part attempts to map out the practice of IGAs in Canada. It seeks to answer questions such as: "What are they; where do we find them; how are they negotiated, and what is the role of legislative assemblies in the adoption of IGAs?"

The second part tackles the issue of the status of IGAs in Canada. The main objective here is to examine their justiciability from a variety of angles. Indeed, while they are undeniably the result of political negotiations and manoeuvring between orders of government, IGAs intersect with the legal and judicial systems in many ways. I explore various elements of this intersection, and I hope to show that contrary to popular opinion, IGAs can create legally binding obligations between the governments which sign them. This being said, even when an agreement is binding on the governments that sign it, the legislative assembly of each order of government may legislate so as to counter it. In this context, the chapter examines the challenge posed by the principle of parliamentary sovereignty to the stability of intergovernmental relations, as well as various avenues that could allow for a greater *legal* protection of those relations. I then briefly examine the legal effect of IGAs on those who are not party to them and consider how third parties are resorting to the courts to challenge the way IGAs are concluded or implemented, notably when they impact on fundamental rights. The following subsection canvasses — also very briefly — the issue of the proper judicial forum in which the intersection between IGAs and the law occurs, as well the question of the legal remedies which can be expected.

The third part attempts to challenge the myth that IGAs are ultimate tools for a "non-constitutional" reordering of the federation. IGAs cannot officially alter the distribution of powers, but they can modify the *exercise* of these powers. They can also blur lines of constitutional competences, even as they clarify administrative roles and responsibilities. As tools of *realpolitik* in the federal system, they reflect and consolidate power games between federal actors. IGAs are undoubtedly used to avoid constitutional reform. In none of these contexts is the use of IGAs constitutionally "neutral."

Given these numerous and momentous functions of IGAs in the workings of the Canadian federal system, shielding them from any sort of judicial review seems counter-intuitive in a country that prides itself on its commitment to the rule of law. While the legal and judicial systems may not always be well-suited to controlling what is often the result of harsh, complex, lengthy negotiations, their intervention can contribute to greater transparency and accountability with regard to an instrument of executive federalism par excellence. In any event, whether they want it or not, and irrespective of the opinion of governments that are party to agreements, the courts *are* increasingly challenged by problems related to IGAs. In brief, the main thrust of my analysis is that IGAs are not — and often *should* not — be shielded from law.

A PORTRAIT OF INTERGOVERNMENTAL AGREEMENTS IN CANADA

THE CHALLENGE OF DEFINING AND LOCATING IGAs

"Intergovernmental agreement" is a generic expression in Canada and it includes all formal agreements between executive branches of government. With the exception of very limited provincial legislation concerning the authority to conclude agreements and signature requirements, no legal framework governs IGAs.[2] Exact criteria for identifying them can be elusive. The present section seeks to demonstrate the importance, both in numeric and political terms, of such formal agreements in the Canadian federal system.

The number of intergovernmental agreements concluded between the different members of the federation over the years is difficult to assess. The same is true of agreements currently in force.[3] At the federal level, and in most provinces, no legal or administrative text governs the conclusion, registration or publication of agreements. For decades, departments in Ottawa have concluded agreements without any kind of archival system. Until 1995, the Federal-Provincial Relations Office published an inventory of activities, which included major federal-provincial agreements. In its annual reports, the Canadian Intergovernmental Conference Secretariat (CICS) lists some agreements concluded in the context of the conferences for which it assumes logistical responsibilities. However, the CICS does not keep a complete register of agreements.

In 1998, the Privy Council Office (PCO) launched an initiative to create a central registry of all federal-provincial agreements. After the defeats of the Meech Lake and Charlottetown accords, and the 1995 Referendum on Quebec sovereignty, "administrative" agreements were hailed as the solution to unattainable constitutional reform. Yet no one in Ottawa could actually take stock of the body of existing agreements. With some exceptions, they were scattered around the country and in the filing cabinets of various departments in Ottawa. Moreover, it is not uncommon for the regional office of a federal department to conclude an agreement with a provincial authority without even formally informing the main office in Ottawa. There was no complete list, let alone comprehensive archives.

The PCO project is ambitious. It seeks to locate as many agreements as possible to which federal authorities are party, whether those agreements are in force or not. A relatively sophisticated research tool was developed, which allows for the retrieval of agreements according to a series of criteria (ranging from the province or the federal department involved to the expiration dates, and including second language or dispute resolution clauses).[4] A rough estimate sets the number of federal-provincial agreements at 1,500 to 2,000. At the end of 2001, nearly 1,000 had been located and the registry contained over 880 of them. The estimate is bound to remain just that because some agreements have not been located, or for a variety of reasons, have not been transferred to PCO. This may result from a lack of resources, the inadequacy of filing systems, or the reluctance of some departments to see a highly political entity involved in federal-provincial arrangements which function smoothly at the policy level, but which may be stalled if they become embroiled in more traditional intergovernmental bickering. Another factor that makes the creation of a comprehensive registry difficult is the variety of terms used to describe an intergovernmental agreement. In the PCO registry only, I identified 36 different designations in French and 39 in English.[5]

To this large — but imprecise — number of federal-provincial agreements, we must add interprovincial agreements, which are not included in the PCO registry and which most provinces do not systematically classify. One of the exceptions is Quebec, where for decades copies of IGAs concluded by Quebec have been kept at the Secretariat for Canadian Intergovernmental Affairs in Quebec City.[6] Set up much earlier than the recent federal one, the Quebec registry is much more complete in terms of agreements to which Quebec is party. At the end of 2001, this registry contained over 1,600 agreements, 534 of which were considered to be in force. Because this archival system was established much earlier, the research tools are not as sophisticated in the case of the more recent federal registry, but remain very useful.

PARTIES TO IGAs AND MAIN POLICY AREAS COVERED

Few policy areas are free from intergovernmental agreements. They deal with the environment, health, education, service delivery to Aboriginal communities, transport, natural resources, water management, the promotion of official languages, support to immigrant populations, the labour market, and road constructions. They are particularly common as tools for channelling federal funds for programs managed by the provinces. Because a particular agreement may cover a variety of fields (a construction deal involves both infrastructure and the environment, for instance), both the federal and the Quebec registry file agreements pursuant to departments which are official signatories, and not to policy areas.

Despite the general uncertainty concerning the exact number of IGAs in Canada, it seems likely that there is a greater proportion of "vertical" agreements (federal-provincial ones) than "horizontal" ones (interprovincial agreements). This is partly because IGAs are regularly used as instruments for the federal spending power. Even when federal-provincial agreements have similar objectives, it is not uncommon for the federal government to negotiate bilateral agreements with each province individually, to complete a "framework agreement," for instance. For example, of the 880 federal-provincial agreements found in the PCO registry at the end of 2001, nearly 85 percent were bilateral, and only 13 were actually "Canada-wide"; that is, concluded with all provinces and territories.

NEGOTIATION AND CONCLUSION FORMALITIES

As a general rule, at the federal level, agreements are negotiated by the civil servants who have a functional responsibility for a particular policy area. Only agreements which have a strong symbolic value, are politically sensitive, or involve significant sums of money, will also involve central agencies. An emotionally charged agreement, such as the Quebec-Ottawa one relative to the Millennium Scholarships, would largely be handled by central federal-provincial entities. On the other hand, a local arrangement on fisheries may be handled in a decentralized federal office, in British Columbia, for instance.

Similarly, the level of signatories varies greatly, depending on the strategic significance of the agreement. Some are signed by the prime minister and premiers, others by ministers responsible for the sector at issue, others by senior civil servants. Some agreements are not actually signed, and in a surprisingly large number of cases, the original signed copy cannot be located.[7] The situation is somewhat different in certain provinces, where, with a few exceptions, an agreement may not enter into force until it has been approved by Cabinet and signed the Minister for Canadian Intergovernmental Affairs.[8] This raises interesting legal issues since — technically — an agreement could be considered as in force in another order where there are no such formalities, and not yet in Quebec or Alberta, until the double signature has been obtained.

THE ROLE OF LEGISLATIVE ASSEMBLIES

It is relatively common for legislation to authorize ministers to conclude intergovernmental agreements. This authorization is not a formal legal requirement: the Crown has the inherent power to conclude contractual arrangements, be they of a "private" nature (a deed of sale, for instance) or of a public one (a clarification of roles and responsibilities between governments, for instance, or even international treaties). The authorization serves essentially to identify the minister of the Crown who can act on behalf of the whole executive.[9] Even when they have authorized their conclusion, legislative assemblies are not systematically informed of the negotiations and signature of IGAs. When — exceptionally — they are called upon to approve or ratify an agreement, legislative assemblies are essentially reduced to rubber-stamping a text negotiated by their respective executives. They cannot modify the result of fragile and/or complex intergovernmental political bargaining.

THE PUBLICATION OF IGAs

As a general rule, there is no obligation to publish an intergovernmental agreement. However, if an agreement is implemented through a statute, it may be annexed to it in official publications. An unpublished IGA is subject to the federal *Access to Information Act* or the equivalent provincial legislation. Access may, however, be restricted if it threatens intergovernmental relations.[10] Given the importance of agreements in the conduct of public administration, subjecting public access to this type of procedure raises concerns of democratic accountability. Neither the federal nor the Quebec registry is directly accessible to the public. Plans to put the whole PCO registry on the Internet are on hold for the time being.

This being said, it is obvious that the Internet phenomenon has had an impact here as well. Indeed, as all departments seek to communicate with the public, we now find on web sites agreements that would have been hidden in the filing cabinet of the responsible civil servants only a few years ago. Again, this change of attitude occurred relatively spontaneously, pushed by technology and the new public management ideology, in the absence of a clear legal framework. In other words, for each agreement accessible on the web, dozens of others may not be. Furthermore, nothing ensures that such virtual publication is kept up to date, or that different versions of a document do not circulate on different sites. In other words, IGAs are clearly not subject to the same degree and quality of control as traditional legal norms. To the extent that some agreements are central to policy-making, these discrepancies are problematic.

Again, the practice is somewhat different in Quebec. As was mentioned earlier, with a few exceptions, a government decree is needed for an agreement to enter into force. Decrees are published, although the agreements to which they refer rarely are.[11] Pursuant to the provincial access to public information legislation, anyone can apply to Quebec's Secretariat for Canadian Intergovernmental Affairs (SAIC) for a copy of the agreement. Again, access could be denied if "disclosure would likely be detrimental to relations" between the government of Quebec and another government.[12] The procedure is not simple, but it is nevertheless more transparent than the unsystematic process in place at the federal level.

THE "JUSTICIABILITY" OF INTERGOVERNMENTAL AGREEMENTS

The general purpose of this section is to challenge the general assertion that IGAs are not justiciable. The notion of "justiciability" is a fluid one. An issue will generally be deemed "justiciable" if it is "suitable" or "appropriate" for judicial determination.[13] While the question of the legal enforceability of agreements partakes of the enquiry into the justiciability of agreements, those two notions are not coterminous. As we shall see, some IGAs are binding, while others are not. Yet even when IGAs are not legally binding, they can still play a significant role in the judicial process, as instruments of interpretation, or background for challenged acts of government authorities. The term "justiciable" tends to obscure all these distinctions. Taking "justiciability" in a wide sense, this section examines various ways in which IGAs and the legal and judicial systems intersect. First, I will examine whether IGAs can create legally binding obligations between their signatories. Second, I will consider whether IGAs are binding on third parties, notably citizens, and how citizens have used courts to challenge governmental action relating to IGAs. These first two sub-sections deal essentially with the rights and obligations created, not with the means through which they can be "enforced." The third subsection briefly deals with the issue of the courts of competent jurisdiction, and even more briefly with available legal remedies.

THE STATUS OF IGAs BETWEEN THE GOVERNMENTS WHO SIGN THEM

Are intergovernmental agreements binding in law? Do they create legal — as opposed to political, or even moral — obligations for the governments who sign them? What is the role of courts with regards to IGAs? The blunt and short-cut answer often given by politicians or top civil servants is that intergovernmental agreements are basically "gentlemen's agreements" and that disputes involving IGAs ought to be resolved through the political process. This assertion is generally based on a 1991 Supreme Court reference concerning the *Canada Assistance Plan*. While it is true that in that case, a unanimous court refused to enforce a federal-provincial agreement, it did not deny that agreements can — in some circumstances — be binding between their signatories.

In fact, it is crucial to distinguish between different aspects of the problem. The status of an agreement between the executives who concluded them must be analyzed separately from the power of legislative assemblies to modify or denounce such an agreement unilaterally. Indeed, it is not because Parliament can adopt a law that counters an agreement that the latter is not binding. It may be "fragile" from a legal perspective, but that does not, in itself, preclude it from having some legal force.

SOME ARE, SOME AREN'T

IGAs are not all the same. While most of them are drafted in relatively formal terms, their content varies greatly. In fact, there is a broad range of agreements spread over a wide spectrum of legal status. Some are clearly non-legal, while others are clearly legally binding. The vast majority would appear to fall in the grey zone in between. The determination of their status requires an analysis of their terms, of the context of their conclusion, or the way in which they have been applied. A particular agreement may contain both binding and non-legally binding clauses.

At one extreme, there are "constitutionalized" agreements, which generally governed the "Terms of Entry" for new provinces in the Canadian federation.[14] While there can be serious debates about the exact content of these agreements or the contemporary significance of a particular nineteenth century undertaking, there is no doubt that they have a supra-legislative status.[15] A modification requires the consent of all parties.[16]

Also legally binding are agreements that are very close to "normal" contracts by public authorities: loan agreements, contracts of sale, of lease and so on. The PCO registry lists some — but by no means all — of them. Most of these types of agreements are governed by the law of contract of the province involved (civil law for Quebec, the common law in other provinces). In some cases, the agreements themselves provide that a dispute can be resolved in a court of law. Even when that is not the case, I see no reason why a court would refuse to enforce a loan agreement between two governments, assuming the case is filed before the proper court.

At the other extreme, we find undeniably political agreements, which everyone understands to be fragile until couched in more formal legal instruments. The Meech Lake and the Charlottetown accords were political undertakings, not meant to become law, even between the signatories, until a specified legal process had been followed. As Jacques Bourgault recalls in his contribution to this volume, Frank McKenna, who became premier of New Brunswick after the signature of the Meech Lake Accord, did not feel bound by the "word" (*"la parole donnée"*) of his predecessor Richard Hatfield, and no one claimed that the change of position in New Brunswick violated a legal undertaking.[17]

Agreements drafted in very general terms — such as declarations of intentions, promises to collaborate in the future and so on — are not legally binding either. Again, an analogy can be drawn with private law contracts. A certain number of conditions must be met before an agreement between two private parties constitutes a legally binding contract. Some are drafted in such general terms that they are not enforceable in a court of law. Similarly, vague undertakings by governments to co-operate in a particular field of activity do not create legal obligations by virtue of their content; not because agreements between governments can never be binding.

In between these clearly binding and clearly non-legal agreements lies a vast zone of uncertainty. The status of IGAs depends on a combination of factors that are clues to the "intention" of the parties to the deal to create legal obligations or not. These factors include:

- The subject matter: Some things can never be the object of a binding contract. Individuals cannot sell their organs. An executive cannot contract so as to bind the exercise of its discretionary power to act in the public interest.[18] It cannot contract not to levy taxes, for instance. Nor would an undertaking to promote a particular legislation or to limit the legislature's power to repeal a particular Act be legally binding.[19] However, over the years, courts have given a more nuanced interpretation of the principle pursuant to which an executive cannot "fetter" its own discretion. This is particularly the case in matters that have a commercial connotation, or that bear a close resemblance to the types of contractual arrangements that private parties can engage in.[20] Hence, undertakings couched in very precise terms, particularly if they involve an exchange of money, are more likely to be legally binding. I see no reason why a deal such as "you build a bridge, I give you so much for it" would not be legally binding.

- The kind of language used: Clauses can be drafted in contractual jargon. Others use more "aspirational" language ("X agrees to build a road" *versus* "X undertakes to inform Y in due course concerning any development in this matter"). As a general rule, the use of the verb "shall," in opposition to "will," connotes a legal undertaking, although this is only a guideline.[21] Moreover, there are no standard rules of drafting IGAs, or even guidelines for civil servants, who usually do not have legal training. Consequently, drafting style must be used with caution as an "indicia of legal status."

- Dispute resolution provisions: Another indicator of the parties' intentions to bind themselves in law — or not — is the explicit provision of dispute resolution mechanisms. Explicit resort to a court of law or to arbitration creates a strong presumption that parties intended to create legal obligations. On the other hand, in a large number of agreements, parties agree to resolve their disputes through negotiation, by submitting them to a joint committee and so on. This does not necessarily exclude an eventual recourse to a court of law. But it may. Sometimes "alternative" dispute resolution mechanisms simply take precedence over judicial solutions. Sometimes they oust them. The precise drafting of the clauses must be analyzed in light of all the other indicia.

Courts may be more inclined to find that an agreement is binding between parties if one of them has relied on it to its detriment. In such a situation, concluding that the agreement is not binding in law could result in denying any legal recourse to the "injured" party, sending it back to the political arena. The courts, which are not immune from result-oriented reasoning, can conclude that an agreement is legally binding in such a case, to avoid an outcome that strikes them as unfair. In this case, of course, the determination of the agreement's status would not depend primarily on its drafting, but on the behaviour of each party with regard to that agreement.

In summary, nothing precludes IGAs from creating legal obligations between their signatories; that is, the executive branches of two or more governments, in appropriate cases. The nature of the agreement will depend on the intention of the parties, determined through the types of undertakings, the language used, the means of resolving eventual disputes, or even subsequent conduct (did the parties treat the IGA as binding?). There are certain things that executives can never promise to do, or not to do. Otherwise, executives can contract legal obligations through IGAs. This being said, the doctrine of parliamentary sovereignty can intervene to deprive these intergovernmental "contracts" of their legal effect.

THE IMPACT OF PARLIAMENTARY SOVEREIGNTY

Regardless of a particular IGA's legal status, it is clear that pursuant to Canadian public law, a legislative assembly can always legislate so as to denounce it unilaterally, or adopt statutory instruments that contradict the content of the IGA, provided it does so in clear and explicit terms. In other words, in the Canadian legal system, unilateral legislative action takes precedence over bilateral or multilateral agreements. Again, this does not mean that the agreement does not bind its signatories. It means that nothing precludes a legislative assembly from acting in violation of this agreement. This situation would be unthinkable in some other federal systems.[22] It flows from a very classic interpretation of the principle of parliamentary sovereignty by the Supreme Court of Canada in the *Canada Assistance Plan Reference* in 1991.[23] In order to assess the actual scope of the court's opinion, which is sometimes exaggerated, a brief summary of facts may be useful.

In 1967, a federal Act authorized the government of Canada to conclude agreements with the provinces concerning the federal contribution to provincial social assistance and welfare programs. The federal Act — the *Canada Assistance Plan* — provided that federal contributions would cover half of the provincial social welfare costs. It placed conditions on certain expenditures, but generally left provinces free to establish programming and spending. The Act also provided that the agreements would remain in place as long as the relevant provincial legislation (implementing the agreements) was in place. Within one year, ten federal-provincial agreements had been concluded. Among other things, the agreements dealt with the timing and methods of payment. The formula for calculating the federal contribution was not, however, reproduced in the agreements: it was only included in the federal legislation.

Costs covered by the Act and agreements increased exponentially over a period of 20 years. With half of their costs covered by the federal Treasury, wealthy provinces instituted costly social services. In 1990, wishing to limit this form of "consumer federalism," the federal government unilaterally modified the arrangement, by changing the contribution formula contained in the federal Act. It did not actually modify the agreement, although it was clear that the whole system was altered without provincial consent, and the changes were made without regard to the delays specified both in the Act and in the agreement. Indeed, the federal-provincial agreement provided that each party could terminate it by mutual consent, or after a minimum one year notice. The Act did not, of course, address the rules governing its own amendment. The federal government tabled a bill which set a ceiling (thus the *"Cap on CAP"*) on its contribution to Alberta, British Columbia and Ontario, the three provinces which did not receive equalization payments.

The government of British Columbia tried to stop this unilateral action by addressing two questions to the Court of Appeal of the province, through a reference procedure. The Court of Appeal ruled that no "statutory prerogative or contractual authority" entitled the federal government to modify its obligations pursuant to the federal provincial agreement unilaterally. Furthermore, it found that the doctrine of "legitimate expectations" actually prevented the federal Government from introducing legislation limiting its obligations without the consent of British Columbia.[24] Seized of similar questions by the federal government, a unanimous Supreme Court of Canada gave exactly the opposite answers.

For the Supreme Court, the doctrine of parliamentary sovereignty, which benefits equally the federal and the provincial legislatures, is only restricted by two elements: the constitutional distribution of legislative powers and the charter of rights. Otherwise, legislative assemblies are fully sovereign and can legislate so as to counter the acts of their respective executives. The irony here, of course, is that it was a contracting executive that was tabling the Act that unilaterally modified the federal contribution.

Before the Court of Appeal, the federal government had admitted that it could only challenge an intergovernmental agreement through a legislative instrument. It did not pursue its original argument that the federal government could unilaterally modify its obligations on the basis of the prerogative or principles of government contracts. If the federal government could get out of its obligations, it had to do it by legislative means. In other words, executives may be bound by the terms of an agreement, notably by denunciation clauses that govern the way an agreement may be modified. However, such a clause does not bind legislative assemblies.

The Supreme Court's decision put great emphasis on the fact that most of the wording of the federal Act was replicated in the various IGAs, with the exception of the formula setting the federal contribution, which was only placed in the federal Act. For the court, the parties had to know that putting the contribution formula in the federal legislation, and not in the agreements

themselves, made it subject to (unilateral) amendment. Similarly, the contribution formula was not inserted in the regulations that were — exceptionally —
subject to provincial consent, but in a federal Act, which was not. For the
court, this scheme implies that:

> In lieu of relying on mutually binding reciprocal undertakings which promote
> the observance of ordinary contractual obligations, these parties were content to
> rely on the perceived political price to be paid for non-performance.[25]

This is so, *not* because an IGA cannot bind the governments that are parties
to it, but because of the particular arrangements in this case, which put one of
the fundamental clauses of the "deal" not in a "contract," but in a unilateral
statute. In other words, the court held that the complex federal-provincial arrangements that involved an IGA as well as federal and provincial legislation
could be modified by unilateral legislative action. It did not make a general
statement that no intergovernmental agreement could ever be legally binding.
It stated the obvious, that such an agreement is not an "ordinary contract,"[26]
but it did not deny that in other circumstances, an IGA could give rise to legal
obligations or that courts could have jurisdiction to rule on a conflict arising
from the implementation of an IGA. In other words, it is not because legislative assemblies are "sovereign" that executives cannot be bound at law.
Executives only have the significant advantage of being able to introduce legislation to put an end to their obligations.

This ability does not negate the legal status of the agreements, although it
leaves this legal status ultimately fragile. In fact, this possibility of using the
legislature is consistent with rules governing clearly legally binding government contracts. In Canada, a legislative assembly can always legislate so as to
put an end to a contract concluded between the executive branch and a private
citizen, a company, another order of government or a foreign power.[27] An
executive, however, cannot adopt regulations to put an end to its own contractual obligations unless it has express legislative authority to do so.[28]

This trick in the hand of the executive was recently criticized by Supreme
Court of Canada in a case that did not involve an IGA, but an employment
contract between a public official and the government of Newfoundland. Some
of the findings are, however, of interest for our purposes. Very briefly,
Mr. Wells, a member of a Public Utilities Board, lost his job when the legislature restructured the institution. The Supreme Court admitted that the
legislature could legislate so as to abolish the board, and thus the Commissioners' positions. It held, however, that the executive, which sets the legislative
agenda, could not argue that it was impossible to honour Wells' labour contract on the grounds that the law had changed. The Newfoundland government's
argument seemed particularly cynical since it could have reappointed Wells
to the board that replaced the one that was being abolished, and chose not to.

The court recognized that the separation of powers is an essential feature of the Canadian constitutional system. However, it added:

> The government cannot ... rely on this formal separation to avoid the consequences of its own actions. While the legislature retains the power to expressly terminate a contract without compensation, it is disingenuous for the executive to assert that the legislative enactment of its own agenda constitutes a frustrating act beyond its control.[29]

Moreover, the Newfoundland government had issued a directive pursuant to which the complainant would not receive compensation. True to its interpretation of the principle of parliamentary sovereignty, the Supreme Court held that a *legislature* has the "extraordinary power," through clear and explicit language, of legislating to deny compensation for the breach of a government contract.[30] But the *executive* party to that contract could not do so, especially not through a directive. The discretionary power which governments enjoy to act in the public interest does not imply that an injured party may not receive proper compensation. The party may not be entitled to the "specific performance" of the contract (in this case, the job), but to financial compensation (which is what the complainant was seeking anyhow).

Are the *CAP Reference* and this decision reconcilable? In *CAP*, precluding the federal government from introducing a bill risked paralysing the legislative process, which raises obvious problems in a democracy. Governments — and legislative assemblies — must be allowed to alter policies. This does not imply, however, that they can do so with impunity, and that parties to government contracts are not entitled to compensation for these changes of policy. In *Wells*, the Supreme Court clearly stated that Newfoundland was fully entitled to abolish a board, and as a consequence, to terminate an employment contract. What it could not do was to act so as to deny compensation for a clear breach of contract, unless it did so through a very clearly worded statute. For the court:

> There is a crucial distinction, however, between the Crown legislatively avoiding a contract, and altogether escaping the legal consequences of doing so.... In a nation governed by the rule of law, we assume that the government will honour its obligations unless it explicitly exercises its power not to.... To argue the opposite is to say that the government is bound only by its whim, not its word. In Canada, this is unacceptable, and does not accord with the nation's understanding of the relationship between the state and its citizens.[31]

How this analysis could eventually affect a dispute relative to an IGA, as opposed to a contract between a government and a private party, is open to speculation. What is particularly striking, however, is that in *Wells*, the argument that the executive constitutes an integral part of the legislative process was reinterpreted so as to avoid a result that appeared abusive. Governments can, notably through their control of the legislatures, get out of contracts. However, in so doing they may be liable to pay damages.[32] Again, to the extent that an IGA was held to create legal obligations as elicited through the language of the agreement and the behaviour of the parties, I would argue that the court's concern with the rule of law should extend to legally binding intergovernmental agreements.

CONSTITUTIONAL CONVENTIONS, PRINCIPLES OF FEDERALISM AND
LEGITIMATE EXPECTATIONS

In the *CAP Reference*, several provinces intervened to support British Columbia's position. They argued that a convention existed pursuant to which neither Parliament nor the legislatures would legislate so as to "unilaterally alter their obligations" with regard to cost-sharing agreements.[33] The court replied that the questions to which it was asked to respond did not include the existence of a constitutional convention, with the exception of the doctrine of legitimate expectation, which of course it found to be inapplicable to the facts of the case. For the court, Justice Sopinka declared, rather abruptly, that "the existence of a convention, therefore is irrelevant and need not be considered further." The court did not actually deny the existence of such a convention: it simply refused to consider the issue. This refusal suggests that the court was uncomfortable with the argument, particularly since it did reply to two questions which — the court expressly admitted — had not been properly raised either.[34]

Before the court, Manitoba also argued that an "overriding principle of federalism" precluded unilateral federal legislative action. The argument went as follows. Since federal authorities have no constitutional power in matters of social welfare, their financial contribution to the provinces can only be founded on the federal spending power. Once it has agreed to spend money in an area of provincial jurisdiction, the federal authorities cannot unilaterally revoke its support without that province's consent because of the disruption caused in this sphere of provincial jurisdiction. The court rejected this argument in a summary fashion, noting that it could not control the use of the spending power. It refused to delve any further into the role that "federal principles" may have played in the matter.

Again, this summary dismissal by the Supreme Court does not imply that it would never find such principles of federalism in other contexts. In fact, "principles of federalism" made a noted *grand début* (or coming back) in the *Secession Reference*, together with the "duty to negotiate" which was certainly not included in the questions that the federal government had addressed to the court.[35] Some cynics could intimate that federal principles could not be found in the interstice of constitutional law to limit federal power in its dealing with provinces, but that they could be discovered to restrict the autonomy of a province, admittedly in a more dramatic political situation.

In my view, the *CAP* decision raised fundamental *constitutional* as well as political questions concerning the workings of a federal system, and the court's refusal to consider the existence of federal principles or constitutional conventions is regrettable. Indeed, the federal government's unilateral action has had a serious impact on the conduct of federal-provincial relations since then, and perhaps even more on the spirit that guides them. It also explains the genesis of the interprovincial initiative to harness this unilateralism through the original Social Union project.[36] There is no doubt that the Supreme Court's decision strengthened the power of each order of government to "go it alone," to the extent that it has the financial capacity to do so. This is strangely dissonant with the rhetoric of interdependence that prevails in federal circles.

However, as I have sought to demonstrate, it is important to take into consideration the particular fact pattern of the *CAP Reference*. The crucial financing clause was not contained in the intergovernmental agreement but in a federal Act. Moreover, the "injured" parties in that case were "rich" provinces that had more sophisticated social programmes than "poorer" ones, partly because those programmes were financed in half through transfers from federal coffers. This did not make them particularly sympathetic, as demonstrated by their opposition to Wells, for instance. Nevertheless, it bears pointing out that Saskatchewan and Manitoba, provinces which were not directly affected by the modification to the funding formula, as well as Aboriginal groups, intervened in favour of the three "rich" provinces. They sought to strengthen respect for the "given word" (and even more for the "given written word") in intergovernmental relations. I would not exclude that in other circumstances, and with the renewed interest in the principles of federalism, the court could render a more nuanced opinion.

In the *CAP Reference*, a majority in the British Columbia Court of Appeal held that the province had a legitimate expectation that the federal government would not unilaterally alter its obligations by the introduction of a bill into Parliament. The Supreme Court was much more circumspect. First, it rejected any application of the substantive legitimate expectation, which would give an order of government a substantive veto on legislative action of another one. Secondly, it also rejected the "procedural" version of the doctrine, pursuant to which a party with a reasonable expectation that a certain conduct will continue, or a certain procedure will be followed, is entitled to be consulted before any alteration to this conduct or procedure. For the court:

> It is fundamental to our system of government that a government is not bound by the undertakings of its predecessor. The doctrine of legitimate expectations would place a fetter on this essential feature of democracy.[37]

In the context, it is difficult to determine whether the "essential feature of democracy," which the court alludes to here, is parliamentary sovereignty or the rule against the fettering of *executive* discretion. It bears repeating that the

BC government had not suggested that Parliament could not legislate so as to counter the agreement. Rather, it sought to prevent the executive from introducing a bill that had that effect. With regard to the rule against the fettering of discretion, the quotation from the court overstates the case. What is impermissible is not for the executive to contract, but for it to contract not to introduce legislation, or to contract to introduce specific legislative measures. As we saw in the previous subsection, an executive can bind its successor, but not in all matters.

In *CAP*, the Supreme Court did not speculate as to the application of the doctrine of legitimate expectations when an executive is not acting as a conduit in the legislative process, but in its purely executive or administrative function. In other words, the case does not deny that a government party to an IGA could have legitimate expectations that the other party would respect it. It is interesting to note that the architects of devolution in the United Kingdom admitted that while intergovernmental agreements concluded in the wake of the devolution process would not be legally binding per se, there would a legitimate expectation that they would be respected.[38] Statements by British and Scottish politicians are obviously not binding on Canadian courts. However, it is worth considering whether the potential influence of the doctrine of legitimate expectations in the UK in the context of intergovernmental agreements could eventually lead to a reconsideration of the issue in Canada.

CONSTITUTIONALIZING IGAs

The potential evolution of judicial interpretation raises the possibility that conventions, principles of federalism or legitimate expectations could eventually strengthen the status of IGAs. But my advice to policy-makers and government negotiators would be not to bet on such an evolution. For the time being, while IGAs bind their signatories, they remain fragile in the face of the sovereignty of the various legislative assemblies. A few options could be envisaged to consolidate the status of IGAs. One of them lies in the "constitutionalization" of IGAs.[39]

If IGAs are granted a "constitutional" status, the hierarchy of norms would have to be altered. IGAs would be located at the same level as other constitutional norms (if they are completely constitutionalized), or located "below" the constitution, but above legislative norms. This way, parliamentary sovereignty would no longer be restricted only by fundamental rights and the formal distribution of powers, but also, in some cases, by agreements concluded between orders of government. Placing IGAs "below" the constitution would ensure that IGAs are subject to the *Charter of Rights and Freedoms* and would preclude orders of government from formally altering the distribution of powers without due respect for the amending formula.

Such a "constitutionalization" could be done on a case by case basis by placing a particular agreement in the constitution. This was envisaged both in the Meech Lake and Charlottetown accords with regard to federal-provincial immigration agreements.[40] This process gives a relatively permanent character to agreements, as their modification would have to follow a process similar to a constitutional amendment.

Alternatively, or in addition, a general clause could be inserted in the Constitution enabling parties to grant a special "supra-legislative" status to a particular IGA. Parties would state in the agreement that they wish it to be subject to the relevant clause of the constitution and then submit the agreement to their legislative assemblies. The ensuing "entrenchment" could be set for a fixed period — five, ten, or twenty years, for instance, to strike a balance between legal security on the one hand, and democratic flexibility on the other. In the meantime, an agreement would be binding on executives and legislative assemblies. It could be modified, but only by mutual consent. This was the approach advocated in the Charlottetown Accord.[41]

The 2001 constitutional programme of the Quebec Liberal Party favours — in the "long term" — both the firm "constitutionalization" of the Quebec-Ottawa Immigration Agreement, as well as the insertion of a clause in the Constitution that would allow it to opt for a "supra-legislative" status on a case by case basis, for a period of five years.[42] This "constitutionalization" à la carte would thus require parties to reflect and agree on the degree of entrenchment they wish to confer on an agreement.

IGAs AS "SOFT LAW"

So far, this section has been devoted to demonstrating that IGAs can — under certain circumstances — legally bind the governments that sign them. This being said, it is crucial to note that even when agreements are not formally binding as law, they can have an effect very similar to that of ordinary legal norms.

An agreement may not be legally binding because the parties' intention *not* to create legal obligations is undeniable. For instance, they may have even written that their agreement binds them "in honour only." Or its status may be doubtful because a required formality was disregarded. It may not have been signed,[43] or its official expiration date may have passed. Officially, an agreement may provide that it only enters into force following a certain event or a certain period, yet be applied before that.

Agreements that are not binding because they lack the "indicia of legal status," or because some formality has not been complied with, may nevertheless have a "soft law" status. They are negotiated, drafted, interpreted, implemented and respected as if they were legally binding.[44] IGAs govern the behaviour of civil servants and of all actors involved, including third parties. In fact, the majority of civil servants I interviewed were convinced that the agreements they were working with were legally binding, while the majority of senior civil servants thought the opposite! Regardless of the actual legal status of the Quebec-Ottawa Agreement on Immigration, all potential immigrants are governed by its content: Quebec selects and favours French-speaking applicants, while Ottawa applies security and health conditions. Until a "hard" legal rule is used to counter it, an IGA can have the same impact as legislation, without having that formal character and often with far less public scrutiny.

CITIZENS, INTERGOVERNMENTAL AGREEMENTS AND THE LAW

There is no doubt that IGAs have an effect on third parties, notably citizens. An IGA to fix the border between federal land (a harbour) and provincial land (the surrounding area) will determine which legislation applies. So would an agreement to set a maritime boundary between two provinces. An egg producer may be affected by quotas set up through co-operative schemes, in which IGAs play a key part. And, as was just mentioned, potential immigrants to Quebec are clearly affected by the Quebec-Canada Immigration Agreement. When agreements are concluded between public authorities, there is always an impact on the public. That impact may be more or less direct. This is true whether the agreement is legally binding between its signatories or not.

Given that the focus of this book is intergovernmental institutions, this chapter deals primarily with the status of IGAs between government parties that sign them. However, the slow, hesitant, but in my view, undeniable evolution of the courts' attitude concerning intergovernmental agreements warrants a short foray into their status with regard to third parties, notably citizens. While governments may wish to keep agreements out of court, citizens and interest groups may force them to justify their actions before judges. In this section, I will only sketch some of the ways in which courts have allowed third parties to resort to the legal system to control what are often deemed mere "political instruments."

Citizens may engage judicial institutions on a variety of issues concerning intergovernmental agreements, although procedural and financial hurdles are significant and sometimes prohibitive. Over the years, courts have permitted third parties to challenge the way agreements are concluded, interpreted, implemented, or the impact they have on the formal distribution of powers. The logic of allowing citizens to challenge instruments that affect them may be patently obvious to any student of public policy. However, this logic offends the conventional judicial understanding of agreements, which oscillates between denial of legal status (leading to judicial refusal to interfere) and the application of classic rules of contract law, which would leave very little remedy to those who are not direct parties to an agreement. It is therefore not surprising that the relevant case law has mostly — though not exclusively — developed since the adoption of the Charter, which has heralded a more interventionist attitude on the part of courts with regard to governmental functions. I will outline four different ways in which citizens have managed to bring agreements to the attention of the courts.

First, third parties have successfully argued that they are not bound by the terms of an intergovernmental agreement, unless it has been incorporated into a formal legislative instrument. In other words, governments cannot modify legislation through IGAs. In the *Anti-Inflation Reference* of 1976, the Supreme Court of Canada denied that an agreement could render federal norms on wage control applicable to the Ontario public service.[45] The Supreme Court admitted that governments can conclude agreements that legally bind them without specific legislative authorization. However, a proper statute is required to make the content of the IGA binding on third parties. Otherwise, governments would be able "to legislate in the guise of a contract."[46] The actual legislative technique and language required to render an agreement formally binding on third parties is still subject to controversy. There are no clear drafting guidelines and the case law on the subject is limited.[47] In 1999, a Quebec Court ruled that the simple legislative approval of the Internal Trade Agreement by the legislative assembly did not amount to a proper incorporation. As such, the agreement did not have supremacy over provincial legislation and regulation.[48] The uncertainty concerning the status of agreements that *may* have the same normative value as formal legislation is astonishing.

Second, while not party to the "contract," third parties have nevertheless been granted standing to challenge the interpretation and implementation of an intergovernmental agreement. In 1986, the Supreme Court of Canada recognized that citizens may have a stake in the execution of an agreement, even when the governments that are party to it tacitly agree to derogate from it, or at least when one of the parties closes its eyes to a loose interpretation by the other one.[49] In fact, third parties are more likely to have an interest when governments agree on a particular interpretation of an agreement that seems to deviate from their initial intention or from the text. In this case, a recipient of social assistance argued that the Manitoba authorities did not respect the terms of the *Canada Assistance Plan* agreement concluded between the federal government and the province. While Mr. Finlay lost his case after nearly two decades and a string of court rulings, a significant development resulted from his judicial adventures.[50] The Supreme Court admitted that, under certain conditions, citizens may resort to the legal system to interfere with a course of action by governments that is essentially political.

Third, an interest group has recently sought judicial intervention to prevent a federal minister from concluding federal-provincial agreements, which implied, so the argument went, an abdication of federal responsibilities in the field on environmental protection.[51] This group also lost on the merits of the case. The Federal Court of Canada ruled that the impugned agreements contained such vague undertakings that they did not amount to an actual surrender of competences. What is significant for our purposes, however, is that the court did allow the group to state its case: it did not reject the application on grounds of lack of interest or standing. It did not rule out that the legal system could interfere in what the federal government argued was, again, a purely non-legal arrangement. The case shows that fairly classic administrative law doctrines can be invoked by third parties to challenge agreements that are not formally legally binding on them, but which clearly affect them.

Finally, citizens have successfully argued that intergovernmental agreements may not have the effect of encroaching upon their fundamental — in this case, linguistic — rights.[52] Since the early 1990s, the federal government has delegated to provinces and municipalities that are willing, the responsibility to issue contraventions and prosecute violation of federal Acts. At issue was whether the federal *Official Languages Act* and the linguistic protection found in the federal Criminal Code continued to apply, or whether the process would henceforth be covered by provincial second language legislation. The Federal Court of Canada ruled in favour of the first option.[53] In other words, when the federal government transfers the exercise of some of its own powers to a province, the latter must respect the linguistic rights that were heretofore protected through federal legislation.

The situation is much more complex when the field of activity that is "transferred," or more precisely "re-transferred" to the province through an agreement, is not a clearly federal matter, but a matter in which the federal government had previously been involved on the basis of its spending power. In such a scenario, it is the provincial linguistic regime that will apply, because the matter falls within provincial jurisdiction.[54] The formal distribution of powers thus has a significant impact on linguistic rights. In that context, drawing clear "constitutional" boundaries has concrete consequences for the public, even when governments actually prefer to maintain blurred lines. This is another illustration of judicial intervention catching up with political actors.

FINDING THE RIGHT COURT ... AND REMEDY

While the judicial system is not closed to disputes concerning IGAs, one of the challenges is to find the appropriate forum. Here again it is useful to distinguish between challenges to the validity or the implementation of IGAs by third parties on the one hand, and disputes concerning the violation of an IGA by one of the signatories. The first would raise administrative, and occasionally constitutional, principles. In the second, the issue is more clearly "contractual." In the first case, issues of "legal standing" of the person (or body) who wishes to contest an issue related to an IGA may be raised. In the second, courts will easily admit that parties to an IGA have standing to request its application, but may raise doubt as to the legal nature of the instrument.

The Canadian federal system is essentially dualist, meaning that each order of government is independent from the others in institutional — if not in policy — terms. Each has its legislative assembly and its own administration.[55] The position of courts in this scheme is more intricate. Ordinary legislative or administrative instruments or decisions made unilaterally by any order of government may be challenged in a number of ways before specific judicial or administrative courts. When such norms and acts result from a concerted action of several orders of government, there may be a "judicial vacuum." Complex alternatives must then be sought.

At this stage, a minor technical incursion is needed to explain the deficiencies of the judicial system in dealing with intergovernmental agreements. In addition to the provincial courts that each province is free to set up, and the Federal Court, which the federal government has created largely to oversee the legality of federal administrative action, there are provincial Superior Courts that enjoy very broad general power. Provincial Superior Court and Appeal Court judges are named by the federal government, but they originate from the province in question. The Supreme Court, whose nine judges are also appointed by the federal government, reigns in final appeal over all of them.

This complex web of divided jurisdiction is poorly adapted to challenge co-operative schemes. In the *Canadian Environmental Law Association* case discussed above, the federal court weakly hinted that it may not have jurisdiction to hear a direct challenge concerning the legality of an IGA. However, it held that it had jurisdiction over decisions of a *federal* minister concerning the *conclusion* of an *intergovernmental* agreement. Unilateral acts of provincial authorities relative to an IGA can similarly be challenged through the regular administrative law process applicable to review the validity of provincial administrative acts and decisions. Finlay had to attack the Manitoba government's decision to recoup the overpayment before the Manitoba courts and, then he had to challenge the federal government's decision to transfer funds to Manitoba before the federal court.

Litigation between parties to an agreement on the existence, interpretation, validity or implementation of that IGA is even more complicated. Here, it is crucial to distinguish between two aspects of the question that are often conflated: the determination of the "justiciable" nature of the agreement on the one hand, and the identification of the court of competent jurisdiction on the other. In the first case, the question is whether the dispute is purely political and should be shielded from judicial intrusion. In the second one, the question is one of the proper judicial forum for hearing the actual case.

Assuming that an IGA is legally binding between its signatories — because it meets a sufficient number of criteria for legal status — which court would have jurisdiction? As a rule, and in a very sketchy manner, an action between provinces should be launched in the Superior Court of the defending province. The same would be true of an action by the federal government against a province for violation of a federal-provincial agreement. An action against the federal government by another government may be launched before the Federal Court.[56] Particular problems would arise if a challenge were to be initiated against several provinces, or against both the federal and a provincial government.[57]

Luckily, some IGAs outline specific dispute resolution mechanisms. Hence, the Internal Trade agreement contains its own detailed process for resolving disputes that circumvents the "traditional" judicial system.[58] Other IGAs contain arbitration clauses. For instance, a Canada-wide agreement on milk pooling provides for a variety of dispute resolution schemes, ranging from reference to a management committee, to conciliation and finally, to arbitration panels.[59] In fact, one of the first decisions concerning an IGA — the wartime taxation agreements — was rendered by a three member arbitration tribunal.[60]

Other IGAs confer jurisdiction to "regular" courts to resolve disputes, if non-judicial methods have failed. This is the case of a number of IGAs through which the federal government finances legal services offered by the province in relation to criminal law and the *Young Offenders Act*. The agreements contain financial clauses as well as standards of legal services to be maintained. All agreements contain clauses pursuant to which non-judicial avenues should first be sought to revolve "disagreements." Failing that, however, a dispute can be referred to the Federal Court or the Superior Court of the province.[61]

Finally, Article 19 of the *Federal Court Act* provides that "controversies" between the federal government and a province, or between provinces, may be submitted to the Federal Court, to the extent that a provincial legislative instrument has recognized this jurisdiction. This is a fairly old attempt to circumvent the dualist nature of the Canadian judicial system.[62] In this way, the Federal Court acts as a sort of arbitrator of intergovernmental relations. Recourse to Article 19 is rare, but does occur. The limited recourse to Article 19 may be explained by a number of reasons.

First, the judicial resolution of disputes in general, and of intergovernmental disputes in particular, is not frequent to start with. Second, Article 19 is only available to governments, not to third parties. Third, many of the "actors" involved do not even seem aware of the possibility of filing an application to the Federal Court in this context. Fourth, while judges of a provincial Superior Court are named by the federal government, as are judges of the Federal Court, at least the former originate from that province. A province may be reluctant to submit a "controversy" between itself and the federal government to judges named by the latter and who may not even have a connection with the province. Arguably, in the case of an interprovincial disputes, submitting the case to a court outside provincial jurisdiction instead of filing it with in the Superior Court of the defending province, could appear advantageous. Yet resort to the Federal Court in this context is not frequent either.[63] Nevertheless, despite the scarcity of cases submitted pursuant to this section, this "intergovernmental forum" has the virtue of existing.

It should be underlined that the federal court's jurisdiction is not limited to legally binding agreements. The dispute could be political in nature, to the extent that it needs to be resolved "in accordance with some recognized legal principles." In other words, it would appear that the Federal Court could have jurisdiction to hear a dispute based on the doctrine of "legitimate expectations," for instance. While in the *CAP Reference* the Supreme Court denied that the doctrine could apply to prevent a government from introducing a bill, it did not pronounce on the applicability of the doctrine to other acts of government. The Federal Court could also have jurisdiction to clarify constitutional issues such as a determination of the constitutional foundation of responsibilities that are "administratively transferred" to a province pursuant to an IGA. In other words, through an Article 19 application, the Federal Court could apparently have proceeded with an analysis similar to that of the *Contravention* and the *Lavigne* cases, which had been initiated by third parties (assuming, of course, that the province at issue has officially recognized the jurisdiction of the Federal Court).

Finally, of course, governments can use the reference procedure to seek a judicial opinion on an issue relative to an IGA. A province can address constitutional questions to its Court of Appeal, and the federal government can directly ask questions to the Supreme Court. This, of course, is what happened in the *Anti-Inflation* and the *CAP* references. In the latter, the court held that the issues had "a sufficient legal component" to justify judicial intervention. Principles of constitutional and administrative law were involved, as well as the interpretation of a statute and of a federal-provincial agreement. In other words, the interpretation of an intergovernmental agreement is a proper judicial function, at least when they are implemented through legislation. The Supreme Court also noted that its decision would assist in resolving the controversy by settling the legal questions and that "there is no other forum in which these legal questions could be determined in an authoritative manner."

Finding the proper court is not, however, the only problem. Once the proper forum has been identified, which remedies are available? When third parties challenge the implementation of an IGA, it would appear that classic administrative remedies should be accessible. This includes, for instance, the annulment of a decision made to implement an IGA, and even potentially an injunction against the government acting in contradiction to the terms of an IGA.[64] In the *Contravention case*, the Federal Court ordered that the agreements be amended within one year to include explicit language rights protection, lest they become "void." The court also issued a declaration that the federal government had not complied with the *Official Languages Act* in delegating the exercise of certain competences to a province without guaranteeing language protection. In the *Canadian Environment Law Association* case, the interest group was similarly seeking a declaration that the minister had acted without proper authority.

When a case raises contractual issues between parties to an IGA, remedies could range from traditional contractual ones (such as the payment of damages)[65] to a "declaration" that one party violated its terms of an agreement. This could include a declaration that government B is entitled to some financial compensation. Such declaratory judgements cannot be executed by a court. In other words, even if a court found in its favour through a declaratory judgement, wronged province B could not seize property of province A in satisfaction of this judgement. Nevertheless, judicial "declarations are invariably honoured by governments."[66] Of course, the remedy in a reference procedure is the court's opinion, which although not binding, is also (almost) invariably respected by governments.

IGAs AS TOOLS OF PARA-CONSTITUTIONAL ENGINEERING

Intergovernmental agreements can play a variety of functions in federal systems.[67] They are central to most fields of public activity in multi-layered political systems. The policy areas in which they are commonly used is apparently endless. They can used to articulate the exercise of exclusive — but closely connected — competences. This is the case of arrangements linking the federal power over unemployment insurance and the provincial power over labour training, for instance. They can also be used to sort out responsibilities, in order to avoid duplication, in the case of concurrent or shared powers. IGAs on environmental protection would largely fall within that category. They can be used to co-ordinate policy initiatives. They are used to co-finance projects, and are key instruments for channelling federal funds in areas of provincial jurisdiction. As such, they are the nuts-and-bolts of the spending power. In fact, policy coordination appears to be the primary function played by IGAs in Canada.

While the main purpose of IGAs is to coordinate and finance policy initiatives, others outline procedural mechanisms of co-operation. In this case, the question is not "Who does what?" or "Who pays for what?" but rather, "How do we each exercise our own competences? How do we consult, communicate and resolve our disputes?"[68] Of course, many agreements will involve both substantive and procedural aspects. Of the 880 agreements classified in the PCO registry, 595 contain "management committee" clauses. The Canada-wide Accord on Environmental Harmonization is a prime example of an IGA which sets out general principles of co-operation meant to guide governments in the elaboration of more precise arrangements.

In this final section, I would like to explore another role played by IGAs in the Canadian federal system, that of constitutional engineering. Indeed, apart from these policy coordination and procedural roles, agreements also play a number of latent, less transparent, "para-constitutional" functions. First, IGAs can alter the *exercise* of constitutional powers. Second, IGAs are useful instruments for blurring constitutional boundaries, even when they delineate administrative responsibilities between orders of government. Regardless of their official status, IGAs are products of negotiations. As such, they can reflect power game and constitute tools of federal *"realpolitik"* between orders of government. IGAs also serve as alternatives to unattainable constitutional reforms. Finally, I will conclude by arguing that no matter how hard parties to an agreement may seek to avoid difficult constitutional issues, when an IGA modifies constitutional practice, it plays an undeniable "constitutional engineering" function. Circumventing the constitution is never constitutionally neutral.

MODIFYING THE EXERCISE OF CONSTITUTIONAL POWERS

As the *Anti-Inflation* case illustrates, governments cannot modify the formal distribution of powers through an IGA. Hence, provinces could not, individually or collectively, transfer jurisdiction over education, health or intraprovincial transportation to the federal government. However, agreements can enable governments to delegate functions to one another, thus modifying the *exercise* of constitutional competences.[69] An IGA may also structure a trade off through which one order of government confers some benefit — generally financial — on another, in exchange for an undertaking to respect a number of conditions.

While a scheme pursuant to which the federal government mandates a province to ensure compliance with certain federal statutes is not unconstitutional, it does involve a certain degree of constitutional remodelling. It transforms an essentially dual federal system into an administrative one.[70] No constitutional rule is violated. Yet, because of the essentially dual nature of the Canadian federal system, this type of arrangement raises a number of complex issues, ranging from ministerial responsibility (which of the federal or provincial minister would be responsible for the error of a provincial officer applying federal legislation?) to civil liability (who would be liable if the fault of this officer causes some injury to a citizen?).

Another way in which IGAs serve to modify the exercise of constitutional power lies in the use of IGAs as conduits for the spending power. By making transfers conditional on the respect a certain conditions, the federal government does not directly legislate or regulate a provincial matter. However, in so doing, it can undoubtedly influence the actual exercise of provincial powers by their rightful holder. Again, examples abound and range from previous conditional grants in the field of social security (the *CAP*) to infrastructure projects and second language programs in schools.

IGAs AS INSTRUMENTS FOR BLURRING CONSTITUTIONAL BOUNDARIES

While IGAs can serve to sort out roles and responsibilities between orders of government, particularly in areas of shared jurisdiction (as should be the case with the environmental agreements), they can also have the effect of blurring the lines of the formal distribution of powers. In the era of "multi-level governance," where interdependence is seen both as a practical necessity and as a value, clarifying constitutional borders is often considered an obsolete or passé exercise. Surprisingly, the strongest proponents of interdependence are the orders of government for whom a particular distribution of powers is either an obstacle (because they want to get involved in an area over which they do not have legislative authority) or irrelevant (because they are unable or unwilling to assume full responsibility for a matter falling within their jurisdiction). For them, IGAs can serve to sort out "who does what" regardless of who actually has the formal constitutional competence to act. Again, in this context, Quebec is often the odd one out, clinging to a more classic and dual view of the Canadian federation.

In some cases, opposition on matters of principle may be set aside if a text is drafted so that each party can interpret it in a way consistent with its official constitutional position. In some cases, the conclusion of a particular IGA may depend on a certain degree of constitutional ambiguity. Ambiguity may be a virtue for the parties to the agreement. Again, the Canada-Quebec labour-market agreement offers an interesting illustration. Parties do not characterize the agreement quite in the same way. The federal government maintains that parts of it serve to implement the federal *Employment Act*. With a minor exception, Quebec disagrees and posits that the policy areas covered are not founded on the federal power relative to unemployment, but on the provincial powers over education and labour policy for which Quebec receives federal funds grounded on the federal spending power. In fact, the federal *Employment Insurance Act* is not even mentioned in the Quebec-Ottawa agreement. For Ottawa, this does not mean it is irrelevant. For Quebec, this omission has symbolic and constitutional significance.

Through this negotiation strategy, parties have agreed to disagree on characterization, and elaborated a text that they could both interpret in view of their own constitutional and legal positions. IGAs are sufficiently pliable to allow for this "double-reading" phenomenon. Yet, as we have already seen with the *Lavigne* case, even when parties to an IGA prefer the blurred solution, the need for constitutional clarification may be unavoidable, if the rights and interests of third parties are affected.

IGAs AS TOOLS OF *REALPOLITIK*

The law of contracts and of international treaties are both founded on an assumption of equality between parties. The schism between theory and reality can of course be tremendous. Contractual arrangements of any nature are potentially subject to power relations. In most cases, the agreements that result will reflect the power of signatories, in terms of material, financial, legal or political resources. The same is true of IGAs. Regardless of their actual legal status, they are negotiated as contractual arrangements and they can reflect power games between orders of government: "You have the money; we have the constitutional power; you need public visibility, we need infrastructure; you want to be involved in a particular policy area, we need more autonomy in order to put another policy in place...."

But as is the case with any contractual arrangement, inequality of bargaining power may result in one party making an offer to another one "which it cannot refuse." Agreements used in the context of the spending power are particularly prone to this type of bargaining. Rejecting such an arrangement may result in depriving the population of services, for which it may even have paid taxes. This could be costly in terms of electoral politics, and have negative consequences in terms of social policy.

Given the permissive attitude of the courts regarding the federal spending power,[71] and given the needs of their populations, provinces find it hard to resist a federal incursion into their sphere of jurisdiction when it is accompanied by significant financial contributions. Principles yield to *realpolitik*. The threat of the spending power acts as an incentive for provinces to reach agreements. From that perspective, IGAs reflect actual imbalances in the federation. They can also exacerbate such imbalances.

On the other hand, even when the federal government can "go it alone," it may find that politically, it is preferable to reach an agreement with a province. This would appear to be the case with the agreement between Quebec and Ottawa regarding the Millennium Scholarships. Even if the Quebec government objected to the Scholarships scheme, it probably could not have stopped the federal government from actually putting it into place independently, in parallel to its own bursary program. Politically, however, both parties felt that an agreement was preferable. In the end, Quebec managed to avoid most direct transfers to individuals and to ensure that the federal funds were used to complement its own means-tested system. *Realpolitik* is not necessarily a one-way street.

IGAs AS AN ALTERNATIVE TO CONSTITUTIONAL REFORM

Because of their flexibility and the limited degree of parliamentary and public scrutiny to which they are subjected, IGAs are often called to play another "para-constitutional" function: that of alternatives to constitutional reform. This is frequent in some federations, in which constitutive units will conclude agreements to avoid the transfer of a competence to central authorities. IGAs of this type play a certain "defensive" function: they serve as an "antidote" to centralization.[72]

Of course, in Canada, where constitutional reform is considered beyond reach in the foreseeable future, IGAs cannot serve as an alternative to a real threat of constitutional amendment. They can, however, be used to obviate the need for such a transfer. In other words, intergovernmental agreements enable governments to structure their relations so as to bypass hard constitutional issues, or to find pragmatic solutions that would be inaccessible in more visible and politically charged constitutional negotiations. Paradoxically, one may wonder whether the very existence of IGAs may not actually reinforce the belief that constitutional reform is both impossible and unnecessary. IGAs can thus not only serve as an alternative to constitutional reform, but also as a pretext for avoiding them.

The labour-market agreements demonstrate another "para-constitutional" function of IGAs. The regime put in place is remarkably asymmetrical, with provinces able to opt for one of three models of varying degree of decentralization.[73] In the current political context — in which "asymmetry" is officially anathema — such a system could never have been established through official constitutional reforms. IGAs have an opacity and an apparent temporary nature which enable governments to actually do what they cannot officially endorse. Moreover, this can be accomplished without much public or parliamentary scrutiny (in fact, it may be possible precisely because of this limited public scrutiny).

"NON-CONSTITUTIONAL" STRATEGIES ARE NOT ALL
"CONSTITUTIONALLY NEUTRAL"

In her contribution to this present volume, Julie Simmons notes that the Canada-wide Accord on Environmental Harmonization, the National Child Benefit, the labour market agreements, the Agreement on Internal Trade and the Social Union Framework Agreement have become synonymous with the non-constitutional rebalancing approach.[74] While I agree with the diagnosis, I would not term this trend as "non-constitutional," an expression which suggests that constitutional norms are irrelevant.

In fact, the transformation of federal practice through which partners rearrange responsibilities outside the framework of official constitutional rules is not constitutionally "neutral." "Administrative" agreements to that effect do not necessarily clarify constitutional powers. In the long run, even IGAs that are not legally binding can, through their "soft law" impact, modify constitutional practice and legitimize the role of one order of government in a particular field over which it does not actually enjoy official jurisdiction. Some critiques of SUFA argue that by agreeing to minor restrictions on the exercise of the federal spending powers, provinces that have signed the agreement (all but Quebec) have actually consolidated further the legitimacy of a federal presence in some areas of exclusive provincial responsibility.[75]

All the IGAs that gravitate around the SUFA initiative partake of this "para-constitutional" engineering process. In many cases, a blurring of the constitutional distribution of powers coincides with a certain clarification of administrative responsibilities. In other words, it is possible for governments to decide on "who does what" regardless of "who is constitutionally competent to do what." This can lead to a marginalization of sections 91 to 95 of the *Constitution Act, 1867*. Circumventing the distribution of powers — even an admittedly gravely dated distribution — is far from constitutionally neutral. It is one thing to hail the era of a new "collaborative federalism"; it is another to modify the dualist nature of the Canadian federation. If policy imperatives favour an evolution from the dualist system, we have seen that tools of political and legal accountability have not quite followed. The tension this informal reordering is creating is not constitutionally neutral.

Similarly, the use of IGAs to introduce asymmetrical solutions is not constitutionally neutral for those who seek an *official* recognition of the legitimacy of asymmetrical federalism. Nor is it constitutionally neutral for those opposed to asymmetry as a matter of principle. It is a constitutional ordering that either does not speak its name or that develops completely outside the official process of constitutional rule making. These "para-constitutional" engineering techniques may be effective from a policy perspective, and they are certainly preferable to complete paralysis. Nevertheless, in my view, they raise serious concerns in term of legal stability, respect for the constitutional ordering and the (federal) rule of law.[75]

CONCLUSION

Intergovernmental agreements govern a wide spectrum of co-operative schemes in the Canadian federal system. In addition to being helpful devices for co-ordinating service delivery and procedural co-operation between various orders of government, IGAs also play a number of para-constitutional functions: they are used to modify the exercise of constitutional powers, to avoid clarifying frontiers of constitutional jurisdiction, and to make asymmetrical arrangements that would be politically difficult to sell were they to be constitutionalized. Indeed, they are used as alternatives to constitutional reforms that the partners in the federation cannot — or do not wish to — pursue. As one of the main conduits for the federal spending power, they are undeniable tools of *realpolitik* in the federation.

The flexibility of IGAs is their main virtue. They are almost infinitely malleable and can be modelled to respond to particular technical needs and political constraints. As instruments of executive federalism par excellence, however, IGAs do have the effect of strengthening the executive at the expense of the legislative branch. The significant recourse to intergovernmental agreements, both from qualitative and quantitative angles, raises a number of concerns in terms of the stability of intergovernmental relations, accountability, and transparency. While unilateral legislative instruments follow a complex and well-known process, and are examined in parliamentary commissions, IGAs are more prone to bureaucratic arrangements and back room negotiations. The effectiveness of this approach is not to be underestimated. But neither should the costs in terms of public accountability.

IGAs and the law already intersect in a number of ways. Depending on the legislative technique used, IGAs can be binding on third parties. Even when they are not formally binding, the vast majority of IGAs affect the interest of citizens in some ways. Transferring administrative responsibilities from one order of government to another may seem like a simple internal, administrative, and technical arrangement. But, as we saw, such a transfer can have significant consequences on the language rights of citizens, or simply of the clarity of administrative and political responsibility. Of course, intergovernmental agreements often result from harsh, prolonged negotiations, and translate fundamental political interest. Yet, to the extent that IGAs have a significant normative value, there is no reason in principle why these "cooperative norms" should be better protected from judicial review than are regular (unilateral) administrative acts.

Over the last two decades, the courts have shown a greater openness towards third parties that seek to challenge the conclusion, implementation and even content of IGAs, all of which is to be encouraged. In an age of "Charter citizens" who have learned to appeal to judges to protect their rights, it seems plausible that citizens and public interest groups are increasingly going to turn to courts as a means of controlling the ever-growing impact of executive federalism. Whether parties to an agreement want it or not, and whether judges themselves welcome the trend or not, IGAs are finding their way to court. Increasingly, judges are struggling to find ways of providing effective judicial review in relation to instruments which used to be understood as contracts from which third parties were considered uninterested outsiders, or as political devices to which judicial deference was owed.

In the recent past, courts have had fewer opportunities to refine their positions on the binding character of agreements between the governments who sign them. Agreements range from aspirational, political, general undertakings, which can hardly be enforced in a court of law, to contractual arrangements, which the courts (assuming the proper forum is identified) should not have any difficulty in executing. The determination of the status of the large number of agreements that fall somewhere between these two extremes is a matter of interpretation, which is not an unusual judicial enterprise.

Regardless of their actual status between the parties that conclude them, there is no doubt that pursuant to the actual Canadian system, legislative assemblies may always legislate so as to explicitly counter an agreement. Options for securing agreements against unilateral legislative modification or denunciation include a more sophisticated judicial treatment of IGAs than has been provided so far — notably through a recourse to unwritten principles of federalism — manner and form limitations, and "temporary and voluntary constitutionalization." Enshrining agreements implies granting them a supra-legislative status. This would obviously strengthen the role of courts in guaranteeing that unilateral legislative and regulatory norms of each order of government comply with the terms of a co-operative agreement.

This being said, the Canadian judicial system, which has effective mechanisms for controlling the legislative and administrative action of each order of government acting independently, is particularly ill-equipped to control co-operative schemes. Unless governments, legislators and courts were to collectively and explicitly determine that IGAs should be protected from judicial interference, these significant technical difficulties will have to be addressed.

Judicial review to protect the rights of citizens, eventual court actions by parties to administrative agreements, or legal challenges to ensure respect for eventually constitutionalized agreements are all essentially *a posteriori* interventions. The potential contribution of law to the practice of IGAs could also be envisaged *a priori*.

For instance, an explicit legal framework governing the conclusion, ratification, modification, publicity and archiving of IGAs would increase their visibility. This would not resolve all outstanding legal difficulties and uncertainties. It could, however, assist negotiators in addressing a number of issues that would render the process and the end-product more predictable and transparent. Such a legal framework could lead to the development of more a careful, precise and standardized use of language in the drafting of IGAs. Provisions for systematic (or at least widespread) publicity should be made. A number of potential dispute resolution mechanisms could be outlined.

The role of legislative assemblies with regard to IGAs should be clarified. Provisions concerning the circumstances requiring parliamentary assent would be helpful. So would the specification of the legislative language required for agreements to have a particular standing *inter partes*, as well as with regard to third parties. Should IGAs be explicitly discussed in parliamentary commissions? In this context, it bears pointing out that the recent and innovative Quebec legislation pursuant to which major international agreements touching upon provincial powers must be approved by the National Assembly does not extend to IGAs.[77] Hence, Quebec parliamentarians may be called upon to vote on international trade agreements, but not on labour market agreements with Ottawa, or on an agreement with Ontario concerning the mobility of construction workers. Should not this laudable legislative initiative be extended to IGAs? Even more ambitiously in terms of democratic control would be a process pursuant to which parliamentarians could actually be associated in their negotiations, so that their role is not limited to rubber-stamping *faits accomplis* by the executives.

Of course, improved accountability, transparency and legal stability come at a cost, in terms of flexibility and speed of process. There is little doubt that given the opportunity, the executive branch of government prefers to act without public, parliamentary or judicial scrutiny. In the face of dogmatic opposition to what is perceived as an assault on the "equality of provinces," asymmetrical arrangements may be more difficult to conclude if they become "entrenched" albeit for a limited period of time. Finally, foreign experience shows that even when agreements are governed by a clear legal framework, parties may attempt to circumvent the process in order to escape the very controls and publicity that attach to formal agreements. In other words, responding to concerns of stability in intergovernmental relations and public accountability through a more defined legal framework is not a panacea, but it may partake of the overall treatment. Nor am I suggesting that the judicial route is to be favoured over political or "new public management" methods of public responsibility. I am simply arguing that legal techniques also are, and should be, part of the accountability arsenal.

Law and IGAs already intersect in many, but often misty, ways. The main thrust of this chapter was to identify some of these points of intersection. In a country founded on the rule of law, instruments that are used to blur constitutional boundaries and reorganize the federation on the margins of the constitution, even in the name of effective governance, ought to be taken seriously. In a federation, the (federal) rule of law ought to be paramount. In this context, the crossroad between intergovernmental agreements and the legal system should not only be acknowledged, but also welcomed.

NOTES

A number of officials have generously shared information with me and answered endless questions. I thank them for their time and trust. I particularly wish to thank the Privy Council Office in Ottawa and the *Secrétariat des Affaires intergouvernementales canadiennes*, in Quebec City, for giving me access to their respective data banks of intergovernmental agreements. My thanks also go to two anonymous reviewers, and to Hamish Telford and James Crawford for helpful comments and suggestions. Finally, I wish to acknowledge the financial support of the Social Sciences and Humanities Research Council of Canada, the International Council for Canadian Studies and the University of Montreal, which enabled me to conduct this research, as part of my doctoral dissertation.

1. Some authors have addressed particular legal aspects related to IGAs: Katherine Swinton, "Law, Politics and the Enforcement of the Agreement on Internal Trade," in *Getting There: The Agreement on Internal Trade*, eds. Michael J. Trebilcock and D. Schwanen (Toronto: C.D. Howe Institute Toronto, 1995), pp. 196-210; Nigel Bankes, "Co-operative Federalism: Third Parties and Intergovernmental Agreements and Arrangements in Canada and Australia," *Alberta Law Review* (1991):792-838 and "Constitutionalized Intergovernmental Agreements and Third Parties: Canada and Australia," *Alberta Law Review* 30 (1992):524-55; Lara Friedlander, "Constitutionalizing Intergovernmental Agreements," *National Journal of Constitutional Law* 4 (1994):153-67; Steven A. Kennett, "Hard Law, Soft Law and Diplomacy: The Emerging Paradigm for Intergovernmental Cooperation in Environmental Assessment," *Alberta Law Review* 31 (1993):644-61; Susan Blackman, *Intergovernmental Agreements in the Canadian Administrative Process* (Ottawa: Department of Justice, Research and Statistics Directorate, 1993); Andrée Lajoie, *Contrats administratifs: jalons pour une théorie*, (Montreal: Editions Thémis, 1984).

2. Notably in Quebec, Alberta and Newfoundland, see *infra*.

3. At this stage, the expression "in force" is not limited to the legal status of IGAs, but also refers to the status of non-binding agreements that are properly concluded and — apparently — respected by parties to them.

4. Given the elaborate research tools developed with the PCO data bank (and the numerous criteria through which agreements can be identified) it is regrettable that there is no reference to applicable legal provisions or even to case law dealing with particular agreements.

5. Including "licensing agreement," "co-operative action framework," "transfer agreement," "memorandum of agreement," "memorandum of understanding," and "loan agreement."

6. There is also a centralization process in Alberta and Newfoundland.

7. Puzzled, a Federal Court judge described a written but unsigned agreement between the Ontario and federal governments as an "oral" or "draft" agreement: *Commissioner of Official Languages* v. *Canada (Department of Justice)*, F.C.T.D., T-2170-98, 23.03.2001, par. 68 and 193 [hereinafter referred to as the *Contravention* case].

8. In addition, where relevant, signature by the minister responsible for the particular matter at stake may be required: s. 3.9, *An Act Respecting the Ministère du Conseil Exécutif*, S.Q., c. M-30. Along the same lines, see Schedule 6 of the *Alberta Government Organization Act*, RSA 2000, ch. G-10, which also provides that an IGA must be approved by the Department of International and Intergovernmental Relations in order to be enforceable, and s. 7 of the *Intergovernmental Affairs Act*, RSNFL 1990, ch. I-13.

9. This was a crucial element in the *Canadian Environmental Law Association* v. *Minister of the Environment*, T-337-98, F.C.T.D., affirmed without reasons by the Federal Court of Appeal: 05.06.2000, A-446-99, discussed in the Impact of Parliamentary Sovereignty section earlier in this chapter, hereinafter, the *CELA* decision.

10. S. 14, *Access to Information Act*, R.S.C. 1985, ch. A-1.

11. The SAIC web site now lists IGAs to which Quebec is a party.

12. *An Act Respecting Access to Documents Held by Public Bodies and the Protection of Personal Information*, R.S.Q., ch. A-2.1. The government could also refuse access on the basis that "disclosure would likely be detrimental to relations between the Gouvernement du Québec and another government: *ibid.*, s. 19. Similar procedures are no doubt in place in provinces which keep systematic copies of IGAs as well.

13. Lorne Sossin, *Boundaries of Judicial Review: The Law of Justiciability in Canada* (Toronto: Carswell, 1999), pp. 2 ff.

14. See also the "Natural Resources Agreements" which were constitutionalized in 1930. Bankes, "Co-operative Federalism: Third Parties and Intergovernmental Agreements and Arrangements in Canada and Australia." Because of their particularities, this chapter does not deal with agreements of various sorts (treaties, conventions and so on) concluded between governments and Aboriginal groups.

15. Bankes, "Co-operative Federalism." See, also for instance, *The Queen (Canada) v. The Queen (P.E.I.)*, [1978] 1 F.C. 533 (F.C.A.), on the nature of the federal obligation to provide ferry service. See also *B.C. Railway case, supra,* in which an agreement annexed to a federal Act was held not to enjoy "constitutional" status.

16. And may require a formal amendment procedure (art. 43 of the *Constitution Act, 1982*): Bankes, "Co-operative Federalism," pp. 529 and 533.

17. Jacques Bourgault, "Quebec's Role in Canadian Federal-Provincial Relations," in this volume. Although it could also be argued that the Meech Lake Accord was not binding not because of its content, but simply because the procedure agreed upon for its entry into force was not complied with.

18. *Rederiaktiebalaget Amphitrite* v. *R.*, [1921] 2 K.B. 500; *Commissioner of Crown Lands* v. *Page*, (1960) 2 All E.R. 724 at 735; *R.* v. *Dominion of Can. Postage Stamp Vending Co.*, [1930] S.C.R. 500; Perry v. Ontario (1997) 33 OR(3d) 705 (Ont. CA).

19. G.H.L. Fridman, *The Law of Contracts in Canada*, 4th ed. (Toronto: Carswell, 1999), p. 29.

20. *South Australia* v. *Commonwealth* (1961) 108 C.L.R. 130 at p. 154. On this question, see Sue Arrowsmith, *Government Procurement and Judicial Review* (Toronto: Carswell, 1988), pp. 126-130.

21. In French, this distinction is reflected in the use of the present as opposed to the future tense. For the Supreme Court of Canada, the verb "shall" can be "directory" and not "mandatory": *B.C. Railway case, supra.* See also par. 16 of the Federal Court's decision in *CELA, supra.*

22. Such as Switzerland (through a combination of constitutional norms and case law) or Germany (through the principle of federal loyalty).

23. *The Canada Assistance Plan,* [1991] 2 R.C.S. 525 (hereinafter referred to as *CAP Reference*).

24. *Re Canada Assistance Plan*, 1990], 46 B.C.L.R. (2d) 273 (B.C.C.A.).

25. *Re CAP Reference*, p. 554.

26. Ibid., p. 553.

27. *Wells* v. *Newfoundland*, [1999] 3 S.C.R. 199.

28. *Cité d'Outremont* v. *Commission de Transport de Montréal*, [1955] Q.B. 753; Patrice Garant, *Droit administratif*, 3d ed. (Montréal: Yvon Blais, 1991), p. 465.

29. *Wells* v. *Newfoundland*, p. 220.

30. Patrick Monahan argues that the rule of law may act as a proper limit on parliamentary sovereignty in this context: "Is the Pearson Airport Legislation Unconstitutional? The Rule of Law as a Limit on Contract Repudiation by Government," *Osgoode Hall Law Journal*, 33 (1995):411-52.

31. *Wells* v. *Newfoundland*, pp. 216, 218.

32. Of course, one may wonder if the risk of incurring damages may not thwart public policy. This raises issues of balance between legal certainty and democratic governance. On this, see Peter W. Hogg and Patrick Monahan, *Liability of the Crown*, 3rd ed. (Toronto-Calgary-Vancouver: Carswell, 2000), pp. 220-29.

33. *CAP Reference*, p. 561.

34. The issues of "manner and form" (raised by Aboriginal groups) and of the federal legislative competence (raised by Manitoba): *CAP Reference*, pp. 561-67.

35. *Re the Secession of Quebec*, [1998] 2 S.C.R. 217.

36. Up to the Saskatoon consensus: text reproduced in Alain-G. Gagnon and Hugh Segal, *The Canadian Social Union Without Quebec: 8 critical analyses* (Montreal: Institute for Research on Public Policy, 2000), pp. 227-41.

37. *CAP Reference*, p. 559.

38. Richard Rawlings, "Concordats of the Constitution," *Law Quarterly Review* 16 (2000):257-86 and Johanne Poirier, "The Functions of Intergovernmental Agreements: Post-Devolution Concordats from a Comparative Perspective," *Public Law* (2001):134-57.

39. Another possibility may be the adoption of certain "manner and form" limitations through which Parliaments may bind their successors not on substance, but on procedure. See Swinton, "Law, Politics and the Enforcement of the Agreement on Internal Trade."

40. Meech Lake Accord, proposals for insertion of new ss. 95A to 95E to the *Constitution Act, 1867*.

41. Charlottetown Accord, 1993, art. 26, which would have inserted a new s. 126A in the *Constitution Act, 1867*. The Beaudoin-Dobbie Commission had made a similar recommendation. Note that only federal-provincial agreements were envisaged. I see no reason why the process could not be made available for interprovincial agreements.

42. Parti Libéral du Québec, *Un projet pour le Québec: affirmation, autonomie et leadership*, Rapport final, Oct. 2001, pp. 83-85 and 160.

43. In the *Contravention case, supra*, the Federal Court appeared mystified by the status of an agreement, which should have been signed, but was not. The court nevertheless ordered that his "oral" or "draft" agreement should become void unless it was amended within one year so as to explictly provide for the linguistic protection of the Criminal Code and the *Official Languages Act*: par. 193-194. The official explanation for the absence of signature was that both parties "thought it preferable to test the procedures before signing the agreement"!

44. Whatever the status of the Canada-Ontario agreement in the *Contravention* case, it was undoubtedly being applied by both parties.

45. In that case, a provincial minister had been authorized to sign the agreement by an Order-in-Council, rather than by an Act: this, held the court, was insufficient to alter the Ontario labour legislation. *Re Anti-Inflation Act*, [1976] 2 S.C.R. 373.

46. Ibid., at p. 435 (emphasis added).

47. Hence, a year after the pronouncements of the majority in the *Anti-Inflation Reference*, another slim majority of the Supreme Court ruled that general statutory language authorizing the conclusion of an IGA was also insufficient to alter Manitoba's legislation. *Re Manitoba Government Employees Assoc.* v. *Manitoba*, [1978] 1 S.C.R. 1123. The Supreme Court has also held that an IGA approved and ratified by statute does not necessarily acquire the same status as the Act: *B.C. Railway case, supra*.

48. *U.L. Canada Inc.* v. *A.G. Québec*, [1999] R.J.Q. 1720 (S.C.). On the variety of drafting techniques to implement agreements (and their respective normative impact): see Bankes, "Co-operative Federalism," pp. 813-33.

49. *Finlay v. Canada (Minister of Finance)*, [1986] 2 S.C.R. 607. Contrast with: *Re Lofstrom and Murphy*, (1971) 22 D.L.R. (3d) 120 (Sask. C.A.).

50. The first decision of the Manitoba Court of Appeal was rendered in 1976, while the final pronouncement on Finlay's situation was made by the Supreme Court in 1993: *Re Finlay and Director of Welfare (Winnipeg South/West)* (1976), 71 D.L.R. (3d) 597 (Man. C.A.) and *Finlay v. Canada (Minister of Finance)*, [1993] 1 S.C.R. 1080. In the meantime, he had been before the Manitoba courts and the Federal Court of Canada.

51. This was a crucial element in the *CELA decision, supra*. For a discussion of these agreements, see Julie Simmons in this volume, "Securing the Threads of Co-operation in the Tapestry of Intergovernmental Relations: Does the Institutionalization of Ministerial Conferences Matter?"

52. Linguistic rights enjoy "quasi-constitutional" status in Canada: *R. v. Beaulac*. [1999] 1 S.C.R. 768 at pp. 788-89.

53. *Contravention* case, supra.

54. *Lavigne v. Human Resources Development et al.*, 2001 FCT 1365 (F.C.T.D.).

55. Although, as we saw, delegation of administrative functions to another order of government is permissible.

56. In some cases, claims of limited financial value can be filed before provincial courts.

57. Because of the doctrine of "interjurisdictional immunity": Hogg and Monahan, *Liability of the Crown*, p. 352. This doctrine is slowly evolving, however: Janet Walker, "Interprovincial Sovereign Immunity Revisited," *Osgoode Hall Law Journal* 35 (1997):379-97.

58. Art. 1702-1710, *Internal Trade Agreement*. With one exception: the constitutionality of retaliatory action may be submitted to a court of law: art. 1710(10). Available at <www.intrasec.mb.ca/index-he.htm>.

59. Multilateral Agreement on All Milk Pooling.

60. *Re Taxation Agreement Between the Government of Saskatchewan and the Government of Canada*, (1946) 1 W.W.R. 257.

61. For instance, art. 22(2) of the *Alberta-Canada Agreement Respecting Legal Aid in Criminal Law Matters and in Matters Relating to the Young Offenders Act*, Jan. 1997, provides that a dispute may be referred to the Federal Court. In the case of Quebec, disputes can be brought before the Superior Court (same article of the Canada-Quebec agreement).

62. There may be some doubt at to the constitutionality of this section: Hogg and Monahan, *Liability of the Crown*, pp. 362-63; Lajoie, *Contrats administratifs*, pp. 176-181.

63. The Federal Court may even lack the constitutional power to rule on interprovincial disputes.

64. In *Finlay no 2* (1993), *supra*, Justice McLachlin diss. but not on this issue, at pp. 1120-21. On the possibility of judicial injunctions against governments, see: Pierre Issalys and Denis Lemieux, *L'action gouvernementale*, ed. Yvon Blais (Cowansville, Canada, 1997), p. 1006ff.

65. In *Re Taxation Agreement Between the Government of Saskatchewan and the Government of Canada* (1946), 1 W.W.R. 257, the arbitration tribunal applied the doctrine of "set-off" (compensation of one debt by another).

66. MacGuigan J.A. in *Finlay* v. *Canada (Minister of Finance)*, [1990] 2 F.C 790 (F.C.A.) at p. 816, cited with approval by Justice McLachlin, diss., in *Finlay no. 2 (1993)* at p. 1120, without opposition on this issue by the majority.

67. I have explored elsewhere in greater detail the multiple functions — both explicit and implicit — played by intergovernmental agreements in federal regimes: Poirier, "Concordats of the Constitution," *supra*.

68. See, for instance, the Canadian Intergovernmental Agreement Regarding the North-American Agreement on Labour Cooperation at <http://labour.hrdc-drhc.gc.ca/psait_spila/aicdt_ialc/nao/cia//index.cfm/doc/english>.

69. While the delegation of legislative function is unconstitutional law, this is not the case of delegation ,of administrative responsibilities from one order of government to another: Joseph Eliot Magnet, *Constitutional Law of Canada: Cases, Notes and Materials*, 7th ed. (Edmonton: Juriliber, 1998), pp. 85-107.

70. This includes the German or the Swiss federations, where the federal government has a limited civil service, federal laws being mainly implemented by the bureaucracies of the constitutive units.

71.   Over the years, courts have established only one condition: the spending by one order of government must not "in its essence" amount to regulation of a matter falling within the competency of the other order. See *YMCA* v. *Brown* [1988] 1 SCR 1532 at 1549.

72.   The most recent example is the inter-cantonal *Conférence universitaire suisse*, meant to avoid the transfer of competence concerning university education from the cantons to the federal government.

73.   Provinces can opt for one of three models: T.R. Klassen, "The Federal-Provincial Labour Market Development Agreements," in *Federalism, Democracy and Labour Market Policy in Canada*, ed. T. McIntosh (Montreal-Kingston: McGill-Queen's University Press, 2000), pp. 158-203.

74.   Simmons, "Securing the Threads of Co-operation."

75.   André Tremblay, "Federal Spending Power," in *The Canadian Social Union Without Quebec: 8 Critical Analyses*, eds. Alain-G. Gagnon and Hugh Segal (Montreal: Institute for Research on Public Policy, 2000), pp. 170-71.

76.   For a similar argument, see Jean-François Gaudreault-Desbiens, *The Canadian Federal Experiment, or Legalism without Federalism? Towards a Legal Theory of Federalism*, forthcoming.

77.   *An Act respecting the Ministère des Relations internationales and other legislative provisions*, RSQ, ch, M-25.1.1, s. 2.2.

16

Inter-Legislative Federalism

David Cameron

Signalant la domination de l'autorité exécutive dans la conduite des relations intergouvernementales au Canada (fédéralisme exécutif), le chapitre suggère que la législature y contribue. Il fait état de plusieurs réformes possibles, et conclut qu'une telle initiative pourrait renforcer modestement la démocratie canadienne en améliorant le fonctionnement du fédéralisme, favorisant la performance gouvernementale et accroissant l'unité nationale.

INTRODUCTION

This chapter has its origins in an article Richard Simeon and I wrote for the Canadian Centre for Management Development a couple of years ago on intergovernmental relations and democratic citizenship.[1] While struggling with ways in which the Canadian intergovernmental system might be reconciled a bit better with democracy, open government and public accountability, we wrote a couple of paragraphs on enhancing legislative federalism. Noting that powerful institutional forces — in particular, the tyranny of party discipline and the failure of the Canadian Senate — sharply limited the capacity of legislatures to play a role of any consequence in monitoring intergovernmental relations, or to act as arenas of public debate about federal issues, we proposed several modest reforms aimed at strengthening the role of legislatures in intergovernmental relations.[2]

It was some time after that that I came across C.E.S. (Ned) Franks' excellent paper, "Parliament, Intergovernmental Relations and National Unity." Originally prepared in 1997 for the Privy Council Office, it appeared in amended form as a Queen's Institute of Intergovernmental Relations Working Paper in 1999.[3] Happily, a revised version appears in this volume as "A Continuing Canadian Constitutional Conundrum: The Role of Parliament in Questions of National Unity and the Processes of Amending the Constitution." Franks' work is a thorough and creative consideration of what might be done to strengthen Parliament's role in intergovernmental relations and its contribution to national unity. Recognizing the structural tensions between parliamentary government and federalism, it focuses on the weakness of Parliament and the consequent feebleness of Parliament's intergovernmental role, engendered by, among other things: the domination of the executive and party leaders; excessive partisanship; short-term amateur membership in the legislature; and the well-known problems associated with the Canadian Senate. Franks puts forward some proposals for reform, none of which require formal constitutional amendment. He divides his reform proposals into two categories: incremental improvements designed to make "the present structures of national decision-making work more effectively"; and a far-reaching set of revisions designed to shift the whole system in the direction of a more consensual form of government.[4]

Franks is far from naïve; he is not inclined to concoct abstract schemes with little connection to real-life concerns. Writing originally in the aftermath of the Charlottetown debacle and the 1995 Quebec referendum, there was a sense of urgency in his analysis, and he made a convincing case that our institutional constraints shackle our capacity to cope effectively with many of the federal and national-unity challenges we face. As he says:

> Canada has made the least reforms to its machinery of parliamentary democracy of any of these countries [Britain, Australia and New Zealand], yet it also suffers from the worst stresses and risks of disintegration. These two phenomena are not unconnected.[5]

Nevertheless, he cites sympathetically Donald Smiley's pessimism about expanding the capacity of Canadian legislatures to influence the processes of executive federalism,[6] and his rejection of proposals that would require formal constitutional amendment is a sign of his effort to keep ideas for improvement in the realm of the possible. Franks' remark, however, that, in terms of institutional reform, "Canada has proven to be the most conservative of all parliamentary governments,"[7] is intriguingly ambiguous: it might be understood as an indicator of pessimism, or alternatively as a comparative indicator that Canada ought to regard itself as having a wide latitude for innovation should it develop a genuine taste for reform.

PROPOSAL

It was clear to me upon reading "Parliament, Intergovernmental Relations and National Unity" that I had nothing useful to add to this sophisticated study. It had pretty systematically canvassed the ways in which our federal Parliament might be given an increased role in the practical management of the federation. But that study and my work with Richard Simeon got me thinking. What if it were possible for federal, provincial and territorial legislatures to find a means of working in concert on certain common issues, thereby supplementing the dominant processes of executive federalism? What about what might be called "inter-legislative federalism"?

Let me explain. The business of the federation is currently carried out via the fluid processes and lightly institutionalized organizations of executive federalism, in which first ministers, Cabinet ministers and public officials negotiate — or fail to negotiate — arrangements providing for the matters in which both orders of government have an interest and responsibility. Stéphane Dion, Minister of Intergovernmental Affairs, makes the point well in a speech comparing the German and Canadian federal systems:

> In Canada, the absence of a parliamentary forum that would institutionalize the relations between the two orders of government means that federal-provincial co-operation is conducted almost exclusively by the executive branches: the first ministers and the federal and provincial ministers meet regularly to coordinate their actions. They consult and inform one another of legislative or other initiatives they intend to take.[8]

Much of what Canada's governments have achieved over the years has been accomplished through these mechanisms of executive federalism, but no student of the Canadian federation would fail to acknowledge their serious deficiencies. Donald Smiley's searing critique still rings true more than two decades after he wrote it:

> My charges against executive federalism are these:
>
> - First, it contributes to undue secrecy in the conduct of the public's business;
> - Second, it contributes to an unduly low level of citizen participation in public affairs;
> - Third, it weakens and dilutes the accountability of governments to their legislatures and to the wider public.[9]

Roger Gibbins is not alone in contending that the recent trend toward more collaborative forms of executive federalism — reflected, for example, in the negotiation of the Social Union Framework Agreement in 1999 — has, if anything, worsened the problem by obscuring yet further what is effectively one of the country's critical decision-making processes, and by removing it still more from effective popular and legislative control. Parliament is locked out; the provincial and territorial legislatures are locked out; and so are Canadian citizens.[10]

Inter-legislative federalism — that is to say, the development of relationships among Canadian legislatures, perhaps focused on key intergovernmental issues — might be of some assistance in opening up the enclosed world in which federal, provincial and territorial politicians and officials conduct the business of the Canadian federation. By so doing, it might also in time contribute to shifting our executive-driven legislatures at least a short distance along the continuum toward a legislative-centred model of legislatures.

As Franks points out, a central problem with our system of intergovernmental relations, and one that many believe is getting worse,[11] is the degree to which the processes of executive federalism escape the legislative accountability which lies at the heart of our system of responsible government. This is related to the strength and autonomy of the executive branch in our system — at both levels. And a central problem with our legislatures — federal, provincial and territorial — is their general weakness and their incapacity to impose accountability on governments and leaders. This too is related to the strength and autonomy of the executive branch in our system. Given the high importance of intergovernmental relations in Canada, then, the search for stronger lines of accountability linking intergovernmental processes back to legislatures is a top agenda item for reform. In addition, there exists the problem of the accountability of both executives and legislatures to citizens and to the public — accountability in another form. This tangle of accountabilities, then, is at the core of the issues I am seeking to address in this chapter. Inter-legislative federalism could open up both the intergovernmental relations system and the legislative processes to some extent, making executives more accountable to the people's representatives in their respective legislatures, and making the political system itself more open and accountable to the public.

What are the prospects for this reform idea? *Prima facie*, there is little reason to believe that its fate will be any different than that of a dozen other reform proposals in the general area that have fallen victim to Canada's institutional conservatism and the natural preference of its political leaders to retain a system of which they are the prime beneficiaries.

- There have been impressive analyses of our electoral system and our party system, and their deleterious impact on responsive government and national unity, but the old ways live on in splendid contempt for the vain attempts to make some positive change.[12]

- I read my first proposal on Senate reform when I was a callow undergraduate at the University of British Columbia; I cannot count the number of proposals for Senate reform that have passed before my glazed eyes since then. Yet the Senate endures, untainted by renovation.

- There have been frequent measures proposed for the improved operation of Parliament itself, designed to invest it with more autonomy, and greater life and purpose, but the changes actually effected in response to these proposals have been modest, and laments about the irrelevance of Parliament have continued unabated.[13]

A reforming zeal appears for the most part to have passed our provincial assemblies by as well. Franks makes the following comment:

This paper has considered parliamentary government at the federal level, but much of what has been said also holds true, indeed is more true, for the provincial level. Executive domination, amateur short-term membership, weak opposition, ineffective committees, in many ways are exacerbated in provincial legislatures. This, when coupled with the importance of provincial premiers and a few key ministers in executive federalism, gives rise to a federal-provincial dynamic that does not properly or truly reflect the complexity and divisions of opinion within the provinces.[14]

The partial exception to this rule seems to be the National Assembly of Quebec. For many years, it has been my belief that Quebecers have operated the British parliamentary system — adapting it to their own unique needs while respecting its genius — better than any one else in the country. At moments of high importance the National Assembly has been the unquestioned, central institutional focus of the people of Quebec, and the cockpit of democracy in that community.[15] The National Assembly has also, I think, exercised its duty of holding the executive to account better than have other legislatures in this country.[16] It has innovated in some of the institutions and processes it has established.[17]

As Peter Dobell points out, Quebec has adopted a number of practices that are "carefully designed to enhance the opportunities for deputies to play a meaningful role and to promote a more co-operative relationship between government and opposition parties."[18] Contrasting the very limited contribution that Canadian legislatures make to institutional innovation with the more substantial role played by legislatures in Great Britain and most European countries, Dobell singles out Quebec as an exception. A reform package approved by the National Assembly in 1984 overhauled the committee system. Members of the opposition chair four of the National Assembly's ten committees. Chairs and vice-chairs are elected by a double majority, which is to say, by separate majorities of both government and opposition committee members. The plan for the committee's business, developed by the chair and co-chair, who are from opposite sides of the assembly, is again confirmed by a double majority vote. Committee membership is stable, usually lasting for the life of the assembly. Unlike Ottawa, the relevant minister usually joins the committee for its deliberations when his or her legislation is being discussed. As Dobell remarks, these and other reforms have "generated a more co-operative relationship between the parties, more frequent amendment of legislation in committee, and greater 'job satisfaction' for deputies."[19]

Quebec aside, however, the prospects for reform *within* Canadian legislatures have, until recently, appeared to be dishearteningly poor; all the more difficult, then, is it to believe that the introduction of unfamiliar innovations *between and among* legislatures is possible to achieve. If Parliament and our provincial assemblies are unequivocally executive-dominated, rather than legislative-centred, and if, further, Canadians and their governments have consistently displayed a rock-ribbed resistance to innovation, then proposals for deepening and expanding relations between and among legislatures face forbidding odds. Indeed, given that the initiatives considered in this chapter would be more readily accomplished to the extent that the participating legislatures inclined more to the legislature-centred end of the continuum than to the executive-centred end, we seem to have multiplied the difficulty, rather than diminishing it.

Yet there are some signs of change. For starters, there appears to be a growing interest among our political and policy elites in democratic reform, including the reform of our central political institutions. Conferences, projects and reports assessing the state of democracy in Canada and prescribing modest to far-reaching change are legion. Only a few can be cited here. The influential Institute for Research on Public Policy (IRPP) has devoted considerable resources to conferences and publications on the theme "Strengthening Canadian Democracy."[20] Under the auspices of the Canadian Studies Programme at Mount Allison University, a large team of researchers is producing a multivolume series examining Canadian government and politics under the rubric of "The Canadian Democratic Audit."[21] The Law Commission of Canada has a major project underway on electoral reform,[22] while organizations as diverse as the Fraser Institute, Elections Canada, the Centre for Research and Information on Canada, the Canada West Foundation and the Canadian Policy Research Networks have organized conferences or commissioned reports to assess Canadian democracy and attempt to improve it. Among the groups actively lobbying for democratic reform are Democracy Watch, Fair Vote Canada and the Canadian Taxpayers Federation. A steady stream of books — including contributions from left- and right-wing writers, prominent journalists, academics, engaged citizens and others — address questions of democracy in Canada: Gordon Gibson's *Fixing Canadian Democracy*, Judy Rebick's *Imagine Democracy*, Jeffrey Simpson's *The Friendly Dictatorship*, Donald Savoie's *Governing from the Centre* and several of the volumes in the "Underground Royal Commission" series, such as Patrick Boyer's *Just Trust Us* and Paul Kemp's *Does Your Vote Count?*[23]

Clearly, members of the policy community in Canada are concerned with the contemporary state of our political institutions and practices, but what of the public? Reforms that directly challenge the position and prerogatives of those holding political power are unlikely to progress far in the absence of citizen interest and solid popular support. Public opinion data suggest some grounds for hope on this score. In reviewing these data it is important to distinguish generalized ideas of democracy from attitudes about the actual practice and institutions of democracy. A national study conducted in 2000, for example, found 71 percent of Canadians satisfied with "the way democracy works in Canada" but only 58 percent similarly disposed to "government" and 53 percent towards "politics."[24] According to the public, the most significant determinant of discontent with democracy in Canada is political inefficacy — i.e., the feeling that citizens have no real impact on decision-making in the polity. Fifty-five percent of Canadians cite political inefficacy as the explanation for low voter turnout, as compared with 23 percent who believe it is caused by lack of political education. In this same survey, 77 percent of respondents agreed with allowing free votes in Parliament, up from 72 percent a decade before, while the percentage of Canadians who say that the first-past-the-post electoral system is "unacceptable" because of "wasted votes" has risen from 39 percent in 1990 to 49 percent in 2000. Between 1974 and 1996, confidence in the House of Commons fell from 49 to 21 percent and the percentage of Canadians expressing "a great deal of confidence" in political parties dropped from 30 to 11 percent.[25]

Certainly politicians — both in and out of office — believe Canadian democracy needs work, and hope to reap political benefits by putting forward proposals for democratic reform which will find favour with Canadians dissatisfied with their system. Both Canada's outgoing prime minister and the country's putative prime minister-in-waiting have stepped up to the plate. Prime Minister Jean Chrétien has made political party finance reform one of the signature pieces in his heritage agenda, facing down substantial opposition from within his own caucus. Paul Martin has made dealing with the "democratic deficit" a prominent plank in his policy platform.[26] The former Parti Québécois government created a Cabinet portfolio entitled "Minister Responsible for the Reform of Democratic Institutions" which, significantly, has been retained by the new Liberal government. Serious investigations into major electoral reform — possibly encompassing a shift to an electoral system based on proportional representation — are underway in Prince Edward Island and British Columbia. In British Columbia, the government has committed itself to hold a referendum on whatever proposal for reform of the province's electoral system a citizens' assembly recommends. Premier Gordon Campbell's government has also introduced fixed provincial election dates, and has been holding Cabinet meetings in public, with the information posted on the Government's web site. In Ontario, the three major political parties all featured democratic reform in their manifestoes in the 2003 general election.[27] The Ontario Liberal Party under Dalton McGuinty, for example, announced while in opposition a number of significant democratic reforms it said it would introduce if elected to office. These include: fixed provincial election dates; spending limits for parties, elections and leadership contests; "citizen juries" to examine policy ideas; more freedom for Members of Provincial Parliament and more clout for legislative committees; and a referendum on the electoral system.

There are, then, some grounds for believing that a taste for democratic reform has been growing in this country, and that the reduction of the power of the first ministers together with an increase in the autonomy and responsibilities of the members of Canada's legislatures, is a significant part of most reform proposals. If that is so, a proposal to develop the idea of inter-legislative federalism fits well into the current policy environment.

SOME IDEAS FOR PUTTING INTER-LEGISLATIVE FEDERALISM INTO PRACTICE

Before bringing forward some thoughts about how one might introduce elements of inter-legislative federalism, it is worth pausing to consider what kind of legislative work would be susceptible to this kind of process. The closer the work is to the formal law-approving functions of the chambers, the less likely that this kind of inter-legislative contact would be appropriate. It would seem that activity involving several legislatures would make the most sense at an early, general stage in the policy-making and legislative cycle, when governments have not yet committed themselves to a specific course of action, but are in a position to receive advice and guidance from members of the legislature. Indeed, at the start of any inter-legislative reform effort, there may be a real advantage in restricting the focus chiefly to information sharing and broad, general topics. It would surely make sense in the early going to stay clear of the more sensitive domains of public policy in which executives have an especially active interest. As we will see below, this appears to be the general practice of bodies that perform these sorts of functions in other parliamentary contexts.

Let me now list some ideas for consideration that would, if implemented, introduce an inter-legislative component into the operation of the Canadian federal system.

PERIODIC MEETINGS OF FEDERAL AND PROVINCIAL REPRESENTATIVES WITHIN A GIVEN PROVINCE

In every province there are two sets of representatives serving the same set of citizens — more than two, if you include the municipal realm. It would be useful for all the people's representatives of a given territory to meet periodically to exchange information and ideas. The socio-economic conditions and development opportunities specific to a given province would naturally offer a central focus for discussion, given that all elected officials in a province — federal, provincial and municipal — have to confront these matters as part of their responsibilities.

As it happens, British Columbia has held a meeting of just this kind. Convened by the Gordon Campbell Liberal Government, the so-called Provincial Congress was held on 26 February 2002, the second of a series of four dialogues planned by the province. It brought together all members of the BC Legislature, all BC Members of Parliament (MPs) and Senators, mayors of the 15 largest cities in the province, the presidents of the five regional municipal associations in BC, the President of the Union of BC Municipalities, and Aboriginal leaders. It explored future directions for the province, and held sessions on the economy, the province's demographic prospects, health care and the environment, and Aboriginal issues. With representatives from all spheres of government, the Congress was, in Premier Campbell's words, designed to "discover what it is we share, and how we can work together to provide our citizens with the services they need in a thoughtful way."[28] Premier Campbell judged this to be a useful and positive event, and his Government plans to hold others of the same sort in the future.

THE PARTICIPATION OF REPRESENTATIVES FROM ONE JURISDICTION IN
THE PROCESSES OF THE OTHER

When a legislature is examining a topic with significant extra-jurisdictional impacts, it would be possible to invite the participation of representatives of other jurisdictions. At first blush, this sounds strange, but in fact we have a concrete example of this, with Quebec being, again, the innovator. The Commission on the Political and Constitutional Future of Quebec (The Bélanger-Campeau Commission) is known more for its proposals than its process, but in fact it was a highly unusual body that exemplifies the distinctive and often creative fashion in which Quebec has adapted the British parliamentary system to its own needs and preferences. Established in September 1990 in the wake of the demise of the Meech Lake Accord, its mandate was to examine the political and constitutional future of Quebec.

Its composition was remarkable. Half of the 36 members appointed by the National Assembly were members of the National Assembly; the other half were not. Both the Premier of Quebec, Robert Bourassa, and the Leader of the Opposition, Jacques Parizeau, were members. The co-chairs, Michel Bélanger and Jean Campeau, were prominent Quebec businessmen. There were representatives from the municipalities, from the business and trade union sectors, and from the co-operative, educational and cultural sectors.

In addition, and of particular relevance to the topic of this chapter, three federal MPs were named as members.[29] They were Lucien Bouchard, then leader of the Bloc Québécois; Jean-Pierre Hogue, a Conservative backbencher representing Outremont; and André Ouellet, Liberal MP for Papineau-Saint-Michel.[30] Neither the Liberal nor the Conservative representative signed the final report, which is not surprising, given its contents.

The commission offers an intriguing example of the way in which political leaders from both federal and provincial jurisdictions, in conjunction with citizens from many walks of life, can lead a broadly based process of public discussion engaging significant sectors of the larger political community — and do so with respect to an acutely divisive issue.

THE CREATION OF A FEDERAL-PROVINCIAL-TERRITORIAL PARLIAMENTARY
ASSOCIATION

The Parliament of Canada is engaged in a fairly wide range of international relationships with foreign legislatures. Given that a federation is a system with multiple legislatures, it would be possible to establish a similar domestic inter-parliamentary association, and, in developing it, draw on the extensive international experience that decades of federal parliamentary participation provides.

The Parliament of Canada has membership in 10 official parliamentary associations — five bilateral and five multilateral.[31] The bilateral associations are with the United States, France, Japan, the United Kingdom, and China. The multilateral associations are the following: the Commonwealth Parliamentary Association; *Assemblée parlementaire de la francophonie*; the Inter-Parliamentary Union; the Canadian NATO Parliamentary Association; and the Canada-Europe Parliamentary Association.

Members of the Senate and the House of Commons are involved in all of these. For each, members elect an executive committee to plan and coordinate activities with their bilateral counterparts or with the international secretariat of the multilateral organizations. Each executive committee is supported by an executive secretary who is responsible for the day-to-day operations of the organization. Additional support staff from the Senate and the Commons assist as necessary. A Joint Inter-Parliamentary Council, functioning under the authority of the two Speakers, oversees general budget and administrative matters. Financial allotments are approved by the Senate Standing Committee on Internal Economy, Budgets and Administration, and by the House of Commons Board of Internal Economy. Association budgets are about 90 percent for travel; there is relatively little money available for staff support and research.

The only international inter-parliamentary association to have assumed an "executive oversight" role is the *Assemblée parlementaire de la Francophonie* (APF). Section 2.1.5 of the APF constitution establishes a formal link with the *Conférence des Chefs d'État et des gouvernements ayant le francais en partage*. The APF has given itself the mandate to oversee plans and decisions made by the annual summit of the heads of state and governments of the Francophonie.[32]

The bilateral inter-parliamentary associations of which Canada is a member typically have the general and anodyne goal of exchanging information and promoting better understanding. They normally meet once a year, but sometimes organize special working sessions on specific or urgent issues. The multilateral associations tend to pursue more specific objectives linked to the character of the relationship, such as the promotion of peace and co-operation through the United Nations, the increase in knowledge of the concerns of the North Atlantic Alliance, or the promotion of the French language and co-operation among francophone countries.

There is a Canadian branch of the Commonwealth Parliamentary Association (CPA). Its annual meetings, rotating among the various capitals, bring together legislative representatives from Ottawa, the provinces and the territories, but the focus is on how the legislatures work, not on policy substance. Regional parliamentary seminars are also held, but again, the focus is on process. The Canadian branch of the CPA also supports the Centre for Legislative Exchange, established in 1971 and closely associated with the Parliamentary Centre. It serves all Canadian legislatures, and arranges annual visits to Washington or to a US state capital, sponsoring discussion of such issues as border problems, transportation, and the like. Separate from the CPA, speakers of Canadian legislatures meet annually in January, as do house table officers, who meet normally in the summer.[33] In addition, the Public Accounts Committees of the Canadian legislatures meet annually, and these meetings with federal, provincial and territorial participation, might serve as an example to build on.[34]

A Canadian version of an inter-parliamentary association would be quite different from the international versions, given that all participating legislatures would be members of the same country, but models and guidance could nevertheless be drawn down from Canada's extensive international experience. The budgetary, administrative and management arrangements used currently by the two houses of Parliament could provide a point of reference for an all-Canadian initiative, but a more substantial business agenda could surely be developed, given that the time spent in international associations simply familiarizing oneself with the other's political system would not be required, and participants could therefore concentrate more directly on substantive matters of common interest. In the early 1980s, there was an initiative of this kind. The Parliamentary Centre obtained funding to organize some meetings of federal and provincial legislators. There were several such meetings, each lasting three to five days, involving ten to 12 participants, and discussing matters of substance. Legislators with expertise in the given area were invited to attend. Each meeting involved sessions in Ottawa and events outside of Ottawa. The first was held on rail abandonment, and the group travelled by rail to some of the sites being considered. The second was on fisheries, and the group went to St. John's.[35]

THE ESTABLISHMENT OF A NATIONAL CONFERENCE OF CANADIAN LEGISLATURES

The United States, with its congressional dispersal of power at both the national and state levels, has generated a rich array of highly sophisticated organizations to express the diverse relations among the federated units, both interstate and state-federal. The National Governors' Association and the National Republican Legislators Association are just two examples of the many that exist. Many of these are peculiar to the American system, and would have little applicability elsewhere.[36]

Nevertheless, one such organization is worth mentioning here as one thinks about how inter-legislative federalism might be developed in Canada. The National Conference of State Legislatures (NCSL) is "a bipartisan organization dedicated to serving lawmakers and staffs of the nation's 50 states, its commonwealths and territories."[37] Founded in 1975, with offices in Denver and Washington, the NCSL is a substantial and sophisticated organization, holding meetings and seminars, providing consulting services, undertaking research and publications in areas of concern to state legislatures, and facilitating the exchange of information on a wide array of issues of concern to American state legislators.

There is no reason why many of the functions it performs would not be of equal benefit to Canadian provincial legislators and staffs. Canada is endowed with 13 provincial and territorial legislatures. A fuller appreciation of how these democratic systems are evolving could only help to improve the vigour and level of democratic discourse in this country. A Canadian legislative web site could support the exchange of ideas and the circulation of information about best practices. An association of Canadian legislatures might start modestly, and concentrate initially on institutional and procedural matters, but, as confidence and mutual knowledge among the participants grew, and common staff resources were established, it would become possible for the association to move into more substantive areas. Such an organization could be established as an intergovernmental body only involving the provinces and territories. However, given Canada's specific circumstances, the arrangement should also be extended to include the federal Parliament as well.

CONCLUSION

The introduction of a degree of inter-legislative federalism could make a modest contribution to the strengthening of Canadian democracy by expanding the role, perspectives and the effectiveness of the country's legislators; to the functioning of federalism, by supplementing the dominant practices of executive federalism with the addition of a legislative dimension; to governmental performance, through greater information exchange among jurisdictions on innovations, experiments and best practices; and to Canadian unity, by offering an additional integrative bridge across regions and provinces — one, moreover, which is not focused on turf or status, as executive intergovernmental institutions tend to be.

Were some or all of these proposals judged to be desirable, they could be implemented at the will of Canadian legislatures and political leaders. None of them, of course, requires constitutional change, and, in fact, a single legislature could get the process started by taking an initiative on its own. But these ideas run up against the same obstacles that Ned Franks identified in his paper on parliamentary reform in Ottawa — namely, the institutional conservatism of Canadians, and the self-interest of first ministers and executive bodies in the federation. It can be argued that the need to get a multiplicity of federal actors on board for much of what is proposed here further complicates the situation.

Yet, despite the historical dominance of parliamentary traditionalism, there are, as we have seen, hopeful signs in the public and in a number of jurisdictions of a growing taste for reform. There are several promising initiatives that seek to improve democratic government in Canada, and inter-legislative federalism fits in well with some of the ideas for institutional innovation. There are a number of possibilities to get the ball rolling. One jurisdiction could commit itself to an initiative, and invite the others to come. It all could start with an invitation and a first meeting. British Columbia's Premier Gordon Campbell has already done this in a small way. As well, the long experience in Canada's Parliament with various inter-parliamentary associations, and the degree to which the organizational and budgetary arrangements for these bodies have been institutionalized within the structure of Parliament, may give federal parliamentarians some capacity for autonomous action, if they choose to exercise it in this way.

In addition, if these ideas, and others like them, are deemed to be of some potential utility, civil-society institutions might take the first step in organizing some critical review and further development of them. Reform proposals could be further refined and more carefully explored, as could the means of bringing them into being. As I have said, the Institute for Research on Public Policy has been running a very useful series of meetings and publications on strengthening Canadian democracy and parliamentary institutions;[38] a think tank such as the IRPP, or the Parliamentary Centre, or a university with strength in legislative studies, might convene a conference or a series of working sessions, involving legislators, to test these ideas further.

I would not wish to be misunderstood. I do not believe that such initiatives as these, even if they were fully implemented, would radically alter our executive-dominated parliamentary democracy or transform the pattern of executive federalism. Regard them, rather, as sites of modest legislative self-assertion with some potential, in time, to enliven and reinvigorate our desiccated system of responsible government — not to mention the arcane pathways of Canadian intergovernmental relations.

NOTES

1. "Intergovernmental Relations and Democratic Citizenship," in *Governance in the Twenty-First Century*, eds. B. Guy Peters and Donald Savoie (Montreal: McGill-Queen's University Press, 2000), pp. 30-58.

2. Ibid., p. 95: The establishment of standing committees on intergovernmental relations; the holding of debates or committee hearings on intergovernmental

issues before First Ministers Conferences; legislative ratification of all major intergovernmental agreements; and the participation of Opposition members on governmental negotiating teams.

3. C.E.S. Franks, "Parliament, Intergovernmental Relations and National Unity," Working Paper 1992(2) (Kingston: Institute of Intergovernmental Relations, Queen's University, 1999). For convenience, I will quote from this version of the paper.

4. Ibid., p. 31.

5. Ibid., p. 36.

6. Ibid., p. 27.

7. Ibid., p. 34. Clearly, the introduction of the *Charter of Rights and Freedoms* in 1982 was a very substantial reform of our institutional arrangements and has profoundly affected Canadian government, but I presume that Franks is referring specifically to the operational machinery of Parliament itself.

8. "Germany and Canada: Federal Loyalty in the Era of Globalization," notes for an address to members of the Atlantik-Brücke, Feldafing, Germany, 28 October 2001.

9. "An Outsider's Observations of Intergovernmental Relations Among Consenting Adults," in *Confrontation or Collaboration: Intergovernmental Relations in Canada Today*, ed. Richard Simeon (Toronto: Institute of Public Administration of Canada, 1979).

10. Roger Gibbins, "Shifting Sands: Exploring the Political Foundations of SUFA," in *Policy Matters/Enjeux publics,* 2, 3 (Montreal: Institute for Research in Public Policy, July 2001).

11. Keith Banting, "The Past Speaks to the Future," in *Canada: The State of the Federation, 1997*, ed. Harvey Lazar (Kingston: Institute of Intergovernmental Relations, Queen's University,1998); Roger Gibbins, "Democratic Reservations About the ACCESS Models," *Assessing ACCESS: Towards a New Social Union* (Kingston: Institute of Intergovernmental Relations, Queen's University, 1995); Ghislain Otis, "Informing Canadians — Public Accountability and Transparency," in *The Canadian Social Union Without Quebec: Eight Critical Analyses*, eds. Alain-G. Gagnon and Hugh Segal (Montreal: Institute for Research on Public Policy, 2000). Writing in the mid-1980s, Paul Pross argued differently. He contended that the diffusion of power within the executive branch and the increasing role of interest groups have led to the enhancement of Parliament's role in the policy process. "Parliamentary Influence and the Diffusion of Power," *Canadian Journal of Political Science* (June 1985):235-66.

12. For example: Alan Cairns, "The Electoral System and the Party System, 1921-66," *Canadian Journal of Political Science*, 1,1 (March 1968):55-80; *A Future Together: Observations and Recommendations*, The Task Force on Canadian Unity (Ottawa: Queen's Printer, 1979), pp. 104-06; Michael Cassidy, "Fairness and Stability: How a New Electoral System Would Affect Canada," *Parliamentary Government*, 42 (August 1992).

13. In addition to Franks' work, see Canada, House of Commons, 1985. *Report of the Special Committee on Reform of the House of Commons* (The McGrath Report).

14. Franks, "Parliament, Intergovernmental Relations and National Unity," p. 31.

15. The National Assembly has performed this central role, for example, during the referendum processes, at moments during the patriation of the constitution in 1980-82, and on the occasion of the failure of Meech Lake. At critical moments in the life of Quebec society, Quebecers turn quite naturally to the National Assembly, whose televised proceedings are, at such times as these, among the most heavily watched television in the province.

16. Quebec, for example, was the only province to review and approve in its legislature the draft of the Meech Lake Accord before the agreement was accepted by all governments in its final form at the Langevin meetings in the spring of 1987.

17. Ironically, it is the Government of Quebec that has recently raised the possibility of a complete overhaul of its legislative processes. On 21 March 2002, Jean-Pierre Charbonneau, the minister responsible for the reform of democratic institutions, announced the creation of a reform secretariat. Stating that *"nous sommes mûres pour une grande réflexion nationale,"* the minister raised the possibility of a substantial "congressionalization" of Quebec's parliamentary system: direct popular election of the head of government; separation of the legislature and the executive, giving MNAs greater freedom of action; the selection of ministers from outside the National Assembly; and fixed provincial election dates. He also floated the idea of introducing proportional representation. (*Communiqué* c3062, 23 March 2002.) Whether the minister's grandiose call for the creation of *"un grand et vaste chantier de réformes fondamentales"* was seriously intended or a desperate pre-election sally will, in the light of the Parti Québécois' electoral defeat, remain unknown. What is clear is that it responds to no passionately expressed desire on the part of Quebecers to change the system by which they are governed — certainly none that I am aware of.

18. "Reforming Parliamentary Practice: the Views of MPs," Institute for Research on Public Policy, *Policy Matters* 1,9 (December 2000):12, 25-26.

19. Ibid., p. 12.

20. Much of this material is available on the Institute for Research on Public Policy web site at <www.irpp.org>.

21. For an overview see <www.mta.ca/faculty/arts/canadian_studies/demaudit_overview_15aug.pdf>.

22. See <www.lcc.gc.ca/en/themes/gr/er/er_main.asp>.

23. Gordon Gibson, *Fixing Canadian Democracy* (Vancouver: The Fraser Institute, 2003); Judy Rebick, *Imagine Democracy* (Toronto: Stoddart, 2000); Jeffrey Simpson, *The Friendly Dictatorship* (Toronto: McClelland and Stewart, 2002); Donald Savoie, *Governing from the Centre: The Concentration of Power in Canadian Politics* (Toronto: University of Toronto Press, 1999); Patrick Boyer, *"Just Trust Us": The Erosion of Accountability in Canada* (Toronto: Breakwater

Productions, 2003); and Paul Kemp, *Does Your Vote Count?* (Toronto: Break-water Productions, 2003).

24. Paul Howe and David Northrup, "Strengthening Canadian Democracy: The Views of Canadians," *Policy Matters*, 1,5 (July 2000):7. Unless otherwise indicated, all data in the paragraph are taken from this survey.

25. Patrick Boyer, "Reconsidering the Role of Citizens — The Case of the *Underground Royal Commission*," paper presented at the Annual Meeting of the Canadian Political Science Association, Halifax, 6 May 2003.

26. See his speech to the Osgoode Hall Law School, reported in *The Globe and Mail*, 22 October 2002; see also, Paul Martin, "The Democratic Deficit," *Policy Options* (December 2002-January 2003):10-12. Martin's reforms are designed to give backbench MPs more freedom to amend or reject government bills and to review prime ministerial appointments.

27. See Ontario Progressive Conservative Party, "The Road Ahead: Premier Eves' Plan for Ontario's Future," pp. 50-52 <www.ontariopc.com>; Liberal Party of Ontario, "Government that Works for You: The Ontario Liberal Plan for a More Democratic Ontario" <www.ontarioliberal.com/2000/PDF/democratic/democratic.pdf>; Ontario New Democratic Party, "Publicpower: Practical Solutions for Ontario," pp. 67-72 <www.publicpower.ca/our_platform/publicpower_platform.pdf>. The previous three paragraphs are drawn in part from a report on democracy in Ontario prepared by David Cameron, Celine Mulhern and Graham White for the province's Panel on the Role of Government.

28. Premier Gordon Campbell, Address to the Federation of Canadian Municipalities, Toronto, 18 October 2001.

29. "Three members of the House of Commons of Canada appointed on a proposal of the Prime Minister [Premier of Quebec] after consultation with the Leader of the Official Opposition, who were elected at the last general election to represent an electoral district in Québec, and who continue to do so." In *An Act to Establish the Commission on the Political and Constitutional Future of Quebec*, S.Q. 1990, ch. 34.

30. It is worth noting that the participation of the federal MPs was not sanctioned by the House of Commons. It was a political decision made by the party leaders at the time.

31. Information in these paragraphs is taken from the Parliament of Canada web site at <www.parl.gc.ca>.

32. I am indebted to an anonymous reader for this information.

33. Interview with Peter Dobell, Parliamentary Centre, 20 December 2001.

34. I am indebted to an anonymous reader for this suggestion.

35. Interview with Peter Dobell, Parliamentary Centre, 20 December 2001. This initiative eventually petered out. Peter Dobell notes that these sorts of meetings need to be carefully designed, to ensure that they do not simply become a forum for intergovernmental or interjurisdictional squabbling. This touches on an important point made by Dr. Tsvi Kahana, executive director of the Centre for

Constitutional Studies at the University of Alberta, in correspondence relating to an earlier draft of this paper. He argues that one of the reasons that Canadian legislatures have a bad name is their poor deliberative performance, and worries that a proposal that offers legislators the capacity to do more of that which gave them a bad name in the first place — namely, engage in debate — might exacerbate the problem in the public mind, rather than alleviate it (email to author, 23 January 2002).

36. To display how different the constitutional and political context is from that of Canada, one need only consult the National Governors Association web site, at <www.nga.org>, where it is stated with pride that *"Fortune* Magazine recently named NGA as one of Washington's most powerful lobbying organizations." Canada's provincial premiers do not see themselves or their interprovincial organization, the Annual Premiers Conference, as Ottawa lobbyists, but as constitutionally grounded federal actors, in this sense equal to their federal counterpart, the Government of Canada.

37. The information for these paragraphs comes from the National Conference of State Legislatures web site at <www.ncsl.org>. Interestingly, paralleling the observation of the National Governors Association, NCSL asserts that it is "recognized as the states' most effective lobbying voice in Washington, DC."

38. The series is called "Policy Matters/Enjeux publics."

VII

Chronology

17

Chronology of Events
January 2002 – December 2002

Adele Mugford with Aaron Holdway

An index of these events begins on page 513

8 January 2002
Health

The Premier's Advisory Council on Health releases the Alberta-commissioned Mazankowski Report on health care reform proposals. A major recommendation includes a new health "debit" card that automatically displays a patient's medical history and the cost of health services used. The hope is that this will deter further abuses to the system, while introducing a blended health care system. Also included in the report are recommendations to delist non-essential services from medicare and to increase health care premiums. Federal Health Minister Allan Rock praises the report, but Roy Romanow — who is heading a separate but similar commission at the national level — is critical of its abandonment of medicare based upon an assumption that it is unsustainable.

16 January 2002
Atlantic Canada

MP Gerry Byrne of the Barbe-Baie Verte riding is sworn into Prime Minister Jean Chrétien's Cabinet as minister of state responsible for the Atlantic Canada Opportunities Agency, and will replace Brian Tobin as regional minister.

17 January 2002
British Columbia

The British Columbia government unveils a three-year restructuring plan aimed at reducing operating costs and delivering services more efficiently. These plans include a 25 percent reduction in departmental funding as a means of addressing a $3.8-billion deficit, revitalizing investment, and creating new economic growth to sustain and renew public services. In addition to funding cuts, the government also introduces revenue-making measures, including user fees and the selling off of BC land assets.

21 January 2002
New Brunswick

Premier Bernard Lord announces that the province will ensure that all municipal bylaws are available in both English and French. The province of New Brunswick became officially bilingual in 1969 but until a recent court decision, only provincial laws were required to be available in both languages.

22 January 2002
Alberta

Alberta Premier Ralph Klein announces that his government will adopt all 44 recommendations of the Mazankowski Report on health care reform. The sweeping changes are expected to take three to five years to implement, and will remain consistent with the five principles of the *Canada Health Act*.

24 January 2002
Agriculture

At their meeting in Toronto, federal and provincial agriculture ministers — with the exception of Quebec — report that considerable progress is being made toward a formal agreement on a twenty-first century agricultural policy to boost the long-term success of the industry. The ministers also commit to exploring future-oriented and nationally integrated directions in risk management for the sector.

24-25 January 2002
Premiers' Meeting

The premiers' meeting in Vancouver reiterates the connections between the federal government's inadequate funding of health care and a declining ability to sustain its quality. They agree to establish a Premiers' Council on Canadian Health Awareness, expected to be operational before 1 May 2002, with a mandate to gather and disseminate information to Canadians on health care issues in all jurisdictions. Premiers also ask Ralph Klein of Alberta to work with the federal government to finalize a dispute resolution mechanism — for the purposes of clarifying the *Canada Health Act* — by 30 April 2002. Other significant outcomes include: an agreement (excluding Quebec) to follow the lead of the Atlantic provinces and develop a common review process for new pharmaceutical drugs, as well as a process for streamlining generic drug approvals; an agreement — excluding Quebec — to develop Sites of Excellence in various fields across the country to ensure higher quality care and more efficient spending; and a call on the federal government to fulfil commitments to Aboriginal health services made in last year's Speech from the Throne.

25 January 2002
Health

The provincial and territorial premiers, after a two-day meeting, issue an ultimatum to Ottawa to reach an agreement on settling disputes under the *Canada Health Act*. The provinces and territories have set 30 April 2002 as the deadline for a federal-provincial and a federal-territorial agreement. They further suggest that a failure to meet this deadline would indicate that Ottawa is abandoning the Social Union Framework Agreement.

30 January 2002
Quebec

The Parti Québécois' new Cabinet is sworn in with a view to strengthening its chances for re-election in the upcoming election that must be called within the next year. Notable appointees include former Speaker Jean-Pierre Charbonneau as minister of intergovernmental affairs, Montreal anglophone David Levine as junior health minister, and André Boisclair as House leader and minister of municipal affairs (which are added to his environment responsibilities). Sylvain Simard drops the Treasury Board in exchange for the education portfolio, François Legault moves from education to health, and two young rookies — Stéphane Bédard and Jean-François Simard — are added to the now 36-member Cabinet. The Cabinet has been increased in size by 13 members.

6 February 2002
Health

The interim report of the Commission on the Future of Health Care in Canada, headed by Roy Romanow, is released, setting the stage for the second phase of the commission: consultation and dialogue with the Canadian public. The report is intended to promote understanding of the issues by Canadians, as well as engage the public in a national dialogue. It also stresses that medicare must be remodelled instead of dismantled, and asks that all reform options be considered in the coming debates.

7 February 2002
Aboriginal Peoples

Quebec Premier Bernard Landry and Cree Grand Chief Ted Moses sign an agreement to recognize a new relationship between the Cree of Quebec and the provincial government. This marks the first time that recommendations of the Royal Commission on Aboriginal Peoples have been applied in Canada. In particular, the agreement will see the Cree drop all lawsuits against the province and consent to the construction of the Rupert-Eastmain hydroelectric project in return for payments totalling $3.4 billion over the next 50 years. A deal made outside of the agreement with Hydro-Quebec guarantees $862 million in contracts to the Cree for building and environmental cleanup.

13-14 February 2002
Justice

Federal, provincial, and territorial ministers responsible for justice meet in Moncton, NB, to discuss a wide range of issues. They discuss implementation of the *Anti-Terrorism Act*, expressing general support for new hoax offence provisions; cost-sharing of the *Youth Criminal Justice Act*, agreeing, with the exception of Quebec, to a target date of April 2003 for the new Act to come into force; the creation of two new offences under the Criminal Code concerning acts of criminal voyeurism and distributing visual images through the Internet and by other means; and further measures to create a national approach to sex offender registration for police use.

15 February 2002
Municipalities

A dozen mayors from Canada's largest cities gather in Ottawa in connection with ongoing efforts to pressure senior governments for more powers. The agenda centres upon building the advocacy process for urban needs. Several federal Cabinet ministers are also involved in this conference, which the Federation of Canadian Municipalities has organized with a view to facilitating improved federal-municipal relations.

19 February 2002
British Columbia

In addition to announcing that its fiscal plan is ahead of schedule, the British Columbia government's budget reveals the deficit and the debt will be $600 million and $3.5 billion lower, respectively, than had been anticipated. Vowing to stick with its original fiscal plan to balance the budget by 2004-2005, the BC government will further realize the BC Heartlands Economic Strategy and will complete and implement economic development plans across the province. These plans include new partnerships with First Nations groups; new investments in transportation and infrastructure; new opportunities for tourism, sport, and recreation (via the 2010 Winter Olympics bid); and a restructured forest industry.

20 February 2002
Northwest Territories

Boasting a strong economy and increased opportunity for residents and businesses, the Northwest Territories budget reviews its investments and developments with respect to employment, literacy, its Social Agenda, transportation infrastructure, and non-renewable resources. It also alludes to concurrent pressures, including housing shortages, increased demand on community infrastructure, and social and environmental issues. Ultimately, however, the budget's main theme is about balance — in terms of revenues and spending, economic and social investments, resource development, and environmental protection.

21 February 2002
Trade

Prime Minister Jean Chrétien and the provincial premiers wrap up a trade mission to Germany by acknowledging the imperative of eliminating interprovincial trade barriers in connection with attracting European investment. Further to this acknowledgement, New Brunswick Premier Bernard Lord and Alberta Premier Ralph Klein agree to head a federal-provincial committee on trade barriers.

28 February 2002
Equalization

Federal Finance Minister Paul Martin suspends cuts to equalization payments due to a change in calculation methods of residential real-estate values for Quebec, but will go ahead with changes to the indices used to calculate payments. Originally Quebec would have been short $800 million, but will now incur a loss of $334 million. Newfoundland and Labrador also have a $6-million cut suspended, while all other provinces benefiting from the change do not have their new funds suspended.

5 March 2002
Environment

Federal Minister of the Environment David Anderson outlines his plan to implement the Kyoto Accord, stating that the biggest greenhouse gas producers must reduce emissions or purchase emission credits from other domestic or international companies. He also suggests Ottawa purchase credits from abroad to distribute to industries or parts of the country that have trouble meeting the Accord's targets, as well as measures designed to reduce emissions from other sources, such as municipalities.

7 March 2002
Ontario

James Bartleman is sworn in as the 41st Lieutenant Governor of Ontario, becoming the first Aboriginal person to hold this position. He leaves his post as the head of the Mission of Canada to the European Union and a distinguished career spanning more than 35 years in the Canadian foreign service. Born in Orillia, ON, Bartleman grew up in Muskoka, ON, and belongs to the Minjikanig First Nation.

7 March 2002
Aboriginal Peoples

In the case of *Benoit* v *Canada*, the Federal Court of Canada rules that an oral agreement made during the signing of Treaty 8 (encompassing northern Saskatchewan, Alberta, and British Columbia, and the southern Northwest Territories) is equal to treaty terms. The decision means that Aboriginal peoples within the Treaty 8 territory, whether they are living on- or off-reserve, are exempt from all taxes. This ruling is expected to have implications on treaty rights all across Canada.

9 March 2002
Ontario

The Ontario government implements a series of tough new regulations affecting Quebec construction workers as a means of countering conditions in Quebec which do not allow Ontario companies fair access to its construction market. Under the new regulations, Quebec workers will have to meet certain criteria to document their competency and register with the Ontario Jobs Protection Office in order to legally work in Ontario. Additionally, Quebec companies wanting to set up an office in Ontario will be required to register and post a bond as proof of financial stability. Any contracts signed before 9 March 2002 will not be subject to the new rules. Earlier in the year, talks between the Ontario and Quebec governments dedicated to renewing the agreement that governed access rules over the past two years, broke off after Ontario Labour Minister Chris Stockwell accused Quebec officials of being unco-operative and inflexible.

12 March 2002 *British Columbia*	British Columbia Attorney General Geoff Plant introduces the eight questions that will form the basis of a provincial referendum on the Aboriginal treaty process. Ballots will be mailed out on 2 April and must be returned by 15 May. The results will be binding on the government if more than 50 percent vote the same way. Critics claim this process is a waste of time, saying that answers to the referendum questions have already been determined.
13 March 2002 *Parliament*	Electoral boundaries will begin to be rewritten today as the number of seats in the House of Commons will rise from 301 to 308 by 2004. Ontario will have three new federal electoral districts, and Alberta and British Columbia will each have two new electoral districts.
13 March 2002 *Aboriginal Peoples*	The British Columbia government announces it will kick off its referendum on Aboriginal treaties with an apology. Attorney General Geoff Plant explains that the government wishes to introduce the issue of reconciliation at the negotiation table, including an expression of regret by the government.
19 March 2002 *Newfoundland and Labrador*	The Newfoundland and Labrador government appoints a Royal Commission to review the province's place in Canada, with a view to securing a better deal with Ottawa. Premier Roger Grimes further explains the importance of this Royal Commission as a means of renewing and strengthening Newfoundland and Labrador's place in Canada and reinforcing its contribution to the Canadian fabric. The details of the Royal Commission and the terms of reference are to be announced at a later date.
19 March 2002 *Alberta*	The Alberta government announces its new budget. In addition to forecasting a balanced budget, continuing to pay down the province's debt, and maintaining Alberta's tax advantage, spending priorities include health, education, and "those in need." The Department of Health and Wellness and Learning and Children's Services received the largest influx of new funding. With a view to avoiding

any erosion to the "Alberta Advantage," this budget scales back on a promise of $275 million in corporate tax breaks until oil and gas revenues stabilize.

19 March 2002
Quebec

The Quebec government announces a $300-million anti-poverty plan — the centrepiece of a revised provincial budget — including tax breaks for low-income families and more money for welfare recipients. The money for this plan comes from an increase in tax revenue of $586 million since the budget was first tabled in November 2001.

21 March 2002
Newfoundland and Labrador

The Newfoundland and Labrador government announces its new budget. Highlights include strong economic performance forecasts for 2002, a greater emphasis on youth, and continued high priorities for health, jobs, and economic growth. Funding remains stable for families, municipalities, and infrastructure.

21 March 2002
Trade

Negotiators fail to meet the deadline to resolve the two-year-old softwood lumber dispute between Canada and the United States. Talks between the two countries subsequently collapse in the face of what Minister of International Trade Pierre Pettigrew describes as an "unreasonable" eleventh-hour offer. As a result, Canadians must now prepare for the new permanent duties of up to 32 percent on their annual $10 billion in lumber shipments to the US. It is estimated that this will cost the industry a minimum of $1 billion per year. British Columbia, Quebec, Ontario, and Alberta — the four largest lumber-producing provinces — will be most affected by the US duties being imposed in connection with claims of provincial government subsidies and unfair dumping.

23 March 2002
Ontario

Ernie Eves is elected to replace Mike Harris as leader of the Ontario Progressive Conservative Party and becomes the 23rd premier of Ontario. Although currently without a seat in the legislature, Eves served as Ontario's deputy premier and minister of finance from June 1995 to February 2001. Eves was born in Windsor in 1946 and attended the University of Toronto and Osgoode Hall Law School at York University. He was called to the bar in 1972 and was made a Queen's Counsel in January 1983.

27 March 2002
Aboriginal Peoples

Mi'kmaq chiefs sign a proclamation directing Ottawa and Newfoundland and Labrador to recognize that treaties signed in 1760-1761 cover all Mi'kmaq. The impetus for the proclamation comes from demands made by the Maritime Mi'kmaq chiefs that treaty rights, including access to the fisheries, be extended to 800 to 1,000 Mi'kmaq living in Newfoundland and Labrador.

4 April 2002
Nova Scotia

After experiencing a $106-million deficit for the 2001-2002 fiscal year, Nova Scotia Finance Minister Neil LeBlanc unveils Nova Scotia's first balanced budget in 40 years. The surplus projection is attributed to increased revenues — chiefly from increased taxes on alcohol, gas, and tobacco — and reduced spending.

9 April 2002
Aboriginal Peoples

Quebec Premier Bernard Landry; Minister of State for Population, Regions, and Native Affairs, Rémy Trudel; President of the Makivik Corporation, Pita Aatami; and Chairman of the Kativik Regional Government, Johnny N. Adams, sign a $900-million partnership agreement between the government of Quebec and the Nunavik Inuit of northern Quebec. The agreement promises to accelerate economic and community development in northern Quebec. The 25-year deal was reached during the annual general meeting of the Makivik Corporation, a forum for bringing together representatives from 14 Inuit communities and Nunavik's major socio-economic stakeholders to address issues related to finance, governance, public services, and infrastructure in Nunavik.

9 April 2002
Political Parties

Canadian Alliance leader Stephen Harper and Progressive Conservative leader Joe Clark announce during separate media briefings that efforts to unite their parties have failed. Each claims different reasons for the inability to find common ground. Critics suggest this failure raises questions about Clark's tenure as Conservative leader.

9-10 April 2002
Education

At a meeting in Toronto, the Council of Ministers of Education, Canada, declares 8-14 September International Adult Learners Week, to coincide with the worldwide event established by the United Nations Educational, Scientific, and Cultural Organization (UNESCO). The focus of discussions is placed upon the importance of adult learning and innovation in this sector, as well as a call on government to amend the *Copyright Act* so as to increase reasonable and equitable access to materials on the Internet.

15 April 2002
Political Parties

François Corriveau wins the former Parti Québécois stronghold of Saguenay in today's byelection and will join Action démocratique du Québec (ADQ) leader Mario Dumont in the Quebec legislative assembly.

15 April 2002
Ontario

Ontario Premier-designate Ernie Eves appoints a new Cabinet, naming Elizabeth Witmer as both deputy premier and minister of education and Janet Ecker as minister of finance. Jim Flaherty becomes responsible for a new "super-ministry" to replace the Ministry of Economic Development and Trade that will also include portions of the Ministry of Energy, Science, and Technology. Chris Hodgson, who remains minister of municipal affairs and housing, will assume control over some of the province's $20 billion SuperBuild public-works infrastructure program. Tony Clement remains minister of health.

24 April 2002
Health

All provinces and territories, with the exception of Quebec, accept a proposal on third-party dispute resolution regarding the *Canada Health Act*, submitted by federal Health Minister Anne McLellan. The proposal states that the two levels of government will discuss differences before going to a panel. The panel will consist of one member chosen by the federal government, one chosen by the provincial government, and a chairperson agreed to by both parties. Resolutions are non-binding, however, and the power of final decision resides with the federal health minister.

1 May 2002
Aboriginal Peoples

The Federal Court of Canada orders a stay of judgment on the *Benoit* v *Canada* case giving Treaty 8 Aboriginal peoples absolute tax-free status. The stay — deemed a victory for the federal government — gives officials time to adjust to the changes in government revenues and tax-free goods.

7 May 2002 *Quebec*	The Quebec government introduces legislation to tighten its French Language Charter to address what Premier Bernard Landry calls a "loophole" in the current law. Bill 104, which includes new guidelines to make it more difficult for immigrant and francophone children to attend English public schools, will be passed by spring. More specifically, children will no longer gain eligibility to attend English public schools after spending one year in an English private school, nor will the government continue to provide Quebec-based companies written communication in English.
9 May 2002 *Ontario*	Ontario Premier Ernie Eves' first Throne Speech claims a new era has begun under a new government with new challenges and new solutions. The Eves government explains that it wants to listen to and work in partnership with educators, health care workers, parents, and any other identifiable groups. There are suggestions of increased per-student funding and promises to review the funding formula via a special task force, which is expected to report back in November. In addition to renewing commitments made during his leadership campaign — to establish three-year base funding for school boards — the Eves government is promising to spend more money on the search for a cure for cancer and to more fully utilize MRI machines.
9 May 2002 *Finance*	Prime Minister Jean Chrétien promises to apply the year's entire federal budget surplus — predicted to be about $10 billion — to reducing the $540-billion national debt.
21 May 2002 *Climate Change*	Federal and provincial energy and environment ministers (with the exception of Alberta) meet in Charlottetown to discuss climate change and Canada's options to address the implications of the Kyoto Accord. Ministers agree to a National Adaptation Framework, which will assist jurisdictions to adapt to the impacts of climate change. They also release *Canada's National Climate Change Business Plan 2002,* which outlines governmental and non-governmental initiatives designed to address climate change.

29 May 2002 *Ontario*	Ontario Energy Minister Chris Stockwell announces new legislation to enable the sale of the Hydro One power grid and other provincial assets. The legislation — the *Reliable Energy and Consumer Protection Act* — will make changes to the *Electricity Act* and will secure the Ontario government's ownership of the lands underneath the hydro transmission corridors with a view to keeping them available for public use. The government further suggests that leasing the power grid to the private sector may prove to be a viable alternative to selling the utility outright. Other features of the new hydro legislation include increasing consumer protection by providing the Ontario Energy Board with more power, establishing a new energy consumers' bill of rights, tightening the rules surrounding marketing of energy contracts to consumers, and prohibiting false advertising.
30 May 2002 *Affordable Housing Agreement*	The federal and Ontario governments sign an Affordable Housing Program Agreement that will help to increase the supply of affordable housing in the province through increased funding. The federal government will provide $244 million, which will then be matched by a collective of the Ontario government, municipalities, and private and non-profit partners. The money will be made available over the next five years.
30 May 2002 *Prince Edward Island*	The Prince Edward Island government announces that it will fight to overturn a federal fisheries decision to shut out 28 lobster fishermen from their fishing grounds. (The fishermen had been informed they were illegally fishing in Quebec waters and were forced to remove their traps.) PEI will argue that the area in question — located roughly nine kilometres off its coast — is much closer to PEI than to Quebec.
31 May 2002 *Social Services*	Federal and provincial social services ministers meet in Toronto to discuss the success of the National Child Benefit over the past few years, as well as how to facilitate continued program progress and how to improve and expand programs and services with respect to the commitment made to Early Childhood Development in the Annual Premiers' Conference of 2000. Each participating government has agreed to work

autonomously in this effort in order to best meet each province's particular needs. Governments will issue progress reports in the fall.

4-6 June 2002
Western Canada

The Western Premiers' Conference takes place in Dawson City, YT. Most notably, the premiers address the significant progress on Early Childhood Development since last year's conference, as well as an agreement between the federal government and Alberta, on behalf of the provinces and territories, establishing a dispute resolution mechanism regarding the *Canada Health Act*. The mechanism includes an important role for independent third parties to provide publicly-released recommendations. Other topics of discussion include subsidies provided by the United States to its farmers. Accordingly, the provinces are looking to the federal government to provide a trade injury payment to Canadian farmers to offset the impact of the trade-distorting practices. These demands are coupled with a request for the federal government to take aggressive trade action through the World Trade Organization by challenging these subsidies. Climate change is another major area of discussion, resulting in an agreement to pursue new and emerging energy sources and technology. Infrastructure, trade, health, and education are also discussed at the conference.

7 June 2002
Municipalities

Following a week-long meeting in Montreal, QC, the C-5 — mayors of five of Canada's largest cities; Toronto, Montreal, Vancouver, Calgary, and Winnipeg — issue a unified call for increased federal funding and for the federal government to make changes to the way municipalities are funded. These demands go hand-in-hand with the C-5's requests for a seat at the table during the next First Ministers' Conference, with hopes for a discussion of new revenue-sharing ideas, and of gaining recognition as an order of government.

12 June 2002
Ontario

Ontario Premier Ernie Eves reverses the Conservative government's intentions to sell Hydro One through a public stock offering, thereby ending the initial public offering and possibly the largest privatization move in Canadian history.

15 June 2002 *Aboriginal Peoples*	The federal government tables Bill C-61, the *First Nations Governance Act* — the first major overhaul of the 126 year-old *Indian Act* — which proposes to amend sections of the *Indian Act* relating to financial and operational accountability, powers and authorities, elections and leadership selection, and legal standing capacity. The new Act requires Aboriginal bands to establish stricter standards for choosing leaders and managing financial affairs. In the event that rules are not tightened in prescribed areas, the federal government reserves the right to design and impose stricter rules for the band councils. Minister of Indian Affairs and Northern Development Robert Nault explains that Bill C-61 makes band councils directly accountable to the people they represent. Critics of the bill, however, suggest that the Act will not only infringe upon Aboriginal and treaty rights, but will further entrench, not limit, the minister's power over Aboriginal peoples. This Act, if passed, will not apply to bands with self-government agreements.
17 June 2002 *Political Parties*	The Action démocratique du Québec (ADQ) wins three of four byelections in Quebec and 45.4 percent of all votes cast in the four ridings. The victories include Berthier, Joliette, and Vimont ridings and boost the ADQ's presence to five of the 125 seats in the National Assembly. The Liberals finish second in one of the byelections, and the Parti Québécois finishes second in the other three.
17 June 2002 *Ontario*	In his first budget, Ontario Premier Ernie Eves boosts spending on health care, education, and environmental protection. Relying on tobacco taxes and gambling revenues to finance these spending increases, the Eves government also follows through on corporate tax cuts and the phasing-in of tax credits for parents of children attending private schools. Moreover, both income and residential education property taxes will be reduced.
20 June 2002 *Agriculture*	The federal government unveils a farm aid program. In addition to committing $5.2 billion — including $1.2 billion in emergency aid — over the next two years, the federal government is hoping to sign an agreement with

provincial agriculture ministers when they meet the following week in Halifax. Alberta, Saskatchewan, and Manitoba are all critical of the proposal, however, saying it provides yet more inadequate emergency funding. They point to the way in which it divides farm groups along regional lines to create program cost inequities (Saskatchewan residents, for example, will pay $80 while Ontarians will pay $8), and to the criteria requiring the provinces to contribute 40 percent of the total $8.2 billion in aid. Despite these criticisms, the Canadian Federation of Agriculture welcomes the package, praising it for helping to move producers past current challenges and into the long-term policy framework.

24 June 2002 *Housing*	The federal and Alberta governments sign an Affordable Housing Agreement with a view to addressing the housing crisis. The federal government will provide $67 million, which will be matched by a combination of provincial, municipal, private, and non-profit funds, and will go towards affordable housing projects in high-need areas throughout the province. Beneficiaries of the affordable housing initiatives include low-income families and individuals with special needs.
27-28 June 2002 *Agriculture*	In Halifax, NS, agriculture ministers from both orders of government sign the Federal-Provincial-Territorial Agreement on Agriculture and Agri-food for the Twenty-First Century. Saskatchewan, Manitoba, Quebec, and Nunavut do not sign, but retain the option of doing so at a later date. The agreement represents a long-term commitment to ensuring the sector's profitability, and sets the stage for implementing the five-year Agricultural Policy Framework discussed at last year's meeting in Whitehorse, YT.
28 June 2002 *Housing*	The federal and Saskatchewan governments sign an Affordable Housing Agreement. The increase in funding amounts to a total of $45.8 million, with half coming from the federal government and the other half provided by a joint consortium of provincial, municipal, private, and non-profit donors. The funding will allow 1,000 new affordable housing units to be built over the next five years.

1 July 2002
*Supreme Court of
Canada*

Supreme Court Justice Claire L'Heureux-Dubé steps down from the bench as the longest-serving judge on the high court. With a career spanning more than two decades, L'Heureux-Dubé is further recognized as the second woman to sit on Canada's most senior bench. L'Heureux-Dubé served 15 years with the Supreme Court and was appointed by former prime minister Brian Mulroney.

3 July 2002
Aboriginal Peoples

British Columbia Premier Gordon Campbell announces the success of the government's mail-in referendum on Aboriginal treaties. British Columbians, Campbell explains, are overwhelmingly in support of the eight proposals outlined in the referendum, given that of the more than two million ballots the government mailed out, 763,000 were returned. Native leaders announce, however, that more than 40,000 British Columbians sent their ballots to them in protest of the referendum. The results of the mail-in ballots are legally binding on the government under the *Referendum Act*. Aboriginal peoples in British Columbia are waiting to see how Premier Campbell will interpret the referendum results. However, Herb George — an executive member of the First Nations Summit that is representing Aboriginal groups involved in treaty negotiations — says that if the inherent right to self-government is not on the table, neither party will be at the negotiating table.

15 July 2002
*Federal Court of
Canada*

Saskatchewan Aboriginal leaders filed a Federal Court challenge against the *First Nations Governance Act*, which was tabled by the federal government in June. The challenge says the Act contravenes section 35 of the Constitution — the right to self-government — and argues that it turns band councils into legal corporations following federal rules.

16-18 July 2002
Aboriginal Peoples

Approximately 900 delegates gather for the Annual Assembly of First Nations meeting in Kahnawake, QC, and almost unanimously reject the *First Nations Governance Act* tabled by the federal government in June. The rejection centres on claims that Bill C-61 weakens the relationship between the government and First Nations upheld in the Constitution, in treaties, in the courts, and in self-government agreements. Assembly of First Nations National Chief Matthew Coon Come further suggests that the Act ignores First Nations priorities — specifically poverty and unemployment. Despite the near-complete rejection of Bill C-61, the 200 chiefs with voting rights at the meeting are unable to reach a decision of how to proceed in fighting the Act.

30 July 2002
Trade

Nova Scotia Fisheries Minister Ernie Fage accuses New Brunswick, Quebec, and Newfoundland and Labrador of unfair trading practices with respect to the crab industry. Mailing letters to all three of the accused provinces last week, Fage is initiating an appeal under the Agreement on Internal Trade.

31 July-2 August 2002
Premiers' Meeting

At the 43rd Annual Premiers' Conference in Halifax, NS, the provincial and territorial leaders agree on the necessity of a First Ministers' Conference in the near future to directly discuss and negotiate contentious issues, such as health care and climate change, with the prime minister. Insufficient federal funding, health care, climate change, and trade — issues raised in a recent report from the Conference Board of Canada — all receive the premiers' attention. The premiers address Canada's fiscal imbalance and projections of federal surpluses and provincial-territorial deficits, and their plans to call on the federal government to restore health and social service spending to at least 18 percent with an appropriate escalator, to remove the ceiling on equalization, and to stand by constitutional, fiduciary, treaty, and health service obligations to Aboriginal peoples. The premiers recognize the importance of negotiating Canada's trade relationship with the United States to ensure fair and secure access to markets, but stress the importance of pursuing appeals against market-distorting subsidies through the World Trade Organization and the North American Free Trade Agreement. The premiers also cite the importance of a federal initiative to assess domestic damages caused by these international trade actions, as well as the provision for appropriate trade injury payments to those negatively affected.

1 August 2002
Aboriginal Peoples

Burnt Church First Nation and Fisheries and Oceans Canada sign an agreement-in-principle three years following the conflict at Miramichi Bay, NB. In 1999, the Supreme Court of Canada affirmed through the *Marshall* decision a treaty right to fish to achieve a moderate livelihood. Of the 34 First Nations affected by the Supreme Court decision, 31 are in agreement with the provisions for access to commercial fisheries, which include licensing, vessels, gear, and other capacity-building measures.

12-13 August 2002
Municipalities

British Columbia Minister of Community, Aboriginal, and Women's Services George Abbott hosts the two-day annual meeting for ministers to exchange information concerning local governance priorities and discover new ways to work with local governments.

19 August 2002
Municipalities

At a gathering of over 500 mayors and councillors in Toronto, Ontario Premier Ernie Eves announces the creation of a $1-billion account to assist struggling municipalities in paying for infrastructure and other projects. The purpose of the account is to generate a pool of capital for municipalities to access at low interest rates. The provincial government says it will also research ways to share its tax revenues with municipalities to pay for specific initiatives. Other announcements include promises to continue upgrading water and sewer works, to improve public transportation, and to establish a stable, multi-year funding agreement with local governments.

21 August 2002
Prime Minister

Prime Minister Jean Chrétien announces that he will retire in February 2004. This comes as a surprise to his Liberal Party, but is intended to put an end to the leadership civil war plaguing his party since June 2002. Chrétien explains that he will focus on governing and fulfilling his mandate from now until February 2004. Although Paul Martin supporters may not be happy with Chrétien's departure date, the only way to enforce an earlier retirement date would be for Martin to defeat Chrétien in a party-wide vote of confidence on his leadership.

27 August 2002
Fisheries

One day after suggesting the sockeye salmon fishery would likely remain closed for the rest of the season, Fisheries and

Oceans Canada reopens the commercial fishery in British Columbia's lucrative Fraser River. This decision comes one day after protests by commercial harvesters in BC's Johnstone Strait resulted in 40 charges being laid. Denying any links between today's decision and the charges laid, Fisheries and Oceans Canada explains that the commercial sockeye salmon commercial fishery is reopening after new numbers increased the run size from 5.8 million to 6.5 million.

4-5 September 2002
Health

The federal, provincial, and territorial ministers of health meet in Banff, AB, to discuss efforts to improve publicly-funded health care and to ensure that the needs of Canadians continue to be met, now and in the future. The core issues on the agenda include a common drug review, accountability, human health resources, nursing, healthy living, tobacco, quality health services, emergency preparedness, and the future of health care. Commitments range from establishing a single, common drug review to continuing to make the Nursing Strategy of Canada a priority, to working together on pan-Canadian "healthy living" strategies emphasizing nutrition, physical fitness, and healthy weight.

7 September 2002
Quebec

Quebec Premier Bernard Landry sets a deadline for achieving Quebec independence within 1,000 days or three years, provided the Parti Québécois is re-elected the following year and there is growth in sovereignty support. Landry further outlines his intentions not to call an election for another 300 days. These announcements are made in the context of a drop in support for sovereignty, anti-referendum sentiments, and historic lows in support for the PQ. Moreover, the PQ's chances of winning a third straight term are questioned in the face of history: the last time a party won three consecutive terms in Quebec was in 1956.

17 September 2002
Geoscience

Federal Minister of Natural Resources Herb Dhaliwal and Manitoba Minister of Industry, Trade, and Mines, Mary Ann Mihychuk, sign a renewal of the Intergovernmental Geoscience Accord, which defines the complementary roles and responsibilities of governments with respect to geoscience. Originally signed in 1996, the purpose of the accord is to encourage good working relationships among government geological survey organizations within Canada. It seeks to harness their strengths and increase their effectiveness by defining different but complementary roles and responsibilities, outlining principles of co-operation to optimize the use of their resources, and establishing mechanisms for co-operation and collaboration among the organizations.

23-24 September 2002
Women

Federal, provincial, and territorial ministers responsible for the status of women meet in Whitehorse, YT, to discuss ways to advance women's equality and to exchange information on a number of important issues affecting women in Canada. Items of discussion include ways to achieve women's economic independence, to address violence against women, and to improve women's health.

24 September 2002
Forestry

The Canadian Council of Forest Ministers — composed of federal, provincial, and territorial ministers — meets in Halifax, NS, to discuss sustainable forest management and measures for ensuring the future competitiveness of the forestry sector. The ministers express support for a proposed new joint initiative called Forest 2020, which calls for innovation and investments in fast-growing, high-yield tree plantations and intensive silviculture. This would provide a means of significantly boosting the country's supply of wood fibre, as well as contribute to forest ecosystem conservation and greater community sustainability grounded in the smart use of forest resources. Commitments are made to move forward on the direction of the Strategic Plan for the Renewal of the Canadian Forest Fire infrastructure. The ministers also review the progress of the National Forest Strategy Coalition toward the development of a new National Forest Strategy, which is to be released in May 2003.

25 September 2002
Biodiversity

Federal, provincial, and territorial forestry, wildlife, and fisheries ministers meet in Halifax, NS, to discuss ways to protect biodiversity. The meeting comes 10 years after the Rio Earth Summit, and one month after the World Summit on Sustainable Development in Johannesburg, South Africa. The ministers renew their commitment to work together to implement the UN Convention on Biological Diversity; review progress on priorities for action under the Canadian Biodiversity Strategy and, as part of this review, approve a national blueprint for addressing the threat of invasive species; approve Canada's Stewardship Agenda, which will increase participation by Canadians in biodiversity conservation; review a number of initiatives in support of the objectives of the Accord for the Protection of Species at Risk; and release statements on steps their jurisdictions will take to protect 32 species designated threatened, endangered, or extirpated by the Committee on the Status of Endangered Wildlife in Canada in 2001.

26 September 2002
Saskatchewan

Saskatchewan Provincial Auditor Fred Wendel announces a $483-million deficit for the province's New Democratic Party coalition government. This announcement comes in the wake of the government's prediction in early August that it would have a $100,000 surplus. Premier Lorne Calvert blames the drought for its financial situation.

26 September 2002
Fisheries

The Canadian Council of Fisheries and Aquaculture Ministers, which is composed of federal, provincial, and territorial ministers, meets to discuss concerns and review progress regarding a number of joint initiatives. The focus is on balancing the use and management of the oceans in connection with global concerns voiced at the recent World Summit on Sustainable Development in Johannesburg, South Africa, for protecting ocean resources and rebuilding depleted fish stocks. The ministers agree to work toward implementing Canada's Ocean Strategy objectives, which entail a broad strategic approach to oceans management and emphasize the need for collaboration and co-operation between and among governments. Revisions are also made to a plan for the development of a comprehensive Canadian Action Plan for Aquaculture. This aims at ensuring that provincial, territorial, and federal policies and regulations are complementary and sets out objectives for strengthening the industry's competitiveness. The ministers give an approval-in-principle to the updated National Freshwater Fisheries Strategy and the delivery of the intergovernmental implementation plan for 2002-2003, which set out co-operative objectives and actions for the conservation and sustainable use of freshwater fisheries and habitat in Canada.

27 September 2002
Fisheries

Federal Fisheries Minister Robert Thibault introduces a new policy to put an end to over-fishing on the edge of Newfoundland and Labrador's Grand Banks. In particular, the new federal measures will penalize individual vessels caught breaking international fishing rules outside Canada's territorial waters by denying them access to Canadian ports. Critics find the new policy weak, saying that many of the over-fishing problems stem from European Union ships that do not use Canadian ports.

30 September 2002
Supreme Court of Canada

Marie Deschamps is sworn in to replace Justice Claire L'Heureux-Dubé, who retired on July 1. Deschamps joins two other women on the bench and represents Prime Minister Jean Chrétien's fifth Supreme Court appointment since he came to power in 1993. A well-respected Quebec Court of Appeal judge, Deschamps has served on Quebec's high court since 1992 and is well known as a tough but fair jurist specializing in commercial litigation. Born in Repentigny, QC, and educated at the University of Montreal and McGill University, Deschamps was called to the bar in 1975.

30 September 2002
Softwood Lumber

The federal Cabinet approves an aid package to help workers and communities across Canada deal with the economic and social impacts of the US-imposed duties on Canadian softwood lumber. The assistance will be largely directed to the provinces and the industry through the Employment Insurance program to help companies offer training and job-sharing to displaced workers. Ottawa will also help the British Columbia government and forest industry deal with a pine beetle infestation. The federal Cabinet refuses, however, to help cover the legal fees stemming from the softwood lumber court battle.

3-4 October 2002
Francophone Affairs

The annual federal-provincial-territorial Ministerial Conference on Francophone Affairs takes place in St. John's, NL, providing a forum for governments to reaffirm their commitments and priorities relating to the delivery of

French-language services and the development of francophone and Acadian communities. Discussion of provincial and territorial governments' key role in the implementation of certain components of the federal action plan is important in connection with the upcoming renewal of federal-provincial-territorial agreements on the promotion of official languages. Moreover, a review of current and planned initiatives and approaches concerning health services, early childhood development, visibility of French, dialogue with the community, and provincial-territorial co-operation on regional activities further underlines the importance of the intergovernmental agreements and suggests where and how improvements can be made.

4 October 2002
National Parks

Prime Minister Jean Chrétien announces that 10 new national parks and five new marine conservation areas will be created over the next five years. The parks will protect more than 100,000 square kilometers of wilderness and marine habitat in British Columbia, Manitoba, Ontario, Newfoundland and Labrador, Nunavut, and the Northwest Territories. Negotiations with provincial, territorial, and Aboriginal leaders will take place over the next few months.

8 October 2002
Health

In her most recent report, Auditor General Sheila Fraser criticizes the federal government over its administration of health care delivery. The report accuses the government of not knowing how much money it contributes to the health care system, and charges that the government is not adequately enforcing compliance with the *Canada Health Act*.

8-9 October 2002
Education

The Council of Ministers of Education, Canada, meets in Winnipeg, MB, to discuss issues of assessment, student mobility, and online learning. The ministers adopt a ministerial statement that will lead to a pan-Canadian system of credit transfer among colleges and universities. The primary purpose of such a system is to increase access to post-secondary education and to improve student mobility. The ministers also agree to set up a pan-Canadian portal on online learning and to move forward with the federal government on exploring potential improvements to student financial assistance programs. At the end of the meeting, education and labour market ministers release a paper entitled *Working Together to Strengthen Learning and Labour Market Training,* presenting their shared visions and immediate priorities for post-secondary education and labour market training.

16 October 2002
Immigration

Federal, provincial, and territorial ministers responsible for immigration hold their first meeting in Winnipeg, MB. This represents the beginning of a new partnership on immigration with a number of agreements for co-operation in several different immigration-related areas. Discussions focus on the need to enhance Canada's ability to attract more skilled immigrants to address skill shortages and further develop the Canadian labour market and economy, approaches to increasing the benefits of immigration in all parts of Canada, attracting immigrants to smaller centres and other regions, developing broad principles for guiding the implementation of regional strategies, and removing the barriers that many immigrants face in integrating into the labour market. Of particular note is the establishment of a working group to guide the implementation of strategies focused upon supporting and assisting immigrants in concert with Human Resources Development Canada.

28 October 2002
Northwest Territories

Northwest Territories Premier Stephen Kakfwi succeeds in fending off a second backbencher challenge to his leadership, albeit with reduced political support, in a 10-5 vote.

28 October 2002
Climate Change

Provincial and territorial ministers of energy and the environment gather for a joint meeting on climate change policy. In addition to reiterating a call for a First Ministers' Conference on climate change policy prior to any federal decision, the ministers announce a set of 12 principles to be followed in the drafting of a national climate change plan. This list is in response to the federal framework and the federal government's announcement that it will ratify the Kyoto Accord before the end of the year.

30 October 2002
Economic and Fiscal
Update

Federal Finance Minister John Manley delivers his 2002 Economic and Fiscal Update speech to the House of Commons Standing Committee on Finance. Manley says Canadians are reaping the benefits of sound economic and fiscal management, pointing to five consecutive budget surpluses, the paying down of more than $46 billion of the national debt, and a debt-to-Gross Domestic Product ratio that has fallen from 71 percent in 1995-1996 to 49 percent, the largest decline of any G-7 country. He also notes that Canada avoided recession during the global slowdown of 2001 and posted strong economic growth in 2002. Manley says Canada's economy grew at an annualized rate of more than 5 percent in the first half of 2002, from January to September the economy created 427,000 new jobs, and real personal disposable income per person rose 2.9 percent over the previous year. A survey of private sector forecasts shows that economic growth is expected to average 3.4 percent in 2002 and 3.5 percent in 2003, with Canada leading the G-7 in both years, Manley adds. The minister also notes that for 2001-2002, Canada recorded a budget surplus of $8.9 billion, which went to reduce the national debt. The average private sector projections of Canada's fiscal-planning surplus, he says, are $1.0 billion for 2002-2003, rising steadily to $14.6 billion for 2007-2008. Manley warns, however, that Canada cannot be complacent, and says his government will remain prudent by continuing to balance its budget and pay down debt.

4 November 2002
Yukon Territory

Yukon Party leader Dennis Fentie becomes premier of the Yukon Territory. The Yukon Party wins a 12-seat majority over the Liberals, who drop down to a single seat, and the New Democratic Party, who see their seats increase from four to five in the 18-member legislature. Fentie's inaugural promises include reviving the territory's struggling economy; working to formalize relationships with the Yukon's Aboriginal governments, especially those with settled land claims; and a more inclusive governing style that would see all 18 members of the legislature contribute to the policy-making process.

4-6 November 2002 *Justice*	Federal, provincial, and territorial ministers responsible for justice meet in Calgary, AB, to address a wide variety of items. Topics range from legal aid, to intoxicating inhalants, to the *Youth Criminal Justice Act*, to anti-terrorism, to streamlining the justice system. Agreements among the ministers include developing strategies and/or legal changes to allow for improved legal aid funding, improved protection of children from sexual exploitation, reforms to family law, secure ongoing and enhanced funding for family law services, sustained and enhanced funding for Aboriginal justice issues, the creation of new criminal offences of sexual voyeurism and distribution of voyeuristic materials, a sex offender registration system, more research into the nature and scope of organized crime activity, the adoption of the Canada Public Safety Information Network data standards as national standards, and greater efficiency within the justice system as a way to reduce costs and delays while simultaneously respecting victims and witnesses. The ministers also agree that spousal abuse should be made a regular part of the agenda for future meetings.
15 November 2002 *Aboriginal Peoples*	Federal, provincial, and territorial ministers responsible for Aboriginal affairs and the leaders of five national Aboriginal organizations meet in Iqaluit, NU, to discuss ways to strengthen Aboriginal participation in the economy, especially that of Aboriginal women and youth. The ministers and leaders commit to an ongoing focus on improving the entrepreneurship opportunities for Aboriginal women. Those gathered also approve the work done on two practical tools for facilitating Aboriginal women's participation in the economy: the Aboriginal Women's Business Planning Guide and a comprehensive federal-provincial-territorial-Aboriginal (FPTA) resource guide listing employment and entrepreneurship programs and services available to Aboriginal women. In connection with the National Aboriginal Youth Strategy, the leaders and ministers endorse the National Aboriginal Organizations Youth Committee, which will in turn advise and work through the FTPA Working Group on the development and implementation of Aboriginal youth programs and services.

18 November 2002 *Aboriginal Peoples*	The Anglican Church of Canada agrees to pay $25 million toward a special federal fund to compensate Aboriginal people who were abused as students in residential schools. In exchange for this payment, which is to be made over the next five years, the federal government agrees not to seek additional funds from the Church. The government's share of the compensation is estimated at more than $1 billion. The new government-church agreement — resulting from more than two years of negotiations between church bishops and federal bureaucrats — awaits ratification by both parties.
19 November 2002 *Environment*	Alberta introduces controversial legislation that will reinforce its constitutional claim over natural resources and expand the province's jurisdiction to include environmental management, an area typically shared between the provincial and federal governments. Claiming provincial ownership over carbon sinks (stands of forest and tracts of agricultural land that pull carbon dioxide out of the atmosphere), which are applied toward meeting greenhouse gas reduction targets, represents another area of federal-provincial dispute.
19 November 2002 *Aboriginal Peoples*	Matthew Coon Come announces he will seek to be-elected as National Chief of the Assembly of First Nations with the intention of continuing the battle with Ottawa over native rights. Coon Come's three-year term, perforated by conflict with Indian Affairs and other chiefs, ends in July.
22 November 2002 *Social Services*	Federal, provincial, and territorial ministers responsible for social services meet in Moncton, NB, to discuss the National Child Benefit, the Early Childhood Development initiative, and benefits and services (including labour market services) for persons with disabilities. The ministers also agree to work together to develop options to address the federal government's recent commitments made in its Speech from the Throne to increase access to early learning opportunities and quality childcare.
30 November 2002 *Quebec*	Quebec Premier Bernard Landry introduces tax breaks on donations to a new sovereigntist organization, the Council for Sovereignty, in an effort to kick-start the independence movement. Contributions to this new group

will be treated as charitable donations, allowing the Quebec government to indirectly fund pro-sovereigntist ad campaigns and counter what Landry deems "federalist propaganda." The Council for Sovereignty will immediately receive $250,000 from Parti Québécois coffers, Landry says.

2 December 2002
Aboriginal Peoples

Minister of Indian Affairs and Northern Development Robert Nault introduces the *First Nations Fiscal and Statistical Management Act* in the House of Commons. This legislation will establish four national institutions to improve Aboriginal peoples' capacity to improve the social and economic well-being of their communities. The First Nations Tax Commission is intended to provide more transparency, stability, and regulatory certainty to Aboriginal peoples and to Aboriginal governments that collect property tax on-reserve. The First Nations Finance Authority will allow Aboriginal peoples to issue their own debentures using property tax revenues as security, enabling them to build a competitive economic infrastructure. The First Nations Financial Management Board will certify community financial management practices and systems in an attempt to build the confidence of Aboriginal peoples, investors, and other governments. Finally, the First Nations Statistics Institute is set up to improve the quality and timeliness of Aboriginal statistics, with the purpose of enhancing community planning and reducing decision-making time.

2 December 2002
Fisheries

The Atlantic Council of Fisheries and Aquaculture Ministers, which is made up of ministers from the Atlantic provinces, Quebec, Nunavut, and the federal government, meets in Gatineau, QC, to discuss the Atlantic Fisheries Policy Review and cod stocks. The policy framework has been developing over the past three years and is nearing completion. It is intended to provide a foundation for the long-term sustainable management of the Atlantic fisheries. The second phase of the collaboration process will concentrate on developing and implementing plans and programs to put policies into action.

4 December 2002
Ontario

Ontario Finance Minister Janet Ecker confirms that her government will sell off more than $2 billion in public assets over the next four months to help balance this year's provincial budget. The asset sales include a small rural savings bank, the government's share in an electronic land registry company, publicly-owned real estate, and a 49 percent share in Hydro One.

7 December 2002
Tourism

Federal, provincial, and territorial ministers responsible for tourism meet in Victoria, BC. The purpose of the meeting is to discuss ways to help ensure the tourism industry expands the economies of communities in all regions of Canada, while at the same time keeping in mind the need for strong border security measures. The ministers agree that quick action is crucial in increasing Canada's competitiveness in the global tourism industry and in resolving concerns related to air transportation policy, tourism funding, cross-border travel, and Northern and Aboriginal tourism.

9 December 2002
Health

Roy Romanow unveils his landmark 356-page report, *Building on Values: The Future of Health Care in Canada*. The central message of the report is that Canada's health care system must remain publicly funded. The report's recommendations include a $15-billion increase in federal health care funding by 2006. The report says that the funding increases — $3.5 in 2003-2004, $5.0 billion in 2004-2005, and $6.5 billion in 2005-2006 — should come from future federal surpluses, not new taxes. Other recommendations include the creation of a national drug prescription plan to cover catastrophic costs, the creation of a national home care strategy, and the creation of a Health Council of Canada to act as a public watchdog on the health care system.

10 December 2002
Environment

Parliament approves the Kyoto Accord to reduce greenhouse gases. The vote was a clear majority for ratification of the treaty, with 195 MPs in favour — the Liberal majority, backed by the Bloc Québécois and the New Democrats — and 77 against — the Canadian Alliance and the Progressive Conservatives. The government unveiled its revised plan for the ratification of the Kyoto

Accord in the House of Commons on 21 November. In addition to announcing that Canada could cut 240 megatonnes of emissions by 2012, the report stated that the effects on the economy would be negligible. While calling on individual Canadians to reduce personal emissions by 20 percent through energy savings and other means, the plan targets five areas for emissions savings: transportation, housing and commercial/institutional buildings, large industrial emitters, small- and medium-sized enterprises and fugitive emissions, and international emissions. Critics warn the effects on the economy will be substantial, and further charge that the government has no clear plan on this issue.

18 December 2002
Governor General

Former governor general Ramon John Hnatyshyn dies at the age of 68 following a lengthy battle with cancer. Hnatyshyn served as Canada's 24th governor general from 1990 to 1995. He was known for bringing warmth and openness to his post, which included reopening Rideau Hall to tours. He also created the Governor General's Awards for the Performing Arts. Born and raised in Saskatchewan, Hnatyshyn was first elected as a Conservative MP for Saskatoon West in 1974. In addition to his position as minister of energy in Joe Clark's 1979 government, he was also House leader and minister of justice under Brian Mulroney.

19 December 2002
Supreme Court of Canada

The Supreme Court of Canada rules 5-4 that Canadians do not have a constitutional right to guaranteed state welfare support. Countering activists' arguments that constitutional protection for "security of person" under the *Charter of Rights and Freedoms* should include a guaranteed standard of living, the ruling appears to confirm the federal government's right to control the public purse. The decision was handed down to Louise Gosselin of Montreal, who argued that Quebec's welfare rules in the 1980s violated her Charter of Rights guarantees to equality and life, liberty, and security of person. The governments of Ontario, New Brunswick, British Columbia, and Alberta argued that the provinces should design social policy, and that they should not be limited by the courts to simply handing out cash payments.

Chronology: Index

Ontario 7 March, 9 March, 23 March, 15 April, 9 May, 29 May, 12 June, 17 June, 4 December

Parliament 13 March

Political Parties 9 April, 15 April, 17 June

Premiers' Meeting 24-25 January, 31 July-2 August

Prime Minister 21 August

Prince Edward Island 30 May

Quebec 30 January, 19 March, 7 May, 7 September, 30 November

Saskatchewan 26 September

Social Services 31 May, 22 November

Softwood Lumber 30 September

Supreme Court of Canada 1 July, 30 September, 19 December

Tourism 7 December

Trade 21 February, 21 March, 30 July

Western Canada 4-6 June

Women 23-24 September

Yukon Territory 4 November

Queen's Policy Studies
Recent Publications

The Queen's Policy Studies Series is dedicated to the exploration of major policy issues that confront governments in Canada and other western nations. McGill-Queen's University Press is the exclusive world representative and distributor of books in the series.

School of Policy Studies

Canada Without Armed Forces? Douglas L. Bland (ed.), 2004
Paper ISBN 1-55339-036-9 Cloth 1-55339-037-7

Campaigns for International Security: Canada's Defence Policy at the Turn of the Century, Douglas L. Bland and Sean M. Maloney, 2004
Paper ISBN 0-88911-962-7 Cloth 0-88911-964-3

Understanding Innovation in Canadian Industry, Fred Gault (ed.), 2003
Paper ISBN 1-55339-030-X Cloth ISBN 1-55339-031-8

Delicate Dances: Public Policy and the Nonprofit Sector, Kathy L. Brock (ed.), 2003
Paper ISBN 0-88911-953-8 Cloth ISBN 0-88911-955-4

Beyond the National Divide: Regional Dimensions of Industrial Relations, Mark Thompson, Joseph B. Rose and Anthony E. Smith (eds.), 2003
Paper ISBN 0-88911-963-5 Cloth ISBN 0-88911-965-1

The Nonprofit Sector in Interesting Times: Case Studies in a Changing Sector, Kathy L. Brock and Keith G. Banting (eds.), 2003
Paper ISBN 0-88911-941-4 Cloth ISBN 0-88911-943-0

Clusters Old and New: The Transition to a Knowledge Economy in Canada's Regions, David A. Wolfe (ed.), 2003   Paper ISBN 0-88911-959-7 Cloth ISBN 0-88911-961-9

The e-Connected World: Risks and Opportunities, Stephen Coleman (ed.), 2003
Paper ISBN 0-88911-945-7 Cloth ISBN 0-88911-947-3

Knowledge, Clusters and Regional Innovation: Economic Development in Canada, J. Adam Holbrook and David A. Wolfe (eds.), 2002
Paper ISBN 0-88911-919-8 Cloth ISBN 0-88911-917-1

Lessons of Everyday Law/Le droit du quotidien, Roderick Alexander Macdonald, 2002
Paper ISBN 0-88911-915-5 Cloth ISBN 0-88911-913-9

Improving Connections Between Governments and Nonprofit and Voluntary Organizations: Public Policy and the Third Sector, Kathy L. Brock (ed.), 2002
Paper ISBN 0-88911-899-X Cloth ISBN 0-88911-907-4

Institute of Intergovernmental Relations

Federalism and Labour Market Policy: Comparing Different Governance and Employment Strategies, Alain Noël (ed.), 2004
Paper ISBN 1-55339-006-7 Cloth ISBN 1-55339-007-5, ISBN 0-88911-845-0 (set)

Institute of Intergovernmental Relations
Recent Publications

Political Science and Federalism: Seven Decades of Scholarly Engagement, Richard Simeon, 2000 Kenneth R. MacGregor Lecturer, 2002
ISBN 1-55339-004-0

The Spending Power in Federal Systems: A Comparative Study, Ronald L. Watts, 1999
ISBN 0-88911-829-9

Étude comparative du pouvoir de dépenser dans d'autres régimes fédéraux, Ronald L. Watts, 1999   ISBN 0-88911-831-0

Constitutional Patriation: The Lougheed-Lévesque Correspondence/Le rapatriement de la Constitution: La correspondance de Lougheed et Lévesque, with an Introduction by J. Peter Meekison/avec une introduction de J. Peter Meekison, 1999   ISBN 0-88911-833-7

Securing the Social Union: A Commentary on the Decentralized Approach, Steven A. Kennett, 1998   ISBN 0-88911-767-5

Working Paper Series

2003

1. *Too Many Cooks? Dealing with Climate Change in Canada* by Matt Jones, Bob Masterson and Doug Russell

2. *The Web of Life* by Elizabeth Dowdeswell

3. *Aboriginal Governance in the Canadian Federal State 2015* by Jay Kaufman and Florence Roberge

4. *Canada 2015: Globalization and the Future of Canada's Health and Health Care* by Michael Mendelson and Pamela Divinsky

5. *Implications for the International and Canadian Financial Services Industry and their Governance of Varying Future International Scenarios* by Edward P. Neufeld

6. *The Impact of Global and Regional Integration On Federal Systems Domestic Case Study-Agriculture and Agri-Foods* by W.M. Miner

7. *Federalism and the New Democratic Order. A Citizen and Process Perspective* by Thomas J. Courchene

8. *Understanding the impact of Intergovernmental relations on public health: Lessons from reform initiatives in the blood system and health surveillance* by Kumanan Wilson, Jennifer McCrea-Logie and Harvey Lazar

9. *Le Québec et l'intégration continentale: Les stratégies caractéristiques* by Nelson Michaud

2002

1. *Redistribution, Risk, and Incentives in Equalization: A Comparison of RTS and Macro Approaches* by Michael Smart, Department of Economics, University of Toronto

2. *Revisiting Equalization Again: RTS vs Macro Approaches* by Robin Boadway, Department of Economics, Queen's University

3. *The Stablization Properties of Equalization: Evidence from Saskatchewan* by Paul Boothe, University of Alberta and C.D. Howe Institute

4. *The Case for Switching to a Macro Formula* by Dan Usher, Department of Economics, Queen's University

5. *Using GDP in Equalization Calculations: Are There Meaningful Measurement Issues?* by Julie Aubut, C.RD.E. and François Vaillancourt, Département de sciences économiques and Fellow, C.R.D.E., Université de Montréal

6. *What Do We Already Know about the Appropriate Design for a Fiscal Equalization Program in Canada and How Well Are We Doing?* by Paul Hobson, Department of Economics, Acadia University

7. *Macroeconomic Versus RTS Measures of Fiscal Capacity: Theoretical Foundations and Implications for Canada* by Stephen Barro

8. *Quiet Cooperation: Relations Among Labour Ministries in Canada* by Ronald Saunders

2001

1. *Tax Competition and the Fiscal Union: Balancing Competition and Harmonization in Canada.* Proceedings of a Symposium held 9-10 June 2000, edited by Douglas Brown, Queen's University

2. *Federal Occupational Training Policy: A Neo-Institutionalist Analysis* by Gordon DiGiacomo, Consultant in Workplace Relations, Greely, Ontario

3. *Federalism and Labour Market Policy in Germany and Canada: Exploring the Path Dependency of Reforms in the 1990s* by Thomas R. Klassen, Trent University and Steffen Schneider, University of Augsburg, Germany

4. *Bifurcated and Integrated Parties in Parliamentary Federations: The Canadian and German Cases* by Wolfgang Renzsch, Otto-von-Guericke Universität Magdeburg, Germany

5. *The Two British Columbias* by Phillip Resnick, University of British Columbia and *The West Wants In! (But What is the West? and What is "In?")* by Peter McCormick, University of Lethbridge

6. *Federalism and Labour Policy in Canada* by Gordon DiGiacomo

7. *Quebec's Place in the Canada of the Future* by Benoît Pelletier

8. *The Evolution of Support for Sovereignty – Myths and Realities* by Claire Durand, Université de Montréal

For a complete list of Working Papers, see the Institute of Intergovernmental Relations Web site at: www.iigr.ca. Working Papers can be downloaded from the Web site under the pull down menu "Research."

These publications are available from:
Institute of Intergovernmental Relations, Queen's University, Kingston, Ontario K7L 3N6
Tel: (613) 533-2080 / Fax: (613) 533-6868; E-mail: iigr@qsilver.queensu.ca